For Julie, May and Pablo

Popular Politics in the Making of the Modern Middle East

The waves of protest ignited by the self-immolation of Muhammad Bouazizi in Tunisia in late 2010 highlighted for an international audience the importance of contentious politics in the Middle East and North Africa. John Chalcraft's ground-breaking account of popular protest emphasizes the revolutionary modern history of the entire region. Challenging top-down views of Middle Eastern politics, he looks at how commoners, subjects and citizens have long mobilized in defiance of authorities. Chalcraft takes examples from a wide variety of protest movements from Morocco to Iran. He forges a new narrative of change over time, creating a truly comparative framework rooted in the dynamics of hegemonic contestation. Beginning with movements under the Ottomans, which challenged corruption and oppression under the banners of religion, justice, rights and custom, this book goes on to discuss the impact of constitutional movements, armed struggles, nationalism and independence, revolution and Islamism. A work of unprecedented range and depth, this volume will be welcomed by undergraduates and graduates studying protest in the region and beyond.

JOHN CHALCRAFT is an Associate Professor in the Department of Government at the London School of Economics and Political Science. His publications include *The Invisible Cage: Syrian Workers in Lebanon* (2009), *Counterhegemony in the Colony and Postcolony* (co-edited with Yaseen Noorani, 2007) and *The Striking Cabbies of Cairo and Other Stories: Crafts and Guilds in Egypt, 1863–1914* (2004).

Advance praise for *Popular Politics in the Making of the Modern Middle East*

'John Chalcraft is the Howard Zinn of Middle East studies and has devoted his career to rescuing workers and their agency from the neglect of pundits and chroniclers of the elites. His synthetic treatment of these themes is essential for understanding how the region came to be so fraught in our own era.'

Juan Cole, Professor of History, University of Michigan

'John Chalcraft's *Popular Politics in the Making of the Modern Middle East* is awe-inspiring in its breadth, depth and richness of theoretical nuance and empirical texture. Unparalleled in both its ambitions and its achievements, this book provides not only a brilliant synthetic re-interpretation of the role of popular politics in the making of the modern Middle East, but also a source of inspiration for historians of other regions of the world interested in contentious politics. In all the right ways, this is a very big book.'

John Sidel, Professor of International and Comparative Politics, LSE

'This book makes an outstanding contribution to the study of the recent history and politics of the Middle East. By focusing on the struggles, ambitions and passions of popular politics, Chalcraft brings out the rhythms of political contention over an impressively wide range of countries throughout the past 250 years. This is a major achievement, restoring agency to those who have often been written out of the dominant narratives of power, obliging us to think again about the location and the outcomes of the political conflicts that continue to shape the region.'

Charles Tripp, Professor of Politics, SOAS

'Media analysis of the Middle East and North Africa portrays the region as the land of fallen tyrants brought down by unfocused mass street violence until yet another despot seizes power. John Chalcraft's book tells us otherwise. Ranging geographically from Morocco to Iran and the Balkans, and covering the late eighteenth century to the present, his study demonstrates the workings of mindful, strategic and organized collective populism. In its comparative and theoretical approach, this work is unmatched.'

Julia Clancy-Smith, Professor of History, The University of Arizona

Popular Politics in the Making of the Modern Middle East

JOHN CHALCRAFT
The London School of Economics and Political Science

CAMBRIDGE
UNIVERSITY PRESS

CAMBRIDGE
UNIVERSITY PRESS

University Printing House, Cambridge CB2 8BS, United Kingdom

Cambridge University Press is part of the University of Cambridge.

It furthers the University's mission by disseminating knowledge in the pursuit of education, learning and research at the highest international levels of excellence.

www.cambridge.org
Information on this title: www.cambridge.org/9780521189422

First published 2016

Printed in the Unites States of America

A catalogue record for this publication is available from the British Library

Library of Congress Cataloguing in Publication data
Names: Chalcraft, John T., 1970– author.
Title: Popular politics in the making of the modern Middle East / John Chalcraft.
Description: New York : Cambridge University Press, 2016. | Includes bibliographical references and index.
Identifiers: LCCN 2015037119 | ISBN 9781107007505 (Hardback : alk. paper) | ISBN 9780521189422 (Paperback : alk. paper)
Subjects: LCSH: Middle East–Politics and government–1945– | Middle East–Politics and government–1914–1945. | Middle East–Politics and government.
Classification: LCC DS62.8 .C46 2016 | DDC 956–dc23 LC record available at http://lccn.loc.gov/2015037119

ISBN 978-1-107-00750-5 Hardback
ISBN 978-0-521-18942-2 Paperback

Contents

Maps

Preface and acknowledgements

Sometimes a striking phrase will not go away. It seems to contain a vital but elusive idea. This research project has been dogged and inspired by such a phrase: 'The people defied the authorities and took matters into their own hands.' This was what some Palestinians in the late 1980s said to doctoral researcher Sonia Nimr about their uprising of 1936–9 (Nimr 1990: 3). My aim has been to write a history of this kind of transgressive mobilization in the Middle East and North Africa since the eighteenth century. Along the way, I have incurred many debts.

The research was made possible by a two-year ESRC Mid-Career Development Fellowship which bought out my teaching during 2009–11, and by a term's research leave granted by the London School of Economics (LSE) during 2011–12. Thanks are also due to the Archives du Ministère des Affaires étrangères at La Courneuve, in France, the Archives of the Hoover Institution in Stanford University in the United States, the Institut Français du Proche-Orient in Syria, the Bibliothèque François Mitterrand in Paris and the British Library in London, where much of the research was conducted. I would like to thank the academics, journalists, activists and intellectuals in the region who were generous with their time during the research, especially Abd Al-Aziz Al-Arab, Yasser Alwan, Naira Antoun, Mustafa Bassiouny, Ralph Bodenstein, Vittoria Capresi, Khaled Fahmy, Dina Makram Ebeid, Sameh Idriss, Philip Rizk, Tamer Wageeh and Muhammad Zahid. Among LSE colleagues, Fawaz Gerges' good sense and support has long been important to me. John Breuilly and Martha Mundy's intellect and erudition have been a source of engagement and learning. Thanks are also due to George Lawson and the Global Historical Sociology Workshop where there were useful discussions and presentations. I am grateful to John Sidel, whose wisdom, mentoring, good humour and engagement with the manuscript have been important throughout. This book has been enriched by the presentations and discussions in the LSE-based seminar series, Social Movements and Popular Mobilization in the Middle East. I am grateful to the Middle East Centre and the Government Department for supporting the series, and to paper presenters and discussants Maha Abdelrahman, Gilbert Achcar, Charles Anderson, Fadi Bardawil, Claire Beaugrand, Joel Beinin, Marie Duboc, Salwa Ismail, Charles Tripp and Frédéric Vairel. My Ph.D. students have taught me much: I have been inspired and enriched by Michael Farquhar's subtle and intelligent commentary, Neil Ketchley's strong-minded engagement with social movement literature and Alia Mossallam's originality, imagination and activism. The research and acuity of Amélie Barras, Francesca Biancani, Jann Boeddeling, Yasmine Laveille, Suzanne Morrison, Fuad Musallam, Anastasia Nosova and Reza Pankhurst have in different ways contributed to this study: it has been a privilege to work with you all. This book has also developed alongside two masters courses at LSE: The History and Politics of the Modern Middle East, and Popular Politics in the Middle East. I would like to thank the students on these courses collectively: their energy, good humour and application has surprised and energized me year on year. Some took the trouble to read and comment on parts of the manuscript, especially Cecilia Rossler, who helped me cut down on the waffle, and also Joseph Leigh and Cécile Rossi. I would like to thank the journal of *International Labor and Working Class History* for allowing me to reproduce parts of my article 'Migration and Popular Protest in the Arabian Peninsula and the Gulf in the 1950s and 1960s' (79 (2011), pp. 28–47) in the present volume. Cambridge University Press allowed me to reproduce the two maps from Joel Beinin's book *Workers and Peasants in the Modern Middle East* (2001). I want to thank Laleh Khalili for suggesting Mosa'ab Elshamy's photography for the cover image. Alaa El-Mahrakawy gave me some useful references towards the end of the writing-up process. I would like to thank Karim Eid-Sabbagh for convivial intellectual conversation. Anne Alexander has been an enduring source of engagement and kindly helped me with contacts in Egypt. I would like to thank Zachary Lockman for his encouragement of this project at an early stage and his support since. I am grateful to Michele Filippini for discussions and references on hegemony.

I am particularly thankful to colleagues and students who went out of their way to read parts, and sometimes all, of this weighty 'beast' in its near-final incarnation: Julie Gervais, Michael Gilsenan, Neil Ketchley, Nawal Mustafa, John Sidel, Charles Tripp and the anonymous reviewer at Cambridge University Press. These readers saved me from errors large and small, and played important roles in both maintaining my morale and refining the presentation and overall argument. I am grateful to the whole team at Cambridge University Press, especially Maria Marsh, the Commissioning Editor, whose enthusiasm and support have helped enormously in turning this manuscript into a book. In sum, it is a pleasure to acknowledge here how very collective is the whole process of writing a book, while of course I must take responsibility for the remaining errors and misjudgements. Finally, I would like to extend heartfelt thanks to my partner Julie Gervais, whose intellect, passion, joy, gimlet eye on parts of the text and unstinting encouragement and support in regards to the burdens and demands of book-writing have been a fundamental source of support, pleasure and inspiration.

Introduction

In late December 2010, in a Tunisian provincial town, familiar patterns of protest developed in new directions. Self-immolations, such as that of the soon-to-be well-known vendor, Muhammad Bouazizi, on 17 December 2010, were nothing especially new. Desperately trying to make a living and provide for families in survivalist enterprise, several men had in previous months protested the corruption and brutality of the police and the indifference of the authorities by setting themselves on fire in public. Not much had come of it. Familiar enough, in turn, were demonstrations and strikes, such as those over unemployment, government neglect, unfair contracting, and the indifference of much of the union leadership that briefly inspired the Gafsa mining basin of Tunisia in 2008. In late 2010, however, the confrontations with police that typically accompanied such protests only sparked wider mobilizations. New constituencies were drawn in: bloggers, lawyers, ever larger numbers of labour unionists, educated youth in the cities, satellite media, gang members, journalists, smugglers, women, and even members of the ruling party (Allal 2013; Hmed 2012). Someone, somewhere, started to demand that the people should bring down Ben Ali's long-entrenched regime (*al-sha'b yurid/isqat al-nizam*). This new slogan, its import unthinkable only weeks before, was taken up and roared all over the country with extraordinary force. Those who flooded into the streets signalled their disgust with a *status quo* declared unendurable. Suddenly, the well-worn poetry of Tunisia's national anthem took on a new life:

> If, one day, a people desires to live
> Then fate will answer their call
> Darkness must dissipate
> And must the chain give way
> (Colla *et al.* 2012)

1

Those on the streets called not for Islam, the most common (but not the only) protest frame in the region for decades, but for bread, dignity and freedom. Once the demonstrations were joined, and pitched battles with police successful, continuous occupations of key, urban public spaces emerged: the people would not go home until their demands were met. When the army refused to shoot on these masses of civilians, Ben Ali, strong-man president since 1987, boarded a plane for Saudi Arabia and never came back.

The region was electrified. No one had seen the fall of an entrenched Arab 'president for life' (Owen 2012) as a result of mass protest. All but one of the ruling regimes in the independent states of the Arab world had endured, with personnel changes only, since Colonel Gaddafi's Free Officer's revolutionary coup had seized power from King Idris in Libya under the banners of pan-Arab national liberation in 1969. The only exception was Iraq. Saddam Hussein's strong-man rule there since the Ba'thist coup of 1968 had been broken by the US-invasion of 2003. This was an exception that seemed to prove a simple rule – the people could *not* bring down the regime. Indeed, the mass uprising of 1991 in Iraq had been smothered in blood. The last great popular uprising in the region, the *intifada* of 1987–91, had not resulted in a national state for the Palestinians. It was, in any case, directed not at a domestic dictatorship but a colonizing occupation. Nor had the Bahrainis won a constitution or an independent parliament through the long protests of the 1990s. Bread riots and crowd actions in the 1970s and 1980s had at best been only able to slow the pace of IMF-led structural adjustment programmes. The resurgence of strike action among workers and civil servants in Egypt after 2004 had likewise only blunted privatization. The vast energies of Islamist movements had not been able to topple a single regime, with the major exception of non-Arab Iran in 1979. The assassination of Egyptian president Anwar Sadat by Islamists in 1981 had not sparked the anticipated popular uprising or dislodged the rule of the military. Many among the poor had hunkered down, thinking less of revolution or reform and more of migration opportunities abroad and survivalism at home. This meant 'weapons of the weak': the use of informal networks, the 'quiet encroachment of the ordinary' (Bayat 1997), and everyday modes of resistance in order to acquire goods and services and make claims on the propertied and powerful. These were interstitial manoeuvres in the gaps and fissures of the power structure that avoided overt, organized collective action, doctrine or programme.

In spite of this recent history, or perhaps because of it, the months following Ben Ali's fall on 14 January 2011 witnessed an outpouring of contentious mobilization which included mass uprisings in Egypt, Libya, Bahrain, Yemen and Syria and protests in many other parts of the region. In little more than a year, three more dictators fell or were dislodged, albeit in increasingly complicated ways, from power. On 11 February 2011, it was the turn of Hosni Mubarak of Egypt, president since 1981. On 20 October 2011, Colonel Gaddafi of Libya, president since 1969, was killed. On 27 February 2012, Ali Abdullah Saleh of Yemen, president since 1990, finally ceded power. In Bahrain there was repression; in Syria a civil war and the advent of a new, rival Islamic state; in Egypt, elections, a Muslim Brotherhood presidency, at least one more popular uprising (30 June 2013), quickly followed by a counter-revolutionary military coup (3 July 2013). In Tunisia, there were elections and forms of liberal democracy. In Saudi Arabia, around 8 per cent of the country's GDP was re-distributed to head off dissent by socio-economic concessions. Within and without the region, elites and regime incumbents remade their calculations, manoeuvred for influence, and sometimes sent in their militaries. In the aftermath of these uprisings, whether for better or for worse, nothing was quite the same as it had been.

Puzzles and goals

The 2011 Arab uprisings are only the most proximate reminder of the rationale for researching and writing a wide-ranging history of protest in the Middle East and North Africa (MENA). Even if they did not announce the new millennium, or cause a fundamental rupture with the past, they still serve to demonstrate that contentious politics is an important topic, raises a variety of puzzles, and intensifies the sense that not enough research has been carried out. They showed to a wider-audience than usual that it is not adequate, in writing the history of the region, to ignore contentious politics, or to cede the basic dynamics of change to external powers, securitocracies, ruling monarchies, the politics of ruling parties and their clients, or crony capitalism. They emphasized the revolutionary modern history of the region. And they vivified questions about the complex role played by contentious politics in the history of the MENA.

No straightforward narrative of progress and popular emancipation could be attached to the Arab uprisings as a whole. The mobilization already led by the end of March 2011 to a NATO military intervention in Libya (Prashad 2012). Even before then, Saudi Arabia had sent troops to crush the popular uprising in Bahrain. This was by no means the first time that protest movements had precipitated the arrival of foreign armies. Britain occupied Egypt, for example, in the wake of the 'Urabi movement in 1881–2. The uprisings on Mount Lebanon in 1821, 1840 and 1858–60 also brought in French imperial intervention. The repression wielded by the Syrian regime, which started to carry out air-strikes on its own population by the end of 2011, had also been seen before: in Hama, for example, in 1982. The Syrian president Asad's response to the uprising of 2011, meanwhile, bore similarities to the French response to the anti-colonial, patriotic armed struggle in Syria of 1925–7. On the other hand, there were surely gains in 2011. The fall of dictators was not nothing. Both Algeria and Saudi Arabia stepped up their rent-fuelled provision of socio-economic goods. There were political concessions in Algeria, Morocco and Jordan. Tunisia made progress to liberal democracy. Egypt for a time was under the control of no one, and a whole generation was politicized. Gains had been seen before in the region likewise. Nasserist and Ba'thist land reform, labour rights, and women's literacy and education pro-grammes in the 1950s and 1960s followed decades of protest over the need for social and economic reform. Hizbullah had managed to force Israel to terminate its illegal occupation of south Lebanon in May 2000. British and French imperialism had been dismantled in South Yemen (1967) and Algeria (1962) respectively in the wake of popular and nationalist armed struggles. In short, the Arab uprisings were a reminder that the role of contentious politics in the region had been complex. Neither a modernist narrative of progress, democracy, liberation and socio-economic redistribution, but nor some Orientalist story of chaos, violence and hatred. Historians, and social scientists, nonetheless, by no means had the kinds of histories at their disposal that had tried to pursue, on a broad-canvas, the complex role that contentious mobilization has played.

The Arab uprisings also vivified a subtle paradox in regard to the explanatory strategies scholars have used to understand contention:

how to explain, without explaining away? On the one hand, the episode of contention had exhibited innovation, creativity and surprise. New constituencies and new groups had undoubtedly been politicized and made a forceful entry into the political arena, for whatever reason. Football fans, and smugglers, for example, had not been seen on mass demonstrations and protests in the region for years. New sorts of identities and frames had been activated and constructed amid these new mobilizing projects. The idea of the people was suddenly infused with activist meaning. New claims were made to bread, dignity and freedom. New goals emerged: very few had called in any half-way realistic fashion for the 'overthrow of the regime' at least not in secular mode, and in mass protests, for many years. New modes of coordination, through the Internet, for example, and new forms of leaderless organizing had come into being. And there were new strategies and tactics, such as the determined occupation of major public squares and spaces, and pitched battles against the police. There were also amazing, immediate achievements, such as the fall of dictators, that no commentator or government had predicted. Innovation, moreover, was nothing new in the history of the region's contentious politics, as this book will make abundantly clear.

On the other hand, these innovations, as many pointed out, did not drop from the sky. New liberal protests had become more common in the region in recent times; new groups, such as educated students and liberal militant bloggers, had appeared, as well as liberal figures and movements contesting dynastic succession in putative republics. The labour movement had been moving *en masse* in Egypt since 2004. And, in Tunisia, the lower ranks of the major union, the UGTT, had kept up a steady stream of mobilization on social and economic rights. Indeed, perhaps the Arab uprisings were merely the expression of these trends? There are also many ways to explain these uprisings in more structural and contextual terms. The spread of the new media, including satellite television, Internet and mobile phones, the economic crisis, corruption, police violence, and so on, were invoked as factors which created grievances and provided reasons for mobilization.

There is a problem here. Genuine creativity on the one hand, and complete explanation on the other, add up to an explanatory paradox. How could creativity co-exist with such explanation? How can we explain innovation, without explaining it away? How can explanatory strategies be developed that do justice to forms of innovation, and figure out how to understand how they come about, without turning them into an epiphenomenon of something else? We note, of course, that explaining 2011 in terms of prior rounds of contestation is to beg the question. It leaves aside the question of what could explain those prior rounds of contestation. It also occludes the forms of innovation that did take place. The question revolves in part around the extent to which scholars should pay attention to initiative, agency, appropriation, attribution and the like, and to what extent to the solidity of pre-existing forms of organization, structure, objective opportunity and so on. The resort to 'anti-explanation' and the construction of 'the lived experience of the moment' (Kurzman 2004), however provocative and interesting, is ultimately an unsatisfactory answer to this conundrum, because protests happen in inherited contexts, and are not completely random, unfathomable or absolutely unpredictable. If so, then what explanatory strategies exist in which creativity can be allowed for? How can one avoid explanations for the new which resort to one form or another of immanence – i.e. the idea that the result was already lurking in complete form somewhere in the start conditions? How could we be surprised, but not perpetually so? How can creativity be satisfactorily situated? This is an important conundrum, highlighted by the debates over the Arab uprisings, but never satisfactorily resolved. It is a puzzle that has been lurking for some time in the long history of the region's contention.

A third and final question was vivified by the uprisings. The leaderless, relatively spontaneous, and even horizontalist organizations of the urban youth scored an impressive success in evading security services and organizing protests, and helped to bring down a regime or two. On the other hand, their capacities and powers dissipated rapidly, at least in Egypt in the aftermath of the uprising, and pyramidal-type organizations, such as the Muslim Brotherhood, made major gains in subsequent elections. Then, partly because the Brotherhood, anxious to secure its place in the state, had abandoned popular mobilization and the revolutionary coalition to its fate during 2011, it was in turn left without allies when it needed them on the streets in the wake of the 3 July 2013 military coup. These events certainly implied that spontaneity, informalism and so on were no panacea. More importantly, they brought to the fore basic questions about the role of leadership, organization and mobilization in the study of social movements. The question of leadership can be posed in relation to mobilizations all over the region: it is hard, for example, to explain the prolongation of the first *intifada* in the Occupied Palestinian Territories in 1987–1991 without taking into account the way leaderships mobilized amid the initial uprising; conversely, why was the Egyptian uprising of January 1977 so short-lived? Perhaps this had something to do with the reluctance of the Left and liberals to engage in building up mobilizing structures. To what extent, in fact, have leaderships in the region, and the characteristics, strategies and tactics of the mobilizing projects with which they are associated, played a role in their own successes and failures? Can leadership be safely ignored in the face of other forces? How can leadership be understood without recourse to the unsatisfactory and voluntarist reliance on the existence of thinkers and heroic individuals?

These puzzles can be summarized in the basic questions posed in this book. First, what contribution did contentious mobilization make to overall patterns of historical change? Second, to what extent can we speak of innovation and creativity in relation to contentious mobilization? If there is creativity, then where does it come from, and how can it be characterized, understood and situated? And, third, to what extent did the nature of what I will call mobilizing projects, complete with forms of leadership, organization, identities and principles, goals, strategies and tactics, determine the course and outcomes of contentious mobilization? The main goal of this study is to explore and shed light on these three basic questions. The book also aims to gather together a rich-array of new and quality scholarship, leavened by primary research, to provide a wide-ranging introduction to the important but under-studied history of contention in the MENA from the late eighteenth century to the present.

In answering these questions, the book makes a pitch for the existence of unruly, transgressive and creative contentious politics in the history of the MENA. At certain points there have been new entrants into the not-fully-policeable boundaries of the political field; these new entrants take political matters into their own hands, and, once they get organized, push forward a mobilizing project that is innovative above all in relation to the collective subject it proposes. In contrast with top-down and power-institutional histories, the book aims to explicate the many ways in which protest has mattered in the political struggles and dynamics involved in the making of the modern region. Against conventional views, the book aims to show that contentious

mobilization is not merely about the reactions of Muslims and Arabs
to the impact of the West, an epiphenomenon of socio-economic
change, or an expression of prior processes of colonizing discursive
inscription. To do justice to the role played by agency, this book aims
to show that the dynamics and vectors of transgressive mobilization
owe a good deal to ideas and intellectual labour, translocal appropriation, normative commitments, leadership strategies and contingent
interactions. Against purely constructionist and agency-laden
accounts, however, the book suggests that transgression does not come
out of nowhere, but above all finds enabling conditions in the failures
and weaknesses of hegemonic incorporation, the dessication of sites of
articulation, and the contraction of existing forms of hegemony at the
level of the political community as a whole. Borrowing in unconven-
tional ways from the Italian thinker, Antonio Gramsci, the book steers
between objectivist historical sociology and subjectivist social constructionism to offer a new history of the MENA, couched in the
dynamics of hegemonic contestation.

Survey histories

No wide-ranging history of protests, social and political movements,
uprisings and revolution in the region in modern times exists. Edmund
Burke's research pioneered this kind of work (Burke 1990) but he
never wrote a book-length survey of the sort attempted here. Readers
will find much that is complementary in our approaches, but probably
conclude that the analysis presented here breaks with the structuralist
historical sociological tradition that is so vital in Burke's work. Joel
Beinin has offered the only survey history of workers and peasants, an
invaluable resource (Beinin 2001). The present study aims to be a lot
more inclusive of a wide variety of collective action, and to pursue a
much narrower thematic focus on mobilization, leadership, identities,
principles and interactions in the political field, as opposed to political
economy, class formation and the like. The overlap between the two
books is therefore not that great. This book constructs a history of
contentious politics which is much more acculturated and political
than Beinin's. Tripp's landmark study of resistance in the region,
The Power and the People (Tripp 2013), situates contestation firmly
in structures of domination; it considers not just economic, but also
coercive, administrative, gendered and discursive power; it offers a rich

exploration of the intersection of contestation with space, performance, communication and art. In contrast with Tripp, the analytic core of the present book, in order to sidestep too heavy an emphasis on the sometimes amorphous figure of power, is rooted less in domination/resistance, and more in hegemonic articulation/re-articulation. This book is more concerned with change over time, its structure is more historical than thematic, it is more 'eventful', foregrounds specific leaderships, what they believed, and what they did, and it covers a much longer period.

Many of the other surveys of the history of the region, regardless of their other strengths and riches, do not give a strong sense of the role played by contentious mobilization. Diplomatic and political histories (Holt 1966; Lewis 1961; Vatikiotis 1969; Yapp 1987, 1991) tend to see politics as a matter for Europeans, diplomats, officials and modernizing elites. There may be outbursts of local popular anger from time to time, but these are mere bush-fires in a landscape otherwise carved out from above. Holt's key study of the Mahdi of Sudan in the 1880s, from which this study draws much, was an exception to this (Holt 1970). Other important surveys of Arab politics, such as those that focus on modernization and political legitimacy (Bill and Leiden 1979; Hudson 1977), while suggesting that modernization unleashed a wide variety of social demands, do not focus on those demands or related social or political movements, but rather on rulers' capacity to engage in political development in order to keep order. While Albert Hourani's well-known history of the Arab peoples pays serious attention to social and economic history, popular contentious politics is more or less absent (Hourani 1991), just as it is in his intellectual history (Hourani 1962) and seminal work on the politics of the notables (Hourani 1994). More recent political histories of the region certainly give a fuller view of social forces (Cleveland 2004; Gelvin 2005; Kamrava 2005), but they do not explore the role of contentious politics in any systematic way. In survey analyses of state power and political economy (Ayubi 1995; Luciani 1990; Owen 1981, 2004a; Richards and Waterbury 1990), popular politics is almost invisible. These studies tend towards a 'hard' power, institutional view in which hegemony, consent and contention are residual matters compared to concentrations of military, economic and political power. Agency became much more important in Owen's later work (Owen 2012) but it was that of elites learning from each other to construct ruling systems.

Orientalism and neo-Orientalism

There is a long Orientalist and now neo-Orientalist tradition of writing about protest in the MENA. After 1945, this tradition gradually migrated away from the university as its colonial assumptions of civilizational and racial superiority, and its ethnocentrism, exceptionalism and cultural essentialism, became ever harder to defend among serious researchers (Lockman 2004: 66–98). Nonetheless, this tradition is important, because blended and modified, it still has a powerful presence among pundits, think-tanks and the media, and enjoyed a revival in universities, especially in security and terrorism studies, during the War on Terror in the 2000s (Lockman 2004: 215–67).

Nineteenth- and twentieth-century colonial officials, sometimes those directly involved in repressing anti-colonial protest, set the tone. According to Mercier, for example, a figure high in the French political establishment in the late nineteenth century, the mass-based Algerian rising of 1871 was simply about the personal opportunism of a key leader, Al-Muqrani, who was styled as 'a rebel, an ingrate, and a traitor' (Mercier 1901: 31–2). Or, the millenarian uprising of the Mahdi in Sudan in the early 1880s was seen by Sir Francis Wingate (1861–1953), a highly decorated British colonial official, and Governor General of Sudan after 1899, as being about a 'dangerous group of religious fanatics out to conquer "infidel" countries' (cited in Tschacher 2011: 74). For British colonial officials in Egypt in the 1920s, liberal nationalists, most of whom were land-owners, Pashas or lawyers, and sought to achieve independence by legal means, were simply known as 'Extremists'. In Libya in the 1920s, the Italian general Graziani saw the inhabitants of Cyrenaica as little more than beasts (Atkinson 2000). During his attempted conquest of Egypt (1798–1801), Napoleon told one of his generals:

The Turks can only be led by the greatest severity. Every day I cut off five or six heads in the streets of Cairo ... It is necessary to take a tone that will cause them to obey, and to obey, for them, is to fear (Cole 2007: 104–5)

It was a violent trope that was to echo in the corridors of power from the France of elusive Oriental glory to the Israel of the Iron Wall (Shlaim 2000).

The idea that protestors were backward, uncivilized, chaotic, irrational, violent, opportunistic, fanatical, recalcitrant and dangerous has been a staple of the Orientalist and neo-Orientalist scholarship. Bowden, for example, saw the uprising in Palestine in the 1930s as a mixture of the medieval and the modern fought by 'feudatory retinues of bandit marauders only marginally inspired and motivated by loosely held, inchoate notions of liberation and *jihad*'. It involved a 'set of smaller wars', often of the fratricidal variety, and lacking 'a single, binding political objective'. It was parochial, immature, politically 'under-developed', and lacking even 'moderately sophisticated structures'. Its peasant protagonists were 'reactionary', and won adherents through 'intimidation at the point of a revolver', just – and here Bowden quotes a British colonial source to make his point – '[a]s in Ireland in the worst days after the [First World] war or in Bengal' (Bowden 1975: 147–9). Orientalist tropes made surprise cameo appearances in more advanced scholarship. Tignor's introduction to a translation of one of the texts of the famous Egyptian chronicler Al-Jabarti, for example, characterized the resistance to Napoleon's invasion of Egypt in 1798 in general as a matter of a sometimes 'aggressive', 'recalcitrant population'. In Cairo in October, 'hot-headed recalcitrants' supposedly 'filled the population with rumor and inaccurate information' (Jabarti 1993: 6, 8–9).

During the Cold War, Orientalism was often blended with a psycho-social version of modernization theory (Lockman 2004: 133–47). Movements of the Left in this view were irrational and hostile threats to order and stability. They were often explained in terms of the psychological strains of rapid modernization with which the inhabitants of the region clearly could not cope. In such views, the only constructive role was played by new, aspirant middle classes and modernizing, authoritarian militaries (Halpern 1963; Huntington 1968; Lerner 1958; Perlmutter 1970; Salem 1994). In this context, Muslims were often seen as submissive to authority and thus as useful allies for Washington (Sadowski 1993). This view shaped action, such as in Iran in 1953, when the CIA made links with conservative Shi'a clergy (Abrahamian 2001). In the 1990s and 2000s, the view of Muslims as submissive switched with the prevailing political wind, as Muslims were increasingly identified as terrorists (Said 1997). Muslims did not so much protest but 'rage', and they did so because of fanaticism, resentment, self-pity, sexual repression, or hatred of Western-style freedoms (Lewis 1990). Huntington suggested that Islam had 'bloody borders', and that

Muslims, as a matter of civilizational conflict, were bound to fight the Judeo-Christian West (Huntington 1997).

Fascinating as a case study for the analysis of the relationship between culture and imperialism (Said 1994), and occasionally yielding some usable information, Orientalism nevertheless does not contribute any theoretical content to the study of contentious politics. Its fundamental interpretive, as opposed to normative or political, flaws are rooted in its inflexible, ahistorical and homogenizing cultural and civilizational essentialism and exceptionalism. Orientalists see protest as part of the stirring up of ancient prejudice, but seem only themselves to express a prejudice constructed in modern times. They identify violence in the Other, blaming the victims (Said and Hitchens 1988), while whitewashing from the figure of 'Western civilization' of all traces of such violence. No history of settler colonialism, racial slavery or industrial genocide seems to disturb this view. There is no ontological or explanatory value to the notion of Oriental, Muslim, Arab or Middle Eastern contentious mobilization. Tilly showed, for example, that terror tactics have been used in many countries, by a wide variety of groups, in and out of government, for a wide variety of reasons (Tilly 2004), and that the exceptionalist and essentialist insistence by terrorologists that terrorism was a separate ontological category, and terrorists were a breed apart, deserving their own special mode of explanation, was indefensible. Other detailed research has made the same point in regard to the MENA (Beinin 2003; Halliday 2000: 71–87). In the MENA, there are certainly forms of 'cultural-historical specificity' (Zubaida 1993: 179), understood outside the essentialist choice between a universal West or an exceptional Orient. These specificities and diverse histories, like that of Christians, whiteness, or of, say, France (Zeldin 1997), are not determined by some transcendental, historical essence, impossible to define concretely, and impervious to history, context, power, economics, class, society, gender and contestation. The social movements of the MENA past and present, as a matter of empirical fact, have never been hermetically sealed from other influences, regions and connections, from Maoism to liberalism to Islamic revivalism.

Finally, it is worth noting the basic interpretive weakness in the distinctively Orientalist brand of exceptionalism. If, as Orientalism holds, the West is exceptional – progressive, freedom-loving, peaceful, open and so on – and if, as it also holds, the East is exceptional – decayed as a civilization, backward, freedom-loathing, violence-prone, closed and so on – then how could any Westerner purport to develop an interpretive framework capable of studying such a radically different civilization or culture? The Man of the West would always have to be 'discomposed', in Conrad's word, fumbling around in the dark, and unable to develop a satisfactory set of methods for something that was, at root, an inscrutable 'Chinese' puzzle (cf. Sartre 2001: 18). Civilizational exceptionalism falls on its own sword. By proposing basic epistemological, onto-logical and etiological distinctions between Eastern contention and Western contention, it accepts its own failure to understand. In many ways, this is the key to this discourse: much like a long-line of colonial would-be conquerors, it endlessly repeats its own exasper-ated incomprehension. As Napoleon expostulated amid his failed conquest of Egypt, 1798–1801, who were these people (in this case inhabitants of Alexandria) who must be blind, ignorant or 'extremely presumptuous' to resist (cited in Cole 2007: 23)? Such a failure to understand, a gesture that closely shadows the morphing of mean-ingful explanation into cultural essentialism, is no basis for the understanding of protest.

Marxism and historical sociology

Historians and social scientists influenced by Marxism and historical sociology have contributed the most substantial body of research on protest in the MENA. This tradition roots protest in the development of capitalism, the onset of modernity, urbanization, the spread of new communications, state formation, colonialism, new forms of property rights, the rise of new social classes, material interests and socio-economic change.

Joel Beinin, for example, explained growing protests in Egypt in the 1930s and 1940s in the following terms:

elements of the social impasse ... became sharper and more persistent: increasing unemployment among the urban intelligentsia, continuing agrar-ian crisis due to concentration of agricultural land in the hands of a small number of large land-owners and increasing population pressure on the land, rapid urbanization, accelerated growth of an industrial working class, and intensification of the industrial conflict that had appeared in the first decade of the twentieth century. The socially conservative Wafd proved as incapable of resolving these issues as it was of achieving Egyptian national liberation (Beinin 1988: 207).

Here the lead note is socio-economic change and the rise of new social classes. Doumani's discussion of peasant protest in nineteenth-century Palestine echoes this kind of analysis. Peasants evinced a 'nascent class consciousness' (Doumani 1995: 180), and their protests were rooted above all in the 'slow dissolution of patronage ties between peasants and long-time ruling sub-district chiefs, as well as the transformation of the latter into agents of urban interests' (Doumani 1995: 172).

Laroui's explanation for Morocco's rural revolts of the nineteenth century ultimately involves 'general impoverishment, itself resulting from the pressure of foreign economy' (Laroui 1977: 158–60). Edmund Burke's rich account of pre-colonial protest in Morocco concurs:

The incorporation of Morocco into the modern world-system produced unprecedented strains upon the society and resulted in widespread movements of protest and resistance. This book is a study of the ways in which Moroccans coped with a time of rapid changes and social disruption (Burke 1976: xi).

Batatu's work on Iraq and Syria saw transformations in property rights and the rise of capitalist forms of accumulation as the most basic processes lying behind new forms of protest. Class formation accounts for a good deal of its political content. Hence, 'the triumph in Syria of advanced ideas on the peasant question' resulted, at bottom, from 'the coming to the political forefront of military elements of peasant origin' (Batatu 1999: 38). Abdallah Hanna's work on the labour movement in Syria likewise takes class and capitalism as the most important explanatory categories (Hanna 1973). This is the conventional view in studies of labour protest in the region in general (Beinin and Lockman 1998; de Smet 2012a; Quataert 2006).

Abrahamian's seminal work on Iran roots the revolution in socio-economic development of the 1960s and 1970s, arguing that the forces unleashed thereby eventually came into contradiction with an under-developed political system (Abrahamian 1982). Cole sees the 'Urabi movement of 1881–2 as explicable in terms of 'social mobilization': i.e. the 'movement of the population into cities, the building of connective links such as railroads and telegraph lines, increases in literacy, and the rise of privately printed newspapers' (Cole 1999: 110). Social mobilization did not necessarily cause protest in this account, but it greatly facilitated co-ordinated, revolutionary action at the national level. For Al-Khafaji, the age of revolution in the Arab world, between the 1940s and the 1970s, came about as a result of the crumbling and impasse of the *ancien* régime under the pressure of capitalist development, rural–urban migration, and the break-up of semi-feudal forms of land tenure (Al-Khafaji 2004). Halliday's work explained protest in the Arabian peninsula in the 1950s and 1960s in terms of the combined and uneven development of capitalism (Halliday 1974). For Achcar, the Arab uprisings of 2011 stemmed from fettered development: contradictions between economic development and the relations of production (chiefly the state and the law) (Achcar 2013a).

This body of research is a major challenge to Orientalism, and forms the most sustained contribution to the study of protest in the MENA. Historical sociology is surely persuasive in founding its analysis not on cultural essences but on struggles and contradictions. It is convincing, moreover, to situate protest within unequal power relations, in a landscape laden with material and strategic interests, and within political communities which are both stratified internally according to access to goods (wealth, power and status) of near-universal desire, and positioned in larger forms of supra-state political economy. This research has also paid useful attention to the place of elite political failures, the importance of organization and strategy in regards to mobilization, and the role of the state.

Nonetheless, historical sociology has often suffered from a Eurocentric teleological modernism, and structural, processual, material and class determinism (cf. Chalcraft 2005b; Lockman 1994b). The content, form, direction and even consequences of contentious mobilization are too often given in advance by the modernist teleology: there is the coming into being of true class consciousness (in the tradition of 1917), or the gradually emerging liberal protest of the proto-bourgeoisie (in the tradition of 1789). Protest is too often conceived as an epiphenomenon of capitalist development or socio-economic modernization – explained away as much as explained. Subjects are expected to take up certain pre-established positions within the larger social formation rooted in their material interests or class position. Cultural factors are either ignored, or referenced *ad hoc* (Zubaida 1993: 64–82). This is one of the reasons why definitions of social movements, contentious politics, or even 'protest', are missing from this historiography

(Barker *et al.* 2013: 23). Protestors can react to their situation, or develop their awareness and sophistication in regard to their predicament, such is the meaning of agency, but they can do little to define creatively the situation (except more 'correctly', as Lenin used to say) or propose creative, alternative diagnoses of their forms of oppression or the solutions to it. The importance of the specific characteristics of mobilizing projects, of forms of hegemonic incorporation, and the explanatory role of leadership, normative commitments, and ideas is heavily occluded. Materialism makes Islamism difficult to grasp outside of some form of exceptionalism: that it is, unlike other protests, about opportunism, the sly support of states, monies from the Gulf, or it simply represents a traditional and even ultimately irrational recrudescence. Hence the insistence by important scholars such as Achcar on the term 'fundamentalism' (Achcar 2013b: 40–67). This book, while drawing heavily on the riches of historical sociology, strives to eliminate teleological modernism, materialism and class essentialism from its study of protest.

Cultural history, gender, transnationalism and power/culture

Cultural history, the study of gender, transnational approaches, and work on power/culture have all made an important impact on the study of protest in the MENA since the 1990s. Research paying attention to subjectivity, representation, cultural creativity, identities, frames and principles has had important consequences (Tripp 2013: 219–309). In the light of this work, for example, it is no longer justifiable to read Tanyus Shahin's movement on Mount Lebanon in 1858–60 purely in terms of political economy (Makdisi 2000), to depict the rise of nationalism as a kind of inevitable teleological excrescence of political modernity (Gelvin 1998), to see Islamist protest in Saudi Arabia as a simple extremism (Lacroix 2011), or to grasp Algerian resistance in the nineteenth century in terms of culture-free demographic and/or socio-economic change (Clancy-Smith 1994). Cultural history has shown that contestation is laden with principles and identities, and that it involves a crucial degree of social and political construction. Culture can be incorporated into the study of protest in the MENA without entrapment in Orientalist cultural essentialism.

Gathering strength since the 1990s, the study of gender, the social and cultural construction of masculinities and femininities, adds a vital layer to this (Tripp 2013: 176–218). Womanhood has always been at stake in the making of protest and quiescence, whether among the tobacco and silk workers of Lebanon (Abisaab 2009; Khater 1996), the militants of Hizbullah (Deeb 2006) or of the DFLP in the Occupied Palestinian Territories (Hasso 2005), among women's activists in Egypt in the 1990s (Ali 2000), in the construction of nationalism in inter-war Egypt (Abu-Lughod 1998; Baron 2007), or in protests over political representation and social rights in Syria in the 1940s (Thompson 2000). The construction of male status honour played a role in the contention surrounding the Lebanese civil war (Johnson 2002). It helps to explain the impact of repression during the first year or two of the Palestinian *intifada* (Peteet 1994). It sheds light on Egyptian nationalism in the inter-war period (Wilson 2011). This research ensures that a gender-blind approach to politics in general, or, worse, an approach that assumed the maleness of the subject of protest, is no longer possible.

Third, in the 1990s and 2000s, there was a marked increase in different forms of transnational history, reflecting a sensitivity, amid the practice and theory of globalization, to the connections between sub-state actors across national and imperial borders that shape contentious politics (Chalcraft 2011a; Chamberlin 2012; Khuri-Makdisi 2010; Kurzman 2008; Takriti 2013). Palestinian nationalism, Khalili shows, was indebted to Third Worldism (Khalili 2007a); Egypt's labour movement, Lockman demonstrates, drew on European imaginaries of social class (Lockman 1994a); Louër linked politicized Shi'ism in the Persian Gulf, and the face-to-face ties that helped to transmit it across borders, to the seminaries of Najaf, Karbala and Qom (Louër 2008a). This work greatly develops historians' sense of the regional and international political, cultural and ideological contexts in which contentious politics plays out. It underlines the important ways in which transnational connections shape protest. And, considering that none of the best of this work gives up on the importance of domestic and national politics, it broaches important debates about the extent to which such connections across borders matter in explanatory terms. The history offered in this book pays considerable attention to 'transnational' and translocal connections across imperial, regional and national borders in the contentious politics of the MENA.

Finally, the emphasis placed by some theorists on the power/ knowledge nexus, the importance of the control of information, and

the importance of cultural production and immaterial labour in late
capitalism (Castells 2000; Hardt and Negri 2004; Jameson 1992;
Mandel 1975; Touraine 1971), has stimulated work relating protest
to discourse, information and the media. From the late 1990s, more
attention was paid to the new media in the region, Internet, mobile
phones and satellite television (Lynch 2007). Some have gone so far as
to argue that it was the 'networks of outrage and hope' developed
outside of state control, on the Internet above all, that could explain
the Arab uprisings of 2011 (Castells 2012). These approaches have
generated important insights, but are limited by their grand, processual
and teleological explanatory core. Just as in theories of modernization
and capitalist development, to link contentious politics fundamentally
to some systemic property or unfolding process is to see it as an
outcome of some prior set of primarily socio-economic determinations,
as usual rooted in some 'advanced', normatively approved, West-
initiated development. Unevenness, creativity, indeterminacy, local
agency, social construction, dynamic interactions and reversals are
thus occluded in ways that this history finds problematic.

A discursively determinist route is taken by a significant group of
more Foucauldian theorists who see discourse as part of an overwhelming mechanism of social control rather than as a stimulant to protest
and contention (Massad 2001; Mitchell 1988; Shakry 2006, 2007;
Wedeen 1999). These authors have generated key insights regarding
the discursive construction of subjects. But where protest merely reflects
colonizing discursive inscription, contradiction, struggles over power
relations and subaltern agency are occluded. A focus on the languages
of the nineteenth-century Egyptian *effendiyya*, for example, even when
coupled with a great sensitivity to the erasure of popular voice, wound
up ignoring that popular voice (Gasper 2009). Brower's book on the
French 'civilizing mission' in Algeria, for all its sophistication, is so
focused on colonial discourse, and on ambiguities in regards to resistance, that initiatives from below are erased, or even start to reappear in
the guises through which their French interrogators saw them, as
violent and superstitious (Brower 2009). In much of this discursively
determinist literature, the subaltern ends up speechless indeed
(cf. Sarkar 2000; Spivak 1988). Sophistication in matters of discourse
and narrative can in fact be combined with the study of peripheral
groups, agonistic contest, violence and political economy as Gilsenan's
masterful historical anthropology shows (Gilsenan 1996).

Noorani's focus on re-articulation points against discursive determinism, and has informed the approach taken here, where the assumption is that subject formation is a contentious and constructed process (Noorani 2007, 2010). Determinists have in practice bracketed the fact that the discursive approach is premised on a postulate of revolutionary agency. Michel Foucault, no less than Edward Said, was inspired by the revolutionary desire to get beyond, unpick and deconstruct the normalizing discourses they both did so much to uncover. In other words, the original impulses of discourse theory actually lead back, eventually, to a reconsideration of the significance of political creativity and the study of resistance. If not, then where do such revolutionary impulses come from, and what do they add up to? It is not only elite, deconstructionist intellectuals who are entitled to pierce the veil of discursive mystification and thereby monopolize the history of contentious creativity. Discursive determinism is caught up in a contradiction of its own making: how to deconstruct without a place to stand? How to construct amid an ever-receding horizon of the real?

Classical social movement theory

A distinctive sub-field within social science, social movement theory (SMT), took shape in the United States and Europe in the 1970s. Rather like historical sociologists faced, in Middle East Studies, with Orientalism and modernization theory, social movement theorists premised their work on a sharp criticism of existing exceptionalist and conservative theory. Scholars of collective behaviour in the 1950s and 1960s, drawing on notions of the mob and the 'madness' of crowds (Le Bon 2014 [1896]), understood protest in terms of deviance and group emotion (Blumer 1951), social dysfunction and integrative failure (Smelser 1962), and/or frustration-aggression stemming from perceived relative deprivation (Gurr 1970). Such psychology-oriented structural strain theories were heavily and convincingly criticized as mechanistic in positing a one-to-one correlation between strain and protest, and as viewing protestors in exceptionalist terms as irrational, deviant and emotionally and psychologically disturbed (Edwards 2014: 10–41; McAdam 1982: 5–20).

Social movement theory aimed to eschew mechanistic determinism by seeking to account for the passage from grievances, apathy and fragmentation, conditions that were said to be widespread, and instances of coordinated action for change, which were not. Over time, social movement theorists built up, not an overarching theory, but a series of concepts with which to tackle this key conundrum in ways that depicted protest in rational terms. Broad social change processes fed into the existence of three key 'intervening variables': (1) mobilizing structures, wherein resources were coordinated and made use of by activists who built up organizations capable of sustaining mobilization; (2) more or less objective political opportunities, in which incentives for action were raised or lowered by factors such as the relative institutional openness of the polity, the relative level of repression, the existence or absence of elite allies, the level of international pressure and so on; (3) cultural framing processes: referring to the capacity of activists to link their cause to frames that resonated with wider constituencies. These three factors fed into repertoires of collective action, the embedded and historically learned means by which claims were made and action pursued, while all of the above were linked together by contentious interaction (McAdam *et al.* 1996). Over time, these intervening variables have been supplemented by others, but the basic puzzle (accounting for the gap between grievance and action) and explanatory form (specifying intervening variables) has shown considerable continuity.

These concepts started to have an impact on Middle East Studies in the 1980s and 1990s (Burke 1990; Denoeux 1993; Ibrahim 1982). The scholarship reached a certain critical mass in the 2000s (Clark 2004; Hafez 2003; Rosefsky Wickham 2002; Schwedler 2006; White 2002; Wiktorowicz 2004), provoking important debates and showing how protest can be re-described and compared in sometimes interesting ways. The basic concepts of SMT are often, but not always, useful orienting and descriptive devices. Organization, resonance, and links to the opportunities and threats extant in the political context are regularly at stake in the construction of transgressive collective action, and the idea of repertoire of contention can often help describe the set of learned means by which people protest in given contexts. The importance of these concepts should not be jettisoned in a rush to constructionism.

The overall problem, however, is that these concepts do not get us very far, while they are too often treated as if they do. The most widely recognized issue is that the explanatory power of classical SMT is in almost constant danger of being overstated: its basic concepts are criticized for objectivism, determinism, structuralism and rationalism (Goodwin and Jasper 1999). Where objectivism reigns, cultural frames resonate, and organizations are built up like businesses, creative dynamics are occluded. Description is presumed to be explanation. Yet, all of SMT's key concepts beg anterior causal questions. Openings and closures in levels of political opportunity have indeterminate and ambiguous effects on contentious actors (Opp 2009). Likewise, formal mobilizing structures, as they acquire vested interests and a stake in the *status quo*, may be just as likely to conform, and to eschew transgression and contention as they are to pursue it. A similar stricture must be applied to the concept of cultural framing where it is used in strategic and instrumental ways: when cultural frames resonate widely, then to what extent are they contentious? In short, the creative excess that is especially present in transgressive forms of contention is occluded by approaches rooted in classical social movement theory.

The other basic problem is less remarked, but no less important. It has to do with a fundamental weakness in dealing with power relations, context and history. The concept of 'political opportunity', for example, is either too narrowly defined, or it is stretched too broadly and vaguely to cope with the whole complex question of the external environment in which movements happen. This history finds a wide variety of reasons for mobilization rooted in contexts. These reasons have not just to do with political opportunity but also with economic, social and cultural forms. The core of the problem is classical SMT's deeply problematic insistence, based on an internalization of the free-rider problem bequeathed by a problematic methodological individualism, that tensions and grievances are everywhere and thus can be discounted as a basis for contentious mobilization. Comparing imprisoned and tortured Islamists with high-ranking members of statist unions, or Palestinians under occupation with recipients of *rentier* largesse in Kuwait, or oasis dwellers facing large-scale colonial violence in nineteenth-century Algeria with careerist technocrats in Egypt, one is forced to conclude that tensions, injustices and grievances are not everywhere of the same kind, depth or quality and cannot be treated as if they are. History and power relations count. The denial of national self-determination, for example, was a recurrent reason for mobilization in the twentieth-century Middle East. In this sense, the problem for classical SMT is not structuralism at all, but a lack of a sufficient attention to the depth and complexity of structure, history and context.

Contentious mobilization: contained and transgressive

While problems of a-contextuality and descriptiveness remain in more recent theories of contentious politics, this book makes some use, especially for purposes of definition, of the dynamic, relational and socially constructionist approach to social movements laid out by some of the founding figures of SMT in their book *Dynamics of Contention* (DOC) (McAdam *et al.* 2001). Conventional SMT is criticized here for its objectivism, and for a too-static and hydraulic account of mechanisms and sequences. DOC stresses social appropriation and the activation of informal networks rather than the bureaucratic pre-existence of organizational resources; it delves into the perception and *attribution* of political opportunity, rather than the objective political openings and closures that characterize conventional SMT; it gives more weight to the generative capacities of the continuous processes of re-interpretation that accompany and are intertwined with all contentious episodes, rather than focusing on the strategic cultural framing by established movement actors. These are important creative vectors, describing pathways of change, which we will see on many occasions in the book that follows.

DOC also pays more attention to the interpretations and actions of those outside of the movement, and to the role of elite collective action, and the interactions between polity members, bystanders and challengers: this is a useful approach because it takes the whole, interacting political field as its referent, seeing contentious politics as a sub-set of collective political struggle in general. DOC considers the importance of the improvised evolution of contentious performances and takes matters like sequencing and 'eventful politics' into more account, pointing to the ways in which alignments and splits can sometimes emerge not from pre-existing vested interests, but from the dynamics of contentious interaction itself. This point is of major importance in grasping both contingency, as well as understanding the generative capacities of contentious politics. DOC pays attention to the role of heightened uncertainty in episodes of contention, which brings new or reinforces existing actors, shakes the *status quo* and causes calculations and diagnoses to change on all sites, causing new contests which would not otherwise have taken place.

DOC started to have an impact in Middle East Studies in the 2010s (Beinin and Vairel 2013; Ketchley 2014). Emphasis on informal modes of organization has a clear rationale in authoritarian contexts where formal and legal overt opposition is very difficult to sustain; this emphasis also chimes with the way informal networks played an important role in the initial mobilization of the 2011 uprisings in both Tunisia (Allal 2013; Hmed 2012) and Syria (Leenders 2013). In addition, aside from the supposedly explanatory concept of mechanisms, DOC resonates with the 'anti-explanation' that Kurzman put forward for the 'unthinkable' Iranian revolution of 1979 (Kurzman 2004), which occurred without a prior state breakdown. Here, all determinist and objectivist causes are rejected as the false wisdom of hindsight, retroactive prediction is eschewed, and unpredictability, informality and confusion are stressed. Kurzman recommends that scholars try to re-construct the lived experience of the moment before rushing to offer one or other deterministic theory. There is no doubt that constructionist approaches have started to point towards important dynamics in the MENA that are occluded in more determinist and mechanical forms of social movement theory.

From the perspective of this study, social constructionism is vital because it draws attention to the existence of creativity in contentious mobilization. For example, new interpretations are expected, along with the creation of new organizations, and constructionism allows for the adventure implicit in the idea of a perceived, rather than a real, political opportunity, and takes into account the potency of political interactions and unpredictability. The DOC programme, for all its problems in regards to context and explanation, helps us to define and describe the moments of becoming and the constitution of new political subjects that play such an important role in contentious politics: the key here is the notion of transgressive mobilization.

McAdam, Tarrow and Tilly make a useful contrast between contentious politics and more transacted and negotiated forms of the political:

Is all of politics contentious? According to a strict reading of our definition, certainly not. Much of politics the majority ... consists of ceremony, consultation, bureaucratic process, collection of information, registration of events, and the like. Reporting for military service, registering to vote, paying taxes, attending associational meetings, implementing policies, enforcing laws, performing administrative work, reading newspapers, asking officials for favours, and similar actions constitute the bulk of political life; they usually involve little if any collective contention. Much of politics takes place in the internal social relations of a party, bureau, faction, union, community, or interest group and involves no collective public struggle whatsoever. The contentious politics that concerns us is episodic rather than continuous, occurs in public, involves interaction between makers of claims and others, is recognized by those others as bearing on their interests, and brings in government as mediator, target, or claimant (McAdam *et al.* 2001: 5).

This study follows this way of nominally identifying contentious politics. Such a domain is marked out by contentious action and claimmaking that bears on the interests of others and is episodic, public, collective and enacted in the political field in interaction with political authority. There is an analytically useful distinction between the routinized, transacted and negotiated politics of those with regular access to the polity, a politics that remains non-public and scheduled within the corridors of power, and a contentious politics which includes claimants excluded from routinized decision-making within powerful institutions, and becomes public, episodic, and involves mobilizing features that challenge, disrupt or influence highly formalized and routinized political transactions. The public face of transacted politics is a mere façade, a matter of PR intended to reinforce immanent morale and secure pre-existing agenda; the public face of contentious politics, by contrast, makes mobilizing appeals which are supposed to influence meaningfully the agenda and power relations in play.

This book makes use of a modified version of DOC's important distinction between 'contained' and 'transgressive' contention. This distinction was dropped, somewhat confusingly, in Tarrow and Tilly's next framework-delineating volume (Tarrow and Tilly 2012), but then reappeared in the 2015 revised edition. Contained contention is more institutionalized (McAdam *et al.* 2001: 6). 'Contained contention is waged by constituted (that is, self-defined and publicly recognized) political actors' (p. 315). Crucially, in contained contention, 'all parties to the conflict were previously established as constituted political actors' (p. 7). Contained mobilization involves what can be usefully conceived of as the politics of pre-constituted actors. Such actors are less innovative in regard to the extent to which they challenge or innovate in regard to existing networks of associational life, norms of political conduct, the distribution of material interests, and dominant discourses. These projects initiate a politics of articulation: they engage in recombination via processes of mobilization which add to, rather than fundamentally alter, existing subjects and agents.

Transgressive contention, on the other hand, 'commonly introduces previously unorganized or apolitical actors into public conflict processes' (p. 315). In transgressive contention 'at least some parties to the conflict are newly self-identified political actors, and/or ... at least some parties employ innovative collective action' (p. 8). Transgressive contention

incorporates claims, selects objects of claims, includes collective self-representations, and/or adopts means that are either unprecedented or forbidden within the regime in question (p. 8).

To stress transgressive contention is to lay emphasis on actions that are 'sporadic rather than continuous, bring new actors into play, and/or involve innovative claim making' (p. 8). The vectors of transgressive mobilization can be grasped in terms of innovation in regards to identities, principles, goals, organization, strategies and tactics. Above all, while contained mobilization wins new adherents and resources for existing, albeit fragile, political subjects, transgressive mobilization generates new collective political subjects, initiating a politics of re-articulation.

There is no reason to suppose that both transgressive and contained forms of mobilization, while analytically separable, do not co-exist, often but not always in tension, even in a given movement (cf. O'Brien 2002). Just as charisma routinizes in Weber, transgressive mobilization, as it starts to build up group solidarity, material interests, and commitments to given identities and goals, can start to operate more strategically, routinize, and increasingly act in a less transgressive way. Actors that originate in transgressive mobilization often wind up in more contained forms, as we shall see from Egyptian trade unions in the 1950s to Hizbullah in Lebanon in the 2000s. On the other hand, as this process of routinization and political recognition goes ahead, or as opponents move to co-opt or neutralize transgression, the movement may splinter as elements dissatisfied with such co-optation breakaway to form more transgressive movements. This is a familiar pattern in the history of the Muslim Brotherhood, as we shall see.

The distinctions between transacted politics on the one hand, and contentious politics on the other, and between contained and transgressive mobilization appear throughout this history: in nineteenth-century Algeria, for example, local chiefs of holy or notable lineage, and religious notables of various kinds, carried on a transacted politics behind closed doors through correspondence and face-to-face meetings with the French colonial authorities and then tried to put the best spin on what they gained or lost to their followers. At other points they made appeals to constituencies in order to put pressure on the French and to take forward their agenda. These were cases of contained mobilization. At still other points, partly because of the public appeals of the notables, and partly because commoners with charismatic, religious and millenarian agenda entered the fray with agenda of their own, a more transgressive mobilization was at play, and notables were pushed into outright confrontations with authorities that they had not sought (Clancy-Smith 1994).

The authors of the DOC programme make a remarkable and under-appreciated claim to justify their focus on transgressive contention. They suggest that 'substantial short-term political and social change more often emerges from transgressive than from contained contention, which tends more often to reproduce existing regimes' (McAdam *et al.* 2001: 8). The potency of transgressive mobilization, it is argued in this history, stems from the fact that it involves politicization around new or relatively subordinated subjects. Its surprising force originates in the fact that suddenly there are new and unexpected entrants into the political field, the boundaries of which are porous, and not always possible to police, to restrict to formal and pre-constituted actors, or to contain within set norms and limits. In other words, new energies, numbers and resources are newly deployed and start to weigh in the political balance in unpredictable ways. At its most extraordinary, such transgression can be revolutionary in the sense indicated by Leon Trotsky:

The most indubitable feature of a revolution is the direct interference of the masses in historical events. In ordinary times the state, be it monarchical or democratic, elevates itself above the nation, and history is made by specialists in that line of business – kings, ministers, bureaucrats, parliamentarians, journalists. But at those crucial moments when the old order becomes no longer endurable to the masses, they break over the barriers excluding them from the *political arena* [my emphasis], sweep aside their traditional representatives, and create by their own interference the initial groundwork for a new regime. Whether this is good or bad we leave to the judgment of moralists ... The history of a revolution is for us first of all a history of the forcible entrance of the masses into the realm of rulership over their own destiny (Trotsky 1997 [1932–3]: 17).

Trotsky here puts with great eloquence a sense of the importance of the weight and capacity of new-entrants into the political arena, even if he then went on to explain the overall course of events in terms of the combined and uneven development of the capitalist mode of production. Consequences are tracked here in terms of how fragile collective subjects are given extra weight through contained mobilization, and how new political subjects are brought into being through transgression: moves that change the nature of political contest. As Gramsci has it, 'the balance of forces ... is in process of transformation, as the new movement demonstrates by its very coming into existence' (Gramsci 1971: 166).

While the debt to the DOC programme on definitions and vectors is clear, basic problems of context and explanation remain. At the root of this is the shapelessness of DOC's weightless, interactionist ontology, which makes history and context very hard to identify, and creativity and dynamism very hard to situate. Structures of power, along with attention to excluded positions and asymmetries (Gamson 1975; McAdam 1983), are hard to indicate amid the profusion of interacting mechanisms and processes. The importance of inherited contexts and slow-moving structures (Tripp 2013) becomes elusive. The invocation of 'resource disparity' between 'claim-making pairs' is insufficient in regard to the thickness of the problem: claims are not always autonomous, and subjects are already implicated in power relations, not abstracted from them. Regimes are left standing rather arbitrarily as the only structure in town (Tilly 2006), while the status of regime as structure is vexed, difficult to reconcile coherently with the interactionist ontology that governs the overall approach. The capacity of established and potent actors, whether oppositional or not, is also occluded amid a focus on interactions; there is a danger in fetishing informalism, as the Arab uprisings have shown. The subjectivist reading of political opportunity in DOC is, moreover, no panacea, but instead an even narrower version of an already too-narrow concept when it comes to grasping explanatory context, as opposed to delineating descriptive expectation. This study has found it difficult to derive an adequate account of history and context from the DOC programme, and thus has found inspiration elsewhere.

The second key problem has to do with the DOC programme's 'workhorses' of explanation: mechanisms. This concept is unclear and very difficult to use. It is comprehensible enough, if vague and all-encompassing, that mechanisms are environmental, cognitive or relational factors which change the relations between relevant elements. That mechanisms can concatenate, or interact to produce new outcomes is trickier to grasp because outcomes may be better seen as resulting from the interaction of actors, not the interaction of mechanisms. Why outcomes should be seen as processes or trajectories, rather than as fixes or provisional settlements, is also not necessarily clear. Clarity is further lost because mechanisms are not clearly distinguished from processes. The core problem is that the concept too thoroughly conflates cause and effect, contention and context, explanans and explanandum. Mechanisms are said to be present in contention itself, and outside of it, in larger processes and in micro-interactions, in the environment and in cognition. Mechanisms are extremely difficult to distinguish from the lineaments of contention that they are meant to explain. Most of the mechanisms that the DOC programme invites us to consider, 'actor constitution', 'brokerage' and so on, might better be conceived as things-which-often-happen during moments of transgressive political struggle. The DOC programme can help us define these things-which-often-happen, but hardly helps us explain them.

One response is to fall back on methodological individualism and rational choice theory to tackle these problems (Opp 2009). This is superficial and cannot do justice to politics because it depends on prior political and social determinations. It is not that relatively autonomous subjects making rational decisions connecting means to ends effectively and maximizing some relatively stable and defined utility function do not exist. They are to be found in Saudi Arabia, Syria and Sweden alike. It is instead that the subject, whether individual or collective, and its form of autonomy, must be constructed, and that these constructions are historically variable. We need to understand where the subject comes from, how it is constructed, and especially how it can be made to cohere and integrate internally and collectively. The assumption that subjects (collective or individual) are stable and internally pre-integrated is an effect of a given form of hegemony, not a satisfactory start point for its examination. To go further in regard to questions of political, power-laden, and inherited context, explanation, subject-constitution, strategic leadership and mobilization, we can profitably turn to the work of Gramsci.

The uses of Gramsci

Antonio Gramsci was a revolutionary communist and strategist whose great contribution to historical materialism was to accord an 'independent and creative role' to human subjectivity (Femia 1981: 1). His most important texts were written in a fascist prison that eventually killed him. His ideas, on the other hand, although sometimes obscured by prison censorship, and the appalling conditions under which he worked, escaped. They made a profoundly original, subtle and complex contribution to understandings of how subjectivity and politics was at work in capitalist development. Debates over Gramsci's legacy, and the meanings of his key concepts, have been the subject of much controversy, especially since the 1970s (Anderson 1977; Mouffe 1979; Sassoon 1987). There are many Gramscis. There is the master strategist (Sanbonmatsu 2003); the post-structuralist radical democrat (Laclau and Mouffe 1985); the theorist of language, popular culture and literature (Hall 1981, 1987; Patnaik 1987; Williams 1977); the Marxist philosopher of praxis (Thomas 2010); the Foucauldian (Massad 2001); and even the reformist, Eurocommunist (San Juan 2009: 56–82) as well as the Gramsci of Subaltern Studies (Guha 1997). Nonetheless, borrowing from Gramsci, while leaving out the co-determining capitalist metanarrative, is not a very Gramscian thing to do. This book is therefore only unconventionally Gramscian. And Gramsci did not try to define contentious mobilization. But debts must be acknowledged. This history makes use of modified concepts of hegemony, strategic leadership, intellectual labour, mobilizing projects, and the collective subject, with clear debts to Gramsci's work. It uses them to assist in stitching culture and meaning into contentious politics (insofar as Orientalism, historical sociology and the cultural turn have failed to do so), and in plugging at least some of the explanatory and historical gaps identified above in regards to SMT and DOC. The idea is to offer one kind of answer to Lockman's vital challenge to Middle East Studies: 'to combine due attention to the question of representation with due attention to social and political dynamics, hierarchies of power and historical contexts, and to explore how these domains are intertwined' (Lockman 2004: 212).

Gramsci's work moved at many levels. He analysed capitalist development, the role of 'fundamental' classes (the bourgeoisie and the proletariat), struggles over meaning in the trenches, earthworks and fortifications of civil society, the role of language and popular culture, and the form of political society, one of his suggestive definitions of which was the 'apparatus of state coercion which legally assures the discipline of those groups which do not consent' (cited in Femia 1981: 28). Gramsci reached for a form of knowledge, a philosophy of praxis, that would not be an 'instrument of government' but the 'expression of ... subaltern classes who want to educate themselves in the art of government and who have an interest in knowing all truths' (cited in Thomas 2010: 452). He was heavily concerned with the study of forms of political, intellectual and moral leadership. It was in regard to the latter that his most famous, and perhaps most vexed concept, was developed: hegemony. In a struggle for hegemony, leaderships, rooted in fundamental classes, but overlapping with political society, supplemented coercion with consent in their attempts to win over allied and subaltern social groups to impose a direction on social life. Hegemony involved the 'complex unity of domination and leadership' (Filippini 2012). It referred to the 'spontaneous consent given by the great masses of the population to the general direction imposed on social life by the dominant fundamental group' (Gramsci 1971: 12). In Gramsci's Italy, that group meant the bourgeoisie, which won consent partly because of the 'prestige' it enjoyed as a result of its 'position and function in the world of production' (Gramsci 1971: 12). Hegemonic projects were carried out in the trenches of civil society. They could also be led by the other fundamental class under capitalism: the proletariat. Both the bourgeoisie and the proletariat had no choice but to try to form blocs to hegemonize subaltern social groups, the peasantry, the petty-bourgeoisie and the lumpen-proletariat, who had not been destroyed by capitalism as many Marxists had expected. It was no use, explained Gramsci, under conditions of advanced capitalism, simply to seize state power as Lenin had done in 'backward' Russia. The institutions of civil society, churches, the media and schools, had to be conquered, and a historic bloc of alternative forces built up, under the leadership of a revolutionary socialist proletariat and its organic intellectuals. This bloc would eventually be able to accede to power in the state as a whole.

Gramsci has only had a limited influence on the study of protest in the MENA. He himself only wrote a few vignettes on Arabia and

Islam. In the 1920s, faced with an Orientalist debate over whether Islam was compatible with modernity, Gramsci's response was promising: he argued that the form of Islam was not immutable and questioned the extent to which *Christianity* was compatible with modernity. He thus struck against the civilizational exceptionalism and essentialism within which the debate was couched (Gramsci 1971: 333). His other notes on Arabia foreground not political economy but descriptions of leaderships and their forms of legitimacy (Gramsci 1971: 278–9, 344–5). As is commonly the case elsewhere, his work has often been used regarding the MENA not for the study of protest or for the study of revolutionary challenges to the existing order, although some work has made a start in this direction (Chalcraft and Noorani 2007; de Smet 2012b), but for understanding the many subtle ways in which the dominant bloc has incorporated and hegemonized other social forces (Davis 2005; Massad 2001; Mossallam 2013; Tuğal 2009). Given that capitalism has not yet been overthrown in the region or elsewhere, the emphasis on hegemonic incorporation and 'passive revolution' is understandable. Gramsci was a Marxist revolutionary, and the capitalist metanarrative, modernist teleology, and economic essentialism, the determination by capitalist development in the last instance, mark his analysis in basic ways. His *œuvre*, nonetheless, is highly suggestive for those inspired by Geoff Eley's call to intertwine cultural and social history in attempts to narrate the aggregate dynamics of society as a whole (Eley 2005: 203).

Gramsci was heavily concerned with understanding the formation and capacity of collective subjects capable of making history and their associated projects of moral, political and intellectual leadership (e.g. Gramsci 1971: 349). This book assumes to be central the fragile, becoming, 'half-articulate' collective subjects associated with movements and contentious mobilization, and the forms of creative and de-sectorized recombination they involve. Crucial is how 'atomized [and subordinated] subjects can transform themselves into collective actors' (Tripp 2013: 132). Collective subject formation, however, is not just about the 'worker Subject' (de Smet 2012b), but a wide variety of collective actors. Interaction as a metaphor is too power-lite to capture the subaltern struggle to become that is often at stake here. Far more suggestive is Dobry's notion of de-sectorization, where new connections are forged between previously relatively autonomous and compartmentalized social logics (in the household, the firm, the party etc.), the particular rules, norms and forms of domination of which are therefore disrupted or suspended (Dobry 1986, 2009). De-sectorized recombination gives subordinated actors leverage to challenge the logics of domination in which they are enmeshed. Contentious mobilization fundamentally concerns heteronomous (other-determined) and/ or coerced subjects who band together collectively to challenge the forms of disarticulation and violence they face. It involves coordinated action, an orientation to achieving some goal, a dose of normative commitment, and a challenge to some aspect of the *status quo*.

In order to flesh out the anatomy of mobilization defined thus, this 'long labour which gives birth to collective will' (Gramsci 1971: 194), and to probe the ways in which collective subjects can cohere or gain traction, this history invokes the idea of mobilizing projects as a 'workhorse' of description. In such projects, as Lockman writes in conceptualizing post-materialist labour history, 'various forces seek to organize some group of people around some pole of identity in order to realize some particular socio-political project' (Lockman 1994a: 158–9). The basic building blocks of mobilizing projects, whether incipient or more developed, are schematically signposted here to be (a) the categories of identity that organize the perceptions of the contentious actors themselves; (b) the principles, beliefs, programmes and ideals that are promoted as the rightful guides for action; (c) the goals that movements espouse; (d) the social relations of association and coordination that develop or exist within movements; and (e) the strategies and tactics that movements deploy in the course of their action. Rooting an ontology of mobilization in a struggle to overcome subordination and fragmentation, this anatomization allows a thicker and more differentiated ontology of 'movement' than the rather behaviouralist and sometime path-dependent concept of 'repertoire', or the overly subject-less concept of 'contentious performance', or the everywhere and anywhere concept of claim-making. All the case studies in this book parse movements in terms of mobilizing projects.

Hegemonic contraction

A modified version of Gramsci's concept of hegemony can make a vital contribution to understanding how mobilizing projects are situated in larger historical contexts. Gramsci sometimes wrote of the hegemony of the state (rather than of a particular social class), and this is taken up here as a way to make sense of the combinations of coercion and consent at work in the construction of political community. To construct a viable political community, capable of monopolizing the legitimate means of coercion, of wielding sovereignty, of making and enforcing binding rules for a whole population and thus sustaining a cohesive legal and administrative state apparatus, and to do so amid gross inequalities of power, status, and wealth, coercion must and has been mixed with consent. The masses are not simply 'organizationally outflanked' (Mann 1986: 7). Domination must be intertwined with moral, political and intellectual leadership. Here, the exercise of power is only carcerally and sectorally about raw domination and naked coercion: at the level of the political community as a whole power must be articulated. The state involves 'force and consent', political and civil society (Gramsci 1971: 170). This is not a result of capitalist development, or French revolutionary concepts, but a familiar feature of empire and state-making over centuries, in the MENA as elsewhere. As Gramsci put it 'in the Renaissance, religion was consent and the Church was civil society, the hegemonic apparatus of the ruling group' (Gramsci 1971: 170, n. 71).

Gramsci has suggested the way in which the exercise of real power involves a supplement to coercion. Social groups seeking to and actually exercising power in the state and acting in the political field must exert not only domination but also intellectual, moral and political leadership (*direzione*); they diffuse their worldview through society, mesh the forms of abstraction and principle they champion with the existing forms of common sense and immediacy, offer concessions on narrow corporate interests, and identify their interests with the general interest, thereby winning the consent of subaltern social groups. The exercise of meaningful political power is always articulated. The relations through which articulation is built up, and means of hegemonic incorporation established are 'intersectional' in that they involve interlocking combinations of meaning, resources and power. Hegemonic expansion, to paraphrase Urbinati, involves both 'cultural work' and strategies of power (Urbinati 1998: 370).

First, there are always questions of legitimacy: sacralization, identification, principled adherence and euphemization are at work in the relations between the agents and structures of the political community, the dominant bloc, and subaltern social groups. Rulers can identify their rule with principles, identities, ideologies, and forms of common

sense and 'spontaneous philosophy' held dear by sections of the population (cf. Patnaik 1987), and confirm these identifications in concrete
policies, in the institutions of civil society, and in rituals, and the
distribution of honours and the recognition of social status. Mossallam's research vividly showed how Nasserism was identified with
popular culture through intimate languages of poetry and song
(Mossallam 2013). Davis showed the subtle ways in which the
re-writing of history – not entirely by party apparatchiks – served the
rule of Saddam Hussein and the Ba'th Party in Iraq (Davis 2005).
Tripp brings out the linkages between struggles over history and
the hegemony of Zionism in Israel and the FLN-state in Algeria
(Tripp 2013: 219–55). Jackson Lears has made expert use of the
notion of cultural hegemony in a US context (Jackson Lears 1985),
just as has Stuart Hall with regard to Thatcherism in the United
Kingdom (Hall 1981).

Hegemonic incorporation is never simply about culture. It always
involves economic and resource-linked questions. State elites can guarantee spaces for money-making, regulate contracts, and enforce and
defend property rights. They can open up these spaces by selling off
public assets, striking trade agreements, protectionism, or through
policies and laws on credit, tax, interest rates and currency. There are
a wide variety of direct and indirect ways to subsidize capital accumulation. States can also redistribute wealth and rents, deliver progressive
taxation, provide welfare, jobs, pensions and protections against
the market, they can offer a wide variety of socio-economic goods,
subsidize basic commodities, and protect against price fluctuations,
whether selectively or as a matter of public good, and whether as a
matter of policy or patronage. In all of these economic matters, states
have the capacity to win the consent of a wide variety of social groups,
a phenomenon vividly brought out in the literature on the *rentier* states
of the Arabian peninsula (Beblawi 1990).

Finally, there are features of hegemonic expansion that are associated with the structure and functions of state power itself: these
features include the guarantee of physical security, the making
and enforcement of binding rules, the protection of civil liberties and
freedoms, and the form of participation, whether in regard to the
existence or not of representative institutions, democratic assemblies,
elections, parties, the functioning of petition and supplication, and
socio-political sites of intermediation. In more de-centralized states,

including empires, the use of intermediaries (notables, tribal leaders, religious leaders, client monarchs and others) to achieve the indirect participation of distant or semi-autonomous constituencies and thus secure their consent has had a long career in the MENA (Hourani 1994).

In regard to the forms of hegemonic expansion considered here, one might say figuratively that, whatever else Caesar does, he cannot be seen to act, or actually act, simply as a tyrant: the expression of martial glory and honour and the capacity to battle down the over-mighty through the spectacular spilling of blood is not at all the same thing as tyranny: this is anachronism at best. Bread and circus once underpinned hegemonic incorporation in imperial Rome just as religious legitimacy and the careful distribution of rents and the exclusion of working populations from citizenship has underpinned hegemonic incorporation among absolutist monarchies in the Arabian peninsula of the present.

The idea here is that ideational, economic and political mechanisms of hegemonic expansion, and the existence therefore of articulation in the political community at large, are intimately linked with the existence of a political field 'understood both as a field of forces and as a field of struggles aimed at transforming the relation of forces which confers on this field its structure at any given moment' (Bourdieu 1991: 171). The dynamics of the political field are not just to be found in the manipulation of pre-existing quotients of direct-state-like, indirect-economic, or diffuse-discursive power, that is in the forms of raw domination and what Michael Mann has called the 'sources' of social power (Mann 1986) and *reactions* to these forms of power (Tripp 2013). If so, where would the power to react come from? Instead, they are to be found in the existing forms of articulation and re-articulation (Chalcraft and Noorani 2007). The assumption is that meaningful politics under conditions of pure domination and coercion is impossible. Where all forms of domination converge, economic, racial, military, gendered, spatial, cultural and so on, in theory there is a carceral vanishing point where meaningful forms of contestation are impossible. This premise may help explain the persistence of racial slavery in the United States, of Stalinism in the Soviet Union, or how genocide, or exterminatory New England-style settler colonialism (Osterhammel 2005) have historically been possible. Contentious mobilization requires resources and capacities. Where hegemonic forms of rule are established, the capacities and resources that such rule places in the hands of subordinates owe their existence to ruling strategies, and thus there is no reason for subordinates to use them to mount contentious challenges. On the other hand, where hegemonic contraction takes place, and sites of articulation break up, reasons for mobilization emerge. Under such conditions, there are reasons to turn existing resources and capacities to new purposes.

Hegemonic contraction often involves those moments when elites, for a variety of reasons, start to undermine existing forms of consent and sites of articulation, without replacing them with satisfactory alternatives. In Gramsci's analysis, in extreme cases, where rulers fail in major undertakings, or where popular masses suddenly make many demands, 'A "crisis of authority" is spoken of: this is precisely the crisis of hegemony, or general crisis of the state' (Gramsci 1971: 210). We will find many such crises in the MENA. Some of the most important were the Napoleonic invasion of Egypt in 1798, the Ottoman and Egyptian debt crisis of 1876, the defeats, partitions and imperial invasions of the period 1911 to the 1920s, the catastrophic dispossession of the Palestinians of 1948, and the military defeat of the Arab states in 1967. Political disincorporation is often less sudden and slower-burning, and can take place at many levels: political, economic and discursive. Elites can shut down forms of participation that were previously allowed – by rigging or corrupting elections or suspending the constitution. This took place in Egypt during the inter-war period, or in Iran in 2009. Groups previously incorporated within the state can be pushed out or neglected. This is partly what happened in Sadat's Egypt in the 1970s. They can suspend political or civil rights in the face of external or internal 'threats', real or imagined. They can act in repressive ways that show their blatant disregard for rights that they themselves have championed. They can withdraw the guarantees that the state used to provide in regard to social and economic rights. They can be derelict in matters of physical protection, in the face of security threats from within and without, as the ruling Mamelukes of Egypt were in 1798. They can undermine the autonomy and authority of intermediaries, as the French did in Algeria during the nineteenth century, or the Israelis did in the Occupied Palestinian Territories during the 1990s, causing them to seek to re-negotiate or completely defect from the existing terms of collaboration. The authorities can also undermine, bypass or ignore existing sites of contained contention, reducing the possibility for the redress of grievances through authorized channels. They can neglect to introduce minor reforms that at least win the approval of reformist challengers and potentially disaffected members of the dominant bloc. They can fail to allow spaces of authorized dissent by heavy-handed security measures.

In more economic terms, rulers can row back on the provision of socio-economic goods and services; or they can make policies that cut into the profits of private capital, or block small business expansion via corruption and heavy-handed regulation. They can shower themselves with privileges and engage in corruption that excludes unconnected economic actors.

Members of the dominant bloc can also build up a site of legitimacy and then go on to act in a way that violates the forms of legitimacy to which they themselves have appealed. This took place in Saudi Arabia at the end of the 1920s. They can also fail to provide a form of political, intellectual and moral leadership that can possibly keep pace with changing demands and times. This is partly what happened in King Idris' Libya in the 1960s.

Elites are capable of acting in ways that strike at the consensual bases of their own rule. This can stem from the way elite collective action is constrained by the vested interests and core values that elites maintain – and that are required in order to maintain the cohesion of the dominant bloc. Sometimes, a dose of blundering is involved. It is hard to read Shakibi's account of the Iranian revolution without accepting the idea that the Shah made mistakes (Shakibi 2007). Hegemonic contraction can also result from the fact that over time elites become increasingly inclined to see their own interests as identical with the general interest. Roger Owen has described this process with regard to Lord Cromer, the increasingly dictatorial colonial ruler of Egypt, 1883–1907 (Owen 2004b). Another route into hegemonic contraction has to do with the fact that hegemonic rule (as opposed to rule by pure domination) must pay attention to the wishes and interests of its key constituencies (which have a dynamism of their own), and offer a stream of concessions beyond their narrow corporate interests. If continuous and proactive elite collective action is not maintained, the dominant bloc will even by simple inertia and inaction, undermine the hegemonic bases of its rule. There are also, of course, many temptations for those in positions of power in the dominant bloc: corruption (the use of public money or regulations for private ends) is only one of these. There are significant countervailing forces among elites to prevent hegemonic contraction. For example, the British quickly moved to replace Cromer in Egypt after his heavy-handed actions in Dinshaway in 1906 were seen to backfire. Here the agency of elites must be taken into account. On the other hand, the vested interests and value commitments of members of the dominant bloc cause them to shy away from radical solutions to radical problems. Such measures might threaten the cohesion of ruling groups in any case. In such situations, pressures from on high to break up and undermine sites of hegemonic articulation are powerful indeed.

Gramsci's explanation for the contraction of bourgeois hegemony relied in the very last instance on the development of capitalism and the rise of the proletariat. The explanation offered here suggests that the hegemony of the dominant bloc is unstable precisely because it is not anchored in a cohesive bourgeoisie unified by its common ownership of the means of production. Usages of the term hegemony relaxing the centrality of the bourgeoisie are conventional in Middle East Studies (Chalcraft and Noorani 2007; Davis 2005; Massad 2001; Mossallam 2013; Tuğal 2009). Such usage admits that the leading powers of decision are in the hands not just of an economic class, but a complex dominant bloc consisting of polity members, those with regular access to the polity, and wealthy and high-status elites with many vested interests, including that of maintaining the ship of state. Polity members, and those domestic and international actors with access to the polity, we should note, can sometimes rise rapidly from humble origins. We will see this in post-independence Syria and Algeria, for example. The dominant bloc is not by any means cohesive or monolithic. Indeed, fragmented among different sources of power, the dominant bloc faces basic problems of cohesion, which can cause it to undermine the forms of hegemony on which it relies. No teleological guarantee secures the reproduction of either ruling groups or their challengers: political labour counts.

Hegemonic contraction is unlike a general economic crisis, or ongoing forms of oppression and exploitation, or generalized resentment against deprivation or corruption, because it specifically shocks and affronts the very constituencies that have become habituated to, and have the capacity to, exercise their agency in the construction of the socio-political order. For this reason, it creates dis-incorporated constituencies, suddenly faced with new forms of repression, with reasons ideal and/or material to mobilize contentiously to challenge some aspect of the (new) *status quo* as well as, often, the capacity, to do so. It generates the conditions for the re-delegation of authority from below (contained mobilization), or the bottom-up seizure of that authority (transgressive mobilization). It captures the key vector of de-structure in a way missed by the language of political opportunity and threat. This idea of what makes persons available for mobilization is also strictly impossible in the DOC programme, because the notion of de-structure has no methodological validity amid a thoroughgoing relational interactionism. Hegemonic contraction is analytically separable from contentious mobilization and thus can be described as an external, inherited or contextual factor relating to the circumstances in which movements find themselves. It is of course not a purely inert element, because it depends heavily on the actions and decisions of those inhabiting the dominant bloc, and is impacted by the nature and form of mobilizing projects themselves. Hegemonic contraction, the failure of political incorporation, and the dessication of sites of articulation, forms the single most important enabling condition for the transgressive contention in which this history is most interested in exploring.

In short, and in more structural and contextual mode than DOC allows, and enabling a richer grasp of political context than that supplied by notions of opportunity and threat extant in classical SMT, a concept of the degree of hegemonic incorporation drawn from a non-teleological and non-economistic reading of Gramsci's *œuvre* can inform an analysis of how consent is secured and lost, and thus an analysis of the contexts within which contentious mobilization can take place.

Leadership, intellectual labour, the translocal and norms

Hegemonic contraction, however, is not enough to explain contentious mobilization. In the face of hegemonic contraction, some of those shocked and affronted may simply exit or withdraw, or channel their energies into some site of articulation that has not yet been shut down. Some might exchange political participation for money-making, for example, or for the exercise of domination itself. Others may emigrate. Conversely, some mobilizing projects get under way well before hegemonic contraction even sets in. There are always ways to imagine otherwise – especially on university campus or in seminaries, or among intellectuals, charismatic individuals, or true believers. Hegemonic contraction thus only forms an enabling condition for contentious mobilization, albeit the most important one. Moreover, the content, form and degree of transgression of mobilizing projects that do arise under conditions of such contraction are very difficult to explain in terms of contextual determinations. Some will persist doggedly with reformist and legal methods in the face of all inhumanity and brutality to hold on to their own humanity, as the activities of Palestinian liberal and legal activist Raja Shehadeh testify. Others may embark on revolutionary action even when conditions seem decidedly unripe, as in the small groups who carried out armed operations in Algeria in the late 1940s, or the Iranian guerrilla groups who attacked regime targets in the early 1970s. The choice of identities and principles, the modes of social association, the goals that movements come up with, the strategies and tactics they adopt, can be highly innovative, or they can be relatively tried and tested. What can explain these original moves, where they are original, other than initiatives taken by activists? What structure can explain why the peripatetic preacher, Izz Al-Din Al-Qassam, for example, took it upon himself to mobilize a relatively lonely armed struggle in Haifa starting in the early 1920s, while other graduates of Al-Azhar were non-armed gradualists and reformists, and most in Palestine looked to the legal and unarmed strategies of the Palestinian notable leadership? Of course, when regimes shut down avenues of contained mobilization, there is a strong pressure on those who want to continue to make an impact to turn to transgressive modes of contention, but there is no lock-step relationship here. Much remains in the hands of particular initiatives and distinctive recombinations of disarticulated elements. In their origins, groups can form relatively spontaneously. Hegemonic contraction forms a key enabling condition, but it cannot explain the precise initiatives that are taken. To understand how mobilizing projects form and cohere, this book has made much of leadership, ideas, norms and the translocal.

Gramsci paid a great deal of attention to the labour, dynamics and strategies involved in the construction of a collective subject capable of making history. That mobilizing projects, especially those in more transgressive mode, must work hard to secure and maintain new or partially new collective subjects is a central analytic principle in this history. This labour for cohesion and sustainability amidst creative re-combination can help account for the ways in which movements develop. In this regard, leadership strategies are important. Leadership, as used here, does not imply simply a fixed group, but all the agencies most active in determining the overall shape of a given mobilizing project. Especially in the early stages of a movement, or where internal democratic procedures are put in place, leadership can be fluid or rotating – with different persons coming to the fore, and other persons or groups receding into the background. The idea of leadership relates to the conscious choices that are made and enforced in the construction of the mobilizing project, and the way a constant stream of dilemmas is resolved. It refers not just to a sole leader, but to the forms of active agency that play a role in shaping the project as a whole. The constituencies that leaderships seek to mobilize are demanding in their own right, capable of discerning their own interests, and having their own commitments and goals, as well as alternative forms of loyalty or apathy. Popular culture, for example, has a relative autonomy that it is perilous to ignore (Hall 1981; Patnaik 1987). In regard to the revolutionary situation in Russia in 1917, Trotsky compared the leadership to a piston box, and the spontaneous energies of the masses to steam:

Without a guiding organisation the energy of the masses would dissipate like steam not enclosed in a piston-box. But nevertheless what moves things is not the piston or the box, but the steam (Trotsky 1997 [1932–3]: 19).

Trotsky here preserves a strong sense of the driving force of what one might think of as the transgressive mobilization of the masses, while pointing out the role of leadership. It is understood here that leaderships must keep pace with the energies of their constituencies if they are not to cede their position to those who are taking initiatives, or if they are not to foster a split in the movement. New or altered forms of leadership can come into being where non-leaderships successfully seize the initiative in regards to winning consent or finding advantage. In other words, leadership refers to all the active agencies giving direction to the mobilizing project as a whole. Nonetheless, leadership exists: movement rank and file, and supporters in the wider society, to the extent that they offer consent to a movement, sign over some quotient of their political agency, they agree to be represented, delegate powers and capacities to leaderships, and look to the latter to deliver on their material and ideal interests. Kurzman's approach, in spite of its clear virtues in relation to understanding crowd actions and spontaneous upsurges, has much less to say about organization and leadership. Yet delegation sets up a tense relationship between leadership and constituencies that produces many dynamics. The problems of cohesion that movements face are profound, more so than in Gramsci, for example, or other immanentist or essentialist accounts, as there is no pre-existing subject, the proletariat, the multitude, the bourgeoisie, the nation, the Muslim, the Arab, Womanhood, underpinning the agency of such projects. Instead, the collective agency associated with movements, especially the more transgressive they are, has to be constructed. Leadership plays a key role in the sustainability and capacity of movements in regard to inward-facing matters of cohesion.

Further, outward-facing decisions taken by leaderships over strategies, tactics, and styles of organizing have been consequential in basic ways in this history. Drawing on Gramsci here by no means suggests that there was only one successful strategy in the MENA, mass mobilization in the earthworks of civil society, although this strategy was vital. The seizure of power (by revolutionary coup, for example) has also played a crucial role in the MENA, among many other strategies. The decision to pick up arms has been hugely consequential for movements in the region as will be shown. Inspired by Gramsci, this study takes very seriously the strategies, tactics and modes of organization of mobilizing projects in order to understand their fate and fortunes.

Second, while refusing the idea of causation in this regard, the framework used here does offer a way to make sense of the initial shape (content, and degree of transgression) that mobilizing projects take. This is where the role of intellectual labour becomes vital. At moments of hegemonic contraction and heightened uncertainty, ideas, at least for small committed groups out of which larger movements often come, can play an important role. They act like railway switchmen, in the Weberian analogy, determining the tracks on which action is pushed by the dynamic of interest. Weber maintained that people formed pictures of the world, or wielded charismatic forms of authority, and adherents signed up to such pictures or forms of charisma, and committed themselves to conscious goals, which shaped action motivated by both material and ideal interests. He maintained that, once people became committed to groups, they established vested interests, which in turn routinized earlier more normative concerns. Tilly sailed closer to Marx than Weber, paying considerable attention to material interests, especially until the 1990s. Nevertheless, he was still compelled by Weber's analysis and refused to dismiss his conceptions entirely. He identified the strengths as follows:

People *do* sometimes group around distinctive definitions of the world and of themselves: why and how? There *is* something about the growth of Temperance or Abolitionism that neither an analysis of whole social classes nor a study of specific associations exhausts: what is it? A group's conception of its aims and rights *does* inform its action and influence its very readiness to act: can't we take that into account? Weber left us an important agenda (Tilly 1977: 2–48).

Such an agenda has rarely been taken up. Weber's work has mostly, and in many ways justifiably, been used for institutional analysis. Historical materialists looked askance. DOC, in which meaning is everywhere, and thus in many respects nowhere, is surprisingly slippery on the specific role played by intellectual labour and ideas. But here was a highly suggestive summary of the importance of ideas in the understanding of how especially early rising and initially inchoate mobilizing projects are shaped. While ideas do not cause activists to launch projects, they are available to be appropriated when activists do. Intellectual labour plays an important role in providing the content of these ideas, whether that of Shi'a Islamists in the 1960s and 1970s, of Hardt and Negri in the 2000s, of nationalists and Third Worldists in the 1940s and 1950s, liberals in the late nineteenth and early twentieth century, or heterodox, millenarian or revivalist thinking in the eighteenth and nineteenth centuries. This book will be full of examples of movements that at the outset drew on ideas from previously marginal intellectuals or sometime heterodox religious figures. What is often interesting is the way that ideas at one point considered absurd or pie-in-the-sky, can become assimilated as 'far-sighted' or even as the conventional wisdom at a later date, obscuring the adventurous and unlikely conditions of their own instantiation.

A third, and closely related point, is the important and agency-shaping role played by the translocal appropriation of co-eval models for collective action. Models for collective action (modes of organization, goals, strategies and tactics) as well as key ideational substance (identities, principles and frames) have been regularly appropriated from elsewhere, and put to work in new contexts. This point can help us grasp real innovation in tactics and strategies, marked by creative appropriation, a point rarely addressed in SMT or DOC. While these forms of appropriation operate most vividly at the early and inchoate stages in a movement, they can play a surprisingly important role, as the initial frames and strategies adopted generate forms of path-dependency which leaderships then find it hard to transform in the face of demanding constituencies and the need to maintain cohesion and credibility.

Finally, normative commitments play a vital and often-slighted role in the making of transgressive contention. Movements without a normative commitment are surprisingly hard to imagine. Leaders may be accused of opportunism or personal interest, and movements may be accused of merely pursuing their narrow, corporate or material interests, but arguably once this becomes genuinely the case, which it does from time to time, and once action is emptied of all normative content, it is more likely that we are dealing with an interest group, machine politics, or simple opportunism rather than a movement. It is hard to read Seale's account of Abu Nidal's faction, for example, without forming the impression that it had completely lost its moral compass and become more a mercenary gang than a movement by the 1980s (Seale 1992). Normative commitments can also help explain why early rising, core leaderships may often adopt a course that seems to cut against their everyday material interests, or their ability to live a quiet life. We need not assume, further, that Marxists, the Left and the labour movement have eschewed normative commitment in their really existing activism. The communist revolutionary, Leon Trotsky, wrote that 'all through history, mind limps after reality' (cited in Knei-Paz 1978: 9). But he also wrote in the late 1920s in disgust to erstwhile comrades:

You, who have not suffered repression, torture, or winter in the work camps, have the possibility of giving up the struggle when it doesn't meet your expectations of success and prominence. But the true revolutionary is born when he subordinates his personal ambitions to an idea. Revolutionaries can be educated or ignorant, intelligent or stupid, but they cannot exist without will, without devotion, without the spirit of sacrifice (cited in Padura 2014: 55).

This was the kind of sentiment that is common in revolutionary movements of the MENA, where risks to life and livelihood for those involved in contention have often been very high. As Noorani insists, counter-hegemony involves a death-defying 'moral investment' that is required to 'turn a particular resistance into a practice of freedom capable of articulating other social resistances to itself' (Noorani 2007: 96). Social movements, even if not revolutionary, tend to be more than just interest groups, pursuing narrow corporate and pre-determined material interests, their politics reflecting the balance of power. In the history of the MENA, the labour movement in general (in contrast to certain trade union leaderships) has been heavily inflected with powerful forms of moral economy, nationalism, social-ism, gender, and even sometimes the corporate vision of the Muslim Brotherhood. Material interests cause hardship and discontent, and they provide reasons for mobilization, but it should be remembered that they take no determinant political shape in and of themselves, nor do they fully define a collective subject. In accounting for this shape, norms, often imbricated with ideas, identities and principles, play important roles.

This book is not a thoroughly Gramscian take on protest in the MENA. He provided no definition of a movement, and his analysis placed too much explanatory weight on the development of capitalism in ways that this book finds too deterministic and teleological. The book does make use of concepts inspired by the work of Gramsci in order to understand the dynamics of contentious mobilization by rooting it in the power-laden contexts occluded in SMT/DOC. Gramsci's work, stripped of economic essentialism, but always includ-ing the dull weight of vested, material and strategic interests, can be drawn on to suggest a focus on subject formation and consent, and develop explanatory strategies that are not purely deterministic, but which nonetheless link contention to wider historical structures and suggest ways to analyse its forms of agency. To embed mobiliza-tion in such contexts is not to study resistance as a reaction to power, but to search for different forms of articulation and re-articulation amid hegemonic contraction. Movements challenge heteronomy and coercion through de-sectorized re-combination in mobilizing projects, whether transgressive or contained. Hegemonic contraction, not simply the elusive figure of 'power', generates enabling and galvanizing conditions for the arrival of new entrants into the political field, and the creation of new political actors, styles of organizing and means of collective action. De-structure makes de-sectorized creative re-combination possible by providing reasons and capacities for mobilization rooted in disarticulation. The latter both generates a gap between is and ought, and unleashes unanchored materials which can be redeployed. Creative agency is made sense of, rather than explained away, with reference to strategic leadership, norms, intellectual labour and forms of translocal appropriation, modes of re-articulation, whose significance is elusive in SMT or DOC. Contentious mobilization reinforces fragile or constitutes new political actors which alter the dynamics of struggle in the political field in a way that is not immanent in the start conditions, and thus cannot be explained away: it must be tracked and given a history.

Periodization, coverage and sources

Historians construct periods at their peril. History is rarely so neat. This book is periodized in terms of the rise and fall of state hegemony, and the nature, achievements and failures of contentious mobilization. Whether these principles actually fit the exact dates offered here as never-completely satisfactory start and end points is a matter for debate. In such a diverse region, these exact dates can also be misleading from one area or state to another. The long nineteenth century (1798–1914) takes up the first part of the book. During these years, the hegemony of the region's three main Islamic states was under threat, and transformed in various ways, but was never entirely or sustainably replaced by an alternative. Crises in the authority of the *ancien* régime were occasioned by the Ottoman defeats at the hands of Russia and others in the late eighteenth century, by the defeat of the Mamelukes at the hands of France in 1798, by the defeat of the Algerian Deys in 1830, and the Moroccan sultan in 1844. A further round of crisis was launched by the debt crises of the new, centralizing Ottoman and Egyptian states in 1876, and by the corrupted, concessionary politics of Moroccan and Iranian rulers alike in the late nineteenth century.

Contentious mobilization involved revolutionary millenarianism, Islamic renewal in colours Sufi, Salafi-Wahhabi, and modernist, a persistent search by commoners for justice, rights and custom, and, after 1876, the growth of new forms of liberal and even patriotic mobilization in search of representation within the state itself.

The second part of the book, 1914–52, takes up the period from the multiple crises of authority set in train by the imperial invasions of the period 1911 to the 1920s to the contentious upsurges that preceded the Free Officers' revolutionary coup in Egypt in 1952. Contentious politics saw the ascendancy of a reformist, liberal nationalism, a remarkable round of rugged and patriotic armed struggles and uprisings, and the rise of new forms of political and religious ideology, whereby socialists, Islamists and liberals established mass organizations. During this period, the dynastic, Islamic states of the region were shattered or capitulated, and new forms of national political community and mass politics emerged.

The third part of the book deals with the national liberation movements, guerrilla warfare, revolutionary coups and Leftist revolutionary mobilization that were so important between the Free Officers'' coup in Egypt in 1952 and the failure of Kamal Jumblatt's democratic socialism in Lebanon in 1976. After the dispossession of the Palestinians in 1948–9, a generation of politicians and parties were shunted aside and new more direct forms of mobilization came into being. During this period, the European empires were finally pushed back, national independence, economic growth and wealth redistribution were achieved in many states, while new forms of authoritarian rule were built up.

The final part of the book deals with the period 1977–2011, when revolutionary Islamism, popular uprisings, as well as new forms of liberal and democratic protest, emerged, amid the attrition of Left mobilization, pan-Arabism and Third Worldism, dessicated on the anvil of authoritarianism. This period witnessed new forms of imperialism and intensified settler colonialism, a contraction in the hegemony of the formerly revolutionary republics, and acute crises of authority in some, signalled to begin with by the defeat of the Arab states against Israel in 1967; coercion was in the ascendant, with dictators marketing themselves as 'necessary' in the face of Islamism; while governments with access to rents found new means of hegemonic incorporation in the exclusion of migrant populations, the politics of sectarianism, and the allocation of resources from oil-rents to minority national populations. This period is book-ended by the Arab uprisings of 2011, the forms of domination without hegemony that they signalled, and the acute crises of their immediate aftermath.

The book aims to give wide coverage to many of the most important episodes of contention in the MENA from the late eighteenth century to the present. Inevitably, however, given the breadth of the topic, and the historiographical context, the book developed various principles of selection over time. The focus throughout is on the Arabic-speaking world, reflecting my own linguistic capabilities and research specialism.

The history is anchored in states. For the nineteenth century, coverage pertains to the three main dynastic states of the region: the Ottoman and Qajar empires and the sultanate of Morocco. Since the First World War, the focus is on the Arab states – while the decision to include the Iranian revolution rests on the fundamental importance of this regional event, its vital relationship to contention in the Arab states, and the key comparisons and contrasts it can give. The focus on states implies that the question of defining the MENA as a region is not of central importance in this history. The MENA is more a label of convenience. The Middle East of course was a term originating in early twentieth century imperial strategic calculations made from London, and referring to the borderlands of India (mostly Iran). Since then the term drifted west, coming to Egypt during the Second World War, again because of British war-time logistical requirements. There is recourse here to a geographic terminology, however, coloured by history, culture, society, economy, statehood and topography: this history repeatedly sees the importance of distinguishing the Maghrib (Libya, Tunisia, Algeria and Morocco); Egypt (and for the nineteenth century Egypt–Sudan); the Arabian peninsula, and the Mashriq (the Levant).

The least conventional aspects of the coverage in the book pertain to the nineteenth century, where defensive, autonomist and revolutionary protest has been given considerable emphasis compared to reformist contention. Morocco, for example, receives more attention than Iran. In part the decision stemmed from a history from below agenda, and the discovery through the research process that the *nahda* of the 1860s, the Islamic modernism of Al-Afghani and Muhammad Abduh, and nineteenth-century constitutionalism had a much more tenuous connection to popular contention than might be assumed.

The book also spends more time on the armed struggles of the inter-war period than is standard, because these forms of mobilization have too often been ignored, although not by an older Arab nationalist historiography, and their study reveals much about connections to the nineteenth century that are otherwise missed and the important ways in which these movements added muscle to liberal nationalism.

Readers will find more on the Arabian peninsula during the 1950s and 1960s than might be expected, but it is important in avoiding the 'history of the victors' to capture the nationalist and Leftist mobilizations there during that period, even though they did not achieve their goals. For the period since the 1970s, the book tries to get beyond the common division between those who write about 'unexpected' (Beinin and Vairel 2013: 1) forms of protest and those who write about Islam and Islamism. This has presented some challenges because of the unacceptably exceptionalist ways in which Islamism is often viewed, not only among neo-Orientalists, but also by some liberal and Left analysis. But the divide had to be bridged to understand the mobilization of this period. Finally, it is obvious that a book of this scope is full of omissions. It is hoped that these have not materially transformed or negated the key arguments offered.

In each part, there are a considerable number of case studies, to illustrate both the variety of movements at play, and to make sure that those of greater significance and weight get the coverage they deserve. The devil is in the detail, and although the main arguments are summarized in the introductions and conclusions to the parts, and in the conclusion to the book, the reader will only be convinced or not, I imagine, by the case studies themselves. The reader may complain that the book has kept the elaboration of the wider historical context to a minimum. This history has been told so many times, and is available in so many places, that repeating some of this context seemed unnecessary and distracting from the main focus of the book. The focus on the contentious action itself also signals an objection to the historical sociological tradition, which often spends so much time on external and contextual factors – class formation, the development of industry, state formation, demography and so on – that the actual substance of protest can sometimes almost completely disappear from view. The emphasis on the action in this book is supposed to act as a corrective to this kind of history and the objectivist and determinist viewpoint from which it stems. The emphasis here is also inspired by the approach of writers like C. L. R. James, E. P. Thompson and Christopher Hill, who never neglected subjectivity and action. Context, as we shall see, also flashes up vividly in the fate and fortunes of movements, a fact which proves a useful guide in deciding *which* context is actually *the* context.

As for sources, this book has leaned very heavily indeed, because of its breadth, on the existing secondary literature in English, Arabic and French. The debts are heavy and multiple and to some extent have already been indicated: cultural history and historical sociology have played the leading role. The main primary materials used were petitions, manifestoes, tracts, pamphlets, memoirs and autobiographies authored by activists themselves. Although the number of cases considered meant that the coverage has been uneven, these materials, which are voluminous in Arabic, were mined for the light they could shed on normative commitments, identities, principles and frames, the subjective dimensions of protest movements that are foregrounded in this history because they have too often been occluded. One problem is that the contention-centred approach adopted here is less evident and doable for the earliest case studies in the book because of the relative lack of source material. Archives, French, British, American and Egyptian, have also been used, mostly to shed light on elite calculations and policies in the face of contentious mobilization, and also because such archives sometimes house the writings of activists.

Terminology

Finally, it is useful to clarify some of the terminology that appears throughout this study. Protest, first, (in Arabic *ihtijaj*), is obviously an inclusive term and is used to indicate simply 'the expression of social, political, or cultural dissent from a policy or course of action [or dominant discourse]' (Oxford English Dictionary). Demonstrations certainly count, although they were not very common in the MENA before the 1900s. So too do petitions, letters, boycotts, shutting shops, crowd actions (riots), arson, graffiti, sabotage, strikes, sit-ins, crop-burning, civil disobedience, occupations, shaming, bombing, assassinations and so on. The focus in the book is on overt and coordinated forms of protest, rather than on more hidden and atomistic 'weapons of the weak', partly for reasons of scope, partly because there is no need to repeat the good work already done on 'weapons of the weak', and partly because these forms of protest present problems of social coordination that are of fundamental interest, and above all because my working hypothesis is that more collective and overt kinds of protest, at the most general level, have had a higher impact in shaping hegemonic forms in the period under study.

The word for movements in Arabic is *harakat*. The first linguistic reference to 'movement' (*haraka*) in the sense used here that I have seen was in regard to that of Tanyus Shahin, a muleteer who led a peasant uprising on Mount Lebanon in 1858–60. He referred to his own campaign as a 'movement' (*haraka*). There may well have been earlier uses. His Ottoman imperial opponents, by contrast, referred to his movement as 'unruly gatherings'. On the other hand, the word *haraka* in Morocco for much of the nineteenth century referred to a sultanic war party sent out to 'pacify' an area and/or raise taxes.

References to uprisings or insurrections (in Arabic, *intifada*) refer to the major collective moment where the mass of the population, typically ordinary people not generally involved in politics or organized movements, or not supposed to be so involved, signal the unendurability of the *status quo* and the established authorities, by rising up *en masse*, armed or unarmed, in such numbers as to paralyse the functioning of the existing order. While Trotsky wrote that such a moment was the most indubitable feature of revolution, this study, taking the long view, finds it crucial to distinguish quite sharply revolutions from popular uprisings. In regard to the latter the Arabic term *intifada* is particularly appropriate, as it literally means 'shaking off', although the term is regularly used to refer to events that are smaller than popular uprisings and thus do not really deserve the title, such as the '*intifada*' of 1977 in Iraq, which, although important, as we shall see, was not a mass popular uprising. The book refers to *commoner* uprisings in the nineteenth century, in order to translate the term '*ammiyya*, or rising of the common people. These were regular enough during the century, where 'common people' (*'amma, re'aya*) referred to the productive classes, with all their bundles of rights and obligations, outside the military and administrative elite (*khasa/askeri*). From the 1900s onwards, the book refers to 'popular uprisings' where these insurrections started to be intertwined with notions of national peoplehood and popular sovereignty. In the nineteenth century, the term *al-sha'b* seems to have referred, among other meanings, to a broad category of populace, assumed to be divided into many groupings of tribes (Bustani 1987: 467). It started to take on connotations of national people and popular sovereignty in Egypt in the years just prior to the First World War (Lockman 1994b). The use of the term 'popular politics' in the title of the book is more general, but insists on the fact that commoners during the nineteenth century and ordinary people since have repeatedly intervened in the domain of the political, whether or not Ottoman, colonial or state officials found this to be a terrible affront. The forcible entry, exit, and demands (whether implicit or explicit) of subaltern social groups, and the dynamics imparted thereby, define the notion of popular politics at work in this history.

Finally, the book makes reference to revolution without any qualification only in the case of Iran 1979, which was comparable to 1789, 1917 or 1949 in that it brought rapid, sweeping and lasting change to the political, geopolitical, economic, social and cultural order of that state on the basis of a massive popular insurrection coupled with a revolutionary leadership. It meant that the study of the Iranian revolution had to be included here. There were other cases where a revolution could be said to have taken place, even if it did not necessarily last. The anti-feudal peasant republican movement of Tanyus Shahin on Mount Lebanon of 1858–60 was revolutionary, but crushed. In 1883, a radical millenarian movement in Sudan created a new state and to a considerable extent a new social order. The liberal-patriotic revolutionary movements and revolutions of 1881–2 in Egypt, 1905 and 1908 in Iran and the Ottoman empire respectively and 1919 in Egypt exhibited many features of revolution. They partially implanted new nationalist and liberal principles within the state. The first use of the term revolution (*thawra*) that I have seen in the region was a pejorative one referring to Colonel 'Urabi's constitutional and patriotic movement and the commoner mobilizations that surrounded it in Egypt in 1881–2. There may have been earlier uses. The revolutionary changes regarding national independence and social transformation in many parts of the Arab world in the 1950s and 1960s owed a very great deal to a wide variety of mobilizations. The armed struggle in Dhofar in the late 1960s and early 1970s, which had anti-feudal, national liberation, socialist, feminist, and secularist aspirations, was clearly a revolutionary movement which enacted elements of revolution in the areas it controlled (Takriti 2013).

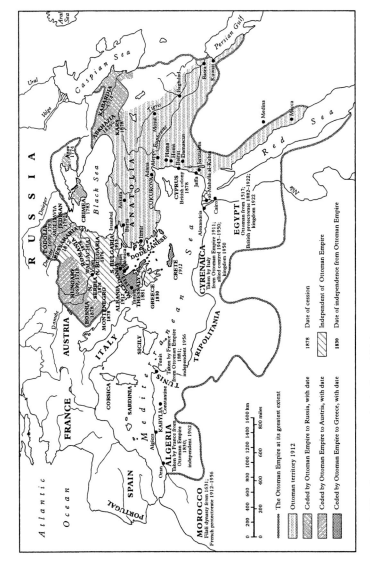

Map 1 The Ottoman empire before 1914

53

I | *Millenarianism, renewal, justice, rights and reform, 1798–1914*

Introduction

The period from the late eighteenth century to the First World War is distinctive because it marked the time when the polities of the MENA region were under considerable pressure from the European powers, but still retained basic forms of sovereignty and relative autonomy, and engaged in various forms of self-strengthening and centralization. These kinds of sovereignty, statehood and hegemony were to be lost or completely transformed in the period surrounding the First World War, when colonial rule became general and new forms of political community based around the national principle came into being. From the mass uprising against the French occupation of Egypt (1798–1801), to the constitutional revolutions in the Ottoman empire (1908) and Qajar Iran (1905), and the revolutionary millenarianism of Al-Hiba in Morocco (1912), diverse strands of contentious mobilization owed much to the crises, reform and transformation of centralizing dynastic states whose hegemony was based on Islamic law, divine favour, the sultan's justice, and guarantees of customary autonomies and practices, cultivation and trade.

During this 'long' nineteenth century, the major, polyglot, multinational, de-centralized, agrarian and trade-based polities of the MENA, the Ottoman empire, Qajar Iran and Alawi Morocco, lost the autonomy *vis-à-vis* Europe that they had previously enjoyed. Some parts of these states were taken over outright by European powers: Algeria after 1830, Tunisia after 1881, and Egypt after 1882. The Ottoman empire also lost territories in the Balkans through nationalist secession. Colonial rule mattered enormously, but was not the key driver of contentious mobilization, in spite of the tenacious protests in Algeria throughout the period from the 1830s to the early 1900s. Instead, the key context had to do more with centralization and even empire-building in the region itself. Partly in response to the changing

54

terms of war and trade, and partly to secure their own power, rulers engaged in major projects of dynasty building and state centralization, and military, fiscal and administrative change. In Tunisia, Egypt and the Ottoman centre, during the first three-quarters of the nineteenth century 'new power states emerged containing centralized bureaucracies, European-style armies, and directed by elites made up in part of men educated in the West'. These states borrowed from eighteenth-century rounds of state-building by provincial dynasts, but they still changed the form of the state decisively.

These states greatly augmented the power of autocratic rulers over their subjects, who became increasingly subordinated to the demands of the central administration (Hunter 1999: 3).

In the eighteenth century, the Ottoman government was de-centralized, minimal, diverse, and with many layers of sovereignty (Shaw 1976: 165; Yapp 1987: 36–7). This point applied with even more force to the Moroccan and Iranian governments. By the early twentieth century, the Ottoman and Egyptian states were ruling with centralized administrative, fiscal and juridical apparatuses, and had autocratic capacity and a depth and breadth of intervention unknown in previous times (Shaw 1977: vii). In Alawi-ruled Morocco after the defeat of 1858/9 and in Qajar-ruled Iran there were attempts at centralization and 'reform', although these were less developed by the time these countries fell under varying degrees of imperial control, Iran in 1911 and Morocco in 1912.

In the Ottoman empire, rulers made a half-hearted attempt to change the basis of their legitimacy. The Tanzimat, the 'auspicious re-ordering' of the Ottoman empire (1839–76), seemed to be aimed at eliminating the priority of Islam in the justification for the state. In a bid to stem nationalist secession (above all in the Balkans) and keep the Europeans at bay, the European-educated men of the sultan's new civil service designed a policy that declared the juridical equality of all Ottoman subjects, regardless of faith or confession. It was a move around which much contentious mobilization was to revolve. Abdulhamid II's long tenure (1876–1909) reversed the policy, in some measure, bringing Islam in new forms back to the centre of the sultanate, a crucial context for the rise of the Young Turks.

During the nineteenth century, the region was integrated into a world economy dominated by Europe. The port cities, including Tanger, Alexandria, Beirut and Izmir, once villages, grew immensely at the expense of the inland cities; merchants, land-owners, usurers and other agents and entrepreneurs of the emerging colonial economy made vast gains relative to other actors in the economy, 'protected' as they were under the Capitulations in the Ottoman empire, and favoured by the Qajar shahs, and to a lesser extent late-nineteenth-century Moroccan sultans. New physical infrastructures (communications, utilities, agro-processing, transport) were built, employing wage-labour. Migration for waged-work became more common. New European-style schools trained middle classes, who staffed new professions and bureaucracies. The social position of the religious establishment was challenged as *ulema* lost the monopoly of the pen, and outside of Iran, subordinated to the new state. Crafts and service trades in the cities were pressured, squeezed and re-structured, the urban guilds were co-opted and in many places disappeared, and many neighbourhood quarters lost their cohesion. In the rural areas, large commercially oriented estates were constructed, share-cropping arrangements multiplied, communal systems of land tenure were eroded, in places a wealthy peasantry emerged, and elsewhere small-holders multiplied.

The eighteenth and nineteenth centuries were also the scene of a too-often-understated religious, cultural and ideological ferment and revival. The spread of Sufi orders where states were inadequate or weak, Islamic renewal, reformist Sufism, heterodoxy of various kinds, millenarianism, *ijtihad*-minded Shi'ism, patriotism, Arabism, Turkism, pan-Islam, Islamic modernism, and ideas of constitutional and representative government appeared in different parts of the region, intertwining with and transforming long-standing notions of Islamic law, justice, rights, and custom. These ideas crossed borders using new and old communications technologies and played important and often under-appreciated roles in shaping popular movements.

Revolution, justice, autonomy and reform

Revolutionary mobilizing projects challenging elites, local dynastic and European colonial rule in Egypt–Sudan, Iran, the Arabian peninsula and North Africa were founded not on nationalism but on religion, whether in millenarian (Mahdist), purist (Salafi-Wahhabi), or neo-Sufi (Qadiri/Sanusi) colours. Millenarianism and Mahdism were above all important in Morocco and Egypt–Sudan throughout the period. In Sudan, Al-Mahdi (the son of a boat-builder) built a new state

(1883–98). In Morocco, the most radical uprisings before 1914, as Laroui rightly argued, were millennarian. These did not seek to replace the *makhzan* (central government) with a perfected *makhzan* or the reigning sultan with a pretender from the same dynasty or even an alternate dynasty. Nor were they about the ambitions of this or that provincial *qaid* or tribal leader, whether to participate in the politics of the central government or to consolidate a 'more or less recognized' sphere of autonomy (Laroui 1977: 160). These were not revolts of those under regulation protesting against the exactions and oppression of this or that governor or *caid*. Millenarian uprisings, instead, such as that of Al-Hiba in 1912, posited that the whole order was broken, at the most fundamental level, and that the new form of rule would redeem that order through a revolutionary transformation. It was about Mahdist uprisings, where 'the poor enrol, the notables stand apart', that contemporary Muslim historians were the most venomous, their orthodoxy usurped; and the sultan most worried, his legitimacy directly challenged (Laroui 1977: 160, and see 158 n. 91).

Elsewhere, Sufism took the lead. In Iran, the Bab movement of the 1840s drew on a stream of heterodox Sufism. In Algeria and in Cyrenaica renewed forms of Sufism were central in the movements of Abd Al-Qadir (in the 1830s and 1840s) and Ahmad Al-Sanusi (after 1911) alike.

Finally, in the Arabian peninsula, Salafi-Wahhabism, a form of purism that declared *jihad* against all other Muslims in the region, and was largely rejected by that region until the last quarter of the twentieth century, was nonetheless central in state-building efforts in central Arabia that broke with Ottoman rule from the mid-eighteenth century onwards.

In sum, it was access to new forms of the divine, not the development of nation-ness, whether through new interpretations of the scriptures, or new forms of ecstatic contact and charisma, that lay in the main behind the capacity to imagine and act in the name of radically new forms of political community and social order in most of the nineteenth-century MENA.

Another vital stream of contention placed less emphasis on Islam, was more defensive than revolutionary, and sought to restore or give altered content to the new and old terms, identities and principles linked to the *status quo*, and to re-interpret these terms in ways more favourable to particular constituencies. Defensive elements within the state, above all Janissaries, mounted rear-guard actions against state centralization in the first quarter of the nineteenth century. Another version of a conservative and defensive mobilization by a member of the Ottoman state, was that of Hajj Ali of Constantine against the French occupation in the 1830s. More subaltern were collective petitions and mobilizations from artisans, townspeople, peasants, wage-workers and others, from Vidin in Bulgaria to Nablus in Palestine to Cairo in Egypt against local exploiters, notables, merchants, land-owners *inter alia* who violated principles related to rich and transformed traditions of Ottoman statecraft and popular culture alike. These mobilizations were more radical, and appealed to the justice of the sultan, the rights of the subjects (*huquq al-ra'iyya*), the welfare of the people (*maslahat al-ahali*), and the demands of customary (*'adat*) and local practice. These movements were neither strictly economic nor strictly political, a fact which had to do with the way economic and political functions and forms of power were merged at a time of incomplete state centralization: local notables, guild heads, village heads, land-owners and others discharged state-like functions. These mobilizations drew on rich political and ideological resources, anchored in existing forms of hegemony, to pursue interests both ideal and material. The period of the Tanzimat was particularly important as it put forward new terms, above all equality, that mobilizing projects sought to claim for themselves, while developing new forms of centralized rule which protestors aimed to draw on in their fight against local exploitation. One of the most radical of such defensive movements, which in general could harbour many different forms of creativity, was that of Tanyus Shahin, a muleteer and Christian from Mount Lebanon, who led a mass, popular uprising against feudal injustice in 1858–60. In general, defensive mobilization, especially when its social bases and leaderships were subaltern, invoked secular traditions of rule, justice and custom, or the innovations of the Tanzimat, more than they invoked Islam. This is an important caution against vacuous or exaggerated generalizations about the all-important role of religion in 'pre-modern' commoner protest. As we will see, defensive mobilization tended to invoke Islam only when it was led by elements from within the state (such as Janissaries or Ottoman officials), or when issues of the defence of the political community as a whole were touched on. Where it was a question of justice amid local stratification, invocations of Islam dropped out, and the language of justice and rights was emphasized.

A third stream of contention throughout the century, especially in de-centralized contexts in North Africa and Iran, where the writ of the central state ran thin, and where local forms of autonomy anchored in tribes, Sufi orders, city quarters, guilds or communal traditions was strong, had much more to do with the defence of pre-existing (or the search for projected) sites of autonomy against the exactions or depredations of a distant state, conceived of as a necessary evil, or as an entity to be avoided as much as possible. As a nineteenth-century 'Iraqi' tribal chant stated: 'It [the government] is a flabby serpent and has no venom' (Batatu 1978: 14). In Cyrenaica, in the mid-nineteenth century, the Sufi leader Al-Sanusi 'appeared to his adepts as a sort of avenger and a substitute for the decadent establishment' (Berque 1972: 35 n. 2). Communal traditions were strong among the peasantry in nineteenth-century Egypt. Some developed direct means of exacting justice; others broke with conventional society and sought to achieve liberty against the law. Autonomist and state-rejecting movements were often led by the poor and the marginal, but not always. The Druze uprisings of the 1890s and early 1900s, for example, represented efforts to generate new spheres of autonomy within Ottoman Syria for the relatively wealthy Druze warlords who had made their money in land and the grain trade in recent times, but who were excluded in other respects from notable Damascene society.

Finally, there were reformist movements, seeking some decisive (but not revolutionary) change in the terms of the hegemony of the dominant bloc, often in the sense of winning representation of, and a place in the state for, new and previously unrepresented groups. The 'Urabi movement in Egypt under patriotic and constitutional banners in 1881–2 was one example. Another was the Committee of Union and Progress (CUP) and the Young Turks in the Ottoman centre from the 1880s until the 'revolution' of 1908. These movements, in partial contrast with revolutionary, defensive and autonomist movements, were very often led by those who had made gains through the political and economic changes of the century, and sought to convert those gains into political power. They were often drawn from the ranks of the urban intelligentsia. New modes of organization, such as the learning, reforming or charitable societies that increasingly emerged in the second half of the nineteenth century in the cities owed their genesis to these constituencies and their movements. These movements aimed to reform the state, but not to replace it, or charge it with new social and economic functions, with the exception, perhaps, of the demand that the state now provide European-style education. These movements were influenced heavily by European liberalism and Islamic modernism alike. Before 1911, at least, nationalism in the sense of an independent and sovereign political community with no allegiance to dynast and rooted in nation-ness rather than religious community was only a very minor key in unruly popular politics. Only in the Balkans or among Armenians and Maronite Lebanese had it come to the fore. 'Urabi sought some form of autonomy under the rule of the Ottoman sultan; the Young Turks, at least before 1908, sought to restore the Ottoman empire not to abolish it, and to prevent nationalist secession, not to encourage it.

Algeria: Sufis, tribes and Janissaries, 1783–1816

Protests arising amid state imposition were by no means an innovation of the nineteenth century or simply a result of colonial encroachment or invasion. Well before the French invaded Algeria in 1830, there was a rich tradition of protest in the entire region against the central government which in late-eighteenth-century Algeria involved the Deys, appointees of the Ottoman sultan.

Weaknesses in the military and oligarchic system of the Algerian Deys before 1830 stemmed from various military and financial prob-lems going back to the mid-eighteenth century. The loss of income from piracy, and the costs of defensive war, notably against Spain in the 1770s and 1780s, reduced the pay and prestige, and sapped the loyalty of the Deys' marines and infantry corps. In a search to keep up rev-enues, the Deys imposed severe fiscal burdens on the tribal population. Here, growing impositions stemmed less from systematic projects of centralization – as with Ali Bey Al-Kabir, a Mamluke leader of Egypt (1760–72), Al-Jazzar Pasha, Selim III in Istanbul and so on, or from factional quarrels, as in Egypt under various Mamluke houses in the eighteenth century, and more from a resort to expedients to shore up the ship of state. These burdens stirred resistance, championed in the countryside by the Sufi orders and joined by major tribes. Algeria's western province, for example, in the second half of the eighteenth century, was 'the scene of constant conflict between the important tribes of the region and the Turks' (Abun-Nasr 1987: 167). The Beys of the western province used harsh methods to subjugate the tribes and force them to pay taxes, as well as extracting large indemnities from them.

This was the background to the rebellion of two Sufi orders – the Darqawiyya and the Tijaniyya – against the Turks. The leader of the Darqawiyya *tariqa* in western Algeria, Abdul-Qadir b. Al-Sharif, became popular with the tribal population, 'through espousing their grievances against the government and condemning the heavy impositions demanded from them'. Abdul Qadir Al-Sharif was in constant rebellion against the Turks between 1783 and 1805. In 1805, he succeeded in mobilizing the whole of the western region against them, and 'declared his intention to conquer the whole of the country'. Major tribes supported him, along with the inhabitants of at least two important towns (Al-Mu'askar and Tlimsan).

The Tijaniyya order, founded by Ahmad Al-Tijani in Ayn Madi, in the region of Al-Aghwat in 1782, was at loggerheads with the Turks from 1784. Al-Tijani was forced into exile in Fez in 1789. After his death in exile in 1815, his son Muhammad Al-Kabir formed a tribal alliance against the Turks in the 1820s with the aim of driving them from western Algeria. At the core of the uprising were the followers of the Tijaniyya order and the tribe of Banu Hashim. The latter were affiliated to the Qadiriyya order, and were the tribe to which the future leader the Amir Abd Al-Qadir belonged. In 1827, Muhammad Al-Kabir led tribal warriors into the plain of Gharis and attacked the Turkish garrison at Al-Mu'askar; but Banu Hashim did not give the support they had promised, and he was defeated, taken prisoner, and later killed by the Turks. The Tijani order then believed that the conquest of Algeria by the French in 1830 was a fulfilment of Ahmad Al-Tijani's prayer for the collapse of Turkish rule in Algeria (Abun-Nasr 1987: 167–8).

The unrewarding task of crushing such Sufi-led and tribal resistance, from the mid-eighteenth century onwards, fell on the discontented infantry garrisoned in the cities. Moreover, the Deys turned to cash raised on wheat exports to plug revenue gaps, exports which stirred further grievances as, first, they took place at a time of famine, and, second, because the control of these exports was given over to two Jewish families from Livorno, whose privileges were resented. Such was the background to the troop rebellions of 1805–16. In 1805, a Turkish soldier assassinated one of the Jewish ship-owners close to Mustafa Dey (1798–1805). On receiving the support of a former *qadi* and senior *ulema*, the troops then assassinated the Dey himself. The troops went on to assassinate six more Deys by 1816. These events

'reflected the disintegration of the system of government of the *deys*
which could function smoothly only so long as it was dominated by a
small number of officers who were obeyed by the troops and trusted by
the *deys*' (Abun-Nasr 1987: 164–7). They were about the incoherent
attempts of a financially and militarily weakened dynasty to maintain
itself by imposing burdens it did not have the wherewithal to impose,
and thus stirring resistance it could not thoroughly repress.

Protest in eighteenth-century Egypt, 1786–1798

The situation during the last decades of Mameluke rule in Egypt bore
some similarities to this, while the depth of the social and economic
crisis in Egypt may well have been greater, with famine and dearth
making regular appearances especially in the last two decades of the
eighteenth century. Especially after the fall of Ali Bey Al-Kabir
(1760–72), protest was in some ways the result of a crisis in the state
itself – it was neither a reaction to state strength nor an attempt to
direct and reform state power. We find in Al-Jabarti a blistering
critique of the multiple failures of the Mamlukes in regards to maintaining the safety and security of the roads for merchants and travellers, and the proper regulation of the markets, including that of weights
and measures. On the other hand, the urban *ulema*, who were often
wealthy through pious foundations and trade, tended not to lead or
inspire popular protests: at best they played a mediating role, or they
would weigh in with condemnation of discord; much of the time they
'preferred to be let alone' (Baer 1977: 228–9). Social historians have
shown that during the eighteenth century the urban crowds, which
included women, rose up to try to put an end to profiteering, or they
opened the granaries through direct action, attacked merchant-
profiteers, opposed exactions, and occasionally set out to seize property from the Mamlukes' mansions themselves (Raymond 1968:
112–13; Raymond 1973: 794). Marsot mentions some examples from
Al-Jabarti where the 'guilds rose in protest at a forced loan' in October
1787, and where 'there was an uprising in protest at the arrest of the
head of the guild of butchers' in September 1790 (Marsot 1966: 275).

In the countryside, while there were plenty of intra-elite conflicts
over the fiscal surplus, there was also a good deal of struggle centred on
the amount of surplus (in taxes) that the diverse elements of the
military-administrative elite could extract from commoners. In the

1770s, for example, after the fall of a local potentate in Upper Egypt, peasants refused to pay grain and land taxes; they were threatened with house demolition by the authorities (Abul-Magd 2013: 37). In 1778, in Tahta in Upper Egypt, the '*fellahs* of the surrounding country had risen in a body, and refused the imposts' (a French naval officer, cited in Baer 1969: 95). Here arms were used and alliances forged with Bedouin. A key weapon available to peasants was flight. Marsot notes of Egypt before Mehmet Ali, an 'entire village could escape into the hills in Middle and Upper Egypt and so avoid paying the taxes' (Marsot 1984: 8). Flight did not only block surplus extraction, but it signalled defiance, and could further imply that a village might enter into the protection of this or that Bedouin tribe, who regularly received substantial payments from Mamluke or other authorities in return for their military quiescence or alliance.

Baldwin's research has shown that ordinary people in Egypt, in spite of the de-centralized nature of the Ottoman empire in the eighteenth century, remained tenacious in their search for the justice of the Ottoman sultan in Istanbul (through petitions) and the correct application of the law (through recourse to the courts) (Baldwin 2010). Standing between the courts, the Ottoman *wali* (governor) and the sultan in Istanbul, however, were an array of vested interests, warring and even rapacious Mameluke households, exploitative tax farmers (Marsot 1984: 7–10), *qadi*s, and merchants (Chalcraft 2007: 182ff.). In 1794–5, the inhabitants of a village near Bilbays in Sharqiyya (Lower Egypt), came to Cairo to lodge demands against the imposts imposed by a prominent '*alim* who was also a tax-farmer. Backed by 'disturbances', these demands won some tax remission (Baer 1969: 96). Others turned away from direct engagement with the authorities and towards neighbourhood solidarities, urban craft guilds and flourishing mystic orders for social, economic and religious succour. The sugar carriers of the imperial refineries in eighteenth-century Egypt, for example, sought to 'distribute guild income equally among themselves' (Ghazali 1999: 64).

The multiple crises in the authority of the Mamluke Beys, and the hopes among the population for better alternatives, are underlined by the events of 1786. In July of that year, the Ottoman commodore Hasan Pasha arrived in Alexandria with a small contingent of troops. He had been sent by the sultan in an attempt to re-establish justice and order – and for a brief period the main Mamluke lords became open rebels against the authority of the sultan. Hasan Pasha sent couriers to the villages of the Nile delta, saying that the Ottoman sultan had decided to reduce greatly their taxes. He arrived at Bulaq, Cairo's chief harbour and crafts district on the Nile, 'to enormous popular acclaim and a cannon salute'. As Al-Jabarti wrote: 'The people were happy and full of joy and took him for the Mahdi [messianic saviour] of the age' (cited in Cole 2007: 96–7). Hasan Pasha, it turned out, was no saviour, and could not bring the Mamlukes to heel. He allowed taxes to rise, the sultan's writ remained weak, and the powers of the Mamluke households continued largely unchecked.

The Janissaries and the urban crowd, 1789–1826

The protests of the townspeople, *ulema* and Janissaries that unseated Ottoman Sultan Selim III (1789–1807) in May 1807, were about resistance to centralization in the shape of a new conscript and centralized army, a major threat to the existing infantry corps (Kafadar 2007; Shaw 1976: 273–4). The threat was new, but the repertoire of contention was not. For more than a century, uprisings centred in Istanbul involving Janissaries and their allies, mostly drawn from the townspeople, had been able to unseat the sultan. The Janissaries of the early nineteenth century could look back to at least two major eighteenth-century precedents for their actions. In 1703, an uprising against the new life-time tax farms deposed Mustafa II (1695–1703) and put Ahmed III (1703–30) on the throne (Shaw 1976: 227–8). One Janissary renegade, a certain Calık Ahmed, had even suggested in that year that the Ottoman dynasty be discarded in favour of a '*çumhur çem'iyyeti*', for which the literal translation is 'popular assembly'. Kafadar notes that *çumhur* could mean 'rebellious crowd' rather than the whole population, and that this rebel probably had a 'Janissary oligarchy' in mind. However, it is not clear why Janissaries would refer to themselves in negative terms as a 'rebellious crowd', and there were plenty of other more conventional terms available to disguise an oligarchical putsch (Kafadar 2007: 133). The uprising of Patrona Halil in 1730 deposed Ahmed III (1703–30) and put Mahmut I (1730–54) on the throne (Shaw 1976: 240). In Izmir in 1788, urban artisans, guilds and townspeople rose against the tripling of taxes stemming from the outbreak of war in 1787, ousting a number of important officials and local notables (Clogg 1973: 24–5). The rising of 1807 can be seen as a continuation of this tradition, one born amid the seventeenth- and eighteenth-century de-centralization of the empire, and based in links between an important section of the military and administrative *askeri* class and the 'flock' – the urban crowd.

The New Order declared by Sultan Selim III shortly after his accession to power in 1789, and prompted by military defeat and territorial loss to the Tsarist empire in 1774, led to immediate resistance from the Janissaries from the 1790s onwards. Notables who had their *timar*-holding seized joined with the Janissaries. Many *ulema* opposed non-Islamic innovations in the structure of the state. Urban artisans also opposed the fact that the sultan had set himself against the monopolistic rights of many guilds (Akarlı 1987: 228). Artisans were sometimes protected by Janissaries, depended on them for their livelihoods, or actually were Janissaries themselves, a legacy of the military de-centralization of the eighteenth century. Artisans sought more secure rights of control and access to the positions, working capital and premises where they worked (Akarlı 2004). The townspeople more generally were discontented by inflation (Shaw 1976: 273). The last minute concessions on officials by the sultan were too little, too late, the movement secured a legal ruling against the New Order and the sultan was deposed and replaced by Mustafa IV (1807–8). For the time being, the powers of the new army were pegged back.

The link between the Janissaries and their urban allies was articulated in the early nineteenth century by the idea that, in borrowing military techniques from Christendom, Sultan Selim III was deviating from the faith. Many believed he was, a position that was potentially explosive on the political level, and certainly brought many *ulema* into these struggles. After supporters of the centralizer Mahmud II managed to get him on the throne in 1808, against popular sentiment in the capital, a new uprising broke out in November 1808, above all against the powerful Bulgarian provincial notable Bayraktar who was the Grand Vizier responsible for bringing in new military corps. Janissaries were outraged by the threat to their position that his policies posed, stirred up by rumours of their abolition and by shock at execution of Prince Mustafa (by the sultan in order to eliminate a rival). The first public appearance of the corps was on the last night of Ramadan (1223 AH/14 November 1808). The Janissaries 'obtained the support of the artisans' (Shaw 1977: 4–5) as well as the urban crowd.

On this occasion, concessions were made. Mahmud II continued to manoeuvre cautiously, and to foster the development of new,

European-style military units at the heart of the state. The last stand of the Janissaries came on 14 June 1826. Objecting to the new corps, the Janissaries rebelled, being joined by thousands of artisans and others on Janissary payrolls fearing loss of salaries, or as *ulema* and others 'offended by the sultan's attempt to innovate one of the most traditional institutions of all' (Shaw 1977: 20). The Janissaries were massacred. The sultan was careful to associate himself with Islam, as opposed to the ways of the infidel, a move that was in some respects an innovation, as the Islamic credentials of Ottoman sultans had rarely been subject to this kind of debate; in more secular mode, the sultan made sure that the Janissaries were linked with corruption and defeat (in the Greek war). Indeed, here the sultan was exploiting public discontent, as the 'Ottomans still were unable to break into the Morea, contributing further to general public dissatisfaction in Istanbul with the Janissaries and the rest of the old army' (Shaw 1977: 17–19). After the massacre, weapons of the weak were a last resort, and fires of unknown origin devastated the old part of city; even the buildings of the Sublime Porte were burned on 31 August 1826 (Shaw 1977: 28).

Uprisings and tax revolts in the Mashriq

The struggle at the core of the Ottoman state was resolved in favour of the forces of a new, European-style army and forms of state centralization. The outmanoeuvring and then the massacre of the Janissaries in 1826 put an end to the contentious capacities of the urban crowd outside the palace, breaking the old linkages between the Janissary military on the one hand, and urban crafts and service workers, certain notables, merchants and tax-farmers, and the *ulema* on the other. The new military order was – at least for the time being – fully under the control of the Porte. The defeat of the Janissaries, paved the way for the re-configuration of the Ottoman state, enabling it to achieve a power to overcome the de-centralized popular politics of the eighteenth century, and unleashing a prolonged wave of centralization, which involved a provocative assault on existing tissues of consent.

After 1826, for many decades, popular resistance would come from outside the centre of the new state. In the years immediately following 1826, 'opposition to the sultan and his reforms began to spring up everywhere, not only among former Janissaries and conservatives but also among *ulema*, artisans, merchants, and even former partisans of reform who were affected in some way or other by the sultan's financial and military policies'. Tax farms, heavy taxes, *ulema* loss of control over pious foundations and new taxes were part of the reason for this. In addition to the fact that promised life-time pensions for ex-Janissaries turned out to be a death sentence for those who applied (Shaw 1977: 28).

After 1833, severe defeats on the Ottoman sultan inflicted by Egyptians and the European powers, paved the way for revolts in Anatolia, Bosnia, Macedonia and Iraq; some were only partially put down. Many lower level *ulema*, who had remained neutral, now turned against Mahmud II, 'attributing the defeat to the reforms and complaining about what they considered to be the sultan's infidel ways as well as the presence of foreigners in the capital.' Mahmud II's use of the Mansure army to suppress unrest only added to discontent (Shaw 1977: 35). There were protests against Ottoman centralization in Baghdad, inaugurating a tradition that continued for decades (Batatu 1978: 470).

French consular correspondence from the late 1820s offers a glimpse of the opposition to new exactions in the cities and towns of the Mashriq: Beirut, Tripoli, Acre, Antoura, Aleppo, Homs, Hama, Damascus and Baghdad. In early 1828, Janissaries in Aleppo tried to forge alliances with townspeople in order to defy the Porte (Correspondence Politique Turquie (CPT) Vol. 258, fols 7–8, 1828). In February, Maronites on Mount Lebanon sought out French protection, presenting letters of protection from Louis XIV and Louis XV, and informing the French that they were crushed by the impositions of the Ottoman Pasha of Acre (CPT, Vol. 258, fols 13–14, 1828). On 25 June 1828, Henri Guys, the major French consul in the region, wrote of 'troubles' in Hama and Homs following a new tax imposed by the Turks (CPT, Vol. 258, fols 23–6, 1828). On 27 June 1828, he detailed the new levies, and announced that 'the towns of Hama and Homs have revolted. They completely refuse to pay their component [of the tax], nor new levies'. Tripolitanians, on the other hand, without taking up arms, have refused to pay a farthing ('un parat') of the new demands (CPT, Vol. 258, fol. 27, 1828). In February 1829, a number of Janissary chiefs 'revolting against authority' were executed (CPT, Vol. 258, fol. 87, 1829). In May 1829, the inhabitants of Baghdad rose against the Ottoman Pasha and put him to death (CPT, Vol. 258, fols. 136–7, 1829). In the same year, more exactions were reported in Acre, and a riot (*émeute*) in Hama (CPT, Vol. 258, fols. 153–6, 1829).

These uprisings may have been stimulated by the new tax burden, but they also built on a prior tradition of resistance to imposts judged excessive. There was an uprising of the commoners ('ammiyya) in Mount Lebanon in 1790, for example, against extraordinary tax levies (Makdisi 2000: 45). In 1821, there was another such 'ammiyya against new poll and land taxes imposed by the amir and considered excessive by the Christian peasantry (Havemann 1991; Hilw 1979). When the amir refused to repeal his demands, 'resistance evolved into a military conflict' (Havemann 1991: 89). A Maronite bishop 'is reported to have initiated the first protest meeting and organized the subsequent campaigns' (Havemann 1991: 89). Some muqata'aji-s, noble tax-farmers who controlled the sub-districts of Mount Lebanon, were also involved. Most of the protestors, nonetheless, were peasants and lower Maronite clergy. Many saw their action as being in the 'interest of the country' (maslahat al-bilad), referring to Mount Lebanon, a de facto tributary principality within the Ottoman empire under an amir, drawn from a noble family, loyal to the sultan. This was a transgressive move, aggregating to commoners the right to judge the interest of the country, something that the Ottoman authorities were completely unable to countenance. In a further departure from hierarchical or genealogical principles, the villages that joined the uprising elected deputies (wukala') from among the commoners to advocate for them. The revolt demanded lower taxation, and that the tax levies come only once a year and after the harvest.

For the authorities this was said to be incomprehensible: as an Ottoman governor addressed the people in 1821, the notables were corrupting the land, using 'intrigue, cunning and deception' to disturb the peace. The commoners, on the other hand, put themselves in a perplexing way at odds with the august authority, order and security of the amir, because they were ignorant, base, stubborn, disobedient, bold and deviant; they had entered a domain for which they were utterly unfit and unprepared; they were easily crushed, not 'an army ready for battle', and should give up on folly. As an Ottoman official declared, subjects 'held in compassion and protection ... should return to your villages and preoccupy yourselves with your own affairs and render what is required of you' (quoted in Makdisi 2000: 47–8). In this view, social rank was a natural fact and an inviolate reflection of 'the will of God'. The French revolution, in this view, bolstered by the French counterrevolutionary exiles, priests and émigré princes alike who took up residence in Mount Lebanon, was an abomination, a breakdown of social order that threw open the 'doors of hell' (Makdisi 2000: 21, 41).

The tax protests in the Mashriq in the late 1820s and early 1830s paved the way to some extent for Mehmet Ali's invasion and occupation of Syria (1832–41) under Ibrahim Pasha, especially as the latter, who defeated the Ottoman forces, made promises of self-rule to the local inhabitants in order to gain support. Such promises resonated above all because they implied some respite from the new and overweaning burdens from Istanbul – but also because the uprisings in the Balkans in particular had suggested new formulae for forms of local rule and autonomy. On the other hand, Ibrahim Pasha, betrayed these expectations: the 'children of Arabs' were despised and treated as Egyptian *fellahin* (Makdisi 2000: 53); heavy taxation was imposed on land and individuals, weapons were confiscated, conscription threatened, and forced labour introduced.

Against this background, there were uprisings against Egyptian rule in Palestine, Syria and Mount Lebanon from 1834 until the military regime was dismantled. On Mount Lebanon, the major event was another commoner rising, mainly involving peasants and lower clergy, which took place in 1840. This time the leadership was drawn from humbler strata, and 'a certain degree of patriotic feeling' (Havemann 1991: 89) was at work. Some Christians were inspired by the 1839 decree of Gülhane, which officially inaugurated the Tanzimat, and stipulated the juridical equality of Muslim and non-Muslim subjects. Merchants and artisans were involved for the first time, and helped provision the movement through the coastal towns. A number of elites were involved for their own reasons: some tax-farmers, French noblemen, Catholic missionaries and British diplomats (Havemann 1991: 89–90). Some muqata'aji-s were present as a means to restore the Ottoman regime and maintain privileges usurped by the amir and the Egyptians (Makdisi 2000: 58). Druze, who had also suffered harsh Egyptian rule, were also involved. In 1840, unlike in 1821, moral backing was given to the uprising by the Maronite Patriarchate itself: after hesitation, and 'fear of the apparently leaderless nature of the uprising' the Patriarch 'finally urged the priests and monks in Mount Lebanon to aid in '*al-qiyam al-jumhuri*', the rising of the masses. He insisted that the popular welfare (*al-salih al-jumhuri*), understood in terms of the flourishing of the populace under conditions of just taxation, could be served only if Egypt's oppressive reign ended (Makdisi 2000: 58). The French government itself, urged by the local consul, considered whether to support the rising as 'protector' of the Christians, but decided against it on the basis of preserving their relations with the Ottoman empire and the British. At a church in Antilyas on 8 June 1840 Christian, Druze, Sunni and Shi'a villagers declared themselves of 'one mind and one voice' (Makdisi 2000: 58).

In 1840, insurgents invoked the interest of the 'fatherland' (*maslahat al-watan*) (Hilw 1979: 35, 91), not just the interest of the *country*, as in 1821. This idea invoked a stronger form of territoriality. It used a translation of the French revolutionary term, *patrie*, drawing on the example of the Greek war of national independence, where Christian peasants and commoners had risen up against local nobility, the Christian church, the Islamic state, and Ottoman rule alike (Hilw 1979: 92).

The goal of the commoners and their backers was to lower taxes, revoke orders to disarm the Christian population, win exemption from conscription, and the abolition of compulsory labour. These goals were reactions to Egyptian measures. On the other hand, there were also political demands: that two members from each religious community should be appointed to an advisory council to help the amir in his affairs (Havemann 1991). Such demands represented a 'first step toward a confessional order' (Havemann 1991: 91). In this altered political context, the Maronite church started to appeal to solidarities of sect more frequently, setting a new context in the mountain.

The British and the Ottomans took advantage of the uprising to issue the ultimatum to Mehmet Ali to withdraw his forces from Syria (Makdisi 2000: 51). Conflicts of a more sectarian character broke out in the aftermath in Mount Lebanon in 1841 'between Druze notables, who were returning from an exile imposed by the Egyptians, and Maronite villagers of Dayr Al-Qamar' (Makdisi 2000: 51, 63ff.), the first major sectarian clashes between Maronite and Druze in Mount Lebanon.

These protests only altered in part the course of the new fiscal policies, and were only able at best to blunt the force of the new exactions; they also had the disadvantage of bringing down repression on the heads of their protagonists. They also, inadvertently, facilitated the intervention of France, as protector of the Maronites, not to mention, in the earlier case, the invasion of Ibrahim Pasha, who posed as defender of the local inhabitants. They also enabled local notables to step in as peace-makers, power-holders who were then in a position to alter the terms of tax-raising to the advantage of themselves and their clients, rather than to the advantage of the mass of the population. On the other hand, on Mount Lebanon certainly, out of these conflicts came intimations of a new concept of territorial autonomy.

Egypt: resisting French occupation, 1798–1801

In July 1798, to cite the chronicler and religious scholar Al-Jabarti, 'the people of the port [of Alexandria] suddenly realized that the French and their ships had reached Al-'Ajami and were advancing on the town ... by land like a swarm of locusts' (Jabarti 1993: 20). Napoleon boasted that he had just 'vanquished one of the foremost Powers in Europe'. He was shocked to discover that the small town of Alexandria, only 8,000 strong, put up a stiff resistance. He thought them blind, ignorant or 'extremely presumptuous' to resist. The struggle was general. Bedouin horsemen fired on the French as soon as they appeared on the coast. Men, women and children called on their friends and neighbours to surge to the rather minor fortifications that the town possessed (Cole 2007: 22–3). When the small detachment of cavalrymen put out by the Mamluke state was defeated, the townspeople 'peppered the French with gunfire'. And where there were no guns or ammunition, the inhabitants 'pelted them with stones' (Cole 2007: 24–5). When throwing stones became foolhardy because of military repression, the Alexandrians showed their opposition by refusing to witness Napoleon's grandiose review of his victorious troops: they either withdrew from the town, fled in fear for their lives, or stayed in their homes (Cole 2007: 25). When the chink of an opportunity appeared, with much of the French army marching south, a short-lived uprising took place at Alexandria, with inhabitants firing from the windows during 10–15 July, 1798 (Cole 2007: 59).

In Cairo, as the Mamlukes set about trying to build up the city's defences, 'gloom spread among the populace and was felt in the market-places and people withdrew to their homes from sunset onward'. Others gathered in groups amid the general 'uproar' and 'chewed their fingers in distress and sorrow'. For others, 'fear and terror waxed greater than ever' (Jabarti 1993: 24, 37, 38). Many expected little but destruction at the hands of the Christian French. Egyptians were not naïve about the intentions of Europeans, they did not greet them as gods, liberators, or civilizers, and most rejected the French project *in toto*. An imperial decree issued by the Ottoman grand vizier circulating in Egypt in 1799 warned that the French would 'seize the goods of the believers; their women and children will be reduced to slavery; and your blood will be spilled (may God preserve us)!' (Cole 2007: 158). Such by no means unreasonable fears were probably widespread among ordinary Egyptians. It was inconceivable for most that Muslim lands could be ruled by a Christian power, or that Ottoman and Egyptian subjects, loyal to the sultan for centuries, could be ruled by Napoleonic France. There was little precedent for this across North Africa, the Mashriq, the Arabian peninsula, Iran and the Ottoman domains since the Crusades. In the Maghrib the struggle against Spanish incursions there had been mostly successful since 1492. What would become of authority, justice, law, faith, custom and rights? What would become of the great institutions and traditions of the Egyptian, Ottoman and Islamic world? French culture and institutions were alien, Napoleon and his army, who were said to have rebelled against and killed their own sultan, were seen as arrogant and deceitful, their talk of liberty and civilization was mostly incomprehensible, and their claims to being supporters of Islam nothing short of a 'derangement of the mind' (Jabarti 1993: 30). Commercial relations with the French, or other circuits of material and affective exchange on which new forms of power could be founded were lacking.

  Al-Jabarti devoted several pages to a coruscating denunciation of the French attempt to legitimate their rule in Egypt. In July 1798, the French distributed a short and supposedly expert tract, written in Arabic by France's finest Arabist, aiming to justify their conquest. The French declared themselves to be acting 'In the name of God, and on behalf of the French Republic, based on liberty and equality' and in opposition to the disobedient, 'corrupt, contemptuous and high-handed Mamlukes', who were given over to 'extortion and violence' and lacked 'reason, virtue and knowledge'. They spoke of Egypt as the 'fairest land that is to be found upon the face of the globe'. They announced that they had come, not to oppose Islam but in order to 'restore your rights', in the service of God and in reverence for the Qur'an and the Prophet. The proclamation claimed that 'the French are also faithful Muslims' and hence they had invaded Rome and destroyed the Papal See. They also maintained that they were friends of the sultan, 'may God ever perpetuate his empire!' They continued:

'Blessing on blessing to the Egyptians who will act in concert with us, without any delay, for their condition shall be rightly adjusted, and their rank raised ... Woe upon woe to those who will unite with the Mamlukes and assist them in the war with us.' The statement closed as follows: 'Every village that shall rise against the French army, shall be burnt down' (cited in Cole 2007: 25–7).

Al-Jabarti was profoundly unimpressed by what Napoleon thought was a daring attempt to divide the local population and win hearts and minds by posing as the defender of sultan and Islam against the tyranny and disobedience of the Mamlukes. For Al-Jabarti, no friend of the Mamelukes, this was simply worthless propaganda combined with a threat of brute force. 'Here is an explanation', he begins coldly, 'of the incoherent words and vulgar constructions which he put into this miserable letter.' Over several pages, Al-Jabarti details the thicket of errors in grammar, syntax and word choice that littered the French proclamation. For an heir to a tradition in which the pen was monopolized by those of deep learning, for a scholar schooled in Arabic, and for a cleric living and breathing the intimate relationship between Arabic, Qur'anic revelation, religious judgment, and Islamic law, the butchery of the Arabic itself was a reason alone to invalidate any meaningful claim to authority.

This was only the foothills of Al-Jabarti's denunciation, which becomes increasingly full-blooded as it progresses. He argues that the French claim to believe in three religions, but in fact they are 'liars' as they do not, nor indeed in any, 'may God afflict them with every calamity'. 'They are materialists', he points out, 'who deny all God's attributes'. Indeed, by destroying the Papal See the French have gone against the Christians, and thus opposed both Christians and Muslims. Napoleon claims that 'I more than the Mamlukes serve God', but 'there is no doubt', Al-Jabarti goes on, 'that this is a derangement of his mind and an excess of foolishness.' Indeed, *'kufr* (unbelief) has dulled his heart'. Napoleon is also lying when he says that he respects the Prophet or the Qur'an – as he clearly does not believe in or respect the *umma* (Islamic community), and nor does he glorify the Qur'an by believing in it, 'may God cast him into perdition'. 'The French', he continues, 'are appointing themselves controllers of God's secrets, but there is no disgrace worse than disbelief.' The French, moreover, had killed their own sultan and rebelled against him. Their women have no modesty, and their men have intercourse with any woman who pleases them; they do not shave heads nor their pubic hair, but they do shave their moustaches and beard; they mix their foods; and they should rightly be treated with 'contempt'. Al-Jabarti concludes in a fairly comprehensive fashion, 'May God hurry misfortune and punishment upon them, may He strike their tongues with dumbness, may He scatter their hosts, and disperse them, confound their intelligence, and cause their breath to cease' (Cole 2007: 27–33).

It was part of a widely known stock of chronicles, legends and common sense that the scholar-leader and dynasty-founder Salah Al-Din Ibn Ayyub (d. 1193) had driven out the Crusaders – and although no such leader existed in Egypt in 1798, and although the Ottoman sultan was initially silent – many responded to the general call to arms issued by the Mamlukes. 'The Shaykhs, the dignitaries, and the common people set out with clubs and arms' (Jabarti 1993: 33). With or without authorization, Napoleon's army was resisted every step of the way south through Lower Egypt to Cairo. Peasants, villagers, fishermen, Bedouin and the inhabitants of market towns such as Damanhour fought back with whatever weapons were to hand. They were not daunted by news of Napoleon's military prowess. 'The officer memoirists often expected peasants to be subservient, but were repeatedly disappointed.' One peasant woman, combining child care and guerrilla struggle, managed with what was described as a pair of scissors, her baby still in her arms, to put out the eyes of a French aide-de-camp who was out in front of the advancing troops. Just as in Alexandria, the town of Damanhour rose up with arms against the French garrison stationed there on 17 July, managing to beat back some of the French forces and killing twenty French soldiers. Kléber, one of the most important French generals, felt under siege there. A similar rising against the French garrison in the provincial town of Bilbeis involved 1,500–1,800 peasants and Bedouin (Cole 2007: 116–17). Market day in Mansura in August 1798 allowed Bedouin and peasants to filter into the town, join with the townspeople, and effect an armed insurrection involving 4,000 people protesting the occupation and the heavy taxes. The French took casualties and the garrison was 'helpless'. The uprising was only broken by major French reinforcements (Cole 2007: 120–1).

In the province of Al-Minufiya, the French faced 'hordes [read large numbers] of insurgent Bedouin', and burnt many villages 'in order to imprint terror on that unruly population' wrote Niello Sargy, fighting with the French (Cole 2007: 122). Some refused to be terrorized. Instead, another insurrection, this time near Mansura in the village of Sonbat, broke out during August and September 1798. Again Bedouin and peasants formed an alliance, the former supplying arms (Cole 2007: 143). As a French soldier admitted, 'instead of being aided by the inhabitants, whom we had ruined ... we found all against us'. As another soldier, by the name of Bourrienne wrote, 'No Frenchman was secure of his life who happened to stray half a mile from any inhabited place' (Cole 2007: 110–1).

The fishermen and grandees of Lake Manzala managed to beat back the marauding French for several months. In September 1798, between 1,200–1,500 armed men and women joined battle. After their defeat, the whole area subsequently suffered terrible repression: in several villages all the inhabitants were killed, while the would-be emperor Bonaparte wrote in martial tradition of the 'honour' that this bestowed upon his troops (Cole 2007: 161–5).

Others tried to resist without picking up weapons and using forms of civil disobedience. On 19 July, for example, all the inhabitants of the small town of Shum assembled and refused to provide supplies to the French (Cole 2007: 63). The French answered with a massacre. As Sergeant Francois's diary has it: 'while firing into those crowds ... [w]e killed about 900 men, not counting the women and children, who remained in their habitations, to which we set fire with our musketry and artillery.' The soldiers then took everything, livestock and food, and before leaving 'we finished burning the rest of the houses, or rather the huts, so as to provide a terrible object lesson to these half-savage and barbarous people' (Cole 2007: 63). The same thing happened in Abu Za'bal. The villagers, notwithstanding the gruesome fate of their compatriots in Shum, nobly refused to provide provisions to the French as demanded. But they suffered the same fate. In the words of the chronicler Al-Jabarti, the French 'attacked them, beat them, broke them, pillaged the town, and then burned it' (Cole 2007: 88).

Cairo was taken because the Mamluke cavalry were unable to defend it in open confrontation against the French. They were defeated at the Battle of the Pyramids, according to Al-Jabarti amid cowardice, arrogance, delusion and disgrace (Jabarti 1993: 36, 38). Many of the former fled after their defeat to Syria or up the Nile, where some continued to fight, joined by volunteers from Arabia and various Ottoman officials, such as Hasan Bey Al-Gadawi, who had been a

Mamluke of Al-Jezzar Pasha (Jahhaf 1975: 102). Al-Jabarti may have bequeathed a too-negative picture of the usually universally reviled Mamlukes. Murad Bey, the chief Mamluke leader, refused Napoleon's offer to rule as a tributary French vassal in Upper Egypt, using an insulting tone and even sarcastically offering Napoleon 'money to go back to France and save the blood of his soldiers' (Abul-Magd 2013: 56). It was this failed collaboration that gave Napoleon no choice but to pursue the French military conquest of the south, greatly increasing the costs of the occupation. The fighting continued in Upper Egypt for some time, with the assistance of various important tribes such as the Hilla and the Juhayna (Jahhaf 1975: 103), as well as of peasants, 800 of whom were enrolled, for example, in one action in Qina province (Abul-Magd 2013: 58). Where local forces were defeated, the French followed up with massacres of the commoners, and destroyed villages that refused to provision their army (Abul-Magd 2013: 58, 60).

In Lower Egypt, resistance with a more civilian leadership developed. In October 1798, after a string of French atrocities and injustices regarding pillage, killings, exactions, and the destruction of tombs, mosques, minarets and shrines, the 'common people' of Cairo rose up with arms against French rule. They were encouraged by the news from Istanbul. At last the sultan had spoken. The Ottoman authorities finally declared a *jihad* to defend Egypt and Islam against the French in September 1798. The Ottomans asserted that the French had betrayed the Ottomans who had stood with them, lied that the Ottomans had acquiesced, and contrary to law, they had set out to conquer and subjugate Egypt, 'the gate to the two holy cities, Mecca and Medina', and hence 'of the greatest importance for all Muslims'. It had thus become a 'personal religious obligation' incumbent on every Muslim to march against the French, and thus 'purify' Cairo and its environs from their 'corrupting presence' and 'liberate the servants of God' (Cole 2007: 155–6). Thus the sultan declared a *jihad*, authorizing guerrilla war in Egypt on the one hand, and eventually, on the other, authorized the Ottoman governor of Palestine, the formidable Bosnian, Ahmad Al-Jazzar Pasha, who was attempting to build a dynasty out of his fortress in the coastal town of Acre, to liberate Egypt from the French. Rumours spread in Egypt that Al-Jezzar's armies had reached Bilbeis in the Delta and were coming to deliver the population. This was a potent cocktail, the sultan had declared war, mobilized

Al-Jezzar, and simultaneously authorized through the highest religious authorities in the empire, that all Muslim individuals now had a duty to take up arms themselves against the French.

The idea of *jihad* was well known, although interpreted in different ways, to every Muslim. In its most simple form, *jihad* meant exertion of whatever kind (armed/unarmed, collective or individual), in defence of the faith. In this context, it meant something like 'just war': Islamic jurists in the early centuries of Islam had worked out a legal doctrine, mandating that, when the Dar al-Islam (House of Islam) was threatened with becoming a Dar al-Harb (Abode of War), then it was incumbent on Muslims as a matter of law to take up arms in the cause of God in order to defend the faith. Charismatic leaders, reformers and would-be dynasts fought various kinds of *jihad* against forms of unbelief and injustice from Mauritania to the Sudan, all along the southern fringes of the Sahara, from the late seventeenth century down to the early twentieth century. Their rank and file included itinerant beggars, slaves, ex-slaves, pastoralists, oppressed peasants, outcasts, young men's gangs, renegades, as well as students, teachers, Sufis and preachers (Lapidus 1988: 510–34). Further afield, an Indian theologian called Shah Abd Al-'Aziz (1746–1824), who was the son of the famous theologian and reformer Shah Wali Allah, was to issue such a legal ruling (*fatwa*) in India in 1803. He reasoned that, in the lands between Delhi and Calcutta, the leader of the Muslims, the Imam al-Muslimin, had no authority, whereas the authority of Christian rulers, in matters of administration, arbitration, punishment, taxation and safe passage, was enforced (Peters 1979: 45). The implication was therefore that India, under the ever more invasive control of the East India Company, had become Dar Al-Harb.

When the news of the invasion of Egypt spread in the Islamic world, volunteers came from Arabia via Jidda to join the forces of the Mamlukes to fight the usurping Christians. In July 1798, for example, a number of women entered the Grand Mosque in Mecca and 'threw down their rings, necklaces and fine clothes before the gathering' (Jahhaf 1975: 87). With this dramatic gesture, these women were challenging men of honour to take up arms. At the same time, by handing over their valuables, they were providing an important source of funds for the fight. The women perceived that the House of Islam was under threat. The Yemeni chronicler Jahhaf (1775–1827) spoke of the French 'entry' into 'the land of Egypt' and how they 'made themselves masters of it' (*astawlu*), and spread the hands of unbelief (*al-kufr*) thereon, bringing forth corruption, dominating over and making the Muslims present there suffer', operating through 'trickery' and 'greedy ambition' (Jahhaf 1975: 87). News of this abominable Christian usurpation, unprecedented since the Crusades, was travelling far and wide. The sultan in Istanbul remained silent. The Amir Ghalib of Mecca sat on his hands, merely writing a polite letter to Napoleon, even after the Porte declared *jihad* in August 1798. The Amir Ghalib was busy in any case trying to hold his own against the Wahhabis and was disgusted with the lack of Ottoman assistance in this regard. Instead it was a Maghribi sharif, a certain Shaykh Muhammad Al-Kilani, who stepped up. Preaching in the mosque that day, he cited the sayings of the revered Prophet of Islam, urged the men and women present that it was a religious duty to take up arms against the enemies of God and faith. Al-Kilani's 'summons wrought in people's hearts what it wrought, and he became known among the people ... so they appeared before him ... with money in their hands ... and volunteers came to him from remote regions' (Jahhaf 1975: 97).

Al-Kilani won the backing of a number of big merchants of the Hijaz, religious and tribal leaders from up and down the Red Sea coast, and some officials, including the Amir of Mecca, an important dignitary, loyal to the Ottoman sultan. Before long, perhaps 4,000 volunteer fighters (the word 'volunteer' was used by a contemporary chronicler) set out on ships from Arabia to Qusayr to join the many Egyptians, military and civilian, battling the French along the Nile. Al-Kilani headed a mixed force of North Africans, Meccawis and the *sharifs* of Yanbo. These forces later joined up with the Mamlukes, and were continuously reinforced through Yanbo and Qusayr (Abir 1971: 192). Also involved in the resistance in Egypt were Bedouin from Libya. Other volunteers came from as far away as Yemen (Jahhaf 1975: 101). French estimates eventually put numbers of volunteers at 6,000–7,000 (Abul-Magd 2013: 57).

In Cairo, a well-known cleric came forward, 'mounted on a steed' in extraordinary, military fashion, leading crowds from the Al-Husayn quarter. The crowd became 'huge' and full of the poor and those of low status, 'ruffians' and 'inhabitants of lodgings' in the ever-critical language of Al-Jabarti (Jabarti 1993: 83–4). They gathered in front of the Al-Husayn mosque, the Al-Azhar seminary and the chief judge's house to demand what faith, law and justice required. A perfumer among them, 'dressed up in the guise of a cleric, with a vest and waist cloth, came forward calling out to the people, incited them and exclaiming "Muslims, God is most great. The clerics have commanded you to kill the infidels. Make ready, stalwarts, and strike them everywhere"' (Cole 2007: 199). Al-Jabarti grumbled about an important popular leader, Al-Maghribi, who

> interfered in things which do not concern him [and] . . . appeared in town like the pasa and the *kethkuda* and the mamlukes . . . What is he that he appoints himself without having been appointed by anybody? It is civil strife which turns any ignoble bird into a vulture, especially when the rabble riots and the mob and riff-raff rises. This is what suits their aims (Baer 1977: 237–8).

Here, then, was a vivid if sour description of the transgressive seizure from below of political and doctrinal agency. Al-Jabarti also despaired, considering that rebellion was futile in the face of French overwhelming military superiority. He wrote that a rebel leader 'forgot that he was a prisoner in the hands of the French, who occupied the fortress and its walls, the high hills and the low; fortifying them all with forbidding instruments of war' (Jabarti 1993: 84). Al-Jabarti noted that women supported the rebels by uttering 'shrill and quavering cries of joy (*zaghratna*) from the windows' and passing rumours and stories around (Jabarti 1993: 89).

The French replied to the uprising with massacre and destruction, by means of the heavy artillery that they had moved into positions above the city. Under shelling, Cairo's main thoroughfares became littered with the corpses of the populace, and sodden with their blood. And as the French started to bombard Al-Azhar itself, one of the oldest and most venerated mosque-universities in the Islamic world, some insurgents drew back in horror lest these hallowed-halls be destroyed. Firepower repressed the uprising. A grim retribution was then exacted by the French: spectacular violence was supposed to patch up political weakness. Prisoners, whether they had been fighters or not, were executed in their thousands. Others were killed in their homes where they sheltered. Pillages, exactions and the destruction of sacred sites increased, partly to pay for the costs of conquest, partly to widen routes for military purposes, and partly out of arrogance and revenge. As Al-Jabarti wrote, these were the 'enemies of the religion . . . malicious victors who gloat in the misfortune of the vanquished, rabid hyenas, mongrels obdurate in their nature' (Jabarti 1993: 93).

That the French 'killed a large number of persons' underscored, in the sober analysis of the prominent cleric Abdallah Al-Sharqawi, how they 'could not be trusted'. Likewise, although the French claimed to be only against the Mamlukes, 'when they came in, they did not confine themselves to pillaging the wealth of the Mamlukes. Rather, they looted the subjects' (cited in Cole 2007: 160). To Sunni *ulema* such as Al-Jabarti, the French presence represented a force of corruption, sedition and criminality regarding order, hierarchy and law. With the French ravaging the land, wrote Al-Jabarti, there was a general outbreak of injustice and evil, 'gangs of thugs looting, as well as other hooligans, thieves, pickpockets, robbers, highwaymen, all having a field day' (Jabarti 1993: 35).

The uprising was not just about resistance to the enormous provocation of French invasion, but it was also stimulated by the dereliction, weakness and dysfunction of the authorities of the Mamluke state. Al-Jabarti offers a swingeing criticism of Mameluke arrogance, ill-preparedness and inability to protect Egypt from European invasion. When news of the French invasion at Alexandria hit, the clerics did not pull their punches. The two principal Mamluke lords, Ibrahim and Murad Bey, met with the princes (amirs), the chief judge (the *qadi*) and the religious shaykhs in Cairo. 'All this', said one, 'is a result of [your] negligence in managing the ports and letting things slide, to such a degree that the enemy could occupy the port of Islam.' Murad Bey then exclaimed: 'What can we do, for whenever we want to rebuild and fortify you claim: "their intention is rebellion against the Sultan", and this is what has prevented us from acting.' But Al-Jabarti was unimpressed. 'Such were their excuses', reads his chronicle, 'as frail as a spider's web.' Al-Jabarti was here citing the Qur'an and the Sura of the Spider (S. 29, v. 41). This reference was particularly appropriate. The full verse reads:

Qaaroon, Pharaoh, and Hamaan: Moses went to them with clear signs. But they continued to commit tyranny on earth. Consequently, they could not evade (the retribution). All those disbelievers were doomed as a consequence of their sins. Some of them we annihilated by violent winds, some were annihilated by the quake, some we caused the earth to swallow, and some we drowned. God is not the One who wronged them; it is they who wronged their own souls. The allegory of those who accept other masters beside God is that of the spider and her home; the flimsiest of all homes is the home of the spider, if they only knew (29: 39–41).

In other words, in making reference to the spider's web, Al-Jabarti was likening the Mamlukes to the tyrants of old who turned away from God, weakened their own houses, and brought down upon themselves a great calamity as a consequence. Al-Jabarti's depiction of the arrival of the French as a 'swarm of locusts' likened their invasion to a tremendous calamity, overseen by God, but brought on by the folly and sin of man, in particular of those of unjust rulers. Here, then, was another version of a pre-nationalist and non-European rejection of the tyranny of the unjust ruler.

His critique was pressed home in more 'secular' mode. He writes of their 'excuses' and failures. 'For since the time of [the Mamluke] 'Ali Bey [who ruled Egypt 1760–72]', he writes, 'not only did they not pay sufficient attention to the port but even removed what weapons and cannons were already there'. Moreover, they did not pay salaries, they deployed useless and 'broken-down cannons'. Worse,

once ... they needed gunpowder to fire the cannon on the Feast [celebrating the end of Ramadan, the month of fasting] but they could not even find enough to load it ... so they had to buy powder from a druggist. All this after Alexandria and its towers had once been extremely well built and fortified with an excellent wall ... maintained by former generations ... Every tower had its own ammunition depot, supplies, and garrison. All these were neglected until nothing remained.

Al-Jabarti was therefore underlining the temporal inadequacies of the Mamluke beys – comparing their activities unfavourably to those of the recent past and the example of the state-builder, Ali Bey Al-Kabir. They were even incapable, in spite of their membership in the military class, of providing the proper ceremonial cannon shot for the popular celebrations of the end of Ramadan, and were reduced to procurement from a humble member of the civilian 'flock'. Indeed, the shaykhs present at the meeting were so scandalized by the Mamlukes that they agreed to write a report about these failings and send it to the sultan (Jabarti 1993: 22–3). Given the momentous events that were engulfing the country, and the uproar rising in the towns, villages and deserts, a report to the sultan was a bookish response indeed. The point to underline here, however, is that the forms of disgust and outrage that stirred contentious action arose not from some putative opportunity in the state, nor because the state had provoked action, but because the state was derelict. The initial target of such protest, at this level, was

not the infidel, but the swingeing criticism of the authorities themselves, and the imperative to act that followed from such dereliction.

The French occupation of Egypt had been a fiasco. Instead of French
glory in the Orient, it meant ignominy for France and destruction for
Egypt. Napoleon could have gone to Ireland in the 1790s to serve the
cause of Irish national self-determination. Instead he chose the chimer-
ical glory of imperialism itself (Morton 1938: 304). His occupation
was done for not only by inter-imperial rivalry, which caused the
sinking of the French fleet, or the strength of the Ottoman empire,
whose fortress at Acre withstood his siege, proving in the process that a
de-centralized empire was not necessarily a completely weak one. An
important and neglected factor, however, in Napoleon's failure, was
the popular politics of the land: the force and tenacity of the unruly,
widespread and many-headed popular mobilizations that resisted the
French: that lost them troops, lowered their morale, disrupted their
supply lines, made them realize that their attempts to win hearts and
minds were failing, and made collaboration by notables extremely
fraught by placing a sea of blood between occupier and occupied.
The Mamlukes may have lost virtually all their legitimacy in Egypt,
but by what hubris or historic precedent did a French would-be
emperor believe that he and his alien, invading army would have
more authority than they? According to the chronicler Al-Jabarti, even
the mere sight of Napoleon, near the great mosque of Al-Azhar,
'almost provoked a riot' (Cole 2007: 158). When people did obey 'to
some extent', as Al-Sharqawi averred, it was not by consent, but
because of their 'inability to resist them [the French] because the
Mamlukes had fled with the instruments of warfare' (Cole 2007:
160). In other words, overwhelming force, and not legitimacy, coercion and not consent, was the rule. Cole notes that Napoleon's 'lack of
legitimacy' was one of his 'chief difficulties' in attempting to rule Egypt
(Cole 2007: 112). In 1799, Napoleon stole out of the country, leaving
a deputy to negotiate a withdrawal. The French were gone by 1801,
the Mamlukes started to filter back into Lower Egypt, from their
sanctuaries up the Nile, and a garrison and governor loyal to the sultan
was installed, with British assistance. The first attempt by a European
power to rule a major territory in the MENA had been a failure. The
region had had its bloody introduction to colonialism, although this
time the Christian attempt to achieve direct territorial control had been
repulsed, in part by a widespread and highly varied resistance.

One negative legacy of the occupation was the association, at least in some quarters, between women and Coptic Christians with the corruption, injustice and unbelief of the Napoleonic occupation. Al-Jabarti made reference to both political and economic collaboration, sexual corruption, and essentialist caricatures about Copts and women. When the French demanded a festival at the top of the Nile flood in spite of 'poll taxes, unrelenting demands, looting of homes, harassing women, and girls, arresting and imprisoning them, and making financial settlements which exceeded all bounds', Al-Jabarti wrote that 'not a single person went out that night for pleasure excursions in boats as was customary except for Shami Christians, Copts, Europeans with their wives, and a few idlers who went as onlookers in the morning, broken-hearted and despondent' (Jabarti 1993: 49). Thus were Syrian Christians and Copts associated with Napoleonic corruption in Egypt, a corruption which was grasped in partly sexual and gendered terms, especially where Muslim women were depicted as consorting in a depraved fashion with French soldiers, and removing their veils. Al-Jabarti also wrote that, to raise taxes, Napoleon appointed Coptic tax collectors 'who went into the country like rulers, wreaking havoc among the Muslims with arrests, beatings, insults, and ceaseless harassment in their demands for money. Furthermore, they terrorized them with threats of bringing in the French soldiers if they did not pay up the determined amount quickly; all this occurred by means of Coptic planning and trickery' (Jabarti 1993: 54). These associations, linking the rights of minorities and women to colonialism and corruption were to echo through the period in different ways all the way to the present day.

Egypt: weapons of the weak and liberty against the law, 1805–1879

Mehmet Ali's accession to power in 1805 took place partly thanks to the transgressive mobilization of Cairean commoners. In May 1805, amid the struggle for power in Egypt in the wake of the French departure, commoners (*al-'amma*), neither controlled or entirely led by the *ulema* or by Umar Makram (Baer 1977: 238–9, 242) assembled and demanded to depose the Ottoman-appointed Pasha and appoint the Albanian military man Mehmet Ali in his stead. The uprisings of the previous decades against Mamlukes and French alike appear to have politicized the population. 'The same enthusiasm reigns here as in France during the first moments of the revolution', wrote the French consul in 1804: 'Everyone buys arms, the children also follow the example of their elders' (cited in Tucker 1985: 141). The Turkish Pasha declared that he would not quit his office 'by order of the *fellahin*' (Baer 1977: 217): but he was forced out. Hajjaj Al-Khudari, the head of the greengrocers' guild, 'a popular leader with great authority and influence in Rumayla quarter and elsewhere', prevented supplies getting to the citadel where the Pasha was installed. When Mehmet Ali was then invested as governor by the Ottoman sultan on 9 July, Hajjaj led a huge demonstration holding in his hand a sword drawn from its sheath as a symbol of his power (Baer 1977: 241). Ibn Sham'a, the shaykh of the butchers of Husayniyya, also figured prominently in the procession (Raymond 1968: 115–16). Artisans, petty traders and service workers may have seen in Mehmet Ali some hope for order and justice, not only after the French occupation, but after years of de-centralized and disorderly politics of exactions, impositions and exploitative intermediaries. This logic was not completely absent in the countryside. Following the abolition of tax-farms by Mehmet Ali in 1814, Al-Jabarti reported that the 'rabble' among the peasants 'insolently' declared to tax farmers who sought to extract their customary forced labour services, 'What is left to you in the country? Your days have finished, and we have become the Pasha's peasants' (cited in Cuno 1994: 5).

The consolidation of power was a different matter. Mehmet Ali was concerned to put the transgressive genie of an armed populace back into the bottle. In 1807, for example, amid the threat of a British invasion of Cairo (British troops had landed at Alexandria in March), Umar Makram, not an *'alim* but a sharif from Asyut who never taught at Al-Azhar or composed *fatawa* or religious commentaries (Baer 1977: 236–7) 'galvanized the population and ... ordered all able-bodied men under arms, even the students of Al-Azhar'. But the new Pasha was unhappy about this: 'like the *ulama* he too feared popular movements that he could not control and remarked sourly that war was not the business of the populace but that of soldiers' (Marsot 1984: 65). The function of the commoners was to supply arms and funds, he told Makram, and asked him to raise a thousand purses to pay the troops who were preparing to lay siege to the city of Alexandria where the British forces were entrenched.

The semi-autonomous dynastic state built by Mehmet Ali (reigned 1805–49) may have removed an exploitative layer of intermediaries, but it also severed the links between the urban crowd, commoners, peasants and tribal shaykhs on the one hand and their potential allies and protectors in the state on the other by eliminating the Mamelukes and the Janissaries, centralizing the levers of administrative and fiscal power, and presiding over an 'unprecedented expansion' of state control in the countryside (Cuno 1994: 199). In town and country alike, the new order brought with it an unprecedented intensification of exactions and burdens to finance dynasty-building and imperial warfare in Arabia, Greece, the Mashriq and Sudan. St John, a British journalist and traveller, wrote of groups of those conscripted in the 1830s by the 'Great Reformer': 'forty or fifty men chained together, with iron bands around their wrists and iron collars around their necks … carried away to fight battles in a cause which does not concern them' (St John 1845: 96). He wrote: 'To the Turks, to the Europeans, are accorded liberty, privilege, licence; to the Arabs and the Blacks, absolute deprivation of all rights. Power is the lot of the first class, subjection of the other' (St John 1845: 15). There was some respite in the 1850s (Toledano 2003), but burdens were ratcheted up again under Ismail (1863–79) to pay for the latter's grandiose schemes of modernization, his extravagances, his re-conquest of Sudan, and to pay off the indemnities and demands of European consuls and bankers, behind whose economic power stood the coercive power of the British navy. Ismail, for example, increased the annual land tax from 6 to 10 to 20 piastres per feddan (Hunter 1999: 39). In the 1860s in particular, the 'burden of the *corvée* [forced labour]' also weighed heavily because forced labour was used extensively in the digging of the Suez Canal and in other public works, and the fiscal crisis of the 1870s 'made taxation both heavy and capricious' (Brown 1990a: 192–3). The spread of money-lending and indebtedness, crop failure, famine and starvation only made matters worse. Ismail's acutely heavy-handed taxation policies were continued under the European debt controllers during 1876–9 (Hunter 1999: 212–13).

In this new context, commoners built up new forms of contentious mobilization. Weapons of the weak and informalism were widespread. In the countryside, peasants fought tenaciously, by collective desertion, evasion, dissimulation, crop burning, and spontaneous, small-scale physical attacks (Fahmy 1997: 101ff.) against a crushing new tax burden, increased doses of forced labour, and conscription of the free-born Muslim peasant *re'aya*. The latter was a startling innovation as the *askeri* (military) class had previously been built up through the Mamluke system as Ottoman statecraft considered it improper to arm the *re'aya*, who existed for cultivation and as a tax-base, and as a fighting force might be disloyal or too socially embedded. '[M]any shaykhs refused to collaborate with the authorities against their fellow villagers [regarding conscription gangs in the 1820s] and often resisted the pressure from above to comply with the system by employing various ways that ranged from a calculated lack of interest in government policies to deliberate attempts to frustrate such policies' (Fahmy 1997: 104–5). A law was passed in February 1844 prescribing death by hanging as punishment for shaykhs who collaborated in any way with villagers who deserted to evade taxes (Fahmy 1997: 101) – a sure sign of the forms of informalism through which incompletely co-opted headmen tried to soften the burdens imposed from above. Marsot mentions setting fire to crops, and connivance with the village headmen to avoid taxes (Marsot 1984: 8). Peasants could act directly to destroy irrigation apparatus that diverted their waters to royal estates (Abul-Magd 2013: 90). Others deserted or fled in order to avoid taxes or forced labour (Gordon 1969: 152–3). In 1836, a group of Upper Egyptian peasants, apparently allied to some headmen, refused to pay their taxes and attacked the official levying forced labour for canal-related public works. Officials seem to have been quite regularly attacked and killed (Abul-Magd 2013: 90).

In March 1867, Lady Duff Gordon remarked that the prisons in Upper Egypt were overflowing with village shaykhs who had exacted too little in taxes. The Mudir of Qena had many beaten for the same reason, and two had not survived the ordeal. Gordon also mentions the strains that conscription put on women, through the loss of their menfolk from the household economy, and of the solitary protests about the corruption and bribery involved that women mounted:

I hear that a plucky woman here has been to Keneh, and threatened the Mudir that she will go to Cairo and complain to Effendina himself of the unfair drafting for soldiers – her only son taken, while others have bribed off. She'll walk in this heat all the way, unless she succeeds in frightening the Mudir, which, as she is of the more spirited sex in this country, she may possibly do (Gordon 1969: 153).

Small wonder, in this context, that there was a 'deep distrust of everything to do with the Government' (Gordon 1969: 157). Those with ailments would refuse to declare themselves to government doctors, and pilloried thieves were readily given employment after their release:

> I inquired whether the thief who was dragged in chains through the streets would be able to find work, and was told, 'Oh, certainly; is he not a poor man? For the sake of God everyone will be ready to help him.'... Our captain was quite shocked to hear that in my country we did not like to employ a returned convict (Gordon 1969: 111).

These popular perceptions of the government may have been exacerbated by the burdens of state-building, but they built on a long and rich history in Egypt (cf. Tucker 1985: 159) and in the region as a whole.

Peasants found a variety of informal ways to resist the expropriation of their lands under the Land Law of 1858, non-payment for labour services, the use of forced labour, extortionate money-lending, or the illegal seizure or use of resources such as trees, water wheels and water. Some released their cattle and sheep into the fields of their tormentors, both to find fodder and to damage crops. In another case, the temporary jobs offered by an offending land-owner and official were boycotted by villagers in the district of Qus (Abul-Magd 2013: 102–4). Others refused to vacate lands that had been sold beneath them; others refused to pay rent; others blocked irrigation canals leading to new, often European-owned estates (Abul-Magd 2013: 110). Others physically prevented the arrival of seasonal labourers. In a case from the late 1850s, dispossessed peasants seized back the lands they had lost and refused to pay rent, to sign a lease, or enter into new share-cropping agreements (Abul-Magd 2013: 111). Workers digging the abortive coal mines in Qina province in the late 1850s deserted as a result of the irregular payment of wages, sometimes coordinating with camel-drivers to return across the desert (Abul-Magd 2013: 107).

A more radical response to the burdens imposed by the state or new forms of economic exploitation involved what Christopher Hill, referring to seventeenth-century England, called 'liberty against the law' (Hill 1996). Some peasants joined groups of bandits (*falatiyya*), who made use of shifting alliances with Bedouin, often carried firearms, and lived outside conventional society and the system of registration and taxation maintained at the local level by the village shaykhs, often in hilly or desert regions (Abul-Magd 2013: 89, 92). They made a living by irregular forms of extraction. 'These gangs frequently targeted government officials and buildings, Coptic treasury clerks, and wealthy Muslims and Copts' (Abul-Magd 2013: 90). A well-known bandit in the 1840s was Haridi Al-Rujayl, whose band ran several score strong, and who recruited in an audacious fashion: 'whenever he passed by *corvée* laborers doing public work, he would call out and take a few of them before the very eyes of the village shaykhs' (Abul-Magd 2013: 93). Haridi also claimed in unlikely but charismatic fashion to have met the Pasha himself and been pardoned of all crimes and given licence to proceed (Abul-Magd 2013: 93). In the 1850s, the steamboats of European companies were important targets for bandits, as were bureaucrats and large estates. A certain Uthman joined an important group of bandits who carried out their irregular exactions and were in and out of prison in the 1850s. Uthman was a former sailboat captain who had apparently lost his transport business due to the dominance of steamers (Abul-Magd 2013: 100). In 1858, 'an uprising led by *falatiyya* [threatening or directly attacking Europeans] broke out in Isna [in Upper Egypt] and forced Sa'id Pasha to reform the ... administrative system in the province' (Abul-Magd 2013: 100). In the 1870s, a 'band of fifty to sixty peasants operating in the region between the two towns [Sohag and Girga] went into revolt because of over-taxation, and sought to attract to their insurgency others discontented with the government's imposts' (Cole 1999: 88).

Urban crafts and service workers also made use of everyday modes of resistance, subverting regulations, bribing officials, persuading local shaykhs to mislead the government, and above all hiding themselves from punitive taxation in one way or another. One of the most effective forms of tax-evasion available to guild members involved illicit alliances with guild shaykhs. This form of evasion appears to have been widespread, involving thousands in Egypt's towns up and down the country. Weapons of the weak were unable to change directly the overall direction of state policy under Isma'il. Sometimes they led to even more invasive forms of regulation. Nonetheless, the treasury found itself weak in the face of such widespread practices – unable to extract the revenues it sought, except through spending more on the extraction than it obtained by the collection, and unable to establish 'reliable' intermediaries among the population. In other words, these 'weapons of the weak' enjoyed some measure of success, disabling state extractive capacity, and playing a minor role as a coral reef of sorts on which the ship of state grounded in the debt crisis of

1876–1879, and contributing to the new direction of colonial tax policy in the 1880s and 1890s (Chalcraft 2004: 67–103, 146ff.).

Egypt: millenarian uprisings, 1822–1865

The millenarian tradition of protest was nothing new in Egypt, but it appeared in particular ways and under new circumstances in the nineteenth century. Cole maintained that, in the eighteenth century, millenarianism abounded (Cole 2007: 96–7). In 1799, for example, during the French occupation 'a man from the Maghrib [claiming to be the Mahdi] had provoked rebellion in a number of villages around Dashur, in the Delta' (Berque 1972: 137). There was a series of millenarian uprisings in Qina province in 1820–4, 1832 and 1864–5. 'Urabi in 1881–2 was to be hailed in the countryside as a deliverer on Mahdist lines. Lord Cromer feared Mahdist risings (inspired by Sudan) in Egypt in the early 1880s (Tignor 1966: 61). The last Mahdi reported in Egypt seems to have been in 1911. Muhammad 'Ali's seizure of the grain crop in 1812 precipitated the first major revolt of this reign when the peasants in Upper Egypt rebelled and were violently suppressed (Tucker 1985: 139).

Between 1820 and 1824 there was a series of uprisings in the villages of Qina province, in Upper Egypt. One was associated with the village of as-Salimiyyah between Qina and Farshut in 1820–1; another with virtually the whole of Qina province in 1824. In all cases, reasons for mobilization were associated with new taxes, conscription and forced labour among the peasantry, coupled with unprecedented state monopolies over trade and agricultural produce that hit the region's merchants (Baer 1969; Marsot 1984). At least one of the key leaders seems to have been a former merchant. The harsh economic conditions faced by artisans and cloth-workers in town and country may also have been a factor (Lawson 1981). Sufism and millenarianism informed the organization and framing of these uprisings, which began with public meetings, and continued with the refusal to pay taxes, followed up by armed confrontation with the state authorities. In 1820–1, Shaykh Ahmad's rebels were able to hold out for two months. They took control of the government warehouse, and engaged in some degree of fiscal redistribution. They established a 'new administration for a separatist state' (Abul-Magd 2013: 79). The urban *ulema* declared Ahmad heretical. The Pasha's army then defeated the rebels, destroying villages and houses. Some soldiers who hailed from the region defected when ordered to kill their own kith and kin. Apparently, Shaykh Ahmad escaped to Hijaz (Berque 1972: 137).

The uprising against taxation in Qina province in 1832 was said to involve up to 15,000 protagonists. The most important source is that of St John, a British traveller who witnessed some of the action (St John 1845: 378–86). Historians have so far maintained that St John's account referred to an uprising of 1822 (Abul-Magd 2013: 70; Baer 1969: 97). This cannot have been the case as St John was not in Egypt in 1822. He only travelled to Egypt for the first time in 1832 (Oxford Dictionary of National Biography). Qina province, therefore, was by no means entirely subdued by the repression of the early 1820s. St John wrote that he was 'not surprised at this outbreak, knowing well the depth of grievance over taxation, and in what detestation the Pasha's rule was held throughout the country', but reckoned it stood no chance of success (St John 1845: 380–1).

The 'uprising was led by a shaykh', a certain 'Derwish', likely a reference to a Sufi shaykh. He was named 'Ahmed Lilwezeer', and 'styled himself a prophet', likely a claim to being Al-Mahdi (the Expected Deliverer). He was flanked by 'enthusiastic' companions who recounted his miracles, presumably indicating Ahmed's possession of *baraka*, blessing from God. The leader began the uprising by marshalling a considerable force of 300–400 'Arabs' (i.e. non-Turks) at the village of Al-Ba'irat. Perhaps the insurrection was emboldened by the fact that much of the Pasha's army were fighting in the Mashriq. Ahmed was said to have allies in addition among the 'Atouni' Bedouin, who joined him after initial victories. Over the course of the following days he was able to muster more than 10,000 followers, some bearing small firearms, some on horseback, and apparently most of the villages in the area were part of the insurrection. No mere attempt at secessionism, Ahmed claimed to have orders from God and the 'grand Signor' (presumably the Ottoman sultan) to dethrone Mehmed Ali Pasha himself.

The revolutionaries evicted and put to flight local representatives of the Turkish authorities, including the governor of Luxor, while assurances were issued by the 'Prophet' to St John himself that Englishmen were to be protected, along with the Copts, contrary to the wishes of some of his more 'sanguinary' insurgents, proposed at a 'large public meeting'. The authorities responded by destroying the village of

Al-Ba'irat, which Ahmed's men had previously vacated, and offering tax remission to those who stayed loyal. The rebels apparently were emboldened by the unaccountable retreat of the government forces from Al-Ba'irat, and inflicted a major defeat on the Ottoman garrison at 'Gammounli' (Qammula), which retreated. St John then recounts that Ahmed lost heart by failing to drive on to take Asyut, while the Ottomans sent a force including more than 2,600 cavalry, which put down the rebellion over the following days through military victories, the destruction of villages, the killing of captives, and the massacre of men, women and children of the villages.

In 1864–5, Ahmad Al-Tayyib of Salimiyya, who seems also to have been a Sufi shaykh and related to previous leaders, pronounced himself the Mahdi (Expected Deliverer), and gathered followers among Muslim villagers as well as *falatiyya* in Qina province. The uprising was more heavily marked by issues of class and sect than in the 1820s and 1830s, when state exactions were front and centre. The revolt was triggered when a pious Muslim woman refused to become the concubine of a wealthy Copt, and sought an intervention from Shaykh Ahmad, which failed, while the government backed the Copt. No sectarian, Ahmad Al-Tayyib was a millenarian with a charismatic heterodoxy who was said to want to 'kill all the [Muslim] Ulama'; he preached a radical economic egalitarianism: one mortified scholar of Islamic law said that he wanted to divide all property equally (Abul-Magd 2013: 113; Schölch 1981: 37). Duff Gordon styled him a 'communist'. Little is known about the uprising, although it was said to involve much of the province. One rebel target involved the plunder of a boat owned by Greek merchants. Al-Tayyib attempted to assume judicial powers over the regions he controlled. The uprising was crushed with massive repression. Fadl Pasha alone was said to have killed 1,600 men, women and children (Abul-Magd 2013: 114). All Al-Tayyib's relations were jailed. According to Nubar's memoirs, 'One old man who ventured to mention the name of the rebel was put to death by Isma'il' (Berque 1972: 137–8).

The Balkans: protest, uprising and secession

Protests and uprisings in the Balkan provinces of the Ottoman empire were a continuous feature of the nineteenth century. They took place in a different geopolitical context than those in Egypt, the Mashriq and

Anatolia, because the Great Powers of Europe were somewhat more able and willing to intervene there, a fact which encouraged separatism and nationalism. The geographic proximity of the Great Powers, in turn, meant there were spaces in which exile politics could flourish. During the first half of the nineteenth century at least, it appears that class power was more entrenched in the Balkans, built up around merchants, local aristocracies, financiers, feudal land-owners and the Church, and protest was therefore more heavily inflected by the struggle against these local power-holders, at least during the first half of the nineteenth century, than it was in the Mashriq and in Egypt, with the important exception of Mount Lebanon, where patterns of protest were similar. The Christian identity of the protagonists was important, not, at least initially, because it pitted Christians *en bloc* against Muslims (we should not forget that the Church hierarchy was a key opponent of Balkan protests, as were Christian merchants), but because it enabled them to seek protection from European consuls, a course of action that was not widely available to Muslim protestors, and which encouraged European intervention, and therefore greatly empowered the protestors, at least in the short term. But these protests were perhaps more comparable to their counterparts in the Ottoman empire than nationalist historians have generally implied. The most popular of these protests sought the justice of the sultan, and protested their loyalty repeatedly. They rose up against impositions and exactions, and against the corrupt and arbitrary way in which those burdens were distributed locally. They were fuelled by local exploitation, by appeals to the equality announced by the Tanzimat, by millenarian tradition, this time in Christian colours, and by forms of liberty against the law. Early mass mobilization, as opposed to the tracts of some intellectuals, was not in the name of national independence; this came later, after other kinds of protest had failed to redress the grievances that protestors had. In some instances, the Ottoman empire was able to defuse protest, and forestall the possibility of secession, by making appropriate concessions. In short, secession was not inevitable, evidence for which view is to be found at the top of the Ottoman state itself, which only finally gave up on keeping what was left of the Balkans with the Albanian uprising of 1910–12. Secession took place, ultimately, because the central Ottoman state was unwilling to confront and dismantle the forms of decentralized class and political power against which peasants and their allies were above all protesting.

Tudor Vladimirescu (c. 1780–1821), lionized by later Romanian nationalists, was the leader of the Wallachian uprising of 1821 and of the Pandur militia. Wallachia was an important region in what is now Romania, originally a principality before the Ottoman conquest. The subsequent rise of Romanian nationalism should not obscure the fact that Vladimirescu's popular movement opposed the entrenched power of merchants, land-owners and Church exercising feudal privileges. He was from a family of landed peasants, was educated, had served with the Russian army, and worked as the overseer on the estate of a *boyar* aristocrat and headed a local official militia. He declared his loyalty to the sultan and his opposition to the Phanariote (merchant) system, that combination of merchant, financial and Church power – based in Istanbul, that exercised considerable influence in the Ottoman Balkan administration, working through the local *boyar* aristocracy. The grip of feudalism in the Balkans had only been deepened in the eighteenth century by the weakness and de-centralization of the Ottoman state. Vladimirescu's movement mobilized mainly the largely Christian peasantry, who tried to exceed the bounds set by Vladimirescu by destroying property – an act that he ruthlessly punished. Vladimirescu believed he had the support of the Russians. He was not interested in the activities of Alexandros Ipsilantis (1792–1828), who was a member of a prominent Phanariote (merchant) Greek family, a prince of the Danubian Principalities, a senior officer of the Imperial Russian cavalry during the Napoleonic Wars, and a leader of the *Filiki Eteria*, a secret organization that coordinated the beginning of the Greek War of Independence against the Ottoman empire (Shaw 1977: 17).

Vladimirescu's movement demanded the elimination of purchased offices in the administration, the introduction of meritocratic promotion, the suppression of certain taxes and taxing criteria, the reduction of the main tax, the founding of a Wallachian army, and an end to internal custom duties. Tudor also sought the banishment of some Phanariote families and an interdiction on future Princes holding retinues that would compete with local *boyars* for offices. In short, this was a programme of opposition to feudal forms of venality, taxation in Wallachia, and the entrenched power of the Phanariotes in Istanbul and their collaborators among the local *boyar* aristocracy. As Vladimirescu wrote to the Porte, the Wallachians have rebelled because of 'the terrible sufferings they are caused by the union between the native *boyar*s and those who have for long been sent as rulers and legislators of this people'. As he told the *boyar* aristocrat Nicolae Văcărescu:

It seems to me that you sir consider the folk, whose blood has been feeding and giving lustre to all the *boyar* kin, to be in fact nothing, and that you only view the pillagers to be the motherland ... But how come you sir do not consider the motherland to be in fact the people, and not the pillagers' clique?

Vladimirescu's army was defeated by the Ottomans in 1821, and he himself was tried, mutilated and killed.

Clogg's study of the popular culture of the Greek uprising (1821–8) emphasizes its class dimensions – targeting wealthy Phanariotes, merchants and priests alike. Phanariotes were regarded by contemporaries as 'instruments of Turkish oppression, indifferent to the plight of the Greeks'. The popular image of merchants was unflattering. The anonymous author of the *Elliniki Nomarkhia* (1806) spoke of an 'ignorant priesthood'. Merchants who had gone abroad were the 'true enemies and worse than Greece's Ottoman tyrants'. References were made to those Greek students studying abroad as reading 'fanciful poems'. The notables and clergy were no better. For example, in the memoirs of Photakos Khrysanthopoulos, widely judged a 'hero of the War of Independence', the Church was seen as being in craven submission to the Ottoman authorities. Indeed, during the Greek revolt in 1821, the Ecumenical Patriarch Grigorios V and the Holy Synod denounced insurgents, and anathematized Alexandros Ypsilantis and his followers as 'traitors, haters of religion and atheists'. Popular anticlericalism was a significant factor, while the Greek intelligentsia remained small and lacked influence among commoners (Clogg 1973: 10, 16–17, 19–20).

Many of those who filled the ranks of the fighters during the Greek war of independence were outlaws, irregular troops, some who acted as social bandits. These were mainly drawn from among *armatoloi* and *klephts*. The former were 'bodies of irregular troops, for the most part Christians, employed by the Porte in European Turkey for the maintenance of local order, the suppression of brigandage [i.e. the *klephts*]', and for guarding important mountain passes. Their origins were in Rumeli in the seventeenth century. They owed allegiance to Porte, but occasionally did 'rise up against their masters', such as in 1770, during the Russian expedition to Peloponnese (Clogg 1973: 8). The *klephts* were 'essentially bandits, who had taken to the mountains for a number of reasons, usually to avoid the payment of taxes or to escape pursuit by the authorities. As their attacks tended principally to be directed against Ottoman officials and tax collectors, and members of the Greek élite, namely, wealthy merchants, primates, clerics and monasteries, they acquired among the Greek population at large something of a Robin Hood image.' They operated in bands of usually around 50 persons, but they could be 200 or 300 strong. These groups were not unique to the Greek lands. In Bulgaria and Serbia they were known as *haiduts*; in Romania *haiduci*. In 1800, up to 10 per cent of the Balkan Christian population, at least in some of the frontier areas 'was organized militarily for the purpose of transforming or abolishing rather than defending the Empire' (Stoianovich cited in Clogg 1973: 8–9, cf. 33). There were echoes here of the '*celali*' tradition, which while understudied and too often dismissed, had clearly been important in different parts of the Ottoman empire in the seventeenth and eighteenth centuries, with its origins in mass defections from the Ottoman army in the 1590s (Griswold 1983; White 2011).

Nish was an important provincial town, now in Serbia, but populated by Bulgars in the nineteenth century. The revolt there in 1841 was not an isolated incident. There were small prior risings in Berkovitsa (1835 and 1836) and Pirot (1836) (Pinson 1975: 104–5). There were three separate risings that were nipped in the bud in 1849. One involved 'a certain Nikola Sr'ndak, who had been active in the Nish revolt of 1841, organized a band in Serbia for the purpose of beginning a rising in Bulgaria, but was arrested by the Serbian authorities before being able to cross the border into Bulgaria' (Pinson 1975: 118). Another was led by a man named Puyo, who had been active in the Nish revolt. In the spring of 1849, he organized a small group to mobilize for a revolt against the agas, which led to a small revolt in Boynitsa (Pinson 1975: 118). In the same year, a group in Belogradchik started planning a larger revolt against the Turks. Serbia offered covertly to supply guns and powder. The final plan, elaborated in a monastery near the village of Rakovitsa, suggested that things begin in several towns while major roads would be cut. But the Bulgarians were heavily outgunned and defeated by the Ottoman forces in ten days (Pinson 1975: 119). The Romanski, conservative Muslim provincials opposed to reforms, were an important factor in the revolt (Pinson 1975: 105). The 1850 revolt in Vidin, a port town on the southern bank of the Danube in what is now northwest Bulgaria, was a broadly comparable episode. According to one report, these revolts left 15 Turks and 720 Bulgarians dead (Pinson: 1975: 125).

These revolts were 'by no stretch primarily ... for national independence ... the petitions of the rebels, while stating their grievances against local officials, repeatedly protested their loyalty to the Sultan' (Pinson 1975: 132). The revolt in Vidin province was over administration, taxation and land-holding. During a parley between the rebels and a delegation sent by the Vali (Governor) of Vidin the rebels declared 'our troubles are due to the tax farmers, village landlords, constables and suchlike' (Pinson 1975: 113). Here was another glimpse of not just a trope of naïve monarchism, but of the realities of the grip of local exploiters amid a weak and de-centralized state. Peasants stated that the courts were controlled by corrupt local officials. Christian peasants 'were still vexed by such legal difficulties as their testimony not being accepted against Muslims' (Pinson 1975: 114). They suffered from the 'weight of the tax burden and the diverse and confused nature of the obligations' (Pinson 1975: 115).

The exact status of peasants' forced labour obligations was indeed confused as the edict of Gülhane (1839) had officially abolished them, but 'failed to create any mechanism for enforcement of the abolition or any revenue replacement, all of which helped perpetuate the exaction of the *angarya* [forced labour]' (Pinson 1975: 115). 'The rapidity with which large numbers joined a movement which from the outset clearly had so little chance of military success was however a significant indication of the extent of discontent among the peasantry' (Pinson 1975: 118). 'In matters of taxation, the peasants not only wanted their taxes reduced, but also wanted the exact amounts stipulated and the collection by *subaşis* ended and replaced by direct payment to the vali'. All such demands pointed to the importance of the class element in the uprising – which was about exploitation by feudal officials and corrupt tax-collectors (Pinson 1975: 129) as well as about tax burdens imposed from on high.

Pinson has shown in detail how much the revolts in Nish (1841) and Vidin (1850) in Ottoman Bulgaria owed to a bottom-up attempt to bring the egalitarian promises of the Tanzimat, new notions of citizenship, and the sultan's justice to bear on the exploitation of Christian peasants by land-owners and tax-farmers and local elites in the province. In April 1841, for example, 1000 Christians from near Nish petitioned the Prince of Serbia that people are not revolting against the legitimate government of the Sultan. Rather they want that the benevolent terms of the *Hatti Sherif* of Gülhane be faithfully and exactly carried out (Pinson 1975: 109).

The various announcements from the centre in regard to the equality of status of all the subjects of the empire, regardless of religion, also led to challenges to the fact that Christian testimonies in court were still not being accepted against those of Muslims, giving rise to accusations in regard to local corrupt officialdom (Pinson 1975: 114). The abolition of *sipahilik* in the 1830s and 1840s 'created in the minds of some of the peasantry the idea that they were now the real owners of the land' (Pinson 1975: 117). This was another reason for mobilization. It also created new land conflicts where agas and small peasants vied for control of land in the wake of the departing *sipahis*. The Bulgarians claimed that the local Turks oppressed in particular those Bulgarians who pressed for application of the Tanzimat (Pinson 1975: 130). Some of the new land codes, moreover, played into the hands of local elites, who were able to inherit land *de facto* rather than have it revert to the state, and thus amass land at the expense of the poor (Pinson 1975: 117–18).

In northwest Bulgaria (in Vidin province) there were villages where local agas had taken control and ownership with the departure of the *sipahis* owing to Ottoman reforms. The forms of rent and share-cropping that they imposed 'were not new; nor was discontent with them. The latter was rather heightened because the vague promises of the Tanzimat had appeared to hold out some relief' (Pinson 1975: 118). The failure of the Tanzimat to deliver on its own promises pushed the protests in a more secessionist and ultimately nationalist direction.

Ottoman policy was unable or unwilling to implement fully the promises of the Tanzimat, to tackle its corrupted administration, and to deal with these questions of class power. Ottomans were aware of the source of the injustice. One official circular issued to officials in Vidin stated that: 'From now on no objectionable conduct and evil deeds by officials and other persons are permitted.' On the other hand, Ali Reza Pasha, who was sent from the capital to put down the revolt, ordered that 'let care be taken not to ignore the legitimate rights of the agas and others who as landlords of any field or partners in any sown plot are obliged to go around to the villages to collect the share which was due to them'. As Pinson argues, 'the latter order largely nullified the former promise' (Pinson 1975: 125). Such official failures can only have exacerbated the discontent among the Christian peasantry, and ultimately opened the door to secession.

Algeria: Sufis, saints and holy men, 1830–1900s

The major drama of resistance to colonialism in the nineteenth century took place in Algeria. From 1830 down to the early 1900s, there was a drawn-out resistance involving some of the most mass-based uprisings in the nineteenth-century history of the region. Sufi orders and tribes of the countryside were pitted against the French imperial state that underpinned a policy of 'colonization without restraint', a near-genocidal military and economic assault on much of the population and the heavy-handed coercive and regulative control that colonizing policies entailed. The French were quite unlike the Algerian Deys, who lurched from one expedient to the next in order to shore up the ship of state, and whose own Janissaries could unseat them. Coercive power at the top was unified and heavily resourced from without. A key distinction between French and Ottoman imperialism in Algeria is that the former eventually sought to conquer and settle the whole country, and imposed a very much more direct form of rule than the Turks who came before them.

Those who were subordinated, dispossessed and fragmented by land seizure and economic domination itself did not have the capacity to resist on their own. Unaided, their struggles remained more fragmented, local, unobtrusive and hidden. These forms were more about everyday resistance, silent defeats and humiliations, 'fire on the mountain' and weapons of the weak than they were about armed insurrection (Prochaska 1986). Nor were uprisings led or even significantly supported by *ulema*, notables and townspeople. The existing state system, the Ottoman Deylik, the Ottoman Sultan and the Sultan of Morocco, were not irrelevant in this struggle as we shall see (Danzinger 1980; Temimi 1978), at least in the 1830s. Nonetheless, the Ottoman sultan was distant, and the Moroccan sultan confronted the French briefly in the early 1830s and again in 1844 only because it appeared that his position at home would have become untenable without it (Danzinger 1980: 65–66).

By far the most important protagonists, over the decades of the century, were the Sufi orders, the holy lineages, and tribes of the mountains, deserts and oases, and assorted holy men and miracle workers (Clancy-Smith 1994; Von Sivers 1982, 1983). The enormous resistance against French imperialism in Algeria was about these *dramatis personae*, their leadership, organization, resources, tactics and ideas. 'Resistance ... came from the religious brotherhoods, the *turuq*. They offered the organizational framework necessary for waging a struggle against a superior enemy' (Peters 1979: 54). The capacity of Algerian society to resist stemmed less from its overall cohesion and more from its many-headed and de-centralized nature. No single authority could control the Algerian population. They could not be handed over to the French by an authoritative intermediary. This situation resulted partly from the fact that the French destroyed such intermediaries rather than built them up. But it existed also because the Algerians themselves had many leaders and many organizations; and they inherited a strong tradition of resistance to central authority from the past.

The French, under Charles X, the last of the Bourbon monarchs of the 1815 restoration, were considering the invasion of Algeria with a view to achieving a foreign-policy success to bolster a flagging monarchical prestige and authority in the face of 'subversive' and republican masses at home (Brower 2009: 9). There were also expectations of commercial gain, particularly among the merchants of Marseille. Whereas the French had faced British and Ottoman opposition in Egypt in 1798, they calculated, correctly, that such imperial objections would be less forthcoming in regard to Algeria, which was hardly viewed by the British as a great geostrategic prize. Algeria was also far less central to Ottoman concerns, who were embroiled in domestic centralization and protest, as we have seen. The French seemed, however, to have forgotten, or ignored, the fact that popular resistance (which the French dismissed as fanaticism and recalcitrance) had played a role in the defeat of the French in Egypt. Knowing the Ottoman forces to be weak, they seemed to assume that the 'wild tribes' of the interior would be easily subdued, divided, or paid off.

The French invaded in 1830 over a pretext, and quickly routed the small forces Dey of Algiers and the provincial governors in west and central Algeria. The Dey, said Hajj Ahmad Bey, the governor of Constantine, the major city in the eastern part of Algeria, in a letter to the Ottoman sultan in 1833, simply wanted to give up, 'saving his person, his family, [and] his goods ... he neglected the destiny of the

Muslims' (cited in Temimi 1978: 220). But authority was so dispersed in Algeria, traditions of local autonomy so robust, and the rule of the Deys so spurned as but a fiscal burden, that various 'rayah' tribes immediately threw off Deylik authority and ceased to pay taxes to the privileged, government-linked tribes who were used by the Deys to collect taxes from them.

Not all the authorities submitted or fled. Like Murad Bey of Egypt and Al-Jezzar Pasha of Acre, the redoubtable Bey of Constantine, Hajj Ahmad, decided to stand his ground. Hajj Ahmed was busy trying to reorganize his military and administration in the face of what he called the 'stupefying fact' of the defeat of the Dey. He was inspired by the reorganizations then afoot in both Egypt under Mehmet Ali (1805–49) and the heartlands of the Ottoman empire under Mahmud II (1808–39). In October and November 1832, Hajj Ahmad declared that he would accept a peace treaty with the French as between equals, or even a truce involving a cessation of hostilities. He would not accept, however, to submit to French authority, cede them the coastal town of Bône/Annaba, send them tribute (to pay for the costs of the French occupation), reduce the number of his soldiers, and raise taxes that used to be raised by the Ottomans on behalf of the French. If the French insisted, he declared, 'we are ready to fight' and would consider it a 'bounty that is sent to us by God'. When the French, amid threats, offered to furnish him with what the Ottomans had previously furnished in troops and money, Hajj Ahmad understood that receipt of such 'protection' would confirm a vassal status, and thus rejected the possibility:

I depend on the Ottoman government, and I have under my authority more than a million Muslims who will not accept submission to the French Christians. To make them [the Muslim population] submit to your authority because of the submission of my sole person, and to become myself a slave ... is out of the question insofar as God has created us free. An imbecile refuses to accept such conditions, what can the wise man do? The signature of a peace treaty has a meaning and an implication well defined; but to be submitted to the authority of a Christian has another implication and another sense.

In the name of God, freedom, wisdom, the wishes of the Muslim population, and the rightful authority of the Ottoman sultan, Hajj Ahmad refused to become a client of the French (Temimi 1978: 212–18).

Hajj Ahmad quickly moved to mobilize material and men, who flocked to his banner, in preparation for the coming French assault. He also tried to obtain help and intervention from the powers, petitioning, with more than 2,000 signatures of religious, tribal, Sufi leaders and urban notables from Constantine to the coast, the British parliament and, in a smaller petition from the Hajj and the 'notables of Constantine', the Ottoman sultan. To the sultan, he underlined the dereliction of the Dey of Algiers, along with the incapacity, maladministration, brigandage and power-seeking of an ex-Bey of Constantine. And he invoked the defence of order and law against the sedition and criminality that the French usurpation unleashed among the Muslim population. The 'arrival of the French in Algeria', he wrote, 'incites the population to sedition', has caused the 'dispersion of the Muslim horsemen ... [who] are struck by stupor and do not know where to direct themselves'. In the absence of authority, the Muslims are 'like the bats who get agitated and who dart around from right to left at the rising of the sun'. Moreover, there was an outbreak of criminality and insecurity on the roads: the Muslims, wrote Hajj Ahmad to the sultan, 'are surrounded and stripped naked by brigands' (Temimi 1978: 220, 225).

In the face of what he saw as sedition, confusion, and brigandage, Hajj Ahmad depicted himself as the one who would restore order, cohesion, and security. He wrote, 'Ahmad the firm, the attentive, regarding whom acts and words reflect a perfect certitude, has called the soldiers, [including the major Arab chiefs], all of whom responded in the blink of an eye ... All the population obeyed, because it is he, Ahmad, who denounces injustices and extinguishes the sources of corruption' (Temimi 1978: 220).

To the British parliament, Hajj Ahmad listed the atrocities of the French. He wrote that the petitioners 'have been informed that the British Parliament has for its objective the respect of the rights of man, the interest of humanity and the consolidation of fraternity between men'. But the French had not respected the treaty they had concluded with the authorities; they deported subjects without good cause; they separated husband from wife and children, and seized people's goods; they caused some to change their religion; they had taken possession of funds consecrated for the poor; they had taken over mosques to sell or rent to merchants; destroyed houses unjustly; killed and massacred without valid reason; imprisoned others; violated graves; impoverished all the inhabitants of Alger; massacred even peaceful Bedouin nearby, including women and children; and they have taken Bône by treason and trickery. Indeed, the French 'claim that they have come to modernize, install justice and suppress barbarism. We reply that today we are sure that the barbarism and the injustice that they practice are more odious and detestable than all the injustice and barbarism known ... since Adam.' Hajj Ahmad and his co-signatories concluded that 'we are submitted to the authority of the Sultan' and 'we will refuse to be his [France's] neighbour'. 'We cannot have confidence' in his undertakings, and thus 'nothing can exist between us except hostility and its repercussions' (Temimi 1978: 228–30).

Like the Melians on the other side of the Mediterranean, two millennia before, Hajj Ahmed's forces were defeated by military force. His downfall came in 1837, when eastern Algeria was mostly occupied by the French. Hajj Ahmad had sought honour and independence, a path of confrontation and uncivilized 'intransigence' in the eyes of his imperialist foe. He was defeated. With his passing, and while the sultan in Istanbul remained aloof in spite of many appeals and reports, none of the officials of the Ottoman era remained to defend the country. Only the Sultan of Morocco, who had no official relations with the Ottoman empire, because both dynasties laid claim to the Caliphate (the rightful successor to the Prophet in leadership of the Muslim community), moved to send help to the tribes in the west of the country, during 1830–2. The Dey of Algiers could be criticized for a self-interested capitulation; Hajj Ahmad for over-playing his hand. In either case, the crisis of the Ottoman *ancien regime* in Algeria was complete.

Amid this crisis of authority, the door stood open to more popular mobilizations. New leaderships and protagonists, drawn largely not from the older military and administrative elites and their staffs, but from among the tribes, Sufi brotherhoods and venerated descendants of saints (*awlad sayyid* or *marabouts*), and the more rugged, wandering miracle-workers of the hinterland, stepped forth across the country to fight the French (Peters 1979: 53–4).

The most well known of these was Abd Al-Qadir (1807/8–83), the learned son of the head of an important Sufi brotherhood, based in the west of the country. Abd Al-Qadir, who had performed the pilgrimage, memorized the Qur'an, and had a reputation for learning and scholarship, won the allegiance of many of the important tribes and notables of western Algeria, received support from the sultan of Morocco, and fought the French from 1832 to 1834, and intermittently until 1837. Hostilities resumed in 1839 when the French and Abd Al-Qadir came to blows over territorial limits, and continued until he surrendered to the French in 1847. He was imprisoned in France and then exiled to Damascus.

The Moroccan sultan sent forces to Oran to fight the French during 1830–2, but on their withdrawal, following French naval pressure against him on the Moroccan coast, he appointed Abd Al-Qadir's father, Muhyi Al-Din – the head of an important Sufi order with a tradition of fighting the central government, the Qadiriyya – as governor of Oran. Muhyi Al-Din then declared *jihad* against the French in spring 1832. Muhyi Al-Din, along with family members and the heads of several important tribes, formally offered their allegiance to Abd Al-Qadir, who had gained a reputation for courage and leadership in battle, as Commander of the Faithful (*amir al-mu'minin*) in 1832 under a tree in western Algeria. The pact of allegiance was in conscious imitation of one made by the followers of the Prophet at a time of adversity in early Islam.

A war led in this way for a reformist version of Sufi Islam against the infidel was able to unite a broad constituency, the backbone of which was the Arab and Berber tribes of western Algeria. Abd Al-Qadir's authority was further enhanced by dream visitations by departed saints affirming his mission. An anecdote also circulated of a mysterious old man who had hailed Abd Al-Qadir as Amir during the latter's visit to Baghdad in 1826. For some of his followers, Abd Al-Qadir was undoubtedly surrounded by a distinctively Sufi aura of divine favour (*baraka*, or blessing).

After two years, although the military record was mixed, Abd Al-Qadir had harassed the French by guerrilla warfare sufficiently for them to agree to a peace treaty in February 1834. While the French presented this domestically as a way of bringing Abd Al-Qadir under their authority, Abd Al-Qadir presented it to his constituency as a recognition by the French of his authority.

However, abandoning the *jihad* and striking a deal with the unbelieving French drew criticism. And Abd Al-Qadir now turned to the government-linked tribes in the way the discredited Ottomans had done in order to collect taxes. Hajj Ahmad denounced Abd Al-Qadir to the Ottoman sultan as an upstart, liar, and a 'hypocrite ... claiming to come from a grand lineage' (Temimi 1978: 260–1). While other government-linked tribes were sidelined by Abd Al-Qadir, causing some to oppose him and even join with the French. Sufi orders who lost their tax privileges under Abd Al-Qadir, and disagreed with his strict reformist creed, were also disaffected (Peters 1979: 54–5). As opposition formed, Abd Al-Qadir actually accepted some military help from the French, who were considering indirect rule, and set about reorganizing his army, with a nucleus of regularly paid and well-trained soldiers instead of relying solely on tribal levies that were commonly raised in times of war (Peters 1979: 54). French influence was present here, but we also know that Abd Al-Qadir had been impressed, in his visit to Cairo in 1826, by the military reorganization being undertaken by Mehmet Ali there. Hajj Ahmed was also doing the same kind of military organization over in Constantine, as was the Ottoman sultan himself in the heartlands of the empire.

Abd Al-Qadir's state-in-waiting was shaped not only by the military technique of a standing army derived from Cairo, the Ottomans, or France. To win loyalty and build up a state organization that transcended this or that tribe or Sufi brotherhood, and to justify tax-raising, and to unify his followers, Abd Al-Qadir leaned heavily on contemporary currents of Islamic renewal and reform. During 1834–9, Abd Al-Qadir secured regular revenues to pay his soldiers by collecting taxes according to Qur'anic prescriptions. This was a departure, in an 'Islamic' direction, from the Ottoman norm, whereby taxation was understood within the general question of justice, and was often subject to sultanic decrees and local customary forms not formally defined by Islamic law. In Algeria, such non-Islamic taxes were often criticized as being unGodly. Abd Al-Qadir tapped into this tradition of criticism by promulgating Qur'anic taxes, including the *zakah* (charitable tax), the *'ushr*, and a special war tax, *mu'unah*. In order to collect taxes and administer justice according to Shari'a, he appointed paid officials (Peters 1979: 54–5).

Abd Al-Qadir, in developing a form of authority that could transcend the tribes and brotherhoods, drew on an uncompromising emphasis on the unity of God and an opposition to polytheism, un-Islamic innovation, deviations from the faith, and the 'superstition' associated with wandering saints, certain forms of Sufi ritual, and miracle-workers. These austere prescriptions bore the stamp of revivalist teachings. The key principle of unity, capable of winning, at least for a time, a measure of consent, was derived, not from local tradition or particular custom, but from how these were combined with the revivalist doctrine of *tawhid*. Islamic renewal was the banner that Abd Al-Qadir held aloft in order to try to win over the loyalties of those who wavered.

In some respects what Abd Al-Qadir was doing here was a very old thing. The idea of renewing and purifying a faith that had become deviant in some way over time by tyranny, superstition, and blind imitation on the part of religious scholars was one of the oldest and most inspiring ideas in Islam. The age of the Prophet and of the rightly guided caliphs (his successors) had been an age of extraordinary worldly success as well as an age of Truth, in which the final, divine revelation had been revealed to mankind via the messenger-Prophet, Muhammad. In other words, the idea of returning to the spirit of the early days of Islam, the ideal community that the Prophet had established in Medina, the example and sayings of the Prophet, as well as the revelation itself, had an extraordinary inspirational power. The Islamic revolution, as-it-were, of the seventh century AD, had meant a time of perfection, one might say, on earth. It was not a paradise lost by carnal knowledge and the Fall, as in the Garden of Eden; nor a paradise yet to come. Instead it was a model of divine will, justice, truth and right that had once combined God and man, power and right, wealth and justice, the divine and the temporal. A pure age that had been corrupted, so the revivalists said, by deviation from the true path.

The Prophet had said 'At the head of every century comes a renewer'. And those hailed as renewers appeared at various points in the long history of Islam: some founded dynasties. Ibn Tumart (1077–1130) was one such example. He was an itinerant devotee-beggar, and son of a mosque lamp-lighter from Morocco. After making the pilgrimage to Mecca and working in Baghdad, he declared himself a renewer and Mahdi and went on to found the strict, puritannical Almohad (*al-muwahhid*) dynasty, which dominated Andalusia and North Africa as far as Libya in the twelfth century. He and his followers were known as the Al-Muwahhidun, those who declare that God is one. They espoused an interpretation of the faith that heavily emphasized the unity of God, meaning that divinity could not be conferred on saints, preachers, prophets, the rich, or existing rulers alike. The Al-Muwahhidun looked for guidance, not to the arcane, orthodox, or derivative interpretations of this or that school of law, but to the original sources of the faith such as the revelation (the

Qur'an) and the authoritative reports of the sayings and doings of the Prophet (the *hadith* and Sunna). They railed against unlawful innovations into the faith, deviation, superstition and saint worship, which was denounced as polytheism. They declared that scholars could exercise *ijtihad*, the independent use of reason, analogy and various other forms, to derive lawful propositions as to correct practice from the original sources of the faith. Such *ijtihad* could provide startling criticisms of convention, orthodoxy, and the existing distribution of power. More recently, the puritannical Qadizadeli movement, which achieved some political power in the Ottoman empire in the seventeenth century, picked up on similar themes (Evstatiev 2013). In many ways, therefore, Abd Al-Qadir's revivalism represented an old gesture in the history of Islam.

In other respects, Abd Al-Qadir's revivalism drew on and transformed themes that were part of a far wider contemporary revivalism at work in many parts of the Islamic world. During the period 1750–1850, as empires ceased to expand, or de-centralized, (or collapsed, as in the case of the Mughals), as the sultan's justice retreated, as local oligarchs usurped customary and divine bounds, and as scholars seemed merely to repeat what their predecessors had decreed, or became lost in arcane disputes, there was a highly diverse and by no means monolithic 'world Islamic revival' (Hobsbawm 1988: 225). Among the key intellectuals of this revival were Shah Wali Allah (1703–62) in India; Muhammad Ibn Abd Al-Wahhab (1703–87) in Arabia; 'Uthman Ibn Fudi (1754–1817) in West Africa; and Muhammad Ali Al-Sanusi (1787–1859) in North Africa (Dallal 1993). The influential Yemeni theologian Muhammad Al-Shawkani (1760–1834) was another important thinker (Haykel 2003). Another key figure who took up permanent residence as an influential teacher in Mecca was the Moroccan born Ahmad Ibn Idris (d. 1837), who through teachings, pupils, family, travels and correspondence had a direct and indirect revivalist influence 'from North Africa to Indonesia' (O'Fahey and Karrar 1987: 205). Pupils from his immediate circle also established the Khatmiyya and Rashidiyya brotherhoods (O'Fahey 1990). Another important teacher, based at the heart of important scholarly networks in Mecca in the late eighteenth and early nineteenth centuries, was South Asian-born Hayat Al-Sindi (Voll 1975), who taught Abd Al-Wahhab. Revivalism was marked by the idea of renewal and reform, of a return to the Qur'an and the *hadith* as the authoritative sources for faith and practice, and by the idea that syncretic, superstitious, or polytheistic accretions or unlawful innovations should be expunged from the faith (cf. Levtzion and Voll 1987; O'Fahey and Radtke 1993; Voll 2008). Unlike the Islamic modernism that appeared after the mid-nineteenth century, or reformist liberalism, revivalism before the 1860s paid little attention to the West: as Dallal has it, the 'Islamic imagination' was yet to be encumbered with the West 'whose challenge was yet to be perceived' (Dallal 1993: 359). Islamic revivalism's cultural dynamic was rooted in the Islamic world (O'Fahey and Karrar 1987: 210).

Revivalism was, at the same time, highly diverse. While Al-Wahhab denounced Sufism as polytheism and even unbelief, Al-Sanusi founded a new and highly influential Sufi order. Ibn Idris, while critical of saint worship, and certain aspects of Sufi practice, pitched for a reformed and Prophet-focused Sufism (O'Fahey and Karrar 1987: 208). While for Al-Wahhab the use of *ijtihad* – the independent use of reasoning on the basis of the sources of the law to ascertain the divine truth – had little importance, it was crucial for Wali Allah and Al-Sanusi alike (Dallal 1993: 350, 358). The latter even enjoined *ijtihad* for every Muslim. While Wali Allah was interested in syncretism and reconciliation, Al-Wahhab pushed 'a grim and narrow theory of unbelief' (Dallal 1993: 351), bent on classifying, aggressively denouncing, and taking up arms against 'unbelief' and 'polytheism', especially among Muslims themselves. While Ibn Fudi challenged local power, and Abd Al-Qadir French power, Al-Wahhab sought an alliance with the warlord Ibn Saud to spread his creed. While Al-Sanusi and Ibn Fudi were taken up with the question of challenging political and economic injustice, Al-Wahhab merely formulated credal distinctions; the only form of tolerance enjoined was that for the excesses of the ruler, to whom obedience was demanded (Dallal 1993: 349). Revivalism was a partner of state-building in Yemen (Haykel 2003), Arabia, and for Abd Al-Qadir, whereas Al-Sanusi's mission 'was to model initiate and structure an ideal society' in places where existing political authority was weak (Dallal 1993: 356).

An Idrisian version of Islamic renewal, coloured by the Sufi milieu in which he was raised, provided a significant element in the shaping of Abd Al-Qadir's state-building leadership in Algeria in the 1830s and 1840s. The Qadiriyya already had 'reformist and revivalist leanings' (Peters 1979: 54). Abd Al-Qadir himself ruled as much as possible in agreement with Shari'a, while emphasizing monotheism (*tawhid*) and violently denouncing polytheism (*shirk*). He strongly condemned as *bida'* the worship of saints (Peters 1979: 55–6). While protests in the Balkans gravitated eventually towards nationalism, Abd Al-Qadir's resistance to empire, and the state-building project that went with it, was heavily intertwined with the tradition of Islamic renewal, with a Sufi colouring.

During the winter of 1845–6, there were so many uprisings in Algeria that the French army was stretched to breaking point. A tribal revolt, acting in defence of customary and tribal autonomy, in January 1845, by a religious chief, Bu Ma'zah, 'the man with the goat', kept the French army busy across the country and gave Abd Al-Qadir a chance to return from eastern Morocco with his men, to score a major victory over the French in September 1845 at Sidi Brahim. His forces managed to kill 384 French soldiers, the heaviest defeat yet sustained by the French.

These striking successes had an electrifying effect on the Algerians. Whole tribes flocked to Abd Al-Qadir's banner, and innumerable new revolts against the French, led by a large number of 'Bu Maza's', sprang up all over the country. The entire French position in Algeria seemed in jeopardy (Danzinger 1980: 67).

When Abd Al-Qadir retreated, even in defeat, in July 1846, he received a 'hero's welcome' by the tribes in the Moroccan borderlands (Danzinger 1980: 68).

Morocco provided official help in the 1830s, offered important sanctuary for Abd Al-Qadir and his men for most of the period, and streams of arms, ammunition, funds and volunteers. His successes after November 1839 generated enthusiasm in Morocco which was 'soon translated into massive transfers of arms, ammunition, and other provisions, as well as the appearance of Moroccan volunteers in Abd Al-Qadir's camp'. The sultan, desperate to avoid a losing confrontation with the French, formally prohibited in mid-1842 traffic with the emir. Nonetheless, support for Abd Al-Qadir continued in Morocco in the tribes, in cities, and also among officials and in the court itself. Abd Al-Rahman's prohibition was largely ignored, and in March 1843, Moroccan soldiers, commanded by the Governor of Oujda, participated in an assault on French units in Algeria' (Danzinger 1980: 64).

Abd Al-Qadir's struggle was conducted across state borders in other ways. The Amir wrote to Egyptian religious scholars in 1846 of the 'legally abominable deeds of the Moroccan Sultan, deeds that one does not expect from any person, let alone from notables'. The sultan, charged Abd Al-Qadir, had acted to 'strengthen the Party of Unbelief and to weaken us'. Abd Al-Qadir received a reply from a Cairo-based jurist that, although not as full-blooded as Abd Al-Qadir might have liked, certainly condemned the sultan in fairly dramatic terms:

Yes, everything you have mentioned is forbidden for the said Sultan ... These prohibitions are axiomatic articles of faith and nobody who has but a grain a faith left in his heart, can entertain any doubts about it. We would never have expected that our Lord Sultan Abd al Rahman (may Allah grant him success) would promulgate such orders with regard to a man like you. But we belong to Allah and to Him we shall return. What Allah has decreed, will necessarily be (quoted in Peters 1979: 59–61).

Certain tribes, with their own ideas about autonomy and just or customary practice, were resistant to the idea of paying new Qur'anic taxes to the state of Abd Al-Qadir. The latter tried to get the chief judge (*qadi al-qudah*) of Fez to rule that collaborators were apostates who might legally be killed. The learned judge refused to oblige, but did rule that helping Muslims who are unable to defend themselves against enemy attack is an obligation incumbent on all Muslims nearby, who would perform this duty in person or by giving financial support (Peters 1979: 59–60).

The ferocious violence of the French assault, who turned from the possibility of indirect rule to 'colonization without restraint' during this period, an imperialism with no problems of re-supply through the ports and seaways, caused Abd Al-Qadir to surrender with a promise of safe passage in 1847, once he realized that, in military terms, the game was up (Danzinger 1980: 67; Peters 1979: 54–5). Abd Al-Qadir eventually lived out his life in Damascus, where he was decorated by the French for saving the lives, true to his ecumenical philosophy, of many Christians during the political and sectarian violence of 1860.

Those who assume that Abd Al-Qadir was merely currying favour with the French, after his defeat in 1847, by compromising, and by saving the lives of Christians in Damascus, may not be familiar with an important dimension of Abd Al-Qadir's pre-nationalist and deeply non-communitarian, and non-xenophobic, thinking. The tract he wrote in prison in France in 1849 gives us a glimpse of a sweeping, egalitarian, ecumenical and inter-racial vision of the relations between countries and peoples – from China to France – a vision rooted in shared genealogies and histories, religious traditions, the legacy of the Roman empire, and the broad possibilities among different peoples for the achievement of learning, virtue and justice (Abd Al-Qadir 1849). Here was a revivalism that owed more to reconciliation and syncretism than to rigid and Manichean binaries.

The French made all sorts of self-justificatory declarations in regard to equality and patriotism. As we know, Charles X had invaded in order to quell republican sentiment and 'seditious words' at home, not to encourage them; and such declarations reeked of hypocrisy in any case for those who suffered invasion, spoliation and slaughter in their name. Abd Al-Qadir signalled that equality and love of country were nothing new, and were of no great interest, because his intellectual traditions already encompassed them. He noted that it was well known that men are all equal, because their origin is sperm, which is not differentiated by reason, science or religion. All men, in any case, were descended from Adam and Eve: as the Prophet said: 'You are the sons of Adam, and Adam of the earth.' Only virtue comes to distinguish men. As for love of country, 'each man habituates himself to his land, as he habituates himself to his mother and his father; he remains always nostalgic for his country'. Indeed, the Prophet said: 'God make us love Medina as we had loved Mecca or more.' And, Abd Al-Qadir continues, the poet said: 'The country is beloved to men / They passed their youth there / When they remember it, They remember their promises' (Abd Al-Qadir 1849: 12–13).

Of far greater interest to Abd Al-Qadir, judging by the number of words devoted to these themes in his treatise, was to establish the broad genealogies and histories that gave different religions (Jews, Christians and Muslims), and national or ethnic groups (Berbers, Arabs, French, Indians and Chinese), a shared basis for the non-conflictual pursuit of faith, justice and virtue. He noted that Caesar of Rome, the Arabs and our Prophet all share a common ancestor: Ismail bin Ibrahim el-Khalil (Abraham). Ham bin Nuh (Noah), the author went on, is also the common ancestor of the Copts, the Berbers, the Sudan, India and China. The Berber tribes, the Zenata and Louwatta, were exiled from Palestine towards the Maghrib (North Africa) after the death of

Goliath. Abd Al-Qadir points out that the Prophet did not support the defeat of Rome at the hands of the Persians, because the Romans were people of the book, and the Persians were atheists; in fact God informed the Romans that they would be victorious over Persia in a few years. He pointed out that the Qur'an eulogizes Christians and considers them as closest to Muslims. He noted that the virtuous Christian king of Ethiopia had warmly welcomed Muslims who had emigrated to his country to escape the atheists of the Quraysh. The latter insisted and sent presents to the king to get them to turn them over to him, but he refused to give them up, and protected them. Peoples, in Abd Al-Qadir's conception, were not static and monolithic, journeying through homogeneous and empty time, but overlapping communities defined by webs of ancestry and genealogy.

Much of Abd Al-Qadir's treatise turned on how the legacy of Rome should be understood. Karl Marx, who had a PhD in Roman law, in his most brilliant political tract, had famously polemicized against Louis Napoleon of France, the upstart nephew of Bonaparte, for borrowing the disguises and ancient lustre of Rome while pursuing narrower and self-aggrandizing goals. Abd Al-Qadir was, like Marx, a political exile, in Europe, and an opponent of Louis Napoleon, and also versed in the history of Rome, but languishing in a French prison. He knew that French pundits were discussing whether anything could be resurrected of ancient Roman glory in North Africa, and whether Roman virtue was still to be found among its people. Abd Al-Qadir's main point seems to have been to turn around the arrogant French enquiry *vis-à-vis* the peoples of North Africa, and wonder instead whether Louis Napoleon and France were worthy of the glories and virtues of Rome. If so, they would refuse injustice towards Algeria and keep their word to release Abd Al-Qadir as they had promised on his surrender.

Even with the loss of Abd Al-Qadir, and the smashing of his newly constructed organizational structures, many Algerians fought on, especially in the name of tribal autonomy, or following the charismatic leadership of one or other preacher, descendant of a saint, millenarian claimant to the status of the Mahdi (or Expected Deliverer) or wandering miracle-worker. The uprising led by Abu Ziyan at Zaatcha in 1849 (Clancy-Smith 1994: 70–1) was joined by commoners of all kinds under millenarian banners, dragging local religious notables into a conflict with the French.

Another kind of uprising was more charismatic, such as that of a holy man, Si Tayeb, in 1862. Holy men were marked not so much by their association with Sufi ritual, belief, or organization, or even by their saintly lineage, but by their status as thaumaturges and possessors of miraculous gifts. 'The most important miracles', writes Brower, 'included locating springs, returning wayward livestock, protecting crops and pastures, and resuscitating dead palms' (Brower 2009: 120). The demonstration of these capacities distinguished such figures from madmen and imposters. They situated such holy men firmly within the economic practices of oasis dwellers and pastoral nomads. In April 1862, Si Tayeb and a group of 50–60 men and boys bearing sticks staged an attack on colonist houses and a coffee-house in Djelfa. In the ensuing scuffle following the encounter, Si Tayeb's men killed two men and a five-year-old girl (Brower 2009: 94). Si Tayeb's men claimed to French interrogators, or at least French interrogators understood, that their actions had been motivated by nothing more than a temporary enchantment brought about by the personal powers of their leader. A more satisfactory history is lacking.

The uprising of the Awlad Sidi shaykh in Algeria in the 1860s, rooted in a saintly lineage, and a respected tribe, stemmed in part not from the sheer fact of their vassal-ship to France, but to the breakdown of that relationship, when France violated it through usurping the shaykhs administrative power, and his sphere of autonomy defined by a sharp limit on mutual contacts involving only a handing over of the tribute and a confirmation of family members in office. Si Suleiman wrote to the French with complaints as to his 'reduction in power, strict supervision and constant interference' adding up to 'French treason' (Von Sivers 1983: 120). When the shaykh called out his men in order to offer a show of force to encourage the French to pull back, a wider and less-controllable round of contention broke out.

The French were prepared to go to extreme lengths to destroy the resistance of the lineages, the tribes and the holy men. The French sought to achieve submission through engineering economic insecurity and subsistence crises, cutting tribes from their grazing grounds and so on (Brower 2009: 98–112, 137). These policies created the conditions for the famine of 1867–8, which involved some 800,000 deaths. Drought was an important part of the picture, but 'the victims of hunger died as a consequence of history rather than climate' (Brower 2009: 106). The genocidal violence faced by Algerians under French 'colonization without restraint' is still little appreciated in the English-speaking world. The remarks of a French general in 1851 offer a glimpse of French tactics:

I left in my wake a vast conflagration. All the villages, some 200 in number, were burnt down, all the gardens destroyed, all the olive trees cut down (cited in Quandt 1969: 4).

As historians now know, almost half the Algerian population was killed directly or indirectly by the French. The best demographic work has shown that 825,000 'Algerian lives were ended because of the violence of the first forty-five years of the French occupation, and an equal number died in the famines and epidemics triggered, in large part, by the colonial-induced economic mutations suffered by Algerian society'. Algeria's indigenous population shrank from 4 million people in 1830 to roughly 2 million in 1872 (Kamel Kateb's work, cited in Brower 2009: 4). The contrast with Tunisia after 1881, where there was settler colonization, but it was done in a less violent and provocative way, and where there were hardly any protests on a scale to compare with Algeria, is suggestive.

The largest uprising of the post-1847 period was led by neither saint, Sufi, Mahdi nor holy man, but by Muhammad Al-Muqrani, who issued a call for *jihad* on 16 March 1871. Al-Muqrani had been the Governor of much of Grand Kabyle with the French administration, accounting perhaps for some of the hysteria of those French who condemned him (Mercier 1901). Al-Muqrani's initiative was new, because until that point no substantial official or *caid* associated with the French-imposed administration had turned towards insurrection. The French had just been defeated by the Prussians, Paris surrendering to the siege on 28 January 1871, implying a moment of objective weakness. Al-Muqrani and others were following these events closely, and read the defeat as a punishment by God for French usurpation and corruption of Muslim lands in Algeria. In addition, decrees giving citizenship to Jews in October 1870 (Schreier 2010) were widely seen as proof of the partiality and discrimination practised by the French authorities, a divide-and-rule device that made a mockery of French universalist pretensions, in regard to a practice deep within the French-Algerian state.

The rebellion spread quickly to encompass an area about 300 km in length, from the suburbs of Algiers to the heights of Al-Qull (Collo), and southwards as far as the desert. An extraordinary 800,000 Muslims, 'involving about one-third of the Muslim population of Algeria' (Abun-Nasr 1987: 267) rallied to the banners of *jihad*. Rumours circulated in the country that the Ottoman sultan would move on the country against the French, or in regard to the imminent return from exile of the Amir Abd Al-Qadir's son to lead resistance to the French (Abun-Nasr 1987: 266). Whether or not Al-Muqrani had limited and personal aims, his actions sparked off a general rebellion which was by no means entirely within his control (Abun-Nasr 1987: 266–7).

The uprising was largely defeated by June 1872, and was met with extensive repression, collective punishment and the imposition of punitive indemnities (Evans and Phillips 2007: 31). The settlers insisted on criminal trials, and economic repression such that Muslims would not have the means to rebel again. A war indemnity of 36.5 million francs was imposed on the region of Kabylia, amounting to ten times the annual tribute. All the lands of the tribes who had participated were sequestrated by a decree of 31 March 1871, invoking 'tribal collective responsibility' for the events. Alsatian and Lorrainian emigrants settled on 100,000 hectares of sequestrated lands in the Summan valley and regions of Sétif and Constantine. Approximately 'seventy per cent of the total capital of the peoples involved in the rebellion was levied from them in the form of war indemnity or for freeing their lands from sequestration' (Abun Nasr 1987: 268–9).

A further uprising, which began in 1881 in the southwest, and continued on and off until the 1900s, was led by Abu Amama, an ascetic, Sufi preacher of reformist colour, whose emissaries declared: 'There is no god but God and Abu Amama is his friend (*wali*); there is no god but God and Abu Amama is the falcon of the Sahara, this guest of God' (Von Sivers 1982). Abu Amama linked tribe to religious cause, the immediate interests of oasis-dwellers and pastoral nomads to a larger organization, and their customs and proverbial wisdom to a wider and more abstract set of principles and identities. Insurrection broke out among the population of southwestern Algeria on 22 April 1881 with the assassination of a French officer, and a period of fighting lasted till summer 1881. The timing was propitious in that the French were partially diverted by their invasion of Tunisia, under way from 28 April to 12 May 1881. After the summer, Abu Amama's forces regrouped, with the former in exile in Morocco; this challenge to the French only definitively ended with the death of Abu Amama in 1908 in exile in Morocco.

These uprisings straddled the border between Algeria and Morocco in important ways. In the 1860s, the Awlad Sidi shaykh in the Sud-Oranais drew into their orbit many of the Moroccan tribes on the southeastern frontier: the Doui Menia, the Oulad Jerir and the Beni Guil. This was the occasion of a French campaign of repression into the Guir valley in 1870 (Burke 1976: 29). The French repression of Bu Amama in the early 1880s brought the French closer to the southwest Moroccan border, involving the creation of a permanent French post at Ain Sefra (Burke 1976: 29). At this point, in the early 1880s, it was the turn of forces based on the Moroccan side of the border to take the lead. Si Al-'Arbi, a Darqawa shaykh, who possessed considerable influence over the tribes in the frontier region, became increasingly alarmed by the steady French advance. The weak response of Mawlay Al-Hasan did nothing to reassure him, and thus he began calling for the tribes in the area to launch a *jihad* against the French in the districts south of Oran. He had a considerable prestige, which meant a substantial following. By 1888, he started to expand the scope of his claims, and challenged the *makhzan* to take action against the French, failing which he would arm the tribes himself and send them against the infidel. But the movement lost momentum when its *marabout* leader died in 1892. The visit of Mawlay Al-Hasan to Tafilalet then worked to de-mobilize the tribes, and re-impose the precarious authority of the *makhzan* (Burke 1976: 29).

Egypt: petitioning in town and country

Not all *fellahin* in Egypt turned away from the centralizing state, kept their distance in silent hostility from state institutions, drew solely on popular traditions and local experiences, or used informal or forceful means of redress. Collective and individual petitions, either made as appeals in person to the ruler (something remarked upon in Mehmet Ali's time), or much more commonly lodged through procedures that were increasingly formalized and bureaucratized from at least 1830 onwards, were widespread in the 1870s in Egypt. There was also an extensive use of the court system in the search for justice. There was no Tanzimat as such in Egypt, but Mehmet Ali's use of the term *al-ahali* (meaning the populace) was a broader category than the more familiar Ottoman term *raʻiyya* (meaning the 'flock') and his claims that his policies were for the 'welfare of the populace' (*rafahiyyat al-ahali*) (Abul-Magd 2013: 87) may have encouraged petitioners. Petitions lodged on stamped government-issued paper, and obeying conventions of address and language, were a routinized and official channel through which grievances of all kinds could be brought, by even the lowliest subject. Petitions were constructed by peasant leaders and their constituencies, and professional petition writers who frequented markets up and down the country. Petitioners' language was not grovelling or mindlessly subservient (Vatikiotis 1969: 160), but nor did it express some underlying and deeply rooted nationalist and revolutionary consciousness (Salim 1981).

Not all petitioners were male. Umm Muhammad from the village of Hamidiyya in Qina province petitioned on behalf of a larger group of villagers against the attacks of a local shaykh in 1846; in the same year a certain Amina from Nagada petitioned to recover palm trees inherited from her mother that had been seized by a certain shaykh Hasan (Abul-Magd 2013: 90–1). Abul-Magd notes that a number of peasant women in Qina province in the 1850s actually sued their husbands in the Shariʻa court for not providing the family with suffi-cient staple foodstuffs (Abul-Magd 2013: 100). Women 'often complained to the courts of arbitrary confiscation of property or even coercion of person [by village shaykhs]' (Tucker 1985: 137–8), while '[w]idows or women whose husbands were absent went to the Shariʻa court to demand payment of their husbands' wages from the State' (Tucker 1985: 138).

In Egypt, elections for village headmen were established in 1866, as part of Ismaʻil's constitution of that year, which was also designed to make local tax-raising more efficient (Chalcraft 2005a). These elec-tions were associated with much petition-writing, and certainly served to widen the institutional opportunities available for this kind of action. Above all, they provided reasons for the active participation of peasants in a politics at the village level that surrounded the local headmen.

Peasants made strategic use of the figure of the just ruler, trying to draw the *khedive* and ministers into their disputes, and lodged some-times assertive appeals to the rule of law and new and old rights in a dangerous and power-laden context. They stuck to the terms of official discourse, while giving it a content, associated with their own interests and forms of moral economy, that it would not otherwise have had.

The peasants invoked the justice of the ruler in order to make claims and raise grievances as loyal subjects committed to justice, order and cultivation, and pitted against the ambitious, the greedy and the tyrannical, whether the latter were members of the government or not. Peasant petitioners in the Egyptian countryside sought justice against unscrupulous shaykhs who had over-taxed them, or against landowners who had evicted them, dispossessed them, or forced them to work for them at exploitative rates. During the summer of 1880, thirty-four cultivators from the village of Kafr Akhsha in Lower Egypt, who were protesting against a tyrannical headman who had seized their land and kept them 'in captivity and slavery', were bold enough to claim that 'the government is not well known for [delivering] justice other than [where] Your Highness [intervenes]' (cited in Chalcraft 2005a: 309), a sweeping criticism, by implication, of the host of mayors, *nazirs*, inspectors and even provincial governors who stood between *khedive* and peasant. In a partially centralized context, where so many local figures had state-like powers, the language of the just ruler and the loyal subject was not a form of 'traditional subservience', but expressed a political consciousness rooted in Ottoman statecraft, and was a strategic move aimed at intervention from the highest levels of the state against local power. And, while peasants asserted that the *khedive* had in mind the comfort, prosperity, and interests of the people (*masalih al-ahali*), they played some role in defining and making reference to what the people's interests actually were. In this sense, petitioners clearly did not believe that only the ruler knew or was able to define the content of the interests of the people.

Contesting local exploitation, peasants laid claim to their rights or dues (*haqq/huquq*), a long-standing term conveying the meaning of 'what is deserved'. The government had a right (*haqq*) to a certain share of the surplus and, by the same token, said the petitions, so did the peasants. The violation of these rights, which could be used to refer to a wide variety of goods and services, was a form of tyranny which peasants were vigorous in protesting. Peasant petitions, further, especially in the context of elections, made regular reference to the wishes and consent of the people, and occasionally made reference to the need for equality (*al-musawa'*) among the people in the face of inequalities meted out by exploitative local figures (Chalcraft 2005a: 317).

In July 1869, one newspaper went so far as to report that 'the Egyptian *fallah* has begun to emerge from the silence of slavery which he has been mired in for centuries and started to supplicate [the powers that be] with complaints, something not yet seen in Egypt' (cited in Chalcraft 2005a). While this report exaggerated in typically modernist fashion the extent of the change, new repertoires of contention were developed where cultivators drew on languages and practices associated with state centralization, and coloured them with their own interests and concepts, in order to make a stream of claims on the authorities couched in assertive, changing and 'secular' languages of justice, rights, and the interests of the people. New concepts were stitched into old through contentious practice. A contentious politics had arisen that tried to make use of, rather than merely to resist, the centralizing state.

Something similar seems to have been at work in Palestine in the nineteenth century. Peasant petitioners in Palestine 'openly adopted the government's public interpretation of the Tanzimat and used it as a weapon against the authority and privileges of their traditional leaders' (Doumani 1995: 18).

under the suffocating weight of both the rural and the urban elites of Jabal Nablus, the peasants' best hope of carving out a political space for themselves lay in involving the state and appealing to its sense of justice (Doumani 1995: 175).

These avenues of participation were explored with remarkable persistence, even though they had mixed results. As Ottoman administrators and technocrats, Tamimi and Bahjat wrote, after their visit to Salfit in Palestine, '[t]he government in their eyes is nothing but sub-district administrators and a number of police ... and a door that does not answer the complaints of the people' (Doumani 1995: 178).

Urban townspeople, merchants, artisans, crafts and services workers, from high to low status, drew up collective petitions to rulers, ministers and governor in order to obtain redress for their grievances throughout the century. Just as in the countryside, centralization brought central agencies closer to the affairs of the crafts and trades, and bureaucratization increased their capacity, heightening the incentive and the practicality of making use of these agencies for the resolution of disputes. Petition submission procedures became increasingly formal. Moreover, the state was busy enacting decrees and orders to which crafts workers and others could legitimately appeal. In 1869, the establishment of elections for guild shaykhs, under police supervision, also created an institutional opening which increased the incentives to engage in petitioning in order to initiate, invalidate or object to candidates or procedures.

Petitions were used by a wide variety of social groups in towns. Not only merchants and notables sent petitions. So did boatmen, porters, weighers, measurers, box-makers, water-carriers, carters, cab-drivers, masons, dyers, retailers, wage-workers in larger enterprises, and many others. Women also sent petitions on occasion. Hejazis, Sudanese, Jews, Christians and Muslims, and others were also involved.

Many members of guilds, by custom, *qadi* judgment, or by agreement, held the right to practice a particular trade in a particular location. Many mobilized when these rights were violated – whether by contractors, guild shaykhs, masters, or outsiders. Others mobilized in regard to the corruption of weights in measures. Others found reason to act in order to reduce the burden of customary dues which weighed on them from within guilds. Others sought to reduce the level of forced labour to which they were subject. Still others objected to the way guild shaykhs carried out their state-like functions – in tax assessments, in assisting the police. In one case, a group of porters petitioned to get the police to carry out a redistribution of wealth. Many of these reasons to mobilize were intensified because of the spread of market relations, the existence of many new entrants into trades, heavier burdens in taxation and forced labour, and because the state co-optation of shaykhs divided the guilds. In competition with European imports and investment, some crafts and service trades were under pressure, and others engaged in labour-squeezing and self-exploitation in order to survive.

Crafts and service workers couched their petitions in a rich language appealing to custom, rights, the justice of the ruler, and the welfare and interests of the people. These languages appealed to official discourses sanctioned by the state, while giving them a content drawn from a long-standing and changing moral economy of the crafts and service workers themselves. They appealed to the state for the sultan's justice, to ensure the flourishing, comfort (*raha*), welfare (*maslaha*) and rights (*huquq*, just shares and dues) of the commoners (*re'aya, 'amma, ahali*), to safeguard and guarantee the demands of custom (*'adat*), law, and regulation against tyranny (*zulm*). This social consciousness owed little or nothing to European liberalism or socialism. Egalitarianism of a non-European sort existed, harking back to older movements, linked to Sufism and asceticism, or linked to customs of the trade. It is important to point out that communistic traditions on the Arabian peninsula hailed back at least to the Qarmatians of the ninth century. The fifteenth and sixteenth centuries saw major movements in the Ottoman empire based around the equal distribution of wealth. Ascetic critiques of luxury and decadence were strongly articulated during the nineteenth century in many Sufi orders, organizations which overlapped strongly with urban guilds, crafts and trades (Baer 1964; Ghazali 1999: 20, 42–3; Raymond 1958, 1968: 107, 1973: 505, 507). The porters at weigh-stations in Alexandria proposed the redistribution of wealth (*al-rukiyya*) in their own guild in order to compensate those who had lost out. Al-Rukiyya referred to a little-known custom involving the redistribution of all the income of the guild among the rank and file of the workers, and was customary in some guilds in Egypt in the 1870s (Chalcraft 2004: 80–101).

On the other hand, reference to state regulations and to bureaucratic procedures was almost certainly on the increase, and petitioners were quick to adopt and adapt the new languages which the state used to justify centralization and self-strengthening – whether of the Tanzimat, of law and order, of civilization and progress, or of regulation. In the context of elections, there was much reference to the desires, wishes, and comfort of the people.

Petitions were written in conjunction with government scribes and were sometimes signed by scores of claimants. In 1871, for example, seventy-seven Sudanese and Nubian cab-drivers petitioned against an Arab shaykh they regarded as tyrannical, possibly for contracting outsiders to a job to which they believed they had a right. Organization was largely informal – at least in Egypt after 1863 – where petitions were signed and organized not by the guild as such but usually by some group within the guild, whether involving the shaykh, the senior masters, or not. Before the early 1900s, however, no new organizations were brought into being, although middle class reformers occasionally suggested that societies or leagues to regulate and reform the crafts and trades should be instituted.

Petitioning as a strategy was rooted in the way it could manipulate dominant terms and practices, giving official politics a certain colour that it might not otherwise have had, and thus enabling petitioners to obtain redress.

These kinds of protests were by no means always successful, even in the short term. The carpenter box-makers of Cairo failed to bring their leadership to book for unfair fiscal practice; the porters of Alexandria, for all the radical daring of their proposal on the redistribution of wealth, failed, and probably never stood a chance of persuading the state to get involved in such matters within the guild. On other occasions, elections could be rigged, voters bought off, and officials bribed. On the other hand, protests sometimes re-instated popular guild leaders; they held to account more powerful masters and shaykhs seeking to manipulate custom in their own interests.

Weapons of the weak, and collective petitioning alike played an important role in the attrition of the guilds. Where guild structures were co-opted, or unable to protect their members' livelihoods, crafts and service workers banded together in informal networks that were either sub-guild, or extended beyond guild boundaries. Guild members, in the search for more adequate protection, were to some extent rejecting their guilds, and forging informal networks in order to pursue their interests. Had guild members remained passive, the government might have retained guilds intact for the purposes of regulation and taxation. But the very resistance of guild members, on a variety of fronts, led to state intervention, which furthered the attrition of guild autonomy.

Urban crowds

From Morocco to Iran, urban crowds, in the face of unfair prices, dearth, hoarding, and monopolistic behaviour engaged in collective action more disruptive and evidently transgressive than weapons of the weak, petitioning and the use of the court system (Abrahamian 1993; Baer 1977; Raymond 1968). In Iran, the tradition of urban protest was marked. The shah declared himself ready to hang his own son to stop rising prices in the 1860s (Abrahamian 1982: 41–2). There were occasionally food riots in Baghdad, when famine threatened, such as those of 1877 (Batatu 1978: 470). In Morocco, this living tradition of protest continued to play a role in the nineteenth century: the rising in Fez of 1873 furnishes an example.

According to Laroui, Moroccan towns, part of the *makhzan*, were usually calm and well administered. Sometimes the *qadi* (chief judge) and the *muhtasib* (market inspector) were opposed to the *qaid* (local lord) and this meant momentary conflicts, but revolts in general were rare (Laroui 1977: 129). Nonetheless, there was a tradition of urban and crowd protest. There was a revolt in Fez in 1818 by commoners (*'amma*) against merchants and *makhzan* which succeeded in thwarting the schemes of Sultan Suleiman (1792–1822) (Laroui 1977: 130). There was a revolt in Rabat in 1844 against Sultan Abdulrahman (1822–1859) and again in Fez in 1873 against the taxes of sultan Hassan I (1873–1894). The last was the longest. It was also carried out by poor and low-status townspeople, and various poorer rural elements integrated into the city economy (such as peasants who sold in the town), and took on the colours of an uprising against the merchants, notables and orthodox religious *ulema* of the city.

The merchants and notables, many of whom benefitted from the *maks* (the tax provoking the grievances) as they served as tax-farmers, viewed the crowds as a ferocious mob, at least in a letter they wrote to the sultan disclaiming responsibility. They spoke of

a day of great tumult ... the city was full of people coming from everywhere, the towns and the countryside, all furious like lions and tigers ... Having no judgment they were not able to be stopped except by a strong army ... they were blind, hot-tempered, deaf, insensible to the existence even of those who exhorted them to calm (Laroui 1977: 129–31).

The *maks* were taxes imposed on primary materials and transactions, imposed by the sultan seeking revenue for centralization and 'reform', and the occasion of irregularities and injustices. The uprising was no elite plot, but a revolt of small artisans (the tanners were involved) and traders already organized in guilds with a sense of brotherhood and solidarity. Laroui observes that the opposition of the corporations to the sultan remained very strong throughout the nineteenth century. In Laroui's terms they were flattened by taxation, impoverished by devaluation, and injured by European competition; nonetheless, these urban economic groups exploited the surrounding countryside, and, as we shall see, the more powerful challenges to the *makhzan* in Morocco were furnished by rural uprisings, involving tribes, brotherhoods, heterodox religious figures and pretenders to the throne. As elsewhere in the region, nonetheless, new impositions and forms of exploitation did not go unchallenged, and were limited by the collective action of those whose consent could not be won.

The people's republic of Kisrawan

In December 1858, a force of Christian Maronite commoners, under the leadership of a humble muleteer, rose up against their feudal lords in the district of Kisrawan on Mount Lebanon, northwest of Beirut. They took the unprecedented step of physically evicting the Khazin family, a Maronite lordly family that dominated the Kisrawan, from their homes and from the region itself. A peasant movement, led by peasants, and acting in the name of the people (*ahali*), 'autonomously sought to carve out their own place ... and to enter the realm of traditionally elite politics' (Makdisi 2000: 97). The popularity of the uprising quickly spread – and impoverished Maronite peasants flocked to its ranks. By late 1859, the republicans were in *de facto* control of most of Kisrawan, and the movement was soon to spread beyond. European elites at the time saw the overall episode in terms of barbarism, fanaticism, of lawless races and tribes (Makdisi 2000: 152). Yet, this was 'the most sustained popular mobilization' in nineteenth-century Mount Lebanon (Makdisi 2000: 97), and surely of the Mashriq as a whole.

At the head of Mount Lebanon's hierarchically organized nobility, and drawn from its leading family, stood the amir, loyal to the sultan. Below the amir were the various heads (*muqata'at*) of the tax-districts (Kisrawan, Matn, Shuf etc.). The leading families belonged to various confessions and faiths. Peasants and artisans, who formed the bulk of the population, whatever their faith, were supposed 'to produce and to do so with diligence' (Makdisi 2000: 43). They also had many obligations. In Kisrawan, 'they presented their shaykhs with a quantity of soap, coffee, honey or tobacco at Easter or on the occasion of the marriages of the shaykhs' daughters, sons or sisters. Villagers could not marry without the permission of their lord' (Makdisi 2000: 43). Holidays on saints days were restricted. And armed men meted out 'onerous' punishments for disobedience.

Tanyus Shahin, who led the uprising from December 1858, was a poor muleteer and blacksmith, a devout Maronite Christian, and almost certainly illiterate, from the district of Kisrawan. He associated with the Lazarist school in Rayfun, obtaining thereby credentials from the French consulate in Beirut allowing him to travel to cities. He kept close company with village priests (Makdisi 2000: 109). His movement – Shahin himself called it a movement (*haraka*), while his opponents, the Khazins, called it an 'excitement' (Makdisi 2000: 102) and Ottoman officials condemned it as 'unruly gatherings' (Makdisi 2000: 122) – had a more subaltern character than the risings of 1821 and 1840, enjoying a 'genuinely popular base' (Makdisi 2000: 110) among Christians of Kisrawan on Mount Lebanon and Christians living in mixed districts in the Shuf. There was some indirect support from merchants and clergy, but '[a]part from wealthier villagers from the northwestern plains of Kisrawan whose commitment was temporary, the bulk of the rebels who permanently adhered to the movement were poor and perhaps landless peasants from the upper south of the area' (Havemann 1991: 90).

The Maronite Church, a staunch supporter of social hierarchy, was paralysed by the movement which threatened its extensive property holdings, and its monopoly on the representation of the Maronite 'nation'. The Church also saw the movement as dividing the Christians (Makdisi 2000: 103).

Peasant grievances existed in abundance in regard to local landlords, noble families and tax-collectors, being related to undue fiscal extractions, irregular fees, levies in kind, *corvée* services and so on. These were intensified by land-owners, who had lost income because of the declining fortunes of handmade silk production, and were making higher tax demands and exactions to make up the shortfall (Havemann 1991: 88). An economic downturn in 1856 must have added to feelings of discontent, and profitable land was in short supply (Havemann 1991: 88–9), making exactions even harder to bear. In this pressured context, the Ottoman imperial decree of 1856 promised equality and freedom for all Ottoman subjects, regardless of religion. Disgust at the fact that the Maronite Church was not necessarily serving the cause of oppressed Christian peasants motivated others. Debilitating feuds among Maronite notables (Makdisi 2000: 96) also may have presented an opportunity of sorts, although the Khazin family united in the face of the commoners in December 1858 (Makdisi 2000: 98). Christian peasants looked back with pride on earlier uprisings – in 1840 and 1821. The grievances of the movement were initially presented as 'the excessive and unjust taxes and humiliating gifts they were traditionally compelled to present to the Khazin shaykhs' (Makdisi 2000: 96).

The uprising was joined in the name of the people (*ahali*) of Kisrawan. The fighters of 1840 were referred to as the 'army of the people of Kisrawan'. Delegates and leaders were referred to as representatives (*wakil*) of the people of Kisrawan. Goods were requisitioned on the authority of the people. Electoral, representative and consultative mechanisms were put in place so that the desires of the people could be implemented. Leaders regularly pointed out that decisions could not be taken without consultation. The movement saw the people not in official terms, as a passive and quiescent flock, represented by others, but as 'an active, unified, discerning and mobilized population willing and able to legitimately represent itself' (Makdisi 2000: 104). Shahin styled himself the 'general representative of Kisrawan' and was addressed as such by partisans in 1859 (Makdisi 2000: 99).

The solidarity of Christians was very much enjoined by Shahin and his armed men. He presented himself, and was perceived as, especially over time, as the 'savior of the common Christian inhabitants of Mount Lebanon' (Makdisi 2000: 97).

One of the most insistent themes of Shahin's uprising was a defence of the rights guaranteed by the Tanzimat, and in particular the 1856 Hatt-i Hümayun, which proclaimed equality to Ottoman subjects regardless of confessional affiliation in regard to law, education, civil service, religious worship and the provision of public security. The Tanzimat implied that the state would no longer discriminate against non-Muslims, but it said nothing about the abolition of social hierarchy or economic equality. Nor were its political implications in a place like Mount Lebanon, where local state power was rooted in genealogy more than confessional belonging, anything but superficial, or at least so elites tended to assume. 'It never occurred to the reformers that the upheavals of reform would provide for a subaltern understanding of the Tanzimat' (Makdisi 2000: 105).

The interpretation taken up in the villages of Kisrawan was far more radical than this at all levels. First, in political terms, Shahin's movement did not push for a more developed notable Maronite representation on the flanks of the Amir. On the contrary, it pushed for the political representation of commoners (who were also Christians) at the level of the district, and the complete political equality of those commoners in regard to the noble families. 'Nobody from the shaykhs' they insisted 'will be an official over us' (Makdisi 2000: 101). These commoners 'represented themselves rather than allowed themselves to be represented' (Makdisi 2000: 97). Although the details never saw the light of day, the implication was a republican and representative system of government.

Second, in more economic terms, feudal exactions and dues were to cease. They aimed at 'the repeal of oppressive customary obligations and payments, the abolition of forced labor [for noble families,] personal levies (such as gifts), [and] more favorable tenancy terms' (Havemann 1991: 91). They 'pressed for an end to the marriage taxes levied by the Khazins, the beating of the *ahali*, and the practice of passing the taxes due from the shaykhs on to the *ahali*' (Makdisi 2000: 100–1). They sought compensation for previous extortions, and an end to encroachment on the common grazing lands in Kisrawan. They even demanded that the Khazins indemnify them for the costs incurred during the rebellion (Makdisi 2000: 100).

Finally, in social terms, titles, honorifics and humiliating modes of address and so on were to be removed. They insisted that the Tanzimat had abolished 'distinctions and disdain in the forms of address' (Makdisi 2000: 101).

Overall, the movement demanded that 'the [social] station (*manzalat*) of the shaykhs be [equal] to ours without exception' (Makdisi 2000: 101). The movement aimed to overturn the feudal relations of political, economic and social subordination that existed between the *muqata'aji*-s and the peasants and institute an egalitarian republic.

An executive council (*diwan*), headed by the general representative (*wakil 'amm*), was formed to take charge of administrative and judicial tasks. Financing remains obscure; what monies there were most likely came from confiscations, as no taxes were levied. Otherwise, villages elected their representatives, who were supposed to look after the 'common welfare', and were recallable (Makdisi 2000: 114). The movement never developed much of an armed force. At most, the fledgling republic could put out a few hundred men, armed with old muskets or daggers (Makdisi 2000: 123). There is evidence that women were involved, for example in delivering water to fighters (Makdisi 2000: 124).

The movement aimed to keep the Ottoman forces at bay by maintaining absolute loyalty to the sultan and the Tanzimat, exhort the Maronite Church to protect them in the name of Christian solidarity, and focus on the iniquities of the Khazin shaykhs, while reshaping the social order in Kisrawan through the mass, forceful but non-violent appropriation of the means of production and the temporary eviction of the Khazin shaykhs.

The mass expulsion from the region of the Khazin family, several hundred strong, was successfully effected in January 1859. This was certainly an innovative and audacious tactic, shocking to elites who had never seen anything like it and who did not know how to react (Makdisi 2000: 97–9). Notables were also physically beaten, but almost never killed. For a long time, the uprising was remarkably non-violent. The only confirmed fatalities occurred in July 1859, when the wife and daughter of a Khazin shaykh were found dead, but the killers were not found (Makdisi 2000: 99). Many petitions and exhort-. ations were sent to the Maronite church and other figures, urging the church to remain faithful to the majority of its flock (Makdisi 2000: 103) and assuring them of the movement's loyalty to the Tanzimat. Shahin's men also cut down Khazin trees, presumably for fuel and other uses, appropriated Khazin harvests, made use of their grazing land, and seized their possessions and weapons. Share-croppers made good on outstanding accounts. Notable houses were not occupied as no one knew when the notables would return, and Shahin's men repeatedly informed them that they were welcome to come back in any case (Makdisi 2000: 100). Booty was taken to Shahin's own house 'by virtue of the authority of the populace', and from there distributed to his followers (Makdisi 2000: 99).

These strategies and tactics had their strengths. The Maronite church was certainly pulled in different directions (Makdisi 2000: 123, 125). For example, under pressure from Shahin's movement, the Church was ready to countenance the abolition of various forms of humiliation, beating, and the institution of elected representatives from villages (Makdisi 2000: 103). Some lower clergy were wooed to the ranks of the rebels. Shahin's growing exhortations to Christian solidarity – 'Return to your religion and stand united' (Makdisi 2000: 108) – were an attempt to win allies among an otherwise indifferent Christian notability. Further, the Ottoman forces, partly restrained by the Europeans for their own reasons, did not immediately move in to crush militarily the uprising (Havemann 1991: 90; Makdisi 2000: 106). Such non-intervention was a *sina qua non* of the movement's survival, as Shahin was not preparing for any sort of guerrilla war.

A popular, largely non-violent, socially radical peasant uprising in the name of the people and a republic gradually morphed into a violent sectarian conflict between Maronite Christians and above all the Druze. This had less to do, arguably, with the absence of the correct structural conditions, or an overdose of false consciousness (Smilians-kaya 1966) and more to do with interactions over time and Shahin's leadership. When the uprising spread to Maronites outside of Kisrawan, by late spring 1859, Christian peasants suddenly found themselves in confrontation with non-Christians, especially the Druze notables. The uprising quickly acquired a confessional colour familiar in Balkan conflicts, that, for all Shahin's personal devotion to the faith, had been absent in Kisrawan. Second, inter-confessional violence, once begun, started to spiral rapidly according to no pre-ordained plan, drawing in Christians, Druze and Shi'a who had nothing to do with the original uprising. A chain of trivial incidents, for example, set off the Druze–Christian battle of Bayt Miri in August 1859 (Makdisi 2000: 112; cf. Porath 1966; Dahir 1988).

Third, Shahin started to embrace rather than resist the Christian confessional colouring of his movement, taking on the title of 'general representative of the Christians' (Makdisi 2000: 110) especially when threatened Christians appealed to Shahin as their hero (Makdisi 2000: 113). Shahin failed to condemn and increasingly condoned confessional attacks against Druze and Shi'a, while accepting the title of 'Bek', in flat contradiction with the egalitarian principles of the original uprising (Makdisi 2000: 124). As champion of a much enlarged constituency, and now outright competitor of the Maronite Church, his prestige was raised, and he may have believed that confession was a potent glue to unify his forces (Makdisi 2000: 110, 123). Finally, amid the intensifying cycle of violence, Christians suddenly discovered that they had brothers in all parts of Lebanon, regardless of genealogy or village, developing a sense of horizontal kinship that implied a unity and strength in the face of their enemies. Not for the first or last time, republicanism and democracy for insiders implied exclusion and hostility abroad. From May and June 1860, there was widespread inter-communal Druze–Maronite fighting. At least 200 villages were destroyed and thousands injured or killed (Makdisi 2000: 127–35; Khalaf 1987).

The Druze emerged victorious following the rout and massacre of the Maronites. The legend of Tanyus Shahin was destroyed as he could not protect his Christian brethren (Makdisi 2000: 140). The Ottoman peace treaty of July 1860 stipulated that 'each person was to return to his place ... and to take back all his property and lands as it was in the past' (Makdisi 2000: 145). In 'one day they [the republicans] went from being masters ... of their own destiny to having not the slightest say in shaping the world in which they lived' (Makdisi 2000: 145).

Shahin retreated to Kisrawan utterly demoralized, without allies, and surrounded by Christian refugees 'for which he could do nothing' (Makdisi 2000: 158). He gave up the cause, denuded of his extraordinary audacity, swore obedience to the sultan, and repudiated his own movement as sedition. A few skirmishes with Ottoman troops, and a threat of excommunication from the Maronite patriarch dissolved what remained of the movement. The muleteer 'who had helped turn a world upside down' (Makdisi 2000: 159), and the people's republic of Kisrawan, was finished. The feudal hierarchy was restored.

The transformation of the uprising into a more general sectarian conflict was, as it turned out, the movement's Achilles' heel, as it changed its character and disorganized its strategies and tactics. For all its proclaimed eagerness to fight, Shahin's movement was not militarily equipped to take on the Druze, let alone confront the Ottoman state. Once a more general sectarian conflict was set in motion, whatever the movement gained in numbers could not – or at least did not – compensate for what it lacked in firepower. In the aftermath of the defeat, a weakened movement lost credibility with its new adherents, and was in no position to come to any sort of terms with the Church, the Khazins, and above all the Ottomans.

The peasant uprising of 1858–60 did bring into being a short-lived *de facto* authority, which by June 1859 was being referred to, even by its enemies, as a republic (*jumhuriyya*), the first of its kind in the Mashriq for centuries. The uprising did not spark wider movements in the region. But it did lay the basis, unwittingly, for the Mutasarrifiyya of Mount Lebanon of 1861.

The 'Ammiyya of 1889

The rising of the common people of 1889 in Jabal Druze involved a group of secondary chiefs and peasants who formed a coalition to challenge the economic and political domination on the Jabal of important sections of the Al-Atrash family. The domination of the Al-Atrash chiefs in the Jabal was itself of nineteenth-century origin – stemming from migration there, especially after the 1860 civil war. The Al-Atrash were involved in the evictions of local peasants, and the subordination of Muslim and Christian villages. They claimed the right to dominate the mountain and plain, in competition with Ottoman authorities and notable families. They thus struck up new dealings with the new grain merchants from the Maydan, on terms favourable to the Druze chiefs, who also established ascendancy *vis-à-vis* the Bedouin. Nonetheless, these chiefs insisted on supervising the communal division of land, thus interfering in customary arrangements, and in grasping larger shares for them personally, moves which led into evictions and dispossessions (Provence 2005: 33–6).

The result of the uprising was that the 'power of the great chiefs declined. Peasants earned secure title to their land, or at least to their shares, and the chiefs gave up half their shares, to bring the amount of land they controlled in most villages to no more than an eighth. Involuntary evictions stopped' (Provence 2005: 36–7). In many respects, this kind of uprising, because of its systemic implications, and its appeal to the state, went further than the moral economy style of protest. Here there were some systemic changes, and the state was more thoroughly a party to the action. Nonetheless, this kind of uprising fell well short of changing the system in a revolutionary way through millennarianism or nationalism.

Insurrections of the Druze, 1899–1910

Between 1899 and 1910, the leading figures in the Druze community mounted six armed insurrections against increased taxation and conscription by the Ottomans (Khoury 1987: 160; Provence 2005: 37). They were defending an autonomy that had been newly carved out through access to property rights and new markets and against the resistance of those they exploited in new ways. These uprisings were thus firmly situated in the political economy of the second half of the nineteenth century, rather than being some defence of the 'old society'. Against the Ottomans they used new firearms, and the new skills associated with them, the terrain (mountains and deserts), tribal alliances, and codes of honour and bravery (Hassler 1926: 143–4).

The Mahdiyya in Sudan, 1881–1885

In Sudan and the Horn of Africa, a good deal of protest was focused not so much on the Ottoman state, or French imperialism, but on the Egyptian administration (albeit one increasingly backed by the British) and its empire-building projects that went back to the 1820s. Mehmet Ali, drawing on centralized state capacities and a large tax base, conquered northern Sudan in 1821 in order to destroy the remnants of the escaped Mamlukes and to acquire gold and slaves and soldiers (Holt 1970: 2–3). A substantial state, the Funj Sultanate (1504–1821), along with its rulers and tribal vassals, was broken in the process. High taxation prefaced the 1823–4 revolt, which was 'smothered in blood' (Peters 1979: 63). Henceforth, Khartum developed as the centre of Egypt's administration in Sudan, with the conquest of much of the northeast completed by 1841.

The advent of Isma'il, who sought to extend dominion in Sudan and to suppress the slave trade, thus aligning himself with British policies, brought a new round of conquest. Isma'il obtained with British support the cession in 1865 of the ports of Suakin and Massawa (present-day Eritrea) from the Ottoman government. The occupation of the hinterland of Massawa (later called Eritrea) then followed in 1874, while the occupation of Harar in 1875 gave Egypt a brief and precarious foothold on the shore of the Indian Ocean. By the later 1870s, Egyptian rule extended to the Upper Nile and the Equatorial Lakes, to the tributary of the Bahr al-Ghazal and the former sultanate of Darfur. 'This growing Egyptian pressure in the east, led, not surprisingly, to a war with Abyssinia and so contributed to the bankruptcy which ultimately overwhelmed the *khedive*' (Holt 1970: 2–3). By the 1870s, tribal leaders in large parts of Sudan had become dependent on the Egyptian administration. They were responsible for the collection of taxes, and could be disposed of at will. Meanwhile, orthodox Islam entered Sudan with the 'Turco-Egyptian administration' and hence was associated not only with wealthy, urban elites linked to the state, but also to a form of foreign and Turkish domination (Peters 1979: 63).

Two years after the deposition of Khedive Ismail [in 1879] the Mahdia began. It was a movement of religious origin which was assisted in its development by political, social, and economic stresses in Sudanese society, and which accomplished a political revolution – the overthrow of Egyptian rule and the establishment of an indigenous Islamic state (Holt 1970: 3).

Muhammad Ahmad (d. 1885), the Mahdi, led a rebellion in the 1880s that was able to defeat both the Egyptian forces and then the British and establish a state from 1883 to 1898. The Mahdi proclaimed himself Al-Mahdi in June 1881. He managed to defeat first the Egyptian and then the British garrisons under Hicks (1883), Samuel Baker and then Gordon (1885). His state was ruled by his successor from

1885 until being broken by the British in 1898. The Mahdist state covered an area almost as big as Egypt. It reached in the west to the borderlands of what is now the Central African Republic, in the north to just short of Wadi Halfa and in the east to Suakin on the Red Sea coast.

The Ottoman–Egyptian administration in Sudan was weak in winning the spontaneous consent of the mass of the population. As Holt has it:

Stronger than the tribal and religious systems of the Sudan in material force and formal organization, the Egyptian administration was far weaker in its emotional appeal to the loyalty of the individual (Holt 1970: 13).

With a few exceptions, the Egyptians ruled indirectly through local, tributary tribal chiefs rather than breaking up the tribes. Most of the northern Sudanese tribes 'looked back to the era of the Funj and welcomed any weakness in the central administration which promised them a partial return to their old autonomy' (Holt 1970: 16). Such memories of statehood and sovereignty were powerful:

During a political intrigue in Kordofan just before the Mahdia, the chief of the Ghudiyat tribe was incited to revolt against the governor by being reminded that he was 'a descendant of the Funj, of the dynasty of the Black Sultanate, the kings of Sennar' (Holt 1970: 17).

The northern Sudanese were frustrated in their political loyalties: they 'regretted the loss of their tribal independence' and sought the regulation of local affairs according to tribal law and custom. 'Egyptian rule was unpopular, not merely by its faults but by its very nature, since it was alien, unremitting, and exacting' (Holt 1970: 17, 22).

Once the Egyptian administration started to back British-led attempts to abolish slavery, the impositions became not only administrative, but cut into the material interests of many sections of Sudanese society in every part of the country. Heavy taxes were imposed on slave merchants. Command was given to a foreign, Christian colonial official, Sir Samuel Baker. It was generally asserted that 'slavery was an institution permitted by Islam, and the appointment of a Christian to suppress the trade aroused the religious resentment of the populace generally' (Holt 1970: 34–5). Baker imposed a series of coercive measures. 'Thus the extension of Egyptian rule and the measures against the slave trade were associated with an increasing European official personnel.' The suppression confronted 'the ramified influence of the slave traders, the suspicions of the southern tribes, and the unwilling co-operation of a lethargic bureaucracy' (Holt 1970: 34–5). These impositions and violations alienated many from the Turkiyya in Sudan. After 1877, the Ottoman–Egyptian authorities adopted an ever more proactive stance on the abolition of slavery, while entering a period of weakness related to the indecisive and expensive war with Abyssinia, bankruptcy, and then the suspension by the Khedive Ismail of salaries to officials in Sudan in 1875 until all taxes were collected (Holt 1970: 37). The European dual control in Egypt after 1876 and the deposition of the Khedive Ismail by the British and the Ottoman sultan, signalled a certain weakness at the centre. Divisions appeared among power-holders: rivalry among elites led to a short-lived rebellion in July 1878 which was suppressed (Holt 1970: 38).

The spread of revivalist Sufism in Sudan contributed a key dynamic. Sufi renewal, as elsewhere, went back to teachers in Mecca and Medina. Of Moroccan origin, Ahmad b. Idris Al-Fasi (1760–1837) was probably the most important of these. His disciples, who moved in North Africa and the Arabian peninsula as missionaries and pilgrims, and their descendants, founded and led what became two of the most important Sufi orders in Sudan, the Khatmiyya and the Mirghaniya (Holt 1970: 19–20). A Medinan-based shaykh, Mohammad Ibn Abdul Karim Al-Sammani (1718–1775) founded another important order, the Sammaniyya, which spread in Sudan through the preaching of Ahmad Al-Tayyib Al-Bashir (1742/3–1824), a renowned *mujaddid* and shaykh. This *tariqa* was especially successful between the Blue and White Niles. Al-Bashir's grandson, Muhammad Sharif Nur Al-Da'im, was the future Mahdi's first Sufi shaykh (Holt 1970: 21). Proselytization was carried out by individuals, not necessarily backed in a formal way by the orders to which they belonged. Successful teachers came to be regarded as saints (*wali/awliya*) and miracles were attributed to them. Saints were revered as transmitters of holiness (*baraka*). Their tombs became places of pilgrimage; their possessions, relics endowed with sacred power. The headship of orders became hereditary (Holt 1970: 17–18).

While urban, scriptural and orthodox Islam was often distinct from rural, experiential, Sufi and heterodox Islam, the 'great gulf' between the personal faith of many Sudanese and the 'official Islam of the Egyptian administration [and the urban *ulema*]' (Holt 1970: 17) was in many ways a result of the Islamic and Sufi revival of the preceding century. Adherence to these forms of the faith, and the organizational structures with which such loyalties were intertwined, were an important element in the background to a 'revolt against a Muslim government' (Holt 1970: 17). This background, however, should not be exaggerated. The Egyptian authorities co-opted and ruled through leading religious shaykhs. The Mirghani family were especially favoured, and the Khatmiya was closely associated with Egyptian rule in the Sudan. There was nothing inevitable about the incidence or shape of the Mahdiyya that was to follow.

Muhammad Ahmad (1844–85) was born at Dongola on the Upper Nile in the land of Nuba, and grew up in Karari just north of Khartum. His father was a boat-builder, while the family traced descent from the Prophet. Muhammad Ahmad devoted himself from an early age to religious learning, going to study under the grandson of the founder of the Samaniyya Sufi order in the 1860s. He was recognized for his piety and asceticism, became a shaykh, and travelled the country for religious purposes. In 1870, he moved with his family to Aba Island on the White Nile near Al-Kawwa south of Khartum, built a mosque, and established a reputation. He fell out with his old master in 1878 after objecting, in Islamic revivalist fashion, to dancing and music at a circumcision ceremony. He became leader of a different branch of the Sammaniya in 1878, and established good relations with the notables of the important provincial town of El Ebeid. He developed a reputation for piety, asceticism and charisma among common people and good relations with a number of important tribes.

Muhammad Ahmad then devoted a period to solitary meditation before disclosing his mission on the island of Aba on 1 Sha'ban 1298 (29 June 1881) (Berque 1972: 142). He wrote letters to various notables, assuming the style of Muhammad Al-Mahdi, and calling on adherents to rally. Initially, he stressed not *jihad* but *hijra*: 'the flight for the Faith from among the infidels to the Mahdi' (Holt 1970: 54). Here was a conscious parallel with the Prophet, who had undertaken a *hijra* (emigration) from a hostile Mecca in 622 AD (1 AH) to depart from those who would not accept Islam, and to gather strength in Medina before effecting a triumphant return. The idea of *hijra* as a means of resistance implied not an outright confrontation with the enemy but a withdrawal from abodes deemed Dar Al-Harb and an emigration to locations within the Dar Al-Islam. It was an idea enshrined in the Qur'an:

They will say, 'We were oppressed in the land.' The angels will say, 'Was not the earth of Allah spacious [enough] for you to emigrate therein?' For those, their refuge is Hell – and evil it is as a destination (4: 97). And whoever emigrates for the cause of Allah will find on the earth many [alternative] locations and abundance (4: 100) (cited in Peters 1979: 41, 47–8).

The idea appeared elsewhere in the contentious history of the nineteenth century. Several hundred Muslims emigrated from the region around Constantine in 1893, and from around Tlemcen in 1911. Here there were economic grievances over land registration, as well as fear of being conscripted – a fate which might have involved fighting fellow Muslims in Morocco. Peters notes that the emigration from Tlemcen was the last instance of typically religious resistance against French colonial domination in Algeria (Peters 1979: 61). Further afield, there was a *hijra* from India in 1826 and the Hijrat movement in India in 1920 'when tens of thousands of Indian Moslems set out for Afghanistan, following a *fatwa* to this effect' (Peters 1979: 41, 47–8).

The sequence *hijra–jihad* announced by the Mahdi was 'characteristic of West African Islamic movements in the nineteenth century' (Holt 1970: 54 n. 2). The bulk of the Mahdi's forces in Sudan in the 1880s were drawn from a nomadic cattle-herding tribe, the Baqqara, whose grazing lands reached as far as Lake Chad. The Baqqara would presumably have been familiar with the West African contentious repertoire, and may even have helped bring it to Sudan. The Mahdi called for *hijra* to be done during the sacred month of Ramadan, adding to its divine association and appeal to piously minded constituencies. The call to *hijra* did not just evoke an abstract piety: it battened onto tissues of common sense and widely known living traditions of protest. Holt notes that this call for *hijra* with Faith was a

sanctified version of a traditional Sudanese reaction to oppression – the mass emigration of a tribal group from its territory (Holt 1970: 54).

Flight was also a widespread response to heavy taxation and regulation among the settled peasantry up and down the Nile Valley: its association with *hijra* turned it into a more explosive and revolutionary act. Only when Egyptian troops were sent to arrest the Mahdi was *jihad* declared:

I am the Mahdi, the Successor of the Prophet of God. Cease to pay taxes to the infidel Turks and let everyone who finds a Turk kill him (Holt 1970: 54).

With this declaration, at once religious and political, the Mahdiyya was definitively under way.

For centuries, a mass of beliefs in an Expected Deliverer 'whose coming will restore the Golden Age' were to be found among the Jewish, Christian and Muslim communities of the MENA (Holt 1970: 22), as well as among Zoroastrian and pagan communities, and in Europe and elsewhere. Mahdi means 'divinely guided one'. The term *mul s-sa'a*/Lord of the Hour was often used in North Africa. The idea is that, in times of calamity or oppression, or when the day of judgment draws near, a messiah-like figure will appear in order to put an end to oppression and establish the rule of justice. The appearance of the Mahdi will have its own precursors – catastrophes, signs, and inspired or charismatic individuals. The spread of non-Muslim rule was one of the signs that would precede the coming of the Mahdi (Peters 1979: 42). Ibn Khaldun's classical formulation of the idea ran as follows:

inevitably there will be manifested at the end of the age a man from the People of the House, who will support the Faith and cause justice to be manifested. The Muslims will follow him, and he will acquire domination over the Islamic realms, and he will be called the Mahdi. The emergence of Antichrist and the subsequent Signs of the Hour, as established in the *Sahih*, will ensue. Jesus will descend after him, and kill Antichrist, or will descend with him [the Mahdi], and assist him [the Mahdi] to kill him [the Antichrist]; and he [Jesus] will take the Mahdi as imam in his prayer (cited in Holt 1970: 23–4).

In Ibn Khaldun's formulation, the Deliverer will be: (1) from the Prophet's kin; (2) called Mahdi; (3) will support Faith and justice and restore the unity of Islam; and (4) his manifestation will be one of the 'Signs of the Hour', that is, 'an eschatological event preceding Dooms-day' (Holt 1970: 24). The idea was derived from *hadith* (sayings of the Prophet) foretelling the Expected Deliverer under certain kinds of circumstances (Holt 1970: 24). The notion had become a staple of Islamic eschatology – the study of end times, the day of judgment, and heaven and hell. Yet, the link with end times was not inherent to the idea of a Deliverer, and had only grown up over time as an attempt by orthodox *ulema* to limit the subversive potential against established authorities of those claiming to be the Mahdi (Holt 1970: 29). Among Sunni Muslims, the line could be blurred between Mahdi and *mujad-did* (the renewer of the faith) (Holt 1970: 30).

Millenarian expectations were not confined to the implementation of justice in the purely legal or political sense, but extended to questions of prosperity and welfare. In one tradition cited by Ibn Khaldun 'a generous ruler shall give abundantly, and neither the heavens nor the earth shall withhold their increase' (Holt 1970: 28–9). In another, '[a]t the end of my Community, the Mahdi shall come forth. God shall send him abundant rain, and the earth shall bring forth her plants. He shall give wealth fairly; the cattle shall abound, and the Community shall be great.' In another, 'He shall fill it [the earth] with justice and equity as it was filled with injustice and oppression. The heaven shall refuse nothing of its rain, nor shall the earth withhold anything of her plants' (Holt 1970: 29).

Sometimes millenarian hopes and expectations were 'passively held as an inner consolation to the individual, or projected into a vague and indefinite future' (Holt 1970: 23). In this sense, this idea could be quietist or actively de-mobilizing, where believers were to patiently endure all wrongs and passively await the coming of the Mahdi. The Tayyibiyyah Sufi *tariqa* in Algeria in the 1840s employed the term in this sense in order to undermine Abd Al-Qadir's position, arguing that mobilization was pointless until the Mahdi actually appeared (Peters 1979: 42). At other times, claimants to the Mahdi went unrecognized – as in the two obscure Mahdis from the Nile valley (Khartum and Upper Egypt) in the 1880s mentioned in a tract opposing Muhammad Ahmad of Dongola (Holt 1970: 30–1 n. 3). In other cases, many expected and hoped for the arrival of a Mahdi, but such a figure never appeared – as in Egypt for a few years after the British occupation of 1882 (Berque 1972).

At times, however, of particular strain, arising from alien domination or from the inner tensions of an unstable society, expectation becomes active: the Deliverer, it is felt, will shortly appear, and the floating beliefs are given precise significance through attachment to, or appropriation by, a claimant to this status. Thus there comes into being a movement subversive of the existing political or social order, led by (or at least propagated in the name of) the Expected Deliverer (Holt 1970: 23).

Eschatology had occupied urban scholars and preachers, but was also well known in legends and popular sayings in town and country alike. It was an idea of near-universal import to very wide-constituencies, and part of the common sense and proverbial wisdom of many

Muslims, Sunni and Shi'a alike, from all walks of life. It seems to have been especially important along the Nile and in North Africa.

In Sudan, Muhammad Ahmad claimed that he had been appointed as the Mahdi by a prophetic assembly (*al-hadra al-nabawiyya*), an idea familiar generally in the Sufi tradition – only prophets could certify a new prophet. There were also local expectations as to signs and portents. Leaders of the Samaniyya order had asserted that the redeemer would come from among them. Shaykh Al-Qurashi, the previous head of the relevant branch of the Sammaniyya, had said that the Mahdi would ride the shaykh's pony and erect a dome over his grave. The idea that the Mahdi would manifest himself at the turn of an Islamic century was particularly potent in the early 1880s, given that 1 Muharram 1300 (the first day of the new century) corresponded to 12 November 1882.

A sign of the revolutionary framing of the Mahdist project was that Muhammad Ahmad adopted the terminology and practice of the Prophet. He referred to himself as a successor to the Prophet, changing the *shahada* (declaration of faith) to indicate this. He also replaced one of the five pillars of Islam (pilgrimage) with the obligation to undertake *jihad*, and added a sixth pillar: belief in the Mahdiyya. He named his four closest deputies after the four successors to the Prophet Muhammad; he named his followers Ansar (after those who had supported the Prophet in Medina following his *hijra* from Medina), forbidding use of the term *dervish* which applied to other Sufis. This framing implied sweeping change of the kind conveyed by the term revolution, as it implied the founding of a new community, a fundamentally new form of socio-political system. Indeed, the Mahdi may have started out in the Sufi Sammaniyya order, but his radical intention was to supersede and abolish Sufi orders. This kind of framing could only be believed on the one hand, or entirely heretical on the other. In regards to these kinds of claims, there was no 'middle ground'.

The Mahdi did not derive his authority to speak from the *ijtihad* of the scriptural authorities, but claimed instead to receive direct inspiration from God. His was a charismatic and prophetic, not a scriptural authority. His proclamations could thus supersede this or that jurisprudential tradition, including the four Sunni schools of law, heresy in the eyes of most urban *ulema*, some of whom were employed by the Ottoman–Egyptian government and were loyal to the Ottoman sultan.

These critics did not deny the concept of the Mahdi, but aimed to discredit Muhammad Ahmad's claim to it.

The Mahdiyya marched under the banners of Islamic millenarianism in opposition to Ottoman–Egyptian domination. Political power and religious inspiration were woven tightly together. As the Mahdi proclaimed:

Verily these Turks . . . thought that theirs was the kingdom and the command was in their hands. They transgressed the command of [God's] apostles and of His prophets and of him who commanded them to imitate them. They judged by other than God's revelation [i.e. the Qur'an] and altered the Shari'a of Our Lord Muhammad, the Apostle of God, and corrupted the Faith of God and placed poll-tax [*al-jizya* – usually reserved for non-Muslims] on your necks together with the rest of the Muslims . . . Verily the Turks would drag away your men in chains, imprison them in fetters, take captive your women and your children and slay unrighteously the soul under God's protection, and all this was because of the poll-tax, which neither God nor His Apostle had commanded. Moreover, they had no mercy upon the small among you nor respect for the great among you (Holt 1970: 42).

Here the corruption of the true faith and political injustice and tyranny are linked tightly together. Unfair taxation, coercion and the violation of honour are intimately intertwined with the corruption of faith, law and prophecy. Indeed, the Mahdi at other points went out of his way to execrate Ottoman and Egyptian officials and soldiers posted to Sudan as part of a tyrannical Turkish government (Holt 1970: 14). It was said that the Mahdi had long before refused to eat the food provided by one of his early religious teachers as that teacher was subsidized by the government (Holt 1970: 45). The Mahdiyya was framed in terms at once religious and political. The Mahdi did not just propose a new religious community, but at the same moment, a new political order and alternative form of government. This point is highlighted where in the terminology of the movement the 'Mahdiyya' was opposed to the 'Turkiyya' – the Ottoman–Egyptian government.

The authorities at the outset understood that this was a profound threat to their temporal power as well as to the established ways in which they turned to Islam to legitimate their rule, deploying troops at once in order to crush the Mahdi. This terminated the previous strategy of co-optation, whereby the authorities had implicitly recognized the growing status of Muhammad Ahmad by ceasing to levy wood from Aba Island. The declaration of the Mahdiyya was something different: no longer were the authorities dealing with a pious ascetic and Sufi with a reputation, but a revolutionary challenge against which the only response was military force.

Muhammad Ahmad's movement was not only framed in opposition to religious orthodoxy and Turkish domination, but, unlike Wahhabism, it explicitly opposed the wealthy, the powerful, the high status, and those who claimed a monopoly of the pen and education, especially in the cities, along with their particular tribal allies. This framing did not rely on the terminology of social class, but drew on indigenous, syncretic and living traditions, in some ways comparable to the rugged 'visions of the people' mobilized against the wealthy in England (Joyce 1993). Powerful languages here involved asceticism, world-rejection, and the corruption and vanity associated with wealth and luxury. A glimpse of this comes in the memoirs of one of the Mahdi's key followers. He wrote that, after the fall of Khartoum in 1885:

they opened for him [the Mahdi] the room where all the gold was kept, and there it was – jewellery and guineas and ingots. But as soon as the door was opened, and all the gold glowed at us, the Mahdi, with whom be God's peace, turned his back on it with the quickness of lightning, and left. I stood where I was, and thought about the gold, and remembered the line of Al-Busiri: 'They tried to tempt him with the hills of gold', and I said to myself, 'Here indeed is disdain for the things of this world' (Bedri 1969: 32).

Thus the reader was to understand the importance of the Mahdi's dramatic repudiation of wealth and its temptations.

Consonant with this was the charismatic defence of his humble followers mounted by the Mahdi himself in response to the demand for submission by Yusuf Pasha Hasan Al-Shallali, a key military commander in the Turco-Circassian administration under Giegler Pasha, the new Governor General, on 4 Rajab 1299 (22 May 1882). In this letter, in a context where urban opinion was prone to seeing pastoral nomads as only semi-civilized at best, he extolled the poverty, ignorance and unorthodoxy of the pastoral nomads of the Baqqara cattle-herders, one of the important constituencies of his movement:

You say that Our only followers are the ignorant Baqqara and the idolaters. Know then that the followers of the apostles before Us and of our Prophet Muhammad were the weak and the ignorant and the nomads, who worshipped rocks and trees (Holt 1970: 58).

In other words, by analogy with the sanctified histories of those who turned to Islam in its earliest days, he was able to frame the 'ignorant', the 'weak' and the 'nomadic' in terms of the highest social value (true belief), and suture this to potency, in that the Mahdi is reminding the Egyptian general here that it was out of these simple true believers that the Prophetic mission and thence the glories of Islam had been constructed. These sentences suggest powerful, innovative and charismatic framing capacities with which Muhammad Ahmad was endowed. They are also highly suggestive of both the social class, in the broad sense, of his constituencies, and those against whom his movement took aim.

The strategy adopted by the Mahdist movement was a radical one indeed. It involved an outright assault on the established political order, the forms of religious orthodoxy, the ruling classes, their tribal allies, and large segments of the wealthy in the cities and major towns. The new order would be brought about by declared, outright assault on and defeat of the existing order. Whether or not these revolutionary goals were achieved is one question, but the radical strategy, both proposed and largely undertaken in practice, was not in doubt. As the Mahdi also wrote in the aforementioned letter:

As for the *'ulama* and the rich and the people of power and luxury, they did not follow them [the Prophet's supporters] until they [the Prophet's supporters] had ruined their palaces, killed their nobles and ruled them by force ... know that Our going is only the command of the Apostle of God (Holt 1970: 58).

This excerpt is a clear enough indication of a thoroughly non-accommodationist strategy of force and defeat, one read into the example of the Prophet, which, in an act of time-space compression, was to be re-enacted in the present. It was comparable to the mode of action adopted by Al-Hiba in southern Morocco in 1912 as we shall see – while a strategy more distant from that of the Islamic modernist Muhammad Abduh, who was accommodationist towards British rule, the Egyptian state, urban and landed wealth and notability, could hardly be found.

As far as is known, the Mahdi had no explicit theory of guerrilla warfare, or how it could be that small, lightly armed, dispersed and mobile groups linked to local populations could defeat a larger, slow-moving and heavily armed alien foe. The tactics followed by the Mahdi in Sudan were effective precisely because they were guerrilla tactics with or without such a theory. The summons to make *hijra* during Ramadan was carefully timed in this regard. The Mahdi's dispersed followers could prepare in one month, whereas the 'dilatory bureaucracy' in Khartoum would not be able to organize countermeasures because administrative and military action would be retarded during the fast. Moreover, in 1881, Ramadan coincided with the height of the rainy season 'when travel by road and navigation by river would be difficult'. Indeed, the second attempt to send a large body of troops against the Mahdi had to turn back in September 1881 because of heavy-rainfall (Holt 1970: 56). In these circumstances, 'the lightly clad, hard-living tribesmen who formed the bulk of the Mahdi's supporters would have the advantage of mobility over the troops of the Egyptian administration' (Holt 1970: 54–5). The forces of the Mahdi were initially armed only with swords, spears, and wooden staffs. They later developed a centralized and disciplined corps carrying firearms. Avoidance of direct, open confrontation on the battlefield, surprise, ambush, harassment, mobility, the knowledge of terrain, the seizure of arms and booty, links to the indigenous population which solved problems of supply and cover were basic to the tactics deployed against the relatively slow-moving and concentrated forces of the Ottoman–Egyptian conscript army, and of the British-commanded columns.

The first military confrontation with the authorities took place when two companies of troops were sent by steamer from Khartoum on 12 August 1881 to arrest the Mahdi. The troops were ambushed, by night, as they filed away from the steamer. They were routed, even though their ambushers numbered only 350 men, and were inferior in firepower, having no firearms whatsoever. The Mahdiyya suffered only twelve casualties (Holt 1970: 55). This was an important victory: it seemed miraculous to the Mahdi and his followers; it triggered the *hijra* into Kordofan (Holt 1970: 55–6). Ambush was again important in securing victory in the second major encounter with the authorities. On 9 December 1881, Rashid Bey of Fashoda's force was ambushed and overwhelmed. Rashid Bey was killed and a large quantity of arms and other booty accrued to the Ansar. The victory was hailed as a miracle and the prestige of the Mahdi was again raised (Holt 1970: 57). It was fortuitous for the Mahdiyya that appeals by Khartum to Cairo for reinforcements from December 1881 to March 1882, made while Egyptian imperialism was paralysed by the 'Urabi movement, went 'almost unheeded' (Holt 1970: 57). In spring 1882, once Cairo realized the seriousness of matters in Sudan, 'the Mahdi had already won his first successes' and attained a strong position (Holt 1970: 41).

One of the distinctive strengths of the Mahdist movement in Sudan had to do with the revolutionary ideas that stitched it together: what Holt refers to as 'moral strength' (Holt 1970: 42). Mahdist ideas, far from being part of the backwardness and weakness of the movement, were in fact capable of rallying a broad constituency under one banner; they were capable of inspiring a deep commitment and motivation. As Holt argues, a key problem for Cairo was precisely that the Mahdiyya was not a mere civil rebellion, like those of Al-Zubayr, Sulayman, or the pretenders in Darfur. Instead, the Mahdi was primarily a religious leader. He had 'arisen to purge the Muslim world of its faults and to break the power of the infidels'. In other words, he led a *jihad* claiming support of all Muslims (Holt 1970: 41) – drawing on foundational, radical forms of Islam, putatively universal in the social formation as a whole. Such claims, credibly made, gave the movement a powerful spine. For the Mahdi's followers, these ideas brought into the present, in an act of appropriation and time-space compression, a deliberate re-enactment 'in their own persons [of] the sufferings and the triumphs of the early days of Islam ... their consciousness of playing a part in this great drama was an inspiration to them' (Holt 1970: 54). It is not clear how else it is possible to explain the Mahdi's refusal of British and Egyptian attempts to turn him into a vassal of the Turco-Egyptian administration, in a region full of such figures, tempted by the seductions of power. Through client-status, guns and means of statehood could be obtained, interests and profits pursued, and prestige acquired: but such vassal-ship would have violated the basic principles and identities on which the Mahdi built his movement. A figure no less august than General Gordon, representing the world's largest empire, sent the Mahdi in March 1884 a pacific letter appointing him Sultan of Kordofan, urging him to release European prisoners, and giving him a red robe of honour and a tarbush. As Holt writes, the recipient was 'no puppet prince in exile' but a 'religious leader and political master of half the Sudan'. The Mahdi replied:

Know that I am the Expected Mahdi, the Successor of the Apostle of God. Thus I have no need of the sultanate, nor of the kingdom of Kordofan or elsewhere, nor of the wealth of this world and its vanity. I am but the slave of God, guiding unto God and to what is with Him ... As for the gift which you have sent Us, may God reward you well for your good-will and guide you to the right ... It is returned to you herewith (Holt 1970: 93).

Gordon's policy vacillated between accommodation and aggression: the Mahdi as Hajj Ahmad of Constantine had done in the 1830s and as Abd Al-Krim was to do in the 1920s, stood firm. The principles which united his movement could not be violated so lightly.

The appeal of the Mahdiyya sapped the loyalty and morale of the Ottoman Egyptian troops:

Against the Mahdi the troops of the Egyptian government fought with divided hearts and uneasy consciences, particularly since the Mahdi's victories seemed to them to bear witness that his was indeed the cause of God (Holt 1970: 42).

Here was a moral strength, capable of motivating and mobilizing an important constituency, whether or not it was dismissed in London as fanaticism (Holt 1970: 42) and by urban modernists as irrationalism and backwardness. Ill-omens and signs of God's will appeared to dog the authorities' campaign. When, for example, the contingents of the Ottoman–Egyptian forces paraded near Khartoum under the German official in Egyptian service Giegler Pasha in preparation for a new attempt to crush the Mahdi in March 1882, 'its well-wishers shuddered to see the great drum of Abdallah Dafa'allah [a tribal chief allied to the Egyptians] fall to the ground from the camel which bore it ... [and] the men of El Obeid marched out with heavy hearts' (Holt 1970: 57). Like the rainfall which had fallen to stymie the army, this was read in religious mode as an ill-omen and a sign that God was on the side of the Mahdi. When some of the Mahdi's spies were hacked to death in front of the paraded troops 'they embraced martyrdom with such fortitude that the spectators were deeply impressed' (Holt 1970: 57).

The loyalty and adherence that such a mobilizing project could inspire in the local population could generate important intelligence about the enemy. The only reason that the Mahdi was able to ambush the forces of Rashid Bey in December 1881 was because news of their advance was 'brought in by a woman of the Kinana tribe' (Holt 1970: 57). This was not purely a matter of links to an indigenous population considered as monolithic, because the population of Sudan was heterogeneous and often divided.

Once the Mahdist forces created a state, they became, paradoxically enough, easier to crush by conventional military superiority, because at this point they now defended fixed points, and were forced into open confrontations against superior weaponry – in this case machine guns.

The Mahdiyya had attracted attention, from Morocco to Singapore. It demonstrated that a revolutionary religious project could stitch Sufi orders, pastoral nomads, peasantries and townspeople together into new forms of community and state. In the end, this new political community succumbed like Abd Al-Qadir's to colonial violence.

Morocco: tribes, Sufis, pretenders and millenarians

The central government in Morocco was less able to exert sovereignty, or impose new kinds of order and taxation, especially outside the country's cities, than most states elsewhere in the region in the nineteenth century, with the possible exception of Iran. Even though attempts made by the *makhzan* (the central government, literally, 'the treasury') to centralize power, in alliance with various, mostly urban groups, were relatively modest, at least compared to Egypt or Istanbul, a wide variety of mostly rural-based groups (tribes, Sufis, provincial lords, pretenders and heterodox religious figures), were able to hold even these forms at bay, resisting centralization, attempts to raise taxes, and the sultan's effective collaboration with urban *ulema*, merchants, and European geopolitical and economic interests that increasingly accompanied them. When the sultan finally handed over formal sovereignty of the country to the French in 1912, boarding ship to escape the consequences as he did so, even then the levers of power were not in place to guarantee a stable handover to the new rulers.

The authority of the Makhzan in Morocco had long been limited, opposed and sometimes came close to disintegration. In the early seventeenth century, an uprising had played an important role in putting an end to a state-led attempt to impose a Spanish–Caribbean-style sugar-plantation economy based on black slave labour (Le Tourneau *et al.* 1972: 78). The short-lived republic of Bu Ragrag was founded by Andalusian Muslims near Rabat in the 1610s. One group 'formed a self-governing community, ruled by an elected governor who held office for a year with the assistance of a *diwan* of elders'. These citizens also engaged in piracy and were reputed to hate Christians (Abun-Nasr 1987: 221). During the first half of the eighteenth century, the Alawi dynasty, which originated in the seventeenth century, became the plaything of the slave troops who were originally brought in to protect it. It was during these years that the well-known notions of bilad *al-makhzan* (the lands under the control of the sovereignty, taxation and regulation of the central government), and the *bilad al-siba* (the lands outside of that direct control), came into being.

On the other hand, the centralization of the second half of the eighteenth century under Mawlay Muhammad b. Abdulla (1757–90) was relatively successful. At that time, when European consular and debt pressure was less, and where different models of state power prevailed, centralization was armoured by important forms of consent: for example, during 1775–82, a period of conflict, plague and famine 'The sultan had large amounts of wheat imported and sold without profit. He reduced taxes, had bread distributed free to the poor, and gave money to tribal leaders in order to enable them to cater for the pressing needs of their groups' (Abun-Nasr 1987: 240). No 'savage God' of liberal economic doctrine impeded, as in British India and Ireland in the eighteenth and nineteenth centuries, the sultan's readiness to 'interfere' in market forces to engage in provisioning during a time of famine. On the other hand, Mawlay Suleiman's (r. 1792–1822) high-handed treatment of certain Berber tribes and religious figures, and his flirtation with Wahhabist doctrine, was a cause of resistance to his powers by tribes and various Sufi orders in the 1810s. Under royal sponsorship, there was an attempt to reinvigorate traditional theology and purge it of heterodox influence. The court launched a campaign against Sufi brotherhoods as decadent and prone to excess, and against saints' cults, and strove to 'prevent religious shrines from granting protection to refugees from *makhzan* justice' (Burke 1976: 37).

The sovereignty of the sultan as ruler of Morocco and as caliph and Amir Al-Mu'minin of the Muslim community at large was important in accounting for the overall coherence of Morocco as a political community. But underneath such an over-arching principle, the central government was weak and the forms of local autonomy strong. It was widely held and practised, for example, that the shrines and mausoleums of holy men or the founders of revered lineages, offered sanctuary to those sought by the *makhzan*. The shrine of Mawlay Idriss, who brought Islam to Morocco in 789 AD, for example, in the hill-top town of Meknes, was a place of pilgrimage and of sanctuary for those who had incurred the wrath of central authorities (cf. Laroui 1977: 160). The bureaucracy was relatively small throughout the century (Burke 1976: 17). State power, in turn, was limited by the low degree of urbanization. In Morocco, the cities, which were identified with the *makhzan*, were relatively small in demographic terms. As late as 1905, it was estimated that Morocco's population of around 5 million included an urban population of only 230,000 souls (Burke 1976: 3). Urban notables were very far from controlling the countryside through effective access to property or rights to the surplus, as in the Mashriq and much of Egypt. In place of a settled peasantry in easily patrolled plains fed by navigable rivers, and railways used by the forces of coercion, administration and taxation (as in Egypt), in Morocco were mountains, hills, desert regions, non-navigable rivers, rugged coasts, powerful provincial lords and numerous clans and tribes. These areas were protected against incursions from without by the low capacity of the transport infrastructure, and endowed with a strong sense of the ways in which their own forms of power and consent, tribal leaderships and tribal customs, holy lineages and local ways of living, should determine how things were done.

Forms of local cohesion were enhanced by the fact that there was no entrenched hereditary aristocracy – 'few families or groups enjoyed substantial power for more than three generations' (Burke 1976: 15). Class conflicts were moderated by the 'obligation of wealthy patrons to defend even their humblest servants, the traditional rivalries between notables, and the periodic re-division of land among the adult males of the clan that was practised in many tribes' (Burke 1976: 9). The fact that Morocco's capacities to disrupt the economic interests of Europeans who appeared there deterred those interests from coming in the first place. After the 1880s, tribal uprisings were greatly assisted by the use of smuggled Remington and Winchester repeater rifles, which stripped the *makhzan* of the one advantage it had traditionally had – superior firepower (Burke 1976: 32–3). In general terms, military engagements between the government and this or that tribe or movement were by no means decided in advance.

After the death of Mawlay Suleiman (r. 1792–1822), there was a period of heightened conflict, just as there was after the defeat at the hands of the French at the Battle of Isly in 1844. On that occasion, the sultan showed himself as Amir Al-Mu'minin (Commander of the Faithful) and caliph (head of the Islamic community) to be incapable of protecting the Muslim faithful against the power of the Christian French; his more temporal duty to provide security and protection to his flock was also in doubt. The sultan had been drawn into the battle by the resistance in Algeria to the French. The defeat meant the dishonourable imposition of the humiliating 'infidel' Treaty of Tangier

(10 September 1844). Article 4 of the Treaty declared Abd Al-Qadir, a hero in the eyes of many, to be an outlaw. As a result of the Treaty, 'serious tribal revolts sprang up in many parts of Morocco, forcing the sultan to focus his efforts on putting them down' (Danzinger 1980: 66–7). This pattern was repeated following the defeat of Tetouan at the hands of the Spanish in 1860, except that, on this occasion, the tribes were more significantly bolstered by heterodox religion in the shape of one of the most important Mahdist uprisings for a long time. For this radicalism, '[t]he criticism of the inertia of the Sultan seems to be the fundamental reason' (Laroui 1977: 158 n. 91).

After this defeat, the Moroccan elite started to make more significant efforts to centralize power and to strengthen the administration, which in turn linked it more closely to European geopolitical and economic interests, not to mention European ideas, and involved it in an assault on spheres of autonomy that it did not in reality have the capacity to take on (Burke 1976: 20). The 'reforms' were provocative not only because they were launched by a weak centre aiming to extend its power, but because they signalled to many a deviation from the faith. As one scholar who opposed them, Al-Nasiri, put it of the reformers: 'They want to learn how to fight to protect the faith, but they lose the faith in the process of learning how [to protect it]' (cited in Burke 1976: 38–9). Not only this, but in practice 'reform' was carried out selectively, involved double-standards and violent repression.

In the 1890s and 1900s, incidences of extortion and corruption in the collection of taxes increased and, in the early 1900s, 'The needs for tax revenues of the *makhzan* ... caused the rural administration to become progressively harsher and more unjust in its collection of taxes. Movements of rural protest appeared with more frequency' (Burke 1976: 34). There was a small-scale and mostly successful *jihad* repulsing a Spanish territorial incursion from Melilla into the Rif in 1893 (Burke 1976: 30). The sultan, Mawlay Hassan (1873–94), failed to support it for fear of being drawn into a losing military confrontation with the French (Burke 1976: 30). His authority and prestige took a beating as a result. With the death of Hasan I in 1894, tax rebellions became more frequent in the countryside (Burke 1976: 36). This was a deployment, under new conditions, of a familiar repertoire of contention acting to check over-weaning extraction as noted by Burke:

The local *qaid* tended to exact as much in taxes and extraordinary levies as the population under his control would put up with. The principal check against abuses of this system lay in the revolt of the people, or in the alienation of the local notables. Tribal administration thus often consisted of a familiar cycle of 'squeeze', 'revolt' and 'repress' (Burke 1976: 15).

Older traditions of protest were thus drawn on in the face of new and more systematic pressures over taxation.

The increased burdens that the *makhzan* was imposing upon the population, and its weakness in the face of French power, especially after the French were given a free hand in Morocco after the Entente Cordiale of 1905, and thus accelerated their commercial and military penetration, along with various economic problems, were important in driving the three great uprisings of the early 1900s, led in turn by the heterodox and charismatic Abu Himara, during 1902–3, the pretender to the throne, Al-Hafiz, during 1905–8, and the millenarian of Mauretanian origin, Al-Hiba, during 1912.

The rising of Abu Himara or El-Rogui as he was also known, ran from autumn 1902 to January 1903. Abu Himara was a skilled thaumaturge, claimed to be Al-Mahdi, and propounded the necessity of *jihad*. He had also been a student engineer in government service, had links to a *qaid* (provincial governor) by marriage, and claimed to be none other than the usurped but 'rightful' sultan, Mawlay Muhammad, whose claim to the throne had been usurped by Abd Al-Aziz (r. 1894–1908). His attempt to seize and transform the reigns of state power was defeated militarily in 1903, but he maintained a zone of independent rule until 1909 (Burke 1976). His ultimate demise did not owe above all to the power of the *makhzan*. Abu Himara 'was really defeated by the local tribal alliances, not by the sultan. The tribes were unwilling to submit to direct rule [and taxes] from outside' (Pennell 1986: 33).

The rising of Abd Al-Hafiz ran from 1905 to 1908 and succeeded in deposing Abd Al-Aziz and putting Al-Hafiz on the throne. His uprising proposed a better model of what existed but not a new model. The movement developed amid the recession of 1905–1907, crop failures, livestock deaths, and the lack of rainfall in 1906 which led to widespread famine and epidemics. 'At Fez, rioting was averted only by the massive importation of grain from Marseilles' (Burke 1976: 90). This concession was only a palliative. The 'fierce opposition' to the sultan in the mosques and brotherhoods broke out finally in the most substantial urban uprising of the period in Fez against Abd Al-Aziz in December 1907 and continued into 1908. Just as in 1873, the Sufi brotherhood was important, in this case the Kattani order, which recruited numerous new members (Laroui 1977: 130). The reigning sultan, Abd Al-Aziz, was also seen as a Europeanized dilettante, who played with European trinkets, engaged in foolish dalliances (such as riding bicycles), and handed out concessions to European opportunists, when he should have been protecting the state. The crisis was sharpened by the fact that, by 1904, French policy had shifted from encroachment to conquest (Balfour 2002: 6), posing an intense threat to the Moroccan state itself. Abd Al-Hafiz carried half the country with him on his ascent to the throne on the promise of the protection of Morocco and Islam from the French.

In the event, Sultan Abd Al-Hafiz signed over Morocco to a French protectorate in March 1912. Once in power in 1908, he discovered that the Moroccan *makhzan* was more or less in the hands of European creditors and the ascendant military power of France, no longer obstructed by British or German manoeuvres, to whom recourse was no longer effective. He turned his back on his erstwhile supporters, even in ideological terms, eschewing the heterodox and religious concepts which had mobilized the uprising which put him in power, and drew somewhat on Arab liberal currents and the constitutional movement in Istanbul to legitimate his rule. This was something new in Morocco: a sultan turned not to the traditional *ulema*, nor to the Al-Muwahhidun, nor to Islamic modernism and pan-Islam, but to constitutionalism and liberalism. In this case, it signalled little more than a willingness to co-operate with France. But, unlike in Egypt, the Moroccan urban elite drew far less wealth from European-linked commerce and investment, meaning that those ready to go along with a policy of collaboration were far fewer in number.

The sultan's betrayal of the Moroccan sultanate, of Islam, and of his own supporters triggered a mutiny at Fez and the *jihad* of Al-Hiba in the south. The betrayal was so profound because it eviscerated the very meaning of the most universal principles of authority in the state: it implied at once the renunciation of the temporal powers and religious meaning of sultan-caliph. The crisis of authority may have been more intense in Morocco, because its ruler combined the positions of sultan, caliph and sharif (descendant of the Prophet). The sharifian claim had been important to the Alawi dynasty since its inception in a way that had not applied to previous Moroccan rulers. In Egypt in 1882, for example, these posts were divided between Istanbul (sultan and caliph), *khedive* in Egypt (viceroy of the sultan) and *ashraf* (descendants of the Prophet) – a group which included neither Ottoman sultan-caliph nor Egyptian *khedive*. Thus in Egypt in 1881–2 one could be a supporter of both the sultan-caliph and Colonel 'Urabi, but an opponent of the Egyptian *khedive*. In Morocco, the sultan's position could hardly be so minimized. Holding all these positions, his dereliction was felt profoundly. Nor could the sultan claim that he was seeking protection from the French against powerful neighbours as the ruling families of the Persian Gulf could as they struck deals with the British, because of the real threats posed by Saudis, Ottomans and, to a lesser extent, Iran.

Al-Hiba was the son of the renowned Mauretanian religious and tribal warrior, Ma' Al-'Aynayn, who had defended the emirate of Adrar against the depradations of French colonialism from the 1880s onwards, only succumbing to defeat in 1910. Al-Hiba's movement was the most revolutionary of all the Moroccan movements so far. '[I]t was a revolution', writes Burke, 'aimed at nothing less than the overturning of the existing political regime, that of the great *qaid*-s and the *makhzan*, and the substitution of a new society modelled on the early Islamic community of Medina' (Burke 1976: 202). Extraordinarily, the sultan Abd Al-Hafiz, who had betrayed the movement that brought him to power, notified Al-Hiba of his abdication, implicitly passing him the baton of *jihad* against the French usurpation. The radicalism of Al-Hiba's movement was a mark of his origins and beliefs, but it also reflected the depth of discredit to which the *makhzan* had sunk. It was no longer a new pretender to the sultanate that Morocco required, as Abd Al-Hafiz and Al-Rogui had declared, but an entirely new socio-political order. That Al-Hiba was able to win support for such a project owed much to the crisis in the authority of the *makhzan* that the French protectorate provoked.

Tunisia before 1881

Where state centralization was less violent, and where it took more 'national' forms, such as in Tunisia in the eighteenth and nineteenth centuries, protests against central power were less marked. The

Husaynid dynasty, which was to rule Tunisia until 1957, was founded in the process of repulsing the Algerian invasion of 1705. The dynasty developed the Beylicate less as a 'foreign military caste' – as in Algeria – and more as a 'quasi-national monarchy', ruling through local leaders (Abun-Nasr 1987: 173). The drawing up of the constitution of 1860 was an elite affair, resulting not from popular mobilization. On the other hand, the rebellion that broke out in Tunisia in spring 1864 was the exception that proved the rule: it was a direct response to the decision of the Tunisian government in December 1863 to increase revenue by doubling the poll-tax. The uprising began among the tribes and spread among the urban population whom the Bey had alienated by his decision in 1864 'to levy the poll-tax on the inhabitants of towns usually exempted from it: the capital, Susa, Munastir, Sfax, and the religious capital of the country Qayrawan'. In addition, categories of people previously exempt from taxation were now taxed, including the *ulama* and soldiers. Britain, France and Italy sent squadrons to 'protect' their subjects and interests in April 1864. The Bey made promises seeking to control the situation: the reduction of taxes, the appointment of local chiefs as governors in place of Turkish officers, and the abolition of secular tribunals which *ulama* resented. By the end of the year, several of the tribes that took part in the rebellion had been induced to give up their arms (Abun-Nasr 1987: 280–1).

Istanbul, debt crisis and constitution, 1876

The fiscal crisis of the Ottoman state in 1876, rooted in indebtedness to European financiers, threatened the hard-wiring of the Ottoman state and called into question the basis of its administration and the high-handedness and autocracy of those who ran it. It simultaneously raised the spectre of European control over some section of the finances of the Ottoman state, which posed basic questions about the integrity and autonomy of the empire. Before payments on the debt were suspended in July 1876, however, a socio-political crisis more political than fiscal struck. News of the Bulgarian atrocities hit the new Istanbul press in May 1876. Massacres of helpless Muslim villagers were perpetrated as a result of the territorial designs on Ottoman territory of expansionist European powers, the Russians foremost among them – massacres which vivified the dereliction and weakness of the Porte in protecting fellow Muslims and its own subjects threatened by European imperialism. A popular sense of injustice was stirred further by the distortion of events in a European press seemingly thirsty for Muslim blood. The crisis mobilized both liberal and conservative opponents of the Tanzimat. The former opposed autocracy and demanded a constitution – just as the Porte tried to censor the clamouring press; the latter opposed un-Islamic innovation and demanding a pan-Islamic policy and a renewed Caliphate. Both constitution and Khilafa were touted as the basic ways to save the ship of state from European intervention and internal break up and secession.

Students of religious schools (*softas*) left classes on 8 May 1876 and joined mass meetings attended by *ulema* and townspeople at the main mosques and public squares of Istanbul, denouncing the government for cowardice in the face of large-scale massacres of Muslims and European intervention (Shaw 1977: 163). Sultan Abdulaziz attempted to appease the movement by appointing a new şeyhulislam, but this only encouraged the students' demands. To obtain popular support, the new ministry rejected the recent financial arrangement with foreign bankers (Shaw 1977: 163). The army then moved to depose Sultan Abdulaziz by surrounding his palace on 30 May with two battalions. He was replaced in short order by Murat V. The latter mentioned the will of the people in his accession speech. It was the first time since 1807 that a sultan had been deposed in a politics that went far beyond the palace. All payments on the foreign debt were suspended in July 1876. Midhat Pasha was pushing for a constitution with encouragement from the British ambassador (Shaw 1977: 164–5). In August 1876, Murat V in turn was deposed as insane. Abdulhamid II succeeded him on the promise of a constitution which was duly promulgated under Midhat Pasha, who argued in instrumental fashion that the constitution would serve as a foil to deny the Europeans a pretext for intervention (Shaw 1977: 157–74). The first Ottoman constitution was granted very much on the basis that it would defend the sultan's domains against Great Power machinations. Although there was a link to the uprisings and protests over the massacres of Muslims in the empire, in every other sense, the constitution descended from on high. Those protesting under the banners of constitutionalism remained an elite minority, and it was the popular call for pan-Islam that Abdulhamid II was to take up and make the basis of his legitimacy.

Strikes before unions, parties and socialism

In 1863, coal miners staged a walk out over pay and conditions at the Zonguldak coal mines on the Black Sea coast of Anatolia. It was perhaps the first labour strike in the history of the region (Karakïşla 1995: 20). In February 1872, there was a strike by telegram workers in the Beyoğlu Post Office in Istanbul, and during 1872 and 1873 there were strikes involving hundreds of workers on Ottoman railways and in the Maritime Arsenal in Istanbul. In October 1878, workers employed in tailor shops in Istanbul left their jobs, demanding a wage increase of 70 per cent (Karakïşla 1995: 20–1). In the 1870s, there were a number of substantial strikes by journeymen weavers over wages paid by masters operating within merchant-dominated putting-out systems in Damascus (Vatter 1994). In 1882, coal-heavers working in the docks of Port Sa'id in Egypt went on strike over wages and conditions (Beinin and Lockman 1998). There were strikes by porters on the docks in Beirut, Istanbul and Salonica in the early 1900s. In 1907, the cab-drivers of Cairo organized and carried out a strike involving thousands over a heavy-handed regulatory intervention into their trade by the colonial state (Chalcraft 2004). By the first decade of the twentieth century, strikes, walk outs and labour stoppages, whereby workers of various kinds protested in order to negotiate the pay, conditions, organization, regulations and extra-economic coercion that they encountered in work-places or at the hands of the state, addressing those who organized and controlled their labour, whether bureaucrats, private capitalists or state officials, became a by no means atypical or peculiarly new occurrence in the Ottoman empire and Egypt.

Early strike action and work stoppages and other forms of labour protest were undertaken by a wide variety of social groups of varying backgrounds in town and country alike. Highly stigmatized silk-spinning women, often from low-status village families, organized some strikes on Mount Lebanon in the 1890s to improve their 'appalling sweat-shop conditions' (Beinin 2001: 64; Khater 1996). Machine-breaking, which first appeared in the Ottoman empire in 1839, was pioneered by women, and was used by female textile workers on a number of occasions, for example, in 1851, at Samokov (Karakïşla 1995: 20). Jews were prominent in Ottoman Salonika (Quataert 1995). Several factories employing conscripted peasants were burned

to the ground by suspicious fires in the 1830s and 1840s in Egypt
(Tucker 1985: 144). The coal-heavers of Port Sa'id were rural–urban
migrants, closely connected to their villages of origin, and mostly
Nubian or Sudanese (Chalcraft 2001). Many of the coal-miners of
Zonguldak were provincial villagers and minors drafted as conscripts
to provision the state (Quataert 2006). The cigarette-rollers of Egypt,
who struck in 1899 and subsequently, were mostly Greek-protected
subjects. The telegram-workers of Istanbul were minor civil servants.
The strikers in the weaving sector in Damascus were mostly journeymen whose wages and chances of obtaining a master-ship had been
reduced.

Lockman has suggested that various forms of social consciousness
informed workers' collective action in Egypt before the early 1900s:
guild solidarity, popular Islamic notions of justice, notions of equity
and concepts of masculinity (Lockman 1994a: 186). For such a diverse
sociology, what Beinin called '[t]heir radically different life experiences
and mentalities' (Beinin 2001: 69), an emphasis on variety must be
plausible. Studies of the sorts of identities and principles that informed
early strike action, nonetheless, are rather thin on the ground, as well
as sources. The existence of new forms of heteronomy associated with
new large-scale enterprise did not necessarily translate in any auto-
matic way into new forms of worker consciousness. The most plausible
hypothesis must be that, prior to the 1900s, at least among Ottoman
subjects, it generally did not: workers already had access to a rich
moral economy, and it was this that informed their protests. The term
for worker – '*amil* – continued to mean something like agent, someone
charged with carrying out a task (Lockman 1994a). Strike action was
most likely undertaken according to similar sets of principles and
identities that obtained among other townspeople and peasantries
who faced tyranny and injustice in town and country alike. The
evidence cannot bear a back-projection of labour socialism into the
nineteenth-century MENA region. The justice of the ruler, the pro-
testor as loyal subject, the search for redress in the face of violations of
faith, justice, state regulations, custom, egalitarian tradition and forms
of local autonomy, and opposition to injustice, tyranny, treachery,
greed and ambition, were the by no means flimsy identities and principles that informed and drove the emergence of this new repertoire of
contention. Such indeed were the watchwords of a number of petitions
and reports submitted by the coal-heavers of Port Sa'id to the central

authorities in the 1890s and later (Chalcraft 2001). The Cairo cab-drivers presented themselves to the government as those who were wronged by arbitrary punishments, heavy fines, and an inability to carry out their trade or eat decent food. During the nineteenth century, few strikes were carried out by those who saw themselves as workers, or as belonging to the working-class, or still less by those committed to revolutionary socialism. Strike action preceded these forms of consciousness, and was most likely rooted in the ways that new forms of production and state control violated existing tissues of moral economy.

Strikes were a highly transgressive act. They were banned, along with all forms of labour organization, almost everywhere in the region. The Ottoman Police Regulation Law of 1845, for example, stipulated that 'the associations of workers must be removed, and ... [the possibility of] revolutionary events should be prevented' (Karakişla 1995: 30). The law was a word-for-word translation of the French police law of June 1800, and was used for suppressing labour strikes and demonstrations. While revolution may have been far from the minds of those who protested, the authorities, not for the first time, exaggerated the level of the threat, fearing socialism, and acted accordingly. Strike action in the Ottoman empire before 1908 was invariably met with repression. Under Abdelhamid II, even the use of the words for strike (*tatil-i eşgal*) was forbidden in the press.

Moreover, educated opinion had little time for strike action. In Egypt, the renowned jurist Muhammad Abduh expressed a relatively benign view when he suggested in 1904 in Egypt that strikes should be judged on their merits according to Islam and the public interest (Lockman 1994a: 175). More common among Egypt's educated classes was dismissal. In 1894, for example, on hearing of a strike in Port Saʿid, Muhammad Farid, then an official in the prosecutor's office at the national courts and later Mustafa Kamil's successor as leader of the Nationalist Party, commented in a highly unfavourable judgment that 'this European disease has spread to Egypt' (Lockman 1994a: 171–2).

The organization of protest was relatively informal and fleeting. 'Trade unionism was very weak, almost non-existent [in the Ottoman empire] before 1908' (Karakişla 1995: 26). There were some Ottoman workers' aid societies, formed in the 1860s and 1870s, mostly by Italians or Greeks, but these do not seem to have played a role in organizing strikes, at least among Ottoman subjects (Karakïşla 1995: 26). Instead, strikers had to rely on their own means of informal organization, and visibility or continuous organization was neither tolerated nor possible. The first worker's organization that also exhibited signs of class consciousness was established illegally in 1894 by workers in the Tophane factories, employing 4,000 workers, at the Ministry of War. The Ottoman Workers' Society (*Osmanlï Amele Cemiyeti*) elected a board of eight from among their number, and made contacts with Young Turks exiled in Europe. In 1895, its activities were discovered by the regime and the board exiled. Before 1908, further attempts to organize were also repressed (Karakïşla 1995: 26). Strikes in Egypt among local subjects were organized on an informal basis and without organizations until the turn of the century. Before the 1900s, strikes, stoppages, or acts of machine-breaking, arson or sabotage were not formally organized by unions or parties, and they were more likely to be dismissed than encouraged by the urban intelligentsia.

Urban retailers and artisans had a tradition of shutting their shops in protest at taxes or regulations, a work stoppage of sorts, a tactic which must have informed new forms of strike action. The tradition of flight from over-taxation and conscription was also important among workers who were drafted in to work in Mehmet Ali's factories in the 1830s and 1840s. Some 'ran away' from their places of work, stating that their taxes exceeded their wages. In a case from Qina province in Egypt in 1844, the governor of Isna responded to the absconders by raising daily wages for workers' 'comfort' and to end the problem of flight (Abul-Magd 2013: 91–2). This model of collective action was close to strike action, and surely informed the strike repertoire. Later strikes were complemented by other, less overt, and sometimes less collective strategies: flight, failure to show up for work, avoidance of dangerous tasks, individual refusals to work under given conditions, and so on (Quataert and Duman 2001). While repression was often meted out, strikers did have genuine powers of institutional disruption. They could not be ignored because employers needed their workers to work in order to realize profits; governments could only avoid at their peril their responsibility to maintain systems of extraction and provision. Dismissal was costly for employers and not always a viable option. Workers were able to win concessions on numerous occasions on pay and conditions, although sometimes at the cost of the repression of their incipient leaderships. In Damascus in 1879, for example, more than 3,000 of the city's 4,000–5000 journeymen weavers struck to protest a cut in piece work rates. 'To ensure that all journeymen honoured the strike, militants threatened potential strike breakers and cut threads mounted on looms to keep them from working' (Vatter 1994: 3). After a four-week stoppage, the masters re-instated the old pay rates, and the journeymen returned to work. Workers in the abortive Qina coal-mines protested their irregular wages in 1858, successfully obtaining the promise of regular wages from the governor of Qina, and, following accidents, instructions from Sa'id Pasha to the foreign concessionaire to improve safety (Abul-Magd 2013: 107–8).

We should not miss the way labour protests went in search of the state, which they hoped would be the main agent that would resolve their problems, amid the failure of local or de-centralized organizations, such as guilds. Migrant coal-heavers in Port Sa'id, for example, looked increasingly to the state to regulate disputes over labour-contracting, the rates paid by the shipping companies, the miserable and over-priced state of the food that they were forced to purchase in the docks, and the exploitative practices of their labour contractors (Chalcraft 2001). Such mobilization, no less than petitioning, contributed to, rather than hindered, the ongoing centralization of the state and the development of its powers.

The 'Urabi movement, 1881–1882

In July 1882, a patriotic and constitutional movement led by an Egyptian-born colonel in the army, Ahmad 'Urabi, stood at the helm of the Egyptian state. The *khedive*, Egypt's now only nominal ruler, sought refuge with the British, who were occupying Alexandria. Popular mobilizations were breaking out all over the country in the face of a looming British occupation – *'ulema* were calling the faithful to arms, peasants were seizing land, artisans were demonstrating in the streets, and urban crowds were seizing European property. No more was the dynastic and modernizing rule of the Khedive Isma'il, seemingly impregnable in the mid-1870s, backed by the Ottoman sultan, a rubber-stamp Chamber of Deputies, the European powers, and a strong, Turco-Circassian elite. In its place was a Common Law Assembly (*majlis al-'urfi*), arrogating to itself the powers to govern, justified by reference to the will of the Egyptian people, horrifying the Great Powers, and led by an Egyptian *fellah* from the army and his allies among Egyptian-born merchants and wealthy provincial farmers.

The revolutionary situation was triggered by the debt crisis of 1876, and the divisions and manoeuvring within the state, and the European control that ensued. But it was pushed forward by the coming together of the 'Urabi movement by September 1881, the gains made by that movement over subsequent months, the threat and then the reality of a British bombardment and invasion in June and July 1882, and the popular mobilizations, well beyond the control of the 'Urabists, that arose in this *status quo*-shaking context. The revolutionary situation did not, as it turned out, contain a cohesive revolutionary movement adequate to the moment, and was terminated with indecent speed. The (second, much larger) British invasion of early September 1882 defeated 'Urabi's forces at Tal Al-Kabir and all too easily repressed the scattered popular mobilizations that remained.

For at least the first five years of the drama, from 1876 to 1881, it is not possible to speak of an 'Urabi movement as no such cohesive socio-political movement existed. Instead, the pre-history of the movement was marked by the crisis of Khedive Isma'il's state which, egged on by consuls and European businessmen, had spent its way into a debt default by 1876. The debt crisis paved the way for sharpening divisions and manoeuvres among ruling elites and segments of the state, and the advent of European control of the treasury, which taken together operated, partly inadvertently, and certainly dialectically, to develop on the one hand the forces of the Chamber of Deputies (established 1866), the fledgling liberal and patriotic press, and notions of constitutional government, and, on the other to upset the army, which had grievances of its own.

First, the Debt Commission directly threatened Isma'il's previously uncontested control of the state, and, because it meant European and Christian control over Egypt, heavily damaged his prestige. This led him to make new alliances as he fought for his position. In seeking to claw back revenue and power in the face of European control, Isma'il reconvened the Chamber of Deputies in 1876 (Hunter 1999: 210–11), a Chamber that he had largely ignored (and failed to convene) in the early 1870s. The *khedive* even temporarily supported (in 1879) aggrieved junior officers in the army, and sponsored journalism 'in hopes of gaining help in his battle against Egypt's creditors' (Hunter

1999: 192). Isma'il proved too independent for the Europeans, who had him deposed in 1879 via a *firman* from the sultan. The puppet Tawfiq (1879–92) was put in his place.

Second, the debt crisis precipitated grievances in the army because pay and privileges were cut amid austerity and 1,600 officers were threatened with the sack. A satirical song circulated in Cairo: 'The Egyptian troops, Because of lack of payment, Their tails [are] hanging down, Let their ears drop, They separated from their wives' (Schölch 1981: 65–8). Likened to donkeys, and seen as incapable of providing for their wives, the army was also a site of considerable discontent, focusing on the tension between the senior and privileged ranks of Turco-Circassians, and the junior ranks of Egyptian born soldiers and junior officers, who faced discrimination and were often contemptuously referred to by the Turks as *fellahin*/peasants. In February 1879, petitions were written and a demonstration was organized, with the soldiers focusing much of their ire on the European debt controllers (Schölch 1981: 65–8, 90–1; Hunter 1999: 179, 215). These grievances could not simply be ignored, Isma'il was in any case in tacit support, and action was promised.

In convening the Chamber, and appealing to ideas of popular consultation, Isma'il created more substance than he intended (Cole 1999: 30–1). The Chamber of Deputies (*majlis shura al-nuwwab*) had been established in 1866 in the crucible of centralization and extraction: through it, Isma'il sought to diffuse the responsibility for the imposition of heavy burdens on the population (Hunter 1999: 39, 51–4). It was, as Rifa'i Al-Tahtawi (a major Egyptian writer, educator and intellectual) saw it, an instrument to lighten the burden of rule (Schölch 1981: 14–17). But from 1876 onwards, the Chamber gradually became a site through which meaningful demands for representation within the state were made by Egyptian-born provincial notables and merchants, made wealthy by the new cotton economy, but chafing against the political and other privileges of the Turco-Circassian elite. Members of the chamber had started forging alliances with cabinet members opposed to the European control from at least 1878.

The leading figures in the chamber, one a Cairean merchant, Abd Al-Salam Al-Muwailihi, signalled their intent at the convocation of the Chamber in January 1879. First, Al-Muwailihi's speech hailed the *khedive* as the leader on the path of progress and civilization. More significantly, he went on:

we, the delegates and representatives of the Egyptian people, the defenders of its rights, and the promoters of its welfare which is at the same time the welfare of the government ... [thank the *khedive* for the convocation of the Majlis which] ... represents the basis of civilization and order ... [and] the necessary means for the achievement of freedom (which is the source of progress and advance), and the true driving force for the development of legal equality, which in its turn brings about the essence of justice and the spirit of equity (cited in Schölch 1981: 80).

The Chamber thus staked its place in the state on the basis of its representative function, and its claim to promote the welfare of the people (*maslahat al-umma*), the advantage of the fatherland (*manfa'at al-watan*) and the rights of the subjects (*huquq al-ra'iya*). Similar principles had been at work in the Tunisian constitution of 1860, in the thought of the Young Ottomans, and the short-lived constitution in Istanbul in 1876, but in Egypt this was innovative talk indeed. The key criticism made by the Chamber, furthermore, in 1879, was of 'the heavy load of taxes being laid upon the country, and, in particular, their collection in advance of the harvest when the country was suffering a severe famine' (Hunter 1999: 212–13). The reality of what the Chamber actually demanded only amounted to control over half the government budget by February 1882, the beginnings of a fully fledged constitution as 1882 progressed, and nothing relating to socio-economic equality or rights for the people. Nonetheless, it started to play a role in the elite politics of the state in a way that it had not done before.

Isma'il's deposition only fanned the flames of patriotism against the collaborationist Tawfiq. The press was increasingly assertive, invoking the rights of native-born Egyptians, the unity of the Islamic *umma* in the face of the European threat, the role of representative government, and the need for a constitution.

In this context, senior politicians, the provincial notables and merchants of the Chamber, and their allies in the press, and the army officers led by Ahmad 'Urabi, slowly started to come together, united in their opposition to Turco-Circassian privilege, the autocracy of the *khedive*, and European control. These alliances were made, partly in response to the solidifying positions of others; they did not simply happen because of the weight of pre-existing interests. Campaigns were launched in the press, secret meetings were held in the houses of key figures, such as Muhammad Sultan, a leading provincial notable, who also showered 'Urabi with hospitality in order to win him over to the cause. The French invasion of Tunisia through the spring and summer of 1881 was a key galvanizing moment, as it urged action in the face of the European threat. Through the summer of 1881, an alliance between the army and the leading elements in the Chamber was formed, with 'Urabi coming out into the open for the first time in the demand for a constitution in September.

'Urabi now cemented his position as the leader of a movement, which, under the banners of representative government, pan-Islam, and Egyptian patriotism linked merchants, provincial notables and army together. While mainly operating within the corridors of power, the movement also appealed to crowds through demonstrations and speeches, and to the educated public through the press, and to wider constituencies through the extraordinary eloquence of the poet Barudi. 'Urabi spoke not formal Turkish, nor French, nor did he use stereo-typed Friday-sermon rhetoric. Instead his eloquence 'excited the crowd'. According to Berque 'the revival of the native idiom proved the strongest ally of these men in their struggle against inhuman forces' (Berque 1972: 109). 'Urabi's language now encompassed a wide variety of grievances in the country. He indicted khedivial conscription, forced labour and taxation as oppressive insofar as its fruits were bestowed on pampered Circassian officers, privileged by birth, and bypassing meritorious Egyptian junior officers. Such favours, 'Urabi noted, were 'sucked from the blood of the poor Egyptians and the sweat of their brows' (Schölch 1981: 23). Egyptians who, as 'Urabi had to explain to Colvin (Tawfiq's right hand man) in November 1881, were 'imprisoned, exiled, strangled, thrown into the Nile, starved, robbed, according to the will of their masters' (Schölch 1981: 185–6). 'Egypt for the Egyptians!', indeed, the slogan raised for the first time by 'Urabi, was directed as much against the Turco-Circassians as it was against the Europeans (Schölch 1981: 41), and it was sutured to widespread socio-political grievances.

This campaign clearly had support in the country, especially through the activism of intellectuals such as Abdullah Al-Naim. Villagers near Tanta demonstrated their support of 'Urabi in early 1881, as did petitions from village notables in February and the summer of that year, who also called for the convening of the Chamber of Deputies. Some of these had been printed and circulated by Abdullah Al-Naim (Cole 1999: 261–2). While some *ulema* opposed 'Urabi, on the basis that he had no authority to oppose a representative of the sultan, others supported him. They saw in him the chance to establish a government that could limit the influence of European powers, rebuild ties with the Ottoman empire, assert Egypt's Islamic identity at the heart of the *umma*, and defend the country against the infidel occupation (Mirza 2014). Certain key Islamic modernists, notably Muhammad Abduh, threw their weight behind the movement in late 1881.

The 'Urabists were able to form several governments, and force several climb-downs by Tawfiq, above all because 'Urabi was able to command the loyalty of the army, to the growing horror of the European consuls, who were not reassured by 'Urabi's insistence that he posed no threat to the Suez Canal or the bondholders. Whereas the British had urged a constitution, in the absence of mass mobilization, in Istanbul in 1876, they looked on and acted with increasing hostility as a more popular constitutional movement developed in Egypt. The idea of the 'Urabiyyin was to cement the place of the Egyptian officers within a strong army, to diminish Turco-Circassian privilege, to maintain control over half the Egyptian budget, and to subject the *khedive* to some constitutional guarantees. While there was rhetoric about wider forms of oppression and exploitation, concrete demands or proposals in this regard were wanting. The movement expected to achieve its goals through the institutions of the state, notably the army and the Chamber, and through appeals to the populace.

This was a programme both radical, in that it sought to introduce a representative principle of legitimacy into the body politic, and limited, in that it promised political reform, but without uprooting the system, or offering social or economic transformation. In this regard, 'Urabi's speech to the crowd in Bab Al-Hadid, Cairo's railway station, on 6 October 1881, was significant. He spoke eloquently to the crowd, who were supposedly listening raptly, of

> the end of tyranny, the opening of the gate of freedom for the rights of the people, and also of obedience to the Khedive, of faith in the government … and of the need for unity and fraternity (Schölch 1981: 183).

On the one side, the rights of the people, which in reality meant the rights of the Chamber, on the other, obedience to the *khedive*. 'Urabi, meanwhile, sought to curb European control, but not to throw it out completely. Moreover, 'Urabi did not oppose the Ottoman sultan, or the notion of dynastic authority *in toto*: indeed, he was 'horrified' to learn, on 6 September 1882, the eve of battle, that the sultan repudiated him (Berque 1972: 107). 'Egypt for the Egyptians' was conceived in terms of autonomy and not national independence. Certainly, the idea that the 'Urabi movement represented the first time in centuries that Egyptians had taken their destiny into their own hands is a modernist hubris, substituting destiny for constitutional government and a limited patriotism, and taking the predictable hysteria of the Great Powers far too much at face value.

The bombardment and invasion of Alexandria by the British gave the *khedive* his chance on 20 July 1882 to dismiss 'Urabi, who could be held responsible as Minister of War. 'Urabi promptly convened the 'representatives of the people' at the Interior Ministry to form an entirely new body, a Common Law Assembly (*majlis al-'urfi*), which decided to favour 'Urabi over the *khedive*, but without specifying in detail what this meant or declaring a new government (Schölch 1981: 270ff.). This assembly went on to try and govern the country and ignore the *khedive* for almost two months before the British invasion.

'Urabi's challenge to khedivial autocracy, and his airing of wider grievances, presented a political opportunity of which more popular forces now sought to make use. What created a revolutionary situation, however, was that, on the one hand, the British embarked on an invasion, sending the navy in the spring, then bombarding and occupying Alexandria in June and July 1882, while failing to advance beyond that in the face of popular resistance. And, on the other hand, groups far from the 'Urabiyyin, peasants, village headmen, urban townspeople, with grievances and beliefs of their own, started to mobilize amid the opportunities provided by the divisions among different groups within the state, the threat of British invasion, and the hope that 'Urabi may be a leader who would respond to their claims.

The situation for the mass of the rural population in Egypt in the late 1870s was appalling. The peasantry had been beaten out of its surplus to the limits of its endurance, and a famine was causing deaths by starvation in the thousands. Probably around 10,000 people starved to death in Qena and Isna alone in 1878–9 (Schölch 1981: 60; cf. Tignor 1966: 17). Until around 1880, the Debt Commission only intensified the tax burdens suffered by the peasantry. Rivers Wilson was 'authorizing tax-collecting forays into the countryside without regard to the means used' (Hunter 1999: 212–13). Village shaykhs were starting to appear in the towns, furnished with petitions with ever lengthening lists of petitioners, demanding tax remission (Hunter 1999: 212–13; Schölch 1981: 36–7). This was an innovation. Demands almost always revolved around injustice and oppression in tax procedures and allocations, not an absolute reduction in the level of taxes, which challenged the highest levels of the state, who were responsible for setting these taxes.

The 'temporary triumph' of the 'Urabi movement (Brown 1990a: 192–3) was a formidable mobilizer for the peasantry and townspeople alike. The *status quo* was crumbling, and the foreigner was at the gates. 'Urabi, who set about trying to lead his army at Kafr Al-Dawwar against the British, now had recourse to the doctrine of *jihad* for 'a merely mobilisatory and propagandistic purpose' as his movement was not dominated by religion and had 'no framework of puritanistic and revivalist Islamic ideology' (Peters 1979: 154–5). Nonetheless, this call was received among ears more receptive in the countryside and among the *ulema* alike. The latter began to issue calls to arms from the minarets. Moreover, the rumour spread that 'Urabi was the Expected Deliverer, the Mahdi who would inaugurate a reign of justice in symmetry with Muhammad Ahmad of Dongola, much further up the Nile. The auspicious date of 1300 AH played a role in stirring millennial sentiments. Cobblers, coffee-servers and tailors ran into the streets shouting 'God, destroy the army of the infidels' (Cole 1999: 250). Fisherman and coal-heavers demonstrated, as did railway workers in Bulaq. In Mahalla Al-Kubra, violent protests broke out when the British bombarded Alexandria on 11 July. 'Urabi sent troops to quell them (Cole 1999: 258) 'Uthman Hasan, the headman of the village of Abu Husaybah in Al-Minya was accused of having announced the 'return of the *çiftlik* land grants back to their original villages; the sugar factory would belong to the people, and the lands bought by Tal'at Pasha and Sultan Pasha near his village, from the viceregal lands, would belong to the people' (Cole 1999: 260). Another village headman said that the lands of the nobles would be confiscated and 'made available for homesteading, and the government would be a government of village headmen not of "Turks"' (Cole 1999: 263). The British consular agent in Luxor spoke of the 'most seditious and frightful language' as well as of banditry on the roads. Some peasants refused to pay debts, and resisted the arrival of debt collectors.

'Urabi had been concerned earlier to reassure Europeans of the safety of their investments, but the conjunctures of peasant renunciations of debt and the British landing pushed him and his colleagues toward a more radical position (Cole 1999: 264).

In summer 1882, the 'Cairo-based government pledged that peasants would not have to repay their loans'. This pledge was then quoted for several years, much to the exasperation of British officials (Cole 1999: 264). There were peasant attempts to arrest officials loyal to the *khedive*. There were, moreover, land invasions, one at Samhah in Buhayra, another at Dilga near Asyut. Property division took place elsewhere. Volunteers came from the countryside to serve in the army (Cole 1999: 267). There was talk of an Arab kingdom, and the opening of government jobs to the sons of village notables.

For the 'Urabiyyin, these popular mobilizations, far from signalling the arrival of a revolution which the 'Urabi movement could lead, more likely signalled that movement's downfall, because the 'Urabists had no plan or strategy for a popular uprising. The 'Urabi movement expected the crowd to follow it, not to mobilize on its own. It sought the rights of property, not their usurpation. It sought to counter accusations that it was stirring chaos, not give them credence; and, above all, it sought to avoid a pretext for a European intervention, while the crowd actions against Europeans and their property in Alexandria in June 1882 gave Britain the pretext to bombard and then occupy the city. 'Urabi's army could never take on the British colonial army: 'Urabi was a poor military leader indeed by Schölch's account (Schölch 1981: 292ff.) and was still trying to come to an agreement with the powers even after July 1882 (Schölch 1981: 299). On the other hand, as Berque pointed out, 'Urabi was not the leader of a peasant uprising capable of 'baffling' the British military, even if he may have made some confused gestures in this direction in the summer of 1882 (Berque 1972: 122). 'Urabi had not planned to be the head of a Common Law Assembly in the midst of a revolutionary situation. He had sought a position in a constitutional monarchy, and had pursued much of the battle in the corridors of power. The recourse to *jihad* was a desperate expedient. As were the contradictory responses to peasant demands and protests. When the British arrived, the military confrontation was a rout, the 'Urabi movement fell apart, and the scattered and uncoordinated mobilizations in the countryside were easily repressed.

'Urabi was not a revivalist preacher, scholar, saint or Sufi. Nor was he a Janissary or tribal leader. He had no genealogy such as the Awlad Sidi shaykh of Algeria. In fact, he was a product of the state central-ization of the nineteenth century, a native born Egyptian peasant who became an officer. The 'Urabi movement of 1881–2 was not an attempt to reject the state in libertarian or millennarian ways, nor to resist its advance in the name of local autonomy or vested interests, nor to alter its terms of regulation in reformist mode by appeals to justice and custom. Nor yet was the 'Urabi movement a matter of religious renewal, nor a peasant upsurge from below after the manner of Tanyus Shahin. The movement he led was an attempt to re-organize the state and to institutionalize the political representation in the polity of new groups under the banners of new ideas. It was a movement flanked by more subaltern mobilizations that it did not control. The 'Urabi move-ment was not undertaken by challengers from outside the polity, but by polity members, and those with regular access to the polity. It developed out of the manoeuvrings of established actors within a crisis-ridden state, who then came together to create a movement making appeals to, and to some extent developing larger links to, wider constituencies in the press, the urban intelligentsia and the modernist *ulema*.

The key constituencies of the movement, the officers, the Deputies, the merchants, the provincial notables and much of the urban intelli-gentsia were the product of the new order: the incomes of the cotton economy, the emergence of a wealthy peasantry, their property rights entrenched by state guarantees, and the rise of state-sponsored educa-tion, journalism and the press. The 'Urabi movement was thus led by those seeking change from within the new order, not those who had been marginalized or ousted by it. As such, it was the first time in the nineteenth century that those who owed their existence to state cen-tralization and the new, dependent economy had arisen to change substantially the state. This fact may help explain why the movement was so easily scattered. As Schölch has it:

The provincial notables were anything but revolutionaries, and the major-ity of them also were no firm patriots. They were concerned about the protection of the socio-economic positions they had acquired in the context of the emergence of a dependent agrarian capitalism. When they were not able to secure their positions against the European control, they were prepared to consolidate and to improve them with the European control, i.e. under British rule. In the face of military intervention they deserted the 'Urabiyin (Schölch 1981: 314).

The movement was, nonetheless, a watershed, signalling in contentious politics for the first time deep, political contradictions *within* the state-strengthening and modernizing projects of the nineteenth century. Perhaps, therefore, it was no accident that a new word was applied to the 'Urabi movement, initially by its enemies. One of the great mobilizing notions of the twentieth century received one of its first mentions here. A hagiographer of Khedive Tawfiq spoke of how 'he [Tawfiq] came, stirring all hearts and bringing happiness by extinguishing the flaming torches of the *thaura* [the revolution]' (Berque 1972: 111). The idea of *al-thawra* (revolution) was born in the midst of a constitutional, Islamic, and patriotic challenge to privilege, autocracy and European control. It was an idea that was to matter all over the region for more than a century to come.

The constitutional movement in Istanbul, 1908

The Ottoman constitution had been presented in 1876 by Midhat Pasha as a way to prevent European intervention and to save the empire. Many of those who mobilized under the banners of the constitution in the period leading up to the grant of the constitution in July 1908 also thought that the constitution would save an empire facing a crisis; above all, limiting the rights of the sultan was supposed to solve the problem, ever more pressing, of minority rights, autonomism, separatism and nationalism, which by the early 1900s presented the empire with a ticking time bomb: the gunpowder the polyglot and multi-ethnic population (Bulgarians, Albanians, Armenians, Greek Orthodox, Maronites, Kurds, Assyrians, Arabs and others), and the fuse the ever-rising currents of separatism and nationalism, typically linked to the machinations of the European powers. The constitution would, in the eyes of many of the Young Turks, provide rights to minorities both religious and ethnic and thus ameliorate their grievances on the one hand, and, by providing a reason to remain loyal to the sultan and the Ottoman empire as a homeland for all, defuse the minority drive for national independence on the other. At the same time, it would diminish European encroachment, by demonstrating that the 'sick man' of Europe was actually reforming in terms that

Europeans could understand, and stripping Europe of the pretext of intervention to 'protect' oppressed subjects of the sultan (Shaw 1977: 266).

Constitutional ideas were backed by a Young Turk ideology that was 'scientific, antireligious, and elitist' (Hanioğlu 1995: 26). Rejecting any Young Ottoman attempts to reconcile Western civilization and science with Islam and traditional values, the Young Turks drew particularly on the ideas of the German philosopher, physician and scientific materialist Ludwig Büchner (d. 1899), who pitted progress emphatically against religion. The true poets, wrote one Young Turk, were scientists who 'invented ships and the telegram' (Hanioğlu 1995: 19). Such science underpinned Western superiority, and had to be taken on without compromise against all forms of religious 'fanaticism'. A Young Turk banner held aloft during the celebrations of the 1908 revolution, 'le salut de la nation c'est la science', expressed their deepest feelings (Hanioğlu 1995: 20). Darwin's theory of evolution, in addition to social Darwinism, loomed large in Young Turk thinking: the Egyptian branch of the CUP justified a new committee on the basis that the 'law of evolution' had made the old one redundant (Hanioğlu 1995: 22). Young Turks drew on and were heavily impressed by the racially determined anthropology of Charles Letourneau (d. 1902) and especially the works of the French psychologist and sociologist Gustave Le Bon (d. 1931), who wrote key tracts on the madness of crowds and claimed that through phrenology (the measuring of skulls) intelligence could be determined. Intellectuals turned out to have larger skulls than servants or workers, and were thus entitled to lead and to educate.

Young Turks chafed against the personal loyalty demanded by the sultan, preferring instead to pledge loyalty to the state or the fatherland. Many of the Young Turks were frustrated Young Ottomans, who lamented the failure of Midhat Pasha's constitution and had rejected Abdulhamid II's Islamic turn from the outset. Much discontent was expressed in the late 1880s by intellectuals, students and bureaucrats when censorship was not so strong, especially when budget-balancing staff cuts in the ministries created unemployed graduates who felt they had a right to government employment (Shaw 1977: 256–7). In May 1908, the CUP stated to the Great Powers that all the peoples of Macedonia were suffering from the sultan's oppression, that they sought the recall of parliament to provide equality before law which would enable all elements of the empire to work together for the common good (Shaw 1977: 266).

The aim of the Young Turks was to submit the empire to a constitutional regime, limiting the powers of the sultan, and to bring back a parliament and associated representative institutions. The Young Turk Congress of December 1907 clearly enunciated that the sultan had to be deposed and constitutional and representative government established (Shaw 1977: 265).

The mobilization for the short-lived uprising that led to Abdulhamid II's grant of the constitution involved mostly a relatively small, and relatively high-status, band of educated students, officers, teachers, civil servants, intellectuals and some members of the *ulema* (Shaw 1977: 257); most of the *ulema* and the soldiery, and the overwhelming majority of peasants, crafts and service workers, shopkeepers, tribesmen and artisans, stood to one side. This was certainly not a mobilization by an industrial bourgeoisie. Many of the Young Turks had been educated in the greatly multiplying European-style schools of Abdulhamid II; they were not necessarily native Turkish speakers, self-identified Turks, or Turkish nationalists; they came from very varied ethnic and national origins; they felt the centrifugal forces that were threatening the empire and the need to do something about them. Many were drawn from the lower ranks of the officers: educated, politically minded, and drawn from the ranks of the *re'aya* (the subject class). These were new entrants into what had long been conceived of as a military class (the *askeri*), comparable to Colonel 'Urabi in this sense. They were frustrated by long years of unsuccessful struggles against Macedonian and Armenian separatists, who they regarded as 'terrorists', a sentiment especially marked in the Third Army at Salonika, where the young Mustafa Kemal was stationed, although he remained in the background; Young Turk officers were willing to use force to change the system and remove ineffective courtly politicians; they felt that Abdulhamid II put limits on the army because he was afraid of its power (Shaw 1977: 264).

Other Young Turks were civilian men of position, wealth and respectability. Ahmet Riza (1859–1930) was an important early leader among them. Against many a more conservative land-owner, he believed in the education of the peasantry. He had spent much time in Europe. He was wealthy. He espoused a positivist, Comte-like dream of order and progress. He justified the demand for a parliament on the basis of old Islamic and Ottoman traditions of consultation (*meşveret*). Mehmet Murat Efendi (1853–1912) was a Caucasian Turk with a Lycée education from imperial Russia. He wrote history, taught in the Civil Service School, issued reform proposals to the sultan, and published a newspaper, *Mizan*. He also spent time in Egypt (Shaw 1977: 256–7).

The CUP was an underground organization based in the officer corps and colleges, with sympathizers outside. The CUP was only the most important of a number of secret groups with similar aims that appeared in the army garrisoned in towns such as Damascus, Jerusalem and Jaffa, especially after 1905. Military barracks provided some protection against the sultan's secret police. The Ottoman Liberty Society was organized in small cells on the model of Bulgarian 'terrorists'. These secret groups and 'societies' were also organized among students, such as those of the Imperial Medical Academy in the 1880s. Young Turks and their sympathizers made use of the new print media to disseminate their views. *La Jeune Turquie* was a small newsletter published by Halil Ganim, a Lebanese Maronite and former deputy to parliament of 1877. Secret groups often encountered repression at the hands of the state, driving them into exile. This move stamped politics into their social being, and, although intended to terminate their political activities, could also imply new spaces in which to communicate and mobilize, in Alexandria, Bucharest, Cairo, Geneva, London and Paris. Abdulhamid did all he could to either entice exiles back with promises of high office, or to get Europe to suppress them, 'but a sympathetic public opinion and the Young Turks' ability to travel freely from one place of exile to another frustrated these efforts' (Shaw 1977: 257, 265). The suppression of the Istanbul group after the failed coup of 1895 increased the strength of the movement elsewhere. In Egypt, for example, Ishak Sükûti organized a new chapter, and published several newspapers. There were also links between army groups and exiled liberals in Paris, such as the Ahmet Riza faction. The Young Turk Congress of December 1907 was held in Paris.

Their main strategy was to use a show of military force, coupled with demands, and some large meetings and demonstrations. The army had deposed Sultan Abdulaziz when two battalions had surrounded the palace in May 1876. 'Urabi had shown that officers in Egypt could draw concessions from the *khedive*: the *khedive* had only been saved by turning to the British, whereas such a move was impossible for

Sultan Abdelhamid II, whose reign was built on Islamic resistance to European imperialism. The CUP drew lessons from their failed coup attempts in 1895 and in 1902–3. The idea of 'revolutionary violence' popularized by the Armenians had increased the Young Turks' willingness to contemplate the use of force. The CUP also aimed to organize strikes, the refusal to pay taxes, the circulation of propaganda and arrangements for a major uprising if all else failed (Shaw 1977: 265). After their declaration of intent in May 1908 and clashes with the sultan's men, some of whom defected to the CUP, the latter's cells withdrew to the hills to start guerrilla operations. Incidental factors such as bad harvests, which meant slow taxes, and thus salaries in arrears and the suspension of promotions, generated a wider appeal among civil servants (Shaw 1977: 266). Joint military and civilian uprisings took place at Monastir, Firzovik, Serez, Üsküp and in other towns and cities. Mass meetings held between 20 and 23 July proclaimed support for the constitution. Telegrams were sent to the sultan expressing demands. The CUP in Salonica was not planning open revolt, and was now caught unawares, and hastily planned for an uprising on 27 July.

At this point, Abdulhamid II, the 'master politician', anticipated the next move, and recalled parliament on 23 July 1908. 'Without any real revolution, then, without any soldiers storming the palace, and without bloodshed, the Young Turk Revolution in fact had taken place' (Shaw 1977: 267). Abdulhamid II now gave up most of his powers; he quickly issued further decrees abolishing espionage and censorship, and he ordered the release of political prisoners. For a moment it seemed to many – or at least to those celebrating on the streets – that a panacea had been achieved and that the empire would be saved as one community, with rights for all and minority allegiances secured. Shaw speaks of 'a wave of mass demonstrations, without equal in the empire's long history, in Istanbul and other major cities. Happy mobs of Turks, Arabs, Jews, Greeks, Serbs, Bulgars, Armenians, and Europeans embraced in the streets and made eternal vows of brotherhood for the common good.' Armenians, Greek nationalists and Young Turks had co-operated in Paris, and together brought about a major change to the Ottoman polity with a remarkable lack of bloodshed. It seemed to many as if the ticking time-bomb had been defused (Shaw 1977: 273). A memoirist wrote that: 'Men and women in a common wave of enthusiasm moved on, radiating something extraordinary, laughing, weeping in such intense emotion that human deficiency and ugliness were for the time being completely obliterated.' It 'seemed that the millennium had come, the tension was over, and the empire would in fact be preserved' (Shaw 1977: 273). A period in which a 'freedom of the press and political association hitherto unknown in the Ottoman empire' was inaugurated. Newspapers and political parties blossomed (Shaw 1977: 276). And peasants and workers, who had not made the uprising and for whom very little had changed, started to mobilize in large numbers, making use of new political liberties and the promise of progress, in order to attempt to improve their social and economic conditions.

The Young Turk movement drew much strength from the fact that its liberalism and elitism stitched liberals (including civil servants, students, and others) not to any (largely inexistent) industrial bourgeoisie, but to important elements (especially the rising officer corps) in the army. For liberals, constitutionalism, science, progress and social Darwinism was a creed; for the military it was a way to save the empire in the face of minorities and 'terrorists'. Liberalism and patriotism were not thus merely 'frames' that could be discarded at will, or bent to any purpose: they served to unite otherwise disparate groups in hegemonic ways that could form a basis for a powerful movement, a basis that would outlast setbacks and transformations in the political landscape. Indeed, as Hanioğlu argues, the Young Turk *Weltanschaaung*, which continued to exert a profound influence well after 1908, formed 'the underpinning and the single relatively constant element' in an otherwise shifting organizational and factional and political environment (Hanioğlu 1995: 6).

The uprising in the name of Islam, 1909

Yet, the euphoria was not as widespread as some have maintained, and it was short-lived. One key problem was that the constitution and the recall of parliament was in fact no panacea for the dilemma of multi-ethnic empire in an age of nationalism. Minorities of all kinds thought their demands for autonomy and for rights would be satisfied by the new arrangements: they were sorely disappointed when their demands were refused. The CUP thought that minorities would be appeased by the new regime: they, in turn, were completely mistaken when minorities went on fighting armed struggle in the name of what seemed to the

CUP to be excessive demands. Parliament was no magic wand. Territorial losses in the Balkans continued. By October 1908, the Bulgarians had declared independence, the Austrians had annexed Bosnia and Herzegovina, and the Greeks had announced a union with Crete. The external debt continued to press. In addition, there were those who directly lost out under the CUP: dismissed officials, palace spies and army officers (Shaw 1977: 279). The new regime, seized of an elitist ideology in any case, handed out mostly repression to newly mobilized peasants and workers. Divisions among the Young Turks – between the conservative Liberals, favouring de-centralization and Great Power tutelage and the Unionists favouring a stronger role for the state and a more unified nationalism – now came to the fore once these figures attained power. The social base of the Young Turks movement was far narrower than it might have seemed, and there were many who had rallied to Sultan Abdulhamid II's stand on Islam and Caliphate, who saw ways to achieve progress, unity and order under the banners of Islam, and viewed the turn to a European-style constitution as an unnecessary and un-Islamic deviation from the traditions and faith of the empire, a course which would only lead to ruin and collapse.

Opponents of the CUP, especially after the Unionist elements in the CUP took the upper hand in early 1909, viewed the constitution as a basic threat to Islamic law on which the polity was thought to stand. As Blind Ali, the muezzin of a mosque in the Fatih district of Istanbul, who mobilized crowds in October 1908, maintained, the Shari'a orders that the 'flock be led by its shepherd'. The rise of the Young Turks implied external Christian domination over the polity, and at best the equality and at worst the internal superiority of non-Muslim subjects over Muslims within the polity; it enacted an unwarranted and secular separation of Islam and the state; it provoked the appearance of a decline in morality and values, manifested by the appearance of unveiled women in the streets. The contention here was that the empire's decline was in fact caused not by an insufficient liberalism, but by a departure from its basic Islamic foundations. Islam could be adapted to meet the needs of the modern age. Indeed, Islam could provide laws to regulate every aspect of empire's social and political life. Only Western technology need be borrowed (Shaw 1977: 279–80) and, in this context, Islam would provide the cohesion and the unity required to withstand the European onslaught, and its manipulation of minorities and the question of the constitution, which was in fact a trojan horse for European power.

Hafiz Derviş Vahdeti's movement, that spearheaded the mobilization, propounded a Sufi and popular Islam opposed to government secularism and the influence of minorities and foreign representatives. The movement sought to replace the constitution with the Shari'a, and to use Islam to modernize and rescue the empire. There were echoes of pan-Islam here also as the movement declared its intention to free Muslims all over the world from the tyranny of non-Muslim oppression. They sought to promote the interests of Muslims, while supporting the Islamic principle of consultation as the basis of government. They sought a wider application of Shari'a in the Mecelle code used in secular courts, and to encourage the development of Muslim morals and traditions in daily lives (Shaw 1977: 280). The position of *Volkan/ The Volcano*, Vahdeti's newspaper, founded in December 1908, was initially

liberal and humanistic, supportive of liberty and the constitutional order. At the same time, Vahdeti was anti-Unionist and a supporter of Kamil Pasha's 'English policy'. But after the founding of the Muhammadan Union on 5 April [1909] when *Volkan* became its official organ, its tone changed dramatically. At this point, Vahdeti began to receive subsidies from a number of anti-Unionist sources: some [Young Turk] Liberals [by now opposed to Young Turk Unionists], a group in the Palace, and possibly the British embassy. *Volkan* abandoned its liberalism and adopted Islamist polemics, denouncing the Unionists as freemasons, a code word for the anti-religious and the secular (Ahmad 1991: 4–5).

Whether the changed ideas were a result of the subsidies, or the subsidies were a result of the changed ideas, is not clear. The ideas, nonetheless, were clearly of considerable importance in defining and building up the Islamic position against the constitution in 1909.

Volkan attacked the constitutional regime for bringing with it tyranny (*zilum*) and the 'age of devils' (*seytanlar devri*). The Ottomans were now in a sad state, everywhere there was hunger and poverty. Thanks to the importing of western values, general morality was in decay and the empire crumbling as a result. *Volkan* claimed not to be opposed to the constitution; on the contrary it was a supporter provided 'the constitution was made the guardian of the sharia'. However, 'four or five people ardent for European morality' could not undertake such a task. This could be undertaken only by the army in alliance with the *ilmiye* class. The soldier must know soldiering and remain a soldier; the army must therefore withdraw from politics. In the Assembly, the source of law must be the sharia of Muhammad; laws which did not comply with the sharia could not be considered legally binding (Ahmad 1991: 5).

In sum, *Volkan* maintained that the army should withdraw from politics, the basis of CUP rule was too narrow, the Assembly must not pass legislation that contravened the Shari'a, morality was in decay, and hunger and poverty stalked the land.

The narrow base of the constitutional movement stood in contrast to the broad and subaltern sociological base of the movement in the name of Islam. Sympathizers of the Islamic movement were found everywhere: among the *ulema*, the religious students, the bureaucracy, the army, the Sufi orders, and the mass of Istanbul's Muslim population – artisans, merchants, coffee-house proprietors, public bath-keepers, porters, fishermen, peasants staying in the capital to sell their crops, and the tribes of eastern Anatolia chafing against conscription and centralization. Vahdeti was born in Cyprus where he became a *hafiz* and, at some point, he joined the Naqshbandi order. In 1902, he moved to Istanbul (Ahmad 1991: 4):

The counter-revolution of 13 April was not the work of a few *hojas*; this time virtually the entire *ilmiye* class allied with the troops of the Istanbul garrison and non-academy trained officers (the *alayli*) joined forces. They were supported by the Naqshbandi order, the most extensive and influential Sufi order in the late Ottoman period. The Bektashis had been crippled by Sultan Mahmud II (1808–39) because of their ties with the Janissary corps whose power he broke. Bektashi revival began only after the fall of Abdulhamid. As a part of his Islamist policy, Abdulhamid had patronised the Sufi orders popular in the Arab provinces. But the Naqshbandis, well known for their loyalty to the dynasty, also received his patronage (Ahmad 1991: 5).

The movement in the name of Islam sought the end of constitutional rule, the restoration of the absolute authority of the sultan, the closure of drinking places and theatres, a ban on printing pictures in newspapers, and on the appearance of Muslim women in public (Ahmad 1991: 4). Some called for a *jihad* against European Christian powers in order to resolve the external crisis (Ahmad 1991: 4).

The organizational networks of Sufi orders and mosque imams were present in the mobilization under the banners of Islam, but the movement was actually spearheaded by a new type of organization – a sign of things to come – not a Sufi order, not a mosque imam and his flock, not a *marabout* or tribal network or a guild, but a 'society', the Society of Islamic Unity (*ittihad-i Muhammadi*) (est. 5 April 1909). This Society was organized, under the leadership of Vahdeti, amid the mobilization. Like other societies, committees, and organizations seeking to organize subaltern constituencies, it had its own newspaper (Ahmad 1991: 4).

The active elements in the mobilization were mosque imams, and the Society of Islamic Unity, founded and led by Vahdeti, with rank and file in the urban crowds. Blind Ali had led crowds, whose appearance was spontaneous in that they were not the result of major prior organization, to the sultan's residence in Yildiz Palace in October 1908. There was a mass meeting organized by the Society of Islamic Unity in the Aya Sofya mosque in April 1909. The celebration of the birthday of the Prophet was used to gain further popular support. The sultan refused to finance *Volkan*, and his links to the movement are unclear (Shaw 1977: 280). Chapters of the Society of Islamic Unity, which had members in the First Army, opened in other cities. Petitions demanded further application of the Shari'a.

There were impromptu meetings of students of religion to demand an end to the constitution. Army soldiers grumbled openly in the barracks, many artisans and labourers, themselves adhering to orthodox and mystic religious leaders, talked with increasing fervour about the threat to the Shari'a and the danger of Christian domination (Shaw 1977: 279).

The demonstrations of October were ruthlessly repressed: 'The religious demonstrations were crushed and their leaders punished, Kor [Blind] Ali being put to death' (Ahmad 1991: 4). The Young Turks thought they were avoiding being dragged into a dangerous *jihad* against European powers. But repression of this kind multiplied those protesting the tyranny of the new rulers.

The uprising to restore Islam to centre stage came on 13 April 1909. Shaw speaks of a '[a] groundswell of mass support [that] soon pushed the conservatives to open action' (Shaw 1977: 280). During the night of 12–13 April, soldiers of the First Army and students of religion assembled at the Sultan Ahmed mosque. They marched to parliament and surrounded it. One of their demands was that Ahmet Riza be removed as president of the Chamber of Deputies and a 'true Muslim' be appointed in his place. The crowds began flooding into the parliament buildings, and two deputies were killed. The Minister of War refused to order the army to disperse the rebels, and so the government faced a crisis. Abdulhamid II accepted the resignations of the cabinet and all the demands of the movement.

The CUP members in Istanbul fled, and party and newspaper head-quarters were sacked (Shaw 1977: 280–1). The CUP tried to rally supporters round the empire – appealing also to minority national groups with whom it had co-operated in 1909. Instead, there was an Armenian uprising in Adana, which was severely repressed. After massacres and then some counter-massacres, 20,000 people of all religions were killed in April 1909 (Shaw 1977: 281). The Armenian question, coupled with the secessions in the Balkans of autumn 1908, had confounded the whole 'empire-saving' rationale of the constitu-tional movement. A new policy would have to be found. Meanwhile, the question of power pressed, and the senior officers of the Third Army moved in to seize it under the rubrics of restoring order (Shaw 1977: 281–2). They deposed Abdulhamid II on 27 April 1909 and inaugurated a formal constitutional regime controlled by the army, with the CUP initially in the background. Thus began an army role in 'politics that has been exercised from time to time ever since' (Shaw 1977: 281–2)

The insurrection was crushed by the modern, academy-trained officers of the army (the *mektepli*), men who were committed to saving the empire through constitutionalism and reform. The CUP, which shared the same ideology, continued to operate from behind the scene until it seized power in January 1913 (Ahmad 1991: 5).

The CUP and the senior officers of the Third Army became the effective rulers of the Ottoman empire. Where popular support was lacking, coercion did its work. The fact is that the so-called counter-revolution had a good deal more popular support than the so-called constitutional revolution.

The failure of the constitutional and multi-ethnic path under a sultan-caliph with newly limited powers set the stage for what came to be known as Turkification – and the increasing application of Turkish nationalism at the highest levels of the state. The central authorities, just as in the Balkans, proved unable to resolve the ques-tions of class power that oppressed townspeople and peasantry. From now on, the core of the Ottoman empire would start to fragment on ethnic and national lines, and the Arab world would start to chart its own path in terms of political sovereignty. This direction was confirmed with the Albanian revolt of 1910–12, when claims for autonomy and then national self-determination were bolstered by resistance to centralization, fortified by armed bands operating in the mountains with a long tradition of independence, and emboldened by the Italian attack on Ottoman Tripoli in 1911. Defeats in the Balkans precipitated protest in the empire itself. In November 1912, hard on the heels of Ottoman defeat, unpaid bureaucrats and teachers led 'a series of violent demonstrations which soon spread to the other major cities of the empire' (Shaw 1977: 294). These demonstrations nudged rulers to deliver new formulae. We have already seen how, in the Balkans, it was the inability of the Ottoman polity to resolve the movements of peasants and minorities that paved the way for Balkan nationalism. By the same token, it was the failure of the reformed dynastic form of political order, a failure that turned less on inexorable socio-economic change, and more on the by no means entirely predetermined grind and spark of contentious politics, that above all set the stage for the rise of Arab and regional nationalism. The relative capacities of movements now joined under the banners of nationalism would play a vital role in determining the generalization of nationalism in the Arab world.

The Albanian revolt of winter and spring 1910, in Shaw's words, 'was as much a campaign against the new efforts at efficiency and centralization as it was a national movement'. Shaw continues, 'the new census and tax regulations struck especially at mountaineers who had long treasured their independence and avoided conscription'. Laws against vagabonds and national societies 'struck Albania in particular because of its traditional armed bands, which had dominated the mountain for centuries'. These 'laws transformed general resentment against government controls into open support of the nationalists'. Harsh repression by Mahmut Sevket only 'won new supporters for the nationalists'. The concession of June 1911 were not enough, because the Italian invasion of Tripoli (Libya) now emboldened the Albanian movement, which now demanded 'a united Albania, fully autonomous, administered by and for Albanians' (Shaw 1977: 288).

Centralization was not just problematic because of the debts it incurred. It also stirred up resistance that made its continued viability, at least on an imperial scale, extremely problematic. The euphoria of

1908 (Shaw 1977: 273) reflected the idea that the constitution would solve the problem of minorities and secession by giving them a place in the empire and brought new grievances linked to new forms of economic exploitation to the fore. But the authoritarian powers required to keep the constitution in place meant that such inclusionary forms became unworkable.

Egypt: nationalists, workers and peasants, 1882–1914

The crushing of the 'Urabi movement by the British invasion was followed by a marked absence for at least two decades of mass move-ments confronting colonial rule (Baer 1969: 101). This was in marked contrast to the tenacious and mass-based protests that confronted the French occupation of the same country more than eighty years before. It was also in contrast to the protests that were so prolonged and intense in Algeria, Morocco, Sudan, Libya and elsewhere in the face of occupation from foreign parts, as well as in contrast to the armed struggles that broke out following the partition of the Mashriq after the First World War. Indeed, Egypt was comparable only to Tunisia after 1881 in this regard. The collapse of the 'Urabi movement has already been discussed. Economic interests could be pursued with or without a Chamber of Deputies and a constitution. British rule in Egypt was despotic, especially under Evelyn Baring (1883–1907), but relatively indirect. Formal sovereignty belonged to the Ottoman empire. A head of state had not been formally removed: Isma'il had been deposed in 1879 by a *firman* from the sultan. The Egyptian *khedive*, his palace, prime minister, cabinet, government and ministries remained in place, albeit attached to British advisors who wielded real, if vaguely defined, power. When Cromer over-reached himself with the executions that followed Dinshaway, he was gone within a year, and replaced with the more concessionary Gorst.

More important still was tax remission. The policy of abolishing taxes felt to be oppressive but yielding little or no revenue became increasingly important in Egyptian and British policy from 1880 onwards (Schölch 1981: 53–6). During 1876–9, the European control sought to collect at all costs, but this policy changed. Hunter suggests that perhaps Mustafa Riyad Pasha – from around May 1878 when he moved into the European camp – 'regarded co-operation with the Europeans as an opportunity to curb the power of a tyrannical ruler and introduce long-needed changes into the country', especially where European intervention would not last for ever. '[H]e disliked the *corvée* and detested arbitrary and heavy taxation' (Hunter 1999: 191). Tax remission was implemented after 1882, going some way to meeting one of the most important popular demands in recent living memory. For more than two decades, mass protests directed at the state were virtually non-existent. Islamic modernists hoped for gradual progress under British rule, and many among the growing ranks of the *effendiyya* that went on to challenge the British after the war did little or nothing to oppose them before it. Most of the Sunni *ulema* stuck with their books.

Small groups of urban notables, professionals and salaried middle classes started to espouse nationalism in Egypt from the 1890s, and, under the direction of the orator Mustafa Kamil, looked to bring pressure to bear on the British occupation through the diplomacy of the powers. When this strategy failed with the Anglo-French Entente in 1904, some turned towards thoughts of mobilizing more domestic constituencies (Beinin and Lockman 1998: 66). Such a strategy was powerfully suggested by the outpouring by the literate, urban classes of sympathy for the peasantry that followed the British repression at Dinshaway in 1906. Egypt's urban intelligentsia had already paved the way for such a moment by articulating a discourse that figured themselves and peasants as occupying the same national, political community (Gasper 2009).

In 1906, Cromer insisted that the courts hand down egregious punishments – including executions and floggings – for a number of peasants from the village of Dinshaway. The peasants were guilty of nothing more than self-defence against British, occupying troops, who had shot their pigeons for sport and set fire to a village threshing-floor. Further, when the local branch of the British Royal Society for the Prevention of Cruelty to Animals engaged in a heavy-handed and in practice rather arbitrary attack on the livelihoods of Cairo's cab-drivers, many of the newspapers of the educated were sympathetic to the cause of the low-status cab-drivers who joined a mass strike in March 1907 (Chalcraft 2004).

Responding to these developments, the circle around Mustafa Kamil, following his death, formed the National Party (Al-Hizb Al-Watani) in 1908 under the leadership of Muhammad Farid, a lawyer. Farid aimed to build a base among the masses, and thus engaged in organizing among workers and others, forming night schools for artisans that impacted thousands, unions and agricultural co-operatives (Lockman 1994a). Muhammad Farid sought, among other things, to raise their standard of living, 'to teach them [workers] their rights and obligations' and to improve their speaking skills, as he put it in 1910 (Beinin and Lockman 1998: 70). The National Party's organ, *Al-Liwa'*, told the tramway workers after their strike in 1911, that it welcomed the workers' desire to be 'men like other men' (Beinin and Lockman 1998: 71). This was a dramatic innovation on the Egyptian scene, and an important precursor of forms of mass mobilization that were to become much more general during the 1914–52 period.

When press censorship directed at the nationalists followed, there was a demonstration in protest in 1909 of around 4,000 printers, whose livelihoods were also threatened (Beinin and Lockman 1998: 78). Nonetheless, the National Party was not as resolute as it might have been regarding mass mobilization, and, after serving a six-month prison term in 1910, Farid left the country in 1912 (never to return) to avoid serving a one-year sentence. The strategy of mass mobilization was dropped for the time being by the National Party which in any case was repressed in 1914 with the imposition of martial law.

Relatively unorganized attempts to make socio-economic gains by workers, mobilizing under the banners of an older moral economy and the precepts of Ottoman statecraft, had existed in the region from the 1860s and in Egypt from the 1880s. In Egypt too, a number of strikes were carried out among foreign workers, beginning with the Greek cigarette-rollers in 1899. Over the next decade and a half, labour organizing entered a new phase as nationalist organizers connected with workers' grievances and started to mobilize them for the first time.

In Egypt, a wave of strikes begun on the initiative of workers, who still sought the justice of the *khedive* and lodged demands linked to the customs of their trades (cab-drivers, carters, butchers, bakers, fishermen and various other trades), took place between March and April 1907 (Chalcraft 2004: 164–87); it was followed up by strikes by tram and railway workers in 1908, 1910 and 1911. Workers' consciousness was diverse. It drew on the search for the justice of the *khedive*, the demands of custom, and common sense, and spontaneous philosophy from a variety of sources. In the railway workshops of Cairo in 1908, workers discussing a strike sought rules not arbitrariness, merit not nepotism, dignified treatment not beatings, and an end to economic misery. 'There is absolutely no system', they maintained, 'the energetic worker is denied all rights and the bootlicking fool rises quickly' (cited in Beinin and Lockman 1998: 73). These railway workers characterized themselves as human beings not animals, and thus as having 'courage and culture and concern for … [their] happiness and future' (Beinin and Lockman 1998: 73).

Egypt was not alone on the regional stage. In Ottoman lands, more than strikes involving 'virtually every category of labour in the empire' (Quataert 1995: 72) took place between the July revolution of 1908 and the end of the year. In Iran, the 'labor movement followed on the heels of constitutional government' (Ladjevardi 1985: 2). Print workers organized a trade union in Tehran in 1906, opened a newspaper, and carried out one of the first strikes in Iran in June 1910.

The colonial state in Egypt after 1882, like its predecessor, continued to try to count, police, tax, register, and reorganize the peasantry. The British, after crushing the 'Urabi movement, dismantled the elections that had been instituted for village headmen in 1866, and thus put an end to the elections that had surrounded these posts. Authorities both Egyptian and British, pursuing their own agenda, unsuccessfully attempted to repress the peasant bands that continued to attempt to live outside the law. These bands benefitted from the non-co-operation of peasants with external law-enforcers (Brown 1990b). Peasant millenarian politics, which appeared on several occasions during the nineteenth century, for all Cromer's fears, and for all the inspiration of the Mahdiyya in Sudan, dwindled and then more or less vanished from the scene. On the other hand, urban middle classes and intelligentsia started to take an enormous interest in Egypt's peasantry, as a repository of authentic national identity, as an object for reform and uplift, and also, to some extent, especially after Dinshaway in 1906, as a rights-bearing subject. Such interest almost never translated into direct mobilization of peasants by unions and parties, as it did in the case of urban workers, and the diffusion into the countryside of new political ideologies was limited. Certainly peasants had to rely on their own political resources during these years in particular, especially as many village mayors, for whom property qualifications were raised, signed up to a British colonial strategy of co-optation. There was no respite whatever from the pressures that commercialization, the spread of debt, or the weight of feudal obligations placed on the poorer strata of the peasantry (Abul-Magd 2013: 122ff.). In this context, a good deal of peasant collective action was relatively spontaneous and direct, locally and informally organized, and governed by forms of moral economy. Nonetheless, peasants continued to press demands on central and regional authorities in petitions and complaints.

Individuals and small groups carried out direct attacks, sometimes fatal, on locals doing the bidding of the state, government property, officials, or on transport or communication infrastructure (Brown 1990a: 7) especially when these forms were associated with the collection of taxes, the organization of forced labour, or with unwanted forms of policing, reform, enumeration and reorganization (Brown 1990a: 88–9, 215). More than 100 such atomistic attacks took place in some years (Brown 1990a: 90). Sabotaging the railway, for example, was sometimes actually about an attack on the reputation of the local *'umda*, as it would show that he was incapable of keeping order, and this might lead to his dismissal (Brown 1990a: 92). Banditry, the uprooting of crops, arson, cattle-poisoning, and attacks on 'landlords or their agents' (Brown 1990a: 7, 1990b), were also part of this repertoire. While such actions appeared to the authorities as crime, depending on their intent and on the wider reaction, they could be judged political (Brown 1990a: 7). Women in particular were charged and fined for 'insulting' behaviour and comportment with British soldiers (Tucker 1985: 146).

Peasants also had more communal ways of applying their own standards of justice, taking matters into their own hands, bypassing authorities, and redressing wrongs. Here, larger groups took direct action, taking 'matters into their own hands to enforce their will' through land invasions, rent strikes, attacks by large groups on landlords and officials, and so on (Brown 1990a: 7). Such actions of which there were hundreds in the Egyptian countryside between 1882 and 1914, could involve 'entire villages, estates, or significant sectors of them' (Brown 1990a: 111). These repertoires were not the result of formal organization or planning. Most, instead, were

immediate responses to specific threats or offenses to a community. These threats or offenses included events such as the confiscation of land, raising of rent, or arrest of a member of the community (Brown 1990a: 111).

Some communal actions, judged by the authorities to be forms of disorder, were based on long-standing disputes, others from a more specific confrontation. They involved conflicts between renters and landlords, or moments where a villager's land was seized for failure to repay debts, where most residents were in debt. Such conflicts could spark confrontations with authorities or the wealthy that made use of physical assault. 'Crowds gathered and took violent action when a member of the community was defending rights that villagers felt were theirs' (Brown 1990a: 111). Brown writes that 'peasants had definite ideas about when they deserved land, water, or lower rents and acted communally to enforce these ideas' (Brown 1990a: 116). He argued that 'a common political outlook grants peasant communities the ability to act communally in the face of formidable obstacles' (Brown 1990a: 127).

Peasants achieved a degree of success in keeping the state at bay. Clément's study of Egypt's law courts in the late nineteenth and early twentieth centuries demonstrates the extraordinary opacity of the peasant village world to police, prosecutors, lawyers, bureaucrats and officials (Clément 2012). The intense frustrations that these officials experienced, the fact that peasants would dissimulate, the fact that testimonies in court would change or contradict one another, were less an indication of some inherent peasant peculiarity, irrationality or lack of competence, and more a reason to believe that the *fallahin* treated the new court system, especially when it arrived to judge them in capital cases, as at best a necessary evil and at worst an unwanted intrusion from distant parts into their lives and conflicts, which in general were better dealt with and settled through other means. It is not always clear who was using whom, and who was making a fool of whom, when winding through these cases. Elites found the peasant voice incomprehensible. In some sense, just as in the court rooms of colonial India, the subaltern could not speak (Spivak 1988). In another sense, however, the subaltern did not want to speak. Silence and dissimulation was a way of keeping police and judges at bay. Looking from below, it is possible to discern some of the ways in which peasants maintained forms of relative autonomy in their own forms of contentious politics.

Peasant contentious politics, however, was not hermetically sealed from the wider world. Just as in the 1860s and 1870s in Egypt, or on Mount Lebanon in 1858–60, peasants seized on languages and potential opportunities stemming from ideological and political transformations. One illustration comes from the protests of the peasants and

small-holders of Diyarbakir in Eastern Anatolia in 1910. Here petitioners referenced the 'sun of liberty' that was supposed to have risen
with the constitutional revolution of 1908. To this they appealed in
their search for justice against the destruction of their houses, seizure of
their land, the harassment of their womenfolk and the killing of their
children by feudal land-owners (Özok-Gündoğan n.d.: 1). Here, in a
labour-repressive context were customs were violated by profit-making
land-owners who had not abandoned their feudal attitudes, local
moral economy was intertwined with a local interpretation of wider
events.

Conclusion

The foregoing account offers only a synoptic glimpse of some of the
protests, uprisings, movements and truncated revolutions of the long
nineteenth century. Nevertheless, it is reasonable to argue, on the basis
of the evidence submitted here, that it is impossible to understand the
long crisis of the dynastic and Islamic states of the region from 1798 to
1914 without some grasp of the role played by contentious mobilization. In matters of centralization and reform, contentious politics was
always at stake. Even the implementation of the Tanzimat, usually
conceived of in highly top down ways, was fraught for imperial power-
holders thanks to the ways in which it unleashed mobilizations in its
name, especially in the Balkans and on Mount Lebanon. These mobilizations could transform into secessionist and nationalist movements.
One reason that this did not happen on Mount Lebanon had to do
with the transformation of Tanyus Shahin's popular uprising into a
sectarian conflict, a shift which did not take place purely because of
circumstances, but owed something to Shahin's own decisions and
proclamations that put him at the head of all Christians. Not for the
last time in world history, we find an example of the dangers for the
dominant bloc, and opportunities and potentials for subaltern social
groups, of projects of reform from above that work significant changes
on the hegemonic bases of rule.

We note that Egyptian imperial power in the Sudan was always
confronted with resistance, was broken completely for almost two
decades by the Mahdiyya in the 1880s and 1890s, and only restored
through British power, which in turn had been foiled for the same
period by heavy losses in the ranks of the colonial army. The Greek

uprising, as well as those in the Mashriq, not to mention the movements of the Al-Muwahhidun in Arabia, raised the costs of Egyptian expansionism and Ottoman rule alike. The Al-Muwahhidun continued to regroup throughout the period in spite of suffering military defeat. The Ottomans could not prevent secession in the Balkans, which owed not just to European machinations but also to tenacious, contentious mobilization. Revolutionaries under the banners of Islam brought two new states into being, one in Sudan, the other in Arabia, while Abd Al-Qadir in Algeria and Al-Hiba in Morocco also instated new forms of statehood, albeit temporarily.

Ottomans and Moroccan rulers had to be careful lest their tax-raising went too far and provoked uprisings or protest, or evasion which reduced tax revenues. Weapons of the weak could blunt the force of the burdens imposed by the centralizing states. Merchants, land-owners and others could not always get away with land dispossession, profiteering, or exploitation without finding themselves confronted with collective mobilization, whether of the transgressive-communal or the contained-petitioning type. These tenacious efforts sometimes acted to restore the terms of the *status quo ante*, while working changes on that *status quo*, and to entrench subaltern claims to rights, welfare and protection, and define these terms in ways which were coloured by the interests and ideas of peasants and townspeople. The 'Ammiyya in the Hawran of 1889, for example, was successful in winning back rights for cultivators against Druze overlords. Strikes by wage-workers from the 1860s proved themselves capable of winning socio-economic concessions. Mobilization around elections for headmen and guild shaykhs alike pushed forward representative and electoral principles in Egypt in the decade or so before 1882. Appeals to the state also helped to consolidate state centralization itself. On the other hand, Sufi orders, tribes, guilds and peasants proved themselves capable on various occasions of defending their forms of autonomy in the face of depradations from without.

The uprising in Egypt against French imperialism played a role in the ignominious exit of the French in 1801. Protests in Algeria constantly put the French on notice that they could only push violence and domination so far. Heavy-handed dual control in Egypt after 1876 provoked challenges to the existing order which in turn occasioned a British invasion, a blow against Whitehall's (and Lord Salisbury's) wish to combine mastery with indirect rule and empire on the cheap if possible. Protests in Morocco blocked the advance of European investment and made European economic encroachment and direct rule very difficult to secure. Mining concessions and infrastructural works were always difficult to obtain and take forward in the face of many-sided forms of Moroccan resistance. Even the sultan of Morocco could not deliver the country securely to the foreigner, as the French and Spanish discovered after 1912. The tobacco boycott in Iran in the 1890s was remarkably successful in causing the cancellation of the corrupt concessions handed out by the Qajar shah.

Urban and liberal reformists, sometimes with the support of wider groups, established the principle of representation in the state on at least three occasions, in Egypt during 1881–2, in Iran in 1905 and Istanbul in 1908. In Iran, *ulema*, bazaar, and urban intelligentsia forged alliances in the name of the Iranian patriotism, won representation in the state through an elected parliament (*majles*), and limited at least for a period the absolutist powers of the corrupted and relatively weak Qajar shah (Afary 1996). These were dramatic achievements. Even though short-lived or truncated, they challenged the principle of dynastic sovereignty, subjected *khedive*, sultan and shah to a constitution, and brought into being parliaments that were supposed to represent the will of the people and ensure binding consultation. They left an important legacy for the future in all three major states.

Likewise, while the revolutionary mobilizations of the nineteenth century were often eventually crushed, their legacy too was not simply dispersed. The Mahdist revolution, as we have noted, was no local, tribal affair. Holt writes that 'the form which the revolution took proved in the end more hostile to tribalism than either the Egyptian rule which preceded it or the Condominium which followed' (Holt 1970: 17). Above all, perhaps, before the Mahdi's successor put a Ta'ishi tribal stamp on the Mahdist state, before means of administration based on the Egyptian model were borrowed, the Mahdist movement integrated tribal elements on a new basis. None of these movements (the Mahdi of Sudan, Abd Al-Qadir in Algeria, Al-Hiba in Morocco, Al-Sanusi in Cyrenaica and the Al-Muwahhidun in Arabia) were tribal in the sense that they all counter-posed a new principle of authority that could unite different tribes under one banner, and they undercut the authority of tribal chiefs in various ways. By mobilizing around principles that could unite tribes, these revolutionary movements developed a principle that nationalism was later to take up, but not to invent. They also developed a mode of integration which indirect forms of imperial rule were usually unwilling or unable to bring about: either because imperialism ruled indirectly through local tribal shaykhs, as in Iraq, and especially in the Persian Gulf; or because imperialism, when it engaged in heavy-handed forms of centralization, such as in Jabal Druze in the early 1920s, provoked such resistance as to make the experiment unworkable.

In other words, far from being 'backward' and 'peripheral', the great movements of the 'Arid crescent' played a role in the development of centralized forms of statehood and integrated and horizontal notions of political community. The legacy of these movements too stretched into the twentieth century.

On a great many occasions, however, the picture was not so positive, protest attracted repression and even imperial occupation, and had numerous unintended consequences. Uprisings in the borderlands of empire regularly had the unintended consequence of increasing the extensity and intensity of colonial rule. Colonial invasions took place with or without protest, such as that of the French of Algeria in 1830. Nonetheless, protest could provide the pretext and even an important reason for invasion. This took place in southern Algeria and Morocco after the 1840s, on Mount Lebanon after 1858–60, in Tunisia in 1881, in Egypt in 1882, in Sudan in the 1880s and 1890s, and in Iran in 1911. Not for nothing did people in Egypt mutter '*ya 'Urabi ya khurrabi*' ("Urabi you destroyer') after his movement played a role in precipitating the British invasion of 1882. Where contentious mobilization did not challenge British clients, as in the Persian Gulf, highly indirect rule remained the norm. There is something indeed in Robinson and Gallagher's excentric theory of empire.

In the face of the constant threat from without [their colonies], which also affected the attitude of the Moslems under their rule, [empires] … felt compelled to extirpate these inimical movements and to enlarge their territory (Peters 1979: 153).

In other words, repressive and reactionary elements at work within the structures of imperial power were activated against movements in the region. The Moroccan sultan Mawlay Hassan (r. 1873–94) understood this logic well. It was for this reason that he failed to support the small-scale *jihad* that broke out in the Rif in 1893 against a Spanish armed attempt to seize territory outside Melilla. He feared that the

French would then use such a challenge as a pretext to establish a protectorate, to bring in the apparatus of direct colonial rule, as they had done in Tunisia in 1881 (Burke 1976: 30). Resistance, in short, had a highly mixed record in keeping out direct colonial rule. It was a dynamic that was to invert itself between 1914 and 1976, as we shall see. The revolutionary, religious mobilizations were generally crushed and failed to achieve their objectives, in part because of the way Europeans found their threat to be intolerable.

An important consequence of this dialectic, nonetheless, was a crucial contribution to the crises of the states that remained standing, beset as they were by colonial encroachment, the causes of which came from both above and below. Likewise, the breakdown of constitutional movements, and the moments when spheres of autonomy and defensive gestures were not respected, which were many, thinned out the hegemony of the dynastic states guaranteed by divine favour, Islamic law, sultanic justice and customary autonomy, and fuelled reasons to countenance new measures of how these failures were to be judged. Mobilizing projects were neither able completely to replace, escape, sustainably reform, nor adequately defend the state. Thus, the crisis of the Alawi, Ottoman and Qajar states in the early twentieth century, and the combinations of coercion and consent that they used, was not brought about solely by European pressure or the activities of elites, but also by the tenacity, partial success and perhaps even more regularly the failure of a great array of contentious mobilization.

In order to understand and explain this contentious mobilization, the argument here is that we must pay significant attention to the dynamics of hegemonic expansion and contraction on the one hand, and the content and dynamics of the mobilizing projects and their forms of leadership on the other. Protests were not rooted in some pre-existing set of Oriental, Arab or Muslim essences: above all because Islam, justice, reform, and custom were defined in widely divergent and changing ways. Nor can any modernist, teleological reading suffice. We are not dealing here with primitive, archaic, or elementary forms of protest: immature, 'somewhat inchoate and naïve', stymied by the 'dye' of 'traditional culture' that was yet to 'wash off', and alienated by an irrational attachment to religion (Guha 1983: 10–13, 76, 170, 277). This reading of South Asian protest cannot be grafted onto the history of the MENA because it cannot capture the peaks and troughs of protests, their geographic origin, their diversity and creativity, what they owed to 'secular' state-craft and custom, as well as their strengths and weaknesses and their consequences for political struggle. We must be careful, moreover, before conceiving of protest in terms of objective contradictions, or ascribing contestation to the arrival of new forms of 'social mobilization', or emerging social classes and groups, the urban intelligentsia, wealthy peasantry, middle classes and wage-workers. Centralization in itself did not always stir protest. Neither, even, did colonial rule or world economic integration. And where new social groups were able to find a place in the state, or were given the liberty to earn a living without interference or exploitation, or found that their ideas were in consonance with ruling projects, their rise was not associated with significant protest either.

Instead, protests were much more likely to be associated with the dynamics of hegemonic contraction and expansion. Where authorities broke up existing sites of consent without replacing them with new ones, and thus altered the existing balance of coercion and consent in favour of the former, protest was commonplace, especially in transgressive mode. Heavy-handed forms of state centralization, involving excessive and unfair taxes, conscription and regulation were crucial here, especially in Egypt, for example, in the 1870s and early 1880s. Equally important in stirring protest was the dereliction of the state. This history was particularly marked in North Africa (from Morocco to Cyrenaica) and in Iran, where the central authorities were weaker on the one hand, and repeatedly seen as derelict in the face of colonial encroachment, on the other. The inability of the forces of successive Moroccan sultans to protect the Dar Al-Islam against European political and economic intrusion, and their successive military defeats, particularly the retreat from Algeria in 1832, the defeat at Isly in 1844 at the hands of the French, and the defeat against the Spanish in 1858–9, and the capitulation of 1912, drove protest and mobilization throughout the period. Egypt's debt crisis in 1876 paved the way for the 'Urabi movement and to a lesser extent the revolutionary Mahdiyya in Sudan.

On the other hand, when the authorities opened the door to authorized sites of contention and grievance, such as petitioning in Egypt from the 1820s and 1830s, or elections among shaykhs of guilds and villages there from the 1860s, the populace were often quick to make use of these sites, often for forms of contained contention, insofar as they provided meaningful sites of articulation and participation in the socio-political order.

Hegemonic contraction and expansion is not enough to explain the dynamics of protest. When were burdens deemed 'excessive'? Who judged the state to be 'derelict'? How could effective organization for change be organized? Much depended on mobilizing projects, their social bases, leaderships, ideology, goals, organization, strategies and tactics. The 'Urabi movement and the Mahdiyya, for example, may have drawn on a similar over-arching crisis, that of the Egyptian state in the wake of the debt crisis, but they were completely different, and had different dynamics and consequences, in part as a function of the mobilizing projects that they organized, and the sharply contrasting ideas and frames that were stitched into their contentious actions. While 'Urabi is usually seen as modern and the Mahdi as traditional, the latter was the more effective military leader, emerged from a much humbler position of complete exclusion from the state (unlike 'Urabi), and managed to create a new (albeit short-lived) state where 'Urabi largely failed. As we have seen, it is hard to ignore the point that Al-Mahdi's revolutionary project was stitched together at its centre by a set of very powerful normative commitments; such apocalyptic certainties played hardly any role in the 'Urabi movement itself. On the other hand, the 'Urabi movement unwittingly created an important political opportunity for Al-Mahdi because it worked to diminish the military capacity of the Egyptian empire for several important months. Ultimately both movements precipitated the colonial occupation and rule of their respective countries.

The use of guerrilla war *avant la lettre* was a surprisingly powerful strategy in the face of slow-moving, centralized colonial armies operating in remote areas and facing difficulties of re-supply. They were among the only military forces in the MENA capable of actually defeating European invaders in battle. Berque was right to speak of the 'striking power' of this kind of revolt. Just when 'coastal Islam' was collapsing, 'inland peoples ... from the borders of the Sahara to the verge of the equatorial forest resisted the advance of the colonizers under the banner of religion'. He cited Ma' Al-'Ainain in Mauretania who fought off the French from the Adrar Valley in northern Mauretania in the 1890s and 1900s, Al-Sanusi, Al-Mahdi and the Al-Muwahhidun. He noted the 1881 defeat of the Flatters Expedition at the hands of Tuareg near Bir Al-Gharama, and the 1883 death of Hicks along with 10,000 men in Darfur (Berque 1972: 36–9, 139). Von Sivers points out in regard to the rising of Abu Amama in southwest Algeria in 1881 that the 'French troops were barely superior militarily to the insurrectional Algerian contingents', but that the latter broke up before colonial peace was threatened (Von Sivers 1982: 145). The guerrilla tactics of the Mahdi in Sudan were able to defeat Anglo-Egyptian forces.

The comparison with the ease with which the large, centralized, wealthy and populous state of Egypt was conquered by Britain in 1882 is striking. While Egypt, which compared to Sudan had a significant military capacity, could be taken over in late 1882 with a peculiar lack of military confrontation, the same could not at all be said of Sudan, Algeria, Morocco and so on. The weaknesses of 'Urabi's military leadership and strategy have already been examined. While the urban and European-educated classes may have rather derided the rural forms of resistance against colonialism, it was in many ways guerrilla tactics, borrowed from a forgotten nineteenth-century drama, that urban groups ended up taking up, to some extent in the 1920s, but above all after 1945. In the case of Al-Mahdi, it was, counter-intuitively enough, the journey towards statehood that turned out to be a weakness, not a strength – as it involved the loss of all the tactical advantages of guerrilla warfare, and made the Mahdi's position and forces vulnerable to open confrontation with more numerous and better-equipped colonial forces.

Guerrilla tactics were not invulnerable. According to Peters, the main reason for the ultimate defeat of the Qadiriyya, the Sanusiyya and the Mahdiyya was the military and technical superiority of colonial adversaries (Peters 1979: 151–3). This superiority boiled down above all to a question of re-supply and the sheer numbers of soldiers that the empires could put into the field. All these movements operated away from areas where the colonial armies supply lines were stretched thin or disrupted. The success in Egypt was only possible because Napoleon's army was cut off there because the fleet was sunk. The Mahdi was successful in part because the British were stretched thin in Sudan because it was difficult to get there, and because Egyptian political will to 'get there' was paralysed at a crucial moment (1881–2). The Algerian countryside, but not the cities, were defensible up to a point thanks to topography. In other words, mobilizing projects could only account for so much. The will and capacity of colonial empires to put soldiers in the field eventually was able to overwhelm most of the guerrilla movements of the nineteenth century.

The strengths of normative commitment, on the other hand, are illustrated by the dogged continuity of the Arabian Al-Muwahhidun of the eighteenth and nineteenth centuries. They were far harder to suppress – in Shaw's judgment – than the Anatolian notables. This was partly due to the fact that they made use of geography, remoteness and the use of organizational bases far from Ottoman control. But it was also because they had a cause; they promoted an alternative principle of order which could serve as an effective basis of cohesion. The key weapon that the Ottomans had against the Al-Muwahhidun was the Egyptian army. In the face of superior military force, Abdullah Ibn Saud surrendered on September 1818, ending the early Saudi state; during 1818–20, Egyptians occupied most of Nejd and Hejaz with only distant provinces remaining outside their control. But after Ibrahim's return to Egypt in 1822, the Egyptian presence disintegrated. Wahhabism as an idea endured, even when its immediate political and economic achievements had been destroyed. The Saud were then able to rebuild their state and army in Nejd under the leadership of Turki Ibn Abdullah Ibn Muhammad Ibn Saud (1823–34) (Shaw 1977: 15). On the other hand, as we shall see, normative commitments aside, it was only when the Al-Saud decided to play the game of accommodation with the British empire, not to mention develop new forms of organization, that they managed to secure statehood in the 1910s and 1920s.

One of the key weaknesses of the urban reformists was that they lacked a popular constituency. In some respects, this owed to the fact that they were generally unwilling to develop or mobilize one. Indeed, the reformist milieu often took a dim view of popular protest. Butrus Al-Bustani, for example, a key literary figure of the *nahda*, the Arab 'enlightenment' centred on Beirut in the 1860s and 1870s, saw the Bedouin as only semi-civilized, who fell outside the purview of an emerging, perfectible and progressive 'society' (*al-hay'a al-ijtima'iyya*), defined by its lack of fanatics and troublemakers, its more complex socio-economic organization and its more advanced needs and wants (Bustani 1999). Other elites, given a European-style schooling, were typically highly detached from and opposed to popular mobilization. The engineer and technocrat and government official Ali Mubarak was 'strongly opposed to public disturbances' (Berque 1972: 107): he characterized the millenarian Ahmad Al-Tayyib as 'a sinful, subversive man who led people to disobey God', and transgress the Shari'a because he disobeyed the 'imam' of Muslims, the *khedive* (Abul-Magd 2013: 112). 'Urabi was very different, and did appeal to wider grievances and attempt to mobilize popular support. Nevertheless, he mainly manoeuvred within the state, and had few strategies, goals, ideas or forms of organization that could genuinely link his movement to larger constituencies. The CUP detested the 'mob', imposed their constitution by force in the end, largely against the wishes of the wider and more popular constituencies that opposed them in the name of Islam. They in turn did not do very much to develop the means of mass mobilization and took fright at strikes and popular protests. The liberals of the *majles* in Iran in 1905–11 also lost the support of the urban crowd at an early stage because of their failure to pursue social and economic rights (Abrahamian 1993; Afary 1996). For this reason, we cannot ignore the weakness of reforming mobilization that stemmed from its own inability and unwillingness to build stronger links to wider constituencies.

By the same token, revolutionary, defensive and autonomist movements, especially in Egypt and the Ottoman centre after the marginalization of the urban crowd in the early nineteenth century, often lacked significant allies among urban, educated classes. Islamic modernists, for example, for all the attention they have garnered, were not really to be found among the ranks of defensive, revolutionary or autonomist forms of mobilization. After the idea of armed struggle for the faith lost ground to more accommodationist interpretations of the faith, many an Islamic modernist promoted reform not rebellion. Al-Afghani's goal was to create a more united and cohesive Islamic world capable of eliminating the scourge of Western imperialism, direct and indirect. For all his influence, what he actually did was produce words and urge rulers to do certain things. His emphasis on imperialism drew him away from the central drama of nineteenth-century commoner mobilization, which revolved around the state. He urged the Afghans to make a deal with the Russians against the British; he urged Iran to withstand the British, the Ottoman sultan to stand up to the Russians, and sought British help for Iran at another point. In other words, Al-Afghani acted as an advisor to monarchs and powers, albeit a radical one who frequently fell out of favour and was permanently in exile. He did not build a movement. Acknowledging his lack of success, he also came to oppose at the end of his life the edifice of royal despotism, wondering if he might not have been more effective had he spent more time mobilizing among the mass of the population and less time on the 'sterile soil' of royal courts (Abrahamian 1982: 62–5). Pan-Islam in Morocco in the early 1900s, indeed, was by and large about small groups in the pay of the Ottoman state trying to win adherents but without much success (Burke 1972). It was not a popular movement.

Almost all movements, especially outside of Iran, suffered from a lack of support from the religious establishment, especially the Sunni *ulema*. The urban, scriptural *ulema* waded into the stream of contentious mobilization only rarely, and almost never *en bloc* or on an institutional basis. They moved in Istanbul in the 1800s, in Egypt in 1798–1801, and again, to some extent, in Egypt in 1881–2. Only in Arabia did an important section of the *ulema* side with the state-building project of the Al-Saud, although we note that the intellectual architect of Salafi-Wahhabism, Abd Al-Wahhab, was opposed by even his own brother. But the *ulema* stayed quiet in Morocco, Algeria, Sudan, or for the most part in the Mashriq, Egypt and Anatolia. Even in 1909 in Istanbul, it was a Sufi and a member of a reforming society that led the uprising in the name of Islam. It was no wonder that so many forms of protest (Islamic and secular) took as their point of departure the inertia, rigidity, silence or political irrelevance of the religious establishment. Many of the movements under study were actively opposed to the scriptural *ulema* of the cities, whether in Sufi or millenarian clothes. The conservatism in regard to the *makhzan* of the Sunni *ulema* of Morocco, for example, was apparently a nineteenth-century phenomenon, linked to the nexus of interests between urban merchants, pious foundations, and the central state which developed over the century (Abun-Nasr 1987). The situation was markedly different in Iran where the religious establishment had more financial autonomy, where it was not headed by an appointee of the state, and where Shi'ism in turn, especially in the eighteenth and nineteenth centuries, had developed a tendency to stand in independent judgment on the state through *ijtihad*. These factors weighed in the tobacco boycott, and contributed to the success of the constitutional revolution. They were to matter in Iraq in 1920 as we will see. There can hardly be any doubt that the scriptural Sunni *ulema* of the cities commanded the loyalty and attention of significant sections of the populace, and they also seem to have played a role in constraining that populace from contentious mobilization. In addition to economic interests and state control, quietist, conservative interpretations of the faith stressing obedience and order and opposing chaos and disturbance played an important role in this inactivity. The Sunni *ulema* contributed thereby in no small way to the long crisis of the hegemony of the Islamic state: only radicals and renegades from their ranks sought to re-formulate the meaning of such a state. Most maintained their silence on these matters, and failed to seize the initiative in theorizing a new form of Islamic politics. It was a failure that lay Islamists in later years were determined not to repeat.

II | *Patriotism, liberalism, armed struggle and ideology, 1914–1952*

Introduction

The years surrounding the First World War were a watershed. The dynastic, Islamic states of the region foundered, or were completely transformed, and the outlines of a new states system emerged. The shape and dynamics of the political field, and the forces contending within it, changed in far-reaching ways. Between 1911 and the early 1920s, five European powers (Britain, France, Russia, Italy and Spain) tried to rule directly or partition the great majority of the region's territory. This twentieth-century assault dwarfed the scale of nineteenth-century colonialism. Italy invaded the Ottoman provinces that became Libya in 1911. Britain and Russia invaded Iran in 1911. France took official control of Morocco in 1912, bringing about the submission of the sultan-caliph. Spain started to impose a military dominion over the Rif mountains in the north of Morocco during the 1910s. Britain declared Egypt a protectorate in 1914, terminating the fiction of Ottoman sovereignty and imposing heavy burdens through war-time mobilization. The victorious powers in the First World War, which involved many privations including famine in its own right, tried to carve up the Ottoman empire (which surrendered in 1918) and its Arab provinces in the Mashriq between 1918 and 1922. In 1917, the British promised Mandate Palestine to a third party, the European Zionist movement. This move directly implied the mass dispossession of the existing Arab-Palestinian population. Yet, the British also made contradictory promises of national self-determination to their Arab allies in the Mashriq during the First World War. In the early 1920s, Fascist Italy ripped up the autonomy agreements it had struck with Cyrenaica and turned towards an exterminatory settler colonialism. The Ottoman surrender and the rise of Turkish nationalism defying the colonial settlement turned much of the region into the scene of a rush to seize territory, draw boundaries, and opened the possibilities for new forms of political community and mobilization. It was these opportunities, extraordinary provocations, crises of authority and the desperate need for re-thinking occasioned by the collapse of the Ottoman sultanate and the capitulation of the Moroccan sultan-caliph that served as the immediate context for contentious mobilization surrounding the First World War and the new states and boundaries that emerged from it. It soon became apparent that the long crisis of the Islamic states of the region was finally over. The question of how to construct new forms of political community and mobilization now became general.

The emergence of the outlines of a new state system and national politics in the region is too often depicted as an invention of colonial statesmen or modernizing elites, or the outcome of socio-economic change. These views have paid insufficient attention to contentious mobilization. Colonial invasion may have cracked the existing order, but it accounts for less of what emerged than standard views allow. Nationalist mobilization pegged back direct colonial rule and contributed to carving out a new kind of state-wide political field. The diverse and rugged armed struggles and uprisings that mattered across the region, especially in the 1920s, levered a partially autonomous national political field into existence. The rather elitist secular, reformist tradition of the nineteenth century, mobilizing under the banners of patriotism, liberalism and limited measures of social reform, came of age in the immediate aftermath of the First World War, finding mass constituencies, and for a time hegemonizing the political field. This process was exemplified by the history of the Wafd in Egypt, but also relevant in many other parts of the region. New forms of mobilization did not simply confront and displace existing defensive and autonomist forms of protest, but made use of them, joined hands with them, and derived their great capacities for mobilization from these new articulations. In Morocco and Iraq, for example, tribes were stitched into the centralized state as a result of their own contentious mobilization under new banners. And in Syria, by providing a significant element in the armed struggle of 1925–7, tribes, in greatly altered form, wrote themselves into Syrian nationalism. Nationalism was able to inspire commitment and to unite highly diverse constituencies. It took on the mantle that had been constituted by the wide varieties of more evidently religious mobilization in the nineteenth century. During the 1920s, the marked ascendancy of *political* nationalism, as opposed to socio-economic nationalism, was not because society and economy had not yet developed and leaderships were 'backward'; it was because it was above all the re-making of the political community that was at stake during these years.

Nationalists, liberals, socialists, Islamists and others developed a raft of new forms of mobilization that played a role in the making of a new version of mass politics, associated with attempts to achieve representation and lodge changes within the institutionalized form and permanent policy of the state itself, and the use of new forms of organization, ideology and political programme. New permanent mobilizing vehicles, parties, societies, unions and the like were built up, along with new repertoires of collective action, including congresses, newspapers, pamphlets, strikes and demonstrations. The clubs, learned societies, charities, and leagues of the pre-1914 reformers were replaced with parties, unions and syndicates and mass societies. These were new forms of mass mobilization in that they created permanent links between higher-status figures and subaltern constituencies in the name of trying to generate new state policies and lasting change in the structure of the polity and society at large. These forms of organization proposed a systematic connection between the people and the political, and thus promoted new notions of popular sovereignty, altering the nature of the political community. These new forms of mobilization were rooted in the dynamics of hegemonic contestation: they cannot be understood simply as discursive 'colonial effects' on the one hand, or as epiphenomena of socio-economic change on the other.

The Arab revolt, 1915–1918

In early 1915, the clandestine Arab societies, Al-Fatat (formed by Arabist urban notables in exile in Paris in 1911) and Al-'Ahd (formed by 'Iraqi' military officers in the Ottoman military in 1913) 'decided to combine activities and to prepare for a joint plan for a general revolt against the Ottomans'. The revolt was to be centred on Syria and based on Arab soldiers there. Since the 'planned revolt was to spread to the Arabian Peninsula, the societies chose Sharif Husayn of Mecca as their partner in it and even as its supreme leader'. In response to their queries, Sharif Husayn sent his son Faysal to Damascus in March 1915 'to determine the seriousness of the intentions of the societies' (Tauber 1995: 6). Sharif Husayn, the Amir of Mecca, was an important provincial ruler in the Ottoman empire, with religious credentials based on his claim to descent from the Prophet. His interest in the activities of the secret societies stemmed from his own ambitions to become the leader of a new Arab state – ambitions that were to extend, after the collapse of the Turkish Caliphate in 1922–4, to the mantle of the Caliphate itself.

The planned uprising proposed something new: an incipient alliance between nationalist, educated urban notables, Arab-Ottoman officers of often humbler origins, a Hejazi would-be dynast from the Hashemite line, and various tribes who had links to both Arab-Ottoman officers and Sharif Hussein. Such an alliance thus included reformist and autonomist currents from the pre-1914 period – and promised to put them together in new ways under the banners of Arab nationalism. The real possibility that the Ottoman empire would break up because of Turkish nationalism and potential defeat in the First World War added an incentive to act. Another key factor was that the British, who were fighting against the Ottomans in the First World War, could be tapped for support. The secret societies 'formulated a list of conditions under which they would agree to co-operate with the British' against the Ottomans. The Damascus Protocol, as these conditions were known, became the basis of the Husayn–MacMahon correspondence (Tauber 1995: 6), which formalized the link to the British, winning the latter's support for nothing less than an Arab state in the Mashriq after the war.

Beginning in the Hejaz in 1916, the planned uprising took the form of a military campaign, based on tribal levies and volunteers, and supported by the British, which took Ottoman positions up the Red Sea coast and into the *bilad ash-sham* from the south. The fact that tribes could carry on a war from the deserts, oases, mountains and semi-settled regions leant them a crucial importance against forces relying in logistical terms on mechanized infantry, field artillery, the main ports, key cities, and railways for transport and mobilization. The successful assault on the Red Sea port of Aqaba, for example, came from its undefended landward side, a particularly arid stretch of desert. The relative strengths of this kind of warfare were on view elsewhere: the British had been defeated by the Ottomans (drawing on tribal volunteers) at Kut in 1916. We have also seen the power of this kind of uprising in Sudan and North Africa during the nineteenth century. The facility with which tribes could be mobilized owed a great deal to the long-standing traditions of autonomy linked to tribal custom and law, and opposition to central government and Turkish rule that had become especially vivid during the previous decades of centralization.

The forces of the Arab revolt entered Damascus in 1918. On arrival, Faysal, son of the Sharif Husayn and key field commander, along with his ex-Ottoman officers and soldiers, began setting up the promised Arab state with the collaboration of sections of the urban notability and through links of patronage to tribes in the countryside. The model was one of political independence, led by a dynast with sharifian credentials, and supported by urban notability, merchants, urban land-owners, and Arab officers of the Ottoman army, and based around a version of centralized government complete with some limited representative institutions – a consultative assembly – and a politics of congresses, newly forming political parties, and the press. The Independence Party, for example, seeking Arab independence, was founded by Al-Fatat, the secret society of Arab-Ottoman officers, on 5 February 1919 (Tauber 1995: 49), to give it a more public face. While the state-building projects of Mehmet Ali, Mahmud II and Reza Shah were *against* so many of the tribes, the Arab revolt – like Abd Al-Qadir, Al-Mahdi, Al-Hiba, Al-Sanusi and Al-Saud – proposed the nucleus of a new state *with* the tribes. The innovation here was twofold: first, this had not yet been tried in the Mashriq, where the tribes had typically figured, during the nineteenth century as before, as opponents of the central state, urban elites, and settled peasantry, in spite of, and sometimes because of, the economic links that bound them together. Second, for the first time, this was to be done under secular nationalist, not religious, banners. The national principle was just another way to create cross-cutting alliances *between* tribes, and between tribes and other social forces. The process worked fundamental changes on the tribes themselves; it established a link between the tribes and important urban classes, urban land-owners and merchants, a link between the central state as an institutional apparatus and the tribes, and a link between the tribes and the national principle of independence and self-determination. The institutionalization of the tribes within the state that was to follow was thus not just a top-down and colonial process, as it has sometimes been depicted (Massad 2001).

Libya: the Sanusi *jihad*, 1911–1931

It is not hidden from any critic what has happened to the condition of the Muslims and the domination (*tasallut*) of the enemy over them in the Levant (*mashariq al-ard*) and the Maghreb (*mugharibuha*). They have raped (*ghasabu*) their countries and eaten their wealth and caused the scattering of the Islamic community (*al-jami'a al-Islamiyya*) and wiped out Muhammad's law (Ahmad Sharif Al-Sanusi, 1921, quoted in Wahab 1967: 105).

Ahmad Sharif Al-Sanusi was in 1921 the exiled head of the Sanusiyya of Cyrenaica, and here he was exhorting the tribes of northern Iraq to unity against the British. His words express well the dramatic crisis of the Islamic state, now vivified by colonial invasion, and are couched in thoroughly pan-Islamic terms. But the *jihad* declared by the Sanusi order against the Italian invasion of Tripolitania in 1911 was not waged for purely pan-Islamic reasons. It was clearly a response to the threat that the Italian invasion posed to the Sufi Sanusi order itself in the lands where it was entrenched. This is emphatically suggested not only by the timing of the *jihad*, which was launched in the wake of the invasion, but also by the fact that, although the *jihad* call spoke of a threat to Muslims posed by conquest, the Al-Sanusi order had in fact preferred during the nineteenth century to avoid conflict with the European powers if at all possible, failing to join or offer meaningful support to Abd Al-Qadir in the 1830s, Muhammad Ahmad of Dongola in 1883, or Colonel Ahmad 'Urabi in 1881–2 (Gazzini 2004: 15–18). Clearly, colonial conquest in its own region was the provocation that made the difference.

The Italian declaration of war on 29 September 1911, and the subsequent invasion of the coastal town of Tripoli in 1911, was '[u]rged onwards by a growing colonialist lobby, the patriotism stirred by the fiftieth anniversary of the Italian state, and, some argue, to deflect attention from increasing domestic problems, Prime Minister Giolitti authorized the move with rhetoric about seizing Italy's fair share of colonial Africa. There was also talk of reclaiming the former granary of ancient Rome, and settling Italian emigrants' (Atkinson 2000: 99–100).

During the nineteenth century, the Tripolitanians of the coastal cities for the first time accepted the harsh rule of the Ottomans as the only remaining means of warding off the Christians (Abun-Nasr 1987: 248). The constitutional revolution of the Young Turks in 1908 only widened the gulf between the Sanusiyya and the Porte (Abun-Nasr 1987: 319). The Sanusiyya viewed the CUP with misgivings, but stepped up co-operation in the face of the Italian invasion from the north, not to mention French encroachments in the south (Abun-Nasr 1987: 320). Sanusis and non-Sanusis, the latter including Berber chiefs, form the Jabal Nafusa in Tripolitania (Del Boca 2010), enlisted to fight under Turkish command. The sons of various important tribal chiefs went for training in Istanbul, and returned to fight under Ahmad Al-Sanusi, the head of the Sanusiyya (Abun-Nasr 1987: 321). The Italians incurred heavy losses and material costs over the first year: 3,380 soldiers were killed, and 4,000 men wounded (Abun-Nasr 1987: 321). The combination of religious order, tribes, and the Ottoman army was clearly a powerful one, just as it was to be in a rather different guise in Iraq against the British.

The Italo-Turkish treaty of October 1912 left the Tripolitanians and Cyrenaicans to fight on their own. The remaining Ottoman officers were withdrawn by the end of 1913. The British, meanwhile, prevented help coming from Egypt. From the end of 1912, the Sanusi order laid claim to be the legitimate rulers of the whole of Libya, designating themselves an Amirate authorized by the Ottoman sultan. This was the first invocation of a Libya uniting Fezzan (in the south), Tripolitania (in the west) and Cyrenaica (in the east) for centuries. It came not from colonial officials, but from a *jihad* rooted in a neo-Sufi order. The retreat of the Ottomans enabled the Italians to take coastal positions but no more (Abun-Nasr 1987: 322–3). In this context, various autonomy agreements were hammered out between Italy and the Al-Sanusi order, including the Tripolitanian Republic. Subsequent to this, various forms of uneasy co-operation grew up between the Sanusi order and the Italian would-be empire.

With the advent of the fascist Mussolini, any 'notion of sharing power in the colonies with African 'subjects' fell far short of ideal' (Atkinson 2000: 100–1). Colonial forms of indirect rule were broken from above. Under Volpi, the re-conquest of Tripolitania, Cyrenaica and Fezzan was launched in March 1923, when the Italians attacked the joint Italo-Sanusi camps (Abun-Nasr 1987: 399). Sanusi authority was delegated to a devoted adept of the order, a teacher and tribal leader, Umar Al-Mukhtar, under whose banner the tribes fought 'to defend their lands and their customary life' (Abun-Nasr 1987: 399). The Sanusiyya 'were the organizational pivots of anti-colonial resistance' (Peters 1979: 151). As Evans Pritchard has it: 'the Sanusiya comprised a symbol to which the Bedouin clung and which enabled them to withstand twenty years of privation, near-starvation and death, during the resistance to the Italians' (cited in Atkinson 2000: 103). The settled peoples of coastal towns and cities (the *sottomesi*) were often sympathetic to the resistance, but seldom actively involved. There was no clerical link to the towns as in Iraq, or a link via Ottoman officers to towns as in Syria. Nor were the Libyan towns host to an urban, nationalist intelligentsia. Some semi-nomadic and settled Bedouin tribes further inland were likewise largely peaceful.

After initial battles, the Sanusi-Bedouin forces, 'seldom ... more than a thousand [in total] ... were divided into small, mobile groups ... [t]he sustained and effective manner of their resistance was based upon their flexibility and their mobility in the Sahara desert' (Atkinson 2000: 104). They maintained a guerrilla struggle until 1932, using their advantages of mobility, invisibility, surprise and popular support to hold up far larger forces. The Italians had 20,000 colonial troops, mostly Christians from Eritrea, were professionally trained, and equipped with aeroplanes and chemical weapons.

Italians, in spite of, and perhaps partly because of, their inability to score a rapid victory, saw their foes as barbarians and little more than beasts – and treated them accordingly. Graziani saw the whole of Cyrenaica as 'a poisoned organism'. Starting in late 1923, as the Italians were unable to locate and destroy the Bedouin armed groups (*muhafiziya*), they turned to the indiscriminate killing of those found in Bedouin camps. They destroyed herds and food stores, bombed and strafed camps and dropped poison gas on some of them. They targeted the families of the *muhafiziya* and their herds. These measures only stiffened the will of the Bedouin to resist. Rather than change policy, the Italians built from January 1930 'a series of concentration camps that would eventually contain over 100,000 people and 600,000 livestock'. By the summer, the entire population of Cyrenaica was systematically rounded up and marched into barbed-wire encampments. These camps were intended to stop the flow of arms and popular support. The herds on which the pastoral economy was based died *en masse* through lack of grazing land, leaving the population without any means of subsistence. As Graziani noted in 1930:

the government is calmly determined to reduce the people to most miserable starvation if they do not fully obey orders. The same severity will be meted out to all those outside who act on their behalf (Atkinson 2000: 114).

As a result of this policy, mortality estimates through disease, ill-health, malnutrition and typhus range from 30,000 to 70,000 (Santarelli *et al.* 1986: 97). As in Morocco, an embattled colonial army was a highly oppressive one. By September 1931, the Italians also built on the border with Egypt a 282 km-long barbed-wire barrier, 30 feet wide and 5 feet high. This stopped 'arms, food, and other goods from across the Egyptian frontier, where sympathetic groups, Sanusi lodges and the covert support of the Egyptian authorities combined to provide assistance to the rebels'. Without access to support or supplies, the resistance was physically crushed. Umar Al-Mukhtar was captured, tried and executed in September 1931, before an audience of 20,000 Bedouin forced to attend (Atkinson 2000: 107, 112–13, 115). His trial was a 'tragic farce, highlighted solely by the extreme dignity and restraint of Omar Al-Mukhtar' (Santarelli *et al.* 1986: 92). Perhaps between half and two-thirds of the Cyrenaican population died between 1911 and 1932 – most in the concentration camp system. This was, in the words of the Italian historian Del Boca, 'genocide' (cited in Atkinson 2000: 117). The fortitude of Umar Al-Mukhtar, and his tribal warriors, nonetheless, had given a future Libya a powerful symbol of its national existence. It was the Al-Sanusi who were to be invited to rule the post-independence state by the UN in 1951.

Egypt: the insurrection of 1919

The First World War made British rule in Egypt more direct and burdensome. Even before 1914, the British had increasingly turned to censorship and arrests in the face of urban nationalism. In 1914, the British terminated Ottoman sovereignty, imposed formal rule, and deposed the pro-Ottoman *khedive*, Abbas Hilmi II, who had won considerable popularity for his independent stance. Martial law and censorship struck at urban nationalists. The war brought an assault on the peasant population: forced labour to serve in the Camel Corps and the Labour Corps, serving not only in Egypt, but also in Palestine and even in France; the extensive requisition of grain and livestock, and indirect and often corrupt methods of conscription.

Money was extorted for the Red Cross – seen as arrogant and offensive especially in a Muslim country ruled by Christians (Holt 1966: 293). Cotton prices were kept artificially low for British factories, upsetting many land-owners. Egypt's administration and economy was geared to serve a British war that Egyptians did not choose to wage against the very sultan-caliphate to which many Egyptians still felt loyal. War-related inflation and food shortages brought further privations and intense distress to urban and rural constituencies alike. The tax remission of the 1880s and 1890s was now a distant memory. The demands of imperial war had created a more direct form of rule in Egypt. And, far from planning a relaxation in the aftermath, the British aim, behind closed doors, was 'to strip Egypt of what remained of her independence' (Goldberg 1992: 275).

A group of wealthy, secular, nationalist notables decided to raise the demand to terminate the protectorate and gain representation at the Paris peace conference. They would form the Egyptian delegation (Wafd) to Versailles, representing Egypt's desire for national self-determination. These were men of society and of status. With an initial core several hundred strong, they met in the palaces of sympathetic land-owners such as Hmad Al-Basil (Berque 1972: 306–8). The Ottomans had surrendered. And had the whole country not served the British empire – and been a part of the allied victory? Was not President Wilson of the United States, who spoke of self-determination for the small nations, to play an important role at the conference? 'Why should what was true of Czechs and Slovenes not be true of Arabs too?' (Berque 1972: 270). The Wafd found in the lawyer Sa'd Zaghlul a man who could also speak well and passionately in an Egyptian Arabic that many ordinary people could understand and relate to. Zaghlul and others toured the country mobilizing support for a demand for independence, which could be interpreted in secular or religious colours, and to which few ordinary Egyptians were opposed, and for which many were passionately in favour. The Wafd quickly garnered an immense popularity.

The British saw the Wafd as 'Extremists' and responded to their demand on 8 March 1919 with the arrest of Sa'd Zaghlul and his deportation to Malta. This was the trigger for a relatively spontaneous, uncoordinated, and unplanned uprising that engulfed much of the country and took the British by surprise. Students in the capital were the first to move: they began by demonstrating, and by 10 March virtually all were out on strike. Clashes with security forces on 10 March led to deaths among the protestors. Widespread demonstrations then broke out in Egypt's cities, usually resulting in bloody clashes with the British military. Trams, symbols of foreign domination, were attacked and destroyed (Beinin and Lockman 1998: 92). Strikes in the cities and peasant sabotage in the countryside were so widespread that they now paralysed the economy and state. Everywhere 'violence, sabotage and riots challenged the established order, which had lasted for nearly two generations' (Berque 1972: 307). This was a popular insurrection, a forceful and relatively spontaneous intervention of the masses that signalled on a national scale the unendurability of the existing order, and a demand for national independence.

Incipient links between workers and nationalists, forged before 1914, were now reactivated and developed. The tramway workers were the first to join a nationalist strike within days of 8 March. The cab-drivers, and mule-drawn omnibuses, and the railway workers then came out, paralyzing public transport in the capital and beyond (Beinin and Lockman 1998: 92). British troops laid siege to the popular quarter of Bulaq in Cairo, where railway workers were on strike, but residents and workers broke through the troops and marched on downtown. The colonial army opened fire, killing and wounding many, and foiling the procession (Beinin and Lockman 1998: 97). The railway repair shop workers in Alexandria, where the nationalist MTWU was active, also went on strike after 16 March. The wave of strikes then became unstoppable. Workers at the government press, the Arsenal, the Alexandria tramways, the Hilwan electric railways, the Cairo electric company, postal, port, lighthouse and customs employees, taxi and carriage drivers all walked off the job in solidarity with the nationalist insurrection (Beinin and Lockman 1998: 98). The Wafd hailed the strikers as patriots as the 'work stoppages contributed materially to the campaign against the occupational regime' (Beinin and Lockman 1998: 99). Strikers were celebrated in song and poetry on the streets by well-known performers as pure patriots backing the demand for Zaghlul's rights, independence and a constitution (Fahmy 2011: 158). Before 1914, cab-drivers had generally sought the justice of the *khedive*; now they sought national independence and a new form of political community.

School teachers in villages announced to their pupils that their schools were closing indefinitely as they and their *effendi* colleagues were off to work for the revolution (Calvert 2010: 49–50). Some of the very lawyers who had approved the sentences at Dinshaway and had faithfully served the British in the name of law and reform were now to be found on strike and at the front of mass demonstrations, which were joined by other segments of the population from shopkeepers to Copts and *ulema*. Christians and Muslims marched determinedly together – a powerful show of inter-faith unity under national banners. High-status women joined public demonstrations in what was seen as a bold innovation: many read these moves as showing the ways in which women now represented the authentic core of the new Egyptian nation (Baron 2007). On 2 April 1919, even the civil servants, not known for their audacity, joined a major political strike, demanding an end to martial law, an end to the protectorate, and official status for the Wafd as representative of Egypt. Their *ad hoc* committee aimed at a 'general strike, of the sort which was disrupting European countries' (Berque 1972: 308). The British, contemptuous of the *effendiyya* (Berque 1972: 306–8), were shocked. Disruption was on such a large scale that the British gave way and released Zaghlul on 7 April 1919 (Berque 1972: 306). But with the national movement no closer to achieving its demands, the mobilization continued. On 17 April 1919, a general strike broke out. The post no longer functioned. The streets were no longer swept and watered. The atmosphere became intolerable (Berque 1972: 309).

In the countryside, peasants started to move within days of the exile of Sa'd Zaghlul. On the night of 15–16 March 1919, a large band of peasants, quickly joined by the peasant-workers of the Hawamdiyya sugar refinery south of Cairo, attacked the railway station there (Beinin and Lockman 1998: 98–9). Over the following two months, some 60 railway stations were burned down and tracks were damaged in more than 200 places around the country (Beinin 2001: 86–8). Peasants also destroyed some 'one hundred villages, police stations and large estates' (Beinin 2001: 87), including nearly every *'izba* (large commercial estate) in Daqhaliyya province. Banks were also robbed, fields flooded and irrigation works wrecked. Telegraph lines and government buildings were attacked (Brown 1990a: 213; Schulze 1991). Peasants cut railway lines to protect their food which was being sent to the cities, and to disrupt British troops on their way to repress them (Goldberg 1992: 272). They also did it to strike at symbols of foreign and Christian occupation, to aim a blow at the government that taxed and regulated them, and to resist local notables whose reputation

depended on maintaining security. Peasants also forcefully expropri-
ated basic commodities, sheep, fodder and foodstuffs from wealthier
groups who had amassed them during the war, and launched at least
one direct attack on British officials (Goldberg 1992: 272–3). In Zifta,
peasants and urban, educated nationalists declared an autonomous
republic, which lasted several weeks (Berque 1972: 308). In March
1919, the British undertook the burning of villages as collective punishment, aerial bombing, and the machine-gunning of crowds in the
countryside (Beinin and Lockman 1998: 93; Fahmy 2011: 138–9).

The reports of the British Agency on 1919, betraying a paranoia
about October 1917, stress the Bolshevik character of the peasant
movements, noting the attacks on private property and the peasant
rising against landlords (Berque 1972: 307). But this was no communist movement. But nor was it, on the other hand, a mere 'upsurge of
activity' resulting from 'propitious circumstances' and the 'opportunism of both peasants and notables' (Brown 1990a: 194). Whether or
not some notables acted opportunistically, the idea that largely conservative rural notables with vested interests in property were ready to
enjoin *en masse* an uprising which unleashed what they saw as 'chaos',
'pillage' and the destruction of their own property by peasants and
British reprisals alike is not very plausible. There is little reason to
assume that peasant actions, rooted in a tradition of communal action
and petitioning, were predominantly notable-led. Nor does it seem
reasonable to describe peasant activism as 'opportunistic': opportunities may have been seized, but principles were not necessarily sacrificed. Peasants joined the general insurrection in an informally and
locally organized way as an expression of a well-developed moral
economy armoured by nation and religion and chafing under the
economic and political burdens imposed by the local propertied classes
and the state during the previous decades, and above all those of the
war imposed by the British; that they entered into a nationalist uprising
more likely signalled not opportunism but a broad solidarity with an
anti-colonial uprising in nationalist and for them surely Islamic clothes.
Justice, rights, nation and a prior tradition of protest were mixed
together. It is noteworthy, in regard to the secular colouring of the
insurrection, that no Mahdi appeared among the peasantry as had
happened on many occasions since 1798. Indeed, the last Mahdist
uprising was in July 1910 at Kafr Al-Shaykh in Gharbiyya (Brown
1990a: 132).

This was not an *effendi* insurrection in any simple sense, even if key *effendi*, such as civil servants and school teachers, played important roles. In fact, the class basis of the insurrection was far more diverse, encompassing land-owners, notables, workers, lower middle classes and peasants, as well as *effendi*. We should not assume, moreover, that all *effendi* were identical in point of social status or class, or all born to be nationalists. Those of early twentieth-century Egypt, for example, were by no means nationalist *en bloc*. The new generation of lawyers, for example, virtually without exception drawn from relatively wealthy and high-status families, whether prominent-urban, rural-notable, or Turco-Circassian, who made their way through the new professional schools and forged careers in the legal system prior to 1914, men like Ahmad Bey Fathi Zaghlul (1862–1914), Muhammad Tawfiq Nasim Pasha (1874–1938), Ahmad Bey Lutfi Al-Sayyid (1872–1963) and Saʿd Zaghlul Pasha (1859–1927) himself, were polarized on the national question, and their positions changed, sometimes radically, over time. Some were markedly pro-British; others were fixed on building legal careers and making their way into politics; others published clearly nationalist opinions, especially after 1906. Saʿd Zaghlul was married to the daughter of the pro-British Prime Minister Mustafa Fahmi Pasha, and presided without complaint, as Minister of Justice (1910–12), over the sentencing of the nationalist Muhammad Farid to six months in prison for having written a foreword for ʿAli Al-Ghayati's collection of poems, *Wataniyyati* (*My Patriotism*). Other lawyers were complicit in the draconian sentences handed down at Dinshaway, only to recant later. Tawfiq Nasim Pasha, on the other hand, was ever more closely linked to the palace and the British after 1919. He was told by a stone-throwing crowd which gathered outside his house in 1921 to 'eat donkey fodder' (*Tawfiq Nassim! Akl Berseem!*) for his complicity with the occupation. The crowd had parked a donkey outside his house and loaded it up with berseem (clover) in a creative dramatization of their satire. Saʿd Zaghlul, by contrast, went on to become 'father of the nation' (Clément 2012: 281–8). Any simplistic class analysis of these kinds of divergences and change over time is incapable of granting political and ideological dynamics the significance that they deserve.

Nationalism, infused with demands for a constitution, was central to the action. As one of the speakers assembled in front of prominent female political leader Safiyya Zaghlul's 'house of the nation' said to the crowd on 8 April 1919: 'No one must cease from demonstrating, no one must go back to work, no one must rest, until Egypt has her independence ... it is sweet to die if one is dying for one's country' (Fahmy 2011: 143). The insistence on Coptic and Muslim unity under the banners of independence and nation was a marked feature of the insurrection (Fahmy 2011: 134ff.). As a prominent Coptic priest declared in a speech given at Al-Azhar during March–April 1919, with a witty piece of re-articulation:

As a servant of God my duty is to celebrate marriage and funeral rites, and I long to bury the authority of England and to marry Egypt to liberty and independence (cited in Fahmy 2011: 148).

The slogans and poetry of the uprising give the impression of a blanket insistence on national independence, on the one hand a coherent and unified demand, on the other, a rather narrow political one without an apparently very profound domestic political, economic or social content. This latter point should not obscure the major innovation that nationalism of this kind represented. Even demonstrations by those declaring themselves self-evidently to be the 'sons of Pharaohs' (Fahmy 2011: 134), hackneyed to twenty-first-century ears, was an innovation compared to much of the overt protest that this book has reviewed during the nineteenth century. In 1798–1801, mass anti-colonial mobilization occurred without a hint of nationalism or Pharaonism, as far as is known. And the commoner mobilizations surrounding the 'Urabi movement in 1881–2 were about rights, justice and variants of Islam, not nationalism. The latter served to unite the diverse constituencies of the movement. It was abstract enough to include peasants, but it also formed a basis on which notable Wafdists, salaried professionals, urban intelligentsia, urban workers, Copts and Muslims could unite.

The insurrection was forceful, highly disruptive, but basically unarmed. Ease of communications and flat terrain made guerrilla war extremely difficult. Small, 'spontaneous' cells committed to direct action, and engaged in political assassination of British officials, did appear in Egypt during the action. One group was comprised of secondary-school students and a labourer, one of whom reckoned that such actions had obtained for him a reputation (Calvert 2010: 23). Some had secret links to Wafdist leaders (Beinin and Lockman 1998: 93). These groups may have organized a number of acid attacks to ensure solidarity during some labour strikes (Beinin and Lockman

1998: 97–8). But this was no armed struggle, and isolated attacks had very little impact on the overall course of events.

Mass meetings, often held in mosques, served as focal points through which Wafdist leaders connected to the crowds, gave speeches, issued reports, and tried to direct the action. On 16 April 1919, for example, there was a 'sort of national convention', a mass rally of around 80,000, jammed into and around the precincts of Al-Azhar, a place for the majority of the population, and safe from police invasion (Berque 1972: 309; Beinin and Lockman 1998: 102). In the precincts of Al-Azhar 'Coptic priests, women, young students, railroad workers, and even shoemakers delivered speeches, leading some nationalist leaflets to label the daily' Azhar meetings as the 'Egyptian Congress' (Fahmy 2011: 148). This was as close as the insurrection got to the religious establishment: the Sunni clerics otherwise do not seem to have contributed any particular organizational or intellectual content, although their exhortations against sectarianism were important. The palatial homes of the Wafd were also used for rallies, meetings and decision-making. The Wafd, thanks to fund-raising, was able to distribute a trickle of strike money to workers (Beinin and Lockman 1998: 103). City squares, streets and coffee-shops were all made use of in one way or another for relatively spontaneous organization, communication and debate, and, while the official press was heavily censored, illicit periodicals, pamphlets, songs, poems and plays were all important vehicles through which the identities, principles and demands of nationalist independence were expressed (Fahmy 2011: 143–64).

The Wafd showed no real interest in the socio-economic problems of poorer strata, feared disruptive, forceful or violent methods, and sought neither mass mobilization nor revolution (Beinin and Lockman 1998: 89). Their strategy was about contained contention: a legal campaign of pressure and negotiation led by themselves and backed by a popular show of support. The Wafd went further than 'Urabi, in that it started to organize the masses from 1919 onwards through unions, provincial committees and other organizations. In other respects, the two leaderships were not so far apart: the Wafd sought to win over the masses, to use them as a playing card amid negotiations at the top table, to organize them in order that they could show support, but not to enquire too closely into their interests. They made clear that 'attacks on persons or on property are forbidden by divine law and by positive law' amid the upsurge of March 1919, urging all on 24 March as a matter of 'sacred national duty to refrain from any attack ... so as not to obstruct the path of all those who serve the nation by legal means' (cited in Beinin and Lockman 1998: 93). In other words, the Wafd neither planned nor fully embraced the popular insurrection that was done largely in its name.

The Wafd, especially at the outset, had little in the way of a ramified organizational structure, and, while it enjoyed the spontaneous loyalty of the insurrectionary crowds, it had few means of directing and channelling them. Even though peasants for many nationalists represented something authentic about Egyptian identity (Gasper 2009), Wafdists did little to organize those whose activism threatened the land-holdings of many members. In default of mass mobilization, then, the action started to wind down without the goal of independence being achieved, after the initial burst of revolutionary enthusiasm started to wane, and in the face of heavy repression. Moreover, the Wafd was neither able nor willing to pursue means, whether armed or even simply illegal, that would have led to a more climactic, forceful confrontation with the British. The Wafd, in short, were no Leninists, and they sought to win independence through negotiation and 'respectable', legal means, through winning the acknowledgment from the British and in international circles that they represented the Egyptian people, and thus deserved to rule the country. This strategy they did pursue consistently, and their successful boycott of the Milner Mission did underline their strength. Nonetheless, even with much of Egypt's spontaneous loyalty at their feet, the Wafd chose to soft-pedal mass mobilization, and re-start the failed international strategy of Mustafa Kemal prior to 1904. Two years of campaigning in Europe between 1919 and 1921 by Sa'd Zaghlul achieved next to nothing. Conservatism, legal and diplomatic methods, and a failure to do more in regards to mass mobilization, were elements of the Wafdist mobilizing project that might have been otherwise. More forceful forms of confrontation may have been able to exploit the existing situation more effectively.

In the aftermath of 1919, nonetheless, the British, who were seeking to lower the cost of rule, found it more or less impossible to form workable governments. They sought to lighten the burden of rule by ruling more indirectly, and reserving key strategic interests. In this framework, they declared Egypt's 'independence' unilaterally in 1922. Although the constitution that the British and the palace now drew up was deeply flawed, giving too much power to the Palace, in the end the insurrection had made its mark on colonial rule, forcing a more indirect version of colonialism, and thus creating the preconditions for the development of a national political field.

Iraq: the uprising of 1920

The uprising in Iraq in 1920 included at least a small, nationalist, urban intelligentsia, and was hegemonized by those who sought Iraqi national independence. In these senses, it was similar to Egypt's 1919 insurrection. On the other hand, in Egypt there were no Ottoman military officers, whereas in Iraq there were; in Egypt *ulema* did not play very significant roles, whereas in Iraq Shi'a *ulema* did; in Egypt there was no would-be dynast ready to join the struggle, whereas in Iraq there was, in the shape of Faysal. Finally, the Iraqi uprising benefitted from Bedouin and their firepower, who were largely missing from the action in Egypt in 1919.

When Baghdad fell to the British in March 1917, the latter proclaimed themselves liberators of the Arabs from Turkish oppression (Renton 2007). Some Arab nationalist ex-Ottoman officers were ready to believe this talk through confusion or opportunism. In practice, however, this was a fanciful idea unrelated to the real strategic reasons for the British occupation. These had to do above all with controlling the nearby oil fields that supplied the navy, and maintaining British might and 'prestige' before Indian Muslim opinion. The British were also acting in line with the 1916 war-time (Sykes–Picot) agreement with the French concluded in a secret betrayal of the sharifian officers. In fact, the British saw Iraq as a tribal mosaic, and used the language of nationalism precisely because they believed that such a thing could never weigh seriously in such a 'backward' country. Some merchants and notables, especially in Baghdad, supported the British because of their material interests or as a way to preserve law and order, or out of elitist disgust of the old families for the 'upstart' sharifian officers. The British had some collaborators among certain disaffected and heterodox tribes in the countryside, long chafing at the central government. Yet, British control of Iraq and in particular its pursuit of a heavy-handed and direct 'Indian' style of rule brought them into major conflict with key strata of an otherwise heterogeneous Iraqi society. Far from seeking out collaborators and/or arrangements for indirect rule, the British High Commissioner in Iraq, Sir Percy Cox, and his deputy, Colonel Arnold Wilson, set out to establish a British Raj-style direct rule on a diverse land only ever thinly ruled by any central administration – let alone a British colonial one. This intrusion, partly stemming from a British-Indian administration imposing its will against the London-based Foreign Office, and partly from racial and civilizational arrogance, was an important provocation that disaffected multiple constituencies, from clerics, to tribes, to ex-Ottoman officers, to urban intelligentsia. The confirmation that Iraq was not to be part of an independent Arab state but a Mandate with borders drawn from on high was confirmed in the San Remo resolution (25 April 1920), then ratified in the Treaty of Sèvres (10 August 1920).

The key leaderships of the Iraqi uprising of 1920 were drawn from the Shiʻa clergy of the cities, especially the great shrine cities of Najaf and Karbala, the ex-Ottoman Sunni sharifian officers, hailing originally from Baghdad and northern Iraq, and the tribes of the Middle Euphrates, some of whom had links to the officers by (Sunni) origin and others to the clergy by (Shiʻa) faith. These key constituencies also attracted support from townspeople loyal to the long-standing independence of towns and quarters, unemployed civil servants, and some teachers and lawyers, members of the small urban secular intelligentsia. These highly diverse groups united under the banners of Iraqi independence and prosecuted an armed struggle on a national scale from June to November 1920.

Shiʻa clergy and certain tribes had already come together against the first failed British invasion of 1914–16, and the second more successful colonial campaign of 1916–18. Shiʻa *mujtahid*s, influenced by Islamic modernism, the growing need to defend the *umma* against imperialism, and by the Iranian constitutional revolution, and making use of the increased liberal freedoms in the Ottoman empire that followed 1908, developed a Shiʻa Islamic theory of the state during the early 1900s, complete with a notion of what their role should be within it. This enabled them to 'develop their image as leaders of Muslim opposition', paving the way for their increasingly prominent political role (Nakash 1994: 55). The Ottoman army and local irregulars successfully defeated the first British attempt at conquest. This ended in the ignominious surrender in April 1916 of more than 13,000 British and Indian soldiers who had been besieged in Kut, south of Baghdad. The British offensive was renewed in December 1916 under General

Maude. This time the Ottoman and local resistance was defeated and Baghdad fell on 11 March 1917. Kirkuk and Mosul fell in 1918. The British had encountered widespread resistance (Yaphe 2004: 20), especially in the countryside. Common cause was made with the unloved Turkish army by Shi'a clerics in the cities, and tribes without. The Shi'a cleric Sayyid Muhsin Al-Hakim (1889–1970), from a renowned scholarly Tabatabai' family, and future Marja' al-Taqlid (1961) and important figure in political Shi'ism, ruled for *jihad* against the invasion and went personally to the front. His call was an important reason for 'thousands of Arab tribesmen to join the Turkish effort'. These irregular forces were not friendly to, paid, armed, or fed by the Turks. But their actions played a role, particularly in helping to cut off supply lines during the successful siege of the British in Kut (Wiley 1992: 15).

After the fall of Baghdad, the British appointed Captain Marshall as governor of Najaf without actually conquering the city first (Yaphe 2004: 21). He was assassinated on 21 March 1918. The response was repression and a much more invasive form of rule. The British laid siege to the city for forty days. After its surrender, the British moved in: eleven were executed, more than a 100 exiled and other sentences meted out (Bazzaz 1967: 99). What was meant to be a demonstration of the might of empire which would cow Iraqis into submission, what Tauber rosily calls 'force and determination' (Tauber 1995: 5), had the opposite impact. News of the repression in Najaf reached far and wide across the country. According to one source, it struck the inhabitants of the up-country town of Tal'afar like a thunderbolt (Wahab 1967: 12). The impact was evident in Karbala, Iraq's other great holy (Shi'a) city. Prominent Shi'a clerics and civilians began forming groups seeking independence and opposing British occupation. Repressive measures in Karbala amplified the protests. Connections with the tribal leaders of the Middle Euphrates were intensified. And links were made, in spite of ideological and other differences, with Sunni Arab nationalist ex-Ottoman and sharifian officers (Yaphe 2004: 26–8).

Between 1918 and 1920, the drive for Iraqi independence developed what Gertrude Bell called in a secret report to the British in 1919, an unstoppable momentum (Yaphe 2004: 27). Organizational linkages were developed and the secular intelligentsia was drawn in (Yaphe 2004: 28). By May 1920, Sunni and Shi'a clerics were holding mass meetings at Sunni and Shi'a mosques in opposition to British occupation and calling for co-operation in the nationalist cause for Iraqi independence. They sent representatives to Sharif Bin Husayn in Mecca, stating their support for one of his sons as head of independent constitutional government. In other words, Faysal was not simply imposed on Iraq by the British. The contenders of 1918–20 had explicitly called for Hashemite rule. When Ramadan began on 17 May 1920, there were 'huge demonstrations' in the mosques of Baghdad. Sunni *mawlud* celebrations and Shi'a *ta'ziyya* (passion) plays were held in combined services. '[P]atriotic speeches were made and poems recited appealing to Arab nationalism, honor, and Islam.' Even Muslims 'who opposed the nationalist cause' and Shi'a participation in government attended such occasions and helped defray expenses 'lest they be branded infidels and traitors' (Yaphe 2004: 28).

In Karbala, the leading cleric Al-Shirazi issued a legal opinion in late 1918 declaring 'one who is a Muslim has no right to elect and choose a non-Muslim to rule over Muslims'. He effectively deemed service in British administration unlawful (Yaphe 2004: 35 n. 9). Other religious leaders 'threatened excommunication and exclusion from the mosque for anyone voting for continued British occupation' (Yaphe 2004: 27, 29). Only some merchants and prominent secular notables wrote declarations of support for continued British rule.

Two attempts to mediate between British repression and Iraqi constituencies then broke down in June 1920. One stemmed from the arrest and deportation in late May in Baghdad of a young employee of the Waqf Department who recited an anti-British poem. Baghdad notables managed eventually to get a meeting with Arnold Wilson, the acting civil commissioner of Iraq. They petitioned for an elected national assembly to determine the shape of the nation-state of Iraq. Wilson refused, believing that Iraqis were too divided to be able to press their case. The British then began setting up their own rubber-stamp constituent assembly composed of trusted notable collaborators. There was to be no participation in the colonial state, even of the most limited and representative kind.

The other issue concerned the clerics. Representatives from Najaf and Karbala petitioned the British for Iraq's independence under an Arab king limited by a national legislative assembly. The British refused to accept the petition. Demonstrations broke out in Karbala. The British sent in troops and armoured cars, clamping down on dissent there with the seizure and detention of eleven persons, including Muhammad Rida, the son of the revered Shi'a *mujtahid*, Shaykh Taqi Al-Ha'iri Al-Shirazi (Bazzaz 1967: 100). The British imagined that this crude device (hostage-taking) would give them leverage over clerical leaderships in Iraq. They were wrong. When the clerics failed through negotiations to secure the release of the detainees, now held on Hanjam island, the ageing Al-Shirazi issued on 21 June 1920 a fateful *fatwa*:

Demanding rights is a duty for Iraqis. However, they must preserve peace and security in advancing these demands. Defensive force is permitted if the English do not accept their demands.

The clerics regarded 'the occupation of Muslim Iraq by Christian infidels as a sign of the collapse of Islamic civilization' and sought 'an Islamic government in Iraq free from foreign control' (Nakash 1994: 67–8). This *fatwa*, amid other exhortations and sermons, opened the door to armed struggle. Tens of thousands of copies of the *fatwa* were printed and distributed throughout Iraq. Print technology and mass distribution was clearly not just for secularists, or for a purely modular form of European nationalism. As Bazzaz notes, the *fatwa* had an impact in the souls of tribals in particular and the revolt spread in the Middle Euphrates (Bazzaz 1967: 100; Tauber 1995: 301). Sunni clerics signed up to the *fatwa*, inaugurating 'a brief period of unprecedented co-operation' between these clerics (Yaphe 2004: 29–30).

The 300 or so ex-sharifian officers that played such an important role in the Iraqi uprising of 1920 were very much a product, not of social and economic change, but of the Ottoman imperial military system, its disintegration and prior rounds of political contention. These mostly Sunni men, the majority from Baghdad or the northern half of Iraq, had almost all been officers in the Ottoman army. They had defected to the sharifian revolt against the empire in 1916 and in 1918. Most were loyal to Faysal. These were the men – Ja'far Al-'Askari, Nuri Al-Sa'id, Jamil Al-Midfa'i, Ali Jawdat Al-Ayyubi – who ended up holding the premiership at different times in the future Iraqi client monarchy. Their fortunes were made through the Ottoman military system and their subsequent rebellion against it and their collaboration with the British. Almost 'none descended from families of wealth or social position'. Nuri Al-Sa'id, for example, was born to a minor government auditor (Batatu 1978: 319–20). In the 1920s, they were 'scarcely sympathetic to the wealthy or established families' who had acquired their riches, as one of the sharifian officers later said, 'without right and through injustice to others'. According to one of the younger post-1918 sharifians, speaking three decades later, the patriotism of the 1920s in Iraq was associated with 'the middle class, the common people, and the remnants of the leadership of the [1920s] uprising' (Batatu 1978: 320). These officers were later seen as upstarts by Iraq's old-established families, who complained: 'Who is so and so that he should become a minister or a *mutasarrif*? His father was only a sergeant or a grocer' (Batatu 1978: 322). In the context of the First World War, these men were 'rather radical in their temper and ideas'. Just like the military Young Turks, they opposed Abdulhamid II, they were anxious about the dilapidated empire, and they sought reform, looking to European ideas and believing that 'continued adherence to the old modes of life implied futility and frustration' (Batatu 1978: 321).

Armed struggle began in Najaf and Karbala in June 1920 and in other cities in southern Iraq. The British moved pre-emptively to arrest tribal shaykhs, which spread the uprising further (Yaphe 2004: 29–30). Tribal constituencies had been most severely affected by heavier taxation, forced labour and food shortages that had been the direct result of the British campaign and occupation (Coates-Ulrichsen 2007). By late July 1920, the movement for Iraqi independence controlled the Middle Euphrates and districts around Baghdad. Provisional governments controlled by nationalists were established in the Middle Euphrates, organizing taxation and provisioning. Trains were derailed. Arabs who supported the British were 'denied burial in the shrine cities'. '[C]ouncils headed by radical clerics controlled Najaf and Karbala', while tribes and notables controlled other cities and towns.

The Iraqi uprising cost the British in men and material, but it was eventually crushed by force. Karbala, Najaf and Kufa surrendered in mid-October. The revolt was broken by November. The nationalists had run out of arms, ammunition and supplies. The great mosque in Kufa was damaged by British bombardment (Yaphe 2004: 30–1). The Iraqis had trouble with re-supply. The British empire did not. Nonetheless, coercion was expensive – and could not create political order. The British now shifted to a much more indirect policy. The new Iraqi government was to consist of most of the key constituencies of the revolt, minus the Shi'a clergy, whose autonomy and capacities for popular mobilization were feared by the British and Faysal alike, but who also lost credibility at home because they failed to oust the British, and were divided over the issue of religious leadership. The clergy's attempt to boycott subsequent elections led to the deportation of key leaders, decisively weakening their political position (Nakash 1994: 72, 76–7, 80–4). The ex-Ottoman officers got their state, Faysal a throne, and the urban intelligentsia a constitution. The uprising, even if repressed, was thus the *sina qua non* for the political field that opened up in its wake. It became the symbol of the birth of the Iraqi nation.

Syria: the armed struggles of 1918–1927

The political settlement hammered out in Syria in 1927 and after also owed much to a rugged armed struggle uniting town and country that although defeated forced a more indirect form of imperial rule, this time organized by the French, and helped to lever open a space for a new kind of political field.

The imposition of French rule in 1918 on Latakia, their military encroachments in the borderlands of the *bilad al-sham* and Anatolia in 1918–19, their attack on the south and Damascus in 1920, and their imposition of rule thereafter were crucial in provoking a number of uprisings and a state-wide armed struggle during 1925–7. Just like the British in Iraq between 1917 and 1920, the French attempted to impose a heavy-handed and relatively direct form of colonial rule on provinces that had long been free from European direct rule. Like the British, the French were partitioning the Arab provinces of the Ottoman empire as part of the spoils of war, and in accordance with secret agreements made by the would-be victors. And, whereas the French had not promised a 'national home' to any third party, they did have republican ideas which led to more direct interventions against local leaders – such as those of the Druze in the south – than the British contemplated in Palestine. They also sought to divide the country into statelets the better to rule it. Their invasion represented not only a new and foreign imperialism in Ottoman domains, it also destroyed the fledgling Arab state of Amir Faysal, with its capital in Damascus, and on which Arab national aspirations were increasingly pinned with the break up of the Ottoman state. The French in Syria – unlike in Lebanon, where they had Maronite nationalism – had no major collaborator, and aimed to rule by coercion and division, a policy boosted, like that of the English in Iraq, by civilizational, and racial arrogance.

The uprisings of 1918–27 brought together a wide variety of groups under the national banner. The social, economic, confessional and regional diversity of the coalition that formed to fight the French, especially in 1925–7, was unprecedented. Such a broad unity has not been repeated in Syria since. There were the ex-Ottoman and ex-sharifian Arab officers of the Arab revolt and the patriotic clubs and secret societies of the First World War. There were elements drawn from the urban intelligentsia – with figures like the nationalist party-organizer Dr Abd Al-Rahman Shahbandar and the journalist-activist Munir Al-Rayyes. Others came from the urban, notable, bureaucratic and land-owning classes – such as Nasib Al-Bakri from Damascus or Ibrahim Hananu from Aleppo. Also involved were neighbourhood and quarter bosses (*qabadayat*) such as Hassan Al-Kharrat, militant and mountaineering peasants and those of the Ghouta (fertile region) around Damascus, rural warlords such as Sultan Al-Atrash, and minority leaders such as the Alawi Shaykh Al-Ali. Certain tribes of steppe and desert, such as the Ruwalla and the Shallash, played an important role. Before 1921, Turkish nationalists were also involved in the north.

Resistance began as soon as French military force began to make itself felt in the *bilad ash-sham*. The French occupation of Latakia by sea in November 1918 triggered the uprising on the nearby Alawite mountain to the east. Shaykh Salih Al-Ali, 'an Alawite tribal chieftain and venerated religious leader in the district of Tartus' (Khoury 1987: 99) fought in the name of independence and in declared solidarity with nationalists in Damascus. Even this, then, was not simply a 'mountaineer revolt' for autonomy. Salih's force had control of much of the mountain by the summer of 1919. In the face of French military power, however, the Alawis finally surrendered in November 1920 (Khoury 1987: 99–102).

In 1919, the French were threatening the north of the country. Aleppo had many links to Anatolia and the Kemalist movement. Turkish irregulars (*chetehs*) were fighting nearby. In the summer of 1919, for example, they were only 20 miles north of Latakia (Khoury 1987: 99–100). Impressed by the need for a more forceful defence of Syria than that being offered by the congresses and resolutions of Faysal's state in Damascus, an Ottoman-trained official from Aleppo, land-owner, and officer in the Arab revolt, Ibrahim Hananu (b. 1869), left Damascus and started organizing an armed resistance in Aleppo in 1919 (Khoury 1987: 103–11).

Hananu founded in Aleppo a League of National Defence, with rifles
and supplies from prominent merchants, religious leaders and professionals – and 680 recruits by the summer of 1919. Alongside the League
was a political organ, the Arab Club of Aleppo, to 'propagate [through
exhortation and publication] the idea of Syrian national unity', a blend
of Aleppine regionalism and Arab nationalism (Khoury 1987: 106).
Armed operations commenced in autumn 1919 in the countryside
around Aleppo. When the French occupied the city in July 1920, the
revolt spread rapidly: from 800 men in the summer of 1920, their ranks
swelled to a reported 5,000, with volunteers from Aleppo, conscripts,
villagers and Bedouin. Poorly equipped, with only two cannons and
twelve machine guns, the guerrilla bands resumed armed operations in
November 1920, taking advantage of the rugged terrain, and avoiding
the city, where open resistance was impossible due to the presence of
troops. Bands of Turkish and Syrian irregulars outside of Hananu's
control engaged in looting and pillaging (Khoury 1987: 107–8). By
November 1920, the districts and towns from Harim to Jisr Al-Shaghur
were in the hands of Hananu partisans. By repeatedly cutting the rail
and telegraph lines connecting Aleppo with Alexandretta and Beirut,
Hananu's movement briefly held the lead in much of northwestern Syria.

Just like the rebellion of Shaykh Salih, Hananu's forces depended on
aid from Turkish nationalists, who contributed 'men, money, and arms
in large quantities'. The Turks supported a 'wide network' of political
committees and organizations in Northern Syria for the dissemination
of pro-Turkish and anti-French literature (Khoury 1987: 106–7). One
such liaison was carried on by the Aleppine, Jamil Ibrahim Pasha. He
was an absentee land-owner and Arabized Kurd. He had studied
in military college at Istanbul, joined the CUP, and fought for the
Ottomans in the Balkan wars, supporting the unity of the Ottoman
empire until the Ottoman surrender. He visited Atatürk at the end of
summer 1920 to finalize plans for a 'joint military campaign against
the French' (Khoury 1987: 107).

The resumption of armed operations by Hananu's forces against the
French in November 1920 followed quite quickly on the collapse of the
Turco-French armistice of May–September 1920 (Khoury 1987: 108).
The defeat of Hananu's forces, like that of Shaykh Salih Al-Ali, owed
much to the withdrawal of Turkish military assistance. This commenced from late 1920 onwards as the Turkish forces managed to
obtain by negotiation the withdrawal of French garrisons from Cilicia,

as well as parts of Aleppo province, while accepting the French Mandate over Syria. Following a military defeat in December 1920, Hananu retreated to the rugged terrain of Jabal Al-Zawiya and suffered various defeats in the winter and spring of 1921. In July 1921, he was forced to leave the country, taking refuge with exiled Syrian nationalists in Transjordan.

Much to the chagrin of Aleppine nationalists, the Turks now annexed those parts of Aleppo province, the districts of 'Ayntab, Rum, Qal'a, Ma'rash and 'Urfa, from which the French had withdrawn. The Turks then formally accepted French sovereignty in Syria in the Franklin–Bouillon Agreement of 20 October 1921. With the new borders, the economic life of both Alexandretta and Aleppo was also severely disrupted. Many Arab nationalists saw this as a betrayal by the Kemalists, and re-oriented their political direction, embracing wholeheartedly the idea of a unified Syrian struggle for national independence, and began to strengthen their ties to Damascus (Khoury 1987: 110–12). Thus did the dynamics of contention help determine the borders and national entities that came into existence. Scattered bands of insurgents continued to attack the French until autumn 1921. In March 1922, Hananu was tried by French, and surprisingly acquitted: Franco-Turkish relations had improved. The French saw no need to damage diplomatic relations with Turkey. In Syria, Hananu became a legend in his own time (Khoury 1987: 110).

Urban Syrians had already poured onto the streets and organized popular committees to express their anger in the 'July insurrection' of 1920 against Faysal's rule when it became clear that he was not going to organize an armed resistance against the French advance (Gelvin 1998). Faysal's defection from armed struggle carried an important group of sharifian officers with him. Others from his state, however, saw it as their patriotic duty to defend Syria against French colonial rule. Such was the fate of the young Yusuf Al-Azma, Minister of War under Faysal, ex-Ottoman officer who had defected to the Arab revolt in 1916, and who led regulars and volunteers alike to the passes of Maysalun on 24 July 1920, only to be cut down by the forces of the advancing General Gourand. There was a also a widespread and more or less spontaneous mobilization among the townspeople – some volunteering to fill the ranks of the hastily mobilized army (Khoury 1987: 97). Al-Hawrani remembered townspeople from Hama setting out with 'rifles, swords and lances, heading up the road to Homs to face the French', everyone repeating 'God bless Ahmad Al-Jazzar', in reference to Ahmad Al-Jazzar Pasha who had defeated the siege of Napoleon at Acre (Hawrani 2000: 57). There were movements among the Druze and among various tribes. But, unlike in neighbouring Iraq, the links between town and country were not yet secured, the Shi'a connection between tribe and urban cleric was missing. The Islamic reformers of Damascus (known as the *salafiyya*) had no rural constituency, and the Sunni clerics who did stayed quiet. Moreover, with the French invasion, many of the educated, civilian nationalists of Damascus and other towns were forced underground or into exile.

The uprising of 1925 was broader, and more unified and sustained. By 1925, the inhabitants of the *bilad al-sham*, now corralled into a new and unwanted Mandate, had experienced direct colonial rule, and in 1925 many of them came together to resist it. The provocative interventions humiliating shaykhly leaderships in the Jabal Druze by the French, some in the name of republicanism, had much to do with the emergence of resistance there. Liberal nationalist and educated groups sought independence. The figure of Nasib Al-Bakri linked together the Arab revolt, the Druze in the mountain, urban intelligentsia, and even some elite families through marriage. The Druze had connections through the grain trade to the Maydan quarter of Damascus (Provence 2005), and had lost because of the Mandate system the key export route to Haifa. Urban radicals such as Shahbandar, the Zaghlul of Syria (Khoury 1987: 119–24), formed groups such as the Society of the Iron Hand, which had mounted demonstrations in April 1922 in the name of independence. The presence of ex-Ottoman Arab nationalist officers such as Fawzi Al-Qawuqji (1890–1977), who worked for the French until 1925 while plotting a defection, in turn linked to both these constituencies as well as certain tribes. Al-Qawuqji was born in Ottoman Tripoli in *bilad ash-sham* and graduated from the Ottoman war college in 1912, becoming an Arab nationalist during his time in Istanbul. He fought during the First World War with the Ottomans. The tribes had grievances of their own related to Ottoman and French centralization. There were also neighbourhood toughs, who could muster groups of fighting men in towns and the nearby countryside. The celebrations of the Prophet's birthday gathered crowds which could then be mobilized for political purposes (Khoury 1987: 174).

The ex-Ottoman officers who fought in Syria, like their Iraqi counterparts of 1920, were often born in the 1880s or 1890s, from humble or rural origins and their careers had been defined by the Ottoman schooling and military system. The Military Secondary School at Baramka in Damascus was opened in the 1890s. 'A staggeringly large proportion of the leaders of the Great Syrian Revolt received their schooling there' (Provence 2005: 38). From Military Secondary School, these sons of rural shaykhs, village leaders, and middling urban merchants had gone on to the Ottoman Imperial Military College, which differed from the civil educational institutions that were the preserve of the wealthy elite (Provence 2005: 39). Here and in the army they met and made connections with the sons of tribal leaders, major or minor. Such figures had come through the Tribal School, established in 1892 in Istanbul, with students from all over the empire – Libya, Yemen, Hejaz, Iraq and Kurdish regions. At least two of the first eighty-six students there were from the Al-Atrash clan. Graduates of the Tribal School went to the Imperial Military School, where they met other Arab students from similar rural and provincial backgrounds. Ramadan Shallash, for example, an important leader in the uprising, was the son of a Bedouin shaykh from Dayr al-Zur; at the Tribal School he met and became friends with Ali Al-Atrash, from the Suwayda branch of the Al-Atrash family. Shallash became an Ottoman officer after graduating from the Military School for Bedouin Chiefs in Istanbul. He defected and fought in the sharifian army at Medina. In 1920, he led a band of tribesmen against the French and fought alongside Hananu. He fought with Ali Al-Atrash in 1925, along with another former comrade from the Ottoman army, Fawzi Al-Qawuqji. Another important figure was Muhammad 'Izz Al-Din Al-Halabi (b. 1889) in Jabal Hawran. His relatives were locally important Druze shaykhs. From secondary school near Ankara, he had gone on to Military College in Istanbul. He served in the Ottoman Fifth Army, resigning in protest in 1912. He subsequently became a regional official (*qa'immaqam*), was employed by Faysal, and then fought the French at Maysalun. He commanded insurgents in the countryside from 1925 to 1927 'with often devastating effectiveness' (Provence 2005: 39, 41; Khoury 1987: 107–8).

The Ottoman system bequeathed, therefore, military skills and temperament to people who in many cases were also capable of organizing and communicating to ordinary Syrians in a language they could understand. And it forged solidarities among these leaderships that were later to operate in the uprising. Many of the uprisings' leaders had known one another since they were teenagers and had fought in battles in Libya, the Balkans, Anatolia, Gallipoli, the Arabian desert, and then Maysalun (Provence 2005: 41–2). These solidarities, crucially, crossed the divide between tribe and town. Such links had also been deliberately fostered by nationalist officers. Al-Qawuqji, for example, states that he interceded to get a certain Shaykh Dulaim out of a prison (near Mosul) during the British invasion of Iraq. The same shaykh went on to save his life during the Syrian uprising of 1925 (Qawuqji 1995: 27). Indeed, in the months before 1925, networks old and new were mobilized. Al-Qawuqji, for example, met with tribal leaders, particularly Shaykh Salih Al-Harb, in the months before 1925 and secured promises of men and horses (Qawuqji 1995: 106, 110). As it was the Ottoman state that had forged these groups, it was the breakdown of that system that made them available for new forms of mobilization. Amid a direct and intrusive French colonial rule in Syria, in which few of the aforementioned groups had a place, or at least one that they considered honourable, it becomes easier to grasp how these figures would become the leaders of an armed struggle against it.

The Druze warlord, Sultan Al-Atrash, rallied his tribal and peasant troops in August 1925 with appeals to God, country, ancestry, national honour, the will of the people and sacred hopes, and inveighed against French rule as theft, division, and the crushing of freedom of religion, speech and movement – the last point surely bearing on the fact that the important grain trade route that led from the Hawran down to Haifa had been cut off by the Mandate system. Al-Atrash sent letters to villages and towns all over the country in the name of 'independence, liberty, fraternity, and equality' declaring that all Druze, Sunni, 'Alawi, Shi'a and Christians were sons of the Syrian Arab nation – with one enemy in the French (Provence 2005: 1, 87).

Fawzi Al-Qawuqji, who led military forces up and down the country, paid little attention to the Bolshevik revolution of 1917, but he was highly impressed by the contemporaneous exploits of the 'hero Abd Al-Krim' who was fighting the French and Spanish in the Rif mountains of Morocco in the early 1920s. He wrote that '[t]he doings of the hero Abd Al-Karim – truly these were the inspiration to us in our revolution [in Syria]' (Qawuqji 1995: 104).

The armed struggle scored early successes against French columns in the Hawran south of Damascus. For much of the period 1925–6, sections of the country were outside of French control – especially the Ghouta around Damascus. Tens of thousands of Syrians, especially in rural areas, rallied to the cause. The Maydan quarter of Damascus, linked to Jabal Druze through the grain trade, was a major scene of fighting. But the nationalist forces had difficulties fighting in the cities. And their achilles' heel was that, when the French bombarded the cities, the notables took fright, above all concerned with 'ensuring the security of their property against marauding rioters and later from French bombardment' (Provence 2005: 106). It was these notable groups that were most eager to sue for peace. The French started to get the upper hand in 1926 through an intensive campaign of repression and violence. They were able to re-supply their enormous colonial army using ports and railways and the fighters were driven further and further back into the hill country in the north and south. The last guerrilla operations were brought to a halt in 1927.

The uprising cost the French in money and men, demonstrating the difficulty of direct rule. Its dialectics had also thrown up a possible intermediary, the nationalist notables who, although having reformist aspirations (unlike some of the conservative merchants and land-owners), and thus capable of commanding some wider loyalty among the mobilized forces, were nonetheless opposed to armed struggle and 'disorder' and were ready to work with the French and seek representation in their system through reform. Thus what became known as the National Bloc came into being, and the French set up a more indirect form of rule with this Bloc playing the key intermediary role. The armed struggle as a whole was the basic cause of this new and more indirect form, and thus the *sina qua non* of the new political field. Nonetheless, only the liberal and notable nationalists of the Great Revolt came out with any political prize in their hands. Sultan Al-Atrash had not been captured or killed and tried to fight on from Transjordan, but with little or no support now that the uprising had failed. Fawzi Al-Qawuqji, likewise, now went to Saudi Arabia, but, disgusted with Ibn Saud's lack of support for Arab independence, now took up a post in the Iraqi army, and continued to plan an armed struggle to liberate the Arab nation.

The National Bloc and independence in Syria

After 1927, the French turned to liberal nationalist elements among the urban notables: those who sought Syrian independence, and thus had powers of political incorporation *vis-à-vis* wider and more unruly sections of Syrian opinion, but who were also propertied, educated, and liberal, committed to a routinized politics of press, political parties, congresses, resolutions and negotiations. Some version of self-rule (falling short of real sovereignty) in this context, as long as it did not threaten vital French interests, could be countenanced from above. These liberal politicians came to be known as the National Bloc, and they could remain intermediaries between the French and Syrian constituencies as long as they made progress on self-rule and the construction of, and participation in, a political field, characterized by constitutions, political parties and press. Liberal pedagogy over education and Enlightenment dovetailed neatly with the actual narrowness of the new political field.

When the French dragged their feet on notable proposals and resolutions, as they almost always did, these notables organized petitions, demonstrations and strikes to back their cause, especially as the 1930s went on. A major round of protest in 1936 led to a striking success thanks to the Popular Front government in France. France agreed to Syrian independence in principle. Hashim Al-Atassi, who had been Prime Minister under King Faysal, returned from Paris via Istanbul clutching a treaty in his hands. An at least nominally independent Syria nearly came into existence, except for the fact that the French Legislature refused to ratify the Treaty, striking a major blow at the credibility of nationalist leaderships. Syrian independence in 1946 was a product of the Second World War and inter-imperial rivalry, with the liberal-nationalist notables inheriting the apparatus of the state. These groups had nonetheless built links to wider constituencies, who in turn increasingly came forward with their own programmes and ideologies, deepening the meaning of the new political field and linking it to wider constituencies.

Abd Al-Krim in the Rif

The most important challenge to Spanish and French power in Morocco came not from the cities but from the Rif mountains in the north between 1921 and 1926. Abd Al-Krim's forces announced their presence on the global scene by inflicting a massive defeat on the Spanish forces at Anual in the summer of 1921. The Spanish lost a staggering 17,000–20,000 armed men (Ayache 1981: 8). While forces from the deserts and mountains had scored victories in North Africa before, the scale of victory by a non-state force against a European colonial army was unprecedented in the region, and almost unheard of by global standards. After further resounding defeats, the Spanish were all but beaten by the end of 1924, and Abd Al-Krim was poised to take Melilla in the east and Tetouan in the west. Instead of consolidating his gains, Abd Al-Krim made the fateful decision to open a southern front with France (Ayyache 1981: 8). After April 1925, the Rifian forces were fighting not one but two European empires, and with the Spanish making use of mustard gas 'in vast quantities between 1924 and the beginning of 1926' (Balfour 2002: 128), and with a Rif *population* of around 300,000 pitted against at least as many European *troops*, Al-Krim's republic-in-waiting was defeated by 1926 (Ayyache 1981: 8–9).

The importance of Abd Al-Krim's struggle as a guerrilla war may be measured by the fact that Chairman Mao, one of the single most influential practitioners and theoreticians of guerrilla war during the twentieth century, used to open his remarks to visiting Arab delegations in the 1960s by asking them why they came to learn lessons with him when they already had Abd Al-Krim (Ayyache 1981: 13–14). Although the resistance movement drew in crucial ways on the autonomist traditions of the nineteenth century, it was no 'tribal affair' in any unchanging tradition of 'rural and mountaineer revolts' (Laroui's view, cited in Pennell 1986: 227). Nor was it of a piece with the Islamic modernist and liberal reformist urban nationalism of the educated classes that grew up in Morocco from the 1930s onwards. It was a particularly thoroughgoing blend of diverse currents – nationalism and autonomism, urban and rural – and it was precisely this innovative articulation that gave it its enormous strength.

Spanish territorial conquest in North Africa since 1492 had always been highly limited by the powers of different Islamic states and a variety of forms of resistance. They held two enclaves on the north coast – the towns of Ceuta and Melilla – but no more. They were driven back from the outskirts of Melilla in 1893 by a short-lived *jihad*. Mining concessions were struck with Al-Rogui in the early 1900s, but these encroachments were successfully made unworkable by tribes who undercut Al-Rogui himself. In terms of inter-European rivalry, the Spanish claim to a sphere of influence in the Rif mountains was increasingly recognized in European circles by the 1900s (Balfour 2002: 6). The Spanish were impelled in part by a sense of strategic insecurity following their defeat in Cuba in 1898 (Balfour 2002: 7) and in the context of the 'scramble for Africa' among European powers. Morocco was seen by many Spanish elites as 'an advantageous compensation for past disasters' (Balfour 2002: 11). Significant dissent in regards to the path of colonial conquest existed in Spain – whether among conscripts at Barcelona or even elites, such as the Prime Minister before 1902, Francisco Silvela, who considered that Morocco would only mean 'poverty, sterility, and stagnation for Spain' (Balfour 2002: 8). These voices were increasingly marginalized. Their accurate predictions, as objections to conquest, were not bolstered but silenced by the defeats in the early 1920s, which only served to intensify the forces and sentiments of militarism and imperialism, even paving the way, as Balfour has shown, for the rise of Franco's brand of fascism.

Spain acquired formal control of the north of the country by the Treaty of Algeciras in 1912. Their 'prize' was an area even less submitted to the *makhzan* than the French sphere. The treaty was hard to enforce in practice. Collaborators with Spanish rule were thin on the ground, especially where there were few economic links to Spain, and the constituencies that believed that the Rif could benefit from Spanish influence were relatively small, although Abd Al-Krim and his brother were initially among such constituencies. Even if accommodationist tribal or Sufi leaders could be found, the non-hierarchical, egalitarian and 'many-headed' nature of many of the tribes meant that they were very difficult to co-opt. This was because they often had no entrenched leader or intermediary, secure in his position, who could 'deliver' a tribe to the authorities. This was viewed by the Spanish authorities as a major and even baffling 'problem'. As the Spanish Minister at Tangier said despairingly during the Rifian resistance: 'No one could rule these tribes. They are the most intractable people on earth' (Woolman 1969: 21–2).

During the First World War, Abd Al-Krim Al-Khattabi was a high-status head-judge of the Melilla region, working under the Spanish. He was born in Ajdir in 1881. He was the son of a respected local figure, one of the first judges (*qadi*) to work in the central Rif. He hailed from the most important tribe in the region, the Berber Aith Waryaghar. He was, incidentally, the second cousin of Ahmad Al-Sanusi (Gazzini 2004: 86). He laid claim to an important genealogy: descent from Umar Ibn Al-Khattab, the second Caliph of Islam (Hart 1976: 370). He was educated in Qur'an school in Ajdir and at the Qarawiyin university in Fez in the early 1900s, where the currents of political activism associated with the crisis of the *makhzan*, French encroachment, and Abu Himara drew attention away from the remoter exegeses of many of the *ulema*. After learning Spanish back in Ajdir during the time of the Al-Hafiziyya, Abd Al-Krim spent much of the period 1906–19 in Melilla. He worked as a journalist for a Spanish paper, then as a translator, before becoming chief judge for the whole Melilla region in 1914. He became exposed to, and greatly influenced by, Abduh-influenced Islamic modernism (*salafiyya*), and impressed by the doings of the Young Turks (Hart 1976: 372). His initial view seems to have been that Spanish influence and perhaps even some form of rule might have held some benefit for the Rif, developing its mineral resources, and opening the door to technological and scientific advance. After all, Islamic modernism argued that Islam was not opposed to progress and science, which included in this context the development of Morocco's mineral resources and the scientific forms of learning available in Europe.

During his time in Melilla, however, he came to view the Spanish as arrogant, corrupt and incapable. His was a reformism and a modernism outraged. By 1915, he was developing ideas about Rifian nationalism and speaking of organizing a government for the Rif which could treat with the Spanish on an equal footing (Hart 1976: 372). He spoke out against the extension of Spanish sovereignty in the press, and was imprisoned briefly, before being re-instated. He returned to his family in Ajdir in 1919 for fear of extradition to the zone under the control of the French, who he had also criticized. His father was actively opposing Spanish encroachment – the Rif had been slowly falling under Spanish military domination since 1909 – but was killed at the hands of a collaborator in mid-1920. Al-Krim was joined in Ajdir by his brother, who had started a degree in mining engineering in Madrid in 1917.

The Al-Krim brothers formed a 'war party' (*harka*) of 300 tribesmen in late 1920 with the aim of striking a blow at the Spanish that would strengthen the Rifian hand in forthcoming negotiations. As the Spanish continued to advance, its ranks swelled to around 3,000 (Hart 1967: 374). This force cut off, besieged and defeated the Spanish at Anual in July 1921, decimating their ranks by ambush and surprise as they tried to retreat. Almost overnight, the major part of the eastern Rif fell to Abd Al-Krim, who turned in the space of weeks from pragmatic *qadi* to 'charismatic *za'im*' (Hart 1976: 376). After Anual, Al-Krim's fame spread in the region and across the world.

Abd Al-Krim's movement was distinct from that of his predecessors, Al-Hiba or Al-Rogui, and sought an independent, national and sovereign state in the Rif. On the eve of the conflict, Abd Al-Krim said he was searching for a 'country with a government and a flag' (Pennell 1986: 234). He later told the Egyptian, Islamic modernist newspaper, *Al-Manar*, that:

From the first I tried to make my people understand that they could not survive unless they were as closely joined together as are the bricks of a building, and unless they worked together with sincerity and loyalty to form a national unity from tribes with different inclinations and aspirations. In other words I wanted my people to know that they had a nation (*watan*) as well as a religion (*din*) (Interview with *Al-Manar* published in Pennell 1986: 257).

He recounted that he was an admirer of the 'policy of Turkey' and sought to make the necessary changes, borrowing from Europe, that were required in order to create an independent state. His enemies, in his eyes, were those who could not understand this project, or the sacrifices and reforms necessary to bring it about. In this regard, he appeared to reserve as much if not more ire for the Sufi orders, the sharifian families and the *marabouts*, who thwarted his search for independence and national unity, than for the colonial powers themselves. Such was the importance of the drive for cohesion. He recounted that he 'appeared one day in the uniform of an officer' – he seems to have had the example of Atatürk in mind – but was forced to desist by the 'fanatical' opposition of the shaykhs who opposed this as an unwarranted form of Westernization (interview with *Al-Manar* published in Pennell 1986: 258). In keeping with developments in Turkey, Abd Al-Krim announced the formation of the Rif Republic (Dawla Jumhuriya Rifiya) on 1 February 1923. Abd Al-Krim was the president (*ra'is*), as well as president of its parliament (*barlaman*), which was a large-scale and more permanent version of a tribal assembly (*agraw*). This move was not completely exceptional or entirely parachuted in from parts foreign. Tanyus Shahin's movement in the hills of Kisrawan in 1858–60 sought republican forms of government. This book has already mentioned the seventeenth-century republic of Bu Ragrag in Morocco. More pertinently, Hugh Roberts' political-morphological history has revealed the existence in mountainous Kabylia, among Amazigh (Berber) Muslims, of an eighteenth-century form of deliberative, assembly-based self-government, run by armed and 'honourable' (land-owning) men, establishing representative principles, enacting man-made law rooted in custom and usage and attracting the condemnation of *ulema* who saw it as defying the sultan and the Shari'a (Roberts 2014: 283). To what extent Al-Krim was heir to these traditions we do not know. But his project most likely mixed both the inherited and the appropriated. Like the Igawawen of Kabylie, Abd Al-Krim was not a pretender to the Moroccan throne, a position occupied by Mawlay Yusuf (1912–27). He made no claim on the sultanate, and prayers were never said in his name. The implication was secession.

The acid test of Abd Al-Krim's principles came in 1925, after he had opened a second front with France. It was then that he was offered the chance to play the role of vassal: the French and Spanish terms of August 1925 offered autonomy but not sovereignty to the Rif. Had Abd Al-Krim accepted these terms, 'he would have become the grudging tool of both colonial powers' (Hart 1976: 396), sacrificing the principle of sovereignty and independence on the altar of personal power. Abd Al-Krim chose instead to fight on, just as Ahmad Bey of Constantine had done ninety years before, even against extraordinary odds. The cohesion of the movement was very much at stake.

Al-Krim's forces may have been carrying on a guerrilla war, but at the core of the movement was a state-building project. Coercion was centralized and monopolized. Pillboxes and feuding were forbidden. A paid, trained, standing army was created with Abd Al-Krim as its commander-in-chief. A flavour of the professionalizing thrust of this is to be found in a letter from Abd Al-Krim to be read in the markets of Al-Matalsa, Awlad Sittut and Banu Issnasen (in the French zone):

You must not make war, sons of Mohamed, like bandits. We must go to battle in an orderly fashion, beneath a flag. We have the equipment. Each man will receive a Spanish *duro* (five pesetas) in payment as well as food and ammunition. Each will have his part and role in the battle. We must make war as the Prophet commanded. Kill the enemy under arms, leave the old, the irresponsible, the children, the women (Pennell 1986: 97).

Abd Al-Krim surrounded himself with lieutenants and ministers, each with specialized functions. A bank was established which issued the new currency of the Republic of the Rif. Germany had been useful to Moroccans in previous years as a counter-balance to the other European powers. Al-Krim's father knew Mannesman, of German mining interests, from his time in Tetouan in the 1890s. The flow of cash from concession-hunting Germans to the brothers Al-Krim was an important, if as yet unquantified, resource, especially in regards to buying rifles from smugglers and paying for the full-time nucleus of Al-Krim's fighting force. Resources also flowed from the ransoms paid for the return of Spanish prisoners-of-war, and arms and material captured in battle.

Abd Al-Krim's movement thus opposed the more egalitarian system of internal Rifian tribal government, establishing a more hierarchical pattern modelled in part on the Moroccan *makhzan* (Hart 1976: 380–1), minus the monarchic and sharifian claim. In an echo of the practice of Abd Al-Qadir in 1832, or Abd Al-Hafiz in 1908, but under new circumstances, his followers swore an oath of allegiance (*baya'*) to him, especially during February and March 1923 after the proclamation of the Republic. This meant that Abd Al-Krim accepted in some sense the title of Commander of the Faithful (Amir Al-Mu'minin), and was expected therefore to unite Muslims, prevent strife among them, assure the safety of the roads, maintain the Shari'a, protect the country through *jihad* from the enemy, and to establish 'law and justice for the powerful and feeble alike' (Pennell 1986: 123, 125). The would-be existence of an independent state, and the importance of its leader, is very clearly woven into the text of the *baya'*. Amid the more religious sounding language, we also read:

Let our country be happy since its fetters have been cut away, let it [be given to] the man who undertakes its protection, who spares its blood, who suppresses its enemies, who defends it from destruction, makes the law triumphant, and who undertakes to build it (reproduced and analyzed in Pennell 1986: 250).

In other words, the oath of the allegiance, and the *jihad*, were the religious sinews of a project that was linked to a drive for an independent state. Where genealogy and dynasty dropped out, religion, merged seamlessly with nation, became more, not less, important in forging the horizontal ties that bound.

Abd Al-Krim, who came from the central lands of the Waryaghar, where Sufi influence had traditionally been slight, carried on a critique, not only of the *marabouts*, holy men and *sharifs*, but also of the Sufi orders (such as the Darqawa, the Nasiriyin and the 'Aisawa) – all of whom were deeply distrusted by him, and seen through the spectacles of Islamic renewal (*salafiyya*), as superstitious and deviant from the true faith. In a war context, he also saw them as divisive and ineffective. Sufi and *marabout* alms-raising, as well as the funds of the pious foundations, were revenues he sought for his own war-built state: his encroachments here seem to have earned him the enmity of a number of leading families and Sufi orders. He went so far as to ban *dhikr* meetings where the orders' litany was recited. He 'threatened those [Sufis] who violated his laws with being strangled in the markets with their own rosaries' (Hart 1976: 394). He campaigned vigorously against the reverence for saints. He ensured that his own Minister of Justice read the Islamic modernist journalism, written in Arabic, not Berber, of Muhammad Abduh and Rashid Rida (Hart 1976: 394). Abd Al-Krim promoted the Arabization of the Berber tribes and Islamic renewal. He claimed to *Al-Manar* later that:

What I know of its fundamentals is enough to make me declare publicly that Islam as I know it in Morocco and Algeria is very far removed from the Islam brought by the great Prophet (published in Pennell 1986: 258).

His revivalist convictions here served as a state-building principle and a battering ram to cut through diverse forms of resistance, based on custom, local autonomy, and diverse religious practices and understandings, to his movement.

In the state of Abd Al-Krim, the judge and the law (in this case, Islamic law) were to be substituted for customary practice (Hart 1976: 389ff.). The distinctive scalp-locks that had underlined the differences between the tribes were to be cut off. The egalitarianism and non-hierarchical nature of the tribes were denounced, at least later and to *Al-Manar* of Egypt, as 'anarchism' and 'barbarism'. Everyone was affected by a ban on conspicuous consumption at marriages, in an effort to avoid waste in time of war. Women were targeted for the application of Shari'a law as against local customs: women were to be 'protected'; they were to discharge their duties as women; and they were exhorted to pray (Pennell 1986: 144, 147–8). Amid war-time mobilization (rather than as a result of inexorable socio-economic change), crime was now seen as not being just that of an individual backed by a kin group against another individual, but was now transformed into an offence against society as a whole, because it was seen as threatening the order and political unity of the new system. Male same-sex relations were relatively common, apparently, among some of the Rifian tribes (such as the Jibala, Gomara and Senhadja). Against this, Abd Al-Krim made 'sodomy' punishable by death (Woolman 1969: 30). Intimate domains, usually governed by custom, were now brought into the sphere of the governmental: they were a matter for public politics and for state-wide legal process.

Islamic renewal came from the city, and Al-Krim had learned it in Fez and above all in Melilla through journalism and the urban-based court system. But the languages of his movement were capable of a sharp critique of the *'ulema* and merchants of the cities. The historiographical tendency, based on a modernist teleology linked to socio-economic advance, to see the city as being in the vanguard of the rise of political nationalism has sometimes obscured the importance of this. Themes of religious duty, patriotism, asceticism, sacrifice, bravery and even millenarianism were woven into the exhortations posted by supporters of Abd Al-Krim in Tetouan on the back of the victory of Anual in the summer of 1921. In these texts, the rugged *mujahidin* of the hill-country were depicted as being in the forefront of national and religious unity, while those who 'wear silken garments', or who fail to live up to religious or patriotic duty in the city, were those who divided this unity and collaborated with foreign powers, retarding the cause of national independence in the process. As a letter of uncertain authorship fixed to the outer wall of the Darqawiya *zawiya* in the Dar Al-Burud quarter of Tetuan announced in the summer of 1921:

Muslims! What is wrong with you? You do nothing except eat and drink [while] ... your brother Muslims fight ... The pleasures of this life are nothing compared with those of the next world. Is not your religion the same for everyone? Is not our country of Morocco a single country? Where is your care for your religion and your country? ... Friday preachers, incite your brothers with your brilliant quotations from the *hadiths*. Rich men, aid your brother *mujtahids* with your wealth (published in Pennell 1986: 243).

Exhortations to national unity were thus by no means the creation of the cities or of sociological 'advance'. These proclamations went so far as to indict *ulema* who sat on their hands as leaving the ranks of the Muslims.

The actual capacity to mount an armed struggle owed a good deal
to the tribal recruits who filled the ranks of Al-Krim's fighters. The
building-up of an effective fighting force was greatly facilitated by the
fact that, in the Rif of the tribes, quite unlike in the cities, 'every boy
had learned to use knife and gun effectively by the time he reached
adolescence' (Woolman 1969: 26). Martial prowess was sutured to
manhood and masculinity. Rifians also knew the mountainous terrain
intimately. They were lightly armed and thus mobile, especially compared to mechanized infantry, where roads were unpaved, muddy,
steep, narrow or non-existent. Rifian troops presented few clear
targets; their habitations likewise, which, unlike the townhouses of
the notables, were less threatened by heavy artillery because they were
out of range, hard to spot, less concentrated in one place, protected by
terrain, and meant less in terms of vested interests.

While most of the standing army and the war-parties were comprised of men, women played an indispensable role. They provided
resources, food and shelter at the household and village level which
was a *sina qua non* of the resistance. There were also women employed
by the new state in bread factories to provision the army (Pennell 1986:
148–9). Women were active in mobilization, by appealing to male
honour. After the Spanish capture of Shawin, for example, the women
of the Akhmas tribe took a major role in encouraging resistance by
going to the markets of neighbouring tribes. There they would sacrifice
a bull or a sheep as a way of urging them to send menfolk to aid the
Khmas (Pennell 1986: 148–9). Intelligence-gathering was partly done
by Rifi women who operated 'in internal security work in the villages
and as spies'. They could move across Spanish lines without being
molested by the authorities, and thus had a great advantage over the
men. As the Spanish complained in 1922:

The most dangerous and prejudicial espionage of which the rebels in this
tribe make use is that carried out by women, since they are confident that the
(Spanish authorities) will not suspect or punish them simply because they
are women (Pennell 1986: 148).

Women played supply and support roles in battle, and sometimes
fought, taking the place of men, in the front-line. It was the normal
custom of the women of the 'Anjara tribe near Tanger to accompany
their husbands into action, to load their rifles and help them when
wounded. In 1916, some took the place in the firing line of men who

had been killed. Or, in 1920, 'women of a village in the Jibala used guns that they had hidden in the mountains to ambush a Spanish patrol which was burning their houses, while the men were away from the village' (Pennell 1986: 148–9). It may have been that the professionalization of the military carried out by Abd Al-Krim worked to exclude women from the sphere of fighting itself.

Abd Al-Krim's project can be usefully contrasted with the plunder and banditry of Al-Raysuni. Like Abd Al-Krim, the latter was able to build up a power-base amid the crisis of the Moroccan state as it came under French and Spanish control. Unlike Abd Al-Krim, the latter had no project of moral, political or intellectual leadership, and left a far more limited legacy.

The attack on the French in April 1925 was probably seen by Abd Al-Krim as a manoeuvre 'that would hurt the French so much that they would support his claims for retention of the Rif' (Hart 1976: 396). But fighting on two fronts was eventually overwhelming. The French army of occupation in Morocco was comprised of no less than 325,000 men, who were reinforced by 400,000 supplementary troops, all under the command of sixty generals. The Spanish, meanwhile, had 100,000 troops in the field, of whom 40,000 were regular army. Against these forces stood a maximum of 60,000–75,000 Rifian forces divided among the regular army and the tribal war parties (Hart 1976: 398). The colonial troops effected a landing on the coast of the central Rif and forced their way through the mountain, backed by planes, troops, tanks and vast quantities of ammunition. Abd Al-Krim was defeated, thus, by overwhelming military force, the quantities of men and material that colonial empires were able to put into the field because of their demographic weight, their supply lines, and their mechanized transportation. Abd Al-Krim himself later asserted that he was defeated not by outside powers, nor by his own strategic errors, but by religious fanaticism, Sufi orders and *sharifs* (Pennell 1986: 257ff.).

The Rif could only be delivered to the Spanish *because* of Abd Al-Krim's resistance, not in spite of it. This was because the resistance movement, through state-building, had built up a political community that was far more unified than the Rif before the uprising. After 1926:

instead of having to conquer the Rif piecemeal, the Blad l-Makhzen could take over *en bloc*. As a result, until 1956 Spain governed her Moroccan Zone on a pattern laid down not by her own administrators but by Abd el Krim. The Spanish merely substituted their own authority for that of the Rifian leader (Woolman 1969: 219).

Some of Abd Al-Krim's lieutenants now took up positions of power in 'Spanish Morocco', serving as intermediaries to the new colonial overlords. Although Rifian independence was foiled at great cost to its people, the armed struggle generated the forms of more indirect political mediation that were now taken up by the Spanish to rule. Al-Krim brought tribes into centralized forms of administration, transforming them in the process. Al-Krim's reformism had a lasting impact. On the other hand, the uprising had the effect of discrediting the French colonial administrator Lyautey's more indirect methods, and bolstering forms of direct rule in the French sphere. In other words, this was a highly mixed legacy for Morocco as a whole. In the bigger picture, the armed struggle had again served notice on the Europeans that old forms of imperialism were costly and might not last for ever. Abd Al-Krim himself went into exile on French terms, but then jumped ship in Egypt in the late 1940s, setting himself up in Cairo as a dispenser of advice to future Moroccan nationalists and even Egypt's Free Officers.

Palestine: from negotiations and demonstrations to the Great Revolt

In Palestine, the imposition of colonial rule through the British Mandate in contradiction with British promises made to the sharifians, the growing threat of a Jewish state to the indigenous population, and the dispossession of tens of thousands of the peasants from the land by Zionist settlers, provoked crises, alienated diverse constituencies, and thus did groundwork for the movements and protests that culminated in the Great Revolt of 1936–9. Without such a context – unique in the region in that Britain had promised Palestine to a third-party, the European Zionist movement, which laid claim to the territory on historical and religious grounds – it would be impossible to make sense of contentious mobilization under the Mandate. Unlike in Iraq or Syria, or, more distantly, Morocco, Mandate Palestine did not witness a general armed rising in the early years of the Mandate. The pattern of resistance was instead one of initial opposition to the Mandate from 1920–2 ... [then] atomized forms of resistance (e.g. individual transgressions against land regulations), then ... collective action (1929), and finally ... the armed campaign for liberation from British rule (1936–9) (Anderson 2013: 1154).

The diverse coalition capable of bringing together town and country under nationalist banners – what Anderson suggestively calls 'a symbiotic and *generative* alignment' (my emphasis, Anderson 2013: 1142) – only formed in 1936, through rounds of contention, their suppression and inability to win concessions, and the key provocations associated with the rapid and substantial influx of Zionist settlers after 1933, when formerly assimilationist German Jews, under the severe threat posed by fascism and anti-Semitism, threw in their lot with the Jewish state in Palestine.

The British in Palestine were more disposed than in Iraq at the outset to find collaborators on the ground to lighten the burden of rule: 'to allow, until the early 1930s, the state to sustain itself with only a small repressive apparatus' (Anderson 2013: 1152). The Zionists – an 'Ulster-like constituency' (Anderson 2013: 1153) – played the central role, but there was also a space for Palestinian leaderships of the reformist kind, alongside the middle classes that the British drew into the Mandate bureaucracy. The Arab nationalist notables, led by Al-Hajj Amin Al-Husseini (1897–1974), son of Jerusalem land-owners and Sunni religious dignitaries, stepped into this role. Al-Husseini had studied at Al-Azhar, served in the Ottoman army, and supported and was active in the Arab state in Damascus during 1918–20. He founded the Jerusalem branch of the Syrian-based Arab Club (Al-Nadi Al-Arabi) in 1919 and, although not above all a cleric by education and background, he held the British-created senior Muslim post in Palestine, that of Grand Mufti, from the early 1920s. He opposed Zionism and adopted a reformist position in regard to British rule. He and his supporters were dogged by the rivalry of the less nationalist and more accommodationist Al-Nashashibi family, and the way the British and the Zionists tried to intensify these rivalries.

The politics of the notable nationalists in the 1920s was one of publications, exhortations, letter-writing, patronage, 'conferences, meetings, and protests' (Allush, cited in Nimr 1990: 53). They sought to organize peaceful demonstrations to show the strength of their constituencies, and to demonstrate that they were the legitimate representatives of the people to sceptical British colonial officials. They stated that they trusted the good intentions of Britain, and aimed at negotiation with a minimum of institutional disruption, eschewing the use of force or even direct action against persons or property. In this they were similar to the high-status families and notables of the National Bloc in Syria after 1925 and those of the Wafd after 1919. They formed a new organization, the Executive Committee, and worked through leading families, wealthy households, family members, and networks of clients. They did not engage in systematic mass mobilization in unions or mass societies. It was more that they looked to benefit in negotiation from the position they held as mediator and controller of the more 'unruly' subaltern population. As representatives of the Arab and Palestinian independence, they sought a place in the state and indeed to lead it once Zionism and the British were no more. The mufti also increasingly developed an outward facing diplomatic strategy during the 1930s (Mattar 1988). But, if the notables were to maintain the loyalty of wider constituencies, they would have to deliver on the key term of their project: national independence.

Not all demonstrations were organized from above: there were riots, direct actions, incidences of arson, and direct attacks on the property and persons of Jewish settlers, most of which the notables condemned (Nimr 1990: 43–55). Peasant resistance to dispossession at the hands of Zionism began immediately with the first colonization of the land in the 1880s (Khalidi 1997: 89–117). The resistance of Palestinian peasants to Zionist colonization stemmed in part from the fact that their lands were bought up from under their feet by settlers, sold off by Arab absentee land-owners, and peasants were evicted, only to face penury and unemployment, especially in new, urban slums (Khalaf 1997; Khalidi 1997: 89–117; Swedenberg 1993, 2003). Peasants also faced a very wide variety of economic, fiscal, and administrative pressures as a result of British policy (Anderson 2013: 344–590). Bedouin were also pressured by restrictions on their movement, and the grievances of semi-settled Bedouin overlapped with the peasantry. Peasants and Bedouin were one of the key elements in the protests of 1929 (Nimr 1990: 53). Peasant workers seeking off-farm employment were confronted by labour Zionism's drive to exclude Arab labour from a Jewish economy (Shafir 1996), an organized policy that led to overt confrontations where there were, for example, Jewish pickets in citrus groves organized by the Histadrut (Anderson 2013: 551–4).

New forms of social organization, such as the Young Men's Muslim Association, scouting units, sports clubs, cultural organizations, at least one women's association, unions, syndicates and the Youth Congress started to appear in the late 1920s. Political parties started to be organized in the early 1930s, often by the educated sons of notables, and in the wake of the more unruly patterns of demonstrations, strikes, and the use of force against Jewish settlers and their properties. The Istiqlal Party was founded by tireless activist figures such as Izzat Darwazah and Akram Zu'aytir in August 1932 in Nablus, espousing the complete independence of the now-partitioned Arab countries, and the idea that Palestine was an Arab country and a natural part of Syria. As various

social forces dis-identified with the state apparatus, they tended to grow more active, restive, and organized. The movement's gradual divorce from 'stateness' initially made it stronger, helping to provide the conditions for the growth of a revolutionary movement which itself shook up the Jewish National Home policy far more than any role in the bureaucracy or diplomatic tack ever did (Anderson 2013: 1135).

Some of the founders were members of the Istiqlal party founded in Damascus in 1919–20. Nabih Al-'Azmeh, a Syrian nationalist living in exile in Jerusalem, also contributed greatly to the founding of the party (Nimr 1990: 56). But the Istiqlal party lacked mobilized support from above and below. Hajj Amin Al-Husseini campaigned against it from on high. While the party was incapable of incorporating low-status, poor and uneducated elements in the population

it did not gain the support of the masses in spite of its apparent radical programme and militant attitude. This was because it did not include within its ranks peasants, workers or representatives of rural areas. It remained exclusive to the well-to-do urban educated notables (Nimr 1990: 58).

This weakness in point of mass mobilization was a shackle on the capacities of the Istiqlal Party, which was relatively short-lived, and unable to play the role of, for example, L'Étoile Nord-Africaine in Algeria. Nonetheless, through it the urban intelligentsia had made their presence felt in the political arena, and, as Anderson shows, key figures from the Istiqlal played a vital mediating role during the Great Revolt, in the press and especially through the National Committees.

The *jihad* led by 'Izz Al-Din Al-Qassam (1882–1935) was of a different stripe (Nafi 1997; Sanagan 2013; Schleifer 1993). Al-Qassam was a renegade from all of those Al-Azhar graduates and lay exegetes who followed the Islamic modernist line of Muhammad Abduh and before him Al-Afghani, in which armed *jihad* and mass mobilization were more or less invisible, and whereby Islam had to draw on, or prove its ownership of, European concepts of reason, science, civilization and the like. His activism began not in Palestine in the 1930s, nor even with the colonial carve-up of the Mashriq after the First World War, but went back to the Italian invasion of Tripoli in 1911. Al-Qassam, a graduate of Al-Azhar and at that time a mosque imam in the northeast of Syria, raised money and men to join the *jihad* fought from the interior on behalf of Ottoman Muslims in Tripolitania and the north coast of Cyrenaica against Christian Italians, corrupters of the faith. The Ottomans refused permission to this 'jumped-up' and potentially uncontrollable cleric to join their war effort in Tripolitania and Cyrenaica, so Al-Qassam used the money he had raised to found a mosque back in Syria. He fought the French upon their invasion of the *bilad al-sham* in 1920, gaining some guerrilla experience, and was driven into exile, settling in Haifa, where his mobilization for *jihad* against the British and Zionism alike continued (Nimr 1990: 65–80).

This background can help explain the attempt to mobilize an uncompromising *jihad* in a port city which owed its size and wealth to trade with Europe, and in a context where such cities, from Tanger to Izmir by way of Alexandria, had not offered a propitious site for such forms of mobilization during the previous century. This was partly because of pervasive urban Islamic modernism, but also because the wealthy in these cities had vested interests tied up in European trade, but also because their properties were vulnerable to naval bombardment and heavy artillery. The first urban-based *jihad* in many decades was in a crucial sense a continuation of a tradition that had mobilized in the countryside, not the city. But Al-Qassam was drawing also on the new sociology of the city, where notable patronage networks were increasingly limited, where rural–urban migrants, wage-workers in the docks and elsewhere, and unemployed and dispossessed peasants, and newly appearing slums and urban quarters, made low-status groups available for new forms of organization and integration (Anderson 2013: 560ff.). A key innovation of Al-Qassam's, as compared to other movements in Palestine, was to target for mobilization the poor, who he saw as purer and less corrupted Muslims.

By 1935, he had recruited (starting in the late 1920s) several hundred men, tightly organized in cells. Part of the organizational background here was the Sufi order: Al-Qassam was inducted into the Tijaniyya order in the 1920s and 'the handful of locally based recruits to the Tijaniyya brotherhood ... became the core of the fighting force and secret organization that Al-Qassam forged' (Anderson 2013: 570). His cells had firearms and small bombs, which they deployed against Jewish settlements and British railway lines. There were a number of other small, scattered, guerrilla groups aiming at British targets and Jewish settlement from 1920 into the 1930s (Nimr 1990: 61–4), but none compared to Al-Qassam's in point of ideology, size and system. They lacked the ideological core that Al-Qassam furnished his movement. Al-Qassam also used careful vetting procedures for recruits, demanded death-defying commitment, organized his organization according to function, and introduced an intelligence wing, designed to infiltrate the British police (Anderson 2013: 573–4). Al-Qassam frowned on what he saw as the undisciplined riots of 1929, seeking a core of disciplined cadres who would maintain solidarity with local populations and stand at the centre of a popular insurrection. Early defectors from his organization in the 1930s moved directly to a more immediate confrontation (Anderson 2013: 572) and were less successful.

Amid the demonstrations and strikes of October-November 1935, organized by a variety of Palestinian youth, parties, labour and Islamic organizations, to protest Zionist arms-smuggling, Al-Qassam's men, also under pressure to move because of fear of discovery by the British, took to the hills between Jenin and Nablus to begin their *jihad*, assisted by the local population. Caught up rapidly by the British, Al-Qassam refused to be taken alive and was killed in a firefight. His martyrdom made a major impression on a population at once alienated and mobilized, and his funeral was attended by between 10,000 and 25,000 persons.

Mandate Palestine was crackling, and it was now that the diverse constituencies and organizations of the previous decade and a half came together in a national uprising aimed at terminating the Mandate and eliminating the threat of land colonization and the Jewish state. Revelations about Zionist arms smuggling confirmed the Arab community's worst fears that 'the Zionists were secretly preparing for military conflict and conquest' (Anderson 2013: 591). Mass gatherings, demonstrations, strikes and confrontations with security forces were joined with increasing frequency. On 15 April 1936, members of the guerrilla band founded by the now martyred Al-Qassam held up cars and buses near Nablus, killing a Jewish passenger. Two days later, a right-wing Jewish paramilitary group undertook the revenge killing of two Arabs:

Arab protests soon erupted throughout the country, gradually taking on the character of a broad-based anticolonial and anti-Zionist popular uprising (Lockman 1996: 240).

Arab nationalist activists called for a general strike to channel the upsurge from below which spread rapidly, along with new national committees (which sprang up to lead the struggle in all the major towns) and popular committees (which appeared to coordinate it) (Anderson 2013: 625ff.). The general strike hoped to repeat the electrifying success of the fifty-day general strike in Syria, which had just led to the French announcement in March 1936 that they would seek a treaty of independence with Syria (Nimr 1990: 87–8). What Syrians could do, so could the Palestinians – as the reasoning went. Elite politicians were taken by surprise. They nonetheless tried to retain their positions of leadership and ride the wave of popular energy by endorsing the strike call and forming a new Arab Higher Committee on which all the major parties were represented and with Amin Al-Husayni as president. Even the Al-Nashashibi were briefly involved. Insurrection broke out in the countryside with the formation of guerrilla bands by the peasants who faced dispossession. While elite politicians on the Arab Higher Committee consistently looked to diminish the movement's radicalism, although not to sell it out, in service of a diplomatic strategy (Anderson 2013: 651), '[t]he spread of popular revolutionary institutions, from local committees to guerrilla bands, anchored and organized the rebellion while ensuring that it spread throughout society' (Anderson 2013: 596). On one side, the British system of control, rewards, patronage and employment had broken down (Matthews 2006). On the other, the 'notable-led, diplomatically oriented political movement of the 1920s' had given way to the 'radicalized, rebellious and multitudinous formation of the 1930s' (Anderson 2013: 593).

The general strike, a mass rejection of British rule and the threat posed by Zionism, continued until October 1936, 'making it one of the longest general strikes in history' (Lockman 1996: 240). Called by the mostly educated urban leadership, it also served to draw in shopkeepers, merchants, crafts and service workers, civil servants, wage-workers in transport and industry: it tested their loyalty to the cause of Arab independence, and it gave them a tactic by which they could demonstrate such a loyalty. The forces of the labour movement, where organization and strike action among workers had been developing over the previous decade, were engaged. Arab motor transport, for example, was paralysed by the drivers' union, and 'port workers shut down Jaffa harbour' (Lockman 1996: 240). The issue was, as the railway workers of Haifa put it on May Day 1936, in a message to the British High Commissioner, the '[J]udaization of this Arab country, depriving the worker of his job and the peasant of his land' (Lockman 1996: 241).

National committees, often youth-led, played an important role in enforcing the strike on reluctant workers and business owners (Anderson 2013: 641–7). They also 'collected donations from wealthy Palestinians and from sympathizers in neighboring countries', and distributed strike pay, including to the Jaffa dockworkers (Lockman 1996: 241). Even in some urban quarters, autonomous zones of rebel activity were maintained against police incursion by the blockade of 'streets by barricades, nails or bottles' (Anderson 2013: 645), organized by a youth-led National Guard, that appeared in Jaffa in 1936, in coordination with the Jaffa national committee.

The notable 'leadership' admitted to the British that they were no longer in charge of the action, but refused to condemn entirely the upsurge. They walked a tight-rope, balancing between British grumbling that 'extremists' were taking over the movement, and pressure 'from below' to refuse too-substantial a compromise. In the words of Akram Zu'aytir in April 1936, activists acted as 'soldiers watching over the position of the leadership' (Anderson 2013: 624, 655).

In a faint echo of a state that had passed, villagers were able to make use in the first instance of arms left behind by the retreating Ottoman army that they had collected and hidden after the First World War. Other rural groups had their origins among those who had organized and trained for *jihad* under Izz Al-Din Al-Qassam (Nimr 1990: 74). For example, one of the local commanders of the revolt in the countryside was Abu Durra. He was born near Jenin, became a railway worker in Haifa and acted as a messenger for Al-Qassam (Nimr 1990:

Appendix G). Others were drawn from Bedouin, who had skills in fighting. Others were peasants who, suffering or witnessing dispossession and unemployment, picked up arms and joined the fight.

The organization and military skills of the rebels in the hill-country improved with the arrival in August 1936 of a number of Arab volunteers from Iraq, Syria and Transjordan, led by Fawzi Al-Qawuqji (Nimr 1990: 94). Al-Qawuqji was not ready to take the British at their word or to trust them, as notable leaderships and state-builders across the region were doing. He had been planning to continue the armed struggle to liberate the Arab nation (which included in his view most of the Mashriq and the Arabian peninsula) since his defeat in Syria in 1927, and drafting plans for the 'armed defence' of Arabs in *Palestine* outside any framework of negotiation with Britain since 1929 (Qawuqji 1995: 177). He visited Jerusalem in 1934 and 1935 as an Iraqi officer to propose his plan, but it was not taken up. His next visit to Jerusalem came in April 1936, when the idea of the general strike appeared to him and a tiny group of fellow travellers 'as a great means to begin the revolution' (Qawuqji 1995: 178). When Syria moved towards the framework of negotiations, he focused on Palestine, starting preparations in June 1936. Al-Qawuqji recounts a meeting with Al-Hajj Amin Al-Husseini in Baghdad in which the mufti asked for his support (Qawuqji 1995: 185). Al-Qawuqji wrote that *mujahidin* volunteers from Iraq, Jabal Druze, Jabal Lubnan, Damascus, Homs and Hama were gathering by early August to fight *jihad* in Palestine.

On 25 August, these forces fired their first shots from hidden positions at British aircraft in the Jabal Jaraysh, and claimed to bring down two of them. Contacts between these ex-Ottoman officers and village bands were facilitated by the renegade, urban sons of notables, for example the ex-Istiqlal party figure and formidable organizer Akram Zu'aytir (Nimr 1990: 55–6). Al-Qawuqji himself thought that Palestinians only came to trust him after his men took fatalities in action (Qawuqji 1995: 209). Al-Qawuqji's memoirs celebrates the moment in early October 1936 when he and his men discovered that they could take on tanks, previously considered formidable, and come out on top (Qawuqji 1995: 236).

The British Peel Commission, publishing in 1937, gives an adequate list of the reasons behind the mobilization of many who stepped into collective action:

[F]irst, the desire of the Arabs for national independence; secondly, their antagonism to the establishment of the Jewish National Home in Palestine, quickened by their fear of Jewish domination. Among contributory causes were the effect on Arab opinion of the attainment of national independence by 'Iraq, Trans-Jordan, Egypt, Syria and the Lebanon; the rush of Jewish immigrants escaping from Central and Eastern Europe; the inequality of opportunity enjoyed by Arabs and Jews respectively in placing their case before Your Majesty's Government and the public; the growth of Arab mistrust; Arab alarm at the continued purchase of Arab land by the intensive character and the 'modernism' of Jewish nationalism; and lastly the general uncertainty, accentuated by the ambiguity of certain phrases in the Mandate, as to the ultimate intentions of the Mandatory Power (Palestine Royal Commission Report 1937: 363).

It was indeed these reasons for mobilization that had played crucial roles in the widely varying contentious projects which had come into being throughout the 1920s and 1930s. But the diverse contentious projects and their leaderships were united by the banners of nationalism and independence during 1936–7. Their activism was enough to force a thorough reconsideration of the British position in the country and – as we saw above – a by no means completely erroneous view of why it was that Palestinian Arabs were alienated by the Mandate. The dominant bloc had been forced to pay attention, and Orientalist cliché was given less play. In October 1936, the British asked for a truce, winning the backing for negotiations of Arab rulers such as King Abdullah of Transjordan – who wanted territory in Palestine to be the 'West Bank' of his new, but small, East Bank kingdom. The Arab Higher Committee, winning (fickle) assurances from Arab states, called off the general strike, and hoped for independence at the hands of a British re-evaluation. The turn to diplomacy paved the way for the end of this phase of the uprising. Armed operations in the countryside drew to a close, some very reluctantly where trust for the British was scant indeed.

Matters were now in the hands of the British, as they had been several times before. The Peel Commission was appointed in 1936, to investigate the 'causes of the unrest' in Mandate Palestine. The Royal Commission published its report in July 1937. It concluded that the Mandate was unworkable and must be abolished. It recommended partition, proposing an independent Jewish state on the coastal plain from the south and much of Galilee in the north and an Arab state in the remainder. The British were angling for the post-independence support of both entities, imagining that an opportunistic Arab leadership could be made to play ball. The uprising of 1936–7 may have forced the British empire to reconsider drastically, but the partition was a heavy blow to the Arab independence movement which was fundamentally based on the rejection of a Jewish state on Arab-Palestinian land – as the British themselves seem to have known in the Peel Commission. If this principle were to be sacrificed, the credibility of a notable leadership, already under strain, would be shattered, and with it the cohesion of the movement. Moreover, with growing peasant dispossession and activism since 1933 (and above all since 1936), Palestinian activism had become ever-more linked to the fate of the countryside. And the partition scheduled second-class existence at best, and dispossession and murder at worst, for the hundreds of thousands of Palestinian Arabs slated to live in the Jewish state.

Amid news of partition, which carried with it an implicit logic of ethnic cleansing, the many guerrilla bands based in villages in the countryside were reconstituted, and operations increased rapidly in October 1937. These groups forged ahead with or without the mufti's notable leadership, which although staggered by the blow of partition as well as by exile and imprisonment, formed the Central Committee for Jihad, under 'Izzat Darwaza (Anderson 2013: 869ff.), which furnished weapons and money, operated mostly in exile, and exercised varying degrees of control over often independent rebel commanders. The initiative on the ground was with the countryside, where activism was imbued with a strong sense of independence and honour, but had little developed ideological or programmatic content (Anderson 2013: 1006). Rebels continued to swear loyalty to the mufti, nonetheless, in their drive for an independent Arab-Palestine; the mufti reciprocated, backing the rebels 'unreservedly' as late as January 1939 (Anderson 2013: 1104–5). The movement was

a mélange of contending directions: the authoritarian impulses of the field commanders *qua* governors and of ambitious sub-commanders; the contrary drive towards an efficient, independent judiciary; shades of an Islamic reform project (with discomfort for those outside the orthodoxy, including minorities); social reform and uplift of the impoverished and disenfranchised; and a streak of opportunism by rogue rebels and by other predatory forces intent on profit, exploitation, and banditry (Anderson 2013: 1149).

By the summer of 1938, 'rebel bands controlled much of the hill country and many towns throughout Palestine' (Lockman 1996: 260) and British administration was driven out (Anderson 2013: 1006ff.). At the height of the uprising, the rebels numbered 9,000–10,000 men according to Arab sources, 3,000 operating full time in rural areas, 1,000 operating full time in the towns, and, on their flanks, 6,000 auxiliaries in villages and among the Bedouin (Nimr 1990: 133). The nationalist revolutionaries aimed to drive out the British and the settlers, by direct action, bypassing and usurping the political channels of the urban nationalists and creating their own legal and administrative institutions. They declared moratoriums on rents and debts. They imposed the kufiyya and the veil on the towns – to move undetected, to express solidarity, to express a class conflict, and to enforce female sexual propriety in Islamic mode. The 'development of rebel institutions from intelligence to the courts system were instrumental to the rebellion's flourishing and to its success against the colonial regime' (Anderson 2013: 1010). They added up to a 'nascent counter-state' (Anderson 2013: 1010). De-centralized organizing was as much an asset as a hindrance in the early stages of the rising as '[l]ocalized, migratory, and loosely interconnected rebel formations using flexible tactics and, operating with the support of great swathes of the public, brought the colonial state to the brink of collapse' (Anderson 2013: 1011–12).

The guerrillas' repertoire included cutting telephone lines, railways and roads; the seizure of government property; disruption to the Iraq Petroleum Company pipeline; damage to property, and sniping and attacks on troops and Jewish settlements and quarters; armed robbery; abduction; and assassination and attempted assassination (Bowden 1975: 153). There were numerous attacks on Jewish settlers and Jewish property, as well as on British 'installations, transport, communications, and personnel' (Lockman 1996: 240). Women played important roles in stitching together the infrastructure of the revolt. One female activist later recalled that '[m]ainly we prepared food and took it to the fighters because the men couldn't move around a freely as we could, and we acted as couriers and collected money for the movement' (cited in Irving 2012: 91). Women also supported families made destitute by the imprisonment or death of male breadwinners.

In place of urban leaders and programmes, popular poets and poetry played a role in stitching together the mobilization and raising the transcendent morale of fighters. Ibrahim Tuqan, Abd Al-Rahim Mahmoud and Abd Al-Karim Al-Karmi were the most well known of these peripatetic figures, who praised the armed struggle, criticized the traditional leadership, and wove words against land sales. Men like Nouh Ibrahim moved throughout 'the rural areas, singing their poetry in a language which was simple enough to recite and spread' (Nimr 1990: 87).

The uprising drew strength from sub-state connections to the Arab world beyond the Mandate. Funds came to support the strike from other parts of the Mashriq and Egypt. The most important supplies of arms came from Syria, Lebanon and Transjordan. Arms that were used in the Syrian revolt, some of which were smuggled from Palestine at that time, were now smuggled back to Palestine. Certain Bedouin played an important role here. Renowned smugglers included Ahmad Al-Zinati, prince of the Al-Ghazawiyah tribe. In the Jordan valley there was easy traffic between Palestine and Syria, largely due to the help of a Syrian nationalist and friend of Al-Qawuqji, Adel Al-'Azmeh. He was General Director of the Interior Ministry responsible for border guards, who turned a blind eye to the arms traffic. As Darwazah put it:

The four countries of *bilad al-sham* became one, as far as the revolt and the rebels were concerned, with no customs, no police, no army patrols, and no passports between them (cited in Nimr 1990: 144–9).

Fighters and volunteers came from around the Mashriq. Bowden writes, rather disapprovingly, that Al-Qawuqji was a Syrian, and that the 'gangs' involved 'mixed contingents of Palestinians, Syrians, Iraqis, Druzes and Trans-Jordanians' (Bowden 1975: 157; Nimr 1990: 96). Some of these were ex-Ottoman soldiers and officers, who were now officers in the Syrian or the Iraqi army. Some were veterans of the Syrian revolt.

Eventually, after the appeasement of Nazi Germany at Munich made it possible, British forces came to outnumber those of the rebels by ten to one. The uprising was defeated by force. '[M]assive repression, including collective punishment and aerial and artillery bombardment of insurgent villages' (Lockman 1996: 260), the dynamiting of whole neighbourhoods in towns (such as in Jenin), house demolitions, the destruction of food-supplies, and massacres, coupled with mass incarceration, concentration camps, carceral searches, and torture, allowed the gradual return of British control (Anderson 2013: 1054ff.). Just as in the Rif mountains, the imperial foe was capable of putting so many troops on the ground that eventually the insurgents, who were increasingly losing the support of the towns, were destroyed. Just as in the Rif mountains, relatively small numbers of lightly armed men embedded in the surrounding population were able to hold off the concentrated might of an occupying empire. But they were ground down. The costs in bloodshed, misery and the incapacity to continue with everyday life amid pass laws, curfews, food insecurity and so on were extremely high. Military defeats greatly exacerbated internal tensions and rivalries (Anderson 2013: 1015ff.). Effective de-centralization gave way to internal strife (Anderson 2013: 1020). Significant sections of the population had become weary and alienated by that point; rebel extortion, banditry, sectarian conflict with the less mobilized Druze, and abuse of the population by rebels became more common. Urban and educated nationalists had fallen into prison and exile by the autumn of 1938. The Nashashibis and their allies came out openly against the revolt, taking fright at its deepening social and economic content (Anderson 2013: 1012–13): they organized 'peace bands', which attacked the rebels and the villages that supported them. By the beginning of 1939, the uprising was in disarray.

What lay behind the Great Revolt of 1936–9 was not at all that irrational hatred of Arab or Muslim for Jew finally took concrete form, nor so much that smouldering class antagonisms finally came to the surface in a way that set the stage for a social revolution to come at some unspecified point in the future. It was more that the diverse strands of resistance (among urban notables, the educated middle class, and peasants) that had characterized the previous decade and a half came together. To these groups was added a layer of leadership and firepower contributed by ex-Ottoman officers and volunteers. This loose coalition was stitched together by the banners of neither Islam nor socialism, but of Arab independence against colonial partition and Zionist settlement alike. It was above all the latter – settler colonialism – that was decisive in paving the way for the mobilization of the settled peasantry, who suffered dispossession. Workers too suffered above all from settler colonialism, not capitalism. Some of those, for example, who participated in a train de-railment near Ras Al-Ain station on 14 October 1937 had been fired from the Majdal Yaba quarry. The Histadrut had been attempting, against 'vigorous resistance', to impose Jewish labour there since at least 1934. The resistance had failed by the end of 1936 when the Histadrut got its way, 400 Arab jobs were lost, and those who protested were arrested (Lockman 1996: 245). Settler colonialism and British coercion, not capitalism, formed the background to the direct actions of these men. The settled peasantry moved, as in Egypt in 1919, when its interests were directly threatened. In other words, the uprising of the peasantry was not above all about an inexorable process of capitalist development – which led in uneven directions in regard to relations of production on the land, and peasant interests, not to mention in regard to mobilization and political action itself. There was a reason why the analysis of the Palestine Communist Party, based on class, became less not more relevant in the context of the Great Revolt, which was about a colonial encounter based around dominion and violence at the collective level which the Comintern did not seem to understand at all, and the Palestine Communist Party never faced head on, assuming as it did that Jewish and Arab workers could unite against the real enemy, capitalism (Budeiri 2010: xiii–xx). The Great Revolt split the Palestine Communist Party on Jewish–Arab lines and ultimately spelled its collapse as a 'unified Arab–Jewish party' (Lockman 1996: 259). The demand for independence on national lines was the principle under which a mass movement could be united. This accounted for much of the significance of the national principle, which was thus not a creation of 'enlightened' elites nor a simple product of a long sociological preparation.

The uprising, however, was the partial cause of not one but two shifts in the policy of the British empire. The first was the policy of partition, adopted in 1937, which also involved the abolition of the Mandate. The second came in 1939, when the British were as quick to abandon the idea of partition as they had been to adopt it. They now declared that there was no longer a policy of promoting a Jewish National Home in Palestine, that restrictions on Jewish land purchases and immigration would be imposed, and that there would be an independent Palestinian state within ten years. The White Paper signalled the end of the basic alliance between the British and the Zionist movement that had been in place since 1917. It was the most decisive moment in the shift of the Zionist movement towards seeking patronage and protection from the United States. The British aimed to conciliate Arab states with European war in the offing (Lockman 1996: 261), a war in which Britain needed Iraq, Transjordan and especially Egypt.

There was also a Foreign Office fantasy that the Muslims 'of India and the whole of the Middle East would revolt on the eve of the European War of 1939' (Bowden 1975: 170). There was no such pan-Islamic movement in the region. Both changes of policy, nonetheless, involved a premise, that of a future independent Palestinian state. In other words, the uprising seemed to have won a 'great but limited achievement' in the view of 'Izzat Darwazah (paraphrased in Anderson 2013: 1125). Perhaps not wanting to repeat the error of the Wafd in Egypt in 1936, refusing to return to a politics of collaboration with the untrustworthy British, and gambling on a British defeat in the coming war, the mufti and the Arab Higher Committee, in spite of its greatly weakened position, rejected the White Paper, on the basis that it did not meet Arab demands. Where the stakes could hardly have been higher, the extent of the misjudgment here has been debated since (Achcar 2010: 138–40).

The problem was that in some respects the White Paper was merely empty words gesturing at Arab rulers amid the onset of war. What the British had done was destroy the movement in the countryside, arrest much of the urban movement, and went on to maintain links of collaboration with the Zionists during the war, even as Zionists themselves prepared to resist the British and its official policy in the aftermath. Unlike the armed struggles in Syria and Iraq, then, the one in Palestine was unable to generate a new political field involving intermediaries between British and Arab constituencies. Instead, it played into the hands of the Zionists, who now monopolized this role, and who were now inspired and provoked by the Palestinian exemplar of armed struggle, increasingly informed by the Iron Wall thesis of Jabotinsky's revisionist Zionism, and increasingly prone to seeing Palestinians as savages and terrorists (Anderson 2013: 1156ff.). By refusing to compromise, Hajj Amin became too dangerous for the British, who dropped him. Husseini's legacy was thus mixed, too radical for the British, and not necessarily capable of realizing the radical demands of subaltern constituencies. This weakness, emerging from the dynamics of contestation, rather than some inherent anti-Semitism, must form part of the explanation for why he set off to intensify contacts with Germany during the war, contacts that had begun in earnest with Germany's opposition to partition in 1937 (Achcar 2010: 137). In short, the concrete achievements of 1936–9 were drastically limited, and the road was open to the dispossession of 1948. Nonetheless, during 1936–9, the Palestinians had signalled their national existence as never before, and it was a legacy of much symbolic value in later struggles. Transgressive mobilization had made its mark. As Anderson concludes:

The 1930s era – beginning in 1929 if not slightly earlier – was a unique moment in Palestinian history under the Mandate. It was one of the rare periods of upheaval in the life of a society in which popular social forces rose to pre-eminence and non-elites were able, if very briefly, to redefine their own destiny (Anderson 2013: 1133).

Young Algerians and Messali Al-Hadj

There was no major armed struggle in Algeria between the wars. The imperial context from the 1900s to the 1940s in Algeria was completely different to that of Egypt and the Mashriq. The crisis of the Ottoman empire had little significance where Ottoman authority had been non-existent for generations. Colonial France, far from suffering a military defeat, as in 1871, was a victorious party in the First World War. Algeria, unlike much of the rest of the region, was not subject to invasion, partition or intensive war-time pressures linked to the mobilization of troops and materials. Nor did Britain or any other imperial power, unlike in regard to the Arab revolt, court any nationalist movement in the country. Third, French republicanism held out an assimilationist possibility to those high-status Muslim Algerians that were educated in French schools. These political and partly contingent factors help explain, more effectively than forms of causation linked directly to socio-economic change, why Algeria was less the scene of a powerful nationalist upsurge in the immediate aftermath of the First World War.

While the remnants of rural, Islamic revivalist, neo-Sufi, and heterodox resistance to French settler colonization in Algeria were ebbing away, the first mobilizations of the post-1910 period drew on a different sociological and ideological milieu. Far from challenging the French system from without, they emerged in many ways from within the French system itself, seeking representation in the state. The new activism was based around a 'small nucleus of French-educated Muslims who had nearly been integrated into French life who found the remaining [formidable] obstacles to their participation in political and economic activities intolerable' (Quandt 1969: 2). The 1912 manifesto of the Young Algerians, drawing inspiration in part from the Young Turks, who were mostly urban and educated like them, bore a liberal and constitutional stamp, calling for an 'end to the Indigénat, equal taxation, enlarged suffrage for Muslims and representation in the National Assembly' (Evans and Phillips 2007: 42). France moved to conscript Algerian Muslims for the first time in February 1912 – and this was the provocation around which the new movement mobilized. Led by Emir Khaled, a graduate of St Cyr, and a grandson of Abd Al-Qadir, the Young Algerians argued not to reject conscription and with it French rule *in toto*; on the contrary, they suggested that, in return for conscription, the French must be prepared to give citizenship rights to Muslims (Evans and Phillips 2007: 42).

After the First World War, this liberal tradition persisted, strengthened by the sense of entitlement gained by those who sacrificed themselves for France during the First World War. There was supposed to be a *quid pro quo*: citizenship and a more thoroughgoing assimilation. As many as 173,000 Muslim Algerians served in the French army, 87,000 engaged in combat, and 25,000 were killed. 'A grateful French government intended to reward the Muslims, but the settlers forced Paris to retreat' (Abun-Nasr 1987: 328). The Young Algerian Emir Khaled was elected to Algiers municipal council in 1919, but was forced by a settler hate campaign into exile in France in 1923. The Fédération des Elus Indigènes, a coalition of independent elected officials, was founded in 1926. It called for citizenship rights, the abolition of the Indigénat, and native representation in parliament, 'deeply attached' as it was to 'what they saw as the progressive values of 1789' (Evans and Phillips 2007: 42).

The Young Algerians were urban, salaried middle classes and civil servants or professionals – doctors, pharmacists, and teachers. They were personified by Ferhat Abbas (b. 1899). He was from Constantine, and a pharmacist. His father had been born a peasant but became a *caid* (local governor) and was honoured within the French colonial system. Ferhat Abbas, with 'his slicked-back hair and sharp-fitting suits ... ill at ease with Arabic and married to a French woman', had the demeanour of a 'well-heeled French bourgeois' (Evans and Phillips 2007: 42). The Young Algerians tended to come from relatively well-off backgrounds. They were the newly educated scions of those who had found a place in the French system. In sociological terms, there was a vast difference between these groups and those who had led the anti-colonial resistance throughout much of the nineteenth century. The Young Algerians maintained a non-nationalist stance until the late 1930s at least. Ferhat Abbas pronounced in an editorial in February 1936:

I will not die for the Algerian nation, because the notion of Algeria as a country does not exist. I have not found it. I have examined History, I have questioned the living and the dead, I have visited cemeteries; nobody spoke to me about it ... One cannot build on the wind (cited in Evans and Phillips 2007: 42).

The idea that Ferhat Abbas pursued, without building mass organizations to support it, was some form of autonomy for Algeria in a larger French union, stripped of its racial arrogance and exclusivism. Algerian liberals basically accepted the terms of an assimilationist *mission civilisatrice*, seeking participation and representation in the state.

It turned out, however, that one could 'build on the wind'. Or, more precisely, the innovative idea of the 1930s, that Algerian-Muslims formed a nation deserving self-determination, was to become a potent plank in the project uniting diverse constituencies that increasingly hegemonized the political field during the period and beyond.

Messali Al-Hadj (1898–1974) was the first Algerian activist to call unequivocally for national independence. He was the son of a shoemaker and small-holder from Tlemcen, educated in a local French primary school and who also worked on the land as a youth, during which he was an adherent of the Derkawa Sufi order. Through tireless mass mobilization, bouts in French and Algerian prisons, and his formidable qualities as a speaker, he had become by the late 1940s one of the key symbols of Algerian nationalism. In 1917, he did military service at Bordeaux. After the war, he went to Paris, frequented the French Communist Party in its revolutionary phase, and married a French woman. He founded the Étoile Nord-Africaine in 1926. Organizing among the 100,000 Algerians (many from the Kabylie region) in and around Paris, the Étoile Nord-Africaine had 3,500 members by 1927, when links with the French Communist Party were severed. The Étoile Nord-Africaine was banned in France in 1929.

Messali Al-Hadj's programme was distinctive for its outright assault on the French colonial order under the banners of nationalism and its attention to social questions, and its use of mass mobilization. Islam and Arabic were seen as central to Algerian national identity. The

Étoile Nord-Africaine sought the abolition of the discriminatory legal code (the Indigénat), the freedom of the press, a National Assembly for Algeria, the return of confiscated land to the peasantry, the national-ization of industry, the withdrawal of all French troops, and immediate independence.

Messali Al-Hadj made a return to Algeria in 1936. When he reiter-ated his demand for independence at conventions in Algiers in 1936 and 1937, his slogans 'earned a tumultuous welcome from the crowds' (Evans and Phillips 2007: 47). He brought his newly founded Parti du Peuple Algérien to Algeria under the slogan 'Land to the Peasants'. The slogan of the party, announced at its founding in March 1936 in front of 300 workers in Nanterre, was 'No assimilation, no separation, but emancipation of the Algerian people' (Stora 1987: 20–1). These moves attached the land question to the question of national independence, and within the frame of new organizing vehicles, the political party and not the Sufi order, for the first time. At the same time, strike action indicated the possibilities in regards to those who might organize such new forms of popular politics. A wave of strikes, for example, began on 9 June 1936 with the occupation of factories in Algeria. There was also a strike of agricultural workers in the Mitidja (Stora 1987: 16).

An Islamic modernist current in the tradition of Al-Afghani and Abduh, opposing both imperialism on the one side and superstition and *marabout*ism on the other and adopting a nuanced view of West-ern civilization, was at work in Algeria after the First World War. The Association of Algerian Ulama, founded by Shaykh Abdullatif Soltani (b. 1902) in 1931, was led by Arabophone clerics, graduates of the Islamic universities of Zaytuna in Tunis and Al-Azhar in Cairo, where they had been in the orbit of the Muslim Brotherhood, links with which were maintained by figures like Soltani during the 1930s. A key figure was Shaykh Abdelhamid Ben Badis (b. 1889), educated in Tunisia and Egypt, and leading a circle of religious thinkers back in Algeria, founded two theological journals – *Al-Muntaqid* (*The Censor*) and *Ash-Shihab* (*The Meteor*) in 1925. This current was vitally important for the idea of Algeria as a nation, and involved the Sunni *ulema* in a way that analogous efforts in Egypt never did, proving that there was nothing inherent in Sunnism that prevented this kind of mobilization. As Ben Badis claimed, in rebutting Abbas's claim 'Islam is my religion, Arabic is my language and Algeria is my country'.

'This Algerian and Muslim nation is not France ... It does not want to become part of France.' These Islamic modernists also attacked the folk Islam of the *marabouts* and often that of the Sufi orders as heretical, degenerate, superstitious and linked to colonialism. They rejected the distinction between Berber and Arab, who they maintained had been 'United by Islam for more than ten centuries'. They sustained a puritanical view, condemning alcohol, tobacco, music and dancing. Their network of schools had an important impact on tens of thousands of Algerians, although they were dissolved by the French authorities in 1956 (Evans and Phillips 2007: 43–5; Quandt 1969: 36). This thinking worked to diminish the powers of the Sufi orders that had once derived so much from an earlier version of neo-Sufi Islamic renewal.

The moment of imperial vacillation and division in the dominant bloc that accompanied the election of Léon Blum's Popular Front government in France, a political opening followed by a clampdown, acted first as an opportunity then as a provocation on the Algerian scene, and led to a new tone from 1937 onwards. Major hopes were raised on the Algerian side with the election of the Popular Front in 1936. Messali Al-Hajj was amnestied. He made a 'triumphant return [to Algeria] and was acclaimed by the masses'. A political reform envisaged that 5,000 out of 6 million Muslim Algerians would obtain citizenship and voting rights. Even these extremely modest assimilationist reforms were opposed by settlers, and, when the Popular Front government collapsed in 1938, the Blum–Viollette bill went with it, Viollette being later vilified in racist terminology as 'Viollette the Arab'. The Muslim Congress, calling for unity, and comprised of liberals, the modernist *ulema* and the communists, supported the Blum–Viollette reforms. For Ferhat Abbas, they symbolized a fraternal France which through a grand gesture would 'open the way for assimilation'. With their failure, 'it would be very difficult to resuscitate assimilation as a credible way forward' (Evans and Phillips 2007: 47). After 1937, a more thoroughgoing nationalism rapidly began to gain ground 'especially amongst the working and lower middle classes in the large town and cities'. Al-Hajj spoke of 'neither assimilation nor separation, but emancipation', feeling that his faith in reform by the metropolitan Left had been dangerously misguided. As Quandt has it, those involved in this kind of activism were in the process of discovering the power of mass organization, 'propaganda' and 'agitation' – repertoires that the liberals did not have (Quandt 1969: 43).

Important in the early 1920s, the communists did not play much of a role in Algeria during the inter-war years. The Algerian Communist Party was officially created in 1936, being preceded by the Algerian section (founded in 1920) of the French Communist Party. Initially, support for the Party was drawn from settlers and pro-independence elements in the 1920s. The stance of the party became even more ambiguous by 1936, and more concerned with fighting fascism than French settler colonialism. The party did win a significant number of Muslim members after the Second World War.

The Second World War made French rule in Algeria more repressive and added new reasons to mobilize. War-time security measures led to the arrest of many activists. Messali Al-Hadj, for one, was sentenced to sixteen years' hard labour in March 1941. Of crucial importance was the massacre of thousands at Sétif. On 8 May 1945, just as France was enjoying liberation from Nazi Germany, crowds of Muslim-Algerians demonstrated for their own independence, especially in Sétif and Guelma, 'carrying Algerian flags and calling for the release from prison of Messali' (Quandt 1969: 51). Those who had fought and died for France against the axis powers now sought the reward of independence to which they believed they were also entitled. A peaceful demonstration became a battle with French security forces. 'For days Muslims were hunted down, strafed from attacking airplanes, and bombarded from French naval vessels along the coast' (Quandt 1969: 51). The repression was extensive. For many Algerians, it revealed the violence of French imperialism and the hollowness of its professed ideals of equality, fraternity and liberty. As Kateb Yacine (1929–89), a well-known Algerian novelist, essayist and activist, put it:

My sense of humanity was affronted for the first time by the most atrocious sights ... The shock which I felt at the pitiless butchery that caused the deaths of thousands of Muslims, I have never forgotten. From that moment my nationalism took definite form (cited in Evans and Phillips 2007: 52).

It is clear here that repression itself, enacted in the course of political struggle, provided a reason for mobilization.

When the violence came to an end, perhaps 100 Europeans had been killed, alongside perhaps 10,000 or more Muslim Algerians. As the sub-prefect of Sétif boasted to a youthful Francis Jeanson, a Sartrean French intellectual who ended up organizing assistance to the FLN in France after 1957: 'They wanted to get us, those Arabs! Well, we're the

ones who got them! A thousand to one, yes, a thousand to one.' As
Jeanson continued 'it didn't occur to him that he could shock me by
talking that way! That day, the sick feeling inside me became a revolt'
(emphasis removed, Ulloa 2007: 142). As Jeanson noted: 'Their racism
was radical, flawless, so deep-seated that you ran the risk of surprising
them if you made some allusion to it' (Ulloa 2007: 141).

The Algerian settler community ruled by coercion not consent. Unlike
the French in Lebanon, or the British in 1940s Iraq, they had no use for
political intermediaries. There was no place for assimilationist reformism, and no lever for nationalism to advance as it did in Syria, for
example, under the National Bloc in the 1930s, as there was no crack
within the dominant bloc in the settler community that would admit it.
Instead, the cohesion of the dominant bloc was guaranteed by exclusion
and racism. Against this wall of power, even mass mobilization by
figures such as Messali Al-Hadj was ambivalent. It could build up an
immense sense of nationhood in a mobilized population at large, use
new forms of organization and repertoires of contention, but its leaderships were vulnerable to repression and their inability to deliver concrete gains to their constituencies. It was no wonder that defectors from
parties and mass movements started to emerge in the late 1940s, paving
the way for the launch of the armed struggle on 1 November 1954.

Nationalists, Shi'a, peasants, workers and communists under the monarchy in Iraq

In Iraq, still a de-centralized and heterogeneous society, the establishment of Faysal's new state, and its subsequent development and centralization, were by no means a bloodless process. The Shi'a clergy, so
vital to the uprising of 1920, were largely left out of the new, Sunni-
dominated dispensation. There were two tribal rebellions in the Middle
Euphrates (1935 and 1936) and one in Diwaniyya (1937), as well as
the 1935 rebellion of the Shaykh of Barzan (Batatu 1978: 467–8).
There were in addition in 1935 and 1936 tribal protests against big
landlords and conscription in the Middle Euphrates. The Iraqi general,
the Kurd Baqir Sidqi, now ordered the use of planes to bomb the
tribespeople (Wiley 1992: 22) – turning the weapons of international
and imperial warfare inwards. Iraq also saw important movements
against state control and centralization by newly constituted 'minorities'. There were Kurdish rebellions in 1919, 1924, 1927, 1930 and

1931 (Batatu 1978: 467–8). From the 1920s onwards, Shi'a constituencies, re-thinking their rejectionist position which only enhanced Sunni
dominance in the state, increasingly demanded 'representation in the
government and the civil service in proportion to their numerical weight
among the population, and struggled over the nature of education in the
state school system as well as the definition of Arab and Iraqi nationalism' (Nakash 1994: 109). The identification of communal identity with
the apparatuses of state power, a distinctive feature of nationalism in
the region as elsewhere, was a formidable driver of new forms of conflict
against the central authorities, as minorities were newly imagined and
counted, and as they encountered new forms of exclusion.

The client monarchy, while obtaining formal independence in 1932,
was increasingly damned as a puppet of the British. It also failed to
solve the many new social and economic problems that the country
faced. The young, upstart radicals of the 1910s (such as Nuri Al-Sa'id)
gradually became the placemen, feudalists, and hack politicians of the
1950s. Protests and risings against the failures of the government to
bring real independence to Iraq became much more frequent after
1945. The British invaded the country in the wake of the pro-Axis
Rashid Ali coup of 1941, confirming where the reins of power lay
ultimately. As elsewhere, the strategic exigencies of the Second World
War exposed some of the polite fictions about independence that elites
liked to foster.

The Wathbah of 1948 was 'a mass urban uprising against the
monarchic government in the wake of the signing of the Portsmouth
Agreement of January 1948' (Batatu 1978: 467–8), where grievances
were compounded by 'mass hunger'. Indian independence in 1947 had
encouraged nationalists in Iraq (Batatu 1978: 547), and Lebanese and
especially Syrian independence had raised expectations. The Portsmouth Agreement was intended to re-define Iraq's relationship to
Britain at a time of heightened nationalist sentiment in the country
and more generally. In the event, it was a major disappointment, being
concluded with a minimum of consultation and merely confirming
British overlordship (Batatu 1978: 547). In Baghdad, demonstrations
and strikes combined with a mass march. After murderous fire, a more
general rising ensued. The police lost control. On 21 January, the
Regent openly disavowed the treaty. This was too little, too late, and
the rising continued. The Istiqlal Party withdrew, taking with it perhaps one-third of the crowd – especially those who were suspicious of

the communist links to Moscow. But most stayed on in a protest that now took on, under the leadership of the communists, a more socially revolutionary character, amid calls for a Republic and a 'People's Revolution' (Batatu 1978: 553). The *intifada* of 1952 was 'a *wathbah* of lesser proportions' (Batatu 1978: 467–8), while 'popular discontent had dug a deeper course owing to the loss of Palestine' (Batatu 1978: 665) and after demonstrations in Baghdad in autumn 1951, by workers and activists, protesting Nuri Al-Sa'id's 'government by starvation' (Batatu 1978: 664).

Amid this nationalist ferment, workers and peasants increasingly came forward to contest the new political field. Older struggles over customs, rights, dues, tyranny and justice were recast in new more ideological terms, and peasants and workers started to create links to various urban leaderships, and increasingly drew on new ideological forms. Batatu lists eight rural uprisings in Iraq between 1947 and 1958. In 1947, there was a rising of peasants in 'Arbat (a Kurdish village to the southeast of Sulaimaniyya) against their landlord. In 1952, there was an uprising of the peasant-tribesmen of Al-Azairij against their overlords in the province of Amarah. In 1953, a rising of peasant-tribesmen of Diza'i took place in the province of Arbil. In the same year there were risings among the peasants of Warmawah sub-district in the Sulaimaniyyah province, and of the Hurain Shai-khan sub-district in the Diyalah province. In 1954, there was a rising of the peasants of Shamiyyah in the Middle Euphrates. In 1955, there was a peasant rising among the Bani Zuraij at Rumaithah in Diwaniyya province. Finally, in April 1958, there was a rising of peasants in the Dagharah-Rumaithah region in Diwaniyya province (Batatu 1978: 467–8).

Batatu argues convincingly that these rural uprisings were quite different to the tribal uprisings of the inter-war period. They were against their shaykhs, not with them:

The rural rebellions of the last decade of the monarchy were of an entirely different character [to the tribal rebellions of the inter-war period]. They were rebellious not under shaykhs but against them ... and were made by tribesmen whose customary ideas and norms of life had been shaken to their foundation (Batatu 1978: 469).

These risings were in part provoked by the usurpation of communal domains by shaykhs and their acquisition of private property rights.

This meant the end of 'life-furthering' patriarchal relations between shaykhs and tribe members and instead created 'an overlord–quasi-serf relationship which chained ... [peasants] to distress and privation'. This shift also included that from self-sufficiency to sale for the market (Batatu 1978: 469). Peasants were responding to major violations in the tribal and rural moral economy, violations which had taken on a systemic character. Shaykhs had been stitched into the dominant bloc in the state via property rights and position, and their tribes neutered in the process. This was a novel situation for peasant-tribesmen. The systemic and novel nature of their grievances created an opening for urban activists, mostly communists and in 'certain instances' National Democrats (Batatu 1978: 469), who sought to offer new solutions tied to new ideologies. Communists were evident in Amarah, Kut and Sulaimaniyya uprisings. National Democrats were present in the Diwaniyya unrest (Batatu 1978: 469, n. 3). While such risings may have been novel in Iraq in the 1940s, there were commonalities with past mobilizations amid estate-formation, the entrenchment of private property rights, and alliances between land-owners and the central state. The difference in Iraq in the 1950s was the link to new urban forms of activism.

The rising of the peasants at 'Arbat, a village in the Kurdish province of Suleimaniyya was about the violation of customary practices and old regulations, by a land-owning shaykh who imposed dues, exactions and burdens not seen before. He had taken possession of the village in violation of peasant rights. The state had enabled this by guaranteeing the shaykh's property. The peasants then drove the shaykh's men out of the village – but were then severely punished. In the wake of petitions and demonstrations by peasants and communists, the land settlement committee agreed that the peasants owned the land. But the state was unable to enforce this because of the shaykh and his armed men locally. The Wathbah of January 1948 made the political climate more favourable. After intensive mobilization, the shaykh was ordered to leave the village by the government. However, the Communist Party cells were smashed by the government in autumn 1948, and the local *ulema* interceded on behalf of the land-owner, forcing the peasants into a compromise in return for which they obtained their small-holding land rights (Batatu 1978: 610–14).

In late 1952, peasants belonging to the Arab Shi'a tribe of Al-Azairij in Amara in the South dared to defy their land-owning shaykhs. In this case, the government had taken a decision to alienate the 'customary lands of the tribe to the dominant shaykhs and their families' (Batatu 1978: 664). This contravention of custom and tribal convention, and the accompanying betrayal of justice by the government, aroused the 'bitter feelings of the peasants', who refused to pay dues to their tribal leaders. Their stand, it would appear, had the support of the tribal *sirkal* – an inferior chief who had direct charge of cultivation. On 5 November 1952, there was a confrontation during which the shaykh's men killed two peasants. In return, the peasants burned one of the shaykh's armed retainers to death. The tribal chief called up the mobile police force, which 'brutally put down the rebellion', killing many (Batatu 1978: 664). Here communists played no role. In contrast, communists had a direct hand in an uprising in early 1953 in the north, in Arbil among peasants of the Kurdish tribe of Diza'i. The rising was brutally suppressed, at least ten peasants being killed and a few thousands driven from their homes (Batatu 1978: 664).

The primary force behind this 'deep-seated agrarian discontent', as Batatu calls it, seems to have been the way new forms of exploitation were driving a coach and horses through notions of justice, custom and regulation. This was not above all about urban communists arriving to enlighten a backward and superstitious peasantry as to their true interests. Instead, cherished tribal conventions and customary codes were being overturned, the justice of the government was lacking, and property rights established or promised to small-holders almost a century before by the land codes of the Ottoman Tanzimat, were being usurped or withheld by large land-owners. The source of contention was in defence of a rural order of justice, property rights and custom under threat by the actions of its erstwhile leaders and protectors – while here and there communist activism provided an organizational and ideological banner which could shape perceptions of how now to proceed, especially where other organized forces, *ulema* and Sufi orders, for example, were too distant or inadequate to deal with the new questions. Alliances were formed with urban communists, and in some cases their ideas resonated with rural conditions, aspirations and practices, especially where the older forms of leadership were showing their dereliction. Party cells were formed, but then smashed by state repression.

In Iraq the main wave of workers' strike action took place in the 1940s and early 1950s. This involved strikes over wages and conditions by workers in port and railway installations. The Communist Party concentrated its mobilization here because these installations were strategic and foreign-owned (Batatu 1978: 616–27). In other words, class and nation could be made to coincide – a potent mobilizing force. These strikes achieved some concessions, but in Iraq they were typically met with heavy repression. There was an eight-day wage strike involving more than a thousand workers in the strategically significant Schalchiyya workshops in Baghdad in April 1944. A recently established (1944) union for these workers was suppressed (Batatu 1978: 616–27). In Basra port, there were strikes in May 1947 and April and May 1948. This was a trial of strength with the port authorities, but the union was crushed. The protests returned. On 23–7 August 1952, 'widespread protests paralysed the port and water and electric installations at Basrah'. The subsequent repression led to the deaths of three workmen and injury to twenty-nine others (Batatu 1978: 664). On the oil-fields at Kirkuk, there was a strike in July 1946 involving some 5,000 workers. Some wage rises accompanied heavy repression (Batatu 1978: 622). At K3, a pumping station near Haditha, a strike began on 23 April 1948. The workers undertook a march on Baghdad which continued into May. The protest ended in repression and arrests (Batatu 1978: 625). In June 1952, there was a strike, a clash, and casualties at the British military base of Habbaniyyah (Batatu 1978: 664).

In these strikes, grievances over pay and conditions, rooted in preexisting codes and expectations of fair treatment and respect, joined together with new forms of urban mobilization, and new socioeconomic settings. The strikes signalled that a basically colonial economy might not last forever without some significant changes. The violent response of the authorities spoke of an incapacity to think about what kinds of changes and concessions might be necessary to transform the situation.

Communism in Iraq, more successful there than anywhere else in the Arab world, can best be seen not as an epiphenomena of objective transformation in the economy and in class relations, but as a mobilizing socio-political project, integrating diverse adherents in new ways around new principles and poles of identity – one which drew on socio-economic change, but was not ultimately driven by it. Communism was a forceful, popular movement to be reckoned with, but it was about organization, leadership, politics and ideology as much as it was an outgrowth of changing class conditions. The fate and fortunes of communism in Iraq did not march in lock step with the development of capitalism in the last instance: instead they were a matter of ideas and models, international alignments, imperialism, opportunities and threats on the local political scene, and the possibilities of mobilization and the initiatives undertaken by leaderships in Iraq. Communism was one of the key ideological dynamics in Iraq in the 1950s, just as it played a wider role in the region from the 1940s to the 1970s.

Communism in Iraq mobilized a highly diverse sociology. Class was important, but class here did not involve the rise of a new doubly free wage labour stripped of other means of subsistence, and coming to dominate the ranks of the communist revolutionaries. Class relations were important, but far more complex. Batatu argued that the strongest anchorage of the communists lay among the students, not the proletariat (Batatu 1978: 614). But communism was not just a creature of the urban students educated in new European-style schools. A younger generation of Shi'a, excluded from the political process, and searching for a political framework within which they could play a role in national politics, also 'can help explain the massive adherence of Shi'is to communism' (Nakash 1994: 132–3). Credit for reviving the party between 1949 and 1951 owed, on the other hand, to Baha'u-d-Din Nuri (b. 1927), the uneducated Kurdish son of a propertied religious teacher of Sulaimaniyya. As Batatu remarks, his 'grasp of theory was none too solid. His sentiments were rather simple – love for the Kurds and an unquestioning faith in the future of communism' (Batatu 1978: 662). The only school he had attended, as he wrote to his wife, was 'the forest with its huge rocks and high hills, and the savage valleys inhabited by wild boars'. But he left his native village in 1939, discovered communism in the schools of Sulaimaniyya, and adhered to the party in 1944. He acquitted himself well in the Wathba (Batatu 1978: 662). In this trajectory, too, we see the simplicity of the assimilation of communist movements to the rise of an urban, educated, middle class with a distinctive sociology. Instead, this important communist leader had a rural upbringing, no formal education, a religious background, and a Kurdish patriot to boot. What was important, however, was that Baha'u-d-Din Nuri at some point came into contact with communist ideas – which were able to inspire and organize and direct a certain set of basic impulses.

By the early 1950s, the hegemony of the generation of 1920 was in tatters – a fact partly measurable by the way the dominant bloc could only respond to protest with violence and expediency. The armed struggle of 1920 had helped to bring into being a new political field. The energies and initiatives associated with uprisings, and various urban leaderships, especially the communists, gave that field a new depth and meaning in the 1950s, and brought together a wide array of new forms of mobilization. The advent of Nasser in Egypt, however, offered a new model of collective action, especially for Iraq's officers.

The labour movement in Egypt, 1919–1936

The labour movement came of age in Egypt in 1919, becoming an important and permanent feature of the social and political landscape. Strikes established a definitive and routinized presence on the political scene, and were bolstered and transformed by established new forms of organization, unions, political parties, ideology, often organized by middle classes linked to the Wafd. Workers' actions were fortified and infused with new forms of class and nationalist consciousness. Labour strikes were often used by workers to demonstrate their support for larger nationalist movements, and to express the workers' own sense of nationalism. Workers facing low wages, abusive management practices, poor conditions, and job insecurity developed a wealth of experience in how to band together, raise demands, and undertake collective actions such as strikes, in ways that could and did lead to material improvements in their working lives, and made an important contribution to Egypt's nationalist movement.

A fairly wide variety of social groups and persons were involved in one way or another in organizing the labour movement and its primary repertoire, the strike. Wage-workers and employees in government-owned enterprises or major foreign-owned public utilities were particularly prominent. Artisans, such as bakers, and service-workers, such as cab-drivers, were also present at different times. During the wave of strikes of August 1919, both foreign and Egyptian workers mobilized together. Doctors, lawyers, journalists, intellectuals, poets and at least one prince were also involved in the activity of unions and parties linked to workers.

The key leaderships during the period in question, arguably, were two. On the one side were workers themselves, either organized informally, or elected to union boards, and often undertaking strike action in relatively spontaneous ways, without either union or party direction, and scattered in a way that was not centrally coordinated in different factories, plants and trades in Egypt's cities and towns. Of the thousands of strike actions that were undertaken in Egypt between 1919 and 1936, directly involving hundreds of thousands of workers, it seems likely that a great many were initiated and coordinated by those who worked with their hands, whether or not they had acceded to take on union functions, and whether or not most of these workers' names are unknown. The first strike in the huge Misr Spinning and Weaving Company mill (est. 1928) in Mahalla Al-Kubra, for example, was initiated by a then unknown mechanical loom operator, who later became a communist, who simply stopped his machine on the orders of no one while an engineer was walking through his section (Beinin 2001: 105). The wave of strikes in March–April 1919 and in August 1919 all preceded rather than followed the formation of unions. Nationalist strikes – of which there were dozens in March–April 1919 – began when workers without formal organization walked off the job. Thousands of un-unionized workers went on strike between late 1919 and 1922 (Beinin and Lockman 1998: 126). The sturdiest unions were those built from below, not those imposed from above (Beinin and Lockman 1998: 169).

On the other hand, from 1919 until at least the late 1930s, the labour movement was in many ways led, or controlled by (or at least acquiescent to) liberal nationalism. While this had meant the National Party before 1914, and continued to do so to some extent in Alexandria thereafter, after 1919 it referred above all to the nationalist notables of the Wafd. The latter developed, in the 1920s, a ramified national presence through local committees which coordinated with, and in many ways led, trade unions in Egypt's cities and in almost every provincial town. In the 1920s, under Joseph Rosenthal and the Alexandria Group, communism as a political, organizational and ideological current 'made some impact on some of the Egyptian intelligentsia, a few trade unions, and a small number of workers' (Amin 1987: 433). Yet, when communists organized a series of strikes and factory sit-ins in Alexandria in February–March 1924 they were repressed by the Wafd itself, and were not to re-emerge until the late 1930s.

Most workers, most of the time, likely understood their collective actions in terms of a tenacious, popular moral economy, drawing on common sense and proverbial wisdom, and fragments of this or that worldview, suffused with a powerful nationalism (especially after 1919), and endowing them with both rights and obligations, entitlements and deferences. Workers asserted themselves with many diverse aspects of their moral economy. In the textile mill at Mahalla Al-Kubra, workers were upset because a switch to piece rates in the early 1930s implied that 'they're going to make us sweat blood . . . They haven't given us a raise or left us in peace. They've left us with our same miserable life' (cited in Beinin 2001: 105). In the same textile mill, systems of work discipline often appeared 'arbitrary, cruel, and calculated to break the workers' spirit and human dignity. The harsh system of fines deducted from workers' wages for even the most minute infraction, beatings of workers by foremen . . . appeared unreasonable to workers compared to the norms of their villages' (Beinin 2001: 107). Unmet promises made by management or the government in the course of labour negotiations, in turn, were a much-cited cause of mobilization, such as among the tramway workers of Cairo in the run-up to the strikes of August 1919 (Beinin and Lockman 1998: 110). Unfair dismissals were another major source of grievance.

For all the attempts by non-workers to hegemonize worker consciousness, it seems that this was only in part a limited endeavour for the majority of those who joined and organized strikes. In Mahalla Al-Kubra in the 1930s:

workers . . . had little confidence in and no identification with any of Egypt's Cairo-centred national institutions – the government, political parties or trade unions. They believed that bringing their problems to the attention of the government was useless: 'Who does the government belong to? We're in one valley and they're in another. Do we know any of them? What did they do when [our fellow worker] was seized and beaten to death?' (cited in Beinin 2001: 107).

Fikri Al-Khuli, indeed, the narrator in this case, marked his distance also from the callous *effendi* management in the mill: 'They must be different from us. All their lives they've lived apart from us. They live in palaces. They're sons of village headmen . . . No one has ever insulted them or beaten them. They've made their lives by beating up other people' (cited in Beinin 2001: 107).

Workers' pride in a worker identity in the 1920s and 1930s generally did not reside in the notion that workers comprised a revolutionary proletariat poised to enact communist revolution. Nor did it necessarily see workers as a distinct class whose material interests were fundamentally antagonistic to capitalists. To be a worker, more likely, especially after 1919, meant to take pride in one's contribution to building the nation – and to be steadfast against those who would despise their contribution. Hence the popular poem, penned by a worker who became a literary figure, of 1942: 'We are the Egyptian workers, we are the brave, A thousand salutes to you, oh Egypt, mother of all ... Workers are the secret of the beauty of cities ... We are the builders of your pyramids, oh sphinx' (cited in Beinin and Lockman 1998: 319). Such an identity was a powerful and strongly rooted one, and proved to be a force in tenacious forms of mobilization that ran considerable risks to life, limb and livelihood.

As Egyptians, workers, like other social groups, adhered to nationalism (and sometimes not), in its own right, as a political programme that could liberate the Egyptian nation from an imperialist occupation. Nationalism was also reinforced by working experiences, as 'class divisions coincided with ethnic or national divisions in the workplace' (Beinin and Lockman 1998: 90). Foreigners controlled their labour, meted out abusive treatment, enjoyed privileges they did not have, and were backed and protected by a legal, political and police regime underpinned by the British occupation. The wave of strikes of March–April 1919 was evidently saturated with nationalist feeling among the workers. Strikes in predominantly foreign-owned factories and companies were also very widespread throughout the period – although by no means the only kinds of strikes.

The Wafd, on the other hand, saw the workers in highly paternalistic colours. They reached out to the workers to bring them into the nationalist fold, to make them good and diligent citizens, to raise them up materially and morally, and to protect them against old age and sickness through mutual funds, and to teach them their rights and obligations. The worker should be, as a leading Wafdist put it, 'like a soldier on the field of battle ... We want him properly behaved, moderate in his habits, sincere ... pious ... [and respectful of] law and order' (Beinin 2001: 89). In the wake of the wave of strikes of 1919, the Wafd came to see the utility of workers' unions as, in the words of a leading Wafdist, 'a powerful weapon which should not be under-estimated' (Beinin and Lockman 1998: 104), a constituency that could be mobilized as a bargaining lever, not a constituency that had 'legitimate goals and interests of its own' (Beinin and Lockman 1998: 105). In the Wafd's eyes, workers' collective action should be directed towards bolstering nationalism under the leadership of the Wafd.

The key ideological basis of the alliance between the Wafd and the workers was nationalism. In regard to ways of life, material interests and common sense, these groups were very far apart. There is no reason, indeed, to believe that workers, who, even while seeing the instrumental benefits of alliances with wealthy groups linked to government, internalized the worldview of them held by the Wafd. The alliance was forged, as Beinin and Lockman emphasize, in the uprising of March–April 1919, when both movements came of age in ways that were very closely bound (Beinin and Lockman 1998: 119). It was an alliance that played a crucial role throughout the inter-war period. The workers made use of the Wafd in building their instruments of collective bargaining, while the Wafd made use of the workers as a powerful force that could be used as leverage in bargaining within that state. As Beinin and Lockman emphasize, during the period from the early 1920s until the later 1930s, labour activism tended to tick upwards at times when the Wafd was in power, when repression was relaxed, and a certain kind of politics inaugurated, and then to fall back when the opponents of the Wafd formed governments (Beinin and Lockman 1998: 133, 172; see also Abbas 1967; Izz Al-Din 1967–71; Beinin 1989). This pattern continued until the late 1930s.

Women's movements in Egypt, 1899–1956

From the 1890s onwards, there were growing debates over gender roles and sexuality in the press in Egypt, Istanbul and elsewhere in the region. The domestic and child-rearing 'duties' of the woman, the question of the veil and of seclusion, the right of a woman to education, the legal rights of women, especially in matters of marriage, divorce and inheritance and the extent of female involvement in the economy, and in public and political life were all increasingly a matter of debate, and then charitable, social and political activism. Established practices around masculine domination and gender roles were challenged in new ways and women themselves took on new roles. Women and their defenders had to mobilize arguments, and later organizations and political interventions, in a highly diverse ideational and political terrain. The development of women's activism was by no means guaranteed by abstract processes of modernization or capitalist development: both advances and setbacks depended much on ideas, organization and political struggle itself.

New initiatives went well beyond the press. New forms of organization and activism, about and including women, came into existence, especially after 1918. The first half of the twentieth century witnessed 'the development of myriad social, religious, literary, charitable, educational, and in some cases political women's organizations'. The 1920s also gave birth to the idea that there was such a thing as a women's movement – working to reform and transform the systemic functioning of society in regards to the position, role and status of women (Fleischman 1999: 99). Amid the uprising of 1919 came the first 'women's demonstrations', especially those organized by a number of high-status Wafdist women, including Safiya Zaghlul (1876–1946), 'mother' of the Egyptian nation, skilful Wafdist leader in her own right, and wife of nationalist leader Sa'd Zaghlul (Baron 2007; Ramdani 2013). Although sedate affairs, steeped in wealth, status, nationalism and cultural authenticity, these demonstrations staked a claim in regard to the right of women to participate in the nationalist movement in particular and in public and political space more generally. Far more unsung, and under-researched, were the many peasant female martyrs of 1919, who played their role in the cutting of railway and telegraph communications during the March–April insurrection (Sa'adawi 1980: 176).

Female activism was shaped by an important stream of thought that since the 1890s had linked the empowerment and 'liberation' of women to the nationalist cause. A key figure here was the male reformer, judge and notable Qasim Amin (1863–1908). His widely read book, published in 1899, *The Liberation of Woman*, proposed that lack of education, veiling, and female 'slavery' to their husbands were the key causes of women's (and hence Egypt's) backwardness. Progress and national liberation would come about through reform in these areas, starting with the education of women. Amin's critics suggest that his feminism was a blind imitation of a West in regard to which Amin internalized an embarrassed inferiority (Ahmed 1992). This position risks a rather too familiar, identitarian displacement of key questions about the detailed morphology of masculine domination, diverting attention to abstracted civilizational categories that are themselves products of essentialist and exceptionalist discourse. It must be emphasized that the suture between nationalism, progress and women's liberation was the cornerstone of a generation of liberal, nationalist activism around women; Amin's reputation as a pioneer was unsullied in the movement itself at least until the late 1920s (Nelson 1996: 27). Amin, however, was a man, and he did not touch the personal status law or questions of politics, and he had no reform strategy other than persuasion among elites, and he was not simply a voice in the wilderness. Activist women, for example, linked progress and nationalism to women's emancipation from the 1890s onwards. The educated but non-elite woman, Malak Hifni Nassef (1886–1918), for example, was the first woman to publish her poetry in a mainstream journal at the age of thirteen (1899); the first to get a degree from a government school (1900); to lecture publicly; and the first to address the Egyptian parliament with a list of demands (1910). She argued that the education of women and men alike was the key to overcoming the innocence of women and the abusive and shameless character of men (Ahmed 1992).

Education could imply a more autonomous female management of household affairs in raising 'sons of the nation' in a scientific and rational way (Abu-Lughod 1998; Shakry 1998). But it also meant the capacity of women to represent themselves in the urban press and to speak in a way that could compete with male voices, to defend themselves against many forms of masculine domination, and to offer a basis for political activism.

Huda Sha'arawi (1879–1947) was a woman of upper-class birth who set a more radical tone as the most well-known feminist of her day. She began in philanthropy, creating in 1908 the first philanthropic society run by Egyptian women, offering social services for poor women and children. She argued that women-run social-service projects were important, first, because, by engaging in such projects, women would widen their horizons, acquire practical knowledge and direct their focus outward. Second, such projects would challenge the view that all women are creatures of pleasure and beings in need of protection. Fleischman is surely right to argue that these activities promoted autonomous forms of women's organizing, along with particular skills, including in advocacy, and encounters with authorities, and drew women into the political field. Sha'arawi's landmark moment was the founding of the Egyptian Feminist Union in 1923 to campaign for women's suffrage – a political campaign that a number of women writers had specifically eschewed before 1914 (Ramdani 2013: 44), and against which stood a conservative religious establishment who saw women's participation as a source of chaos (*fitna*). The Egyptian Feminist Union's feminist agenda also called for changes in the personal status law (especially for controls on divorce and polygamy), equal secondary school and university education, and expanded professional opportunities for women: all these points were depicted as key building blocks of the cause of Egyptian nationalism itself (Nelson 1996: 28).

The Egyptian Feminist Union, associated with the liberal nationalism of the Wafd, lost its central position over time. Breaking with the Egyptian Feminist Union, Zeinab Al-Ghazali founded in 1936 the Muslim Women's Society, which joined the Muslim Brotherhood in 1948 (Ahmed 1992: 197). On the Left, Ceza Nabarawi and Inji Aflatoun founded the Committee of Young Women to revive the fading Egyptian Feminist Union as it attracted 'pro-communist women who were prevented by the government to establish an organization of their own' (Nelson 1996: 165). The Committee organized women in popular neighbourhoods around health and education in order to raise their political and rights consciousness and provide them with tools to organize themselves (Ali 2002). In the 1950s, while independent women's organizing was crushed, the labour law was changed to guarantee state-sector jobs for all holders of high school diplomas and college degrees irrespective of gender (Hatem 1992: 232). In 1956, the educational system was reformed to increase enrolment, both for primary and secondary education, which particularly affected female participation in higher education (Ahmed 1992: 210).

Alternatively, blending militant feminist action with palace and high-society connections was Doria Shafik (1908–75), who broke with Huda Sha'arawi when the former linked herself to palace circles in the 1940s (Nelson 1996: 123). Shafik showed little interest in social or economic reform, but she engaged in some of the most high-profile and transgressive direct action of the 1940s and 1950s. She founded in the 1940s *Bint Al-Nil*, one of the first Arabic women's journals, which combined charity, feminist consciousness-raising and political protest. Shafik shifted the debate from women's nature to women's rights in late 1940s. As she wrote:

Publicity was my primary aim. Even the attacks in the press, however personal, were helping the *Bint Al-Nil* movement to become widely known. The propaganda made against our movement by our enemies surpassed by far what the greatest publicity agencies could do (Shafik, cited in Nelson 1996, 157).

Shafik was viewed even by the relatively sympathetic as a lightweight, as contradictory and a lady of the salon (Nelson 1996: 167). By her enemies she was often depicted as a 'tool of Western society trying to undermine the society's Islamic [and Egyptian] values' (Nelson 1996: 161). Nonetheless, she organized among high-status women an extra-ordinary storming of the parliament in February 1951 on the basis of the demand for women's suffrage, after the broken promises of the Wafd. Joining with Inji Aflatoun and others, she organized an armed unit after October 1951, the 'Women's Committee for Popular Resist-ance'. She was also responsible for organizing the women who surrounded Barclay's bank as a symbol of British occupation in January 1952, and she went on hunger strike in 1954 to protest the Free Officers' all-male constitutional committee. Egypt's 1956 constitution did declare that all Egyptians are equal regardless of gender, and in 1956 the state granted women the right to vote and to run for political office (Ahmed 1992: 210).

The crumbling hegemony of the Wafd in Egypt, 1936–1952

A partially independent political field had opened up in Egypt in the early 1920s on the back of the country-wide uprising of 1919. But, for a state almost comparable to Turkey or Iran in demographic weight, wealth, and a prior history of statehood and empire building, progress towards independence, after the unilateral declaration of 1922, and the overwhelmingly popular election of Sa'd Zaghlul and the Wafd to government in 1924, was slow indeed. One of the central features of the period from the 1930s until 1952 was the uneven attrition of the hegemony of the Wafd as representatives of the Egyptian nation, their growing incapacity to command the consent of mobilized forces within the political field, and the concomitant enfeeblement of their mass organization, their hold over the new political generation, and their brand of liberal, secular, Pharaonic and Hellenic-Mediterranean nationalism. Over time, movements arose which challenged the Wafd and its forms of legalism and parliamentary politics: some flirted with fascism in the 1930s; from the late 1930s there was a growing strand of politically independent trade unionism in the labour movement; the waves of strike action pushed on by workers themselves in the 1940s were powerful factors in their own right; the rise of the Muslim Brotherhood and its entry into politics from the late 1930s onwards, and its construction of secret armed cells in the 1940s; the split in the Wafd that led to the creation of a socialist Wafdist Vanguard in the 1940s; a student movement that shifted from showing its loyalty to the Wafd in 1935 to demonstrating its disgust in 1946 and after; the rise of communism among urban intelligentsia and its impact on the labour movement; the guerrilla struggle that developed in the Canal Zone in 1951–2; and finally the popular outrage expressed in the Cairo fire of January 1952. While the Wafd, in and out of power, could occasionally muster some revival of its credibility, and even managed to do so as late as 1951, the crisis of the Egyptian state by the early 1950s was expressed in the paralysis of successive governments, and the growing forcefulness of a wide variety of uncoordinated and diverse mobilizations from below – none of which was capable of taking power – on the other. In 1952, amid the repression that followed the Cairo fire, Egypt was a state in which there was neither hegemony nor alternative hegemony. No actor was capable of making the decisive move, until the Free Officers and the army seized the initiative in July 1952.

The machinations within the corridors of power undertaken by the British, the palace, and their conservative and land-owning supporters played a major role in undermining successive Wafdist governments, progress towards political independence, the powers of the constitution and the parliament, projects of economic nationalism, and social reform. At the same time, social and economic change, the development of the press and radio, urbanization, growing inequalities in landholding and wealth, and the incapacity of the cotton economy to generate a rising standard of living for the mass of the population, coupled with the impact of the Depression, the increasing size of the industrial proletariat especially during the late 1930s and 1940s, and the sharp rise in the cost of living during the Second World War, generated a series of social and economic problems and social groups which fed into new forms of mobilization.

Nonetheless, inexorable processes of socio-economic change and the actions of conservative elites must be put in perspective. The allegiances of most of the politically active population were divided between the Wafd and other forces. It would be wrong to under-estimate, therefore, the role of political leadership, ideology, organization, along with the form and nature of new popular mobilizations, and the way they interacted in the political field in determining the shape and quality of the crisis of the state, the attrition of liberal nationalism, and the rise of alternatives. The contentious politics of the period, including the failures of the Wafd, not just elite machinations, modernization, or the development of capitalism, played a vital role in paving the way for what turned out to be a revolutionary coup in 1952 – which in turn was an initiative neither pre-determined, inevitable, nor bound to succeed.

The failure of the Wafd to deliver on the nationalist aspirations of the great majority of its adherents paved the way, probably more than any other single factor, for new kinds of mobilization. The Wafd, on which the hopes of much of the generation of 1919 rested, was supposed to represent the nation. It was supposed to found a new and independent Egypt, on liberal and constitutional lines, complete with a dose of economic nationalism, and measures of social reform in town and country alike. Even the events of 1924, when the hugely popular Sa'd Zaghlul was ousted from government by undemocratic means after less than a year in office, having accepted to play a political game in which the rules were stacked against him (especially in regard to the outsize powers given to the king in the constitution), but persisting in the use of conservative and legalistic tactics, were an ominous sign of things to come. The Wafd, bound by its stake in the *status quo*, its worldview, and the undeniable attraction of a non-negotiated independence, saw no choice but to go along with the political order that the British and the palace handed to them. Wafdist negotiations with the British over the reserved points failed on every occasion because the British refused to compromise and the Wafd failed to come up with a superior strategy. The early lustre of Bank Misr and its projects of economic nationalism was dissipated by the late 1920s. The weak constitution was regularly suspended, a matter of widespread protests among Wafdist students in 1935. That the Wafd, which had never recognized the legality of the British occupation forces in the Canal Zone and elsewhere, effectively did so by signing the new Anglo-Egyptian Treaty of 1936 was an important blow to its nationalist credentials – a capitulation which stained its *raison d'être* (Bishri 1981: 99–100). The outbreak of the uprising in Palestine in 1936, for which much solidarity was expressed by Egyptians, lowered the British stock still further, and exposed the inability of the Wafd to play a positive role. Nothing came of the high hopes that were raised in some quarters for the young King Farouk (r. 1936–52), who turned out to be an extravagant playboy. There were signs of a weakening of Wafdist authority in the labour movement in the 1930s, but the process was slow, becoming more rapid after 1942.

The 1942 incident, in which Egypt's government was changed by a brute show of British force (in the shape of tanks) was a further symbol of Egypt's subordination to the workings of the British empire – and its lack of progress on the road to independence. The heavy presence of British and transit troops during the Second World War was another provocation – a 'second occupation'. Sayyid Qutb, for example, recalled the 'contempt' of the Allied soldiers who 'ran over Egyptians in their cars like dogs' (Calvert 2010: 103). The war caused food shortages, and the cost of living tripled according to some estimates. The Wafd seemed to have no answer to the social and economic problems that were piling up on all sides, along with the claims that new groups were making. After 1946, the Wafd, which had once monopolized the political field, had decisively lost control of new forms of popular mobilization. The publication of the 'Black Book' by Makram Obeid in the early 1940s aired in public in scandalous detail the corruption of the Wafd (Mitchell 1969: 37). Fruitless attempts by Egypt's leaderships to achieve even minor concessions on independence from December 1945 onwards set the stage for growing rounds of protest. As long time politician, constitutionalist, judge and poet Abdel Aziz Fahmi (d. 1951) wondered in 1946, how could a 'still-born' regime continue to function (Bishri 1981: 98). When, in 1951, the Wafd finally made a move, enacting labour legislation and abrogating unilaterally the 1936 treaty with Britain, it unleashed forces for which it had no plan, and for which it was not prepared.

Fascism in Egypt

The inability of liberal, representative and democratic mechanisms to resolve Egypt's multiple problems prompted interest in fascism in the 1930s. Some Egyptians 'were initially open to the possibility that fascist organizational strength, socio-economic restructuring, psychological self-confidence, and success in apparently achieving national revival all represented a positive model that Egypt might emulate' (Gershoni and Jankowski 2010: 268). Young Egypt (founded in 1933), for example, looked to national assertiveness in Egypt's long history: its members were impressed by the models of organizational discipline then in evidence in Italy, Germany and Spain. In Lebanon, Antun Sa'ada's Syrian Socialist Nationalist Party and Pierre Gemayel's Lebanese Maronite Phalange appropriated aspects of the fascist model. The Muslim Brotherhood formed a youth section – the Rovers – who began to denounce Egypt's parliamentary system, adopting a thuggish posture towards taverns, prostitutes and Jews. A paramilitary group, the Green Shirts, was formed, with 1,800 members (Calvert 2010: 86). Yet, this kind of earlier receptivity to fascism had 'largely evaporated' by 1939, by which time 'the bulk of informed Egyptian opinion had come to the consensus that fascist totalitarianism, racism and imperialism represented a manifest threat to Egypt, the Middle East, and the rest of the world' (Gershoni and Jankowski 2010: 268). Fascism did not make much headway in Egypt, and was only the most minor of the radical alternatives to liberal nationalism that emerged in the 1930s. In the Arab world more generally, fascism 'was only marginally an object of (even approximate) imitation' (Achcar 2010: 67). Its more lasting impact in Egypt was to serve notice on the monopoly of the Wafd, and to mobilize criticism of the established order.

Socialism and communism in Egypt

Far more significant was the rise of socialism and communism in Egypt after 1936. While this (internally diverse) current never achieved the organizational weight or adherence of either the Muslim Brotherhood, or the communists in Iraq, they nonetheless played an important role in the student and labour mobilizations of the post-1945 period, and thereby weighed significantly in the crisis of the state that followed. They were the second, organized political force in the country after the Muslim Brotherhood in 1951–2, and they had links with the Free Officers and counted some of them as sympathizers. The Left was significant because it propounded and elaborated a socialist programme, in matters ranging from land reform to labour rights, that exercised considerable influence on substantial sections of unaffiliated opinion, on the labour movement and on students, and was subsequently taken up by the Nasserist state.

Like other ideological currents, communism had no supra-historical immanent guarantee. It was driven as much by activism and commitment as it was by the workings of capitalism. The Bolshevik revolution had its echoes in Egypt in the early 1920s, as we have seen. The victory of the Soviet Union in the Second World War brought that country under closer scrutiny in Egypt: for some it was a modernizing country that had escaped the Depression, thrown off the shackles of backwardness, and defeated Fascism in the Second World War. As the world's first workers' and peasants' state, it also embodied principles that were attractive to others. Communism in Egypt re-emerged in the late 1930s among a radicalized urban intelligentsia, Egyptian and non-Egyptian Jews, students, middle class intelligentsia, as well as foreign subjects and *mutamassirun*, with connections to communist parties in Mandate Palestine and Europe. Marxism could serve as 'an explanation of Egypt's political and economic conditions and a guide to achieving national and social liberation' (Beinin 1988: 207–8). It was distinctive in Egypt's generally more corporatist milieu for advancing the theory that the interests of workers and capitalists were irreconcilably antagonistic and propounding a resolution of such antagonism in a socialist revolution. Before 1952, perhaps as many as 4,000 activists were involved (Goldberg 1996: 179).

There were quite a number of groups and cells, but only two achieved a social base among unions and workers – the New Dawn (formally established in 1945) and the Democratic Movement for National Liberation (DMNL, est. 1938/9), led by Henry Curiel, the son of an estate owner, Egyptian Jew and intellectual. Both had their origins among intellectuals in the late 1930s and recruited students and some workers in the early 1940s. What became the New Dawn, (with a rather limited membership of 25–30 in 1946), forged links with the textile workers unions in Cairo's industrial suburb of Shubra from the late 1930s by offering legal counsel and other services – especially in support of unaffiliated unionism (Beinin and Lockman 1998: 280ff., 315ff., 351). The DMNL played a role among the unions and strike action in the textile mills at Mahalla Al-Kubra after 1945.

Another important current on the Left was the Wafdist Vanguard, founded in 1945 in opposition to the timidity and conservatism of the Wafd, and its failure on social and economic questions. The Vanguard included popularizers of Marxist ideas (Beinin and Lockman 1998: 311–12). It meant an important fracture within the ranks of the Wafd.

In the wider society, there were a good many unaffiliated socialist intellectuals and writers, such as the folklorist Rushdi Salih, or Luis Awad, or Rashid Al-Barrawi, who made an impact in literate circles. They drew attention to the economic dimensions of imperialism, especially the role of native (not just foreign) elites in perpetuating the poverty of the masses.

Finally, there was a section of the Muslim Brotherhood – driven by its own disgust at social injustice, influenced by contact with communists in prison in the late 1940s, and converted by those that they were sent to spy on – that made an important leftward turn. Sayyid Qutb, Muhammad Al-Ghazzali and Al-Bahi Al-Khuli were among those Brothers or affiliated intellectuals who broke with the Brotherhood's prevailing corporatism and started to speak of the systematic oppression of the poor by the rich and the need for the radical improvement of workers' conditions and rights in order to avert cataclysm (Beinin and Lockman 1998: 390–1).

Sayyid Qutb, for example, developed his own Islamism in the later 1940s amid a concern for social justice. He wrote in an autobiography published in 1946 of the low paid migrant labourers from southerly regions in his home village of Musha. He noted that they formed a caste apart and were only paid one piastre per day. Out of concern for this social injustice, he befriended them, wrote their letters, and arranged for the conveyance of their remittances. He wrote that he felt 'shame in the depth of his soul and contempt for himself and his people. He is a robber. He has robbed these "foreigners" and many millions like them who create the wealth of the Nile Valley yet go hungry. He is a robber!' In a hint at asceticism, he found it difficult to enjoy luxuries or simple pleasures 'amidst the millions of deprived'. He thought also in legal terms, of the corruption of the existing law, and the need for a better one, according to which standard he himself would be classed a 'robber' and a 'criminal': 'If there were a just law in the valley', he wrote, 'it would send him to prison before those multitudes who the law counts robbers and criminals' (Calvert 2010: 51).

The leftward turn in the Brotherhood, echoed in some measure in Syria, did have some impact on union organizing and even allowed some forms of DMNL-Brotherhood co-operation in the second half of 1951 (Beinin and Lockman 1998: 392).

The communists sought to develop a base among industrial workers. The strategy, in line with the Comintern, was to organize a 'broad national front of workers and other 'patriotic classes' (including the national bourgeoisie)' (Beinin and Lockman 1998: 329). The New Dawn aimed to downplay the preaching of communism and front-load support for independent, non-political unions. At the outset, the idea was presumably that communists would reach a critical mass capable of paralyzing the economy and generating an opportunity for the seizure of power and a socialist state. But the communists, although playing an important role in the labour movement between 1942 and 1952, never developed enough weight to detail a viable strategy on these lines or to stick with it consistently. This was partly because communists were repeatedly repressed, although not uniquely so. It was also because they were profoundly compromised by their Kremlin-backed line on the Palestinian catastrophe. Most communists supported the partition, which meant they supported the state of Israel, the creation of which was seen by most as a calamity for the Arab world. The DMNL, accused of Zionism and being in hock to Moscow, lost considerable ground between 1948 and 1950 in this context, while eventually managing to regroup.

The idea of a 'broad national front' did imply working with a wide variety of forces on the political stage, including making contacts with Free Officers or other persons expected to force change from above. This strategy, for all its strengths, had the weakness of diluting the distinctiveness of communist politics. It made what communists actually did in practice, as opposed to what they theorized, remarkably similar to what other political forces did in the political field: they provided services to workers, downplayed their own ideology up to a point, entered unions, helped organize strikes, and tried to make alliances with those who might take power. Entering into relations with Free Officers, furthermore, contradicted the idea of taking power through mass strikes. In soft-pedalling their own ideology, the New Dawn also faced the contradiction of supporting unaffiliated unionism while in actual fact standing for a highly political position and being led by those who did not work with their hands – positions which did not always win the trust of workers. Finally, a united front strategy might have been all very well, but communists were wracked by internal splits (Beinin and Lockman 1998: 352, 406; Amin 1987: 433) rooted in position-taking on theoretical questions, in regard to correct strategy, or in regard to conflicts taking place far from Egypt. These splits significantly diminished their organizing capacity.

Independent unionism

Important initiatives in support of independent, and non-politically affiliated, trade unions began in the 1930s. These began with a small group of worker-activists in the early 1930s, who made use of the protection, status and wealth of prince Abbas Halim to foster their own vision of non-Wafdist independent trade unionism (Beinin and Lockman 1998: 214). Veteran Cairo unionists – led by Yusuf Al-Mudarrik, a well-educated erstwhile leader of the shop clerks' union – then launched a new committee in early 1937 to try to drive forward a kind of unionism that would be independent of all political parties (Beinin and Lockman 1998: 225). Such people, who had a real social base, were very far indeed from being the puppets of the communist intellectuals, and had their own reasons for trying to escape the hegemony of the Wafd. Their drive was aided by the weakness of the Wafd's grip on power in 1937. This group was behind a new independent labour federation founded in March 1938 (Beinin and Lockman 1998: 232) which rapidly became important on the Egyptian labour scene, especially with the inactivity of the Wafd. The federation, influenced by the Indian nationalist, Gandhi, pioneered the use of the hunger-strike in 1939 to try to win labour legislation and the full recognition of unions (Beinin and Lockman 1998: 235). Parliament did take up the question, but failed to pass any legislation in 1939. The federation, further, was repressed with the onset of the Second World War. Unions did achieve legal recognition in Egypt in 1942. This movement among the unions was another activist initiative that played a role in shunting the paternalist, liberal-nationalism of the Wafd to one side, and diminishing Wafd organizational control within the labour movement.

The Muslim Brotherhood in Egypt

The Muslim Brotherhood (founded 1928) organized sentiments that had been especially at work since the dumbfounding, to some, collapse in 1924 of a political community guaranteed by Islam, Islamic law and the Caliphate, along with deep discomfort at other kinds of secular, political, economic, social and cultural change. Neither a mosque nor a Sufi order nor a political party, but an urban reform society in religious clothes that became a political movement, the Muslim Brotherhood

was devoted to making what it saw as a morally decadent and religiously deviant Egypt – and in particular the secular, nationalist
Wafdists – a more Islamic society, and ultimately recreating in some
form an Islamic state that had been lost, through piety, charity, persuasion, mass mobilization and reform. By the 1940s, this society had
hundreds of thousands of members and branches up and down Egypt
(Lia 1998; Mitchell 1969). The Muslim Brotherhood was an implacable opponent of the Wafd and its liberal nationalism from the outset,
though it espoused an Egyptian nationalism in Islamic clothes. It was
also thoroughly anti-communist, while adhering to measures of social
and economic reform in corporate and moral mode aimed at reducing
social inequality and injustice. By drawing large numbers of Egyptians,
mostly drawn from the middle and lower middle classes, to an Islamist
alternative, it aimed major blows at the hegemony of the Wafd and the
authority of the parliamentary system, and played an important role in
the contentious politics of the post-1945 period, contributing significantly to the crisis of the Egyptian state. Its role was far more important than this: with its influence and offshoots all over the region, it
was to become the most significant Islamic modernist movement in the
Sunni Middle East and North Africa of the twentieth and even twenty-
first centuries.

The Brotherhood was founded by Hasan Al-Banna (1906–49) in
1928 in the provincial town of Isma'iliyya. Al-Banna was the son of a
provincial mosque imam. He was active as a young boy in religious
and reform societies, influenced by Sufism and the nationalist uprising
of 1919: the latter 'pushed him towards an activist commitment to
religion, differing from the purely academic efforts of his father' (Lia
1998: 27). He was horrified by the political division and secularism
that he saw in Cairo in the early 1920s, and the attacks on the faith and
tradition that he saw emboldened by the War of Independence in
Turkey and the fall of the Caliphate. Al-Banna was shocked at new
gender roles, the appearance of women unveiled or in public, and
anxious about public morality, atheism, alcohol, gambling and lewdness (Calvert 2010: 81). He viewed nightclubs and entertainments as a
Western invasion and a corruption of true Islam and piety (Calvert
2010: 82). Al-Banna graduated from Dar Al-'Ulum in 1927, where he
had developed contacts through his father in prestigious Islamic circles,
some under the sponsorship of the palace, and became a schoolteacher
in Isma'iliyya (Lia 1998: 27–32). He founded the Brotherhood,

reportedly in response to requests for guidance, to do something about the lowly and debased state of Muslims, the mere 'hirelings of foreigners', as one of Al-Banna's early followers said (cited in Mitchell 1969: 8).

The Society proved popular and grew steadily, opening a branch in Cairo in 1932. The society had broad cross-class appeal: it aimed at Muslims, and Egyptians from all walks of life (apart from Copts). Most of the leadership and spokespersons were probably *effendis* of rural origin: professionals, civil servants and students. Most of the adherents were drawn from the educated lower middle class: small land-owners, petty traders, artisans and peasants (Lia 1998: 200). The Brothers did not win a significant student following at Al-Azhar (Lia 1998: 227). Those who worried about the collapse of Islam at the level of the state and of politics, or who were attracted by the Brotherhood's vision of mutual social responsibility in the economy or criticism of foreign companies, or those who were concerned in socially conservative mode over public morality, believed corrupted by the West (Calvert 2010: 81) or who sought to become better Muslims could all find themselves drawn to the ranks of these 'Brothers', who seemed respectable, serious about social improvement, and pious.

Islam, as opposed to nationalism, communism, capitalism or liberalism was the central guiding principle and identity of the Muslim Brothers. Whatever else Muslim Brothers thought they were doing, they saw themselves first and foremost as good Muslims, and first and foremost as implementing the principles of true Islam. The movement cannot be understood through a reductionist or materialist lens that does not give the role of this ideological factor its due. While the Islamic modernism of Al-Afghani to Muhammad Abduh had looked to borrow a key set of goods from 'Western civilization', the crisis of bourgeois liberalism in Western Europe in the inter-war period, and the failures of liberalism in Egypt, set the stage for a more rejectionist and activist posture. Such strands were evident in the thought of Sayyid Qutb, an intellectual of considerable future prominence who grew closer to and joined the Muslim Brotherhood at mid-century. In the late 1930s, he wrote that:

This [Western] civilization that is based on science, industry and materialism operates with crazed speed and is without heart and conscience. Driven by invention and material advancement, it sets forth to destroy all that humanity has produced in the way of spiritual values, human creeds, and noble traditions (cited in Calvert 2010: 89).

Such criticisms drew succour from conservative critiques of Western civilization and modernity in the West – such as those of the eugenicist Alexis Carrel, who wrote much about the de-humanization attendant on Western materialism (Calvert 2010: 90–1). Qutb, like other conservative and romantic thinkers in Europe and beyond, sought to construct a re-moralized, connected, pre-lapsarian, organic community, as against the hollow, atomized, individualist and materialist 'men' of bourgeois civilization. The East was seen as the site of such a project, with its supposed intuition, spiritual insight and deep feeling (Calvert 2010: 95). Sayyid Qutb argued that Western nations acted the way they did because they lacked a moral conscience: they had turned away from spiritual dimensions and adopted policies and attitudes based on material gain (Calvert 2010: 117).

What was required, at least according to Sayyid Qutb in the late 1940s, whose views at this point were close to the mainstream of the Brotherhood, amid social injustice and forms of moral and religious oppression, was a comprehensive programme, a just order, a *nizam* (social system) framed in terms of the Qur'an and the example of the Prophet. This system was a modern idea of a comprehensive and interlocking order, to be articulated not in the elliptical and exegetical style of the orthodox *ulema* but directly in pamphlets and journals and so on, and in competition as an Islamic system not with Christianity or Judaism but with other competing political ideologies and social systems – communism, capitalism and liberal democracy (Calvert 2010: 125–7, 130–1). This system would guarantee liberation and justice because it would release Muslims from the shackles of greed, priest-craft and political sycophancy; belief in God's unity would allow people to rise above their base desires and appetites in order to be able to do what is best for them and for society as a whole. Justice would thus emerge from an inner conviction of the spirit (Calvert 2010: 132). It made sense, then, that the Brotherhood situated the Egyptian nation within Islam, not Islam within the nation. Against the emphasis of the Wafd on the Pharaonic, the Hellenic and the Mediterranean, they hammered away at 'the Islamic–Arab heritage of Egypt and transform[ed] … it into a reservoir for the redefinition of a collective national identity' (Gershoni and Jankowski 2010: 10–11).

In political terms, some of the modernism and constitutionalism of Abduh was still present in the Brotherhood. Al-Banna claimed that the constitutional system – at least in terms of its provisions on personal liberties, the responsibility of the rulers to the ruled, and the limitation of government authority – was the system of government 'closest to Islam' (Gershoni and Jankowski 2010: 228). Much remained unclear. It is uncertain whether Al-Banna ever fully committed to a complete break with a constitutional system in favour of an Islamic state that would impose the Shari'a. Moreover, in the context of the conflict with the Wafd, the champion of the constitution, the Brotherhood's constitutionalism was by no means front and centre. The Society's association with the Palace (Lia 1998: 214–23), especially in the late 1930s, compromised this position further. In general, there is no doubt that Al-Banna judged the constitution according to Islamic criteria. Political parties were firmly rejected: in principle they were seen as factionalist, artificial and negative bodies 'that divided the nation into factions and served the interests of particular segments of society' (Gershoni and Jankowski 2010: 227), leaving the nation weak before the foreign occupier. They were also rejected in practice in Egypt as self-serving, opportunistic and corrupt. Al-Banna criticized the party system (*al-nizam al-hizbi*), seeing it as 'an obstacle on the road of revival and progress' (Gershoni and Jankowski 2010: 228) – and advocated its total abolition. On the other hand, there was no prohibition on entering parliament and participating in elections, as Al-Banna decided to do just that in 1942 and 1945. What the Islamist political system referred to, then, was a new 'patriotic body' (*hay'a wataniyya*) of 'politicians, technocrats and experts, in effect a new supreme national authority that would incorporate all sectors of Egyptian society' (Gershoni and Jankowski 2010: 228) at a time when national unity, above all, was said to be required. Such a system was likely capable of incorporating a monarchy of some kind (Mitchell 1969: 40), although this too was unclear. Presumably, in any new system, the Muslim Brotherhood was to play the starring role.

In terms of economy and social class, the Brotherhood espoused a thoroughgoing corporatism. The various social strata were seen as 'functionally differentiated corporate bodies, and not classes in mutual opposition' (Beinin and Lockman 1998: 376). Their relations were governed by 'mutual social responsibility' (*takaful 'ijtima'i*). Private property, along with entrepreneurialism and commerce was enjoined as long as it was not usurious and complied with Islamic law, and as long as it did not imply mindless materialism or imperialism, which foreign capitalism in Egypt was often seen as doing. The Society 'argued forcefully for all foreign firms to be Egyptianized, and for all foreign capital to be replaced by Egyptian capital' (Lia 1998: 210). The Brothers advocated for education reform, as well as rural agricultural co-operatives to raise productivity, in addition to health, literacy and clean-water programmes in the countryside. As for workers, in return for performing their duties in a diligent fashion, they were entitled to fair wages providing a healthy and clean home, and the necessities of life, and should be free from feudal obligations. At a time of considerable unemployment, the individual's right to work was to be guaranteed by the state. The poor and needy were above all to be provided for by charity, regulated by the state, which could implement progressive taxation to fund this provision if necessary.

At the level of society and gender, the movement articulated social conservatism – in distinctively Islamic clothes. Hasan Al-Banna, for example, wrote that '[A]fter the First World War and during my stay in Cairo, a tide of atheism and lewdness overtook Egypt. In the name of individual and intellectual freedom, it devastated religion and morality' (cited in Calvert 2010: 81). Al-Banna saw the Egyptian University as a main 'purveyor of atheism'. He put it on the same low level as 'the nightclubs that dotted Cairo's entertainment districts'. He was disillusioned by the muted response of the religious scholars of Al-Azhar to what he called this 'harsh Western invasion'. 'In his view, the *'ulama*'s inaction stood in the way of Islamic renaissance' (Calvert 2010: 82). The enemy, here, in other words, was the sexual 'transgression' and the de-stabilization of supposedly fixed gender roles. Via these mechanisms, Egyptians were losing sight of morality and, ultimately, God.

In the same vein, Qutb underwent considerable discomfort in the 1940s with liberal gender relations. He was an advocate of the supposed 'female virtues of modesty and domesticity' (Calvert 2010: 74). Women's roles were changing in Egypt – in the light of education, pioneering feminists, the arrival of women in certain professions, and minor legal changes in 1920 and 1929 which gave women a greater role in divorce. While Wafdists and Islamists alike tended to agree on the model of the educated housewife, who raised good and productive sons for the nation (Shakry 1998), Qutb was opposed to the potential of educated women to engage in public roles, or to violate norms of sexual propriety. He did not want the former seclusion, which he saw as outdated and socially debilitative. Yet, he saw the 'current level of freedom' enjoyed by women as socially deleterious. He made gender relations central to his analysis of the malaise afflicting Egyptian society. He wrote that '[t]he leap made by the Egyptian woman following the Great War is *the* reason for the lack of balance in our social system' (emphasis added). The free mixing of men and women threatened family life and kinship structures. Unmarried men and women should meet only to choose marriage partners, and then under the watchful eyes of their parents. Unchecked women's sexuality had the power to entice men (Calvert 2010: 108). To follow uncritically the Western example in gender relations and women's freedom was to open the door to discord (*fitna*). Qutb drew support for his view from recent 'scientific' findings at the Egyptian University, that claimed to prove women's biological suitability for domestic, rather than public, responsibilities.

Criticism of the entertainment industry drew on similar sources. Qutb, for example, revered Umm Kalthum and Muhammad Abd Al-Wahhab, but he regarded popular music as weakening the moral constitution of the nation. Pop music did not speak of noble love but of debased forms of association linked to the excitation of the animal lusts potentially present in every human. Qutb railed against commercial publishers, who for profit splashed 'naked thighs and protruding breasts' all over their magazines, images which sapped the energy and will of the nation. Indeed, Qutb regarded 'moral propriety in gender relations as an aspect of the national personality'. He believed that men and women had the same devotional and creedal obligations, but they had unique functions in family and society. The husband is the patriarch; his primary duty is to maintain the family financially, and to make decisions relevant to the overall welfare of the family. The role of the woman is that of wife and mother; she should defer to the authority of her husband. To step beyond these divinely ordained roles is to invite disharmony (Calvert 2010: 109–11). As Qutb wrote, '[t]he Islamic social order is family based by virtue of its being a Divinely ordained system for society that takes full account of the essentials of human nature and its basic requirements' (cited in Calvert 2010: 111). As elsewhere, social conservatism was heavily rooted in the sexual politics of masculine domination.

Overall, the Muslim Brotherhood aimed to make Egypt a more Islamic society. The goal was some kind of Islamic state, presumably with the Brotherhood in charge, the abolition of political parties, and the implementation of Islamic law, with some constitutional limits on executive authority and guarantees of personal rights. They sought an economy based on mutual responsibility, with state-guaranteed rights of employment and basic standards of welfare, the eviction or radical reform of foreign companies, and some forms of progressive taxation. They also sought a major reform of the individual and of society, with modest women, pious men, Islamic criminal, inheritance and marriage laws, and a clampdown on entertainment, alcohol, gambling, public manifestations of sexuality and the like. Copts and Jews would be 'protected' – i.e. second-class – citizens. During the Palestinian revolt especially, racist attacks on Jews as Jews (rather than Jews as Zionists), making reference to Qur'anic verses, were published in the Brotherhood's newspaper (Lia 1998: 244).

The Brothers developed a meticulous, centralized, authoritarian and hierarchical organization based on obedience to Al-Banna and zealous commitment to the cause. Al-Banna condemned in his memoirs those who criticized his financial irregularities in the early 1930s as the 'forces of evil' (Lia 1998: 63). Al-Banna believed 'that the Society could never be successful unless it commanded the total confidence and obedience of its members, and all demands for "consultation" (*shura*) and the diffusion of authority were rejected as nit-picking criticism and a lack of understanding of the Society's supreme mission' (Lia 1998: 70). All members were required to take an oath of allegiance to Al-Banna himself (Lia 1998: 104). Internal elections were ruled out. Powers of decision, ideology, implementation and enforcement were vested in Al-Banna and the executive, whose members were appointed by Al-Banna. The executive, and Al-Banna's authority, was then represented by delegates to the lower rungs in the hierarchy, rather than *vice versa* (Lia 1998: 98–9). Tracts outlining the Brothers' creed were distributed for members to read and memorize (Lia 1998: 103): the duty of obedience was again and again emphasized, along with the 'fatal consequences of insubordination' (Lia 1998: 105). This hierarchical structure drew in many ways on the internal morphology of obedience, devotion, progression through the ranks, and spiritual authority familiar in the Sufi orders, from the ranks of which many adherents came, including Al-Banna himself (Lia 1998: 114–21).

The Muslim Brotherhood sought to achieve its goals through a war of position in the Gramscian sense. It was a stagist and gradualist strategy, beginning in the redoubts and trenches of civil society. The first step involved the moral reform of individual Muslims, proselytizing, publishing and charitable works. The second involved organizational development and enrolment, a form of mass mobilization without necessarily much engagement in overt protest (such as demonstrations or strikes), whereby the organization was developed, and societies, libraries, social services, schools, unions and even companies were founded. Friendliness, gentleness and the avoidance of insults and attacks were emphasized and enforced (Lia 1998: 107). In many ways, these strategies were homologous with those employed by the Christian missionaries in Egypt to which Al-Banna was so opposed, and were devised very much to combat the influence of those missionaries (Lia 1998: 112–13).

The final stage, only possible after society and individual Muslims had been reformed, and dedicated cadres shaped, would involve the acquisition of state power by this rising bloc of forces under the control of the Muslim Brotherhood. As Al-Banna put it in late 1937, 'the stages of this [the Brothers'] path are three: acquaintance – formation – execution' (cited in Lia 1998: 173). The Rovers generally, and more particularly the Battalions, were clearly about preparing cadres from among whom the most promising could be later recruited for armed struggle. Exactly how the seizure of power was to be effected, and what any such seizure would actually mean, was rather undefined, at least by Al-Banna. Considerable ambiguity surrounded the activities of the military wing of the Brotherhood, founded in 1940–1. While it was by no means completely restrained, it does not seem to have launched a systematic attempt to seize power either (Lia 1998: 271). In many ways, it was the rock of 'execution', and the ambiguities surrounding it, on which the movement would splinter and eventually be repressed.

Hasan Al-Banna cleaved to the idea that it was vital to reach out to the 'common people' to 'awaken the faith that lay "dormant" in their souls'. To do so he preached in Isma'iliyya's coffee-houses, rather than in a mosque, and used what he himself called 'everyday language' in order to remind listeners of the Qur'an and Sunna (Calvert 2010: 82). This was a programme of moral and religious education which pictured the common people as essentially redeemable, partly because of their distance from a 'Westernized' cultural elite, but who had also strayed into 'ignorance of the reality of Islam', as Al-Banna put it in 1943 (cited in Mitchell 1969: 29; see Lia 1998: 59–60), and needed to be educated back to the truth.

At first the movement ignored the political sphere – the Palace, the British and the Wafd. Beginning in 1933, however, the idea was to gain patronage in the world of notable politics, enlist political figures in the work of Islamic reform directed towards moral and social spheres, while trying, not without tension, to avoid becoming a political faction or party. The Muslim Brotherhood was opposed to the Wafd party, tainted by secularism, Pharaonism, the 'moral laxity' of its women, and its obvious rejection of the sovereignty of God. They had long been associated with the palace through Al-Banna's contacts in Islamic circles in the 1920s. They looked to the monarch, enjoining him, especially in a letter of 1938, to stand behind the Brotherhood's reformist programme. The Palace, in turn, 'tended to encourage the Brotherhood's forays into street politics, regarding the organization as a valuable counterweight to the Wafd' (Calvert 2010: 85). In many ways, Al-Banna hoped to achieve his reforms through, rather than against, the monarchy (Mitchell 1969: 40). Moreover, during the 1930s, the Muslim Brotherhood took another step into politics, where it dealt more explicitly, and in modern languages, with the possibility of establishing an Islamic political order (*nizam*), first in Egypt, and then in other countries. The Brotherhood believed that the existing political institutions should apply Islamic law (Shari'a). Al-Banna decided to run for a seat in parliament in the elections of 1942 and in 1945, but the road was blocked. In the first case, he was persuaded to desist by the authorities on threat of internment, and, in the second, corruption prevented victories. The ruling elite, in Lia's words, failed 'to acknowledge the growing power of the Society and co-opt it into the political system' (Lia 1998: 271).

In 1936, the Muslim Brotherhood had several thousand members. By the early 1940s, it probably had between 100,000 and 500,000 members in more than 1,000 branches up and down Egypt (Lia 1998: 96, 151–4). Clearly, the strategy of patient mass mobilization, the careful training of young, dedicated preachers, and the application of 'the most modern forms of propaganda, education and organization' (Lia 1998: 57) paid off amid the declining popularity of the Wafd, which in turn failed to engage in serious mass mobilization beyond the elite. Lia's work above all demonstrates the extraordinary capacities of

Al-Banna as an organizer, in 'internal structure, modes of action, methods of recruiting' (Lia 1998: 3), which can help explain why it was the Muslim Brotherhood (rather than its more Salafi, more confrontational, or more secular or Leftist rivals) which won a mass following during these years. As a prominent contemporary 'Islamic Left' Egyptian academic Hasan Hanafi has put it '[t]o say the truth, the ideas of Hasan Al-Banna probably may not amount to much … [but] as an organizing power … he was something else' (cited in Lia 1998: 161). It was a development that made the Brotherhood a key actor in the crisis of the state that was to follow.

Contentious upsurge in Egypt, 1942–1952

By the mid to late 1940s, the Muslim Brotherhood, the communists, independent unionism, socialism more generally, women, organized workers suffering from low pay and poor conditions, and increasingly students came out in transgressive contention on the political scene, pushing forward a crisis in the Wafd and eventually the state. Each group had their own tactics: the Muslim Brotherhood increasingly moved to armed struggle (and were joined by others); the communists organized strikes and influenced students; students came out with mass demonstrations signalling a break with the Wafd and which led to bloody clashes; socialists and social reformers published ever more insistently on the need for socio-economic reform; while unruly crowd actions of diverse sorts challenged the capacities of the state to keep order.

The post-1945 period saw a major escalation in the number of strikes and protests carried out by workers. A dress rehearsal of sorts had been held in the summer of 1936, when there was 'an explosion of labour militancy on a scale not equalled for many years past' (Beinin and Lockman 1998: 220). There was a major wave of strikes in 1945 and 1946 – which was heavily repressed under the guise of anti-communism after July. A further wave of strikes extended from September 1947 to April 1948. There was significant unrest in the Misr Spinning and Weaving Company in September 1947 over rumours of sackings, new disciplinary regulations and new fines for violators (Beinin and Lockman 1998: 354). By early April 1948, the wave of strikes 'reached a crescendo and threatened a complete breakdown of public order' (Beinin and Lockman 1998: 360). Strike action, as ever, was powerfully driven by the common sense and moral economy of workers disgusted with their pay and conditions. Some of it was also organized by communists and Left unionists. Also, and just as in 1919, and in some ways in a return to the nationalist strikes of that year, strikes were driven by nationalism, and unmistakably linked to grievances concerning the failure of the state or the Wafd to advance Egypt's national independence. In other words, wave after wave of workers' strikes signified acute social and economic problems among workers, the presence of organized alternatives, and a growing, yet unfulfilled, nationalist demand.

Meanwhile, the students started to move. The students had been mobilized within the framework of the Wafd during the 1920s and 1930s. One of the most significant rounds of public demonstrations in the inter-war period in Egypt was a student-led *intifada* in 1935 – a movement that demonstrated the frustration of the students in regard to the failures of the Wafd, but their loyalty to Wafdist liberal-nationalism. The round of demonstrations was triggered by the careless avowal of British opposition to the return of the Egyptian constitution – in a context of increased British military presence (especially in Alexandria) linked to the Italian preparations for the invasion of Abyssinia (Ismail 2005: 16–17). The uprising was joined in the name of the fatherland, independence, the constitution, and the will of the people – and against British meddling. The ranks of the demonstrators were dominated by Wafdists, in support of Al-Nahhas, and against the current Prime Minister Nasim who was collaborating with the British by failing to return the constitution (Ismail 2005: 98–9). The *intifada* consisted of a series of mass protests, demonstrations and strikes taking place up and down Egypt, led by the Wafd and Al-Nahhas, and joined by the smaller political parties, and above all students from universities, colleges and secondary and technical schools, from November to December 1935. Tens of thousands of persons, including some all-female demonstrations, were involved. Students were responding to Al-Nahhas Pasha's call, on Jihad Day, 13 November, for non-co-operation with the British until they dropped their opposition to the constitution. The young Gamal Abd Al-Nasser, future president, and secondary school student in Cairo, was one of many who were prominent in the student demonstrations, and was wounded. The watchwords of those who turned out to protest were independence, a return of the constitution, an end to British interference, and opposition to the ongoing collaboration of the Egyptian government with the British. Hundreds were injured or killed by security forces all over the country – from Esna to Damietta. One demonstrator died on Abbas Bridge in the heart of Cairo. The protests culminated in a series of major strikes (Ismail 2005; Rizk 2004). On 12 December 1935, the new king, Farouk, issued a decree restoring the constitution.

The '*intifada*' had achieved one of its important goals – but was poisoned the following year by the treaty of 1936. It was an ambiguous moment: a protest in the name of the Wafd, but one that could by no means be sure any more of the power and commitment of the Wafd. It was a protest in which youth had even given up their lives, only to find the Wafd betraying their cause the following year. Especially the younger generation, with only hazy memories of 1919, started looking for alternatives. Among the young and educated there was a real mood of malaise and anger in the late 1930s and 1940s (Calvert 2010: 78). This was new, compared to the upbeat tone of the 1920s, but it was also new, in many ways, compared to the tone of Egypt's secular *effendiyya* since even the 1870s, who in their periodical and publications had maintained an enormously optimistic posture in regard to progress, civilization, liberalism, science and Egyptian nationalist awakening. In the new context, many students were influenced by the Left. Such readings and contacts, meetings, study groups, lectures and so on, paved the way for the student and worker demonstrations of 1946.

On 9 February 1946, in the midst of the wave of labour strikes, several thousand students held a conference at Cairo University. They set out on a march to Abdin palace, demanding the evacuation of British troops, but were attacked by police and army. Several were injured, paving the way for further protest. A National Committee of Students and Workers was formed, with strong links to the Left of the labour movement, and a general strike was called for on February 21, designated 'Evacuation Day'. On that day, up to 100,000 students, workers and others rallied, demanding immediate British evacuation. The British army was called into the streets. Amid the ensuing clashes, where the crowd attacked army vehicles and burned them, 23 demonstrators lay dead and 121 were injured. There were calls for a general strike and actual demonstrations in a dozen provincial cities. The repression was understood as the symbol of British intentions in Egypt and in the empire more generally. Protestors called for a memorial for the fallen – 'Martyrs' Day' on March 4. On that day the action switched to Alexandria where demonstrations clashed with troops leaving 28 dead and 342 wounded (Beinin and Lockman 1998: 342). Newspapers, factories, stores and schools closed in protest in many parts of the country. At Mahalla Al-Kubra on 5 March, 25,000 workers stopped work in solidarity. Nothing like this had been seen in Egypt since 1919. But, unlike in 1919, the Wafd was no leader of these events. Instead, it shrank to the sidelines, while unionists, Leftists, students and workers, non-Wafdists all, drove the action.

In the aftermath, some students turned to armed struggle, hoping to de-stabilize the government. On 16 November 1946, a group of university students formed a 'National Front of Students of the Nile Valley'. They mounted attacks on British stores, trams, trees, English-language books and on British and security forces in all the major towns. Sa'd Zaghlul Fu'ad was a student who became a journalist in the 1940s, and who ended up becoming a peripatetic guerrilla fighter all over the Arab world in the 1950s and 1960s. He relates in his memoirs how he witnessed Wafdist and patriotic students gunned down by security forces in the 1930s. He eventually (it is not clear when) came to conclude, along with a number of his friends and colleagues, that the only way to achieve national liberation was by using arms (Fu'ad 2001: 19–43). He started to carry out a number of actions in the late 1940s and early 1950s. The various assassinations and bombings of the post-1945 period, often involving radicalized students with their origins in the Wafd, or the Muslim Brothers alike, contributed to the gathering atmosphere of crisis – as did the increasing numbers of ordinary people who joined in crowd actions targeting English-language books, stores, trams and trees (Mitchell 1969: 50).

A more important turn towards armed struggle was taking place in Egypt's largest, mass-based movement. Splinters from the Brotherhood, demanding 'the force of the hand' against Al-Banna's preference for 'wisdom and fair exhortation', had already emerged during the period of the Palestinian uprising (Mitchell 1969: 18). During 1940–1, a 'special apparatus' developed within the Muslim Brotherhood for conducting armed struggle aimed at a seizure of power. In some respects, the apparatus may have been based on a sense of strength founded on a growing membership; but it was also rooted in a feeling of weakness in the face of repression (Mitchell 1969: 32). It was also necessary to contain those within the movement who sought more forceful action and were opposed to compromises with the political elite, a highly divisive issue within the movement linked already to one major split in 1939–40 (Lia 1998: 247–56). It certainly sought to hasten the key shift to 'execution'. That the electoral road appeared – and in many respects was – closed (because of corruption) in 1945 boosted those in favour of an armed option. The fact is that the mechanism linking mass organization to the seizure of power had not been clearly defined. Unlike communists on the contemporary scene, or Shi'a populists to come, the Muslim Brotherhood eschewed mass demonstrations, strikes, attacks on property, or disruptive and forceful methods such as civil disobedience, or even the idea of a popular insurrection. Such tactics did not fit with the respectable piety of the Brothers, their corporatist vision of social harmony, their strategy for winning mass appeal among conservative strata who shied away from such repertoires, or their sensitivity to the charge of stirring chaos (*fitna*) that they levelled at other groups who used these 'noisy' tactics. In other words, mass organization, not overt contention, was the watchword of the Brothers, and such a tactic was necessary in many ways for the coherence of their mobilizing project. Crucially, however, this left a strategic gap. How to seize power exactly, if all these classic means for disrupting the state were unavailable? One of the few options remaining was the way of the gun, but Al-Banna would not thoroughly get behind this option, leaving a near-fatal strategic lack of clarity that greatly exacerbated divisions within the movement and vitiated the coherence of its action.

The Brotherhood sent units to fight alongside the Palestinians, and the Egyptian army in 1947–8, a key moment which developed its armed capacity, and radicalized many members who were shocked at the incompetence and double-dealing of the Egyptian civilian and top army leadership. Amid the strikes and demonstrations, and crowd actions of the post-1945 period, elements within the Muslim Brotherhood clearly judged the time to be right for attacks on the regime's political figures and on the Jewish community in Egypt (who were now associated with Zionism), attacks which, it was supposed, would destabilize the situation and allow the Brothers, the largest non-governmental organization in the country, to take power. Such attacks were carried out during 1948, in the wake of the Palestinian dispossession, known as the *nakba*. In December 1948, the government discovered the secret apparatus and repressed the Brotherhood. Within three weeks, the Brothers had assassinated the prime minister, Al-Nuqrashi. In retaliation, the new prime minister's secret police assassinated Al-Banna in February 1949. For a period at least, the Muslim Brotherhood in Egypt was in complete disarray. Ultimately, it had not been able to decide whether or not the third stage of 'execution' involved a revolutionary armed struggle or an ongoing gradualism. The latter possibility was encouraged by the vested interests and contacts that Al-Banna had acquired in elite circles, but was blocked by the failure of the parliamentary road. The former strategy was too risky for Al-Banna to embrace. The movement nearly foundered on the resulting contradictions. The whole episode was another escalation of political tension, another sign of Wafdist weakness, and of the growing capacities of unruly contenders in the political field.

The crisis of the Egyptian state

The Wafd was in crisis, but in power, and desperate to reclaim its authority. It enacted some labour legislation, recognized the Muslim Brotherhood, which thanks to mass mobilization still very much existed, and, in 1951, unilaterally abrogated the Anglo-Egyptian Treaty of 1936. The Wafd had finally broken with polite diplomacy. The move brought the Egyptian state into a legal confrontation with the British troops in the Canal Zone – who were now in *de jure* terms – an illegal and occupying force. Such a confrontation might have been finessed, absent the forces organizing on the ground. As it was, cadres from the Muslim Brotherhood above all, who by now had significant experience, as well as raw recruits from students and elsewhere, moved in considerable numbers to the Canal Zone, forming 'resistance battalions' to fight a growing guerrilla war against the British troops. These fighters received some support from the state. Nonetheless, around 600 Egyptians were killed. The British were now in confrontation with the Egyptian police, who refused to follow orders in the old way, or to suppress their nationalist comrades. This was the background to the British killing of around forty-one Egyptian police in their barracks in Isma'iliyya on 25 January 1952.

The response in Cairo was electric. A crowd found its way to Abdin Palace, to demand action from the king. The latter, who was banqueting, sent troops to disperse the crowd. This was the trigger for an uprising of Caireans, increasingly experienced in crowd actions since at least November 1946, who destroyed by fire in an almost forensic fashion a very good many of the symbols of wealth, government and occupation in downtown Cairo. The crowd may have been only informally organized, and outraged indeed, but they expressed their outrage in a remarkably targeted manner. This was the 'Cairo fire' of 26 January 1952 (Reynolds 2012). Early risers in the crowd action piled expensive goods in the streets and left them untouched while they torched the premises within, demonstrating to anyone with eyes to see – and few had – that they were not looters or thugs. The result was heavy damage to property and the deaths of several foreigners, including eleven British citizens. In the aftermath, there was an extensive crackdown on political mobilization, which put an end to many of the demonstrations, strikes, and attacks of the previous several years. Whereas in Algeria the state was strong and could not be tackled, the situation in Egypt was almost the reverse. The state was in a crisis but no challenger could hegemonize the political field – not the Wafd, the communists, the students, the socialists, the communists, nor the urban crowds and the workers. The peasantry were hardly to be seen in urban mobilizations: they had not found their champion, as for example they did in Akram Al-Hawrani in Syria after 1950. The Muslim Brothers, skittish about seizing power themselves, hoped that the Free Officers would implement their programme – as too did the DMNL. In the event, it was the Free Officers in the army that seized the initiative.

Palestine: the *nakba*, 1948

The uprising of 1936–9 may have stitched Arab Palestinians together in a search for independence, but British repression left 'the Arab nationalist movement in Palestine severely weakened' (Lockman 1996: 265) in large measure because it spelled the 'end of the popular mobilization' within it (Anderson 2013: 1167). The power vacuum occasioned by the withdrawal of the British meant that force of arms at the local level would decide matters. On the one hand, Zionist mobilization was galvanized, and on the other there were faltering rearguard actions by the Arab Palestinians. Many of the notables had long tried to avoid politics or to accommodate the pressures, and work the opportunities of British rule and the Zionist movement. Those who resisted were now exiled, scattered and divided. Many of the urban and the wealthy started to leave, perceiving which way the wind was blowing. The nationalist leadership had in any case done little to prepare systematically for an armed confrontation. Those who had, such as Al-Qawuqji, now returned to the field, hamstrung by regional rulers from Egypt to Iraq who were either ineffective, unprepared, lacked political will, were divided amongst themselves, and who even had territorial ambitions of their own in regard to the dissolving Mandate. The peasantry had already discovered the appalling cost of outright resistance and resorted to what they hoped would be temporary withdrawal in some cases. Where the scope for politics had shrunk nearly to zero, coercive force came to the forefront: the Zionist dynamiting of villages, massacre, rape, eviction by truck and forced marches played the leading role in driving out Arab Palestinians from hundreds of villages and violently preventing their return (Pappé 2006).

The *nakba* was on the one side an appalling defeat that scattered more than a million Palestinians and made many of them destitute overnight, and dependent on charity and clustered in tents and camps. Those thousands of peasants who had opted for withdrawal, or been forced out *en masse*, now found themselves prevented from returning to their homes, villages and lands. They were dubbed infiltrators by the Israeli state and shot on sight. On the other hand, the *nakba* crystallized for a whole generation the definition of a crisis in the existing order, and acted as an extraordinary call for action of the most galvanizing sort. A nascent Arab Palestinian nation had been destroyed by Britain and the Zionists: who or what had allowed that to happen? How had the project of independence that had been launched in the Mashriq with the Arab revolt of 1916 ended in this catastrophic loss of a key section of the homeland? The dispossession of the Palestinian people (1947–9), and the failure of the Egyptian and Iraqi monarchies to stand in solidarity with their fellow Arabs over Palestine, worked further to erode the legitimacy of these monarchies, while the political field was increasingly crowded with communist, socialist, Ba'thist, Islamist and pan-Arab alternatives. Amid this crisis of the Arab order, new forces emerged from unexpected quarters, and changed the face of the political field.

Conclusion

The armed struggles that broke out in Morocco (1921–6), Libya (1922–31), Iraq (1920), Syria (1918–21, 1925–7) and Palestine

(1936–9), and the uprising of 1919 in Egypt, as well as the uprisings of the Kurds in Turkey and Iraq in the 1920s and 1930s, were unable to bring into being independent national states – and in some cases, such as in Cyrenaica, death and concentration camps awaited those who resisted in the name of nation and Islam. By the end of the 1930s, in Mandate Palestine, and in most cases much earlier, these struggles had been repressed, diverted, accommodated or co-opted. Only the most dedicated, such as Fawzi Al-Qawuqji, continued to fight, and even he retired after 1948. A new generation would have to take up the mantle of national liberation. These armed struggles did not achieve their key goals.

Nonetheless, these movements, in complex alliance with urban, liberal nationalists that often hegemonized them, did a great deal to establish the existence, even if not the completed actualization, of a new political community, that of the nation, along with the imperative that the demands of this subject deserved to be realized. Even amid their own devastation, they set the standards by which politicians and leaderships of any stripe would be judged. They greatly raised the costs of direct imperial rule, and changed the ruling formula almost everywhere. The uprising in Iraq of 1920 changed direct into indirect rule and installed a new generation of once radical but increasingly oligarchical Sunni officers and leaders in power in Iraq. Or, it is hard to imagine the arrival of the National Bloc in Syria standing between the French and the Syrian Arab population after 1927 absent the uprising of 1925–7. In Morocco, Abd Al-Krim held hundreds of thousands of colonial troops at bay and inflicted at Anual in 1921 the heaviest single defeat by a non-state entity on a European colonial power yet known. Abd Al-Krim unified the Rif, and, once he was defeated, the Spanish took over the administrative infrastructure that he had created and used it to rule the region. This was obviously a betrayal of what Abd Al-Krim had aimed at. But it was a testimony to the capacity of his mobilization to bring into being state-like structures. The British thought they could control Arab nationalism in 1917: indeed, in what they saw as a backward, mosaic-like, segmented society, such as Iraq, they thought it would serve as useful, abstract rhetoric, to justify their invasion and project of direct rule in that country. The British view was short-sighted. Iraq *was* a highly diverse and non-cohesive society (Batatu 1978: 13–37). But new forms of nationalist unity were forged in the heat of political struggle, and then greatly deepened by Faysal's state-building project thereafter. Urban nationalists wrote copious amounts about the uprising of 1920: it marked for them the beginning of the Iraqi nation. Especially in Mandate Palestine, the British were largely unable to control the nationalism that they had once rhetoric-ally championed. In 1939, as a result of the uprising and the impending world war, the British abandoned their policy of supporting the Jewish national home, the origins of a historic rift with the Zionist movement. In short, it is impossible to understand the changing shape of imperial rule in the region without reference to contentious mobilization.

The collapse of the Ottoman empire, the success of Turkish nation-alism, the submission of the Moroccan sultan-caliph, and the heavy-handed invasion of much of the region's territory by European powers between 1911 and the early 1920s were enormously provoking. In order to understand *what* was constructed amid these multiple crises, we must pay due attention to the role played by mobilizing projects and leaderships themselves. Much depended on liberal nationalist leaderships, and the extent to which they could hegemonize the polit-ical field. The inheritors of the pre-war reformist tradition had to espouse principles and identities, and get organized in such a way as to unite broader constituencies. What was required was some principle that could articulate highly diverse constituencies. This was precisely what the idea of nationalism supplied, the idea that had already been heavily implicit at the very least in much of the reformist patriotism and Arabism of the pre-war period. The generalization of an idea that had been limited to rather small, wealthy urban groups before the First World War had much to do with the way that nationalism could now act as the articulator of the diverse struggles of the inter-war period. The greatly accelerated appropriation of nationalism, especially in the countryside, is noteworthy. The rapidity of the change does point to the dramatically changing political environment and the demands of the moment rather than to slow-moving socio-economic change – especially as nationalism took hold in areas where newspapers, radios, industry, universities, labour movements, salons, societies and unions did not exist. In Iraq, nationalism could form a powerful connecting principle between the tribes of the Middle Euphrates, to the urban intelligentsia, the ex-Ottoman officers and the Shi'a *ulema*. As long as urban, educated groups ratcheted up their ownership of the patriotic principle to demand a full-blown national independence, they could maintain their leadership in the field of mass politics, which was rapidly being re-constructed on national lines. In the Rif mountains under Abd Al-Krim, it is clear that nationalism and Islamic modernism served as the key principle of unity, not only between the tribes, but also between the core leadership and the tribes in turn. That urban nationalists could later on turn to Islam (one example being Sayyid Qutb) indicates that socio-economic change, or European forms of education do not necessarily a nationalist make. In other words, there is no reason that socio-economic change, newspapers, unions, societies and so on *should* lead to nationalism. It is this unquestioned socio-logical determinism, based on a base–superstructure theory of caus-ation, and a certain version of the European experience, that needs to be questioned here. Why, indeed, should the centralization of the political field not lead into Islam, a far more expansive and abstract identity than that supplied by nationalism? As a new and initially fragile collective identity, nationalism gathered strength the more it could serve as the basis for the cohesion and integration of a wide variety of movements, tendencies and social groups. This it seems, in addition to the crisis and collapse of the Islamic and dynastic polity, which had in turn been pushed forward by nineteenth-century mobil-ization, is at least one useful way to explain the timing of the general-ization of the nationalist principle in the Arab world, which as a mere idea, after all, had been around for over half a century *without* being integrated into mass mobilization.

It should be noted that the flip from a fight for the Islamic *umma*, to the national *umma*, at least at the most abstract level, was not neces-sarily the most extraordinary mental leap requiring long education and preparation. The fact that the word *umma* could mean Islamic community and nation at the same time (Gasper 2009) surely facili-tated this shift. Both pointed to highly abstract and certainly not face-to-face forms of identity. The idea of the nation furthermore did not necessarily imply democracy, representation, popular sovereignty and so on, none of which forms featured especially heavily in the early, monarchical Hashemite vision of the Arab fatherland, although they were present (Gelvin 1998). Nor was the old-fashioned *jihad* trad-ition, in its pre-Islamic modernist formulation, completely absent here. Its structure involved armed struggle in defence of the community, involving volunteers and irregulars, and was well known indeed in the region and in popular memory, even if eschewed by many urban elites. More proximately, it was *jihad*, after all, that the Shi'a clerics of Iraq called for. It was also Izz Al-Din Al-Qassam's renegade *jihad* that helped spark and provided some leadership for the Palestinian uprising of 1936–9. *Jihad* was at work in Cyrenaica.

There is no doubt also, that not just reformism, but the autonomist traditions of the nineteenth century fed very directly into the uprisings and rugged armed struggles of the 1919 and later. While millenarians were nowhere to be found, others played key roles. Peasants practised in communal direct action were well placed to heighten the intensity of their action in solidarity with the Wafd amid the nationalist upsurge in 1919 in Egypt. Druze warlords in Syria had a tradition of fighting to secure their own spheres of autonomy and this fed into the uprising on the national stage. Traditions of Rif autonomy and tribal fighting skill played a key role, albeit under new forms of organization, in Abd Al-Krim's armed struggle in Morocco. Tribal arms and smuggling networks far from state control also played an important role in the Mashriq. The Arab revolt was unthinkable without the use, albeit for new purposes, of tribal armed capacity, which also played a key role in Iraq in 1920. Certain Druze chiefs (but not all) supported the Arab revolt and supplied grain to it, opposing the Turks, 'the murderers of our fathers' (Provence 2005: 42–7). Here the support for Arab independence drew strength from the older autonomist tradition. Such traditions were also at work in the uprising on the Alawite mountain of Shaykh Salih Al-Ali in 1920. Al-Ali was a thirty-five-year-old land-owner with a 'reputation for courage and fair-play' built on 'earlier resistance to Ottoman interference in his district'. With this status, Al-Ali 'easily convinced the notables to contribute their respective fighting forces to the guerrilla army he was organizing' (Khoury 1987: 99). In April 1915, the people of Najaf rose up and expelled the Ottoman Turks from the city, whereupon the different city quarters themselves became independent of one another (Batatu 1978: 19). The tribes played a vital role in the Al-Sanusi *jihad* in the 1920s. Finally, the tradition of commoner uprising in defence of the rights of the people before 1914, and the tradition of village alarm and call to arms at moments of collective danger (*faza'a*) fed into nationalist uprisings thereafter.

Modernist teleology dominated by the causal force of socio-economic change cannot do justice to the contribution made by rural groups. The great wave of armed struggles from Morocco in the West to Iraq in the East in 1911–27, and their subsequent *demobilization*, does not fit such a theory. If rapid socio-economic change was the key to contentious mobilization, this cannot explain the fact that the main armed struggles in the region in the 1920s were rooted in rural areas, such as the Rif mountains, the Jabal Druze, northern Iraq, not urban areas, and that many of them were led and staffed not by urban elites, but by warlords, tribal elements, militant peasants, ex-Ottoman soldiers, neighbourhood bosses and the like. As Provence writes regarding Syria, '[c]ontrary to the expectations of the mandatory power, the uprising began in an apparently remote and supposedly backward rural region [Jabal Druze]' (Provence 2005: 12). Provence's answer, meanwhile, was that the region was not so backward after all – which could account for new contention. The best historiography on the Great Revolt in Palestine persists in the same determination that socio-economic change is the fundamental cause, rooting the uprising in an incipient peasant class struggle against landed elites (Anderson 2013; Swedenberg 1993) and occluding therefore much vital political, cultural and popular content. Indeed, opposition to feudal exploitation and dispossession at the hands of notables was hardly a new theme in the hills of Jenin and Nablus or the rural Mashriq more generally. Workers' strike action under the banners of justice and welfare had started up, we recall, in Damascus in the 1870s. The more striking feature of the history of Mandate Palestine, especially if read in terms of what had gone before rather than in terms of a hoped-for future, was that urban groups actually *did* forge alliances with rural groups – a fact symbolized by the not entirely coerced adoption of the *kufiyya* by urban middle classes to assist rural insurgents from being detected when they came into the towns, and operationalized in the existence of the National Committees. These alliances, and the forms of mobilization they sustained, were in many ways the key to the strengths of the development of Arab and Palestinian nationalism. Likewise, these alliances were formed, albeit in a very different way, under the banners of Islamic reformism, nationalism and republicanism in the Rif mountains of Morocco.

The armed struggles of the inter-war period joined hands with vivacious traditions handed down from the nineteenth century. The complete dismissal in much of the English speaking academy of the classical Arab nationalist historiography, which always emphasized decades of Turkish oppression in the Arabic-speaking regions, has in fact turned out to be an obstacle to grasping the links between long nineteenth-century autonomism and inter-war period nationalism. It was not that an Arab nation had long been suppressed and was now stirred into life by the enlightened ideas of urban nationalists. It was, however, that groups involved above all in defensive and autonomist traditions of protest, which included resistance against 'Turks' and the 'Turkiyya', now hegemonized in new ways, added greatly to the muscle of nationalist movements in many parts of the region. In short, there were limits on the rupture with the past: pre-nationalist traditions of resistance gave immense impetus to patriotic and nationalist mobilization.

The weakness of pan-Islam in the tradition of Abdulhamid II, and the lack of a Khilafa movement as in India, may have owed something to the lack of a viable leadership or any strategy of mass mobilization. The Caliphate became a symbolic prize for which various rulers and grandees competed: Ibn Saud, King Fuad (r. 1917–36) of Egypt and Ahmad Al-Sanusi of Cyrenaica (Pankhurst 2013). The Ottoman state in any case had been shattered, and the sultan-caliph had turned to collaboration with the British and the French, and spoke of Mustafa Kemal and the nationalists with dismissive disgust. Under Abdulhamid II, pan-Islam had become thoroughly identified with the now defunct sultan-caliph, it had never engaged in real organization on the ground, and its fortunes went down with the Osmanlï dynasty itself. The weakness of such mobilization, in contrast with that of the nationalists, can help explain why national political community came so much to the fore in this period. As ever, a great deal depended on the content of mobilization, not just on external actors, and not just on the fact of hegemonic contraction itself.

The Sufi orders were in some ways usurped by the reforming societies that now developed in the milieu of the urban educated classes and by new forms of activism that built new networks outside of the Sufi orders. Sufis and ex-Sufis were involved in these new forms of activism. Hasan Al-Banna had been active in Sufism before he turned to reform societies and founded the Muslim Brotherhood. Messali Al-Hadj had in turn been a Sufi of the Derkawa order. Al-Qassam had been initiated into the Al-Tijaniyya. Sufi modes of organization were adopted and then over-turned by the initiatives of activists themselves, who saw them as no longer adequate to the new tasks of more permanent forms of mobilization rooted in altering the policies of a centralized state and new forms of ideology and programme. On the other hand, Sufis themselves became isolated, even when they led the action. The neo-Sufi armed struggle of Umar Al-Mukhtar of

Cyrenaica, for all its dignity and tenacity in the face of genocidal oppression, could not forge alliances with urban groups, who sometimes offered moral and financial support, but otherwise did not take meaningful contentious action themselves. Not all of this can be ascribed to the vested interests of the *sottomesi*, their supposedly inherent lack of martial valour, and the idea that cities were weak and property vulnerable in the face of artillery and aircraft. Urban guerrilla tactics, under the influence of new ideas, were to come to North Africa in the 1950s, after all. These divisions, and the isolation of Umar Al-Mukhtar's men, were also a sign that new ideas would be necessary to unite the country. Shifts towards Libyan nationalism were unmistakably present in this context throughout the period.

Many urban reformists set out to achieve a position in the state, through new participatory, democratic and representative mechanisms: elections, parliament and constitution. They offered up these new mechanisms as ways in which new groups would be able to achieve representation, a process which was to be hastened by education and measures of social reform. In Egypt there was also a dose of economic nationalism, an attempt to build up national capital and industrial manufactured goods in order to break out of the colonial, agricultural, export economy. The whole project was stitched up with the threads of national self-determination and appeals to popular sovereignty. Elements of this project of self-determination, representation, education and industry were clearly put into action: constitution, elections, Cairo University and the Mahalla spinning and weaving mills were all testimony to this. On the other hand, over time, these achievements were truncated, or looked less impressive as the demand for more thoroughgoing social reform grew louder. In the 1940s and 1950s, as liberal nationalism increasingly lost its mass base, new forms of socio-economic nationalism arose.

The main strength of reformist, nationalist and notable leaderships was that at least for a time they were able to hegemonize large sections of the politically active population. The main weakness of reformist and liberal nationalism, conversely, may well have been that it was unable to shake its conservatism and its reformist and legal methods. In some respects, urban liberals were unwilling and unprepared to throw their lot in with the masses. This was at least the case in Egypt. Many urban groups viewed themselves as more enlightened, advanced and politically conscious than their illiterate country cousins. This position, indeed, has been internalized by some liberal historians (Khoury 1984: 515). This idea bolstered such activists' transcendent morale and gave them a sense that it was they who were entitled to take initiatives. But it was a problem when it came to building meaningful forms of solidarity. This was partly because it was wrong: rural groups were just as politically savvy, the fruit of long experience, as their urban counterparts. But it was also because it contradicted ideas of popular sovereignty that also played a role in the construction of rural–urban links. It was perhaps above all a problem because urban liberals needed the force and capacity of armed and rural groups more than they perhaps realized. If the popular committees of 1920 in Damascus were the fruit of long social and economic change, as Gelvin argues, then this cannot explain why they then disappeared for much of the subsequent two decades. Indeed, their very disappearance can be read as a clue to the ways in which liberal mass mobilization was not as sustained as it might have been. The Wafd in Egypt did have an extensive, state-wide network of committees and supporters, a fact which helped to account for the country-wide Wafdist uprising in the name of the constitution in 1935. It can also help account for the Wafd's long-standing hegemony, for example, over the national and labour movement alike. The Wafd was not limited by any shallowness of organization, but rather by the timidity and legalism of its leadership strategy. When this strategy finally wobbled, in 1951, it was too little, too late.

Women's movements, the labour movement, socialists, communists and the Muslim Brotherhood all moved during the inter-war years to contest the now centralized political field, and developed and generalized new forms of organization, political parties, unions, syndicates, mass societies and the like, and new means of collective action. These new forms of activism converted defensive and autonomist forms of protest into new forms of political mobilization based around newly developing forms of political ideology, and gradually pushed aside the old vehicles of collective action in Sufi orders, tribes, and so on, and generated new forms of organization. In so doing, they made important contributions to the rise of a new kind of political field. They also increasingly forged new alliances on more systematic bases with workers, peasants and other subaltern constituencies. If we are to understand the harsh fate of these new forms of mass politics in the 1950s and 1960s, we must look not just at the machinations of elites, but at the new forms of mobilization themselves that were to arise after 1948.

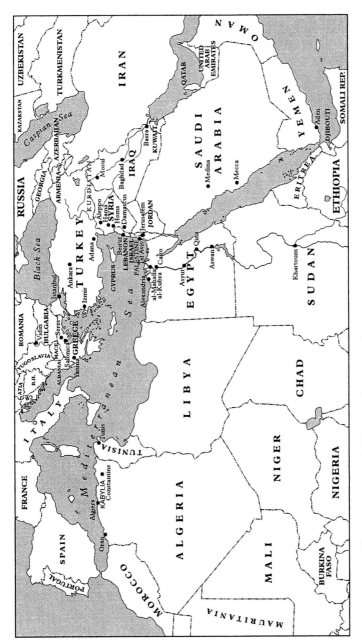

Map 2 The Middle East and North Africa in the twentieth century

311

III National independence, guerrilla war and social revolution, 1952–1976

Introduction

It is difficult to do justice to the energies, the forms of solidarity, and the idealism of the period from the 1950s to the 1970s because contentious mobilization seemed either to dead-end in conservative monarchy, as on the Arabian peninsula, or give rise to corrupt and authoritarian rule, as in much of the rest of the region. It is easy to forget, in the wake of failure and repression, that the mobilizing projects of this period were, for so many, instruments of national liberation and socio-economic uplift. We might do well to remember the judgment of Jacques Berque, who believed that this period involved 'the most violent, and yet deliberate, effort ever made by man to break the chains of weakness, poverty and colour' (Berque 1972: 26). The importance of ideas that were untarnished by history, and that appeared new and powerful, and were thus able to exact normative commitment, is one of the important casualties of hindsight, because it is hard to see how ideas that go on to be discredited could once have commanded intense commitment. The passage of time can fool us as to the importance of initial normative commitments in another way. Where vested interests and group loyalties grow up around meaningful, activist ideas over time, the actual role that ideal interests play starts to diminish, making the latter easier to discredit as having all along been mere instruments in the hands of those who sought power. But this is to put the cart before the horse, and to forget the role played by normative commitments and ideas especially in the early stages of a mobilizing project. The protagonists at the time, just as in previous periods, did not have the gift of hindsight. They read their situation in terms of the present and the past as it was known to them. They responded to the deepening political crisis that reigned in the 1940s and 1950s. Many searched for solutions that could avoid the mistakes of the generation of 1919, those who failed to lead the nation to true independence: Saʻd Zaghlul and Nahhas Pasha in Egypt, Nuri Al-Said in Iraq, Shukri Al-Quwwatli in Syria, Ferhat Abbas in Algeria, and Hajj Amin Al-Husseini in Palestine. The older political generation of 1919 was now confronted with the generation of 1948.

Liberal reformism and rugged armed struggle had played a role in bringing into being a meaningful political field within the new states of the post-1918 Arab order. A measure of this was the fact that in many ways the new movements in the region between the 1940s and the 1960s were reacting almost as much to the failures of liberal-patriotic leaderships and the professional politicians of the existing political field as they were to the forms of injustice meted out more directly by corrupt monarchs, foreign companies and colonial officials. In some respects, it was the contraction of the *alternative* hegemony, one which had never really taken power in the state, that was at stake in provoking new forms of political action from the 1940s onwards. Everyone agreed, or said they did, on the need for national self-determination. The basis of the disagreement was different. The men of action confronted the men of congresses, meetings and statements. Provincial figures, those of humble origins, of few educational credentials, sometimes from stigmatized minorities or refugee camps, confronted the professional, well-educated and well-heeled, liberal notability of the capitals. Those consumed with economic problems and questions of social justice encountered lawyerly figures fiddling with clauses in the constitution. Many of those who grew up on the margins of the political field in the 1930s and 1940s learned an important lesson: that reformism, legal methods, patience, negotiation, demonstrations and letter-writing were doomed to sterility, back-sliding and defeat. What was needed was direct action, forceful methods and the gun.

While liberal reformism went into retreat, identities and principles associated with national liberation, Third Worldism, Arab socialism, pan-Arabism, communism, Baʻthism and Nasserism came to the fore. The new ideologies addressed socio-economic questions above all. While parties, unions and syndicates of all kinds had emerged since the late nineteenth century, cells, fronts and committees emerged as crucial vehicles of transformative political action after 1945. Meanwhile, in many parts of the Third World, the national liberation movements, from Cuba to China by way of India, pushed back imperialism, and brought a rising storm of inspiration, and, by the 1960s, material support.

Islamic activism, which had played such an important role in the
crisis of the Egyptian state, and had been one of the lead non-state
suppliers of fighters for Palestine in 1948–9, dramatically lost ground,
relevance and popularity all over the region after 1952. By the late
1960s, Muslim activism in Egypt, in the words of an important scholar
of the movement, was a matter of 'an ever dwindling activist fringe of
individuals dedicated to an increasingly less relevant Muslim "position"
about society; and of professional malcontents' (Mitchell 1969: xxiii).
Indeed, Islam was subordinated to other principles and identities among
activists. Mehdi Ben Barka, the most important Moroccan socialist
leader, assimilated Islam to democracy (Le Tourneau *et al.* 1972:
86ff.). When Islam was briefly affirmed as the state religion in the final
version of Boumediène's National Charter in Algeria in 1976, 'it was
stated that the only way in which Islam could renew itself was through
socialism' (Evans and Phillips 2007: 97). Hafez Al-Asad 'forgot' to
specify in the constitution he issued in 1973 that the head of state in
Syria must be a Muslim (Alianak 2007: 130). In North Africa, Islamic
modernist *ulema* were important in defining nationhood in the 1930s,
but they did not start any movements that made any meaningful contribution to Algerian independence. Nor did Islamists play any real role in
the Palestinian nationalist movement until well after 1982, when the
PLO was driven out of Lebanon to a deeper exile in Tunisia.

Conversely, secularists condemned Islamists as reactionaries. The
long-time Egyptian activist and writer Adel Hussain, for example, later
told Burgat that supporters of the socialist party, such as himself,
opposed the Muslim Brotherhood as 'just reactionaries opposed to
progress', as 'stupid and weak-willed'. Their refusal to fully support
Nasser was seen in Leftist and nationalist circles as 'strange and
unproductive' (Burgat 2003: 41). As Rashid Al-Ghannushi, who was
to lead the Sunni Islamic modernists in Tunisia, put it, Nasserists and
Ba'thists accused the Muslim Brotherhood of being a reactionary
current tied to colonialism and the Americans (Burgat 2003: 34).
Islamists found themselves in retreat, politically, economically and
socially. As Al-Ghannushi put it: 'There was nothing left for them [this
generation] to do except withdraw and to regroup and to try to control
their rancour at this [cultural] occupation ... by the "Tunisian sons of
France"' (Burgat 2003: 29–31).

Only a few, imprisoned, alienated, or in exile, clung to or developed
Islamist ideas in new ways; there were the writings of Sayyid Qutb, as

yet largely unread; the study circles of Shi'a *ulema* in Najaf, as yet little known. The flurry of activism around the learned cleric and Ayatollah Khomeini in Iran in 1963 seemed an isolated incident at the time. Ali Shariati, future ideologue of the Iranian revolution, was mixing with Third World nationalists in Paris in the early 1960s, his own synthesis of revolution and Shi'ism was still very much on the drawing board. In Saudi Arabia, at least until the early 1960s, the airwaves were ruled by the Nasserist radio, Sawt Al-Arab, and Faysal's initiatives in building up Salafi-Wahhabism there in the 1960s were irrelevant to the contentious scene of these years of secular revolution. The retreat of Islamism, in short, was general.

Another important innovation of these years related to the goals of mobilizing projects. Many of the movements of the inter-war period sought to participate in the state, and re-formulate its forms of sovereignty, its constitution, and establish the existence of a national political community. At most, these movements proposed that the state should be involved in education or this or that project of economic nationalism. The movements of the nineteenth century, outside of this reformist tradition, had sought to escape, replace or moderate the judgments of the state or use its capacity to enforce rules to eliminate instances of injustice. In contrast with all of this, one of the crucial features of the period 1952–79 was the activist and transformative sentiment, which was reinforced until the late 1960s as states started to actually implement social reform, that the state and its apparatuses were now the key agent of social and economic transformation. In some respects, this was the age in which organized contenders in the political field, Ba'thists, communists, socialists, Arab nationalists and Nasserists, proposed programmes which, through the agency of the state, aimed to (and often actually did) shape society and economy in far-reaching ways. This was an age in which the Bolshevik model of 1917, whereby the state was used as an instrument of social and economic transformation, was appropriated as a goal by mobilizing projects.

This statism had another dimension, easily missed because it seemed so obvious. There was a considerable emphasis on how the state was supposed to be the means by which national liberation was achieved. Whatever else nationalism had to do, it had to construct a state, even if one did not exist, as in the case of the Palestinians, the Kurds, and even, to some extent, the Algerians (Roberts 2003). We will explore in detail the question of the Palestinian search for a state (Y. Sayigh 1997). But it is noteworthy that part of the strategy of the Algerian FLN, was that national independence was to be achieved through 'the restoration of the Algerian state, sovereign, democratic, and social, within the framework of the principles of Islam' (Front de Libération Nationale 1954). This was ambitious as in many ways there was no Algerian state to restore. The French had controlled the administration of the country for more than a century, while the Ottoman Deys that preceded them were only an Algerian state in a minimal sense of the term (Roberts 2003). Certainly, no Ottoman Dey had monopolized the legitimate means of coercion in Algiers. But the use of the term 'restoration' was by no means intended ironically. Even though there would be no state, it was necessary for a nationalist movement to create one. The flight from statelessness, the drive to achieve a state, was by no means, therefore, a simple imposition on the region from above. The whole idea of statehood, the drive to create a preponderant, centralized power capable of controlling and regulating a given territory and population, defending its borders and securing order by holding a monopoly of the legitimate means of coercion and enacting change was powerfully inter-woven with nationalist popular movements seeking a political community of their own. Who or what was it that would bring about the changes that were so urgently demanded? Not private capital, not charitable organization, and certainly not the tribes or the Sufi orders that were so important during the nineteenth century, long dismissed as superstitious, devious and backward. It was, in all cases, the state that was freighted with this burden of reform and even emancipation. In this statism, we see both the ambition and the limits on the vision of the national liberation movements of these decades.

That the idea of armed struggle was taken up, and championed by urban and educated figures (such as *hakim al-thawra*, the 'Dr of Revolution' George Habash, a medical doctor), rather than by Bedouin, warlords, Sufis, neighbourhood toughs, militant peasants, mountaineers, radical preachers and the like, was one of the most dramatic innovations of this period. As we have seen, from Tetouan to Damascus by way of Tripoli (in Libya), the secular urban intelligentsia had very rarely advocated for, let alone actually led and filled, the ranks of armed strugglers in the region. This changed. And in contrast with the almost completely male armed struggles of the inter-war period, under the progressive and even feminist banners of these years, women were to play an active role in combat and auxiliary roles. The traditions of some of the Rifian tribes, likely disapproved by Abd Al-Krim, were now taken up again in a completely different milieu.

Another important innovation of these decades, set in motion after the Free Officer's coup in Egypt in 1952, had to do with the fact that nationalist and Leftist movements could count for the first time on the support of powerful regional states. Morocco had briefly supported Abd Al-Qadir in Algeria in the 1830s. Turkish nationalists had briefly supported Syrian anti-colonialism between 1918 and 1921, but then Turkey had turned its back decisively on the Arabic-speaking world, a position that has endured, in spite of a shift after 2011. There had been non-state support for the Arab Palestinians in 1936–9, and some ineffectual and limited state support for them in 1947–9. But there had been nothing compared to the support that Nasser's state was now ready to offer to Nasserist and pan-Arab movements beyond the borders of Egypt – the wealthiest and most populous state in the Arab world, with by far the most developed media apparatus, education system, and literary and film culture. The acute concern, not to say panic, in French official circles in the early 1950s over Nasser's support for nationalism in North Africa is one testament to this innovation (Archives du Ministère des Affaires Étrangères: Maroc 1944–55). Other 'revolutionary' states, such as Syria, Iraq and South Yemen after 1967, followed suit. The latter two states, for example, supported the armed struggle in Dhufar after 1965. After Israel's devastating victory in 1967, state support for Leftist movements moved westwards through Libya (1969) and into the Algeria of Boumediène in the 1970s (Evans and Phillips 2007: 89–91).

Nasser's revolutionary coup

The political impasse was broken in the most old-established, wealthiest, most populous and most culturally influential state in the Arab world by a revolutionary *coup d'état* undertaken by patriotic officers. In the early hours of 23 July 1952, a group of self-styled 'Free Officers', led by Gamal Abd Al-Nasser since 1949, about 90–100 in number, and drawn from every branch of the military except the navy, moved to secure control of army units in Cairo. By the morning, they held the reins of power (Gordon 1997: 48). They promised to restore a sound parliamentary life, purify the political system from corrupt and factional elements, restore national honour, and engage in meaningful social reform. Within days, the Free Officers had deposed the king, turning Egypt into a republic.

The Free Officers took aim at the corrupt, civilian elites, and the monarchy. As Nasser put it in an eloquent speech in 1955, the Egyptian army had not been defeated in Palestine, nor was it responsible for the defeat in Palestine: 'the army should leave the dock and the real criminal [i.e. the corrupt civilian politicians] should be held to account' (Nasser 1973: 4–5). It was not the army as such that moved in 1952. It is important to note that, although the Free Officer networks were built around the charismatic figure of Nasser within the army since the defeat in Palestine, they were mobilized, at least in part, *against* the military high command. Muhammad Al-Gizawi, for example, arrested his commanding officer on the morning of 23 July. In Egypt, it was not the army as a whole that seized the initiative. Indeed, the numbers involved in the army itself were actually quite small: only around 100 officers (Gordon 1997). Nasser's men had had some organizational links to both the communist DMNL and the Muslim Brotherhood – but they were to break with both.

The appeal of Nasser, and 'honourable' and patriotic Free Officers to bystanders and other actors in the political field is not that difficult to discern, where the civilian politicians had failed, especially over Palestine, where competing ideologies could be seen as divisive, and where party politics were corrupted, and associated with a wealthy and out-of-touch elite of land-owners and pashas. Nasser was a son of the nation, a figure who had not been drawn into detailed ideological bickering, an outsider to the existing political and economic elite, and a man of some charisma and eloquence to boot, and who represented technocracy in the military, not privilege, and who promised resolute action on Egypt's corrupted and British-controlled political scene in the name of real national independence and development. On the other hand, Nasser won support because some of the wealthy thought that nothing would change, and some of the revolutionaries and ideologues among the communist DMNL and the Muslim Brotherhood alike thought that Nasser would actually implement their programmes, or could be manipulated. Both the British and especially the Americans thought they could mould the Free Officers in ways that suited their purposes: models of imperialism old and new suggested that a military officer was easier to do business with than a democratic politician or

movement with a meaningful social base. None of the many contending forces in the Egyptian field had been able to hegemonize it, leaving
the way open for a Bonapartist move.

The 23 July Revolution was to inaugurate a revolution 'from above',
and to have profound consequences for protests and political movements across the region, as Nasserism sought to export itself and was
appropriated. Joel Gordon's account is indeed a corrective to the view
that Nasser's coup was the inevitable manifestation of praetorianism
and modernization in an otherwise broken polity, or, on the other
hand, that it was the pre-determined expression of the powers of the
exploited classes against the power of the land-owners and the colonialists. Instead, there was surely, as Gordon notes, a degree of impro-
visation: 'The story of the coup is one of good fortune and near
disaster, and not a small amount of clever extemporaneous acting'
(Gordon 1997: 52). It would seem that the political initiative embedded
in the revolutionary coup is worth considering as a factor in its own
right – while the withdrawal of British troops to the Canal Zone did
provide an important political opportunity, for those who were ready
to spot it, for a military coup to secure Cairo without having to
confront the British imperial army head on. Nasserism drew and forged
new syntheses from many of the currents of activism that had pushed
forward the crisis of the state that had come to a head in 1951–2.

Above all, the initiative of the Free Officers played a key role in
bringing the military into politics in the Arab world. The officers
replaced and displaced political forces rooted in more organic forms
of mass mobilization. By delivering a revolution from above, it eclipsed
and co-opted a great many of the means of popular mobilization that
had been building up in the political field since the 1900s. Real
national and socio-economic change came, but at a heavy cost to the
capacities of independent organization.

The hegemonic incorporation of the labour movement in Egypt in the 1950s and 1960s

A relatively vibrant Left and labour movement, if not necessarily a
cohesive one, existed in Egypt at the time of Nasser's revolutionary
coup in 1952, as we have seen. Communists associated with the
DMNL and other organizations espoused revolutionary ideas about
a workers' and peasants' state. Socialists – such as those associated

with the Wafd Vanguard – articulated strong conceptions of social justice. Journalists, students, and others espoused variants of socialism. There were an array of trade unions, some more independent and radical than others, with a substantial history of committed organizing and strike action. Workers in large industrial firms had their own relatively autonomous grievances and sense of justice, rejecting high-handed and violent treatment at the hands of *effendi* managers and foremen, and seeking better pay and conditions at work, over piece rates, holidays, wages, housing arrangements, social benefits and so on, and had developed a tradition of taking industrial action through their own initiative, whether formally organized or not – principally through strikes and stoppages.

The newly minted Nasserist state, controlled by the military concerned with order and intolerant of independent forms of power, anxious about capital flight, and hostile to communism and class conflict, acted to repress, infiltrate, censor and break up the movement. The new direction was dramatically demonstrated almost immediately after the coup with the heavy-handed repression of a strike at the Misr Fine Spinning and Weaving Company in Kafr Al-Duwwar on 12–13 August 1952. Around 500 workers there, largely on their own initiative, staged a sit-in demanding wage increases and a freely elected union independent of the company (Beinin and Lockman 1998: 421–6). Troops were quickly at the scene, and confronted two demonstrations; a fire was set and shots were fired; the army started shooting and two soldiers, one policeman, and four workers were killed and many others wounded. Five hundred and forty-five workers were arrested, and twenty-nine were charged with offences such as premeditated murder, arson, destruction of property, and theft of police weapons. The military tribunal's death sentence, handed down so quickly that the defendants were unable to appoint themselves a lawyer or generate a defence, led on 7 September to the execution of workers Mustafa Khamis and Muhammad Al-Baqari, wrongly rumoured to be communists. Their executions reflected the 'fear of the political effects of the strike' (Beinin and Lockman 1998: 423). That the demonstrators were almost certainly shouting 'Long live Muhammad Najib' indicated that there was no intention to oppose the new regime (Beinin and Lockman 1998: 423). The Revolutionary Command Council's [RCC's] certification of the death sentences above all 'indicated that the regime would resolutely oppose any expression of autonomous working class organization and collective action' (Beinin and Lockman 1998: 425).

In the wake of Kafr Al-Dawwar, 'the RCC began to take measures to isolate the communists in its own ranks and remove them from all positions of power' (Beinin and Lockman 1998: 426). The Muslim Brothers, still friendly with the regime, participated in this campaign. The DMNL and the FCGFETU (Founding Committee for a General Federation of Egyptian Trade Unions) gritted its teeth and continued to support the RCC, hoping to 'alter the balance of forces within the regime' with some believing that the strike weapon at this time would only 'benefit reactionaries' (Beinin and Lockman 1998: 427). This policy contributed to internal disaffection and splits within the organization. The RCC refused to meet with the FCGFETU until it purged its ranks of Leftists; while these went ahead among the Cairo transport workers, the police in turn infiltrated a number of important unions – such as the Cairo Printers' Union. A number of unionists and others who protested Kafr Al-Dawwar or Left positions were jailed, and further sentences were handed down to workers who went on strike (Beinin and Lockman 1998: 429). Sections of the labour movement continued to protest their loyalty to the regime while asserting their right to organize independently, but to no avail. All strikes were banned by military order in December 1952. In the same month, a law was issued that significantly reduced the scope of permissible trade union action. Meanwhile, the DMNL, into 1953, 'kept relying on its friends among the Free Officers to effect a change in the regime's labor policy', refraining from public criticism or organizing protests – a defensive posture undertaken under a highly limited set of options amid an overwhelmingly corporatist political culture (Beinin and Lockman 1998: 430–3).

The regime decreed the dissolution of all political parties on 17 January 1953, arresting over 100 political figures. Almost half of the arrests were communists, and all Left newspapers were closed (Beinin and Lockman 1998: 433). Locked out of legal political participation, the DMNL turned to opposition. It repudiated its acceptance of the Kafr Al-Dawwar executions amid a textile strike in the Cairo suburb of Imbaba in August–September 1953. It was too little, too late. The strike was put down by tanks, and up to 500 arrests were made. By 1953, most of those favouring independent labour activism had been stripped of their positions, and the FCGFETU and its hopeful successor had been suppressed. Other unionizing efforts, even though legal within new frameworks, were blocked.

The RCC did not demobilize, and probably could not have demobilized, the Left by coercion alone. The key was the stream of policies and concessions offering real material and affective gains to the Left and the labour movement, and positions in newly created corporatist statist institutions for those that would take them – a Nasserist mode of hegemonic incorporation that was completed during the 1960s. The RCC moved quickly to establish a base of support in the labour movement – through a series of entirely top-down measures. The first of these was a comprehensive new labour legislation, enacted on 8 December 1952, and supplemented by Decree 165 in April 1953, which offered increased severance compensation, longer holidays, free transport to remote factories, free medical care, and above all job security, the 'single most important demand of the postwar workers' movement' (Beinin and Lockman 1998: 432). These moves, in addition to the land reform measure of September 1952, 'secured the regime substantial popular support from peasants and workers', enabling the army to repress those sectors rejecting the political deal (Beinin and Lockman 1998: 433).

They also paved the way for the army to organize and co-opt those elements of the labour movement who were ready to play ball by giving them a stake in the regime, a move concretized in the creation of the Liberation Rally in 1953, the RCC's 'single party' with Nasser as Secretary-General. The Liberation Rally brought in a raft of trade union leaders, including the Cairo transport workers. Many of these unionists had only a thin or a recent track-record in independent organizing, and some of the key leaders owed their ascendancy within the movement to the state. Other unionists, critical as individuals of labour policy, were brought in to serve on planning committees. On the other hand, with almost all the communists in prison, independent unionists, the Workers' Vanguard and workers were still able to mount significant protests in favour of Muhammad Najib, parties, parliament and democracy in March 1954 – in Najib's final showdown against Nasser and the Free Officers. But by now the labour movement was split, and 'trade union connections established through the efforts of the Liberation Rally proved critical in allowing the army to mobilize its own mass support' through the labour movement (Beinin and Lockman 1998: 440). The Cairo transport workers strike that paralysed

Cairo, and the general strike call in late March, were thus in favour of Nasser. On 29 March, 'the streets of Cairo were filled with demonstrators opposing Najib and shouting "No parties, no democracy"' (Beinin and Lockman 1998: 443). Nasser carried the day, partly thanks to the labour movement, and Najib was effectively sidelined.

The events of March 1954 secured a deal that was to endure until at least the early 1970s. A section of the union movement

agreed to support a military dictatorship that had repeatedly demonstrated its unalterable opposition to a free trade union movement, the right to strike, and any form of independent initiative and action by workers. In exchange the regime confirmed them in their positions of trade union leadership and agreed to preserve and extend the economic gains that had already been achieved (Beinin and Lockman 1998: 444).

In addition, the bargain was sustained because the RCC 'represented the only viable vehicle for achieving the demands of the Egyptian nationalist movement. The Wafd, and certainly all the other political parties, had repeatedly been proven incapable of forcing a total evacuation of British troops from Egypt, whereas the RCC was on the verge of accomplishing this objective' (Beinin and Lockman 1998: 444).

This form of hegemonic incorporation and co-optation, armoured by coercion, was to continue, and indeed be developed, until the mid-1960s. The radical nationalist dimension was enormously bolstered by the nationalization of the Suez Canal, the successful defiance of the Tripartite Aggression in 1956, and Nasserism's hugely important role on the regional stage, at least until 1967. Many communists and Leftists were brought around to Nasserism during these years (Burgat 2003: 40). The institutional aspects were enhanced with the absorption of the unions themselves into the state occasioned by the creation of the General Federation of Egyptian Trade Unions in 1957, and a Ministry of Labour in 1959, and the associated provision of employment and privilege within a large bureaucracy. Unions no longer existed to promote the independent forms of strike action that had become a standard repertoire among Egyptian workers. The nationalizations of 1960–1 and the official 'state socialism' of the 1960s, and prestige projects such as the High Dam at Aswan, provided a material uplift in jobs, wages, training and social status (Posusney 1994: 216), as well as symbolic recognition for workers, ex-peasants and trade unionists. Standards of living among formal sector workers continued to rise until the mid-1960s – and educational opportunities were greatly increased for the poorer strata. The state subsidized the cost of many basic commodities, including electricity and gas, and enacted price controls. In the 1960s, it was made mandatory that workers comprised at least 50 per cent of the management committees of public-sector enterprises, and that workers and peasants comprised a similar proportion of the membership of the National Assembly. State media, universities and schools provided employment and recognition for a Nasserist brand of Leftism.

The bargain articulated in the National Charter of 1962 was that workers were expected to work hard in return for the economic development that Nasserism would bring (Posusney 1994: 218). Many workers internalized the view that they were working hard in turning the wheel of production in order to build the economy and make the nation great (Mosallam 2013; Posusney 1997: 154) – and that strikes and grievances were distracting, divisive and unproductive. Among workers on the High Dam in the early 1960s, where mortality rates were relatively high, it was commonly said that *'al-marhum kan ghaltan'* (i.e. 'the deceased was in the wrong'): many thought it unacceptable to blame management or the state for these deaths amid dangerous equipment or procedures, as workers were engaged in the manly, even glorious, task of building Egypt and its future under Nasser. These beliefs and cognate Nasserist tropes were circulated in the intimate languages of poetry, story and song (Mosallam 2013).

Egypt's communist parties voluntarily dissolved themselves in 1965, and their cadres 'concentrated on integrating ... into the Nasserist regime: publishing *Al-Tali'a* under the auspices of the semiofficial daily *Al-Ahram*, joining and assuming leading positions in the Arab Socialist Union and its secret Vanguard Organization, and participating prominently in the direction of the regime's mass media' (Beinin 1994: 256).

Finally, there was always repression: 'unions were supervised by government security agencies, and the government invalidated the election of opposition union officials' (Beinin and Lockman 1998: 459), and prison sentences continued to be meted out against elements from the Left that dissented, especially between 1959 and 1964, a wave of arrests that began following the revolutionary coup in Iraq in 1958 (Posusney 1997: 64).

In short, after 1952, an independent if divided Leftist movement was hegemonically incorporated by the Nasserist state through a combination of repression, concession and political inclusion, with both institutional and ideological aspects. Labour strikes and protests, stoppages, sit-ins, and sometimes strikes over pay and conditions, organized on workers' own initiative without official union support, did not completely disappear from the scene, such as a rather solitary strike at the Tanta Tobacco Company over withdrawn bonuses in the early 1960s (Posusney 1994: 223). Yet, organized political opposition in Leftist mode, the critiques of the secular intelligentsia, and independent union activity, were almost completely absent – with these segments now actively involved in the Nasserist state. The labour movement had paid dearly in independence and in repression, but it had exacted real concessions on political position, jobs, welfare and status. This situation was only to change after the defeat of 1967, the loss of momentum in the development of statist socialism in the mid-1960s, Sadat's turn towards neo-liberalism in the 1970s, and a transnational Leftist revival.

The revolutionary coup in Iraq

The 14 July Revolution of 1958 in Iraq was a revolutionary coup which established a republic and overthrew the Hashemite monarchy established by King Faisal I in 1921 under the auspices of the British. King Faisal II, the regent and Crown Prince Abd Al-Ilah, and Prime Minister Nuri Al-Said, were put to death. It was completely different to the coups of the late 1930s, because the military men who undertook it had an important relationship to popular politics. Of the leaders of the coup, Abd Al-Karim Qassim was linked to communists, national democrats, Kurds, and Iraqi nationalism; while Abdul-Salam Aref was linked to Ba'thists, socialists, Nasserism and pan-Arabism. These officers won instant popular acclaim for their actions. During the military coup of 14 July 1958, barring 'light resistance' at the home of the Prime Minister Nuri Sa'id, 'no one tried to defend the British-installed monarchy' (Wiley 1992: 24). Just as in Egypt, the numbers involved in the army itself were actually quite small: in Iraq, about 200 Free Officers on the eve of the revolution (less than 5 per cent of the officer corps) (Batatu 1978: 783).

There can be no doubt of the inspiration of 1952 for the coup of 1958. The first practical step was taken by two officers in September 1952,

inspired by the coup which Gamal Abd-un-Nasir and his little group of Free
Officers pulled against Faruq on 23 July 1952 ... In his reminiscences
Abd ul-Majid explicitly acknowledges the fact, and relates how one day
in September ... he and Sirri agreed to start clandestine work (Batatu
1978: 773).

On the other hand, there was still a long way to go before a coup
could be staged. In 1954–5, after a general increase of officers'
salaries the movement 'ceased altogether' (Batatu 1978: 773). On
the other hand, the Baghdad Pact of 1955 was provocative to the
army because it pushed Iraq into an isolationist and compromised
position *vis-à-vis* the Arab world, while the Soviet Arms agreement
with Nasser, and the Suez Canal nationalization showed what could
be done by a more assertive regional power. For these reasons,
activism picked up again, and, by the end of the summer of
1956, a number of cells of Free Officers were established (Batatu
1978: 773).

The Tripartite Aggression and its defeat then proved decisive:

Nothing gave the reviving movement greater strength than the tripartite
invasion of Egypt in the autumn of 1956. The spirit of revolt rose sharply.
Some of the officers could not conquer the shock to their emotions, and well
nigh embarked upon foolish ventures, but were subdued at the last moment
by their more prudent colleagues. The defeat of the invasion and the further
shaking of the already badly shaken prestige of the government steeled the
Free Officers in their purpose. Their ranks now palpably increased. It was at
this time that Colonel Taher Yahya, a commander of an armoured regiment
at Jalawla and a future premier of Iraq, lent the movement the weight of his
support (Batatu 1978: 776).

The officers were in step with popular feeling on this matter. The 1956
intifada was occasioned by the Tripartite Aggression on Egypt (Batatu
1978: 467–8) – an attack on the 'threatening' Nasser which Nuri Al-
Sa'id had frantically implored the British Prime Minister Antony Eden
to undertake.

In December 1956, a committee of Free Officers assembled for the
first time in a house. Every member took an oath on the Qur'an:

I swear by God, the noble Qur'an, and my military honor: to serve my
homeland with my brother officers who are taking part with me in liberating
it from the imperialists and their henchmen and from the autocratic rule by
which the Iraqi people is oppressed; to act without fear or hesitation in the

interest of the people as my brothers, the Free Officers, will determine; and to guard the secrets of the Free Officers and protect them from harm in all conditions and circumstances, as God is my witness (Batatu 1978: 776).

The Iraqi officers did secure the promise of the Soviets and of Nasser to oppose armed intervention by means of the Baghdad Pact. On the other hand, they hoped to obtain material support from Egypt and Syria in the form of ammunition – although such support, in the event, was not forthcoming (Batatu 1978: 795–6).

The committee met in secrecy in safe houses. They used a cell structure similar to that of Nasser's Free Officers or the Communist Party of Iraq (not to mention the FLN in Algeria), with four members in each cell in order to evade detection (Batatu 1978: 783): 'Where politicians would have crawled, the committee leapt. In one night sitting [it] settled upon a republic' (Batatu 1978: 795–6). Decisive action was prioritized over wide consultation, where the need for clandestinity was paramount.

In the early hours of 14 July, Abd as-Salam 'Aref (b. 1916) disclosed to the officers of the 20th Infantry Brigade:

the aim of the movement and the plan designed to attain it. What he said may have leapt with their own instincts, or some of them, at least, may have been too timid or too passive to offer any obstacle. And then not a few were Free Officers, and must have prepared the ground psychologically for the approval which all now voiced (Batatu 1978: 800).

It is surely difficult to explain such approval in the absence of a thoroughgoing crisis of authority, the legacy of more than a decade of protest and repression.

It should be noted how little coercion or force was actually required to topple the Iraqi client monarchy when the time came. Although the coup is often referred to as 'bloody', only a tiny number, and certainly no one outside the very top of the state, was killed. As Batatu puts it, within hours of the announcement of the coup, 'the will of the revolution prevailed everywhere'. 'The monarchy had come to an end. A few rounds of shelling had sufficed to shake it down. Except for the feeble resistance of the guard at Nuri's house, not a hand had been lifted in its defense' (Batatu 1978: 803). The government had been overturned by fewer than 3,000 troops, while two-thirds of these carried no ammunition at all, and the remainder only held a few rounds per man (Batatu 1978: 805). 'From the outset, Prince Abd-ul-Ilah seemed to lack the will for resistance. Possibly he feared that all or some of the two thousand royal guardsmen would go over to the insurgency if ordered out of their barracks. Probably he realized that the game was up, and that he was face-to-face with an irreversible march of events' (Batatu 1978: 801).

The British, too, seemed paralysed. They were certainly taken by surprise. Both the British and Nuri As-Said thought army officers had 'no real gripes' and were well paid. A sensitively placed Western diplomat just a few weeks before the July Revolution reckoned that the Iraqi army was not politically penetrated and thus the situation was 'nothing like Egypt' (Batatu 1978: 764). In the aftermath of Suez, no British leader was ready to engage in another armed intervention that might go catastrophically wrong, especially in the face of Soviet opposition. Perhaps even more importantly, there were no longer any credible collaborators in Iraq. Moreover, the British, in the wake of Suez and the Eisenhower Doctrine, were to take a back seat to the Americans. They restricted their role to the offer of immediate unilateral support to the US landing in Lebanon on 15 July 1958, which was a direct response to the Iraqi coup, whether or not its declared aim was to 'secure the integrity of Lebanon' against the 'threat of communism'.

The coup drew Iraq out of the clutches of the client monarchy and indirect colonial rule. It thus meant a more thoroughgoing national liberation, paving the way for industrial development and social and economic reform, which was carried out on a wide scale until the 1970s. The conflicts that it unleashed, nonetheless, also paved the way for the slow attrition of party politics, and the rise of the politics of further coups, and eventually the rule of a sole leader.

The rise of Ba'thism and radical nationalism in Syria

Syrian independence in 1946 was achieved with the wealthy, land-owning, urban and liberal politicians of the National Bloc at the helm of state. Lauded at the outset for their leadership of the nationalist movement, these politicians quickly came to be seen as corrupt and inefficient. Their liberal politics was engulfed by a rising tide of activism that set new standards and expectations for what political leaderships and the state ought to do and to achieve. By the late 1940s, the National Bloc were too old, too bourgeois, too comfortable, too much machine politicians, too easily caricatured by the cartoonist (paunchy, perspiring, wearing thick-lenses glasses, a fez, and a broad-striped double-breasted suit like those worn by provincial French businessmen, and fingering a set of amber prayer beads) (Kerr 1971: 10).

A formal national independence for an Arab state, and a parliamentary life, albeit dominated by men of property, would have been considered an achievement by the politically active generation of the 1920s. In the 1940s and 1950s, this was no longer the case. Many a mobilized constituency now sought more thoroughgoing forms of national, pan-Arab and even Third World independence, economic development and industrialization, an end to semi-feudal and inherited privilege, and the redistribution of land and wealth. Newly minted activists would insist on and refer to the inequality involved in a country where before 1958, 1.1 per cent of all land-owners controlled more than one-third of Syria's cultivated land (Batatu 1999: 32). By the 1940s and 1950s, the goalposts had shifted, partly thanks to the mobilization of new and transgressive entrants into the political field, and the content of their demands and projects.

The wider constituencies that were drawn into the new political field were educated just as much in its inadequacies, limitations and failures as its successes. Khoury has shown, plausibly enough, how in inter-war Damascus, rural–urban migration, changing urban space, and the arrival of new quarters undermined the patronage networks of land-owning, position-holding and merchant notables – making urban constituencies available for new kinds of mobilization (Khoury 1984). But these socio-economic changes cannot account for the direction, ideological content, or evolving repertoires of these new forms of politics, nor indeed for the fact that many notables were able to maintain their networks in new forms until the late 1950s at least. Those who came of age in the 1940s and 1950s in Syria adopted new perspectives. The question was less how to create an independent political community, and to participate in the state, and more how to build a state that was independent from all forms of colonial domination, as well as how to use that state to solve pressing social and economic problems.

Michel Aflaq (1910–89) was born in the Maydan, a quarter with a proud tradition of resistance relating to 1925–7. He was the son of a Greek orthodox grain merchant, and had an entirely European education. He re-defined the key terms of the political worldview, rooted in a search for national independence and constitutional, representative government, that had been so important among urban nationalists and the National Bloc during the 1930s and 1940s. He declared that independence without real social and economic reform was just a sham; that Syrian independence was nothing before that of the independence of the Arab nation as a whole. As Aflaq wrote in the newly founded newspaper *Al-Ba'th* in August 1946, the independence just won was but a 'sheer skeleton, bloodless and lifeless'. It was a mere stepping stone on the road to liberty, unity and socialism against oppression of workers, foreign companies swallowing money and wealth, failures on Palestine, conspiracies, and foreign domination (Aflaq 1977: 34). He wrote in 1956 that representative government and democracy was an empty shell if it was not accompanied by socialism: 'constitutional democracy ... not accompanied by socialist legislation is empty and will soon turn into a weapon in the hands of the rich and proprietors so that they may continue their exploitation of the peoples' (Aflaq 1977: 39). Negative liberty and 'freedom from' was associated with corruption, exploitation and disorder, a 'sham liberty behind which the reactionaries hide together with the exploiters of the people and the collaborators with imperialism'. Aflaq advocated instead for 'a positive and creative liberty' – a 'freedom to' complete with a substantive content. '[L]iberty is a principle which should have a practical formula, in each circumstance and at each stage.' Such liberty was not opposed to the use of the state (via legislation and regulation) to curb the exploitation of feudalists, capitalists, or to curb the spread of imperialist agents in the press, or in the state machinery.

Ba'thism was an intellectual current, which reflected new forms of activism and new demands as well as leading them, and was disseminated in schools and in the press, through the emerging party's own newspaper (founded 1946), and then through congresses (the first being held in 1947), and through the founding of a political party as the vehicle to contest state power. The Ba'th Party, which until the early 1950s had concentrated on students and intelligentsia and paid little attention to the peasantry, only developed a mass base once it joined with Akram Al-Hawrani's Arab Socialist Party in 1953. The merger, as Hanna Batatu makes clear, turned the Arab Socialist Ba'th Party into an instrument with a social base. By stitching these ideas into these practical forms of action, the Ba'th Party became a force to be reckoned with in the social formation as a whole.

Al-Hawrani (1912–96), the educated son of a minor provincial notable, was an important figure in Syrian politics from the late 1940s, holding one of the vice-presidencies of the United Arab Republic, until his exile in 1963, a victim of division and fragmentation among the parties and the leaderships. Based in his hometown of Hama, where land-holding patterns were particularly unequal, and feudal privileges were acute, and drawing on early rounds of activism around national liberation, enlightenment, communism and feudal privilege, his was the first among the new, urban-based parties and societies of the Mashriq to engage in the actual mobilization of the peasantry in the Mashriq, drawing them into new forms of political life clustered around participation in the centralized state.

Al-Hawrani's memoirs make clear that he had lived and breathed politics from his earliest youth. The dramas of the inter-war period, the Arab revolt, the uprisings of Shaykh Ali and Ibrahim Hananu, Egypt's uprising of 1919, the songs of Sayyid Darwish, Faysal's short-lived government, a visit from Sati' Al-Husri, the brief rising of the towns-people of Hama in the face of the French advance, Atatürk's war of national liberation, the Great Revolt of 1925–7, a sense of injustice at the poverty and oppression of the peasantry, the rise of what he called the 'popular movement' against feudal privilege, were vividly present in his consciousness and formation (Hawrani 2000). Political consciousness and discussion was centred on newspapers and magazines, cultural clubs, and school, which Al-Hawrani characterizes as full of enthusiasm for Arab national liberation.

Al-Hawrani founded the Arab Socialist Party in 1950, building it around actual challenges to forms of feudal privilege and power. He made the crucial link between Arab national liberation and the abolition of feudalism at the time of the *nakba* (Batatu 1999: 127) – when the Palestinian dispossession and the failure of Arab liberation was blamed on feudalism. The popular movement against feudalism, and Arab national liberation, should march together. Peasants joined his party like a 'flood-tide', and within months there were 10,000 members (Batatu 1999: 128). Al-Hawrani was ready to engage in direct action, helping to organize the coercive redress of peasant wrongs through strong-men (*qabadayat*). The party chalked up some concrete achievements, a secret ballot in elections, land reform, and legislation against peasant eviction (Batatu 1999: 130).

The Communist Party of Syria and Lebanon, active since the early 1920s, and led by Khalid Bakdash since 1937, had put in question feudal privilege on the land. They had put forward a radical demand for a 'Workers' and Peasants' Government in Syria' in 1931. Their programme included ending the control of the wealthy over perennial springs, introducing piped drinking water to villages, abolishing forced labour, cancelling all debts owed by small peasants, exempting them from tithe and other taxes, providing a minimum wage, implementing shorter working hours, instating social security for agricultural workers, expropriating large land-owners, foreign farmers and religious missions, and distributing their estates among the indigent peasants (Batatu 1999: 119). The programme remained just that, and mobilization among peasants and workers was highly limited. The popularity of the Communist Party also took a nosedive when it followed the Kremlin's line recognizing Israel in 1948, further lost out with its negative attitude towards the United Arab Republic, and – even more inexplicably to its own potential constituency – opposed land reform in 1959.

The *nakba* led to the resignation of the government in November 1948, and paved the way for the coup of Colonel Husni Al-Zaim in March 1949. Al-Zaim disbanded all political parties, and the Ikhwan, before being ousted in August 1949 by Colonel Sami Hinnawi who restored civilian government and parliamentary democracy in Syria. The pattern of coups, counter-coups, and the advance of the military within the state was set for the period until strong-man rule was consolidated under Hafez Al-Asad after 1970. Syria's new rulers, who pushed aside the old notability only decisively in the 1960s, did implement, and try to implement, in one way or another many of the social reforms and foreign policies envisaged by communists, Ba'thists, and pan-Arabists. Slowly, nonetheless, ideologues and those engaging in independent forms of political mobilization, and freedoms of speech, association and publication diminished in significance from an increasingly dessicated and stage-managed political field.

Algeria: from parties and politicians to cells, armed struggle and independence

On 1 November 1954, armed units of Algerians, under the banners of a revolutionary nationalism, and declaring a new organization, the

Fronte de Libération Nationale (FLN), carried out attacks on French positions all over the country. Operations against railways, electricity sub-stations, telephone lines and bridges paralysed (temporarily) the movement of French forces. Initial French estimates put the damage at 200 million francs. Few credited the initiative with any chance of success. In November 1954, the FLN fighting cadres, numbering only a few dozen, were only 'miserably equipped and barely organized' (Quandt 1969: 93); the most likely result was 'failure' (Quandt 1969: 6–7). As Hugh Roberts has it:

[t]he extraordinary audacity of the political enterprise begun on that day [1 November 1954] had tended to go unremarked. The Algerian revolution was, in its beginning, an affair of a small, determined and above all adventurous band (Roberts 2003: 36).

Nonetheless, 1 November 1954 turned out to be the first salvo in an armed struggle that after eight often bitter years led to Algerian independence in 1962. The form and content of this revolutionary contentious mobilization, not all of which was determined in advance, have certainly left a major mark on the modern history of Algeria.

Repression and intransigence led a few not towards quiescence but a search for alternatives, and new, more forceful tactics and strategies with which to confront the wall of power represented by the settler-colonial state (cf. Lawrence 2013; Quandt 1969: 2). The news of the massacres in Sétif left Ahmed Ben Bella (1916–2012) and Mohammed Boudiaf (1919–92) ever more sympathetic to the use of arms in the confrontation with the French. Ben Bella had not completed his secondary schooling in Tlemcen, and had risen through the ranks of the French army after volunteering in 1936, and was a decorated soldier for France (and accomplished footballer) during the Second World War. Ben Bella described a fraternal atmosphere in the French army. Algerians were treated with equality and fairness, a factor which contributed to his self-respect. It was the contrast between this respect and the attitude of the *colons* that mattered:

For Ben Bella the realization that all his military decorations counted for nothing in the eyes of the *colons* came upon his return to Algeria in 1945. Coupled with the stories of the brutal French repressions of May 1945, this awareness of the injustices of the colonial system in contrast to the relative equality which marked French military life contributed greatly to the making of at least one Revolutionary (Quandt 1969: 79).

Boudiaf came from a family that had lost land and status during the
nineteenth century because of French rule. He did not complete his
primary schooling because of ill-health, and was early drawn into nationalist activism, joining the Parti du Peuple Algérien (PPA) of Messali Al-
Hadj, and later its successor organization, the Mouvement pour le
Triomphe des Libertés Démocratiques (MTLD). After Sétif, he rejected
electoral politics, assimilation, and the image of metropolitan France as
tribune of appeal: they 'saw violence and direct action as the only way
forward' (Evans and Phillips 2007: 52). Divisions and disputes among the
existing political groups discredited further the existing channels of activism and even the whole idea of political ideology. The men who launched
the armed struggle had experienced the political field as a failure: 'elections, bargaining and compromise seemed futile' (Quandt 1969: 68).
They even believed that the MTLD was insufficiently committed to the
armed struggle (Quandt 1969: 82–3). 'By rejecting colonial politics, the
Revolutionaries were abandoning elections, petitions, competing political parties, mass organizations, and overt political propaganda', as well
as the leadership of liberal and other radical politicians, such as Ferhat
Abbas, Messali Al-Hadj and Benyoussef Benkhedda. These men thought
that they 'were escaping the personal intrigues and struggles for influence
which marked the internal life of the legal political parties'. The 'cult of
personality' forming around Messali Al-Hadj was particularly derided by
the revolutionaries (Quandt 1969: 84).

Almost all of the forty-one initiators of the armed struggle were born
between 1918 and 1928. They were generally better off than illiterate
peasant masses; most had had some education, but education had not
played the dominant role in socialization as it had among the liberal
politicians. Only four out of the forty-one had received university
education. Unlike nearly all politicians, twelve of the forty-one had
only secondary education, while four, and perhaps many more, are
known to have attended only primary school. Many had been
members of Messali's PPA/MTLD, before 1954, and in particular were
members of the paramilitary section thereof, the OS (Quandt 1969:
68–70). These revolutionaries were of lower social status than the
liberal politicians: wage-workers, small businessmen, farmers, traders,
unionists or teachers, as well as conscripts, sergeants and some officers
in the French army (Quandt 1969: 77–8).

The frames and principles propounded by the FLN, involving a
heavy dose of pragmatic nationalism, were by no means dissimilar to

that of Fatah, Yasir Arafat's Palestinian movement, with its origins in the late 1950s, which came to lead the PLO. The proclamation of 1 November 1954, absent a few general references to democracy, Islam and to fundamental freedoms, was almost completely devoid of distinctive political ideology or programme. Instead, it enunciated a straightforward nationalism: it was addressed to the 'Algerian people' and to 'activists for the national cause'. It situated itself at the head of the 'nationalist movement'. It declared itself to be above factionalism and open to all patriots and true Algerians:

We are independent of the two factions that are vying for power. Our movement gives to compatriots of every social position, to all the purely Algerian parties and movements, the possibility of joining the liberation struggle.

The Algerian people was an entity, a collective source of autonomy and sovereignty, that was oppressed, repressed and restricted by imperialism. To throw off imperialism was to be liberated, to seize the right to pursue one's own destiny without hindrance on a collective basis (negative freedom), and to determine the content of that destiny (positive freedom). As the FLN averred: 'At home, the people are united behind the watchwords of independence and action.' The pragmatic young men of the FLN claimed no special ideological or doctrinal insight. They instead justified their leadership on the basis of their character and youth. The national movement, they declared, was 'prostrated by years of immobility and routine' and was 'disintegrating'. Thus, 'a youthful group, gathering about it the majority of wholesome and resolute elements, judged that the moment had come ... to launch it into the true revolutionary struggle'. The FLN envisaged a future world of nation-states, interacting on the basis of equality and respect. They saw in imperialism political domination – and conceived of its end in the termination thereof. They presented no threat to a global order of nation-states – merely wishing to have a seat at the table (Front de Libération Nationale 1954). The FLN invoked Islam, but the guiding concepts of the revolutionary struggle were neither sought nor found in Islamic theology or doctrine. As Quandt has it, these men had in common (only) 'their rejection of the colonial political system and their belief that violence was indispensable for achieving independence' (Quandt 1969: 71).

There were forms of class consciousness at work among the revolutionaries: a sense of identification with the mass of exploited workers or peasants, and the impoverished Muslim masses, rather than with a comfortable or well-off elite. Some of the revolutionaries had indeed spent some years as common workers. Those who had 'known the misery of the masses' were more trustworthy as leaders, according to one well-educated revolutionary. Others, later on in the 1960s, referred to themselves as 'sons of poor peasants', even if this was not in fact the case (Quandt 1969: 79).

While the Islamic modernist associations of the *ulema* had played a role in shaping the thinking of wide sectors of the population since the 1930s, these associations played no direct role in the mass politics or the armed struggle that surrounded the political parties and the revolutionary cells of the post-1945 period. Ben Badis in any case had died in 1940 (Quandt 1969: 37–8).

By August 1956, the FLN had expanded to include various elements from the former political parties – who disbanded in order to join its ranks after considerable scepticism at the outset (Dib 1985: 35). The FLN was a fighting force, but it needed to prove that it had the support of the masses. It therefore announced a boycott by Muslim students enrolled in French schools and an eight-day strike of the entire Muslim population. They also adopted urban terror tactics, targeting colon civilians 'as a more effective use of violence than the guerrilla warfare in the countryside' (Quandt 1969: 105–6). The calculation was 'that urban violence would draw much more attention to the FLN and could oblige the UN and allies of France to recognize the FLN as a major force with which France should negotiate' (Quandt 1969: 105–6). The general strike gave the French the chance to smash the FLN in Algiers, but the leadership, driven into exile in 1957, by repression and the lack of a hoped-for general insurrection, now formed a provisional government in exile in Tunis.

From 1957 onwards, activism was focused on two sites: the political movement rooted in the provisional government in exile in Tunis on the one hand, and the fighters and guerrilla groups in the countryside (the *maquis*) on the other. Quandt's research showed that the latter were different in practice and belief to the revolutionary leadership. They were not as self-centred, but instead showed 'strong feelings of identification' with other *maquisards*. They were more likely to believe that peasant masses, who bore the weight of the war, were the rightful beneficiaries of it. They distrusted and disliked politicians, and were sceptical of the Revolutionaries, especially when the latter tried to direct the war from Tunis rather than from the interior. Instead of the authoritarian tendencies of the Revolutionaries, they 'placed greater value on equality, collective decision-making, and self-criticism' (Quandt 1969: 114–15).

With defeat in the Battle of Algiers, and the completion by the end of 1957 of the electrified Morice Line which 'seriously hampered the flow of supplies to the Armée de Libération Nationale (ALN) units, and the movements of fighters to and from Tunisia' (Abun-Nasr 1987: 347) came a change of strategy. By 1958, the guerrillas in the *maquis* no longer aimed at a military Dien Bien Phu, 'but at providing the foundations of a political victory by the threat of an indefinite continuation of the fighting' (Abun-Nasr 1987: 348).

The extraordinarily violent measures to which the French were willing to resort in their striving to maintain direct colonial rule in Algeria were profoundly provoking for large sections of the Algerian population. Not just the torture, on an industrial scale, of committed and active nationalists, as well as of those who were not. Just as significant, for the wider population, were the euphemistically entitled *Centres de Régroupement*. Two million Algerians, a significant proportion of the entire population of the country, were grouped into concentration camps in the late 1950s, in a French effort to isolate the FLN from their supporters in the population and to defeat the *maquisards* (Evans and Phillips 2007: 62). As Abun-Nasr has it:

The French army did not have an Algerian Dien Bien Phu, and the Algerian Muslim masses did not at once rally round the revolutionary leaders. They became involved in the revolution from about 1956, only after the French army and police became indiscriminate in arresting Muslims and destroying villages (Abun-Nasr 1987: 343).

As much as any other policy, extraordinarily widespread measures of repression contributed to the mass rejection of French rule in the early 1960s.

A crucial ingredient on the international scene was that newly independent states in North Africa, the Arab world, and the Third World more generally were ready to offer direct support to the armed struggle in Algeria. Egypt, even as Tunisia and Morocco after independence stood apart, played the most important role, supplying weaponry, training, logistics, safe-haven, funding and media support. This policy became increasingly overt during 1954–6, and was increasingly endorsed by Nasser in the face of French threats – decisively so in March 1956 (Dib 1985: 145–9). Before moving to outright armed attack, the French tried economic threats over financial assistance and the purchase of Egyptian cotton to stop Egypt's support for Algerian nationalists. On more than one occasion, in private audiences with French officials, Nasser shrugged these threats off (Gillet, Cairo, 6 November 1954: Archives du Ministère des Affaires Étrangères: Maroc, 1944–1955, No. 199). In public, Nasser consistently spoke in favour of national liberation and against the French colonial system, as in, for example, a speech he gave in Kabul on his return from Bandung in 1955 (Brière, in Kabul, 4 May 1955: Archives du Ministère des Affaires Étrangères: Maroc 1944–1955, No. 199). After 1959, Iraq also offered arms and money, China and the Soviet Union likewise after 1956, while other states, such as Pakistan or India, were less fulsome (Dib 1985: 315–16, 339).

The young Ben Bella's frank pitch, delivered at a meeting in Cairo under the auspices of the Arab League in April 1954, impressed the Free Officers, who were committed to supporting national liberation in the Arab world, linking this to the success of their own revolution at home (Abou-El-Fadl 2015). Ben Bella sought arms to supply an armed struggle that would bypass what he styled as the ineffectiveness, posturing, bickering and money-grubbing of the established political parties in North Africa (Dib 1985: 16). The Free Officers were well disposed towards this line of reasoning, partly because of their own background in 'decisive' and pragmatic military action outside of the framework of political parties. They had already sounded out (in March 1954) the old Moroccan resistance fighter, Abd Al-Krim, living out his days in exile in Egypt, on the topic of strategies in North Africa. His analysis, reportedly, was that there were two key problems: first, governments and parties inside and outside of North Africa had failed to unify their action; second, no one would commit to a people's armed struggle, which was the only method remaining. Abd Al-Krim argued that it was nonetheless a good moment for decisive, unified, armed action, as France was pre-occupied with war in Indochina. The Free Officers saw some aspects of Al-Krim's plan, however, as outdated, especially his wish to group all resistance forces in a regular army with a singular command. This idea was not regarded as adequate to the requirements of popular struggle in the 1950s (Dib 1985: 12–13).

Egyptian support, training and weaponry were made available for the armed struggle in Algeria from mid-1954 onwards. Ben Bella was to play a key role in furnishing the supply of arms and money to the armed struggle until his capture in 1956. Egyptian money was used to buy arms in Libya to be smuggled into eastern Algeria in mid-1954. The French were aware of Egyptian support for North African nationalists 'in details' from at least June 1954 (Gillet, 28 June 1954: Archives du Ministère des Affaires Étrangères: Maroc, 1944–1955, No. 199). Egyptian intelligence trained Algerian cadres and was involved in coordinating their activities in Algeria and beyond. By 1956, significant quantities of arms were being delivered by ship, a fact incontrovertibly confirmed by the capture on an Israeli tip-off of the Athos in mid-October 1956 (Connelly 2002: 114). One internal French report estimated that the Arab League was offering US$4 million to support liberation movements in North Africa as a whole (Minister of Interior/Minister of Moroccan and Tunisian Affairs, Paris, 6 October 1954: Archives du Ministère des Affaires Étrangères: Maroc 1944–1955, No. 199).

Egypt's Free Officers moved quickly after 1952 to expand Egypt's (and the Arab world's) relatively restricted radio broadcasting capacity, at a time when the media was dominated by the press and its educated, urban readership. Nasser and others realized that radio could reach a far wider (and non-literate) audience than the press. The Voice of the Arabs was founded in 1953 and became a key media terrain on which the Nasserist message of pan-Arab unity, national liberation and revolution was propounded (Boyd 1975). This was an important innovation on the regional stage. It was a medium that was difficult (but not impossible) for client governments and colonial empires alike to censor and 'snow'. The French were already complaining bitterly through diplomatic channels to the Egyptian authorities about 'incitement to murder and terrorism' carried on the Sawt Al-Arab radio station (De Murville/Rabat, 21 January 1954: Archives du Ministère des Affaires Étrangères: Maroc, 1944–1955, No. 199). Dib recalls in his memoirs that he telephoned the long-time head of the service (1953–67), Ahmad Said, during the night of 1 November 1954 to ensure that the station would broadcast supportive material in regard to the coordinated events that unfolded in Algeria from the early hours of 1 November (Dib 1985: 28).

The French were unable to snow out completely the radio stations that they found obnoxious. In addition to Sawt Al-Arab, there was also

Tetouan's 'La Voix des Fellaghas' and Radio Budapest to reckon with. The latter was conceived via agreement between north African émigrés (Marxist and non-Marxist) to complete the action of Sawt Al-Arab, offering new broadcasts on social questions addressed to worker and unionist milieux. In mid-1954, a French diplomatic note had it that:

A veritable network has just been put in place the coordinated action of which permits the adversaries of the French presence in North Africa to reach at all hours of the day all classes of the Muslim population (Note pour le Ministre, 17 July 1954: Archives du Ministère des Affaires Étrangères: Maroc, 1944–1955, No. 199).

Radio Budapest, indeed, could not be jammed by French emitters at all. Radio was important in Algeria, especially in the towns and villages around which France attempted to impose a *cordon sanitaire* from 1955 and later. Radio could not substitute for concrete organization on the ground, but it meant that colonized populations could not be sealed off from information coming from anti-colonial forces, a channel of information that could provide reasons for mobilization and connect constituencies to leaderships.

The Tangier Conference of 1958, which publicly committed newly independent Tunisia and Morocco to immediate independence of Algeria created 'a new political atmosphere which neither the French government nor the French leaders in Algeria could ignore' (Abun-Nasr 1987: 348).

The emerging non-aligned movement and the UN also played their role on the international scene. In April 1955, FLN representatives were allowed to attend the Bandung Conference, although not with delegate status. Later in 1955, a UN General Assembly resolution declared that the French government was preventing the Algerians from exercising their right of self-determination (Abun-Nasr 1987: 344).

The *colon* community eventually came to blows with metropolitan France and threatened the state with a *coup d'état*. When Zionist settlers had turned their weaponry on British imperial personnel after 1939 and especially after 1945 they were searching for a separate state and their actions played a role in forcing the British to withdraw. The *colons* in Algeria had a far more ambitious, not to say delusionary, strategy, which was that, if the French state would not support them, it would have to be changed, via a military coup if necessary. It was only after the attempted coup of the generals that De Gaulle, already concerned that France would not be able to absorb millions of Muslims as equal citizens, started to shift decisively towards self-determination for Algeria. In many ways, the *colon* leaderships were hoist on their own petard.

French opinion was also finally split by the late 1950s and early 1960s – swinging decisively in favour of giving the Algerians the choice over independence when the extent of the French slaughter there was increasingly well known. The French Left was incapable of siding in any substance with Algerian nationalism before 1956. For example, the French Communist Party issued a sharp criticism of the armed operations in *L'Humanité* on 10 November 1954: 'loyal to the teachings of Lenin, [the French Communist Party] cannot approve the recourse to isolated acts which are the game of the colonialists who are perhaps at the origin of these acts' (cited in Dib 1985: 35). On the other hand, this position changed, as intellectuals such as Francis Jeanson, who became a 'carrier of suitcases' for the FLN in France, published widely on the racism of the *colon* empire and the FLN as a nationalist and socialist force (Ulloa 2007). The idea that French workers, on the other hand, were in solidarity with Algerian workers, even if entertained by Sartre, was more likely an 'illusory dream', as Ulloa puts it (Ulloa 2007: 172).

The stage was set for a negotiated independence at Evian between De Gaulle and the provisional government, which lasted from May 1961 till 18 March 1962, when the French finally yielded on the Sahara, where there was oil, and the future status of settlers. In the referendum of 1 July 1962, 97 per cent voted in favour of independence (Abun-Nasr 1987: 353–4).

The FLN had a strategy of unifying around the nationalist idea, armed struggle, internationalization, and negotiations with the French (Front de Libération Nationale 1954). It is easy, especially with hindsight, to see the strengths in such a bundle of strategies and tactics. The search for negotiations with the French gave a definite terminus to the armed struggle and definite conditions for the French to fulfil – a 'recognition of Algerian sovereignty'. The armed struggle through guerrilla war was capable of harassing the French and neutralizing their superior military power. Nationalism could unify the population. The 'internationalization of the Algerian problem' – as the FLN itself called it – meanwhile seized the available opportunities in the changing geopolitical world of the 1950s and 1960s. The increasing legitimacy of the cause of national self-determination, the establishment of the UN, the appearance of actors on the regional scene (including national states such as Egypt) capable of giving support to the FLN, all weighed in the balance. In other words, here the form of contestation chosen by the FLN, and enunciated in the declaration of 1954, had clear strengths. The FLN, though, ultimately benefitted from the intransigence of the settlers, who decided to take on the French state rather than alter course. This contingency very much played into the hands of the nationalists. Once the French took the political decision to pull back from the massive military repression that holding onto Algeria entailed, the route to negotiations and statehood was open.

The revolutionary coup in North Yemen

A republican *coup d'état* deposed Imam Al-Badr (r. 1948–62) in North Yemen on 26 September 1962. The eighty officers whose tanks rumbled into San'a'were following the model of republican coup made famous by Nasser and the Free Officers in Egypt in 1952. They established the first republican government on the peninsula, alarming the ruling families of the region. Some of the officers had been trained by Egyptian advisers and kept up links to Egypt; they saw themselves as Nasserists, and appealed to the people as the repository of sovereignty. The coup was greeted by various cheering crowds and a measure of 'mass spontaneous approval' (Halliday 1974: 102) based on the hope for progressive change of some kind after decades in which the rule of the imams had kept Yemen isolated from the outside world, delivering neither socio-economic uplift nor political reform. But these officers had no links to any popular organizations or movements in an imamate where secular schools, the press, clubs, underground political parties, unions and labour movements were largely absent. These military men, with connections to the commercial class and tribal leaders, were 'both a representative of the masses and a displacement of them, profoundly suspicious of the people and unwilling to organize, educate or rely on them' (Halliday 1974: 102). On the other hand, the Movement of Arab Nationalists (MAN) was now able to organize in North Yemen, and went on to found a cultural club in Ta'iz, established a union, organized strikes and protests, and developed a base among the workers. In some countryside areas, they also organized in the name of social reform and union rights, forming Peasant

Leagues (*Lijan Fallahiya*) around Ta'iz, Ibb and Radah. The leftward direction of the MAN brought it into increasing conflict with Nasserism after 1964.

North Yemen now became a territory within which the National Liberation Front (NLF), the main force behind the making of the People's Democratic Republic of South Yemen in 1967, was able to take shape and to organize, as nationalist exiles from South Yemen gathered there shortly after the coup. The NLF included 'army officers who had been serving as mercenaries in Saudi Arabia and the Gulf, workers from Aden and the Gulf, [and] intellectuals from the hinterland who had been studying in Aden' (Halliday 1974: 190); its most important organizational component was the South Yemeni branch of the MAN, which had been founded in the 1950s in Aden by South Yemeni students returning from Beirut. It was from their base in North Yemen that the NLF adopted the strategy of armed struggle against the British in Aden, planning actively to enlist the rural hinterland in the armed campaign, where many NLF cadres, as rural–urban migrants, were actually from (Halliday 1974: 190–2, 208; Ghazali 2007: 437–9, 454).

Strikes and demonstrations in Kuwait and Bahrain

The pan-Arab and nationalist leaderships that emerged in Kuwait and Bahrain in the 1950s and 1960s displaced the more conservative merchant nationalists of 1938 as the leading sources of opposition to the Al-Khalifa ruling family in Bahrain, the Al-Sabah in Kuwait, and their British advisers. In the late 1940s and early 1950s, these groups launched an ambitious programme of 'Arab enlightenment', 'rejecting sectarian politics, opposing colonial rule and the tribally controlled regime, and championing the cause of the [popular] classes' (Bahrain Government 1986: Vol. 5, 6; Ghazali 2007: 430–1, 437–40, 454; Khuri 1980: 198). These educated activists were influenced by Nasserism after 1952, communism, liberalism, the ideas of the Arab Socialist Ba'th Party and of the MAN, and the modernist notion of progressive politics, and were familiar with models of labour organization and strike action in Egypt, Lebanon, Palestine and Iraq (Ghazali 2007: 428–33; Mdairis 2004: 12, 14, 22; Smith 1984: 172–3). They were mostly teachers, civil servants, journalists, professionals and technicians, had often been educated in Egypt or Lebanon, and were linked to underground political parties, the most important of which was the MAN, various politicized cultural clubs, and the press, occasionally held positions in the Kuwait National Assembly, and were involved in lectures, publications, organizing workers and staging popular demonstrations.

British imperial control was denounced as isolating the Gulf and as retarding, dividing and exploiting the region. Foreign and non-Arab companies, above all the oil companies, were attacked for exploiting Arab labour. Arab migration, even the abolition of passports, was encouraged as an important element in the pan-Arab project (Mdairis 2004: 15–16). While the rights of Asian and Iranian workers were associated with the schemes of the Shah or British divide-and-rule, the rights of Arab migrants, including the right to form labour unions, and the rights of Palestinians and Palestinian migrants in particular, were championed in the press (Brand 1988: 124, 144; Ghazali 2007: 445–6; Khuri 1980: 198). MAN activists and Palestinian exiles (based in both Kuwait and Egypt), for example, started to organize Palestinian workers in Kuwait at Ford, Mercedes, Fiat, Pepsi-Cola, the municipality and the Ministry of Public Works in 1959 (Brand 1988: 127–9). In Bahrain, demonstrations, strikes (including among bus and taxi drivers) and boycotts were widespread during 1954–6.

The influence and appeal of Nasserism was particularly evident. The Bahraini leadership met with Nasser when he stopped over in 1955 on his way to Bandung, securing a student-exchange programme with Egypt. In the aftermath, the pro-Nasserist press started to cover the movement sympathetically (Khuri 1980: 206; Bahrain Government 1986: Vol. 5, 5). Egyptian activists (based in Kuwait) gave speeches in Bahrain during the crowd actions of March 1956 (Bahrain Government 1986: Vol. 5, 6). Egypt hosted a key Bahraini exile, Abd Al-Rahman Al-Bakir, and aired his speeches on the influential radio station Voice of the Arabs.

The strike at BAPCO (the Bahrain Petroleum Company) in March 1965, with its demands over dismissals and in regards to the right to organize labour unions, and the demands for the dispensation of services of British and other foreign employees, was the trigger for the popular uprising of that year (Fakhro 1997: 172). The struggle at BAPCO intersected with liberal freedoms (the right to associate), nationalism (the removal of British officials), socio-economic rights (terms and conditions of workers' labour) and the drive for economic development against colonial dependency and backwardness. Women increasingly appeared in the ranks of activists in Bahrain in March 1965. In part, this was a sociological change: women's capacities and ways of life outside of the sphere of biological reproduction was developed through education, jobs, and through joining associations (Fakhro 1997: 178). But the active participation of women in the public sphere was also a staple of the mobilizing discourses on the peninsula during these years. Democratic demands were also at work in Bahrain in the 1960s. The widespread popular uprising of March 1965 demanded the lifting of the state of emergency (in effect since 1956), the recognition of freedom of the press, the right to public assembly, and the freedom of expression (Fakhro 1997: 172).

In Kuwait, demonstrations, boycotts and strikes broke out first in support of Nasser's nationalization of the Suez Canal in August 1956 and then in protest against the military attack by Israel, Britain and France on Egypt at the end of September. A similar round of mobilization in Kuwait in February 1959 celebrated the first anniversary of the United Arab Republic. A measure of the appeal of these mobilizations was that the young chief of police in Kuwait refused to use force to disperse the crowds in August 1956. He went on in 1959 to denounce publicly the tyranny of the ruling family, a step which cost him his job and his passport (Ghazali 2007: 452–3).

The armed struggle in South Yemen

In South Yemen, a British naval colony since the 1840s, early reformist nationalists, mainly merchants and Hadramautis, grouped around clubs and newspapers linked to the Adeni Association (established in 1950) agreed to contest the first elections to the tiny Legislative Council in 1955. A more radical coalition with support from the unions, the United National Front (UNF), gathered to demand British withdrawal and reject electoral participation in the unrepresentative and weak council. The UNF included journalists, graduates, and other professionals with political experience, such as 'Shaykhan Al-Habshi, a Hadrami lawyer who was believed to have been a member of the Indonesian Communist Party' (Halliday 1974: 222). Rejecting the unrepresentative and co-opted politics of the Legislative Council, the UNF turned to organizing the trade union movement in Aden, playing a role in the strike action that burst onto the scene in

March 1956 and continued for five weeks. About 7,000 port workers and others joined thirty-three strikes demanding changes in working conditions and protesting colonial employers' dismissal of fellow workers for union involvement. In June–December, up to 18,000 workers came out on strike in a series of about forty protests both linked to local issues and in solidarity with Egypt, which had nationalized the Suez Canal and faced the Tripartite Aggression in October. More than a quarter of the total working population of Aden actually participated in the strikes, and 210,000 working days were lost to employers, and won for the labour movement, severely disrupting the economic functioning of the British colony of Aden. The British tried and failed to model Adeni trade unions on the lines of the apolitical and anti-communist British Trades Union Congress and were suspicious of trade unions 'interfering' in politics. But figures such as Abdullah Al-Asnaj, a younger member of the UNF in 1956 and a future leader of the Adeni Trade Union Congress, saw politicized union organizing not as a crime but as a basic element in a nationalist movement capable of organizing exploited workers and winning concessions for them. Watt argues plausibly enough that workers did not co-operate with leaderships because of shared worker identity. Educated leaders were not proletarians and were not seen as such. The link was instead based on both personal relations (the belief that, with leaders' help, pay and conditions could be improved) and anticolonial national and Arab identity (Watt 1962).

Just as in Bahrain and Kuwait, an exclusionary approach to South Asian skilled (especially clerical) labour in Aden was followed. The nationalist and pan-Arab view was that the British employed these groups to divide and rule the colony. Their employment was also resented by those active and educated elements in the labour movement most likely to be competing with them directly in the labour market. They were identified with British imperialism and heavily stigmatized as a result. The Adeni Trade Union Congress pressed 'very strongly therefore for control of [South Asian] immigration' and Indians suffered verbal and physical attacks (Watt 1962: 448).

The People's Republic of South Yemen was proclaimed at the end of November 1967 after the ouster of the British by a successful armed struggle. The radical Left elements of the NLF in the new republic definitively broke with 'petty bourgeois' Nasserism and sought a revolutionary state run by democratic councils of 'workers, poor peasants and partisans'. This current, especially strong in the Hadramaut, was influenced by regional and international linkages. In the Arab world, there were linkages to radical Left currents in the MAN, as well as with the PFLP and the DFLP. An overlapping but wider transnational geography included the Soviet Union, China and the Third World (especially Vietnam and Cuba). 'The radicalization of the NLF was greatly encouraged politically by the small communist group operating in Aden, the Popular Democratic Union' (Halliday 1974: 208). There was an important visit to China for NLF training in 1967. One of the brigades of the new regular army was named Che Guevara, reflecting the inspiration of the 1959 socialist revolution in Cuba.

It is worth dwelling on the highly developed ideological frames, identities and principles through which the NLF saw itself as joining a mighty, Third World national liberation struggle, led by a revolutionary vanguard, against neo-colonialism, feudalism, colonial rule and reaction, cleaving to the banners of scientific socialism, people's democracy, mass mobilization, and aiming at a comprehensive plan for progress, economic development, and socio-economic and gender equality. This represented a decisive shift to the left in comparison with 'petty bourgeois' Arab nationalism.

'With each day passing' declared the NLF at the height of its post-independence optimism at a conference in October 1968,

> we notice changes in the map of the world with the defeat of colonization, its collapse and the appearance of newly independent countries. However, in spite of the great victories achieved by nations struggling for liberation and freedom, the forces of imperialism and colonialism did not accept the logic of the era.

They were not satisfied with wealth and riches of hundreds of years of colonizing and enslaving. Thus they resort to 'various methods in a desperate attempt' to retain influence and exploitation. In various cases colonialism permitted the surrender of

> political independence to some nations but to retain, in the same time, its economic colonization. That is the new phase of colonization. And wherever it has found any nation determined to resist neo-colonialism, it resorted to resist the new inclination beginning with plotting against the liberal progressive system [a reference to Iran in 1953 and perhaps to Guatemala in 1954] and ending with an open war as it is happening today in Vietnam. This

explains the struggle taking place today in Asia, Africa and Latin America where we see armed revolutions breaking out to stand face to face with international imperialism and old and neo-colonialism (National Liberation Front 1969: 4ff.).

The NLF thus saw the Yemeni struggle for national liberation as going well beyond individual national independence against direct colonial rule, and instead as participating in a wider global and Third World struggle against neo-colonialism.

They stated in the late 1960s that the People's Republic of South Yemen is not just opposed to 'British colonialism and feudal Sultanic rule in our country alone', but is opposed and always has been to 'neo-colonialism and reaction everywhere in the world'. This was a 'natural position because British colonialism represented a part and parcel of international colonialism'. The Front went on: 'Our revolution could not have otherwise succeeded or remained had it not considered itself a part and parcel of the international liberation movement.' Beyond the Yemeni circle and the Arab circle, the Front spoke of the international circle, considering that the fortunes of the latter were bound up with its own. They resolved that

Just as we believe that every liberated nation supports with its liberation our liberation, that it is made up of solid energies added to humanity to partici-pate in ending slavery and exploitation of man, that is has the capacity of doubling its efforts for progress and civilization, we therefore, support the people of Vietnam who, with their heroic struggle and resistance and their escalation of the revolution, give a great example of the people's movements of liberation. We also support the struggle of the people of Angola and Mozambique in Africa and the South Americans in their obstinate persist-ence to rid themselves of the American octopus.

They stated that the NLF 'stands boldly and firmly side by side with the national democratic movements of liberation in Asia, Africa, and Latin America. We oppose all imperialist attempts to strike the democratic progressive forces.' We support, they added, 'movements against the hated, grudging colour distinction in Rhodesia, South Africa and USA. We are with the oppressed frustrated people who were dispossessed by force of their human rights in their great struggle to bring the white man to humanity and to force him to abandon his racialism, exploit-ation and oppression of the black man' (National Liberation Front 1969: 3ff.).

They also linked their activism to pan-Arabism:

> Our revolution is part of the Arab revolution ... We stand now and we shall always stand side by side with the Arab people's movement of liberation in their glorious struggle for freedom from colonialism, international Zionism and imperialism, considering it a responsibility imposed by our faith in the national socialist unity and by the feeling of the continued danger of colonial forces and their bases standing by our doors, on the frontiers of our independent country, and in the heart of the Arab homeland. We are a part of the Arab nation who endeavour to realize unity [against reactionaries].

For the NLF, this meant not only an affirmation of readiness for assistance and support, but also 'strong live relations with the Arab movement of liberation'. This implied support for 'Palestinians in the occupied territory in their just war against Israel and Zionism. We support our brothers in the Arabian Gulf, Dhufar and Arabistan. We support our brothers in the Arabian peninsula against the much hated reaction and the international oil monopoly who exploit Arab wealth' (National Liberation Front 1969: 3ff.).

Liberation would not come through the inexorable workings of monopoly capitalism and imperialism, or the inevitable contradictions or forms of spontaneity set in motion by the rise of new social classes and the appearance of new ideas. What was required instead was a leadership, an *instrument* of change. As the NLF General Command of South Yemen agreed, national democratic liberation requires a 'revolutionary instrument'. This 'leading vanguard' should be developed within the NLF because it had 'led the people's victorious struggle for liberation from colonialism, occupation and feudalism'. This instrument would allow the NLF to morph into a pioneering Party 'leading the people's toiling masses in their revolutionary march' (National Liberation Front 1969: 1–2). Before independence, the central role of the 'Party', the 'Front' and the 'Vanguard' had been to conduct an organized people's armed struggle. The NLF went as far as to argue that the non-existence of the Party in the 1940s and 1950s, and its arrival in the 1960s, was entirely decisive in bringing about an organized people's war in that decade (National Liberation Front 1968: 4–5). Here the party believed that it had played a decisive role in organizing and unifying the previously tenacious but fragmented and overly spontaneous tribal opposition (National Liberation Front 1968: 8–9). As for the post-independence period, while the national economy is the material basis for the protection of political independence, 'the revolutionary instrument ... plays an active and commanding role' in regards to 'economic liberation' and 'social construction'. Indeed, 'failure', 'reluctance' and/or 'retreat' is expected 'without the real well organized masses' instrument and without the strong official authority' (National Liberation Front 1969: 3ff.). The main role of the leadership, the party, or the instrument, would be to implement a 'distinct programme of action' for the whole nation (National Liberation Front 1969: 1–2), a programme inevitably involving the agency of the modern state.

In terms of leadership, the NLF looked very firmly to 1952 and to Nasserism. The revolution of 1952 that had set the question of national liberation on a new footing, responding to the catastrophe of 1948, shunting aside the old part bourgeois, part feudal movements of the previous epoch, and introducing a new dynamic on the road to national liberation and socialism. 'The Arab revolution of the 23rd July 1952 in Egypt was the beginning of the real embodiment of that kind of renaissance in the national liberation movement.' This movement was different to the traditional movements of that epoch, for it was in bitter conflict with 'the reactionary bourgeoisie and feudalist powers allied with the colonialists and subject to their influence'. It went on to destroy colonialist pacts because of 'wealth, loyalty, knowledge and clarity', taking earnest and well-aimed steps, and offering support for the 'movement of national revolutionary struggle in every span of the Arab homeland'. 'Thus the United Arab Republic remained the political cornerstone of the Arab revolutionary struggle based on the foundations of unity and progress.' 'The role of this revolution in the movement of our people's struggle and its support for all the necessary capabilities from the first, is a great historic role which deserves recording and appreciation' (National Liberation Front 1968: 94).

The first priority after political independence was to build genuine economic independence and development. 'After gaining victory and obtaining our independence, the basic task before us today to establish and defend our political independence is to liberate our national economy from being a follower of the international monopoly of capitalism.'

Liberating our national economy is not an easy task. It means that a new difficult and long battle against imperialism and reaction is awaiting us, and that we must depend on the widest masses' energies to serve this inclination (National Liberation Front 1969: 3ff.).

Indeed, the NLF envisaged a class struggle between farmers (the biggest revolutionary forces), labourers, small bourgeoisie (traders, professionals, clerks, intellectuals), on the one side, and the foreign bourgeoisie, the local bourgeoisie connected to foreign capital, and the semi-feudal class (the ruling sultanic families), on the other (National Liberation Front 1969: 3–4). The aim of the NLF was to confront the 'financial crisis left by colonization' by shifting from an 'economy of services' dominated by foreign capital to 'an agricultural industrial productive economy', encouraging national capital, creating a state-owned public sector, generating an industrial economy, engaging in land reform, encouraging capitals available abroad, building roads and balancing the budget' (National Liberation Front 1969: 3ff.). The socialist road was seen as the best way to solve problems of economic under-development while maintaining national independence. They argued that bourgeois forms of development generated the need for loans from the capitalist bloc which came with, first, political conditions, such as in regards to military alliances and military bases, and, second, economic conditions as to how loans are to be used. They argued that loans gave a superficial boost in regard to consumption and unskilled employment, but could not create the conditions for overcoming backwardness. They cited the cases of Iran, Kenya and Ethiopia. Non-capitalist development, on the other hand, without conditional loans from capitalist countries, but via 'economic alignment with the socialist camp and the economic and technical aid forwarded to under-developed countries on the basis of equality', was superior. They gave the example of Egypt (National Liberation Front 1968: 42). Such argumentation was possible at a time when the Egyptian economy was indeed by all measures moving ahead impressively.

The economic shift was to be effected by means of a 'development plan which will direct our national economy' (National Liberation Front 1969: 1–2). Such a plan did not necessarily imply an entirely command economy: a development plan and the liquidation of feudalism 'would enable the private sector to take part in confirming our independence' (National Liberation Front 1969: 1–2). The point was to recruit all of Yemen's 'material and man power to ... rid itself of its backward position to a developing position capable of crowning its political independence with an economic independence'. Such economic independence was necessary 'because the colonial powers depended in retaining their influence in under-developed countries after their evacuation on the economic situation of those countries' (National Liberation Front 1969: 3ff.).

Economic liberation such as this was said to require not terror or Stalinism but a genuine people's democracy. 'The question of democracy is one of the most eminent issues which we should fulfil in this phase. Giving the productive forces of the people their right to practice their rights and to participate in drawing the general policy through a legislative assembly is the gate to democracy on the people's level', involving the right to give opinion freely, and the right to be heard (National Liberation Front 1969: 1–2). Participation and the protection of civil liberties was crucial because:

Victory which could be achieved by under-developed countries in their struggle against the forces of imperialism and reaction depends exactly on confirming the national democratic system ... because [only] this system is capable of mobilizing the entire social productive forces of laborers, farmers, revolutionary intellectuals and small bourgeoisie to perform the principle role in the battle of social construction ... The active participation of the social productive masses' forces in the political life and the spread of democracy in the political system of these productive forces are two inevitable conditions for social and economic progress in under-developed countries.

In short, the Front resolved: 'The national democratic system on the political level is a union of the more progressive forces in the society which fights to confirm complete national independence.' 'On the economic side, the national democratic system works to build up national industry and to protect the country's economy against the control, competition and monopoly of foreign capital. It also works to solve the question of agriculture by liquidating feudalism by means of implementing agrarian reform and developing [agriculture]' (National Liberation Front 1969: 3ff.).

Finally, the NLF sought the progressive emancipation of women. 'Leading courageously the women's sector to take its part in the political and economic life is essential and important not only to enlighten it that the time of humiliation has gone and women should be equal to men but also to point out that it can play an historic role side by side with men in protecting the revolution and building the future.' The idea was that the spread of socialist culture would help '[t]o get rid of the corrupt values which we have inherited from colonialism and the backward society' and embrace new values, on the basis of new social relations which have appeared and which will be promoted by the revolution. These new values in gender relations should be developed in conformity 'with the high values of our legacy and our history ... spirit of sacrifice, truth, sincerity, unselfishness' (National Liberation Front 1969: 3ff.).

The most radical sections of the post-independence Yemeni state actually encouraged peasants and share-croppers to take matters into their own hands in order to acquire land from feudalists and exploiters. This encouragement was an important part of the background to the 'popular *intifadat*' that swept South Yemen in 1970–1, whereby poor peasants, 'armed with forks and scythes', seized land directly from land-owners and set up popular committees to administer it collectively (Halliday 1974: 248). Nonetheless, statism and vanguardism cut against these forms of directly democratic socialism, and statist management supplanted self-management. Indeed, in spite of early, undoubted socio-economic gains, the problem of how to reconcile the existence of an instrument for the class struggle against neo-colonialism and feudalism with popular democracy was not resolved here as elsewhere. This problem, alongside many others, including the regional power of Saudi Arabia, played a role in the development of authoritarian rule in Yemen after independence.

Labour mobilization and attempted coups in Saudi Arabia

Saudi Arabia, the desert kingdom dominating the Arabian peninsula in terms of size, population, and, eventually, wealth, can be contrasted with South Yemen and Oman in that a sustained armed rebellion never broke out. Nor did Saudi Arabia witness a republican coup, as in North Yemen (or indeed as in the oil-rich, pro-Western desert kingdom of Libya in 1969), or a socialist takeover, as in South Yemen. Saudi Arabia can also be contrasted with Bahrain and Kuwait in that the kinds of continuous activism surrounding clubs, underground parties, the press, union organizing, and the resulting fragile establishment (and suspension) of civil liberties and representative institutions never took place. Although various organizations did come into existence in embryonic form, their activities were generally repressed before they could establish themselves on a continual basis. But republican, liberal, Leftist and labour protest developed in different ways in the Hijaz, the oil fields and the armed forces.

Hijazi regionalism had been a source of opposition to the Al-Saud even before the founding of the Saudi state in 1932. Many in the Hijaz had reasons to chafe at their conquest by the Al-Saud. The claims of the Hashemite family, whose scions had directed the Arab revolt against the Ottomans and now occupied the thrones of Jordan and Iraq (the latter until 1958), the holy cities and sites of Muslim pilgrimage of Mecca and Medina, and the relatively cosmopolitan and wealthy merchant city of Jidda on the Red Sea coast, all served as bases for regionalism. As a British security memo put it in 1969, 'sophisticated' Hijazis resented their 'rough' Najdi conquerors (Burdett 2004: Vol. 4, 66). Some Hijazis had obtained higher education in the Mashriq and Egypt from the late 1930s onward. There were jobs for Hijazis and migrants from Egypt and the Mashriq in the oil industry, education, journalism and administration. A certain pan-Arab consciousness, along with progressive views on administrative reform, representative institutions and socio-economic development circulated in private and in the press (Abir 1993: 28–9, 35). Especially between 1958 and 1960, in addition to pamphleteering by opposition organizations, the Saudi press, 'dominated by Egyptians and the Hijazi intelligentsia', openly defied censorship and frequently published articles promoting Arab nationalism – and indirectly attacking the regime (Abir 1993: 40). Until the early 1960s, furthermore, the airwaves were ruled by the Nasserist radio station, Voice of the Arabs, broadcasting from Cairo. Faisal (r. 1964–75) took several measures to repress, control and reshape the media in 1962 and later, including the dismissal of critical Egyptian and local nationalist journalists (Abir 1993: 42–3).

The Al-Hasa region (part of the Eastern Province) had a sizeable population of poor Shi'a peasantry and contained a rather small coastal area where the major oil towns (Dammam, Dhahran and Al-Khobar), work camps and oil installations (especially the refinery at Ras Tanura) were situated. This was another key region of opposition to the dynasty. Building the refinery at Ras Tanura in the mid-1940s had involved 'thousands of . . . skilled and unskilled men from al-Hasa, Basra, and Bahrain' (Vitalis 2006: 92). Palestinians and other Arab migrants, for example, worked in building commercial port facilities in Dammam or on the Dammam–Riyadh railway, which employed 15,000 migrant workers at one point (Smith 1984: 172). In the early 1950s, Aramco employed 20,400 people, including at least 3,000 workers from the Arab world, the Mediterranean and Africa (Rasheed

2002: 97). In 1949, in something of a socio-economic sop to the Palestinian cause, Abd Al-Aziz Al-Saud 'informed ARAMCO of his desire that the company should employ at least a thousand Palestinian refugees'. Aramco sent officials to Beirut, and by 1950 it employed more than 800 Palestinians (Rasheed 2002: 103). By the end of 1953, this number had risen to around 3,000, as Aramco actively sought out Palestinians as foremen because of their skills, their English, and their knowledge of Arabic and Arab customs (Smith 1984: 172).

The first strikes and crowd actions at Aramco over pay and conditions of June and July 1945 are accompanied by references to Iraqi 'trouble-makers' – read activists – deported before the July strike at Aramco over pay and conditions. There was also apparently a consensus among the Americans as to the role of 'the better-educated Hijazi clerks' in organizing strike action in July 1945 (Vitalis 2006: 93–4). A strike over pay and conditions by 1,700 Italian migrant workers followed on 30 July, winning some concessions. Then, on 4 August, 'the entire force of 9,000 Arabs employed in Dhahran, Ras Tanura, and the outlying worksites' – with the support of some of the merchants in Al-Khobar who were contributing to a strike fund – 'defied the Amir and resumed the strike against ARAMCO' (Vitalis 2006: 94–5).

The most important round of worker mobilization (petitions, demonstrations, boycotts and strikes) in Saudi history began at Aramco in March 1953 and continued until June 1956. Thousands of workers – most of the Aramco workforce – appear to have participated. The first period lasted from May to October 1953, and the second dated from May 1955 to June 1956. The timing of these protests overlapped considerably with those in nearby Bahrain, which were a source of inspiration and one or two proven activist links. The main demands articulated by the leadership referred to pay, conditions, equality with American workers, living conditions, the right to elect worker representatives, an end to discrimination against the Shi'a, a more equitable distribution of oil revenues, and closing the American air force base in Dhahran (Smith 1984: 173; Abir 1993: 35). Such demands combined social and economic issues with nationalist and pan-Arab politics challenging US neo-colonialism.

The leaders among the Aramco employees were mostly Saudis, and were the educated or skilled elements, although employees of all status and skill levels, as well as Palestinian, Bahraini and Yemeni migrants, were among the ranks of activists and strikers. The lead name on the petition that started the protests in May 1953 was Abd Al-Aziz Abu Sunayd. In 1949, he began work as a teacher's assistant at Aramco. He was promoted in 1951, and in March of that year he taught at an employees' training camp on Long Island in the United States. He then spent the summer of 1951 at the American University of Beirut – the year when the MAN was being formed. He then became a teacher at Dhahran Training Center – one of the Aramco-linked schools that was to acquire a reputation for radicalism over the following decade and a half. All six of the other Saudis who presented themselves as spokespersons at the first meeting with the company on 30 June 1953 had studied in Beirut in either 1951 or 1952 (Vitalis 2006: 145–7). Abu Sunayd was deported to Iraq in late 1953. He then went to Beirut, worked for a Leftist newspaper, and made his way back to Dammam by 1956 to work at the Labour Office in the Ministry of Finance (Vitalis 2006: 154–5, 172–3). Another Aramco employee, a teacher trainee in his twenties, a certain Sayyid Abdallah Al-Hashim, who had spent time in Lebanon and possibly Egypt, read out at least one workers' petition directly to King Saud in Dhahran in November 1955 (Vitalis 2006: 177–8). Palestinians, Bahrainis, Yemenis and others were also probably involved as activists. Deportations of activist migrant workers from Aramco in November 1953 included 'three Palestinians, a Bahraini, and a naturalized Saudi citizen from Aden ... who was stripped of his citizenship before being exiled' (Vitalis 2006: 154–5). By the end of 1954, more than 160 Palestinian workers had been arrested and deported, and another 100 were arrested in 1955 – for 'unauthorized political activity'. After 1955, 'the number of Palestinians allowed to work in sensitive installations and in the oilfields was reduced considerably' (Smith 1984: 173; Brand 1988: 127)

The workers' committee that emerged during May–June 1953 never quite achieved official recognition as a representative of the workers, although at points Saudi officials directed Aramco to negotiate with it. Unions, indeed, were strictly banned in 1953. But the workers were not completely alone. Links to underground political parties and clandestine organizations came into existence at least in embryonic form during these years. There was some sympathy in the local press and more in the Arab world generally. There was also sympathy from the existing Shi'a population in Al-Hasa. Nationalist and Leftist ideas circulating in the camps supported the workers' cause and linked them to events and personalities in the wider Arab world.

Al-Rasheed writes that, in 1953, Saudi Arabia had its own timid Nasserites, Arab nationalists, and communists, 'all bred near the oil fields and inside "Sa'udi Camp"' (Rasheed 2002: 99–100). A measure of this is that crowds in both Dhahran and Riyadh turned out to give Nasser a hero's welcome in 1956 – while virtually ignoring King Saud (Abir 1993: 37–8). These ideas were linked to clandestine organizations of various kinds, capable of putting out leaflets and inspiring action. A description of a number of underground parties operating in Saudi Arabia and in exile is given in *Al-Hurriya*, the MAN newspaper, in 1968 (Burdett 2004: Vol. 2, 786–91, 796, Vol. 3, 272, 300–1). One leaflet with a hammer and sickle at its head, calling for a workers' democracy and an end to the American 'pigs', the 'days of the Cadillac', and the corrupt and reactionary royal family, was scattered on the streets of Al-Khobar in August 1954 (Vitalis 2006: 157). The National Reform Front was formed in late 1953 and early 1954 by the leaders of the 1953 strike (most notably, Nasir Sa'id), who were in turn linked to Palestinian Arab nationalists and the small Najdi intelligentsia. This socialist and secular group claimed members in the Hijaz and in the armed forces, and was active in the Aramco workforce in 1954 and 1955, before the imprisonment of its leaders in that year (Abir 1993: 34–5). This political activism was the cause of considerable alarm to the authorities, who privately expressed fears that communists were present amid the strike action, citing 'tracts in some of the rooms' and the fact that 'the terms and phrases used by the most articulate had Moscow (via Beirut) written all over them' (Vitalis 2006: 152). The 100 or so Palestinians arrested in May 1955 were under suspicion of belonging to the Parti Populaire Syrien and the Ba'th Party (Vitalis 2006: 161; Lackner 1978: 193).

There were sympathetic figures in the Saudi administration, including in the Ministry of Finance, which dealt with the workers as there was neither a labour nor an oil ministry in the 1950s (Vitalis 2006: 127–93). Abd Al-Aziz Ibn Muammar was director general of the Labour Office within the Ministry of Finance in Dammam. He was called variously a member of the Parti Populaire Syrien, a Ba'thist and a communist. It seems he was behind the scenes in mobilizing workers for the 1955 bus boycott at Aramco in Abqaiq (and spent May 1955 to March 1956 in jail for his pains). He employed at the Labour Office the activist Abu Sunayd on the latter's return from Lebanon in 1956. Another of the leaders of the 1953 strike also worked there in 1956 (Vitalis 2006: 172–3). Ibn Muammar was a Najdi and a close confidant of Abd Al-Aziz Al-Sa'ud. A nationalist, he criticized the American presence, corruption and extravagance by the royal family, and the lack of benefits from oil wealth to downtrodden ordinary citizens. He did have a copy of Marx's *Capital* on his bookshelf. A noteworthy point is that, like so many other reformers and activists of his generation, he was a graduate of the American University of Beirut (Vitalis 2006: 161–2).

Saudi's first oil minister, Abdullah Al-Tariqi (b. 1925), was well known for his reformist views. He was from the Najdi oasis of Zilfi but took his secondary education in Kuwait, and then most of his early higher education in Egypt. From there he entered the Ministry of Finance. He then studied geology in Cairo and Texas. He visited Venezuela, where the oil industry had been nationalized, in 1951. He became oil minister in 1960 with the creation of the Ministry of Petroleum and Mineral Resources (Rasheed 2002: 110–11). His main endeavours surrounded his demand for the nationalization of Aramco and his activities in OPEC on the international scene. His work was far removed from labour activism, but he supported unionization and criticized 'the unfair wages paid his countrymen, the lack of opportunities for Saudi workers, and the firm's substandard native housing' (Vitalis 2006: 134, 181).

Al-Rasheed conducted an interview with a Saudi worker who was a rank-and-file participant in the strikes of 1953. Such evidence is rare and worth quoting in full:

During the second war we almost starved in Qasim. Members of my family were poor peasants who looked after the palm groves of a wealthy local. We had already heard from people that *nasranis* [Christians] were offering jobs in Hasa for cash. My father decided that I should go and try my luck. I travelled with a Bedouin caravan to 'American Camp' and was offered a job to carry goods and material. I did all sorts of jobs. For the first time in my life I found myself with other tribesmen from 'Utayba, Shammar and Qahtan, each had their stories and dialect. We worked together. I met people from 'Asir and other parts of Najd. It was amazing ... The food was awful. But the Najdis would not say anything. They were shy; they would not complain. They would not ask for more money or food. They just left the Indians to eat there. Later in the 1950s they began to demand things from

ARAMCO. When *al-lajna al-'ummaliyya* [the Workers' Committee] told us to ask for more cash and better food, we did not respond. People are not beggars. But when they told us to ask for political rights, we all responded and joined the strikes in 1953. I sent money to my family. All I wanted to buy for myself was a radio. I wanted to hear about what was going on in Palestine and Egypt. Palestinian workers told us about their problems. We listened to the news together (Rasheed 2002: 97).

The most striking part of this testimony is the way that demands related to money and food were framed as begging, whereas the demand for political rights was not. It would appear that some notion of status honour, precluding an undignified and money-grubbing focus on mere cash, was important. Such orientations, arguably, meshed well with the very *political* demands of pan-Arabism, and Nasserism. And it is clear that the speaker was seeking to hear news via the radio of Palestine and Egypt – and his pan-Arab interests here were stimulated and reinforced by mixing with Saudis from other regions and tribes as well as Palestinian migrants. Indeed, the politicization of Saudi's best-known labour activist, Nasir Al-Sa'id (1923–79), may have derived from his contact with Arab workers (Rasheed 2002: 99–100).

South Asian labour, for its part, at least sometimes acted in coordination with other activist groups. At some point before March 1949, with a timing that coincided with a similar movement in Kuwait, Pakistani employees in Aramco 'organized a union to press for improvements in pay and living conditions'. In that month, fifty Pakistanis were suddenly expelled. Once they reached home, they 'began a campaign to publicize their mistreatment at the hands of the Americans' (Vitalis 2006: 102). Nonetheless, it is clear that non-Arab migrants were unable to draw on the same kinds of material and resources in receiving countries as Arab migrants were – a crucial indication of the importance of the ideas, organizations and alliances in enabling workers' protests.

The third main site of contentious politics in Saudi Arabia, apart from the Hijaz and Al-Hasa, was the military and the air force (but never the national guard, composed of Najdi tribesmen and villagers and a pillar of the dynasty throughout the period). There was an attempted coup by a small group of Free Officers in 1955, a number of acts of sabotage (such as the explosions of November 1966 to February 1967), several assassination attempts on leading members of the royal family, and at least one other serious coup attempt in

1969. In 1967, members of the armed forces and the police were accused of organizing, joining, or at the very least failing to prevent demonstrations and crowd actions. The British assessment from the mid-1950s until 1971 stated that a coup was a definite possibility and perhaps even a likelihood (Burdett 1997, 2004). Nonetheless, no would-be Colonel Gaddafi was to succeed in this desert kingdom.

The influence of Nasser's revolutionary coup of 1952, and of ideas and organizations associated with Nasserism and pan-Arabism, was a vital factor in these mobilizations. Disaffection in the armed forces was often among officers who had gone abroad (especially to Egypt) for training or come into contact with Egyptian and other Arab colleagues or their ideas (Abir 1993: 34). The first plot among a 'reform group' of Saudi officers was broken up in Ta'if in May 1955. Lieutenant Colonel Ghanim Madhya Hadi and his comrades were planning to overthrow the royal family. 'Most of those arrested had been trained in Egypt' (Vitalis 2006: 161). When an arms cache was discovered hidden in the king's palace in Riyadh in April 1957, a Palestinian confessed to having secreted them under the instructions of the Egyptian military attaché (Vitalis 2006: 189). Sketchy details in the British documents of a plan to kill Faisal in January 1965 involved Palestinians (Burdett 1997: Vol. 5, 23).

The Arab nationalist organization that claimed responsibility for the bombs of November–December 1966 was the Arabian Peninsula People's Union, operating out of North Yemen. This group was comprised of Saudis claiming to represent all classes of Saudi (not North Yemeni) society (Halliday 1974: 67). They advocated a 'Republic of the Arabian Peninsula' and supported the Arab movement for 'socialism, liberty, unity and democracy'. The Saudi authorities initially blamed these bombings, including one from February 1967, nonetheless, on Egyptian-trained *Yemenis*, seventeen of whom were executed publicly in March 1967 (Burdett 2004: Vol. 2, 507–19). Some years later, the Saudis blamed Egyptian-trained *Saudi* officers for the attacks. The Saudis arrested and beat a number of Palestinians in the wake of a few explosions on 2 June 1967, at American targets in Jedda (Burdett 2004: Vol. 2, 847, 857). South Yemenis from the NLF and the Hadramaut, Egyptian military instructors, and a least one Lebanese, were among those arrested during the clampdown following the coup attempt of 1969 (Burdett 2004: Vol. 4, 4ff., Vol. 5, 59–64). The independence of South Yemen in 1967 gave the MAN, a leading element there, a strategic base for revolutionary activities against Saudi Arabia and the Gulf states (United states Government 1970: 29).

The Annual British Defence Attaché report on Saudi Arabia of 1967 noted that discontent in the army, especially among younger officers educated abroad, was related to the slow rate of material progress in the kingdom (Burdett 2004: Vol. 3, 41, 53). Saudi measures to send its military in the 1950s and 1960s to Britain and the United States rather than to Egypt were interpreted, quite plausibly, in MAN circles in Beirut (for example, in *Al-Hurriya* in June 1968) as an attempt to isolate officers from Arab political influence (Burdett 2004: Vol. 3, 300–1).

The revolutionary coup in Libya

While attempts to pull off a revolutionary coup in the large, oil-rich, desert kingdom of Saudi Arabia were not successful, the same could not be said of Libya. Over the space of about two hours on 1 September 1969, without fatality or even violent incident, a group of about 70 young army officers and enlisted men, led by Mu'ammar Al-Qadhdhafi (Colonel Gaddafi), seized control of the Libyan government. The Libyan army quickly rallied to the cause. Neither the ousted king, his heirs, nor provincial powers did much to resist, unlike in North Yemen after 1962. There was, meanwhile, popular enthusiasm in urban areas and among the youth. Within days, military control was established from Benghazi in the west to Tripoli in the east and across the rest of the country. The Revolutionary Command Council, the twelve-person leadership of the Free Officers Movement, declared the country to be a free and sovereign state called the Libyan Arab Republic, advancing 'in the path of freedom, unity, and social justice' guaranteeing equality to all citizens. Overnight, the fourth-largest country in Africa was transformed from a conservative monarchy supported by British and American military, financial and diplomatic power to a revolutionary republic committed to rapid socio-economic development and seeking out alliances on the Nasserist and pan-Arab stage.

The debt to the Nasserist model of the revolutionary coup under the banners of Arab nationalism, republicanism, socialism, and progress, and involving a mobilization among nationalist junior officers using the tactic of a revolutionary coup within the army, is extremely evident, whether to historians looking back, or in regards to the understanding of both revolutionaries and observers at the time. The great brevity of the episode, its rapid success, and the lack of resistance and bloodshed, all further recall the Nasserist coup of 1952.

As Gaddafi and the other young men who carried out the revolution of 1969 with him were to testify, while at school they became committed to political change under the influence of the Nasserite revolutionary ideology (Abun-Nasr 1987: 414).

The Nasserist model had tremendous appeal to many coming of age in the 1950s and 1960s, and gaining their education in the Libyan school system which developed rapidly after 1961 when oil-rent started to flow. Schooling was a form of upward mobility in itself, but many new students saw no future beyond that in an environment dominated by tribal chiefs and merchants connected to a court guaranteed by British and Americans. Education as such did not necessarily imply Arab nationalism – but the convictions of the teachers mattered. The scarcity of qualified teachers at home meant the 'recruitment [to Libyan schools] of Egyptian and Palestinian teachers in large numbers, who were mostly Arab nationalists by conviction' (Abun-Nasr 1987: 413–14). Schools thus became conduits for ideas that were radically critical of the 'reactionary' and 'corrupt' client monarchy, at a time when progressive and revolutionary changes were being enacted in other parts of the Arab world.

Gaddafi's biography exemplified this context of schooling, blocked upward mobility, and exposure to Nasserism. He was born in 1942 in the Sirta desert to a semi-nomadic family living from pasturage and shifting agriculture. He went to school in Sirta, and then from 1956 to 1959 in Sabha in Fezzan, to where his family had moved. Gaddafi was expelled from Fazzan by a provincial chief, Ahmad Sayf Al-Nasr, because of his participation in demonstrations. He completed his school education in Misurata, joined the military academy in 1963, and encouraged some of his school friends to do the same, including his future right-hand man Abdul-Salam Jallud. 'While at the military academy, [Gaddafi] started recruiting supporters for the revolution, and in 1964 the central committee of the [Free Offices Movement] was formed' (Abun-Nasr 1987: 414–15).

Libya had gained its independence under the auspices of the United Nations in 1951 in the aftermath of the defeat of Italy as one of the Axis powers in 1945.

Economic need, as well as the threat of Arab nationalist forces to the regime, which became especially strong after the Egyptian revolution of 1952, led Libya's rulers to accept the creation of British and American military bases in their country (Abun-Nasr 1987: 412).

Political life in a client monarchy was dominated in the 1950s by rivalry between an oligarchy of politicians and chiefs, and through connections with the royal family. This system had been challenged during the 1952 elections to the House of Representatives. The National Congress Party, led by veteran Arab nationalist leader Bashir Al-Sa'dawi, had accused the government of rigging elections. There were demonstrations in Tripoli and some acts of violence. The NCP, whose support base was limited to urban areas, was repressed and Al-Sa'dawi went into exile.

To the critique of the regime's liberal-democratic failures, was added that of their client status on the regional stage, and their incapacity to manage properly oil-rents in the 1960s, or to use them to promote social justice and development. This criticism drew much power from the demonstration effects of alternative systems in Egypt and Iraq. The rapid decline of cereal production, which meant that by 1969 Libya imported 75 per cent of its food requirements, as well as unemployment in towns, rising prices, and the way wealth flowed to a minority of well-connected privileged families, fuelled criticisms of the system and the policies of the king. While a reform was enacted in April 1963 aimed at making the regional distribution of the benefits of oil less unequal, grievances mounted over 'the government's refusal in the face of popular pressure to espouse Arab nationalist causes' (Abun-Nasr 1987: 414). In January 1964, a number of students were killed by police during a demonstration in Benghazi against Israel's proposed diversion of the Jordan river waters. Public outrage then forced Prime Minister Muhyi Al-Din Fikini, from a family of Tripolitanian provincial notables, to resign shortly afterwards. A new political crisis followed on 22 February 1964 when Nasser demanded in a speech 'guarantees that the foreign military bases in Libya would not be used in an attack on an Arab state' (Abun-Nasr 1987: 414). This put the king at loggerheads with one of his key ministers. The latter, aware of the strong feelings aroused in Libya and elsewhere in the Arab world on this point, informed the United States and Britain that the Libyan government was not prepared to extend military-basing agreements when they expired in 1971 and 1973. The king publicly opposed this line, exposing faultlines at the heart of the state. Further, when the elections of October 1964 elected a parliament that the king thought dangerous, he dissolved the parliament in order to arrange a more favourable vote.

It was amid this year of crisis (1964), divisions at the top, mobilization and repression that the plot of the Free Officers Movement of Colonel Gaddafi took definite shape (Abun-Nasr 1987: 415). As Abun-Nasr avers, the 'political climate of Libya' and the region played a vital role. Figures like Nasser and Aflaq offered to the youth a programme to end their subordination personally and politically. Arab nationalism promised a 'revival of the past glories of Islam with prosperity and national strength through a form of socialism divested of those Marxist aspects which could not be reconciled with Islam' (Abun-Nasr 1987: 414). Colonel Gaddafi also drew on tribal customs and traditions to add another element to the Free Officers' programme: 'direct democracy'. The idea was to make use of oil money, and, less programmatically, the state, to effect a thorough-going transformation of Libyan society, economy, polity and foreign relations.

Rapid socio-economic change occasioned by oil-led development cannot very satisfactorily explain the demise of the monarchy insofar as similar developments on the Arabian peninsula, particularly in Saudi Arabia, did not have the same impact. Indeed, oil-rents are as often associated with monarchical longevity as they are with its demise. Oil-led development since the 1980s, moreover, has taken place in the MENA without any coincidence with a revolutionary leadership – or at least not a leadership in Arab nationalist guise. Certainly, oil-rents were channelled into schools, which then became sites of mobilization for Colonel Gaddafi's group: but the nature of that activism was hardly dictated by the school system itself, which in institutional terms was designed to contain, not to inspire, revolutionary activism. Rather than conceiving of the coup in determinist terms, this section has explored the ways in which the frames, goals and strategies of Gaddafi's movement were very much drawn from the Arab nationalist and Nasserist regional milieu. This milieu may not have caused the coup in any direct or sufficient way, but it very strongly shaped the project that Gaddafi undertook, and thus had an impact on its course and consequences.

Al-Thawra in Palestine, 1964–1982

On New Year's Eve 1964, units of the newly organized military wing of the clandestine Palestinian nationalist organization Fatah, set out to cross the armistice line into Israel to sabotage a water-pumping station used by Israel to obtain the disputed headwaters of the River Jordan. The attack was abortive, but the following day Fatah announced the beginning of the armed struggle to liberate Palestine in Military Communiqué No. 1. Their initial military and financial impact on the Israeli state was negligible. Their small-scale operations, carried out by a handful of poorly equipped volunteers, looked hardly relevant to the many whose attention was rivetted by the conflict between the major Arab states, above all Nasser's Egypt, and Israel. Their actions were seen in most of the corridors of power in the Arab states as a reckless adventurism threatening a war with Israel for which the Arab states were not prepared. Even many committed Palestinian nationalists saw them as 'madmen' (Y. Sayigh 1997: 106). Palestinian fighters in Arab states were typically imprisoned, outlawed and harassed. Their lowly adventure, nonetheless, signalled the beginning of a new phase in the Palestinian nationalist struggle after the crushing of the 1936–9 uprising and the dispersal and fragmentation in the aftermath of the *nakba*.

During the 1960s, the three main strands of the Palestinian nationalist movement, Fatah under Yasir Arafat (1929–2004), the MAN under George Habash (1926–2008), (which was to furnish much of the leadership for the PFLP and the DFLP) and the PLO (founded by Nasser in 1964), initially under the Palestinian notable Ahmad Al-Shuqayri (1908–80) (but taken over by Fatah after 1969), moved increasingly towards armed struggle. A new political generation was mobilized, committed to armed struggle (but usually not drawn from the ranks of the professional military), organizing in factions and fronts, evading the repression of host states, rejecting the mediation of the notables (*wujuha'*), using new means of communication and persuasion, increasingly making use of Palestinian rather than pan-Arab-focused solutions, and often from lowlier social backgrounds than that of the notable leadership in exile, drawing heavily on the ideological currents of the post-1945 era, and building up a Palestinian state-in-waiting. What was initially a very small group of Palestinians and Arabs declared: 'By the gun we will liberate Palestine' (*bi-bunduqiyya bi-bunduqiyya la-nuharrar filastin*). With the shattering defeat of the Arab states by

Israel in 1967, and the bravery shown by Arafat's men fighting along-side regular Jordanian forces at the Battle of Karama in March 1968, the Palestinian armed struggle dramatically expanded, commanding 25,000 armed cadres by 1970 (United States Government 1970: 21–2), becoming an important factor in regional geopolitics. No less an intellectual than Sadiq Jalal Al-Azm declared in 1970 that in the wake of 1967 'the Nasirist revolution proved itself impotent ... and that in the end the Palestinian Revolution must supercede the Nasirist Revolution as the true Arab Revolution' (cited in United States Government 1970: 149). The *thawra* was only to run out of steam in 1982 with the eviction of the PLO from Lebanon following the Israeli invasion (Khalili 2007a; Said 1995; Y. Sayigh 1986, 1997), leaving in its wake a state-in-exile ready to pursue diplomatic means to establish a Palestinian state alongside Israel.

The leaderships and rank and file of the guerrilla movements of the 1950s and 1960s were drawn from a new political generation that with a few exceptions had little or no experience of either notable or grassroots political action in Mandate Palestine and had 'been teenagers, or at most in their early twenties, in 1948' (Y. Sayigh 1997: 669). Their crucial formative experiences were the catastrophe of 1948 'which they witnessed at first hand ... and subsequent life under the [restrictive] authority of different Arab states' (Y. Sayigh 1997: 677). 'Most came from a lower-middle class background, had benefited from the rapid expansion of the education system in the Arab countries in the late 1940s and early 1950s, and were influenced by the new, statist models of political organization and economic development adopted by the host Arab governments' (Y. Sayigh 1997: 669). Most of the new cadres 'came from the smaller cities and market towns of mandate Palestine, as did many prominent members of the post-1967 political class, while a substantial proportion of the long-serving, salaried personnel of the PLO hailed from the rural districts of the West Bank' (Y. Sayigh 1997: 670).

While ex-Ottoman officers, professional soldiers attached to this or that Arab state, or those trained in Ottoman military schools were important in the generation that had led armed struggles in the Mashriq in the 1920s and 1930s, very few of the new generation of Palestinian fighters had professional military training. Salah Khalaf (1933–91) (aka Abu Iyad) was a long-standing second-in-command of the PLO and head of intelligence. He pointed out correctly that Fatah was not made up of professional military men or commanders:

'All combatants in Fatah at all levels were originally university students, engineers, patriotic scholars, or workers', he said. There were no officers. He stated that they were waging a war of liberation, and that the men and the leaders learned to make war 'by actually making war' (cited in United States Government 1970: 22). Arafat's Fatah was to Nasser what Abd Al-Qadir was to Hajj Ahmad of Constantine: when the official military failed in their duties, the volunteers and civilians got into military clothes. The political generation that acceded to leadership positions between the 1950s and 1970s was in many ways new to political action.

Most of the guerrilla fighters, and almost all the top leaderships were men, but by no means all. Here there was some innovation too. Numerous women fought. More typically, women served a plethora of other vital infrastructural functions. Palestinians increasingly recognized, in the words of a letter smuggled out of an Israeli jail by an 18-year-old girl, that woman is 'man's partner in the struggle, joining him in braving danger and defying death and urging him on even with the last breath of life' (United States Government 1970: 80, citing *Al-Jumhuriya*, Cairo, 1 January 1970, p. 6). Palestinian training camps for girls existed, and women were involved in guard duty for the male guerrillas and 'at times take part in military operations, even crossing over into the occupied territories'. In a PFLP camp in Lebanon, girls were shown practising judo, and engaging in hand-to-hand combat with daggers. There was also a parade of nurses in white. Girls have been used on daring missions, planting bombs in a Jerusalem supermarket, and in the Hebrew University, and in hijacking El Al aircraft. 'The woman who entered the supermarket spoke Hebrew and with her blue eyes and miniskirt succeeded in passing as a European Jewess'. A seventeen-year-old girl working for the PFLP was said to have shot dead a Palestinian collaborator on the main street in Gaza. Women and girls in the Occupied Palestinian Territories also took part in demonstrations, and distributed material printed by the resistance organizations (United States Government 1970: 80–1). In many ways, women engaged by asserting their equality with, or becoming like, men. Some were determined 'to prove' in the words of Leila Khaled, 'that we can be equal in [armed] missions and in practice with men' (cited in Irving 2012: 94). This kind of mobilization challenged masculine domination by asserting women's equality, but it left rather intact existing models of masculinity and femininity.

For the activists of the Palestinian resistance, the homeland had been lost, decisively, in 1948, and the goal was to recover it. As the well-known PFLP guerrilla Leila Khaled (b. 1944) put it in her autobiography:

European Zionists occupy Palestine by right of armed force – they drove us out of our fatherland. They live in our homes while we are in exile. They live in my city [Haifa] because they are Jews and they possess power. My people and I live in exile because we are Arab-Palestinians and we do not have their power. But one day ... we will have this power, we will retake Palestine and we will make a human paradise for Arabs and Jews alike and all lovers of Liberty (Khaled 1973: 22).

The recovery of the homeland was conceived in nationalist and statist terms by all currents of the resistance movement. The Palestinians sought a state of their own: they saw themselves as a nation with a common history in search of a state and a territory to call their own. On this 'lowest common denominator' (Y. Sayigh 1997: 679) Palestinians of all political stripes could agree, although they disagreed, often radically, on the form of the polity, socio-economic structure, gender roles, the place of Islam, on relations to the rest of the world, and on the goals, strategies, organization and tactics for achieving national liberation. On the other hand, virtually no Palestinian activists sought to create a neo-patrimonial state-in-exile, which was in many ways the result after 1982. In other words, the outcome here should not be confused with the goal, which is in some respects a danger in Yezid Sayigh's seminal work.

Especially after 1969, Fatah held the hegemonic position within the Palestinian nationalist movement. Fatah's roots were among those who had grown up and studied under Egyptian rule in Gaza and Cairo, many of whom had started their political life in the Muslim Brotherhood and 'later found work in the oil-rich Gulf states' (Y. Sayigh 1997: 677). The idea of forming Fatah crystallized in the wake of 1956, when it became clear to men like Khalil Al-Wazir (1935–88), the son of a grocer from Ramlah who had started organizing resistance in high school, and Yasir Arafat that there were no autonomous Palestinian organizations, amid Egyptian popularity and state strength and the weakness and limited credibility of the Muslim Brotherhood and other groups, that could serve as a focus of support for the resistance (Y. Sayigh 1997: 83). Fatah espoused a thoroughly Palestinian (as opposed to pan-Arab) nationalism, avoiding ideologies of Left or Right, which was less interested in strict organizational discipline or socio-economic transformation, had a strongly pragmatic strain, measuring enemies and friends by their contribution to the basic national cause. As Arafat stated in the newspaper Al-Sayyad in January 1969: 'There is no meaning to left or right in my struggle to liberate my homeland' (cited in United States Government 1970: 24). Perhaps reflecting their origins outside of political parties and domestic Arab politics, Fatah exhibited an acute desire to build up and generate an independent capacity for Palestinian decision-making, in the face of the interference and manipulation of this or that Arab state.

The MAN was established by students in the American University of Beirut during 1949–1951, and became Fatah's most important rival in the 1960s. The most senior cadres of its Palestinian branch 'came mainly from Jordan (including the West Bank) and, to a lesser degree, Syria and Lebanon . . . [t]heir early experiences were of the tempestuous party politics of the Arab East in the 1950s' (Y. Sayigh 1997: 677). The MAN went on to supply most of the leaderships of the Leftist Palestinian factions – primarily the PFLP (est. 1967) and the DFLP (est. as the PDFLP in 1969). By 1970, the PFLP had 1,000–2000 armed cadres (United States Government 1970: 32). These elements of the Palestinian 'opposition' held a more ideological view of the road to national liberation than Fatah. They believed that the road to Jerusalem lay through Damascus and Amman – meaning that their nationalism was more pan-Arab in nature than that of Fatah – and held that reactionary Arab regimes must be overthrown on the road to a socialist state in Palestine. In this the MAN hewed close to Nasserism in the 1960s. The defeat of 1967 was the major catalyst for a leftward shift, whereby petty-bourgeois nationalism was rejected, and the delusions of the 'progressive' military regimes exposed, in favour of Marxist–Leninism. More insistently than Fatah, the PFLP saw enemies in the reactionary Arab governments and reactionary elements among Palestinians themselves, who were now blamed for the defeat of 1936–9. They argued that the economic interests of the Arab governments coincided with those of the imperialists (United States Government 1970: 29). In one camp, wrote the PFLP, is Israel, Zionism, global imperialism, and reaction. In the other is the Palestinian people, the Arab nation, and progressives in the world (*al-taqaddumiyyun*) (PFLP n.d.: 19). As PDFLP leader Nayyif Hawatma declared, Arab nationalism may have been effective in eradicating the old imperialism in Egypt, Syria, Iraq and Southern Yemen – but is ineffective against new imperialism. Effective nationalism had to be led by the working class – as shown in Asia, Africa and Latin America (United States Government 1970: 34). In proposals submitted to a Palestine National Council meeting in Cairo in September 1969, the PDFLP envisaged 'winning the popular war by mobilizing the broad masses of workers, peasants, refugees, students, small merchants, craftsmen and professionals' (United States Government 1970: 38). While the Palestinian pan-Arab Left declared that Arab unity was the road to Palestine, Fatah countered by saying that Palestine was the road to Arab unity, as it would eliminate the key fortress of imperialist divide and rule (Y. Sayigh 1997: 198–9).

The birth of the PLO in 1964 under the sponsorship of Arab states, motivated by the need to contain and control rising Palestinian activism, stemmed from an 'attempt to establish a state-like organization' by 'members of the traditional and upper middle classes of pre-1948 Palestine ... [t]hat had occupied the second echelon in the national leadership under Husayni, and that were effectively denied their chance to govern as a result of the *nakba* and of the subsequent marginalization of the AHC [Arab Higher Committee] and the APG [All-Palestine Government, est. 1948]' (Y. Sayigh 1997: 95). Their leading figures were notables, former government officials and politicians, majors and village council heads, merchants, clergy, lawyers, doctors, engineers and the like, with only a limited representation from women's groups and trade unions (Y. Sayigh 1997: 98–9). The initiative was opposed by Al-Husayni who viewed Shuqayri as an Egyptian stooge, and by the MAN and Fatah who 'warned against an "entity" that was not revolutionary in character and whose ultimate authority was merely nominal' (Y. Sayigh 1997: 99). The PLO adopted a straightforward Palestinian nationalism of politically liberal hue, shorn of a political, economic, religious or social programme, but without advocating armed struggle or adopting the identities and principles of revolution.

The Muslim Brotherhood held a certain place in the Palestinian nationalism of the late 1940s and early 1950s, especially in Gaza, largely thanks to the role played by the armed wing of the Muslim Brotherhood in the 1948 war. Many Fatah activists had joined the Muslim Brotherhood before the establishment of the former. The idea was that the Palestinians should fight as Muslims for the recovery of a homeland corrupted and usurped by unbelievers – and that the struggle for Palestine was above all one for a more Islamic society and state. Another minority version of political Islamism of this kind was embodied in the Islamic Liberation Party (Hizb ul-Tahrir), active in Jordan, whose founder, Nebahani, read the *nakba* in terms of the loss of the Caliphate in 1924. His party's aim, as stated in a rejected application for legal establishment in Jordan in 1952, was to 'restart the Islamic way of life' through the creation of 'the single Islamic State which implements Islam and calls the world to Islam' (Pankhurst 2013: 95).

In complete contrast, a number of smaller movements read the loss of Palestine in terms of capitalist and imperialist exploitation, and considered that the recovery of the homeland should be part and parcel of the liberation of the international proletariat. The principal communist parties, who were linked to the policies of the Soviet Union, were the Jordanian Communist Party (est. 1951) and the Palestinian Communist Organization (Gaza), 1948–82. Communism outside of the direct link to the Soviet Union was embodied in a few even smaller Trotskyist groups.

By the 1960s, scattered Palestinian communities had painstakingly rebuilt a certain sociological space, reviving their social networks, value systems and norms, and cultural symbols (Y. Sayigh 1997: 666). New forms of organization held in common their rejection of notable styles of patronage and conflict resolution, congresses and motions, of the idea that only seniority and genealogy counted, of military hierarchy, and to a large extent the existing political parties, so regularly associated with division, discredited older-generation politics, and an avoidance of direct action. An important trend during the 1960s was 'declining Palestinian affiliation to parties whose ideologies did not commit them first and foremost to the liberation of Palestine. This was obvious in the case of the Islamist movements and the Ba'th Party, and also of the communists of the Syrian National Party' (Y. Sayigh 1997: 95). The new activist groups, of which there were a very great many, were dubbed organizations (such as the PLO), fronts (such as the PFLP), movements (such as the MAN), commands (such as Palestinian Action Command, est. 1964), unions (such as the General Union of Palestinian Students), or councils (such as Abu Nidal's Fatah-Revolutionary Council, est. 1974). Until the defeat of 1967, the armed factions were organized in a clandestine fashion for the most part: only after the defeat were they able to come out into the open.

Shifting styles of political organization are brought out quite vividly in Rosemary Sayigh's oral history of Shatila camp in Lebanon. An older notable politics, based around merchants, notables and land-owners, the patronage of Hajj Amin Al-Husseini, involving conflict resolution, paternalism, the holding of *majalis* to listen to peasant and other grievances, the receipt of tribute, the distribution of employ-ment, and the hallmarks of respect for genealogy and fatherly senior-ity, and indeed the idea that politics was the preserve of notable families, was usurped in Shatila above all in the 1960s by the new forms of activism, fuelled by new forms of education and schooling, new ideological currents, Nasserist radio, along with the political failures of the older generation (R. Sayigh 1994: 50–3, 59–61). Many people blamed Hajj Amin and his style of leadership for the loss of Palestine (R. Sayigh 1994: 50). According to new activists, the older *shuyukh* 'feared that the generation influenced by Abdel Nasser and by nationalism would escape from their control. They tried to frighten us with talk of the state. We considered them an obstacle to our movement' (a Shatila resident and activist in the MAN, cited in R. Sayigh 1994: 51). Many of the younger generation turned to the new political parties and movements which started to appear in the camp in the 1950s and 1960s, including the Ba'th Party, the MAN and the Lebanese Communist Party. Recruitment often took place in schools and workplaces where the older generation had a more limited control. Nasser's popularity – rooted in his speeches defending Pales-tinian rights, his challenges to imperialism, 'the facilities he gave for military training as well as his encouragement of Palestinian insti-tutions (the PLO, the students' and workers' union, the Sawt Al-Filasteeni radio station)' (R Sayigh 1994: 52) – eroded that of Hajj Amin. Al-Shuqayri's tour of Lebanon after the founding of the PLO involved 'mass rallies, the first of their kind [in Lebanon]' (R Sayigh 1994: 73). New activists held demonstrations, they distributed pamphlets and tracts, they wrote extensively in their own group's organs, and they called meetings: these repertoires tended to face the hostility of old men and village notables (R. Sayigh 1994: 78). The new styles of organization were more egalitarian insofar as they broke down the links between political decision and seniority or genealogy. As one MAN activist put it:

If someone like me spoke about politics [the *wujuha'*/notables] would say, 'Who is this? He's only a boy, he doesn't have the right to stand up and speak in front of Hajj Amin Husseini'. They thought that politics is only for certain families ... That's how they were brought up (cited in R Sayigh 1994: 60).

New forms of organization worried the Lebanese state under Chehab, which considered them less easy to control (R. Sayigh 1994: 52). Moreover, when military hierarchies and officer privileges made an appearance with the use of Palestinian officers trained in Arab militaries, problems followed. In 1968, for example, in Jordan, 'many of these officers brought authoritarian attitudes that sat poorly with the guerrillas, who had adopted an egalitarian system that allowed no distinctions in formal rank, pay, sleeping quarters, or other privileges' (Y. Sayigh 1997: 182). They also brought more women, usually by dint of the latter's personal determination and sacrifice, into the ranks of the organized, a matter which provoked considerable resistance.

With the development of military training among Palestinians from the early 1960s onwards, camps were set up, and these, together with existing refugee camps, became important spaces of mobilization, socialization, political education, and the articulation of shared principles and identities. Doctrine and revolutionary practice were developed together:

The guerrilla training camps devote as much as ten hours a week or more to political indoctrination and discussion. Each camp ordinarily has its own library containing Arabic newspapers and periodicals, the Palestinian National Covenant, the numerous publications of the PLO and Fatah, and often the writings of such Leftist guerrilla leaders as George Habash and Nayif Hawatmeh. Instruction is given in subjects such as Arab and Islamic history, the Palestinian cause, the goals of the Palestinian revolution, and the evils of Zionism and imperialism (United States Government 1970: 74).

The military camps were also woven into a structure involving other kinds of mobilization, in which wider constituencies could participate. Fund-raising campaigns, cultural events, donations, auxiliary services and so on played a vital role and mobilized a much wider constituency than the military cadres themselves. In his memoirs, Anis Al-Naqqash, a Lebanese journalist who fought for the PLO as Abu Fakhr in the 1970s, speaks of the cultural centres, the parties, the press, magazines, youth groups and schools that were burgeoning in Beirut in the 1950s and 1960s (Abu Fakhr 2010: 14), the channels of broad mobilization and debate over questions of Arab and Palestinian national liberation.

The take over of the PLO by Fatah in 1969 was an important step in the organizational development of the nationalist movement. The PLO, thanks to the energies of Ahmad Al-Shuqayri, who exceeded his mandate, had built up an important national institution with formal Arab recognition, a developed administrative structure, and various bodies charged with social provision. Rather than eschew armed struggle, as the 1960s wore on, Al-Shuqayri started to jump on the bandwagon, especially by May of 1967 (Y. Sayigh 1997: 141). It was the defeat of the Arab states in 1967, and the guerrilla success at Karama in 1968, that enabled Fatah's Arafat to be elected Chairman of the PLO in 1969. By this time, the Palestinian resistance movement was far more than a clandestine set of armed groups, and had now obtained, because of the way the various struggles had played out rather than by design, an extensive, state-like organization complete with unions and associations, including a mass organization to promote female mobilization, the General Union for Palestinian Women.

The idea that came to dominate the strategic thinking of Palestinian organizations in the 1960s was that of people's guerrilla war, which was to be the crucial means for the recovery of the homeland. This strategy was a decisive break from the politics of notables, party politics or the conventional military. Where home-grown soldiers of the previous generation, such as Abd Al-Krim and Fawzi Al-Qawuqji, were associated with failure – the latter more dramatically and relevantly so than the former – the success of the Chinese (1949), the Cubans (1959), the Algerians (1962), the South Yemenis (1967), and the impact of the Viet Cong (especially after the Tet Offensive of 1968), were the focus of considerable attention in regard to the possibilities of armed struggle (Chamberlin 2012; Khalili 2007a: 11–40) – what the PFLP called 'the way of the armed, organized, conscious masses' (*'tariq al-jamahir al-wa'iyya al-musallaha al-munadhama'*) (PFLP 1970: 4).

Mao's great endorsement of the enormous capacities of guerrilla forces to defeat a technologically and numerically superior foe was a clear inspiration to the Palestinians. But, before 1967, the classical Maoist form of guerrilla warfare by an occupied population against an imperialist occupier did not apply because the Israel of 1948–67 may have occupied Palestinian land, but this directly affected a relatively small number of Palestinian Arabs (around 160,000 at the outset). The Palestinians had been driven *outside* Israel's borders – unlike the Chinese under Japanese occupation, the Algerian Muslims, who lived inside the French-Algerian state, the Libyans under Italian occupation in the 1920s, or the South Yemenis in the 1960s. For the same reason, Palestinian guerrillas could not act according to Cuban *foquismo*, whereby small vanguard guerrilla groups operated from mountainous or inaccessible areas within the domestic state that was to be seized, stimulating a larger uprising by their moral example and capacity to inflict defeat on larger forces. While Mao emphasized how guerrilla forces could bring an occupation to its knees, the Palestinian guerrillas could hope to strike fear in Israel, or to weaken its economy, but not, by themselves, to defeat its army or destroy the state. More suggestive was the Vietnamese model, where guerrilla forces acted in conjunction with state strategy and conventional forces – those of North Vietnam (Y. Sayigh 1997: 200). Mao himself had envisaged the possibility in 1937 of symbiotic arrangements between guerrilla and conventional forces (Mao 1937).

For Fatah, before 1967, 'conscious entanglement' and 'successive detonation' ending in a major inter-state confrontation that would destroy the Zionist state, was the key. The idea was that guerrilla actions by small vanguard groups infiltrating into Israel would entangle the 'strongest force', the Arab masses, in the struggle for liberation. The Arab masses would be drawn in, and their energies detonated, by the daring blows struck by the guerrillas. As the Algerian example was held to show, the popular base would also be united by the resolute action of a small vanguard – which would in turn act as 'a source of political legitimacy and national identity' (Y. Sayigh 1997: 195). And the Palestinian cause would be demonstrated vividly on the international stage. The 'cycle of Palestinian action and Israeli reaction would demonstrate the real threat posed by an expansionist Israel to the Arabs' (Y. Sayigh 1997: 119). The Arab states would either be forced to arm their populations, who would join the 'army of return', or they would be forced to stand with the Palestinians, deploying massive force themselves against the Israeli state. If the Arab states did risk their own legitimacy by turning against the Palestinians, they would lose the support of their people, who would then join the Palestinian struggle (Y. Sayigh 1997: 120, 196ff.). The more Leftist sections of the Palestinian movement added to conscious entanglement and successive detonation another step: revolution in the Arab states, especially the reactionary ones, which would have to come about before such states would join a revolutionary confrontation with Israel. Such a revolution could follow the loss of legitimacy occasioned by the confrontation with the Palestinians.

The Fatah version of this strategy, as it turned out, over-estimated the military strength of the Arab states, and under-estimated these regime's capacity for repression and narrow, statist *realpolitik*. The Leftist version over-estimated the possibilities for popular revolution in the Arab world. Both versions failed to specify how mass mobilization would come about (Y. Sayigh 1997: 120), a difficult task under repressive conditions at the best of times. But, while the tendency has been to see the guerrilla strategy as hyperbolic, vague and chaotically pursued, it was remarkably powerful. The Palestinian cause was indeed placed on the international agenda for the first time in over a decade. The confrontation states were indeed thrown onto the horns of a mighty dilemma – they were caught between Israeli military power on the one hand, and the bases of their own hegemony on the other. To oppose the Palestinians risked civil war and the cohesion of the state itself. To support them risked destruction at the hands of Israel. The Arab regimes could not ignore the Palestinians, and their tool for containing them (the PLO) was increasingly escaping their control. The resistance played a role in dragging Nasser into a war which he had no intention of fighting. As he repeatedly stated, he had 'no plan for the liberation of Palestine', and had made various peace initiatives to the Israeli state, at least before 1956. In some respects, the Palestinian strategy was too successful, too quickly. The expected confrontation came, and the military power of the confrontation states was broken by a pre-emptive Israeli attack in just six days, and Israel quadrupled the territory it controlled.

The shattering defeat of 1967 was predicted by none of the Fatah or MAN activist leaderships, who were temporarily stunned. Only now, with the Israeli occupation of East Jerusalem, the West Bank and Gaza, not to mention the Sinai and the Golan Heights, could the classical guerrilla strategies of Mao or Guevara be put into action, as there was now an occupier and an occupied – with the goal of setting up an independent 'revolutionary authority' that could escape Arab control (Y. Sayigh 1997: 155). Even here, the obstacles were great, as the terrain did not do much to render territory inaccessible to the Israeli armed forces, and strategic depth and supply lines to the outside world were lacking as the territory involved was small and Israel could control much of the Jordan Valley. The attempt by the guerrillas to launch such a classical war was thus abortive, except in Gaza, where the factions controlled the strip by night until the early 1970s. After this failure, whereby an unadapted model was brought to bear, strategies again had to be rethought as the Palestinian movement moved back into exile once again.

At this point, Fatah's continuing grasp of the propaganda of the deed, a temporary weakness in the repressive capacities and change in the policies of the Arab states *vis-à-vis* the Palestinians, and an upsurge from below, breathed major new life into the Palestinian movement. Suddenly it appeared that the Palestinian nationalists, above all Fatah, had been right in seeking an independent Palestinian movement, which would take its destiny into its own hands – because the rhetoric, incompetence and weakness of the Arab states had been definitively exposed. Meanwhile, in spite of the military losses incurred by Fatah in confronting the Israeli forces at Karama in March 1968, it was clear for all to see that the guerrillas did stand and fight, alongside the Jordanian army in this case, and that the recently victorious and seemingly invincible Israelis now suffered some military losses, and that their captured tanks and weapons were paraded for all to see, all of which meant a huge political victory for Fatah. The effect on public opinion, on the nationalist movement, and on the stream of volunteers to the cause, was electrifying.

Abu Fakhr offers in his memoirs an account of his own youthful mobilization to the ranks of the PLO armed struggle at this conjuncture. He notes that the 1967 war was 'a major shock to the whole Arab nation', and 'woke people up to what was going on around them'. This 'defeat took me from just a general [political] interest to a direct political commitment'. He says that he started, in fact, 'to conduct research in political magazines', with a disgust for mere rhetoric and a desire for effectiveness and direct action (*juhud al-mubashir*) (Abu Fakhr 2010: 15). Al-Naqqash writes: 'Everyone started trying to plan a way or a political method or an idea or to find a solution here or there.' Suddenly, all eyes were riveted on Palestine and the Palestinian resistance that rose up on 1 January 1965. 'I was among those young men that were greatly impressed by these *fida'i* actions – and I followed the news of them in the press before I became an openly proclaimed proponent of armed struggle.'

[I]t was the statements of Fatah that impressed me the most. After 1967 I became a Fida'i. But the battle of Karama, 21 March 1968, was the turning point and the point of departure. We organized in the school, campaigns raising money for the camps of the refugees and Palestinian children. And I left school – perhaps because I was most enthusiastic and ready always for adventure – that I went to Jordan with two friends to offer the money raised to Fatah; for me the contact with Fatah was more important than the donation (Abu Fakhr 2010: 16–17).

Al-Naqqash was politicized not by the presence of a pre-existing socio-economic grievance which then translated into political action, but amid a shock at the dereliction of the existing authorities, a journey into politics as a result, and a subsequent adherence to a given political leadership and activism under its auspices. This upsurge resulted from no objective political opportunity, but was more related to a political crisis, and the decisive action of an activist group (Fatah), whose leader certainly grasped the symbolic and expressive value for mobilization of his fighters stand at Karama. Not for the first time a crisis proved hugely galvanizing.

On the other hand, the defeated Arab states, seeking to rebuild their broken militaries, and sometimes favouring guerrilla action as a way to distract and harass Israel while they did so, with their élan in espousing the cause of Palestine blunted for a moment, were less willing and able to engage in the thoroughgoing repression of the Palestinian fighters, and even worked to carve out sanctuaries for them (Y. Sayigh 1997: 147). This was indeed a political opportunity for the revolution. The guerrilla groups shed their clandestinity and came out into the open for the first time, above all in Jordan and Lebanon. In the latter, under the Cairo Agreement of 1969, Palestinian *fida'iyyin* were allowed to carry out armed operations against Israel from the south of the country. These state positions were partly possible because of Fatah's strategy of non-interference in Arab domestic politics and willingness to work with different regimes. In a sign of the times, the much-feared Deux-ième Bureau was finally evicted from Shatila camp in October 1969 by a show of armed force (R. Sayigh 1994: 87–9). One militant recalled this liberation:

Everybody was happy, everybody was singing, everybody wanted to join in. I remember that there were three or four nights when nobody slept. People who had been working in underground organizations revealed themselves. Young men who had nothing to do with it felt ashamed (Cited in R. Sayigh 1994: 91).

In Jordan, the guerrilla camps rode a similar wave of enthusiasm, their ranks swelling with thousands of volunteers. 'This was the heyday of the guerrillas, their "honeymoon" as they called it. A negligible military force before June 1967 ... with an uncertain political future ... they were mounting several hundred attacks on Israel each month by 1969' (Y. Sayigh 1997: 147). As a Fatah poster showing armed young men rising up from a refugee camp declared in 1981 'the giant has escaped from the bottle' (Tripp 2013: 265). If a revolutionary authority could not be established in occupied territory, guerrilla sanctuaries with some extra-territorial rights could at least be carved out in Jordan, Lebanon and Syria, while an institutional framework could be increasingly built up, and a certain autonomy as a regional, if junior, actor, established (Y. Sayigh 1997: 243).

Fatah's pragmatic nationalism should not be under-estimated. Arafat tapped into one of the obvious strengths of guerrilla war for national liberation. As Mao wrote, in a guerrilla war, 'the whole people of a nation, without regard to class or party, carry on a guerrilla struggle that is an instrument of the national policy. Its basis is, therefore, much broader than is the basis of a struggle of class type' (Mao 1937: 48). This point mattered. Fatah's relentless focus on the homeland was a potent force in mobilizing support. As Abu Lutf (Faruq Al-Qaddumi) put it in an interview in the late 1960s:

The exodus of the Arabs from Palestine has generated a new class unknown to Marx and Lenin: the class of refugees [including both middle and working classes] ... When I walk through a refugee camp, I cannot yell, 'Comrades, feudalism and capitalism are your enemies.' They would look at me uncomprehendingly and answer, 'What in the world are you talking about, Abu Lutf? Zionism is my enemy' (cited in United States Government 1970: 25).

In many ways, the central focus on national liberation, distant as it was from theorizing about capitalism and imperialism (or even Islam), provided a direct and clear message capable of resonating with and mobilizing large numbers of those uninterested in ideological debate.

The irony was, however, that now even numerous guerrilla attacks amounted to little more than a nuisance to a much empowered Israel (Y. Sayigh 1997: 202–7), which now had the far more thoroughgoing support of the United States. And with the strategies of entanglement and successive detonation and confrontation having run their course without a victory, the original strategic rationale for a people's guerrilla war, apart from a possible orientation to Arab revolution, was in tatters, just at the moment of its greatest mobilization. Moreover, the Arab states, recovering from 1967, were increasingly driven by narrow *raison d'état*, and as anxious as ever in regard to the threat they saw from the revolutionary option. There was a certain strategic logic, therefore, if a hint of desperation, in the insistence of the Leftists on Arab revolution: but this insistence in turn drove confrontations with host regimes that led to eviction from Jordan after a military showdown with Hussein's monarchy (in September 1970), and contributed to the growing civil war in Lebanon, the Syrian intervention against the Palestinians in 1976, and eventual eviction from there in 1982. From the early 1970s, more implicitly than explicitly to begin with, the Palestinian strategy became less 'total liberation' and more nuisance attacks that would win concessions in some eventual scenario of negotiation over a new partition of the land. The PLO increasingly developed the character of a state-in-waiting, operating in neo-patrimonial ways, relying on rents derived especially from the Gulf countries, rather than a revolutionary guerrilla organization. This outcome had been far from the goals and principles of the young revolutionaries of the 1950s and 1960s, impatient for the revolutionary recovery of the Palestinian homeland. When the PLO was sent into deeper exile in Tunisia in the wake of the Israeli invasion of Lebanon in 1982, the stage was set for the PLO's turn to diplomacy, with this time the road to Jerusalem perceived as running through Washington.

Lebanon: Leftists, Nasserists and pan-Arabists

The tissues of political articulation hammered out in the construction of the Lebanese merchant republic after 1943, the compromise between Maronite and Sunni leaderships at the heart of the state, and the consent that this unwritten National Pact was able to win, came under strain in the 1950s amid new regional developments and new forms of activism. The Tripartite Aggression, pitting Nasserism against Israel, France and Britain's spectacular conspiracy, mobilized Lebanese to protest the indifference or even pro-French and pro-Western positioning of Maronite President Camille Chamoun in regard to this Arab cause. When Nasser emerged with a political victory and uproarious acclaim across the region, the Lebanese position, with its proximity to the Baghdad Pact, and then the Eisenhower doctrine, looked even more invidious. Lebanon's Sunni Prime Minister Rashid Karami came out in defence of Egypt, vivifying a faultline at the heart of the state. Egypt and the Voice of the Arabs radio station denounced the Lebanese position in no uncertain terms. The merging of neighbouring Syria and Egypt under Nasser's leadership into the United Arab Republic in February 1958 increased Lebanese isolation. The rising of 1958 expressed many of these forces and contradictions, but it was followed by a period of reconstruction under Fouad Chehab who at least sought to tackle Lebanese political, economic and social problems.

The hegemony of Lebanese Christian and conservative Sunni financial and mercantile elites, and the 'clientelist structures of the prewar Lebanese state', which had been 'remarkably effective in providing the framework for an overall order' (Johnson 2002: 7) in the post-independence period, were starting seriously to break up by the early 1970s. For all the achievements of Chehabist reform during 1958–64, the Lebanese authorities arguably failed to build a state for all its citizens when this was at least a distant possibility in the 1960s (Sharara 1980). Logics of sect and patronage increasingly asserted themselves at the heart of the state. And the sharp social and economic inequalities exposed by the IRFED report of 1961 were only partially tackled under Chehab, and then left to fester after 1964.

Imam Musa Sadr (1928–78), an Iranian-Lebanese-Iraqi philosopher and Shi'a cleric, created the Movement of the Deprived, rallying the Shi'a of the south and the Biqa'in the name of the grievances of the poor and oppressed against Israeli military strikes and the 'corrupt, monopolistic and socially insensitive establishment that ran the country' (Salibi 1976: 78–9). The Palestinians were content to see Musa Sadr blame the plight of the south on the authorities and the Israelis rather than the Palestinian commandos, and the conservative Sunni establishment were by no means unhappy at his 'demanding full Muslim participation in the Lebanese State in equality with the Christians' (Salibi 1976: 78–9). As the charismatic Musa Sadr put it in 1971: 'We want a share in the economy, the culture and the political power of this country in accordance with our strength' (cited in Hanf 1993: 367). Popular Shi'a revival was a regional, not just a Lebanese, phenomenon, and was about the portable elaboration of new forms of politics and identity as much as it was about modernization processes that uprooted peasantries from existing patterns of land tenure and residency. The organizational vehicles of such Shi'ism linked Lebanon, Iraq, Iran and Bahrain. Ayatollah Al-Hakim of Najaf played a role in sending Imam Musa Al-Sadr to Lebanon. Shaykh Fadlallah, who was born in Najaf to a Lebanese *mujtahid*, began his activist writings in Najaf and continued them in Lebanon. In 1976, Fadlallah wrote *Al-Islam wa Mantaq Al-Quwa* (*Islam and the Logic of Power*), urging Shi'a to abandon their passivity and work for a more just and pious Islamic society. He interpreted the withdrawal from politics that the imams had counselled in earlier times as a temporary expedient, and averred that the time had come to take a stand against oppression (Wiley 1992: 82–3).

The pan-Arab defeat of 1967 gave Maronite isolationists in Lebanon the impetus and opportunity to mobilize, and arm themselves, in the name of a 'Lebanese Lebanon separate from the Arab world' (Jumblatt 1982: 4), while the discredit that 1967 brought to Nasserism was a fillip to an important group of 'new' Left intellectuals and activists. Influenced by French intellectuals critical of official communism on the one hand, and by Maoism and Third Worldism on the other, these militants developed a Left critique of the Arab world's military and 'progressive' regimes. They organized in Socialist Lebanon (1964–70), the Organization of Lebanese Socialists (the Lebanese branch of the Arab Nationalist Movement), and the Organization of Communist Action in Lebanon (est. 1971). They included future prominent public intellectuals such as Ahmad Beydoun, Fawwaz Trabulsi, Nahla Al-Chahhal and Waddah Charara. The latter saw the 'Lebanese entity' as 'the fortified haven for the domination of a financial commercial bourgeoisie that would not have existed if not for the role it plays in the imperialist pillage operation of the Arab region' (cited in Bardawil 2010: 146). In this view, Lebanon's contradiction was that it attempted to profiteer from the Arab region while attempting to isolate itself politically and culturally from it. A socialist revolution would come when this contradiction was detonated. Charara and his comrades saw the Palestinian resistance as the detonator.

In this receptive context, the Arab–Israeli conflict, fought out in Lebanon, was a potent polarizer indeed. On the one side, sectors of Christian Lebanese nationalist opinion feared the destruction of their country at the hands of Israeli reprisals if Palestinians continued to launch raids on Israel from Lebanon, a fear the Israelis did everything they could to confirm by their disproportionate 'reprisals' (Hanf 1993: 3–4). On the other, pan-Arabists, Leftists, the communists, pro-Palestinians, the Druze under Kamal Jumblatt, many Muslims and the Palestinians themselves considered support for Palestinian nationalism in its attempt to regain a lost homeland a non-negotiable issue. Major armed clashes between Palestinian commandos and the Lebanese army began in 1969, ending in the Cairo Agreement that autumn. The Lebanese army itself was hobbled by political divisions, and by its relative weakness, stemming from Lebanon's role as a 'non-confrontation state' regarding Israel. In May 1973, when the second major armed clash with the Palestinians ended inconclusively, the Christian militias, the Kataeb Party (Phalange) of Pierre Gemayel, the Marada Brigade of Suleiman Franjieh, the National Liberal Party (NLP) of Camille Chamoun, and the Guardians of the Cedars of Etienne Saqr, were now more than ever convinced that the Lebanon they knew could not be preserved without eliminating the commandos from Lebanon completely. With the arming by 1975 of tens of thousands of militiamen on all sides, and no political solution in sight, 'Lebanon was ... turned into a powder keg with a fuse attached, and there was no telling when it would be made to explode' (Salibi 1976: 69–70).

After the new bloodshed of April 1975, the time for the coalition of Leftists, progressives, pan-Arabists and communists, the Lebanese National Movement (LNM), headed by the Druze leader, politician, intellectual and socialist Kemal Jumblatt (1917–77), rallying under 'democratic, progressive and non-sectarian' banners, and striking alliances with the PLO, seemed to have come. The movement made great gains on the ground and seemed poised to capture Beirut. Kamal Jumblatt emphasized that 'Socialism without freedom is not socialism: it is blighted by an alienation of the spirit' (Jumblatt 1982: 101), and he mounted a stringent criticism of the 'so-called progressive regimes, which in practice have so much in common with Franco's' (Jumblatt 1982: 97). He noted that most Arab politicians, and sometimes Arab people themselves, fall short in regard to 'the idea of the State in the modern or Graeco-Roman sense'. He wrote that:

Most of these 'progressive' regimes are a clumsy, distorted and ugly copy of the communist regimes on the one hand, the military dictatorships of Latin America on the other: the one-party state, the single legitimate ideology, the intelligence services, the contempt for human rights and civil liberty, the repressive structure of political activity, the empty slogans, the absence of any genuine revolutionary spirit.

He went on, '[a]s for the regimes which are more usually referred to as reactionary, they are even worse; the prince or the rulers treat the State and its revenues as their own property' (Jumblatt 1982: 109). This analysis was obviously developed in part in response to the Syrian military intervention in Lebanon, on which Kamal Jumblatt had not counted. Just at the moment when the LNM controlled more than three-quarters of Lebanese land, 'the Syrians chose to send a regiment with 200 tanks to Masnaa to penetrate our territory' (Jumblatt 1982: 114).

Jumblatt attributed the lack of democracy in the Arab world to foreign machinations, the ambitions of dictators, the preponderant role of the army, while refusing to be pessimistic, predicting (more accurately than Samuel Huntington) that democracy would make progress in the Eastern Bloc in the 1980s (Jumblatt 1982: 101). 'The intelligentsia must, in the long run, win back its rights, and the most important of those rights is freedom of expression, both scientific and political. I cannot believe that the Arab countries will be the exception to this rule. Even Syria will have to adapt' (Jumblatt 1982: 97).

Busy with the war, with concerns over national unity, with no wish to divide Lebanon socio-economically and bring about 'a kind of Korea' (Jumblatt 1982: 118), the LNM did not bring about a social revolution in the areas under its control (two years in Saida, more than a year in Tripoli and nearly six months in parts of Beirut). 'We were too tired, too over-extended, too desperate almost, to undertake a successful social and economic upheaval' (Jumblatt 1982: 118). The 'anarchy of organizations and parties' made it very difficult to do anything (Jumblatt 1982: 91). To push through a social revolution would have required an instrument, which the LNM, many-headed as it was, did not have. The LNM resisted creating a local administration 'so as to avoid encouraging the other camp to do likewise' (Jumblatt 1982: 91). The Vietnamese example, averred Jumblatt, does not apply because of the context. He supported and proposed agrarian reform, and a redistribution of land and housing, but the other Left parties did not agree. 'All the potentates and magnates of the Arab world would have been furious and we would have been gobbled up even sooner, especially by the supposedly progressive Arab regimes' (Jumblatt 1982: 92). Jumblatt reckoned that his movement fought for Lebanese 'unity, the implementation of democratic reforms and the security of the Palestinian movement' (Jumblatt 1982: 92). Jumblatt also cited a lack of support from either China or the Soviet Union, and the fact that the LNM failed to 'interest the people in our economic and social reforms, break up big estates, urban properties, fair rents for tenants and shopkeepers' (Jumblatt 1982: 92).

The long years of civil war changed the calculations of all parties and formed the backdrop to dramatic shifts in the worldview of others. The Movement of Dispossessed became a patronage network and then ceded centre stage to Hizbullah after 1982, when the Palestinians were ousted by the Israeli invasion. The Christian isolationists fought each other as much as their initial enemies and were unable to achieve a Christian state. Syrian control and interference was a constant. While the LNM was mostly defeated, many defected ideologically, often to the Islamist camp (Bardawil 2010), and its Leftist, pan-Arab backbone did not survive the war. Just as the communal clashes of 1860 had buried the egalitarian ideals of Tanyus Shahin, the civil war of 1975–90 was the graveyard of an entire genre of progressive, revolutionary and Left politics. The revolution, in Bardawil's evocative language, had melted into air (Bardawil 2010).

Conclusion

Contentious mobilization during the period 1952–76 played a substantial role in shaping the political dynamics of these decades. It made a vital positive contribution to bringing about national independence and far-reaching political, social and economic change. The armed struggles in Algeria (1954–62) and in South Yemen (1963–7) made major contributions to the end of French and British colonial rule in both countries. The Palestinian armed struggle of 1964–82 transformed a scattered and victimized refugee population into a galvanized national community, with a national leadership (the PLO) able to build up the basics of statehood-in-exile, diminish Israeli security, and obtain considerable international recognition. Revolutionary coups in Egypt (1952), Iraq (1958), North Yemen (1962) and Libya (1969) were decisive in bringing about national independence in these states and putting an end to client monarchies there. Officers who opposed their superiors were only able to seize the initiative in a ruling order shaken loose by more mass-based forms of mobilization, domestically in the case of Egypt and Iraq, and more regionally in the case of North Yemen and Libya. In Tunisia, the nationalist movement did away with the monarchy without a military coup. The extremely popular anti-colonial posture adopted by Nasser in 1956 and later owed something to the ideas and energies of the Left movements that he sought to hegemonize and control.

The far-reaching social reforms that single parties and military men put into place drew much of their content from the principles, identities and demands of Leftist and nationalist mobilization and were part of a bargain through which these new regimes could win the consent of Leftists. Reforms bringing positive benefits to tens of millions – land reform, labour rights, women's rights, education, health provision, nationalization, transport, water, sewerage, electrification – drew strength from the major challenges to neo-feudal forms of power posed by a wide variety of mobilizations. The political field was so dominated by anti-feudal and anti-monarchical positions that land-owners and monarchs only occasionally were able to try mass mobilization, and sometimes were very much of the view that mass mobilization was not an option for them. Nasser's turn to socialism in 1961 was in a certain sense unthinkable without socialist movements in the region and beyond. In Lebanon, movements that eventually linked together Palestinians, Leftists, pan-Arabists, Nasserists and others against conservative, sectarian and isolationist elites made gains from 1958 until the mid-1970s.

Nevertheless, the moment that the military men and vanguardist organizations seized power in the state, they sought to, and as long as they could subvert or eliminate opponent vanguards or prevent *coups d'état*, they could in fact, monopolize the political field. In Egypt and Libya, the military kept power for well over half a century, and at the time of writing is still in power in the former. In Egypt, the Free Officers almost completely crushed the most mass-based organization in the country, the Muslim Brotherhood, and were able to confront and break independent labour and women's activism. In Syria and Iraq, single-party rule gradually became the rule of one, in South Yemen, the rule of a few, and in Algeria, single-party rule became the rule of a more complex array of military and security organizations. In all cases, independent forms of activism were eroded and closed down.

Leftist and nationalist mobilization in Jordan and Morocco was mostly defeated or contained within limited participatory forms; on the Arabian peninsula (apart from South Yemen), it was even more thoroughly put down, only leaving its mark in the rent price of the subsequent co-optation of small national populations. On the Arabian peninsula, however, pan-Arabism was not an effective force in preventing the outsourcing of stigmatized and exploited labour to non-Arab Asians in their millions. The fact that labour movements in the region were rarely able to forge durable alliances with non-Arab labour, or work together, was partly responsible for this situation. In Lebanon, the pan-Arab Left and the Palestinian national movement helped to precipitate a civil war, and the democratic socialism of the Lebanese Nationalism Movement was strangled in 1976 by a Syrian regime committed rhetorically to supporting it.

By transforming the Arab–Israeli conflict into a Palestinian–Israeli conflict, the Palestinian nationalist movement did much to relieve the Arab states of their responsibility for acting on behalf of the Palestinians, just as pan-Arab Palestinians always argued. Under these circumstances, the Arab states were in a better position to negotiate peace treaties with Israel, leaving the Palestinians themselves more and more isolated. On the other hand, in many ways the men of Fatah were proved right, just as 1967 resoundingly demonstrated: any attempt by the Palestinians to rely on the new military and single-party regimes was doomed to failure. In searching for independence here, the Palestinians chose very wisely. They also manoeuvred skilfully on a treacherous regional stage.

Mass-based, unarmed mobilization, without the support of elements in the state at the very minimum, was incapable of driving through national independence or wide-ranging social reform. The Cairo fire of 1952 really was not a highly organized affair. Elections and political parties were dumped in favour of vanguardism, underground cells, and revolutionary committees and fronts espousing ideological and revolutionary legitimacy. The great strength, and a considerable measure of appeal, of the mobilizing projects of these years lay in these new direct forms of action. They all promised, and in real measure delivered on, national liberation and social and economic rights affecting millions. Even with hindsight, it is not plausible to deny that these new forms of mobilization, put together by the initiatives of activists, were able to generate change on the ground in a way that parties dominated by liberal notables were not. The achievements of these years cannot be disassociated therefore from the specific forms of leadership that came into being, and which no structural process guaranteed. Indeed, as this part has argued, the new forms of mobilization were adopted creatively and experimentally in the face of the contraction of the hegemonic promise of existing forms of nationalism. Very few people of political experience, for example, credited the Algerian renegades of 1 November 1954 with much of a chance of success. They were to be taken by surprise. The disgust of Nasser's Free Officers with the failures of the civilian leadership in 1948 are widely known and cited. But, while many were disgusted, only small groups considered and then started trying to organize a revolutionary coup.

The small, committed groups that did adopt these new projects were voracious appropriators of models and principles, and sometimes support, from around the region. The tiny group of men who launched Fatah's armed struggle in 1964 were both inspired by, and borrowed from, the Algerian armed struggle. Although they came to construct a distinctive strategy of their own, at the outset they were influenced by the concepts of guerrilla war, and the fruits that it seemed to offer, stretching from Cuba to China by way of Vietnam. The Iraqi Free Officers started planning for a coup in Iraq only months after the success of Nasser's coup in Egypt. They acknowledged, as we have seen, that Nasser's actions were their inspiration. Nasser, in turn, started organizing not just on the heels of the defeat in Palestine, but during the same period (although the exact timing is unclear) as Husni Al-Za'im's coup in Syria in 1949. The revolutionary coups that followed in North Yemen (1962), Libya (1969) and the attempted coups in Saudi Arabia made their debt to Nasser's example more or less explicit.

A vexing problem regarding these new forms of mobilization was that they had little time for democracy, even if democracy was part of their rhetoric. These were vanguardist forms of political praxis, and they lent themselves to sole leadership and authoritarian forms of command and control. Leftism contributed, only partly inadvertently, to the construction of single-party authoritarian and military rule because it sought strong instruments capable of confronting imperialism and pushing through programmes of social and economic change, and was willing to sacrifice liberalism and democracy for these causes.

In this regard, the remarks of Kamal Jumblatt were telling. He admitted that very little was done to push through socio-economic change during the period when the LNM was in control of significant parts of Lebanon. But he reckoned in the same breath, that the movement lacked the instrument of change. It was instead an 'anarchy' of different organizations. No decision could be taken without reaching agreement with more than a dozen key groupings. Many groupings acted on their own initiative in any case, and this was how the armed struggle was pursued. A single doctrinal line was not to be found in any case. To push through socio-economic change would have required such an instrument. But this was lacking. The implication was that meaningful socio-economic change required a strong instrument. That instrument would have to be tightly organized and disciplined. Such characteristics require non-democracy. What some have seen as Jumblatt's timidity in failing to push through socialist revolution was also linked to his concept that democracy must prevail. Conversely, the elective affinity, at the very least, between these kinds of instruments and authoritarianism was clear.

When the Iraqi communists did come to power, they had little hesitation in calling for the repression of those who deviated from the party line. As early as 1959, for example, and even before they faced a real challenge from the uprising in Mosul, they branded their political foes (who were nationalist and Left-leaning and thus not so very far apart from the communists politically) traitors, plotters and suspicious elements, and called for a 'merciless' cleansing of the army and the state machine and a 'tightening of the screws to the last thread' (Batatu 1978: 890). In this they borrowed from the 'discipline', 'resolution' and political repression familiar in communist parties in many parts of the world. Communism, of course, in some ways offered *the* model in the twentieth century of doctrinal and strategic discipline. In adopting this model, the Iraqi communists participated in and made their own contribution to the logic of purge and elimination, that was to catch up with them brutally, this time with the 'help' of the CIA (actually the lists provided by the CIA often had the wrong names on them, leading to the murder by the state of non-communists), after the Ba'thist coup of 1963.

Another weakness was that the Left was wracked by divisions over doctrine and strategy. In the late 1960s, Nayif Hawatmeh branded George Habash a right-winger and an opportunist, even though the two leaders shared almost all the same enemies. Small differences in doctrine and strategy made the difference. As Zhu Nun Ayyub, ousted from the Central Committee of Iraq's Communist Party in August 1942, complained to a Syrian communist leader, presumably with some exaggeration: 'It is easier for a Nazi and a Communist to agree than for two Communists to work hand in hand' (cited in Batatu 1978: 486). For those on the Left who believed that science and objectivity determined the correct strategy to follow, and then incarnated that correctness in a given doctrine, along with a centrally organized Vanguard, such as the Ba'th Party, it is relatively easy to see how authoritarianism and doctrinal sectarianism could follow. For Al-Shabbi, a Ba'thist possessed of 'objective standards for classifying enemies and friends' (Shabbi 1966: 11), the communist parties were 'merely reformist'; the MAN was a 'caricature' of the Ba'th; the Arab Socialist Union in Egypt was mass only 'on paper' (Shabbi 1966: 9–10) and so on. Of course, the differences between groups and their strategies were real up to a point, but doctrinal correctness did have trouble dealing with difference. This was very far from the more emollient, discredited politics of the notables, where such differences were smoothed over with polite forms of address, clientelism, the acceptance of hierarchy, family name and so on. Division made the broad front extremely difficult to assemble. The implication was that state power, once it was achieved, would likely be exercised on a monopolistic and all-or-nothing basis.

Armed struggles and cells could be intensely egalitarian (from the Algerian *maquis* to Shatila camp in Lebanon), but the forms of internal democracy they occasionally built up tended not to outlast the fighting. These forms of armed struggles were fraternal, they could oppose hierarchy and the power of the father figure, and could and often did accept women, and in this they were feminist. But this acceptance was only on the basis that these women masculinized, and became honorary members of the band of brothers. Women also served many useful roles during armed struggles. But, when the fighting was over, such relatively superficial forms of status shift again did not endure, and more typical gender roles were re-asserted, a retrenchment facilitated by the hyper-masculinity of the armed struggle in general.

It is significant to note that, when many of the movements of these years invoked democracy, they added a qualifier: 'genuine' democracy or 'meaningful' democracy. What these activists meant was that, in a feudal situation, democratic institutions were meaningless and corrupted. In this they were largely right, and were seen to be so. The implication was that, before democratic institutions could become meaningful, there would have to be mass education, social equality and so on. Under such reformed circumstances, a true democracy could come into being. Again, how to fault this logic? The only problem was that, in practice, democratic institutions themselves were deferred, bypassed or thought to be a secondary problem. The key problem became socio-economic. By the time the socio-economic problem had been tackled, states and regimes had built up their powers to the extent that those who controlled them were minded to keep deferring and then quietly to forget the democratic part of their original programme. In other words, here was another elective affinity between the purely socio-economic definition of the problem, and an authoritarian outcome. It was an outcome that would have, and did, horrify the early founders of the Ba'th Party, for example.

The fact that the state was to be the instrument of national liberation and social transformation can also help explain why it was that the state, or at least the militaries, single parties and sole leaders that ended up capturing it, became such an almighty power during these decades. This was not just a matter of regulatory accretion and overweening ambition; it held an elective affinity with the basic goals of so many of the mobilizing projects of these years. The expansion of the state was not merely the result of technical and material requirements: the need to replace foreign capital, or the need to build up schools and hospitals (Owen 2004a). It was also the result of the very principles and practices that were adopted by those seeking meaningful change. In many ways, the means that were taken up to break from colonial rule, to deliver national independence and socio-economic transformation, the revolutionary coup, the armed struggle, and the single party were the very forms that started to become responsible for restrictions on political freedom from the 1950s onwards. The Arab world became trapped in its own means of salvation. Instruments of liberation became fetters of oppression. Under Boumediène's socialist and Third Worldist regime in Algeria, for example, the *Sécurité Militaire* was fine-tuned into an art form (Evans and Phillips 2007: 101). Saddam Hussein's Ba'thist Iraq may have driven forward industrial development, built a utilities and transport infrastructure (from electricity to sewage), pushed forward on schools, universities, women's literacy and so on, but during the same period the country became a 'Republic of Fear' (Makiya 1998), especially for Kurds and Shi'a. The military in politics did away with the possibility of political freedom. The single party formed the vehicle for the steady development of widespread corruption in the relations between government and economy. In the case of Algeria, the single party created a state, 'the armed forces, the civil service, the diplomatic corps and the intelligence and security organs', which in turn took on a life of their own independent of the party, making the latter a 'secondary apparatus, performing public relations, mobilisational and parallel diplomatic functions on behalf of a state machine' (Roberts 2003: 35). In short, the mobilizing projects of these years, and their forms of leadership, as well as taking some credit for national liberation, statist developmentalism and real redistribution of wealth, must also take some of the blame for the growth of authoritarianism, a development that became ever more obvious and problematic as gains in national liberation and socio-economic provision started to dry up in the 1970s.

Signals of a future crisis of authority came as early as 1961. The break up of the United Arab Republic stemmed from the fact that Nasser, following the logic of the rule of military and mass rally, insisted on the dissolution of the Ba'th Party in Syria. No independent powers of decision were tolerable. The defeat of 1967 was crucial, but, as we have seen, stimulated a shift to the Left more than it did to the immediate appearance of Islamist activism, which remained attenuated. The immediate outcome of 1967 was more the rise of attempts to think of Left politics in more proletarian ways, but also in more democratic ways. It was only when the regime of the sole leader, Hafez Al-Asad, turned his powers on the Palestinians, pan-Arabists, Nasserists and democratic socialists of Lebanon in 1976, intervening on the side of the tottering right-wing Maronite isolationists who were allied to Israel, that the crisis of the post-independence order was laid bare for those who had given it their consent. For true believers, direct blows (1967) were easier to take than splits and contradictions (1976). And, by this time, as we have seen, the Palestinian revolution, the pride of the nationalist Left after 1967, had entered a strategic *cul de sac*. Moreover, statist developmentalism and socio-economic redistribution had gone into decline since the 1960s. With the post-independence forms of hegemony contracting, new forms of contentious mobilization increasingly made their appearance on the historical stage.

IV | *Islamism, revolution, uprisings and liberalism, 1977–2011*

Introduction

During 1798–1914, mobilizing projects had looked to escape the state, replace it completely in the name of Islamic radicalism, appeal to its justice, or achieve a limited form of representation in it. During 1914–52, a dominant theme in mobilizing projects was the search for a much broader form of representation in the state in the name of the nation. During 1952–76, revolutionaries and Leftists had sought to capture the state for national liberation and far-reaching socio-economic transformation. In some respects, the climax and final defeat of these kinds of projects on the regional stage came in 'tiny' Lebanon in 1976, when the democratic socialism of the Lebanese National Movement, allied to the Palestinian *thawra*, ran aground on the real-politik of the Syrian dictatorship. This crisis was all the more acute because the Syrian regime claimed to be acting in the name of pan-Arabism, the Palestinian cause, and the Arab socialism of the Ba'th Party, even though it was palpably acting in the name of Al-Asad, and his narrow calculations as to Syrian national security. Partly because the Palestinian guerrilla strategy was ever more threadbare, and because Lebanon was now embroiled in a lengthy civil war, not to mention because of the weakness of the Left revival in Egypt in the 1970s *inter alia*, the epoch of national liberation and social revolution was grinding to a close.

During 1977–2011, the nature of mobilization in the region under-went fundamental changes. Revolutionary mobilizing projects, amid a crisis of the secular state, developed an Islamist politics that sought to replace the corrupted secular state with an Islamic one. Since the 1950s, different strands of Islamism – Shi'a popular, Sunni modernist and Salafi-Wahhabi – had sought to re-group in the face of what they saw as the monstrous, secular usurpation of the true destiny of the independent states of the region after independence. An Egyptian law professor Hussam 'Issa (b. 1939), speaking from an Egyptian perspective, put it very simply: 'After the defeat [of 1967], people would say: we tried liberalism before the revolution in 1952, then we tried Arab nationalism, and then we had to find another form of identity [i.e. Islam]' (Browers 2009: 6). In the 1970s, Islamist groups started to engage in contentious mobilization that went far beyond sermons, publications and occasional demonstrations or attacks. In 1979, Islamism of the Shi'a popular variety took power in the Islamic revolution in Iran. Revolutionary Islamist politics now gathered tremendous momentum on the regional stage. The creation of the Islamic State in Syria and Iraq in 2013 marked the first time, after four or five decades of activism, that revolutionary Sunni Islamists had been able to control state power anywhere in the Arab world.

In the face of the retreat from the provision of socio-economic goods and the guarantee of socio-economic rights, there was a revival of movements of a defensive kind, as, for the first time since the nineteenth century, there was something to defend. A wide variety of groups mounted protests, bread riots, strikes, demonstrations and so on, in the name of the *status quo ante*, drawing on forms of existing hegemony real and imagined, in order to try to arrest the erosion of rights and goods that were thought to be guaranteed by the existing order but were being eroded because of neo-liberal crony capitalism. Just as in the nineteenth century, such defensive protests, which were not about the community as a whole, but sought justice in a context of stratification, made little reference to Islam. These protests brought the return of mass, popular uprisings to the political scene (starting in Egypt in January 1977), a form which had not until that time marked the post-independence order, although it had of course been common under colonial and dynastic rule.

Finally, there was a re-making of forms of protest and contention that were both autonomist and reformist. In regards to the former, the meaning of autonomy meant largely weapons of the weak, informal networks, and the quiet 'encroachment of the ordinary'. These forms of action, although only minimally contentious according to the definition adopted here, did nonetheless seek to carve out spaces that were autonomous from state regulation and control, treated the state as a necessary evil or as a source of individual patronage, and operated to generate alternative networks and norms and undermine the ideological hegemony of the state. In regards to reformism, democratic and liberal traditions were genuinely re-asserted in various quarters in the 1990s and 2000s, playing a role in, but failing in the main to capitalize on, the Arab uprisings of 2011.

Just as in the nineteenth century, a crucial theme reasserted itself, especially in the formerly revolutionary republics: the dereliction, degradation and corruption of the authorities, the contraction of their forms of hegemony, and their almost complete inability to replace older forms of consent with new ones linked to democracy and consumer prosperity. The secular regimes moved from champions of independence, pan-Arab unity, and national liberation, to rent-seeking clients of the United States or of the Gulf Cooperation Council (GCC) states; from drivers of statist developmentalism and economic uplift to bankruptcy, aid recycling, poverty and cuts; from providers of socio-economic services to peddlars of corruption and kleptocracy (Achcar 2013a); from providers of security to manipulators of institutionalized torture. Promises of democracy turned out to be a 'grand delusion' (Kienle 2003). Republics became 'rep-king-lics' (*gumlukiyyat*), in Saad Eddin Ibrahim's word, coined in the early 2000s, reproducing dictatorship and presidents for life (Owen 2012).

The generation that came of age in the 1950s and 1960s had seen national independence, and often experienced forms of social mobility and economic uplift. There had been land for the formerly landless in many parts of the region, a matter not just of property but of an escape from all sorts of semi-feudal restrictions, obligations and physical violence. There had been new educational opportunities, and job security. Many had found good jobs, as engineers, teachers, and so on, possibilities unthinkable for their parents. The generation that was born in the non-oil countries after independence, and that came of age in the 1970s and 1980s, experienced no such thing. National liberation was now simply a story. Unemployment for graduates was just as likely as upward mobility and respectability. Job security was increasingly unlikely. And the public sector, wages and purchasing power were falling in many non-oil countries from the 1970s.

While states ceased to support movements of national liberation and social revolution, they nonetheless borrowed from the regionalism of the previous period by offering support to Islamist movements in other states. The *jihad* in Afghanistan owed a good deal to Saudi support, official and unofficial. Saudi Arabia provided huge backing to the promotion and development of the doctrines of Salafi-Wahhabism on a local, regional and international basis. Various countries of the GCC supported other strands: there was notable Qatari support for the Muslim Brotherhood, for example. Iran supported Hizbullah in the 1980s, contributing directly to its creation. Syria likewise supported Hizbullah, and funded a number of other small Sunni groups. It was a dangerous game to play, as the Syrian regime discovered in the past and the present.

The Islamist challenge to Ba'th power in Syria, 1963–1982

The Muslim Brotherhood in Syria was founded in 1946 by Syrian students who studied at Al-Azhar and developed 'personal ties and shared intellectual sensibilities' with Hasan Al-Banna (Lefèvre 2013: 23). They returned from Egypt and strove to unify the several *jami'at* which had sprung up around the country in the 1920s and 1930s, which had built in turn on the Islamic modernist intellectual trends that had reached Ottoman Syria in the late nineteenth century. Until 1963, the Muslim Brotherhood competed as a political party in Syria's semi-democratic political scene as 'a peaceful group committed to the principles of constitutionalism and political liberalism' (Lefèvre 2013: 19–20, 82–8). While pursuing on social and cultural issues a socially conservative, sexually repressive and moralizing stance, and the rhetoric of a return to Islamic cultural values in the face of foreign cultural invasion (Lefèvre 2013: 32). There was a relatively short-lived socialist colouring to the group – when its most prominent early leader Mustafa Al-Siba'i endorsed land reform in terms of Islam along with social equality. Fasting during Ramadan was read as a kind of socialism (Lefèvre 2013: 34). These socialist elements, echoing the Leftward turn of a section of the Brotherhood in Egypt in the late 1940s, were controversial within the Ikhwan, nonetheless, and links to the pro-business elements disaffected by Arab socialism were reinforced through the 1950s (Lefèvre 2013: 36–7). One of the key reasons for Muslim Brotherhood weakness in the 1950s and 1960s was their dilemma in facing the fact that Nasser, the persecutor of their ally and progenitor, the Muslim Brotherhood in Egypt, was also a hero for much of the Arab world, especially its popular strata (Lefèvre 2013: 20).

Before 1963, the Ba'th Party was one among many leaderships, parties and constituencies with some claim on the direction of the

Syrian state; after the coup of 1963, the Ba'th Party increasingly held a monopoly of power. After 1966, the more military elements within the Party came into the ascendant, narrowing the basis of rule still further. The shift to control by President Hafez Al-Asad himself over and above party mechanisms after November 1970 completed the substitution of the rule of one for the rule of a more polyarchical system, and, while freedom may have been sacrificed, Asad continued to insist on key ideals, in this case Arab unity and a version of socialism. Al-Asad's 'Corrective Movement', nonetheless, reached out to the Sunni Damascene bourgeoisie, put an end to the measures of redistribution and Left radicalism that had characterized the 1966–70 period, while continuing with policies of electrification and infrastructural development and subsidy in the countryside.

The policies of this strong-man alienated many: the increasingly Alawi and sectarian face of the regime; the pro-rural policies; the unprecedented political and economic ascendancy of those from rural and humble origins; the marginalization of urban notables from the seat of power; the measures negatively impacting the fortunes of the wealthy, and of the small traders and artisans of the souks; the ways in which Aleppo, Homs and Hama felt, and to some extent were, excluded from ruling circles; the marginalization of the Ba'th Party itself under Hafez Al-Asad; the steady growth of cronyism and corruption in the ranks of the military and the bureaucracy; the betrayal of the Palestinian and Leftist cause in Lebanon in 1976; the refusal to allow the Palestinian movement any independent decision; and support for 'Persian' Iran against 'Arab' Iraq in the Iran–Iraq war after 1980 – the latter three policies undertaken in spite of the fact that (and perhaps because) Syria considered itself to be the 'beating heart' of Arabism (Lefèvre 2013: 49–61).

In the wake of the Ba'thist coup of 1963, and especially under Hafez Al-Asad in the 1970s, Sunni jihadist movements, whose most important intellectual influence was Sayyid Qutb, emerged on the flanks of, or from radicalized streams within, the Muslim Brotherhood. They were committed to the seizure of state power through armed attacks on the regime, and the establishment of a new Islamic state and society. There were violent protests in Hama in 1964, a growing campaign of attacks on regime and Alawi targets in the 1970s, the killing of the Alawi cadets in 1979 and the urban uprising in Hama in February 1982. These groups, asserting that force was the only language that the regime would understand (Tripp 2013: 52), declared themselves the uncompromising enemies of a Ba'thist government which they asserted had usurped God's sovereignty, corrupted the faith, and led the country to ruin.

The ideological element in the clash between the ruling Ba'th and the Ikhwan in Syria cannot be ignored. The stance of the Ikhwan cannot simply be dismissed in terms of power-seeking, opportunism, sexual repression or backwardness. The basic premise of the Islamist movement was at odds with that of secular, Syrian nationalism. The Ba'th Party, insisted, in line with the formula originally popularized, and perhaps invented, by Faysal at the time of the Arab state of 1918–20, that 'religion is for God, and country is for all'. The Ikhwan maintained, in fundamental contrast, that 'Islam is both religion and state' (Lefèvre 2013: 44). While Michel Aflaq saw Islam as a fundamental component of the Arab nation, with its glorious past and distinctive character, for the Ikhwan this was much too cramping a restriction on the importance of Islam as a political community and a way of life, which they elevated well above what they saw as 'Western' nationalism, unacceptably secular and atheistic. For them, Ba'thists were the morally corrupt agents of the materialist West.

While these principles informed the Ikhwan in general, they could inform and justify a range of activism on the ground, including the Islamic modernist forms, accepting of parliamentary and democratic forms, adopted by the reformist Brotherhood and its Islamic modernist 'Damascus Wing' until the exile of a key leader (Isam Al-Attar) in 1964 and the Ikhwan's eventual espousal of armed struggle in 1979. The jihadist groups, on the other hand, emerging from the 'Northern Axis', 'composed of Ikhwani members from Aleppo, Hama, Latakia and other cities' (Lefèvre 2013: 82) which came to dominate the movement after the leadership vacuum of 1969–72, were inspired directly by Sayyid Qutb's prison writings of the 1950s and 1960s, and were scornful of pluralism and democracy amid assertions of the sovereignty of God (Lefèvre 2013: 119–20). By the 1970s, moreover, there were no meaningful parliamentary or multi-party forms in the Syrian state left to accept, a shift which completely undercut the basis of the modernist wing's philosophy and positioning.

The key figure at the origin of the Qutbist trend was the Hama-born Marwan Hadid (1934–76). He studied agricultural engineering in Cairo in the early 1960s, where he apparently 'befriended' Sayyid

Qutb 'whose advocacy of the need to confront violently President Gamal Abdel Nasser seemed appealing to many Syrian Islamic activists disenchanted by the Ikhwani leadership's peaceful, some said passive, approach to the Ba'th regime' (Lefèvre 2013: 99). A charismatic man who led the Hama 'riots' of 1964, and whose death in Syrian prison in 1976 brought him much fame as a martyr, Marwan Hàdid popularized Qutb's ideology in Syria by the propaganda of the deed. Especially because of the ideological labour of Ikhwan member Said Hawwa, a young Islamic scholar from Hama, whose book *Jund Allah* was widely distributed in mosques and underground religious bookshops in the early 1970s, rulers were seen not only in Qutbist mode as deviant and corrupted Muslims, fallen into *jahiliyya*, but as 'Nusayri dogs', Alawi apostates from Islam from the earliest times, a sectarian reading bolstered by reference to the writings of the Islamic scholar and revivalist Ibn Taymiyya (1263–1328), who had issued a *fatwa* making *jihad* against apostates a priority even over that against polytheists, Jews and Christians (Lefèvre 2013: 98–101). When Hafez Al-Asad issued a constitution in 1973 which omitted to stipulate that the head of state should be a Muslim, the outcry that followed was the occasion of the advance of the jihadist-sectarian interpretation of the Ba'thist regime in the ranks of the Ikhwan.

Marwan Hadid's movement, on the fringes of the Ikhwan, obtained vital military training from Fatah in the Palestinian camps of Jordan in the late 1960s. They observed, if across a vast ideological divide, the armed struggle proposed by the Palestinians, and saw its explosive possibilities on the Arab scene. With only a handful of cadres, they set out on the path of *jihad*, organizing a group called The Fighting Vanguard of the Mujahidin, consisting of a number of clandestine cells, and carrying out 'targeted killings of prominent members of the Ba'th security apparatus' (Lefèvre 2013: 102). Unlike the Palestinians, these Islamists turned their guns directly against the Arab regimes. In the later, undated assessment of an unknown Al-Qa'ida member, it was said that Hadid was impetuous, he 'did not want to wait for the right time' (cited in Lefèvre 2013: 102). Hadid's strategy in fact aimed to 'trigger government retaliation that would ultimately convince the Brotherhood's leadership of the inevitability of armed struggle' (Lefèvre 2013: 102). After Hadid's death, a number of other leaders took up the leadership of the Fighting Vanguards and the targeted killings of personalities representing Ba'thist rule in Syria, security officers, politicians, university professors, and high-ranking civil servants. The largest and most significant attack was that of June 1979 on the Aleppo Artillery School: eighty-three Alawi cadets were killed, and many others were wounded.

Intensive repression followed, involving an all-out assault by the regime, characterized by torture and the arrest and even killing of non-Ikhwan relatives of Ikhwan leaders, on the modernist as well as the jihadist elements of the Ikhwan. In this context, the Syrian Ikhwan as a whole finally, at a meeting of its consultative body (Majlis Al-Shura) in October 1979 in Amman, endorsed the use of violence against the Ba'thist regime. After Hafez Al-Asad narrowly avoided an assassination attempt in June 1980, an estimated 500–1000 inmates of Palmyra prison were massacred by the Defence Brigades. In July 1980, membership of the Muslim Brotherhood became a capital offence.

Hadid's strategy had achieved its goal, especially as in this atmosphere, and amid the need for self-defence against prison, torture and death, wider elements within the Muslim Brotherhood shifted from mere endorsement of armed struggle to action. But their military skills and capacities, and the number of operations they were able to carry out, appear to have been very limited (Lefèvre 2013: 116–17). A short-lived and divided Joint Command was set up, and jihadi elements opposed to democracy and pluralism in the name of God's sovereignty coordinated with newly minted modernist-jihadists who advocated for the rights of religious minorities, the independence of the judiciary, free elections, and the separation of powers (Lefèvre 2013: 120).

The ascendancy of the 'Hama clan' within the Ikhwan partly explains the call for an all-out uprising in Hama on 8 February 1982. The insurrectionist strategy, which seems to have been disputed at the time by the leadership in Amman, was that a full-scale revolt would capture the city, trigger similar uprisings in other cities, general strikes, and the paralysis and subsequent collapse of a regime that was thought to rule through violence. Weapons were distributed to the inhabitants of Hama. On day one, dozens of Ba'thist officials were killed, and violent street protests launched. Approximately 400 fighters were joined by around 2000 citizens who took control of the old city for a few days. The call to arms rang out from minarets; inhabitants were told from which mosques weapons could be picked up. Residency records, an important tool of Syrian intelligence, police stations, security offices and the Ba'th Party headquarters were attacked, some were destroyed, and army units were engaged and forced into retreat after several days of intense fighting.

The regime's most ruthless combat units were now called in, the Third Armoured Division and the Defence Brigades. They forced their way back into the city, engaging the rebels in street battles and house-to-house fighting. Whole residential quarters were destroyed by rockets and shells from helicopters, tanks and artillery. Bulldozers flattened the smoking ruins. Civilians and fighters were killed together, indiscriminately. Mass executions were carried out near the municipal stadium. Between 10,000 and 40,000 civilians and fighters were killed (Lefèvre 2013: 122–8). There was no mass uprising in Syria. The regime stood, no general insurrection followed the Hama uprising, and jihadi and Muslim Brotherhood activism in Syria was brought virtually to a standstill for more than two decades. Syria was the first, but not the last, of the post-independence 'progressive republics' to smother a challenge to its rule in blood. The use of armed struggle, which since the First World War had been used almost exclusively in search of national liberation against the colonizer or their clients, had now been definitively taken up against the post-independence regimes. And the mantle of state terror, involving the indiscriminate killing of civilians in pursuit of a political goal, once a preserve of the colonial powers, had now been donned by the champions of progressive national liberation themselves.

Shi'ism in Iraq: from pamphlets to *mujahidin*

In Iraq, a strong-man securitocracy under Saddam Hussein, with its origins in a single-party Ba'thist regime, ruled over a highly diverse (by region, ethnicity and religion) society, while jealously monopolizing power increasingly on the basis of clan and sect, and violently repressing signs of dissent (Tripp 2000: 193ff.). The dynamics driving the emergence of an armed struggle against the regime in the 1970s, this time under Shi'a populist banners, bore certain similarities to those associated with the development of the Sunni armed movement in Syria during the same period. On the other hand, the movement's origins were by no means a simple reaction to repression but went back to the late 1950s. Moreover, the historical background was different to that of Syria, as no Shi'a version of the Sunni Muslim Brotherhood appeared anywhere between the 1920s and the 1950s. In spite of the prominent political role of the Shi'a *ulema* in both Iran in the late nineteenth and early twentieth century and in Iraq in the rising of 1920, Shi'a constituencies (from Lebanon to Iran via Bahrain) avoided a social activism, a proselytizing or a politics based around Shi'ism, and were either quietist, anti-liberal or anti-Leftist, or engaged politically as individuals through nationalism, communism, Ba'thism and other political currents. From the late 1950s onwards, this changed in the Shi'a world, a shift pioneered in Iraq. Borrowing ideas and strategies from the Sunni movements that preceded them, the leading movements, the Da'wa and the Shiraziyyin, partly thanks to the centrality of Najaf as a shrine city and centre of learning and pilgrimage, were soon to make their influence felt among Shi'a in Iran, Lebanon, Kuwait, Bahrain and Saudi Arabia (Louër 2008a: 67), where histories of exclusion and discrimination also weighed heavily (Jones 2006). Many of Khomeini's ideas were prefigured by these Iraqi clerics and activists. Amid the repression in Iraq that became increasingly heavy in the 1970s, politicized Shi'ism came to declare an armed struggle against the 'criminal' Ba'thist regime in 1979. Arrest, deportation, torture and execution on a wide scale drove most activists into exile in the 1980s, while Shi'a forces joined the failed uprising in Iraq of 1991 in large numbers (Nakash 1994: 274–80).

More so than most of the twentieth-century Sunni movements, Shi'a activism developed in the late 1950s and early 1960s especially through the efforts of clerics (including very senior figures in the relatively centralized Shi'a religious establishment), their families, seminarians and their students themselves. They were based above all in the shrine cities of Najaf and Karbala which stood at the centre of a major transnational network. They saw their religious authority and material resources threatened by secular ideologies and the policies of the newly independent regime in 1958 (Nakash 1994: 134–7). It was this threat, rather than any independent doctrinal revival, that led to the creation of the Hizb Al-Da'wa Al-Islamiyya ('The Party of the Islamic Call') in 1958.

[It] was the direct result of the awareness by the clerical class of Iraq that the *hawza* [the community of those engaged in Shi'a Islamic teaching and learning], as an institution, was in real jeopardy in the face of the rise of secular ideologies (Louër 2008a: 83).

Based in Najaf, Al-Da'wa was led by Muhammad Baqir Al-Sadr (1931–80), a junior but promising cleric of the *hawza*, scion of a prestigious family of clerics, descendants of the Prophet, and student of the leading *marja'* and head of the *hawza* in Najaf, Muhsin Al-Hakim (d. 1970). The latter had a son, Mahdi Al-Hakim (d. 1988), who also played an important role in the founding of the party. Widespread communist mobilization, the overthrow of a monarchy for a republic, land reform, which threatened major land-owners with whom clerics were linked, shrinking numbers of adherents, and a new family law undercutting *ulema* jurisdiction, posed real and perceived threats to the Shi'a *ulema* and their supporters. 'Sons of *mujtahids* were said to leave the turban to embrace the tenets of social revolution' (Louër 2008a: 83). There was alarm over 'Godless' communism, a 'sense that the old faith was receding', that beliefs were weakening, and the place of the *ulema* was slipping (Batatu 1981: 587–8). With the accession of the quietist Al-Khu'i to the head of the *hawza* in 1970, the Da'wa lost its quiet support from above and its association with the highest echelons of the *marja'iyya* in Iraq, while many links remained to the institution in general.

The major rival to the Hizb Al-Da'wa were the Shiraziyyin, a group rooted in Karbala, and chafing at the latter's marginalization in relation to Najaf, and closely linked with the Al-Shirazi family of Karbala, and especially the charismatic figures of Muhammad Al-Shirazi (1926–2001) and his younger brother, Hasan Al-Shirazi (1934–80), prestigious clerics, sons of an anti-communist *mujtahid*, and descendants of the Prophet, who had come to Iraq from Iran in the nineteenth century. Their great uncle was Muhammad Taqi Al-Shirazi, the renowned *mujtahid* of the Iraqi uprising of 1920 (Louër 2008a: 90). The Al-Shirazi family, ultimately led by the charismatic elder brother Muhammad, disputed leadership in matters of religious authority with the Al-Sadrs and the Al-Hakims of Najaf, and conflicted over the control of charitable institutions. The Al-Shirazi placed a central importance on the need to 'reform the *hawza* which risked becoming an ossified institution headed by a handful of gerontocrats remote from public affairs and the concerns of the laity' – and they looked to younger *ulema* who could 'regain the favours of the masses attracted by secular ideologies' (Louër 2008a: 94). They maintained that the party formed in the rival city of Najaf was unacceptable because requiring obedience to a party leader 'entailed the negation of the *marja'iyya*'s supreme authority' (Louër 2008a: 96) – a doctrinal issue which required some finessing over in Najaf. The Al-Shiraziyyin of Karbala also worried that a party would usurp their own power (Abdul-Jabar 2003: 218). Nonetheless, they eventually formed a more formal organization, led by a *mujtahid* nephew of the Al-Shirazi brothers, Muhammad Taqi Al-Mudarrisi, some time after the 1967 rout of the Arab nationalist regimes. The organization avoided the word 'party' as it was seen as un-Islamic, but used terms such as 'organization' and 'movement' before coming to be known after 1979 as the Islamic Action Organization (Louër 2008a: 98).

Shi'a Islamists also included urban Shi'a lay intelligentsia and the middle classes, students, civil servants and some professionals, who for a variety of ideological, religious or material reasons were part of the founding of the Hizb Al-Da'wa, and who came to play a more prominent role after 1963, when some of the clerics withdrew, sensitive to the criticism of their colleagues that they should not meddle in temporal matters. The heavy Ba'thist emphasis on pan-Arabism was not appealing to most Shi'a, who identified pan-Arabism with Sunni domination and instead espoused Iraqi nationalism (Nakash 1994: 136). Iraq had its youthful intelligentsia, indignant at poverty in oil-producing countries, and at the favouritism and autocracy of their government, and the fact that many needed to join the Ba'th Party simply to be favoured with employment (Wiley 1992: 85). Wiley gives the example of Abd Al-Amir Mashkur. He was born into a clerical family in Najaf and joined the Hizb Al-Da'wa in secondary school, organizing a Qur'an study group. Members of this group went to different universities in Iraq, and in 1970 expanded their politicizing efforts to include the masses. Abd Al-Amir was arrested, but in 1971 entered Baghdad University for a science degree. He was obliged to serve with the Iraqi army during the 1974–5 campaign of repression against the Kurds. 'Unwilling to kill Muslim Kurds, he contrived to have the artillery crew under his command fail in its assignments. For this he was demoted to the rank of common soldier.' He was arrested in 1979 and died in prison (Wiley 1992: 87).

Rural–urban migrants, the urban poor living in shanty towns such as Baghdad's Al-Thawra, and recently sedentarized Bedouin, were also among the ranks of Shi'a Islamists in the late 1970s and early 1980s. Al-Thawra's support for politicized Islam was evident when residents of Madinat Al-Thawra poured into the streets to celebrate the Islamic revolution in Iran; they also joined large protests in Madinat Al-Thawra after the arrest of Ayatollah Al-Sadr in early June 1979.

Some important individuals in the movement were drawn from the ranks of the urban poor: Wiley mentions a soldier, a tailor, a vendor and a woodcutter. But the poor were no more numerous in the membership than the young intelligentsia (Wiley 1992: 89–90). Many were young, half were from the holy cities, and they were recruited in the Husainiyat and in mosques (rather than in universities) (Wiley 1992: 92). As Batatu writes, '[t]he conditions that dispose Shi'is of humble background favourably towards the Da'wah or the Mujahidin are quite different than the conditions that actuate their leaders and organizers'. He notes that the poor were drawn from the same townships where communists had been so strong in the 1940s and 1950s (Batatu 1981: 580, 583). These poor were certainly able to contrast the 'socialist slogans' of the Ba'th Party, and the obvious wealth that characterized parts of Sunni Baghdad in the 1970s and 1980s, with their own overcrowded housing, lack of municipal drinking water, poor sewerage, unpaved streets and falling real wages (until 1976). It was 'not until 1980, in response to Islamist successes in Al-Thawra, that the Ba'th government moved to bring essential city services there'. Moreover, the urban poor faced competition in various sectors with imported foreign labour (500,000 strong in 1980) which kept their wages low. As was said on the streets of Baghdad, in a negation of the well-known Ba'thist slogan, *'La Wahda, La Hurriya, La Ishtirakiyya'* ('No Unity, No Freedom, and no Socialism') (Wiley 1992: 89–90, 102).

Small numbers of the more educated, propertied and connected peasants were also involved, while most were dispersed, dependent, immobile and supervised by land-owners and their agents and thus difficult to organize (Wiley 1992: 93–4). The Da'wa, nonetheless, 'was greatly assisted by the drought [affecting hundreds of thousands of peasants] that struck the Najaf–Karbala region and other Shi'a areas in the middle 1970s in the wake of the reduction of the flow of the Euphrates River because of Syria's newly built dam at Tabqah' (Batatu 1981: 589–90). Two cells of the *mujahidin* (which organized at least one attack in July 1982) were established in the 1980s at Dujayl, a planned agricultural settlement northwest of Baghdad. Land had been granted there in the late 1940s to retired army and police officers, civil servants and unemployed graduates of religious institutions (Wiley 1992: 93–4).

Ba'thist female education and literacy programmes, increased rates of female non-domestic wage labour, and male out-migration, all challenged existing patterns of masculine domination. They stoked moralizing fears about the 'corruption' of women, a language that chimed well with some of the themes of socially conservative Shi'a activism.

The inability to afford education for all also worked to bar women from schools. Shi'a prescriptions in favour of polygamy, and against women's rights in the family, in inheritance, and in economic and political spheres, actively upheld by the clergy, had appeal in this context (Wiley 1992: 34).

Nonetheless, women were active at various levels in the movement. In the 1980s, they even acted as fighters (*mujahidat*) via a League of Muslim Women called Um Karar. These *mujahidat* were reported to organize cells, write and distribute pamphlets, transport weapons and ammunition, and play a role in communications between male fighters. In one case, women planted the explosives that blew up a government intelligence building. A number of *akhawat* (sisters) died in prison, including the nineteen-year-old Maysun Ghazi (Wiley 1992: 62).

Muhammad Baqir Al-Sadr, together with Mahdi Al-Hakim, conceived of the Party of the Islamic Call as the 'most efficient tool to fight secularization' (Louër 2008a: 84). Al-Sadr wrote its statutes, defined its programme of organization and action, and took it upon himself to explain the principles of the movement, aiming to define what Shi'ism meant beyond scholarly and doctrinal disputes, and in relation to contemporary politics, economics and society. His key books were *Our Philosophy* (1959), a critique of Marxism, and *Our Economics* (1961), offering an Islamic political economy. The Party opposed nationalizations in the 1960s (Wiley 1992: 31–6). Al-Sadr envisaged that executive and legislative powers would be elected by the people, but placed under the final supervision of a body comprising senior *mujtahidin* ensuring that laws conformed to Islam (Louër 2008a: 86). This formulation echoed in some respects the relationship that the *ulema* sought through the supplementary law in regards to the constitutional revolution in Iran in 1905. It was also a clear forerunner of Khomeinism. It was echoed by the Shiraziyyin during the same period, who affirmed, as Khomeini was later to do, that, in the absence of the imam, the *marja'* were invested with his temporal political power. There is some evidence that Muhammad Al-Shirazi actually called this the *hukumat al-fuqaha* – the government of the jurisprudent (Louër 2008a: 97). This formulation was more precise on the polity and the position of clerics than the Muslim Brotherhood, whose think-ing had arisen in a context where the religious establishment was far more subordinated to the state, and therefore far less inspiring or feasible as a body that could regulate that state.

In the secular Iraq of the late 1950s, and all the more so under strong-man rule in the 1970s, Shi'i Islamist prognostications regarding an Islamic polity were dismissed by many as an absurdity. Few could imagine that, within twenty years, in neighbouring (and apparently even more secular) Iran, some of these 'absurdities' would come to pass.

Sadr's Islamic state, and here the debt was more to the Sunni Hizb Al-Tahrir, which was explicitly mentioned by Al-Sadr in the statutes of Al-Da'wa, would compromise the entire territory of the *umma*, and would claim authority over the rest of the world by virtue of the universal character of Islam (Louër 2008a: 85). These formulations, by no means modest in their ambition, rejected what was seen as the Western concept of the nation-state (although the rejection of nation-alism and statism, of course, was no stranger to radical discourse in Europe and elsewhere). Al-Sadr of the Da'wa, and above all Al-Shirazi (probably because of the particular suspicion which fell on him because of his relatively recent Iranian descent), condemned as un-Islamic, Western and illegitimate the very concept of the nation-state, and the nationalism, borders, and identity cards that it brought with it. A central theme of Muhammad Al-Shirazi's thought was the denunci-ation of 'the game of nationality and identity cards, the game of resi-dence permit and passport . . . the imposture of false geographic frontiers inside the united Islamic homeland' (*watan*) (Louër 2008a: 101).

After the bloody confrontations, deportations and executions of the 1970s and later, the Iraqi regime stood condemned by Shi'i Islamists, mostly driven into exile, as profoundly criminal and illegitimate. In a 1992 tract, for example, the Da'wa accused it of committing all sorts of crimes 'known all over the world'. The regime had 'assassinated thought, values and humanity', murdered Imam Al-Sayyid Muham-mad Baqr Al-Sadr, and extended its crimes to include Kuwait and Iran in 'two senseless wars exposing Iraq and the region to egregious losses' (Hizb Al-Da'wa 1992: 6). The movement identified the secular regimes that perpetrated these crimes against the 'Muslim Iraqi people' and the 'Islamic bases' of society with the West and colonialism (Hizb Al-Da'wa 1992: 5), of which the Ba'thist regime was the agent, above all because it was held to implement Western concepts.

With the threat of advancing secular ideology, Shi'a activists were convinced that political action had to be taken to preserve Islam. Borrowing explicitly from the organizational and strategic models developed in the Muslim Brotherhood in the 1930s, and echoing broader traditions of revolutionary activism (notably the Gramscian emphasis on a war of position advancing by winning positions in civil society), Al-Sadr envisaged party activism as evolving over several steps: first, the dissemination of ideas; second, the shift towards developing organizational capacity and recruiting; third, the seizure of power; and, finally, the establishment of an Islamic polity (Louër 2008a: 85–6). The Hizb Al-Da'wa and the Al-Shiraziyyin broadly set out on this path, achieving elements of steps one and two in the 1960s and 1970s, but reduced to step one at best in the 1980s and 1990s. Nonetheless, the movement, albeit in altered form, was to make progress into step three, ironically enough, after the fall of the Ba'thist regime at the hands of the US-led invasion of 2003.

Sermons, study groups, journals (such as *Sawt Al-Da'wa/Voice of the Call*), and books and pamphlets by the hundred, expressed in accessible and relevant language, were used to disseminate ideas. By the 1970s, tape-recorded messages were quick to be used as the movement adopted the technologies that were to hand and that could evade the authorities. From the late 1950s onwards, professional schools and charitable institutions were founded, notably by the Al-Shiraziyyin. Through these institutions opinions could be shaped, influence exerted, interests entrenched, jobs and status distributed, and recruits found. On the other hand, actual efforts to mobilize the urban poor were not especially extensive, even by the regretful admission of one Da'wa spokesperson in the 1980s (Wiley 1992: 92). The Hizb Al-Da'wa condemned as 'backward' and 'insane' the practice of *tatbir*, whereby adherents annually lamented the martyrdom of Hussein, and the guilt of the faithful therein, by joining public processions while 'making incisions on their foreheads that they hit with a sword to make the blood flow' (Louër 2008a: 94). The Al-Shiraziyyin, in sharp contrast, embraced this practice as a non-elitist demonstration of attachment to Imam Hussein, associated with the people, and made use of Ashura processions as a key site of mass mobilization, out of which direct actions could emerge which suited their purposes – such as the sacking of a Hizb Al-Da'wa-controlled charity in Karbala in 1962, leading to the former's eviction.

Open confrontation with the post-independence Iraqi government
was bound to come sooner or later, but it was the state that made the
first move. The increasingly narrow social base of the regime through
the 1960s, the growing exclusion of Shi'a from leading official positions, and the Ba'thist coup of 1968 which brought Saddam Hussein
into effective power, seemingly validated some of the criticisms of
the Islamists, but they also paved the way for a regime attempt to
smash the movement. Seizing on tension with Iran in regard to the
Shatt Al-'Arab (Iraq's only real access to the Persian Gulf waters),
the government moved to expel some 20,000 so-called 'Iranians' –
i.e. Iraqi citizens of Iranian descent or long-time Iranian-residents
of the shrine cities who had never relinquished their Iranian citizenship – a constituency that overlapped with both the leadership and the
rank and file of Shi'a Islamism. As the dispute intensified, Mahdi
Al-Hakim was arrested and tortured, accused of being a 'Zionist spy'
(Louër 2008a: 87), a Stalinist tactic that was only to be developed over
time. This was only the first step of a campaign of repression,
armoured by xenophobic Iraqi nationalism, the promotion of a secular
history (Davis 2005), territorial disputes with Iran and scare-stories
about Iranian coup plans, a campaign that culminated, following the
Iranian revolution of 1979, in the arrest and execution of Muhammad
Baqr Al-Sadr himself, along with his sister, Bint Al-Huda, in April
1980. During this period, tens of thousands of Iraqi Shi'a, activists or
not, were deported (notably in 1971). Others fled the country in fear of
their lives. 'Hundreds of Iraqi clerics were imprisoned, tortured,
murdered and executed' (Louër 2008a: 87); dozens of others were
exiled; property was confiscated, and homes raided (Wiley 1992:
46–7). The *marja'iyya*, under Al-Khu'i, retreated from politics even
as its ranks were decimated and its sources of funding curtailed (Louër
2008a: 88). As Wiley has it, the Ba'thist Revolutionary Command
Council from 1968 onwards conducted policies against the Shi'a 'far
more inimical to their welfare than had been the secularization of the
British or the Leftist policies of Qasim' (Wiley 1992: 45).

The heavy repression meted out by the 'Republic of Fear' (Makiya
1998), neither crushed nor stimulated protest in any linear or
unalloyed fashion. On the one hand, throughout the period, even in
the face of massive repression, protests continued. There were public
protests by Shi'a clergy in 1974 during the war against the Kurds
which led, predictably enough, to arrests and executions. Pilgrims

undertaking the banned annual pilgrimage from Najaf to Karbala to honour Imam Hussein in February 1977 found the courage to chant 'All the people are against you, Ba'th, we don't accept you'. The procession of 30,000 was intercepted by the army and attacked from the air by military helicopters. Tanks entered Karbala. And, while some soldiers deserted to the demonstrators, sixteen were killed outright, there were 2,000 arrests and 8 were sentenced to death in short order (Wiley 1992: 50–2; Tripp 2013: 76–7). Or, when Baqr Al-Sadr, by now calling for revolution, was placed under house arrest on 13 June 1979, large groups of men arrived from Baghdad, Basra, Nasriya, Kirkuk, Diwaniya, Al-Samawa and Diyala *inter alia*, to proclaim their allegiance to him as *marja'*, while demonstrations were joined in Karbala, Kufa and Madinat Al-Thawra (in Baghdad). The regime responded with killings, mass arrests, torture and execution. Activists were able to continue to demonstrate their own commitment, even escalating their protests, in the face of such repression.

We should also note in passing, that, as elsewhere, deportation and exile did not necessarily put an end to political activism undertaken abroad. Ayatollah Hasan Al-Shirazi (b. 1933), for example, a poet and an authority on Arabic literature, spoke out publicly in Iraq in 1969, and was arrested, tortured and exiled in 1970. He now promoted Islamic activism outside Iraq, teaching in the Hawza Al-Zaynabiyya in Syria, the Hawza Al-Imam Al-Mahdi in Lebanon, and the Hawza Hashimiyya in Sierra Leone. His activism, seemingly stimulated rather than diminished by his encounter with state repression, was only terminated with his assassination in Beirut in May 1980 (Wiley 1992: 78).

On the other hand, the movement's radical opposition to the secular government cannot be simply ascribed to the repression, as it pre-dated the post-1968 period, and the revolutionary seizure of power was envisaged long before. Moreover, the Hizb Al-Da'wa's call for armed struggle in 1979 was as much if not more a response to the inspiration of the Iranian revolution than to Iraqi repression, which both recruited to action and terrorized into inaction. The extraordinary events of 1979 in Iran were intimately linked to Al-Sadr's call for uprising and revolution. 'Many young people, both the educated and the urban poor, were sufficiently encouraged by the success of the Iranian Revolution and affronted by the Iraqi government's methods of violent coercion to join the Islamic groups' (Wiley 1992: 54–5). The movement was 'strongly affected by Iran's popular upheaval, [and] the Mujahidin emerged in Baghdad in 1979' (Batatu 1981: 578).

The execution of Al-Sadr, the continuing violent repression, and above all the invasion of Iran which put the country on a war footing and greatly heightened the fear and the reality of being charged with treason, together put an end to the wider forms of mobilization, including demonstrations and street protests associated with the Hizb Al-Da'wa in Iraq. The movement was driven far more thoroughly underground, and reduced to a number of small groups, based often outside Iraq (for example, in Lebanon or in Iranian Kurdistan) attempting to stage assassinations and even coups but now leaning on the actual assistance of the Iranian state which was attempting to export the revolution (Wiley 1992: 57–66). By 1981, the movement was 'only capable of mounting disruptive acts, suicidal in character and of limited effect', because of the lack of leadership after Al-Sadr's death, internal tensions, and failures at bridge-building, as well as the 'relentlessness of the state repressive machinery' (Batatu 1981: 594). Ironically, it was only once state support from Iran was actually forthcoming for the Iraqi movement that it was actually crushed.

Just as in Syria, the guns and torture chambers of a 'progressive' post-independence regime had been brought to bear against radical Islamist challengers drawn from their own citizens, albeit this time under the banners of political Shi'ism. Just as in Syria, the regime survived, while becoming ever more repressive in the process. And, without any chance to exercise power on the national stage, neither Sunni Islamists nor Shi'a Islamists were discredited, paving the way for their resurgence once their Ba'thist nemesis was destroyed or shaken, in Iraq after 2003 and in Syria after 2011. Worth noting is the quiescence in Sunni Islam in Iraq during these years. Sayyid Qutb may have been inspiring Sunni Islamists from Morocco to the Philippines and, as we have seen, in Syria, but his work had little or no echo among the Sunnis of Iraq. The explanation would appear to lie in the larger political terrain. The Sunnis of Iraq, for the most part, had no Near Enemy to fight, and even the Far Enemy was tilting towards them when it came to the Iran–Iraq war of the 1980s. Ba'thism ruled the social and political field, and it appeared to be, and in many ways was, delivering results for its predominantly Sunni constituency. For the Iraqi Sunnis at least, secularism was by no means a cracked vessel. Yet again, we encounter the importance of hegemonic expansion in securing consent.

In both Syria and Iraq, the Islamist challenge was a sign of things to come in other parts of the post-independence Arab world; whether or not the Algerian or the Egyptian authorities were paying any real attention, or drew any meaningful lessons, was another matter.

Hegemonic contraction: the return of Left protest in Egypt, 1967–1989

From the late 1960s onwards, there was a revival in the labour movement and the Left in Egypt, with increased levels of protest by workers, critique by intellectuals, journalists and students, and organization by Left activists, including at the party level, pressure within the official union structure to do more to represent workers' interests, and one spectacular instance of mass popular protest – the uprising of January 1977. Many on the Left developed an ever sharper critique of military rule, and hoped for a return to some form of popular democracy. The return of Left protest in Egypt had a great deal to do with the political unincorporation of the Left from the regime, which under Anwar Sadat increasingly turned towards neo-liberalism and alternative ruling formulae, generating protests among those who were threatened. The Left revival, which drew on models from within and without the region, was also limited, never really transcending its reactive and defensive origins. The repression handed down by the state can only partially explain this. The weakness of Left leaderships and mobilization, and their continuing, compromising faith in the state, do not seem to have been adequate to the moment, and at least played some role in this failure.

There were a number of worker protests, including stoppages and machine sabotage in 1966 against the renewal of overtime and others against forced salary reductions in 1968. In the wake of the 1967 defeat, amid a revival of Marxism (Hussein 1973), a Leftist critique of a militaristic, repressive regime that had failed to establish a popular democracy emerged after 1967 (Abd Al-Malek 1968). There was a revival in the Left student movement, especially at Cairo University, in the early 1970s. In Helwan, the most industrialized city in Egypt, Leftists at the Socialist Institute held mass meetings in 1969 and 1970, attended by up to 5,000 workers, to discuss economic and social issues. The Institute was promptly shut down by the ministry of the interior (Posusney 1994: 220). In 1971, there were at least five protests, the largest involving 30,000 workers and a sit-in at the Helwan Iron and Steel Company; another involved a sit-in demanding a wage increase in Misr Helwan Spinning and Weaving in May 1971; there was a strike of the Cairo taxi drivers in October.

Beinin lists a series of strikes making socio-economic demands in 1972, 1975 and 1976 in some of the major state owned enterprises – such as a sit-in in the Nasr Transport Company in June 1976, or the three-day strike over work rule changes in March 1975 at the Misr Spinning and Weaving Company in Mahalla Al-Kubra.

The Communist Party was re-established underground in 1975 (in 1977, there were four such parties) and the Tagammu' (National Progressive Unionist Party) was founded in 1976, when political parties were legalized for the first time since 1953.

After an interregnum following the repression of the uprising of 1977, and the lack of mass mobilization in its aftermath, there was a revival of strike action organized mostly by workers on socio-economic issues in the mid and late 1980s. There were dozens of strikes during 1985 and 1986. Beinin singles out

the strike and uprising at the Misr Fine Spinning and Weaving Company in Kafr Al-Dawwar in September-October 1984, the protracted struggle of workers at the Esco textiles firm in Shubra Al-Khayma during the first half of 1986 (including a strike and a sit-in), the strike at the Misr Spinning and Weaving Company in Mahalla Al-Kubra in February 1986, and the exceptionally militant strike of the railroad engineers and stokers in July 1986. The strike and protests at the Egyptian Iron and Steel Company in Helwan in July August 1989 were also part of this movement (Beinin 1994: 262–3).

Strike action was concentrated in large-scale public-sector enterprises in industrial areas.

Much of the labour activism of this period involved a powerful, grassroots determination among workers to hold on to social and economic gains, to contest take-backs, to demand parity and fairness in who was paid what, and to hold companies and managers to the promises that they had made on pay, conditions and benefits (Posusney 1994: 223–31). Such protests represented a push to hold on to the gains that had been made under Nasserism, and implement what Posusney calls the 'moral economy' that workers themselves held. The strike at Kafr Al-Dawwar, which turned into three days of riots aimed at government targets, in September 1984, opposed the recent

government measure to raise the price of basic foodstuffs and double
workers' contributions to health insurance and pensions (Tripp 2013:
155). Sit-ins often demonstrated their commitment to hard work and
national productivity by actually increasing, rather than halting, production during protests (Posusney 1997: 156). Workers at points
accepted sacrifices of hard work and even pay cuts (for an example
of the latter, consider the lack of protest in 1965 following a state-wide
pay reduction), but complained when standards of justice were violated, for example over mismanagement and corruption in unions or
the state.

These strikes were not driven by, or part of, a cohesive, revolutionary movement. Organization was informal and took place at the local
level and was imbricated in a diverse and vigorous popular culture.
Strikes were illegal, although they obtained a certain *de facto* acceptance during the period thanks to the actions of workers; union officials, for the most part, and Left intellectuals and political parties, did
not organize such strikes or engage in other forms of mass mobilization. During the 1989 work-in at the Helwan Iron and Steel Plant,
union leaders fled the factory and urged the authorities to storm it. This
they did, with considerable force, with arrests and even killings
resulting (Posusney 1997: 151–7). At best, Leftist non-workers offered
some material support to strikers, while often (but not always) giving
verbal support in the limited sections of the media where the Left had a
voice. Even these organs, such as *Al-Tali'a* were vulnerable to censorship and closure (Beinin 1994: 249). Veteran labour activists such as
Taha Sa'd Uthman or Ahmad Sadiq Sa'd, who looked back to the pre-
1952 period, and had feet in intellectual, organizational and workers'
milieu were the exception not the rule. And such figures were as likely to
condemn the official Left of parties, unions, and intelligentsia for being
out of touch with 'the working class' as to celebrate it (Beinin 1994:
248–54, 264). The official media in Egypt may have attributed the
uprising of January 1977 to a 'criminal plot' implemented by Marxists
and aimed at the seizure of power, but this was simply not the case:
communists and others had organized neither the demonstrations nor
the property destruction (Beinin 1994: 248–50; Abd Al-Raziq 1979:
22). Some sections of the Left articulated principles and identities that
suggested the need for a return to a popular or workers' democracy in
Egypt. They indicated a faith, if an excessively abstracted one, in the
revolutionary potential of 'the masses'. They were even less convincing

in spelling out what this faith meant in terms of organization, mobilization and strategy, let alone engaging in organization on the ground.

The most significant single protest of the period was the *intifada* of 18–19 January 1977. It was not a strike, but a popular uprising, the most dramatic mass action since the Cairo fire of January 1952. In accordance with IMF structural adjustment prescriptions, Sadat's government announced a 50 per cent cut in subsidies for basic consumer goods, implying steep rises in the costs of bread, sugar, tea and bottled gas, and important rises in the prices of rice, cooking oil, macaroni, gasoline and cigarettes (Abd Al-Raziq 1979: 72). In the capital, protestors increasingly filled the streets, and increasingly violent confrontations with security forces developed. Downtown Cairo was largely in the hands of the demonstrators for two days. Considerable damage was done to regime institutions and commercial private property owned by Sadat's *nouveau riche*.

The first movers of the January *intifada* were the workers of the Misr Spinning and Weaving Company of Helwan. Used to acting collectively on the shopfloor, but now confronted with the sudden price hikes of this magnitude, they led other workers in a march around the industrial suburb

chanting demands for cancellation of the price hikes, the ouster of the government, and expressing particularly enmity to President Sadat and his family (Beinin 1994: 252).

Some workers then blockaded the roads and railway tracks to Helwan against the security forces – while others made their way to join demonstrations in the downtown area, fuelled by hundreds of students from Ain Shams University (Abd Al-Raziq 1979: 80). They were joined by ordinary people shocked at the new prices. In downtown Cairo, protestors raised the Egyptian flag, and tried to win over the Amn Al-Markazi, usually poor rural–urban migrants themselves, by engaging them in discussions about the price rises (Abd Al-Raziq 1979: 81). Illuminated advertisements for luxury goods and display windows of boutiques offering high-priced imports for sale were also targeted. Casinos and clubs were attacked along the pyramids road (Beinin 1994: 248). In the industrial suburb of Shubra Al-Khayma, with its long activist tradition, workers struck and occupied their plants.

Workers at the Naval Arsenal in Alexandria joined demonstrations. Joined by workers from other enterprises, they marched on the Arab

Socialist Union headquarters, 'chanting anti-government slogans and throwing stones at police and security forces' (Beinin 1994: 252). Some students joined in.

Cars, trams and buses on the route were destroyed, as were the rest houses of the president and vice-president of the republic. A police station was stormed; a movie theatre, buildings of large companies, and a consumer co-operative rumoured to engage in favouritism and bribery were set ablaze; and many display windows were shattered (Beinin 1994: 252).

The workers at the Delta Ironworks, fearful of denouncing the government outright, sent the following satirical telegram to Sadat:

We thank you for increasing prices, and raise the slogan, 'more price hikes for more hunger and deprivation'. May you always be a servant of the toiling workers (Posusney 1997: 157).

On 19 January, demonstrations were initiated by workers at the Misr rayon mill and Military Plant No. 45 in Helwan, who walked off the job and started to cut transport links between Cairo and Helwan. Textile workers from at least two other firms initiated demonstrations on that day.

The slogans of the crowd, at least as rendered by a Nasserist academic Abd Al-Raziq, give a picture of some of the conceptions, identities and principles that informed the action. According to his selection, the demonstrators saw themselves as the people, as workers, students and peasants, suffering from poverty and hunger, pitted against corrupt and tyrannical authorities, corrupt, wealthy, exploitative and even decadent elites, and the dangers of capitalism. One chant took aim at the corrupt elites of the open door in the face of popular poverty: 'Thieves of the Infitah, the people are hungry and not satisfied' (*'ya haramiyya al-infitah, al-sha'b ju'an mish murtah'*). Others contrasted the 'whisky and chicken' eaten by the elite while the people went hungry. Another chant pitted workers and people against the 'government of exploitation'. Another chant declared that 'We students are with the workers against the capitalist bloc' (*'ihna al-talaba ma' al-'ummal, did tahalluf ra's al-mal'*). Another chant went: 'He dresses in the latest fashion, while we live ten to a room.' Others chanted that 'It wasn't enough to take our clothes, Now they're coming to take our bread.' Others excoriated the expense of meat. Others denounced the 'security state' (*hakimna bi-l-mubahith*). Both Zionism and the United States appeared as oppressive forces in these chants. 'The Zionists are on my land and the intelligence services are at my door' (*'al-sahiyuni fawq turabi, wa-l-mubahith 'ala babi'*).

The chants of the crowd also gave a sense of the sorts of measures desired from the government. Some invoked Nasser and his protection of the workers. Others called for democracy:

The first demand, oh young men, is the right to a multi-party system/The second demand, oh masses, is the right to publication and expression/The third demand, oh free people, is fixed prices' (*Auwal matlab ya shabab, haqq ta'addud al-ahzab / Tani matlab ya jamahir, haqq al-nashr wa-l-ta'bir / Talit matlab ya ahrar, rabt al-ajr bi-l-as'ar*)

Another chant involved simply a call on 'our rulers in Abdin' for justice and religion (Abd Al-Raziq 1979: 81–2). These slogans were neither communist nor Islamist, in any programmatic way. They did, on the other hand, very much express a Nasserism, but one infused with a democratic content which Nasserism lacked. They illustrate the ways in which at least some of those mobilized saw themselves as poor and hungry, as segments of the people pitted against an elite, as deserving of cheap prices and democracy, and opposed to the corruption, inequality and an authoritarian state. Whether Al-Raziq may or may not have biased his selection of slogans, there was a remarkable coherence between these sentiments and the targets of the crowds' wrath, as we have seen.

Sentiments were further exacerbated by high expectations in the wake of the perceived military victory of October 1973. These expectations had been encouraged by confident prognostications regarding the fixing of prices and improved working conditions in the official press as recently as early January. Sadat himself had said that there would be no sacrifices for 'this generation'. Indeed, when these measures were announced on 17 January in the Industrial Committee of the Majlis Al-Sha'b, they caused an uproar (Abd Al-Raziq 1979: 72–4). The statist Left was also exercised by the undemocratic way in which the measures had been conceived and announced, against government promises on consultation (Abd Al-Raziq 1979: 74).

The subsidy cut was immediately rescinded, and, with the army on the streets, the crowds were driven back by the end of the second day. The mainstream Left now took a rather defensive and law-abiding posture in the face of regime accusations that they instigated the action, seeking to defend their ever more vulnerable position in the state, and unwilling to chance their lives, liberty or livelihoods by entering the fray of mass mobilization to capitalize on the sentiments that were obviously important among significant sectors of the population. The energies of the crowd thus dissipated almost as fast as they had materialized, and for the Left the years after 1977 were marked more by quiescence and intellectual re-evaluation than any deeper mobilization or revival.

The limited posture of the mainstream Left, who were by no means electrified into organization by the uprising, and thus provided no vehicle to sustain the action, had much to do with the attempt to defend the position that the Left had won in the state, and the rights which newly opened up over party organizing in the 1970s – which could be jeopardized if the Left was seen to 'play politics' with strikes and the *intifada* of 1977 (Beinin 1994: 258, 261). It also had to do with the fact that the revolutionary view remained a minority one, and was steadily losing ground among the intelligentsia to more Islamist positions in the 1970s. During the 1970s and 1980s, there was no re-constitution of the more developed links between party, union, intellectuals and workers that had been a feature of the period between 1945 and 1952. The ideal of popular democracy was not given a mass mobilizing content on the ground by activists. In many respects, workers had to rely on themselves, raised demands linked to individual workplaces, and continued to be chary of unions or parties linked to the state, or distant urban intellectuals.

Many authors thoroughly encase the Left politics and labour activism of the post-1967 years in a changing Egyptian political economy. This analysis is important, but needs to be supplemented with ideological, cultural and political factors. The growing disincorporation of the Nasserist hegemony was a key factor. The bargain whereby independent unionism was given up in return for a position in the state, and hard work was offered in return for socio-economic uplift, and intellectuals were offered an often prestigious position in the Nasserist media in return for remaining within the bounds of authorized discourse, started to be disorganized from the mid-1960s onwards.

The union and Left position in the state, although maintained, was subject to competition with the emergence of a multi-party system in 1977 and Sadat's shift away from Nasserist statist developmentalism and his short-lived encouragement of the Islamist movement. The public sector was set to play a diminished role under Sadat's *infitah*. Socio-economic uplift was under threat as real wages in the public sector ceased to rise by the late 1960s, and started to decline in the 1970s and 1980s – while prices of basic commodities such as meat started to rise. Under Nasser, a whole generation had obtained land, rights against 'feudalism', education, training, status, secure jobs and a rising standard of living that their parents had only wished for. Many peasants saw land reform in terms of a seminal moment of liberation from feudalism (Saad 1999). Education and technical training were perceived in similar ways (Mosallam 2013). This experience of upward mobility thanks to the state was not to be repeated for the mass of the population. When delivery from on high failed, questions arose from below.

State officials, looking to reduce redistributive 'burdens' and tackle a balance-of-payments deficit – occasioned not only by macroeconomic difficulties associated with the attempt to raise investment and consumption at the same time, but also by costly foreign policies, especially the war in North Yemen – deducted one-half day's pay per month from all public employee's salaries as early as 1965; there were also some price and tax increases and some factory closures (Posusney 1994: 218). A new round of price and tax increases closely followed the 1967 defeat, with renewed calls to workers to sacrifice for the 'battle' amid an increase from 42 to 48 hours in the work week, an increase in forced savings, and cuts in paid holidays in some cases (Posusney 1994: 218–19).

The Nasserist media and state institutions were not so much purged under Sadat as left unable to square conviction with employment as the state they worked for suffered military defeat, retreated from pan-Arabism and anti-colonialism, and turned to consumption and market economics. Public sector jobs were less remunerated over time, and could be dull and bureaucratic in any case. Others criticized the poor quality and maladministration of public services, while yet others were shocked by growing evidence of corruption among state officials, especially in the context of the sacrifices demanded for the failed war of 1967. Upward mobility in the 1970s and 1980s was supplied not by the state, but by migration for work in the oil-rich Gulf. The shattering military defeat of 1967 had raised a great question over the anti-colonial nationalism that had helped to win over the Left to Nasserism.

The appeal of a Leftist, as opposed to an Islamist solution to these forms of disincorporation needs to be explained, however, particularly as Islamist politics were indeed steadily gaining ground, and won many converts from the Nasserist left. In this regard, the intellectual labour of Egyptian Leftists, as well as the influence of a Leftist revival on the international scene, should not be ignored. The Left in many parts of the Arab world was impressed and inspired by the doings of the Palestinian revolution – which included significant elements considerably Leftward of Nasserism. The MAN in the Mashriq and the Arabian peninsula had been moving Leftward since the early 1960s. Ba'thist critics of the direction taken by 'Ba'thist' regimes denounced the way mass mobilization was stymied by military imposition (Shabbi 1966: 9–10, 31–2). The experiment in South Yemen, a victory against colonialism that came hot on the heels of Nasser's defeat in 1967, proclaimed itself more radical than 'petty bourgeois' Nasserism. The Lebanese Nationalist Movement promoted a critique of military regimes on the regional scene, and advocated for democracy. Mao's 'great proletarian cultural revolution' (Hussein 1973: 11) played a role in influencing students, intellectuals and workers from the late 1960s onwards. May 1968 also impressed some sections of the student movement in Egypt. The possibility of a popular, democratic, political order, a revolutionary alternative to the statist and military-controlled regime and to capitalism in general, appealed to small numbers of intellectuals.

By the same token, the under-development of and contradictions within this Leftist alternative vision, and the lack of meaningful organization and mobilization on these lines, must be held responsible in some significant measure for the decline of Left politics, especially in the wake of the uprising of 1977 when certain intellectuals and activists, including veterans like Ahmad Sadiq Sa'd, perceived a real opportunity. Many sought more democratic forms, while continuing to harken after a single, vanguardist party that could lead and revolutionize the masses (Shabbi 1966: 31–2). Whether democracy could be squared with vanguardism, let alone Maoism, was by no means clear. In the 1970s, the Left generation of the 1950s and 1960s had not lost its institutional position in the state and its institutions, and preferred to cling on to what it had as best it good, rather than to wade into the earthworks and fortifications of civil society to engage in mass mobilization. The call for 'popular democracy' was sometimes half-hearted.

On the one side, it accepted Sadat's liberalization, and thus concurred with, rather than opposed, the state. On the other, it contradicted the bargain that the Left itself had made with the Nasserist state, which was to secure socio-economic rights without democracy. Some were not sure whether to oppose or embrace Sadat's liberalization. Moreover, it is an open question to what extent the Left could bring itself to believe passionately that democracy would actually deliver rather than erode socio-economic rights. Finally, the specific vision of what a 'popular democracy' would look like, as well as the strategy to get there, never came across as highly developed. All this compared rather unfavourably with the convictions and forms of mobilization undertaken by the Islamists, who had no difficulty in condemning outright the secular state.

Left activism during this period made modest achievements in slowing the pace of economic restructuring and winning concessions on subsidies, pay and conditions, at least until the 1990s. But the Leftist generation that had come of age in the wake of the 1967 defeat and played such a central role in these collective actions (Abdallah 2009) was further defeated, demobilized and sidelined by Islamist political currents by the 1990s (Duboc 2011). The work-in at Kafr Al-Duwwar in 1994 met with a repressive response: there is some evidence that the repression really did intimidate and demobilize the workers (Bassiouni 2010), at least in this context. During the early 1990s, worker strike action seems to have reduced.

Sunni Islamist intellectual labour

While the Left in Egypt and elsewhere in the Arab world only had modest success in elaborating a comprehensive political, moral and intellectual alternative to the crisis-ridden Arab order, the same could not be said for the Islamists. During the 1970s and 1980s, a number of important intellectuals, jurists, journalists and activists in Egypt and in the wider Arab world engaged in a major intellectual re-working of Leftism, secularism, pan-Arabism and national liberation – developing a substantial body of Sunni-Islamist discourse around notions of cultural oppression, Westernization, Islamic heritage and endogeneity, secularism, corrupted elites and gender. This body of discourse, disseminated on tape recordings, videos, the print media, television, and increasingly on the Internet, in certain of its general categories and ways of seeing, as well as in regard to the frames and principles developed around particular movements, played an important role in Islamic activism: diagnosing problems, motivating commitment, coordinating behaviour, stitching otherwise diverse sociologies together, defining material and ideal interests, specifying principles and identities, assigning roles, indicating enemies, and prognosticating courses of action (cf. Benford and Snow 2000). The dynamism of this intellectual output can help to account for the ideological content of new forms of activism that arose in contexts of political disincorporation and social, economic and political problems, and the failure of Left leadership. Many of its proponents had been active in Leftist and secular movements in the 1950s and 1960s; others had undergone a conversion to Islamism during those decades or more recently; still others had always been proponents of political Islam.

Just as nationalists in the region in the late nineteenth and early twentieth century had had their Rafi'a Al-Tahtawi or their Husayn Al-Marsafi, neo-Sufis their Ahmad Bin Idris, Muslim Brothers their Rashid Rida, liberation fighters their Mao Tse Tung, and socialists their Karl Marx, Vladimir Lenin, Samir Amin, Mehdi Amil, Anwar Abd Al-Malek, so Islamists had their own intellectual lodestones, whose influence was in important respects translocal. Sunni Islamists had their Tariq Al-Bishri, Adel Husayn, Munir Shafiq and Sayyid Qutb, Salafi-Wahhabis their Nasir Al-Din Al-Albani or Ibn Baz, Iranian reformists their Mohsen Kadivar, and Shi'a revolutionaries and activists their Muhammad Baqr Al-Sadr, Ali Shariati, Imam Musa Sadr or their Ayatollah Khomeini, while Sunni *jihad* groups had their Abu Basir, Abu Qatada, Al-Maqdisi, Abd Al-Qadir, Nasir Al-Fahd, or Ali Al-Khudair.

This intellectual work can help explain the direction that different strands of Islamist organizing took during this period. Yet this has been too easily missed by those who see Islamism in power-seeking, conspiratorial or instrumental terms. Others, viewing Islamism as a monolithic recrudescence of tradition are apt, through their own essentialism and exceptionalism, to miss the innovations and the constructionism that was involved. While those who have dug into this body of thought have sometimes conceded too much reality and cogency to what were in fact new and often fragile, and regularly flawed, and sometimes essentialist and diversionary, political constructions.

One of the most basic moves in this new body of mobilizing discourse was a partly new definition of domination and oppression. This move involved positing that power, subordination and oppression were neither about politics nor about economics above all, but that they were about culture. Tariq Al-Bishri (b. 1933), Egyptian thinker, high-ranking judge and respected legal mind, and 'convert' to political Islam during the 1970s and 1980s, said in Cairo in 1990 that he periodized Egyptian history in terms of movements for political independence until the First World War, movements for economic independence during the inter-war period and after. As for the latest phase, 'I slowly came to realize that the Islamist movement was in fact continuing the political and economic independence movement on the cultural level'. Islamists sought, at bottom, intellectual and cultural de-colonization after post-independence Muslim societies had been taken over disastrously by Western categories and ways of doing things (Burgat 2003: 26). This basic notion, which identified colonialism with cultural oppression, with the corruption and deviation that stemmed from the imposition of Western values, which were in turn considered in homogenous and essentialist fashion, was a key plank in Islamist discourse, from Hamas to the Muslim Brotherhood and beyond. For Anwar Haddam, for example, colonialism was understood not as a matter of economic exploitation, but as an assault on Islam. Anwar Haddam wrote, from his detention centre in Virginia, that 'above all, the Islamic identity of Algerians was the ultimate target' of the French invasion of Algeria. He also averred, citing the exploits of Abd Al-Qadir, Shaykh Al-Mokrani, Shaykh Bou Amama and 'other Muslim scholars', that 'North African Muslims never surrendered' (Haddam 1998).

Adel Hussain (1932–2001) was another important intellectual and activist who made the journey from Marxism to Islamism during the 1970s and 1980s. He was an Egyptian journalist, intellectual and opposition activist. A graduate of Cairo University (1957), he was imprisoned twice for his communism during the Nasser years. In the 1970s, while calling for alliances between Islam and the Left, his central criticism of Anwar Sadat was that he had taken Egypt down the road to dependency. Nonetheless, he made the same discursive move as Al-Bishri, shifting to emphasize above all the struggle for cultural independence, and prioritizing it over other forms of struggle. He told Burgat:

if I support Arab nationalism, if I feel tied to these people in many ways, that must mean that we share a common culture, and this culture should be infinitely more respected than it is at the moment. Nasser stressed integration and economic independence. Of course, these things are important, but not as important as cultural independence and this is where we began to differ. This is when everything started to happen for me.

In other words, in a search for a greater respect for the bonds of Arabism, Adel Hussain looked to Islam, deeming 'cultural independence' to be of more significance than economic or political independence that had been so crucial for an earlier generation (Burgat 2003: 41–2). This was a call for intellectual de-colonization – and it pointed to a new definition of the meaning of imperialism. Not direct political domination (imperialism), not indirect economic domination (neo-colonialism and dependency), but intellectual colonization was the key form of oppression.

A second vital discursive move was also articulated by Tariq Al-Bishri as early as 1972. In a major departure from progressive, secularist thought, Al-Bishri argued that Egyptian history was not just determined by a struggle between progress and reaction, the nationalist movement and imperialism, or a social struggle between classes with different interests. Instead, he noted, it was determined 'by the ideological struggle between that which comes from outside (*al-wafid*) and that which is inherited (*al-mawruth*)'. The recovery of *turath* (heritage, or what was inherited), for Al-Bishri, is profoundly important insofar as imperialism tried to obliterate this heritage. One of the reasons for the weakness of communism in Egypt was its foreign and Jewish origins, which made links to endogenous *turath* highly difficult to forge (Browers 2009: 36). Even the notion of the popular, said Tariq Al-Bishri in 1990, was much less important than the concept of the endogenous (Burgat 2003: 26). The problem was the unthinking imitation of Western models and their crude imposition and slavish imitation in the region.

The sources of the inherited, and the authentic, for emerging Islamists, were to be found in Islamic history, religion and culture – seen as the true force in making contemporary societies. The more I studied Islamic sources, Adel Hussain reported, 'the more I realized that it [Islam] was true and that it was a real force'. So I started to say to nationalists, 'you cannot be seriously nationalist if you are not completely open to Islam. For Islam is the very identity of this nation ... Islam created this Arab nation; that's a historical fact.' While such a proposition was a stock-in-trade of Algerian nationalism in the 1950s, where national identity and being a Muslim were quite closely linked, this proposition was not at all familiar to, for example, the Wafdists of inter-war Egypt, or to Nasserists, Ba'thists, Arab nationalists or communists. He went on, 'This is how I began to convince others', through 'hundreds of discussions, dialogues, seminars and meetings, academic or otherwise'. He then decided to re-enter directly political action by joining the Labour Party (Burgat 2003: 41–2). After the Iranian revolution, Adel Husayn came to believe that socialism was not more relevant to the specificities of Arab-Islamic societies than capitalism, since both were offspring of the West. In the 1980s, Adel Husayn called for authentic models of development and democracy drawn from the particular historical experiences embedded in the Arab-Islamic heritage – models that appeal to, and are anchored in, the religious sentiment of the masses. He made an impact as editor of *Al-Sha'b* and as a member of the Tagammu' (Socialist Labour) Party in Egypt (Browers 2009: 25–7).

This critique of cultural imitation, however, and defence of Islamic heritage, can be contrasted sharply with previous mobilizing discourses. Burgat called Bishri's endeavour a 'spectacular re-reading of the system of references which until then had structured his thinking', a flight from secular nationalism. Instead of a struggle between progress and reaction, the struggle was now defined as between 'the endogenous' and 'exogenous', the 'inherited' and the 'imported', the Arab-Muslim legacy on the one hand, and Western influences on the other (Burgat 2003: 25). The avatars of national liberation, revolution, development and socialism had hardly worried at all about cultural authenticity – or at least they had drawn heavily on Arabism where they did so. The pressing problems of under-development, backwardness, imperialism and neo-colonialism, feudalism and exploitation had to be solved – and, in this context, Islamism was obscurantist, backward, and in league with imperialism to boot – an enemy to be tackled. Many of the activists and intellectuals of the previous period had not worried as to whether they were being true to an endogenous, authentic culture, which they were often likely to read as superstitious, devious or irrational in any case. Franz Fanon's work had plenty of this form of secular modernism, in contrast with that of Ali Shariati. Indeed, those who stayed true to the strands of the previous alternative hegemony, such as the academic and philosopher Sadiq Jalal Al-Azm

(b. 1934), offered trenchant criticisms of the moves away from secularism – which he saw ultimately as 'Orientalism in reverse'. That is, the rejection of both secular nationalism and revolutionary socialism in favour of the authenticity of popular political Islam, he saw as no less 'reactionary, mystifying, ahistorical, and anti-humanist than ... Orientalism proper' (cited in Browers 2009: 42). For many Islamists, nonetheless, Third Worldism and the Non-Aligned Movement were 'tarnished by their recourse' to Western terminology – nationalism, socialism and liberalism (Burgat 2003: 49).

Certain intellectuals came to conceive of Islamic principles as foundational in regards to the very possibility of political community. Tariq Al-Bishri said that 'I realized that Islam was an essential ingredient. If the future of the country demanded it, it was Islam which would make us capable of sacrifices; it was by relying on Islam that we would be able to have a future at the expense of the present, whatever the sacrifices that were necessary in order to overcome the obstacles of the moment.' He noted that rising to the challenges of history requires a psychological underpinning which enables it 'to accept self-renunciation in favour of the motherland' (Burgat 2003: 26). In other words, to be able to shape positive freedom, to achieve collective self-mastery, required a principle – in this case Islam – that would shape, control and transcend narrow and individual self-interests and base passions, and would pave the way for virtue and the common good. As Al-Bishri put it: 'When religious membership was attacked [historically] ... The social fabric was ripped to shreds.' This led to the creation of isolated individuals, who as such could not enter into a relationship with the state. 'The loss of primordial attachments has thus affected all higher attachments. It has affected the capacity of the state itself to manage people's affairs as well as the ability of the individual to belong to the general entity' (cited in Burgat 2003: 27–8). The required principle where primordial attachments were lost was Islam. Islam also protected the Arabism of the Egyptian. Al-Bishri states that this last point occurred to him in the late 1970s, and, '[a]t that moment, I truly felt something very profound, which had a considerable impact' (Burgat 2003: 28). During the epoch of direct colonial rule, the national principle was supposed to achieve the integrative function previously achieved by virtue, as Noorani has so effectively argued (Noorani 2010). In the late twentieth century, Islamists maintained that Islam should play this role – thus transferring the functions of nationalism to those of Islam. Where faith in either the socialist revolution or the 'invisible hand' converting greed into prosperity and the general good was lacking, the workings of capitalism and the 'West' were read in terms of a fallen individualism, materialism, base passion and greed. This is the meaning of Burgat's argument that Islam was the 'reincarnation of an older Arab nationalism, clothed in imagery considered more indigenous' (Burgat 2003: xiv). It was now to serve as the new basis for, as a compelling necessity, political community, just as Arab nationalism had before.

In like vein, Adel Husayn went so far as to read the 'true heritage' of even the Copts as Islam. He spoke of the need for a general ideology so that everything can run peacefully. That general ideology in Egypt was Islam. 'It is the identity of the Muslims but it is also the identity of the Copts. Islam is our heritage, our identity, our soul, whether we are Muslim or Copt' (Burgat 2003: 88). An ambitious position, to put it benignly.

Secularism, emitting the foul stench of cultural retreat, came to be defined as the key political enemy for Islamists in Cairo, Algiers, Sana'a and Amman. While an earlier generation believed that secular ideas could provide the weapons to defeat Western armies, as a remedy for deficient Islamic resistance, many Islamists of the post-1967 generation believed instead that the arrival of secularism had coincided with the triumph of Western armies and thus led to defeat. While earlier Arab nationalists had seen in secularism a way to guarantee a new-found equality between religions in the Ottoman and then Arab world, Adel Hussain and others reckoned that secularism had merely served to guarantee the rights of the foreigners who imported it, and those of increasingly privileged non-Muslim minorities. Most importantly, 'the Trojan horse of secularism is seen, above all, as the most pernicious of the West's ideological weapons, which, at the peak of the colonial adventure, gave legality and respectability to the business of eradicating the normative Muslim system'. By dissolving pious foundations, courts and universities, it denied to Islamic civilization its capacity for producing the rules necessary for its own regulation and reproduction. Indeed, Al-Bishri even saw secularism as working against modernization because of the way it destroyed forms of association capable of subjugating greed and individualism (Burgat 2003: 43–5).

Third, new definitions of oppression and the search for the endogenous and the authentic were given a populist twist as Leftist ideas about social class were re-articulated and given a new, Islamic meaning. Al-Bishri indicated a faith in the 'healthy instincts' of the masses – which he saw as awakening to the call of Islam and the Muslim Brotherhood in Egypt (Browers 2009: 36). It was said to be Westernized, often wealthy political elites, clustered around the post-independence state, who foisted these inauthentic Western concepts onto Muslim and Arab culture. Munir Shafiq (b. 1934), a Christian Palestinian from Jerusalem, developed these ideas more systematically. He moved from Marxist-Leninism, with links to the DPFLP, to Islamism during the 1970s and 1980s. He converted to Islam around 1980 and joined Islamic Jihad and was at points a spokesperson for Hamas. He argued that the Arab world was divided into a modernized, secular, Westernized elite on the one side, and a more traditional or 'original' segment on the other. The former collaborate with the West in order to divide the Arabs and increase their dependence on the West, in contrast with the rural population, who were solidly grounded in traditional Islamic ways of life. This population was a dynamic force with a revolutionary potential. Here was an 'Islamic understanding of dependency theory'. In place of dependency theory's stress on the revolutionary possibilities of the peasantry, the new system of references suggested that the revolutionary revival of Islamic values could mobilize these rural subaltern groups against the centre, the secular West and their representatives, in order to achieve independence and social justice (Browers 2009: 24–5). These intellectual currents worked to replace class consciousness with the notion of an 'authentic' collective identity, rooted in the Islamic heritage and embedded in the hearts and minds of the masses, and contrasted with foreign, imported and inauthentic political and cultural ideas (Browers 2009: 29).

In historical fact, the idea that new forms of political Islam meshed seamlessly with existing forms of popular culture was rather unlikely. Vernacular traditions, folk understandings, mysticism, the occult, everyday ignorance, popular culture – complete with its computer games, video shops, adverts, parties, music and lipstick – inadvertent transgression-in-practice peasant modes of piety, were often at several removes from the Islamist identities and principles that were wielded often enough by urban educated classes, graduates in engineering (such as Al-Faraj), lawyers, doctors (such as Ayman Al-Zawahiri), students, administrators and so on. As Burgat points out, the lack of Arabization in Algeria in the 1980s, and the predominance of the French language and to some extent French categories, were no barrier to Islamist mobilization among Algerian students. Indeed, he notes that the lack of Arabization may have meant an identity gap which Islamists exploited (Burgat 2003: 22–3).

Such an identity gap involved a lack of meaning as to what Muslim-Arab identity was because of an immersion in French, which made it easier for new projects of Islamist mobilization to define anew what it meant to be a good Muslim through their superior linguistic capacities and thus access to a certain selection of scriptural sources of Islam. Here, proverbial wisdom was not the stuff and substance of the mobilization – which did not so much select from existing popular culture but substitute for it.

A homologous factor seems to have been at work in regard to the mobilization in Upper Egypt in the 1980s and early 1990s, of the Al-Gama'a Al-Islamiyya (the Islamic Group), which came out of the Islamist student movement of the 1970s. Burgat interviewed Abdelharith Madani, a member of the second generation of Al-Gama'a Al-Islamiyya, who became a lawyer and was tortured to death by Mubarak's security forces in 1994. Madani made clear that the enemies of Al-Gama'a in Upper Egypt were 'Sufis' and 'family traditions'. He said that even the greeting 'May peace be with you' sounded 'very strange to the locals in Sa'id'. He went on:

Once he had heard this a few times, my great-uncle went to see my father and said to him, 'If your son says that to me once more, I'll swing for him. That kid is always doing something strange, he prays differently'... Really our practices were foreign, as were our way of praying and our doctrinal choice.

Their rejection of Maliki ritual differences, and even beards were contentious on purely religious grounds. Nonetheless, at least according to Madani, this lack of resonance with local forms of popular culture did not prevent their success. He said:

We were arguing with the Sufis over beliefs. We completely dominated them. We exposed them in front of the young ... They came to fear admitting their doctrine in public ... We gained control of the mosques. Our preachers were in such demand that they had to be booked in advance (Burgat 2003: 67).

In other words, in spite of their 'foreign' ways of doing things, Islamists were able to dominate the spaces in which overt collective action could be planned and undertaken. Here the link with popular culture was by no means the source of their capacities.

Secular elites, defined not just by their socio-economic status and corrupted ways of life, but by their positions of power and control in the post-independence states, were increasingly seen as the new enemy and source of oppression. As the Tunisian Aziz Krichen put it: 'The bilingual [post-independence] elite ... announced itself to be ... a harmonious synthesis of opposing cultures. In reality, it was spiritually enslaved by Western values. It internalized its own inferiority and the superiority of others' (Burgat 2003: 47–8). Here the crisis was identified in terms of 'spiritual enslavement'. As Rachid Ben Aissa put it, Algeria had been culturally raped. 'In independent Algeria, there has not been a single example of Islamic education, and when one was finally established, it was a police institution' (Burgat 2003: 47–8). These analyses echoed those of figures like Rashid Al-Ghannushi, who had traversed a similar intellectual journey in the 1960s.

For the Islamist generation of the 1970s and later, born amid the problems of post-independence, and striving to make sense of this situation, the Islamist historical narrative did not assert that Arabs and Muslims had been wrong to fight for liberation from colonialism, but they did assert that the revolution had been betrayed. The Algerian Islamist and key activist for the reformist and modernist wing of the Fronte Islamique du Salut (FIS), Anwar Haddam, wrote that:

Following ... independence, a military group, ex-officers of the French army, who joined the war of liberation just before its end, took over and imposed socialism and one party rule. The authoritarian rulers consolidated their power by physically eliminating anyone opposed to their rule (Haddam 1998).

It was this, according to Anwar Al-Haddam, that could explain the existence of violent military regimes and religious, social and economic hardship in Algeria. The revolution had been usurped by officers linked to imperialism and committed to eradication and power. As Haddam added:

In post-colonial Algeria, the Algerian Muslim people have come to know with full conviction that those in power are nothing more than a regionally affiliated, culturally self-hating elite that cares little for the ethical, moral and civilizational dimensions of Islam (Haddam 1998).

Here was the double gesture, the critique of the culturally self-hating elite on the one hand, and the idea that it is a turning away from Islam that is the problem. It was no major step, in this context, to appropriate Sayyid Qutb's idea, worked out in Nasserist prisons in the 1950s and 1960s, that the real foe was the 'near enemy': nominally Muslim governments, who were so corrupted by the appropriation of Western concepts that they had entered a state of barbarism and pre-Islamic ignorance (*jahiliyya*).

Secular elites stood accused of capitulation, corruption and immorality in regard to their business dealings, ways of life, and their gender norms alike. Present – *sotto voce* – in the programme of the Muslim Brotherhood in Jordan (Muslim Brotherhood in Jordan 1997), for example, was a nationalist and moralizing critique of new economic practices in the kingdom in the wake of the peace treaty with Israel. They pointed to economic deterioration, poverty, unemployment, rising commodity prices and the cost of living, criticized the fact that the 'enemy' can buy real estate, own economic establishments, and compete with national industries, and that multinationals were turning people into 'cheap manpower'. Also under fire was the kingdom's focus on tourism, 'which in turn will horribly contribute in corrupting the society and the public morals ... and the building of hundreds of hotels and night clubs'. Indeed, corrupt elites were also seen as corrupt in matters of gender and sexuality. The Muslim Brotherhood in Egypt, for example, put out on its website in May 1996 a statement on 'The Role of Muslim Women in an Islamic Society':

We completely reject the way that western society has almost completely stripped women of their morality and chastity. These ideals are built on a philosophy which is in contradiction to the Shari'a and its morals and values (Muslim Brotherhood 1990s).

Islamist movements across the region hammered home the idea that men and women were equal in overall value, and in the sight of God, but different in their capacities, roles, and duties. Article 17 of the Hamas Covenant indicated that '[t]he Muslim woman has a role no less important than that of the Muslim man in the battle of liberation' (Hamas Covenant 1988: Art. 17). On the other hand, the woman has particular capacities, roles and duties. She is a 'maker of men' and thus guides and educates new generations. It is because of this very seminal role that the 'enemy' tries to change the Muslim woman. The key role of the woman, as a mother or sister in the home of the fighting family, is in 'looking after the family, rearing the children, and imbuing them with moral values and thoughts derived from Islam', teaching them to perform their religious duties and their housekeeping matters (Hamas Covenant 1988: Art. 18). In other words, Westernized and secular elites were also at fault for allowing the corruption and deviation of women.

The Muslim Brotherhood in Egypt, 1970s–1990s

Amid this Islamist intellectual revival, the Muslim Brotherhood was by far the most important organization on the regional stage to try to bring about a reformist and modernist Sunni vision of a Islamic society and (ultimately) state. When Anwar Al-Sadat let the historic leadership out of prison in the early 1970s (as he hoped to neutralize his Leftist foes and make use of Islamism in his new dispensations), the stage was set for a return to Sunni Islamist activism – which had all but vanished from the Egyptian scene since the showdown of 1954. Unlike the Left, the Muslim Brotherhood were ready to engage in far-reaching charitable, outreach and institutional work in order to develop their social base. The strategy was a way to avoid repression, make use of the mosque network and funds from the Gulf, while offering services and goods to constituencies who saw their statist provision cut. Unlike the Palestinians during the period of the Thawra, or the jihadists in Syria, the Egyptian Muslim Brotherhood rejected armed struggle, arguing for a cautious, reformist and gradual approach. The Brotherhood took up the stagist strategy advocated long before by Hasan Al-Banna – who some of the old leadership had worked with in the 1940s. The attempt to create an Islamic state could only come about in the relatively distant future, after a long period during which, first, ideas were clarified and individual Muslims were reformed, and, second, where a substantial social base had been built up. This reformism put them into complex relations with the authorities, allowing them to operate in a certain semi-legal space, giving them room for manoeuvre in a highly repressive context. Their 'moderation' was also a card that the government might need from time to time, for example in containing jihadists, notably in the 1990s. The emphasis on charity and outreach also created a space in which activists could work in the belief that they were avoiding politics, and merely behaving as good Muslims should.

This apparent rejection of politics was a way to avoid suspicion and repression alike. That the Muslim Brotherhood only very rarely opposed the economic restructuring sought by Sadat and Mubarak, and more often embraced them, also gave them a breathing space in which to operate.

This Islamist movement was energized by the emergence of a new generation which came to be known as the 'New Guard', students in the 1970s, including men like 'Isam El-Erian, who were very active on campus in competition with the Left. The students did not only expect to recruit by winning loyal adherents because of the 'truth' of their programme, or through political victories that would 'rally the masses', or by seeking election on student bodies and societies. They also organized social and economic services, such as campus transport, and cheap books and materials, in order to create a social base. On graduation, these (and other) students entered the professional syndicates in the 1980s, running for election among doctors, scientists, engineers, and other professions and eventually the lawyers syndicate, a former bastion of secularism, in 1992 in free and competitive elections (Rosefsky Wickham 2002: 178). In this way, student activism was sustained into the professional world. The Muslim Brotherhood, although banned, started to field candidates unofficially in national elections from the 1980s onwards, giving them a presence of sorts in state institutions. That these elections were manipulated and corrupted by the regime mattered less insofar as party activity, constitutionalism, and democracy, also closely associated with this brand of Sunni Islam, were not its most fundamental tenet and driving force, just as they were not on the Left either, which could sacrifice parties and democracy on the altar of socio-economic rights, precisely the calculation made by unionists in March 1954.

Islamists expanded their 'summons' (*da'wa*) through study circles and Qur'an groups, and extensive publications. Here, considerable energy was devoted to rebutting, to their own followers rather than the Western press, the idea that *jihad* or armed struggle was necessary in Egypt, especially in the 1990s. Questioners were reminded that the rulers were not infidel (*kafir*) but merely sinners, and that the Brotherhood are summoners (to the faith) and not judges – as their leader Al-Hudaibi insisted from the 1970s onwards. Many reasons were adduced for the undesirability of armed struggle – from the damage it would do to the economy to the poor image of Muslims it would project (Muslim Brotherhood 1990s). Once individuals changed their conduct, so it was held, then their summons would turn outwards, in concentric circles through the family, neighbourhood and eventually the state (Rosefsky Wickham 2002: 127). Hasty or impatient action regarding the seizure of state power would simply lead to new coups and violence by new contenders who sought the same without perfecting their Islam first (Muslim Brotherhood 1990s).

The Brotherhood pursued outreach tactics through charitable activities, building grassroots support for a more Islamic society. They organized kindergartens and health clinics, and provided emergency aid, notably during the Cairo earthquake of 1992 when the state was slow to act. Islamic-oriented, Islamist, and Brotherhood members and supporters opened and ran thousands of new private voluntary organizations, which either had a religious focus, promoting charity or pilgrimage, or provided social services, such as day care for children, health clinics, schools and job training. The Brotherhood not only gained access to existing mosques, but contributed to the building of tens of thousands of new private mosques, funded by Gulf sources or charitable donations. Mosques were spaces for sermons, and were linked to prayer groups, religious lessons, libraries with Islamist books and cassettes, and community services, including bookstores, health clinics and kindergartens.

These actions engaged several constituencies: the urban poor, often of a rural background, who benefited from Brotherhood social services where these specifically targeted the growing informal neighbourhoods. There was some appeal among a downwardly mobile public sector, who were suffering from the withdrawal of state protections and services: its more middle-class segments on long waiting lists for state-guaranteed jobs, and its more working-class segments some of which felt betrayed by a Left that continued to make its bed with the 'corrupted' authorities. Further, an emerging *infitah* bourgeoisie, opposed to the Left by interest and disposition, but finding some succour in the more pious, but often business-friendly, message of the Sunni Islamists, and ready to contribute to mosque building and charitable activity. While the labour movement did little to mobilize women actively, and unions protecting male labour sometimes actively excluded them, the Islamists had strategies for the mobilization and inclusion of women. They offered an array of precepts defining Islamic womanhood, attractive to those seeking to escape the putative cultural inauthenticity of supposedly Westernized women. Second, they provided services that mattered, including childcare, health and so on – areas of biological and social reproduction to which women contributed in overwhelming numbers. Finally, rank-and-file activists could put their energy into the movement believing that they had nothing to do with politics. Instead, they saw themselves as merely 'educating fellow Muslims of their rights and obligations in Islam and forging new kinds of communal solidarity based on Islamic principles of charity and self-help' (Rosefsky Wickham 2002: 102). These Sunni Islamists thus built up spaces and won over constituencies in the context of the retreat of the state from social and economic provision (Rosefsky Wickham 2002; Zahid and Medley 2006).

The Brotherhood added a range of businesses – in banking, construction, manufacturing and trade – to its bloc. Commerce with piety could be an attractive option for business owners. And these businesses also meant employment and sometimes socio-economic provision (where business and charity combined) and developed the resource base of the movement, financed in turn by migrants to the Gulf and some patronage from the Gulf itself, forged through the contacts made by migrants. Many of the latter had sought employment in the Gulf because of the lack of jobs offered in Egypt's economy, which could be blamed on the secular state. Many others, including important leadership cadres, had been driven into exile in Saudi Arabia and elsewhere by the Free Officers' repression of the 1950s and 1960s. Now these chickens could come home to roost, their religious credentials burnished by their contact with the holy cities, centres of pilgrimage and Saudi state-backed Islamic educational institutions, and their wallets and contacts much expanded.

For all the mass mobilization in which the Egyptian Muslim Brotherhood engaged, the actual components of the desired Islamic state were no more in existence in the 1990s in Egypt than they had been twenty years before. Gains had certainly been made along the road, as Islamists saw the highly visible signs of increasing piety and religiosity in Egypt. Nonetheless, those activists who were happy to engage in charitable and other works, or those Egyptians who felt they were perfecting their Islam at the level of characters and manners, did not necessarily have any interest in challenging the regime or seizing power or 'politics' of any kind. Further, socio-economic provision did not necessarily translate into political loyalty. And many in Egypt did not feel they needed to be told how to be good Muslims, or, even where they did, some preferred the religious establishment, or other forms of Islam, for guidance. Islamists alienated Copts in ways that secular nationalism never had. They aroused suspicion and hostility among liberals, secularists and the Left. But leaderships had not promised immediate results: theirs was explicitly and implicitly a long war of position in the Gramscian sense. And, while armed struggle against the Near Enemy had been drowned in blood in 1982 in Hama, for example, and in Algeria during the 1990s, the Muslim Brotherhood was still robust in the 1990s and weathered the measures of repression and made use of those of co-optation wielded by the Mubarak regime in the face of the militant Islamists of the 1990s.

Sunni *jihad* in Egypt

Unlike in Syria, the mainstream Sunni Muslim Brotherhood in Egypt was never drawn into an armed confrontation with the Egyptian regime. But not all of those on the flanks and fringes of the Muslim Brotherhood in Egypt, or who took up the banners of political Islam, were so patient, or so convinced by the long war of position. They, like the 'northern' wing of the Muslim Brotherhood in Syria, wanted to confront the regime, engage in spectacular acts, spark a popular uprising, and seize the citadel of state power, in order to create an Islamic state by force and then use the state to create an Islamic society. Just as in Syria, these activists were influenced by the writings of Sayyid Qutb, and, like Islamists everywhere, were enormously inspired by the Iranian revolution of 1979, in spite of its Shi'ism. The new religious politics trumped sect. Within their ranks were also those who were horrified by what they saw as Sadat's capitulation to the Jewish state when he signed a separate peace on a nationalist basis which left the Palestinians without a homeland, reneged on the desired unity of the Muslim world, and engaged in a peace treaty with a Western and imperialist implant. Many were unimpressed by the silence from Al-Azhar which protested not (Burgat 2003: 53), and the lack of action from the Muslim Brotherhood, which protested only somewhat. A very small number were ready to translate their grievances into militant action.

The long-dormant notion of armed *jihad* was re-discovered. Muhammad Faraj (1954–82) was a graduate in electrical engineering, an administrator at Cairo University, and a mosque preacher. He urged the return of the 'neglected obligation' – *jihad* for the sake of God – as the sole way to raise the 'tower of Islam' anew (Faraj 1980: 4). He led the highly clandestine Cairo branch of the Islamist group Al-Jihad (founded 1979) and was involved in the plan to assassinate the President, which was carried out with spectacular success in October 1981. The idea was to trigger a popular uprising. But, beyond various confrontations with security forces in Asyut, the wider rising did not materialize. Faraj was executed in 1982 (Kepel 1985).

A number of small militant groups committed to withdrawal, vanguardism and armed confrontation survived the repression, and by the early 1990s were able to commence a longer campaign of attacks on regime targets. Some Islamists were strongly opposed to Mubarak's willing co-operation with the US-led coalition of Arab states that ousted Iraq from Kuwait. They read this as the collaboration of a deviant regime with US imperialist designs in the Islamic heartlands of the Arabian peninsula.

These militants stood little chance of achieving their maximalist goals, however, especially when ordinary Egyptians were not convinced of their political programme, and were hit by their attacks on the tourist trade (Rubin 2002). Most of these militants undertook an *ijtihad* renouncing the use of armed struggle from prison between 1997 and 1999, arguing that *jihad* was now a collective duty, determined by qualified and represented *ulema*, and a prerogative of the state. This was a stark reversal of their earlier position that *jihad* could be declared as an individual duty by a dissident leader (Gerges 2005: 200). They simultaneously announced their support for crucial aspects of the regime's neo-liberal programme (Munib 2010), with many leaving prison exhausted (Gerges 2005: 151–65). An important legacy of their militancy was the paramilitarization of sections of the police and security forces (Gunning 2012).

The Iranian revolution of 1979

On 11 February 1979, Tehran's radio station declared: 'This is the voice of Tehran, the voice of true Iran, the voice of the revolution' (cited in Abrahamian 1982: 529). While not one of the post-independence Arab regimes was overthrown by the protest movements – Islamist, Leftist or Palestinian – that confronted them in the 1970s, 1980s and 1990s, Iran was different. Transpiring in one of the largest states in the region, the revolution was an extraordinary, even 'unthinkable' event, notoriously unpredicted by most officials and academics, rapid (with much of the action unfolding in less than six months), and involving sweeping and enduring political, economic, cultural and geopolitical change. The revolution brought down an experienced monarch, a stable regime enjoying rent and wealth from billions of dollars in oil exports, and fortified by a fearsome security apparatus, the largest military in the region, and favoured by the support of the world's most powerful countries (Kurzman 2004: 2).

Unlike 1789, 1917 or 1949, this revolution was unattributable to defeat in war, a financial crisis, a peasant rebellion or a disgruntled military, or the prior breakdown of the state, because none of these things had taken place or existed in Iran. Classical, structuralist theories of social revolution (Skocpol 1979) did not appear to explain everything. The explanatory bottom line, however, in much of the most important scholarship continued to turn on great structures, capitalism, modernization, East and West. Abrahamian, for example, situated the revolution in the great clashing structures of a politics of uneven development:

[B]y 1977 the gulf between the developing socio-economic system and the under-developed political system was so wide that an economic crisis was able to bring down the whole regime. In short, the revolution took place neither because of overdevelopment nor because of under-development but because of uneven development (Abrahamian 1982: 427).

In similar structuralist mode, Halliday and Alavi emphasized the importance of the development of capitalism and tradition:

the main reason why the revolution occurred was that conflicts generated in capitalist development intersected with resilient institutions and popular attitudes which resisted the transformation process (Halliday and Alavi 1988: 39).

Keddie placed a greater emphasis on resistance to Westernization (Keddie 1988), while Arjomand tended to assimilate the revolution to a fundamentalist revolt against modernity itself (Arjomand 1989). Skocpol revised her own theory, paying more attention to both culture on the one hand, and the mass-based movement aiming to overthrow the social order on the other. Nonetheless, the autonomous organizational capacities and resources that Skocpol now saw as fundamental to the revolution were, even in Skocpol's revision, provided by the dense structure of Iran's urban communities and the entrenched power and resonance of Shi'a Islam (Skocpol 1982).

Research in the 1990s and 2000s has often taken aim at this structuralism. Kurzman, especially by focusing on the more spontaneous and informally organized forms of activism, went so far as to reject conventional modes of causal explanation altogether, emphasizing unpredictability and lack of information, and pointing to the importance of the reconstruction of the lived experience of the revolution, looking for the moment when perceptions united around the viability of a revolutionary movement, a powerfully mobilizing perception in its own right (Kurzman 2004). Shakibi emphasized the failures of the shah himself, whose actions created a 'hole' in the centre of the state that led to paralysis and breakdown (Shakibi 2007: viii). The dynamics of contention, including leadership, ideology, the interactions between different segments of the movement, elite actions and contingency clearly played an important role in the making of the revolution in Iran. Whatever else it was, 1979 was a startling demonstration of the revolutionary power of Islamist politics and mass mobilization to overthrow completely an incumbent regime and establish a radical alternative.

The shah spoke to *The Guardian* newspaper in 1974:

Just imagine Iranians, if they are Iranians, demonstrating against their leader after what we have done with them. It is true hegemony that we have in our country. Everybody is behind their monarch, with their souls, with their hearts (cited in Shakibi 2007: 196).

If sincere, the shah was grossly mistaken: a wide variety of social groups had reasons to mobilize in various ways in Iran in the 1970s: the *ulema* whom the shah had denounced as 'medieval black reactionaries' and whose social position and material interests had been eroded since the 1950s; merchants and bazaaris against whom the shah intervened with regulations, invective, and political and fiscal impositions, and who were losing out to the wealthy elite families that surrounded the court; a liberal intelligentsia chafing under authoritarian rule; workers protesting pay and conditions in Iran's substantial industrial sector (Bayat 1987); rural–urban migrants who found themselves in shanty towns and largely excluded from the fruits of the White Revolution and GDP growth of the 1960s and 1970s (Bayat 1997);

peasants who had not been included in the land reform measures or who suffered from a lack of services, or grinding poverty; and poorer women who felt permanently excluded from the models of 'West-toxicated' femininity associated with an urban, upper-class elite (Paidar 1995). The *dramatis personae* of the various leaderships, their rank and file, and the participants in the mass demonstrations of 1978 were drawn from all of these strata – although unevenly – with peasants and slum-dwellers perhaps the least mobilized, and with seminarians, Left and liberal intelligentsia, and workers perhaps the most, or at least the most decisively so.

While the revolution was made by nationalists, liberals, socialists and millions of ordinary people as well as by Islamists, it was undoubtedly the latter under Khomeini who hegemonized the movement even before the seizure of power, and were the main if by no means uncontested architects of the Islamic republic as it developed in the 1980s. Ayatollah Khomeini was, on the one side, a senior cleric from Qom in his late 70s, with great stature in the seminary, and on the other an unwavering, long-standing political opponent of the shah. Khomeini took Reza Shah to task as far back as the 1940s for maltreating the clergy and his first major political work, published in 1943, argued on behalf of establishing an Islamic system of government (Abrahamian 1982: 425). Barely stirring from the seminary during the secular nationalist mobilization of the 1951–3 period, he started to speak out in 1962–3 against the king of kings after the liberal nationalists had been repressed and after the death of his quietist mentor Boroujerdi in 1961. While opposition to land reform and women's franchise of the shah's White Revolution was common currency among the Shi'a clergy, with similar stirrings in Iraq, 'Khomeini, revealing a masterful grasp of mass politics, scrupulously avoided the former issue and instead hammered away on a host of other concerns that aroused greater indignation among the general population' – the lack of democracy, corruption, the economic needs of merchants, workers and peasants, indiscriminate Westernization, and oil sales to Israel (Abrahamian 1982: 425). These concerns were articulated among the crowds who took action, demonstrated and destroyed property in the upheaval of June 1963 in Iran. Khomeini's discourse already presented in embryonic form the development of a popular and revolutionary Shi'ism that spoke in a language that far transcended the corporate interests of the Shi'a *ulema*.

By the late 1960s, in exile, received by the Al-Shiraziyyin in Karbala, and drawing inspiration from the theories of Islamic polity that were already being developed there by both Al-Sadr and Al-Shirazi, Khomeini started to demand an end to the Pahlavi monarchy and the institution of an Islamic government and rule of the jurisprudent (*velayat-e faqih*), lecturing on this in Najaf in the late 1960s, and publishing thereafter. Khomeini acted on his own initiative. And his theories were his own, forged in the context of a Shi'a politicization.

From exile in Iraq, Khomeini devoted himself to bringing such an Islamic government about. He was the head of the militant clerical opposition as it developed in Iran, and directed an 'informal secret network', based in the mosques and seminaries, and led on the ground by senior clerics, such as Montazeri and Beheshti, former students of Khomeini himself, many others from in and around the seminary system (Abrahamian 1982: 475), which had enjoyed long-standing traditions of independence from the state, and offered an important – if by no means free or fully protected – space in which mobilization (meeting, preparation and organization) could take place (cf. Kurzman 2004: 41–3). Khomeini never deviated from the strategy of building a broad, revolutionary coalition with himself at the head. The clearly theocratic themes of his lectures to theology students were soft-pedalled in his proclamations to the public (Abrahamian 1982: 478), which focused on anti-imperialism, full national independence, Islamic justice for the poor, helping the farmers, protecting the working masses, and safeguarding basic freedoms (Abrahamian 1982: 479).

While the communist Tudeh Party never regained the force it had before 1953 because of repression and division, and ceased to play an important role, the remaining significant, organized long-standing opponents of the shah included the 'constitutional' clergy, the liberal-nationalists, the followers of Ali Shariati, and a number of small guerrilla groups.

The moderate clerical opposition were headed by Ayatollah Golpayegani. They sought a constitutional monarchy along the lines of the 1905–9 period, in which the Supplementary Laws had promised a certain, relatively limited place for the *ulema* as overseers of legislation. Active in the 1960s and 1970s, and seeking to preserve the monarchy, they kept open lines of communication with the shah, pursuing a gradualist path and lobbying behind the scenes to protect the interests of the religious establishment.

The repression of Mosaddeq's National Front in 1953 gave rise to a number of movements and organizations – which attempted to continue and develop the nationalist and constitutionalist legacy of Mosaddeq, while struggling to situate these threads within a revitalized attention to religion and socio-economic questions. These included the National Resistance Movement, a reconstituted National Front, and the Liberation Movement, founded amid the relaxation of police controls in the early 1960s (Abrahamian 1982: 460). These movements split at various times, amid divisions, and were repressed, often operating in exile or in secret. Mehdi Bazargan (1906–95), who was to play a key role in 1978–9, was one of the founders of the Liberation Movement. He was trained in engineering, a university dean, religiously devout and anti-communist, he came to oppose theocracy, and sought a more liberal and constitutional arrangement that could include the shah. As such, he was an important figurehead for a vital constituency, both pious and less so, who were opposed to an overblown version of clerical rule.

The other key figure of the Liberation Movement, and its outstanding intellectual, was Ali Shariati (1933–77), who taught by choice in provincial elementary schools in the 1950s, studied sociology and Islamic studies in Paris in the early 1960s, taught at Mashhad university, and then lectured at the Husseineh-i Ershad, a religious meeting hall financed by veterans of the Liberation Movement, from 1967 until its suppression in 1972 (Abrahamian 1982: 466). Ali Shariati was imprisoned from 1972 to 1975, and then kept under house arrest until 1977 when he was exiled to London. He died suddenly, ostensibly of a heart attack, in May of that year. Ali Shariati was vital for elaborating and disseminating the intellectual edifice of a popular, revolutionary Shi'ism, fusing popular sovereignty, Marxism and revolutionary Third Worldism (which he had discovered in the Paris of the national liberation movements in the early 1960s) on the one hand, with Shi'a traditions of protest against social injustice and tyranny on the other. 'Shariati made the case that the essence of Shi'ism, and indeed of Islam, lay in activism in defense of justice and equity' (Chatterjee 2011: 198). This reading was not only a profoundly anti-quietist reading of Shi'ism (against the dominant trend), it also made the people, not the clergy, centrally responsible for revolutionary activism entitled to overthrow an unjust and inequitable government. Further, the content of injustice was deeply coloured by socio-economic questions, the idea of the rich oppressing the hungry and the poor.

A number of small guerrilla groups, in ideological colours ranging from Marxism to Islamism, drawn from the ranks of the urban intelligentsia, and influenced by the theory and practice of guerrilla warfare associated with Castro, Diap and Mao, launched an armed struggle against the shah's government on 8 February 1971, counting on a seizure of power by force and insurrection. They were small in number, and motivated not by economic deprivation but by 'social discontent, moral indignation and political frustration' (Abrahamian 1982: 481). These groups, like the jihadists of Egypt, were unable to trigger wider protests of any substance, and, while their organizations were by no means completely destroyed, the regime more or less prevented them from taking further action until the very last stages of the revolution. As the Pahlavi state began to collapse, however, these groups swung into action to play a vital role, delivering what Abrahamian calls the '*coup de grâce*' to the regime by taking on the shah's Imperial Guard and distributing arms to demonstrators (Abrahamian 1982: 495).

Between the failure of the guerrilla campaign of the early 1970s, and the last moments of the Pahlavi monarchy, three major rounds of protest have usefully been discerned, characterized by distinctive sociologies, ideal and material interests, and effectivity. Each round responded to the way the shah vacillated between repression, paralysis and concession, each round drew in contentious actors in greater numbers, and each ending up confirming rather than contradicting the central place of Khomeini in the revolution.

First, between January and October 1977, a new wave of protest was joined around issues of human and to some extent political rights, especially involving the urban, middle classes and liberal intelligentsia. Open letters were sent, critical reading groups established, and semi-public protest meetings were set up. Hundreds of people were involved. And, while these relatively well-heeled forms of protest still encountered repression, there is plenty of evidence to suggest that there was a limited political opening, a relaxation of some repressive measures, and that this had something to do with the Carterite Breeze of that year. Jimmy Carter's presidential campaign of 1976 did emphasize the promotion of human rights, the shah was anxious about this, and some liberals were incentivized to protest because they believed that the shah would not 'dare jail all of us in the present climate on human rights' (Kurzman 2004: 12, 18). These liberal actions did not on their own, however, produce discernible change on the ground, nor should their size and momentum be exaggerated. As the year drew on, the shah's regime resorted increasingly to repression, while Carter in November 1977 dropped the question of human rights. Poetry readings and moderate oppositionist gatherings were attacked by thugs and beatings administered (Kurzman 2004: 20).

Starting in October 1977, however, in spite and perhaps because of the return to a more repressive stance, protest demonstrations and civil resistance against the shah broke out, drawing in wider and particularly Islamist constituencies. Islamists and Khomeini supporters started to mobilize. Demonstrations were triggered by bad news from Iraq – the death of Mostafa Khomeini on 23 October 1977, the son of the Ayatollah, his aide, and a respected religious figure in his own right. Islamists believed that he was assassinated by SAVAK. 'Death to the Shah' was chanted in public protests for perhaps the first time (Kurzman 2004: 25). Islamists organized the traditional forty-day mourning ceremony for Mostafa on 2 December 1977. The event was not simply a religious ritual but an organized political protest with thousands of attendees, involving long lists of political demands, from freedom of speech to the banning of pornography (Kurzman 2004: 29). Religious activists were joined by those who had never demonstrated before. The mourning ceremonies continued until June 1978 and then were discontinued.

A new phase began in August 1978, when demonstrations broke out on a mass scale, and, together with strike action, they paralysed the country, generating a revolutionary situation. By the first week of November, almost the entire country had walked off the job: newspapers, airlines, railways, customs, banks, and above all the oil industry – on which the regime depended – were paralysed (Kurzman 2004: 76ff.). The non-violent urban demonstrations were among the largest protest events in regional and even global history. The protests of 10–11 December 1978 included perhaps 6–9 million people (Kurzman 2004: 122). Alliances between merchants, intelligentsia and clergy were consolidated. And there were attempts to form a compromise ministry with the veteran liberal politician Shahpour Bakhtiar. It was too little, too late, as, with hundreds dead at the hands of repression, millions on the streets were shouting for the shah to go. 'Neither East nor West, Islamic Republic', went the chant of the crowd.

The shah left Iran for exile on January 16, 1979 as the last Persian monarch. In the resulting power vacuum, Khomeini returned to Tehran, greeted by several million Iranians. Power was held for a mere thirty-seven days by a caretaker regime, which collapsed on 11 February when guerrillas and rebel troops overwhelmed troops loyal to the shah in armed street fighting. A revolutionary regime led by Khomeini was installed. Iran then voted by national referendum to become an Islamic republic on 1 April 1979, and in December of that year voted on a new democratic–theocratic hybrid constitution whereby Khomeini became Supreme Leader of the country.

Much debated, the shah's military and political vacillation was a factor that is hard to ignore. Quite unlike the Ba'thist regimes in Syria or in neighbouring Iraq during the same period (Tripp 2013: 81), the shah did hesitate to unleash the full weight of available repressive capacity against the crowds. Here the stick was used inconsistently, and in reality the shah offered few carrots. Time and again, large unarmed crowds, and substantial protest movements, have either been dispersed, crushed or driven into clandestine armed struggle and civil war when incumbent regimes have unleashed merciless violence. This phenomenon was witnessed in 1982 and 2011–12 in Syria, in Iraq in 1991, in Algeria in 1992, and in Bahrain in 2011. It was witnessed outside the region in Tiananmen Square in 1989 – although arguably the protest movement was not nearly as developed as in Iran. The army deployment in Egypt in January 1977 certainly brought the uprising to a complete stop. The reverse – when the army refuses to shoot and the crowds make gains – was also a marked feature in both Tunisia and Egypt in 2011. It was also at work in Eastern Europe in 1989–90, when Gorbachev made clear that there would be no repeat of the military interventions in Hungary or Czechoslovakia. 'The condition of the success of . . . "people power" revolution', write McAdam and Sewell, 'is that the regimes in power be unwilling to use their superior military force in putting the demonstrations down' (McAdam and Sewell 2001: 115). Given this evidence, it is hard indeed to discount the shah's hesitation in the face of a 'military solution'. Such an attempt might of course have split the army and been catastrophic for the regime. All the more so because the Iranian revolution was not simply a matter of people power, but was also endowed with strong leadership. What actually happened on the ground, for whatever reason, was that the protest movement in Iran was not eliminated with brutal efficacy. On the other hand, repression on a wide scale continued at a level which generated collective outrage, a powerful motivator for public protests (cf. Kurzman 2004: 109–17).

The shah's *political* vacillation was equally important. He acted politically by turns as if everything could continue as before, as if a new and more mobilized and totalitarian single-party system was what he sought, and finally as if there could be a constitutional monarchy in Iran. The abortive attempt to create a one-party state in 1975 'weakened the whole regime, cut the monarchy further off from the country, and intensified resentment among diverse groups' (Abrahamian 1982: 446), especially merchants and *ulema*. While the attempt to reform at the last minute was too little, too late, none was convincing, and none mapped out a political vision adequate to the moment. Indeed, many of the shah's own supporters, sections of the wealthy elite, more worried by the shah's 'weakness' than his dictatorship, decided that the writing was on the wall, and started to leave the country in large numbers in late 1978.

To understand why the shah's politics was not adequate to the moment, however, it is crucial to examine the revolutionary movement itself and its interactions with the shah's policies. For one thing, the shah's reluctance to use the full weight of military repression may have stemmed from a fear that this would fracture the conscript army in the face of the appeal of the protests (Tripp 2013: 81). The unity of the revolutionary coalition under Khomeini, moreover, was not simply a reaction to a despised regime, but arguably owed something to Khomeini's style of leadership. The Ayatollah managed both to conciliate many different groups on the one hand, while coming across as a 'stern and unwavering' idealist (Batatu 1981: 588) on the other. He appeared as a leader with gravitas who stood above the fray (and who some under-estimated as a mere figurehead), as well as a charismatic and uncompromising opponent of the shah. Khomeini refrained from engaging in potentially divisive in-fighting between ideological positions or factions in the broader movement, and he hammered away on themes of universal import, rather than the narrow interests of the clergy. Khomeini refused to oppose Ali Shariati, for example, who was denounced by associates of Khomeini as that 'so-called Islamic expert'. He thus maintained a unifying position, and 'intentionally propagated a vague populist message', factors which subsequently laid the basis for

a broad alliance of social forces ranging from the bazaars and the clergy to the intelligentsia and the urban poor, as well as of political organizations varying from the religious Liberation Movement and the secular National Front to the new guerrilla groups emerging from Shariati's followers in the universities (Abrahamian 1982: 479).

Revolutionary unity also owed something, arguably, to ideology. It was partly that Khomeini had a blueprint which could serve as a frame for organizing ideas and resources and directing energies. This blueprint may have been more important after the seizure of power than before. In terms of revolutionary mobilization, the ideas of Ali Shariati may have played a more decisive role. He certainly became possibly the most popular ideologue, especially among the laity, of the revolution. His importance was arguably in forming a key node of articulation between the more theocratic and clerical activities of Khomeini and his supporters, and the more secular and rights-based concerns of Leftists, workers, subaltern social groups, nationalists and urban intelligentsia. The sorts of conflicts between secular students and the Muslim Brotherhood witnessed on campus in Egypt in the early 1970s (Abdallah 2009), for example, were not as acute in 1970s Iran. That Shariati provided reasons why these conflicts did not necessarily need to exist, as long as Shi'ism was properly understood, arguably played a role in unifying forms of activism that might otherwise have conflicted with one another. Shariati's message also made it easier to politicize Shi'a ritual – an innovation of the 1960s and 1970s (Kurzman 2004: 54). If Shi'ism was in essence popular and revolutionary, as Shariati insisted, then it was only natural that the forty-day mourning ceremonies should be used to stage popular and revolutionary demands. For sections of the urban intelligentsia, a ritual that looked backward and arcane became a site of protest, and an important one in propelling the second wave of protests from 1977 to 1978. This was not just a matter of ideological articulation, but also a matter of tactics. Revolutionary Shi'ism enjoined the use of tactics – mass demonstrations, strikes, civil disobedience and uprising *inter alia* – in which unaffiliated constituencies could participate. These forms of mobilization were open to non-members of this or that group. This was quite unlike the more divisive tactics used by the Muslim Brotherhood in Egypt in the late 1940s. The Brothers eschewed forms of political contention (as opposed to service provision) in which wider constituencies, and non-members, could actively participate. By doing so, the Muslim Brotherhood cut itself off from a wider participation and thus underlined its separateness from the politics of the wider society, arousing division and inhibiting popular unity. In contrast, the revolutionary Shi'ism of Ali Shariati and the tactics deployed by the wider movement, were capable of uniting and mobilizing highly diverse constituencies.

Second, people power, the moment when millions of previously unorganized and relatively apathetic people came out onto the streets or walked off the job to demonstrate their rejection of the existing order, what Trotsky called the 'most indubitable feature of a revolution' cannot be ignored. The revolutionary leadership could not have done what it did without the demonstrations expressing the will of the people, and the institutional paralysis of the economy and the regime that followed the strikes and mass demonstrations of late 1978. The mass insurrection in Iran, based on the decisions of millions of ordinary people forcefully entering the political field, was in many ways, as Kurzman insists, difficult to retroactively predict. It was certainly not sparked by a vanguardist armed struggle. On the other hand, propitious conditions were engendered by interactions with repression, the vacillation of the Shah, memories of revolution (1905) and coup (1953), the one bringing optimism, the other outrage, and wider non-violent campaigns of opposition capable of having broad appeal and encouraging broad participation.

Finally, the more or less fortuitous way in which people power, assorted leaderships and the shah's vacillation worked together to confirm Khomeini's position and reinforce the unity of the revolution, was important. The non-Khomeinist sites of organized opposition in Iran either reached a dead end, were repressed or split, or made important contributions without threatening Khomeini's key position as the protests mounted in 1978–9.

First, Khomeini's main rival among the clergy, the moderate opposition, became untenable in 1975–7 when the shah himself 'slammed shut the doors, mounted the assault on the bazaars and the seminaries, and, through the Resurgence party, pressed to take over the entire religious establishment' (Abrahamian 1982: 475).

Second, the position of those of a more secular persuasion who looked to Bazargan and sought a constitutional monarchy was made completely untenable by the sea of blood that the shah put between himself and the people in late 1978.

Third, Ali Shariati, without being organizationally linked to Khomeini, made a contribution without threatening Khomeini's leadership, partly because he was more intellectual than leader, but also because he was dead, which may or may not have been the work of SAVAK's repression.

Fourth, workers and public sector employees had their own grievances and ideas, and their mass strikes in late 1978 made their own contribution to the revolution – organized by no 'mastermind at the top'. Bayat emphasizes how the relatively short-lived worker-organized *shuras*, forms of shopfloor democracy that spread in late 1978, 'the material expression of their [workers'] strong desire for control over the organization and administration of production' (Bayat 1987: 151), were not invented or led by non-workers.

Finally, the guerrilla groups made their own key contribution at the last moment to the complete collapse of the regime – without challenging Khomeini's leadership. In other words, over the course of the revolution, in a process that was not masterminded by anyone, Khomeini's rivals fell to one side, and other elements made key contributions.

In short, the revolution was made, it did not come. It is hard to ignore the importance of Khomeini's leadership, ideology and people power at the level of the revolutionary movement which, together with a dose of contingency, and in interaction with the mis-steps of the shah, can help account for the unity, force and outcome of the revolutionary upsurge. That these factors came together at the same moment was not a structural necessity, determined by capitalism, modernization, the clash between East and West, between tradition and modernity, or the politics of uneven development. Nor was it the work of this or that all-seeing, all-controlling actor, but in part a contingency. As Kamal Jumblatt said in regard to revolution, this time in the wake of failure, not success, 'there is something adventuristic about the whole thing' (Jumblatt 1982: 15).

Unlike the 'progressive' republics of the Arab world, which came to power through nationalist movements, and who defeated their opponents during the 1970s and 1980s, the Pahlavi monarchy owed its post-1953 existence and basic authoritarian form to a neo-colonial intervention against the nationalist and democratic government that had nationalized Iran's oil industry in 1951. The Iranian revolution of 1979 was in part the unfinished business of 1953, a continuation of the revolutionary politics of national liberation and socialism against the CIA-sponsored coup of 1953 and the neo-colonialism it embodied.

Opposition to the 'Great Satan' (the United States), the main sponsor of the shah, was substantially more developed in Iran in the 1970s, and far more central to activism in that country, than it was in other states and protest movements of the region between the 1960s and the 1980s.

However, the fact that most prominent slogans of the revolution depicted the United States in a religious language (as a 'satan') offers a clue to what was even more important for a history of contentious politics: the overthrow of the Pahlavi monarchy in 1979 was the seminal event in the new regional politics of Islamism. It was the culmination of a mobilizing project launched by a relatively tiny number of Shi'a *ulema* and lay intellectuals in Iraq and Iran from the late 1950s onwards. The post-revolutionary Iranian state bore a remarkable resemblance to the blueprint drawn up years before by Ayatollah Khomeini, Al-Sadr and Al-Shirazi, with a division of powers between an elected presidency and executive on the one hand, and the Shi'a religious authorities having the final say over legislation on the other. Shariati's revolutionary Shi'ism managed to incorporate revolution, popular sovereignty and socialism in a way that the Sunni movements in the Arab world of the same period never did. After 1979, the language of revolution and resistance ceased to be the virtual monopoly of secularists (whether liberal, nationalist or Leftist) and was appropriated by Islamist movements in various parts of the region. The rise of Hizbullah was a case in point.

Lebanon and Hizbullah

Not long after the PLO fighters were evacuated from Lebanon in September 1982, the Israeli forces in Beirut and the south were hit by a series of ambushes and attacks of unknown origin. Then, on 11 November 1982, a Peugeot car laden with explosives struck the seven-storey Israeli military headquarters in the southern coastal city of Sur (Tyre). The explosion levelled the building and killed seventy-five Israeli soldiers, border policemen and Shin Bet agents, almost unprecedented fatalities for the Israeli security forces from a single attack. The tactic was new, a martyrdom operation carried out by a secret guerrilla movement, which was also new: the Party of God, or Hizbullah.

The efficiency of the attack was a sign of things to come. Drawing Lebanese Shi'a from almost all walks of life into its ranks over the following decades, the tightly organized guerrilla movement, with cadres, weapons and training supplied by Iran, and with increasingly strong relations with Syria, added a political party in 1992, developed an array of public and social services, including women's organizations, and increasingly held positions in the Lebanese government and in the municipalities, especially in the southern suburbs of Beirut and the south. In May 2000, it achieved the historic distinction of becoming the only resistance movement in the region to force a full Israeli withdrawal from occupied territory. In 2006, the Party won popularity across the region, but not necessarily in Lebanon, by surviving a devastating US-backed Israeli bombardment and forcing Israel to take casualties and withdraw without achieving its goals (Norton 2007: 145ff.). Just as the PLO was turning to the path of negotiation, Hizbullah took up the mantle of the erstwhile pan-Arab and Palestinian secularists, promoting an uncompromising armed struggle under Islamist banners against the Zionist foe and claiming to stand in solidarity with Palestinians, Arabs and Muslims everywhere (Khalili 2007b).

The Party's leadership was initially furnished by a group of prominent, politicized Shi'a clergy, while cadres were drawn from young men who had gained experience fighting for Palestinians or sections of Amal, ex-members of Musa Sadr's Movement of the Dispossessed, students linked to Amal, pious volunteers for social services at mosques, other recruits from villages who had confronted the Israeli occupation, and contingents of revolutionary guards sent from Iran. Over time, the Party drew in a far more diverse sociology, women active in the many social and public services as well as media activities, research centres, clinics, libraries, charitable and outreach centres *inter alia*, disenfranchised Shi'a from the south and the slums surrounding Beirut, urban professionals, students, academics, journalists, writers, intellectuals, workers, school pupils, rural–urban migrants, peasants and others – almost all Shi'a. Between 1978 and 1982, horror at the Israeli invasions of 1978 and 1982 mingled with inspiration from the Islamic revolution in Iran. After 1979, many Shi'a faithful now looked beyond Najaf to the new religious authority, Ayatollah Khomeini.

One of the co-founders of the movement was Abbas Musawi (1952–92), a Shi'a cleric from the Beqa'a who had spent eight years before his return to Lebanon in 1978 studying in the *hawza* at Najaf, where he was influenced by Khomeini and Muhammad Baqir Al-Sadr alike. The other co-founder, and first Secretary-General, Subhi Al-Tufayli (b. 1948), was another cleric who had studied for almost a decade in Najaf and become a close follower of Khomeini. While the Iran connection to Hizbullah is often thought of solely in terms of geopolitics and weapons supplies, we should not miss the ideological connection to the world of politicized and popular Shi'ism, which transcended the borders of Iran, included Iraq and the Gulf and was just as important as guns, money, and administration, as it helped to form the politics, identities and principles of the founders of Hizbullah even before the Iranian revolution and the beginnings of state support for the movement in 1982. In this sense, the founders of Hizbullah were the heirs of Musa Al-Sadr, who also participated in this transnational revival. Al-Sadr himself was killed in Libya in 1978, and his movement in Lebanon fell apart. But coercion and even the disintegration of a movement did not destroy the cause. The mantle of popular, political, Shi'ism was seized by the new Party of God.

In addition to Musa Al-Sadr, Muhammad Baqr Al-Sadr and Ayatollah Khomeini, two clerics based in Lebanon but not active in the Party were also an inspiration to the founders of Hizbullah, and shaped the perceptions of their constituencies. One was Ayatollah Muhammad Mahdi Shamseddine (1936–2001). From a family of Lebanese origin, he was born in Najaf and lived there until 1969, studying under Muhsin Al-Hakim, and working with Musa Al-Sadr, Muhammad Baqir Al-Sadr and other influential figures of the Shi'a political revival. A cleric in Lebanon, he co-founded the Islamic Shi'a Council in Lebanon in the 1970s. He made a relatively ineffectual attempt to organize armed resistance against Israel in 1983, but was above all an intellectual who avoided politics, published and lectured, and led publishing and cultural organizations. He called for armed resistance to the Israeli occupation, advocated in anti-sectarian terms for a civic state (al-dawla al-madaniyya), and attended to matters of piety, doctrine and faith, winning a following among those who looked to Shi'ism for guidance in manners, morals and everyday life.

More important because of his wider constituency was Ayatollah Muhammad Hussein Fadlallah (1935–2010), a spiritual inspiration to Party leaders and guide to its followers and supporters, but never a leader or member of the Party itself. He was an independent cleric and exponent of the faith in lectures, publications and lessons, who also founded schools and other institutions (a women's cultural centre, for example). He was from a family of Lebanese origin but was born and raised in Najaf, studying in the seminary there, and only coming to Lebanon on a full-time basis in 1966. He spoke out against the Israeli invasion of 1982.

The ideas of these men had an important influence on those determined to act in the new context and dissatisfied with existing groupings and factions. They agreed on three basic principles: Islam as the complete foundation for life in general and the Party in particular; resistance against Israeli occupation; and legitimate leadership rooted in the enforceable rule of the jurisprudent, that is, Khomeini, whose sponsorship was sought and obtained (Qassem 2010: 64–5). The intellectual content of these founding principles owed much to the clerics: Islam as a comprehensive guide, a conviction and a code of law, as enjoining self-discipline, as concerned with politics and justice, together with an endorsement of *jihad* of all kinds (military and otherwise), and the endorsement of Islam as a revolutionary force, a notion that owed much to Fadlallah (Carré 1991: 229–33). The Islam of Hizbullah also involved the prohibition of interest-bearing transactions, and a notion of social responsibility symbolized by charity (*zakat*). Also basic was the need for persuasion and the use of reason, the idea that there is no compulsion in religion, a rather pale echo of Ali Shariati's insistence on popular sovereignty, and the affirmation that piety (not race, colour or background) was the measure of the individual. The Party was also inspired by, and sought to cultivate, a culture of martyrdom, with Imam Hussein as the role model (Qassem 2010: 100). The religious authority of the jurisprudent, which was necessarily political in this context, was considered universal and binding (Qassem 2010: 119ff.). Hizbullah exhorted the need for an Islamic political system (for example, in 1985), but was not very specific about what this meant for Lebanon. The initial disavowal of political sectarianism was certainly a necessary precondition for the development of an Islamic state. With the end of the civil war, and the Lebanonization of the Party, talk of an Islamic state was increasingly toned-down, with the Party emphasizing that such a state could only come about through the free choice of the people (Qassem 2010: 82).

The fundamental goals of the movement were therefore to Islamize Lebanon, at the level of the state if possible, to evict the Israeli occupation, and to institute the rule of the jurisprudent in temporal and spiritual affairs. Following the Ta'if Accords of 1989, the end of the civil war, and Hizbullah's key decision to participate in Lebanese politics via the elections of 1992, attempts to implement an Islamic state or the rule of the jurisprudent increasingly receded into the background, the centrepiece of what is referred to as the Lebanonization of the movement. This move was the background to a greater focus on popular mobilization, and, with the exit from factional struggles that had broken out with Amal and others at the end of the civil war, a return to a thoroughgoing focus on armed resistance. Not for the first time, the goals of a movement changed to fit the moment, to accommodate developments for which no one had planned.

The Party was a organized on a disciplined, hierarchical, pyramidal basis strategically led by an executive committee, the Council (al-Shura), which after 1989 started to elect a Secretary-General, who expressed the Party's official position and had functions in supervision and coordination. The Council came to be at the top of a number of functionally differentiated 'assemblies' – political, executive, military, judicial and so on. Beyond the 'assemblies' were a wide variety of affiliated organizations, each having different kinds of relative autonomy.

This organizational framework ... encompassed those segments comprising fundamental believers in the Party's goals while honouring and maintaining inter-segment differences. It thus avoided the pitfall of excluding 'others' (Qassem 2010: 128).

The party made a strategic effort to avoid the exclusionary aspects of a hierarchical organization by allowing some graded and calibrated autonomy to its component parts. Hizbullah, in contrast to the PLO, took formal organization, functional differentiation and planning extremely seriously. It was distinctive in having a reputation for a lack of corruption within the ranks. Compared to the Muslim Brotherhood under Al-Banna, institutions, not just a sole leader, were vital in cohesion and coordination. While unaffiliated Syrian workers in Lebanon, for example, complained of the indiscipline of the Palestinian commandos, such stories about Hizbullah were absent, and anecdotes indicating the contrary were not uncommon (Chalcraft 2009).

Basic to the strategy of Hizbullah was armed struggle designed to inflict insecurity on Israel, through military casualties in Lebanon and civilian and military casualties in the north of Israel, a policy that Hizbullah reasoned would force the Zionist state to withdraw from occupied territory in Lebanon and allow Hizbullah to build up its forces in Lebanon. Hizbullah believed that this strategy would work because, first, it was feasible, in that Hizbullah assessed the Israeli occupation of south Lebanon to be vulnerable in point of the security of soldiers, and, second, it was effective, in that it would hit Israel at its most sensitive spot, its drive to create security and the protection for its Jewish citizens. Recruitment of fighters was launched in various districts and villages, with different levels of commitment and participation allowed, with all recruits taking part in 'military and cultural training, combat and post-guardianship, as well as any … functions required by the party' (Qassem 2010: 126).

Military tactics were those of classical guerrilla war: ambush, surprise, withdrawal, mobility, invisibility and unit autonomy – which were used in conjunction with advantages of terrain, strategic depth (going back to Iran through Syria), and links to an existing, occupied or bombarded population and constituency, who were ready to support the fighters, some of whom were part-time in any case, and which offered water in which the 'fish could swim'. Hizbullah also obtained from Syria or Iran Katyusha rockets, which, although fragile and slow to re-load, could deliver a high-explosive, and were easy to produce and inexpensive. They had already been used by Israel in the 1982 invasion. Their inaccuracy, when fired into northern Israel, meshed with Hizbullah's strategy of striking at Israel's security, because the killing of civilians would sow fear and challenge the Israeli leadership. Above all, Katyushas were truck-mounted, and so could be rapidly moved before being tracked and destroyed.

The other, even more important tactical innovation was the systematic use of martyrdom operations, one of the most explosive tools in the Party's arsenal. Self-sacrifice for a cause (whether national or religious) was not a new idea in general. Its most proximate use was among the 'mine-sweepers' who fought for Iran against Iraq – young Shi'a soldiers so committed to Iran and the revolution that they would walk into mine-fields in an organized fashion in order to detonate the mines, sacrificing their own lives in order to sweep the mine-fields clean to allow their compatriots to advance. This tactic was transformed into a guerrilla weapon of considerable effect, whereby Party fighters, suitably groomed, would drive a car or truck full of explosives to a key military target and explode it, attacks that were very difficult to stop. The fighter thus martyred would be celebrated, his family honoured and pensioned.

In addition to guerrilla warfare, and arguably as important in the long run, mass mobilization in the trenches and redoubts of civil society was highly ramified and basic to the strategy of Hizbullah, developing extensively from the mid-to-late 1980s onwards. Women's societies were created, often linked to local mosques or local cultural institutions: 'The objective was to achieve cultural and societal recruitment to the end of securing participation in the activities and general call of the Party' (Qassem 2010: 126). Youth participation and recruitment was channelled through the Imam Al-Mahdi scouts, also seen as a method for noting and responding to the 'young generation's needs' (Qassem 2010: 126). Independently run foundations and organizations were set up in education, health, culture, media, agriculture and construction, delivering on social services and public works, often for poorer strata. In construction, for example, the Jihad Al-Bina' Association was set up in 1985, its main task to rebuild homes destroyed by Israeli bombing, a task that it undertook over the following decades on a wide scale across the south with a minimum of corruption. Waste collection in the southern suburbs between 1988 and 1991, water distribution there after 1990, along with services to agriculture and villages in the south and the Beqa'a, ranging from electricity provision, to herbicide, to training in honey production, to cultural clubs, to mosque-building. In 2002, the Party founded the Islamic Health Organization, with a network of health clinics, some mobile to reach rural areas, and provision of free health-care and medication in scores of schools. There were scholarships for students, an institution for treating the wounded, an institution for taking care of families of martyrs, an institution for offering charity to orphans, the destitute and the displaced among other social services and public works (Qassem 2010: 166ff.). Women were particularly prominent in Hizbullah's media operations, which gave them a noteworthy public presence, and sometimes a 'hard-hitting and assertive' one (Baylouny 2013: 96). The Party also undertook recruitment activities targeting secondary-school pupils, university students and academics. It sought a presence in professional associations, syndicates or other societies. In short, Hizbullah was probably the most systematic and carefully organized mass-mobilizing popular movement in the history of the region.

This mass mobilization was linked to the considerable degree of hegemony won among the Shi'a of Lebanon. Hizbullah produced a 'holistic and integrated network' of values and practices, mobilizing a 'society of resistance' (*al-mujtama' al-muqawama*) – the basis of an 'Islamic sphere' (*al-hala al-islamiyya*) (Harb and Leenders 2005). They developed an aura of professionalism and capability in social affairs, and even urban planning and development (Harb 2008), mixing piety and modernity in a way that won the adherence of men and women alike (Deeb 2006). Women's capacity to challenge and push against the boundaries of Hizbullah's discourse, but without crossing certain red-lines (Baylouny 2013) was a part of this subtle incorporation. In this overall context, abstracted denunciations from the Left of Hizbullah's collaboration with neo-liberalism had little impact.

Nonetheless, with the end of the Israeli occupation in May 2000, amid its greatest victory ironically enough, the Party also lost much of its *raison d'être*, that is, to resist the Israeli occupation. Had it remained only a fighting force in the 1980s and 1990s, it is hard to envisage its survival. But, because of its ramified institutional capacities and committed social base, the Party neither dissolved nor relinquished its fighting capacity, now justified in relation to the defence of the south, a task that the Lebanese army was unwilling and unable to fulfil, and the liberation of the Sheba'a farms. In the 2000s, the Party turned more decisively towards obtaining a more secure position in the Lebanese state, gaining a minister in cabinet for the first time in April 2005. After May 2000, Hizbullah could no longer prioritize the resistance above everything else, a prioritization which had always been its formula for avoiding entanglements with factional, political and intra-Arab disputes. With a clear, organizing principle in disarray, entanglement was very difficult to avoid, as other priorities crept to the surface.

Why Hizbullah continued to require an armed wing, especially in the context of closer association with the Lebanese state, was a question in wider Lebanese and international circles that would not go away after May 2000. The armed requirement was only persuasive to the Party and its supporters. Moreover, Hizbullah's position, dictated by strategy not by principle, on the Syrian presence, which by 2005 was widely regarded as an iniquitous occupation long past its sell-by date (given that Israel was, debates over the Sheba'a farms aside, not occupying the south as it had been), also cost the group popularity, not only among non-Shi'a, but also among poor and working Shi'a themselves, whose wages and jobs were pressured by the Syrian workers, whose presence was then wrongly attributed to the Syrian army (Chalcraft 2009). Causes other than 'the Resistance' (monopolized by Hizbullah) were behind the enormous demonstrations that took place in the wake of Rafiq Al-Hariri's assassination in February 2005. Hizbullah was indeed not free from suspicion in the assassination of 'Mr Lebanon' itself. And, while the group survived an Israeli attempt to eliminate it during a large-scale bombardment of the Lebanese south and Beirut's southern suburbs in August 2006, many Lebanese blamed the suffering inflicted on Lebanon by Israel on Hizbullah, especially in the grim aftermath, something which cost the movement much popularity.

While the attempt to avoid being a state-within-a-state (as the PLO had become in Jordan) had been basic to the Party's thinking (Qassem 2010: 192), this attempt looked less plausible in the 2000s, especially when Hizbullah gunmen appeared on the streets of Beirut in May 2008, something the Party had striven to avoid, and which caused howls of alarm among its opponents. In 2011–12, when Hizbullah entered the Syrian civil war on the side of the Asad regime, a move which looked partisan and merely strategic, the popularity of the movement on the local and regional stage took another knock. Diminishing mass appeal locally contributed to making Hizbullah more rather than less dependent on its strategic relations with Iran and Syria, which in turn generated positions that looked more foreign and sectarian from a Lebanese perspective. The post-1992 formula of Lebanonization was seriously compromised. For all its wish to break down sectarianism in Lebanon, Hizbullah, with its exclusively Shi'a constituencies, never transcended, and instead contributed ultimately to entrenching, this logic, a factor which diminished its wider appeal in Lebanon, and restricted its constituency to the Shi'a. On the regional stage, and in absolute terms, the Shi'a of Lebanon were not a very large group, and they lived in a relatively small and militarily weak state. After May 2000, then, the future of Hizbullah, ironically enough, became increasingly uncertain.

While Hizbullah laid claim to solidarity with the Palestinians, the latter's extensive social mobilization in the Occupied Palestinian Territories in the 1970s and 1980s was stitched above all not into religious politics, but into those of secular nationalism, with Islamism, this time in the Muslim Brotherhood tradition, in only a flanking role. This social mobilization, and the repression that it encountered, paved the way for what became known as the first *intifada*.

The *intifada*, 1987–1991

On 8 December 1987, in front of hundreds of Palestinian witnesses, an Israeli tank transporter crashed into a row of cars at the Erez Checkpoint containing Palestinians returning to Gaza from work in Israel, killing four and injuring seven others seriously. Three of the dead were from Gaza's largest refugee camp, Jabalia. The funerals, held that evening, became demonstrations, which were harshly repressed, with at least one Palestinian fatality. The following day, protests and demonstrations spread rapidly in Gaza, the West Bank and East Jerusalem. The previous months had seen a marked increase in contentious incidents across the Occupied Palestinian Territories: there had been organizing, demonstrations, and scattered guerrilla operations which had met with Israeli repression and consequent outrage among Palestinians. Although the Israelis were slow to realize it (Y. Sayigh 1997: 607), however, the latest incident marked a moment at which a scale-shift began. Taking matters beyond demonstrations, confrontations and graffiti, youth now took control of whole neighbourhoods and camps, throwing up barricades of garbage, stone and burning tyres, and repelling soldiers with petrol bombs. Far from standing aside from, or even condemning, these resistant youth, the wider society participated in one way or another: shops were shut, businesses closed, popular committees were formed, students demonstrated and refused to go to classes, Palestinian workers refused to go to work in Israel, and a many-faceted campaign of civil disobedience was launched. The PLO in Tunis reacted slowly (Y. Sayigh 1997: 614–15), and, while the uprising had not been initiated by any of the established political actors, the key factions on the ground, who were numerous, and who had decades of experience, were mobilizing within days.

During what became known as the *intifada*, the mass of the Palestinian population rose up in anger and disgust in an attempt to 'shake off' (the literal meaning of the word *intifada*) an occupation they now signalled as unendurable. What maintained the momentum through at least two difficult years, however, was more than emotion, injustice and 'people power', but existing traditions of protest, prior forms of mobilization, and ongoing leadership, organization, a powerfully articulated set of identities and principles, a wide variety of creative and effective strategies and tactics, and a movement that at least until 1989 was able to achieve an impressive level of coherence. The *intifada* in some sense rescued the PLO, changed the calculations of Israel and other regional and international actors, altered European public opinion, and arguably played an important role, for better or worse, in bringing about the Madrid negotiations in 1991 and the Oslo process in 1993.

The armed struggle of 1968–82 may have produced a neopatrimonial state-in-waiting, now headquartered in Tunis, but millions of Palestinians were still stateless. The Israeli occupation of Gaza, East Jerusalem and the West Bank, territories seized by Israel during the 1967 war, was becoming increasingly permanent and intrusive. The leading factor was the greatly increased Israeli settlement of occupied land after the election of the Likud government in 1977. While settlements prior to 1977 had related to the logic of military control and water extraction, after 1977 they were part of a drive to take over what Israelis increasingly called Judea and Samaria, partly in the name of Israel's growing religious Right. Within a decade, tens of thousands of settlers sought permanent homes in the occupied territories, some 64,000 by 1988. Palestinians were physically displaced as a result, losing homes by demolition, and agricultural land by confiscation, factors provoking protest and repression, as well as encounters with settler violence. It became clear to many after 1977 that the colonization of land was a 'fact on the ground' designed to secure territorial expansion for the Israeli state, not a bargaining chip in a future 'land for peace' negotiation as some wishfully continued to think.

At the same time, the increased wages that Palestinians working over the Green Line (i.e. in pre-1967 Israel) had obtained in the 1970s were now a distant memory for the roughly 125,000 that made the daily trip in the early 1980s. Workers now had to face wage stagnation or unemployment during the economic downturn of the 1980s, increasingly obvious discrimination and inequality in regard to Israeli-Jewish workers, and the levy of taxes by the Israeli state to fund social security systems which did not cover or benefit Palestinian workers. Land and water resources were shrinking as a direct result of settlement, and the heavy integration of the Palestinian economy into the Israeli one implied an increasingly permanent political control (Hiltermann 1991: 31). Defence Minister Rabin's 1985 announcement that 'there will be no development in the occupied territories' (Y. Sayigh 1997: 608) reflected a wider reality whereby Israeli policies de-developed the Palestinian economy (Roy 1995).

During the 1970s and 1980s, in regard to the occupied territories, there was a slow and uneven turn by the PLO, and especially by factions on the ground, away from a focus on militant guerrilla action being carried out by scattered, usually male, armed cells and towards a strategy and practice of grassroots mobilization (Y. Sayigh 1997: 614) in unions, charities, women's committees, schools, universities, women's skills and so on. The DFLP underwent this shift, with notable attention to the mobilization of women: a women's committee, for example, organized health clinics, day care centres, and skills-training sessions during the 1980s (Hasso 2005: 25). In some respects, the factions were now catching up with the Palestinian communists, who, eschewing armed struggle, had long been devoted to such low-profile forms of mobilization.

The shift at the political level dovetailed with the more socially motivated grassroots action, undertaken by women, students, academics, unionists and others on their own initiative, which created 'a vast network of institutions and organizations ... whose dual aim it was (1) to provide services to the local community, and (2) to substitute for the missing state system' (Hiltermann 1991: 210). Even if local income-generation and empowerment relied on external sources of funding and was extremely difficult to achieve (Y. Sayigh 1997: 613), this network created an organizational basis which could be commandeered during the *intifada*.

These changes were partly the cause and partly the effect of another shift: the slow attrition of the domination of the traditional West Bank elite and the rise of a new activist generation composed of middle and lower-middle classes, educated peasants, and refugee camp residents – a development that accompanied a rise in forms of participatory politics, especially for women (Hasso 2005: 21).

It was not that these new civil society organizations spontaneously created the *intifada*, as some readings seem to imply (Hiltermann 1991: 174–5, 208). This is to evacuate the importance of the political field. Instead, heightened Israeli repression during the 1980s was partly in response to these new forms of mobilization and political organizing. Military orders, for example, issued during 1980–2, stated that Israel could dismiss elected union officials and ban candidates, and require university staff to sign a loyalty oath pledging to abstain from political activity, and to ban or confiscate outside funding to charitable societies. And, in 1985–6, Rabin resorted extensively to 'administrative detention, town arrest, dismissal from public sector employment, closure of offices and other facilities, and deportation' to decapitate PLO-backed institutions (Y. Sayigh 1997: 609).

The Iron Fist policy failed as new cadres stepped forward to replace deportees and protests and demonstrations were mounted, the repression of which contributed to the rising tide of tension that preceded the outbreak of the *intifada* itself. Incidents of stone-throwing, demonstrations and armed attacks rose significantly during the middle years of the 1980s (Y. Sayigh 1997: 608). By 1985, an estimated 250,000 Palestinians had experienced interrogation or detention. In December 1986, the fatal shooting by Israeli soldiers of two Palestinian students on campus at Birzeit University provoked demonstrations which were in turn broken up with force. During 1987, graffiti 'denounced the occupation, spoke of Palestinian rights, supported the PLO, and honored the martyrs' (Qumsiyeh 2011: 136). The use of curfew, forced closure of schools and universities, detention and beating became more common, ratcheting up the tension. Demonstrations against the killing of Palestinians during October and November 1987 were met with deadly force (Qumsiyeh 2011: 135–6).

Amid this acute conflict, the PLO appeared to the 'inside' (i.e. residents of the occupied territories) to be increasingly distant from the daily struggles of Palestinians. In November 1987, for example, the Arab summit in Amman focused on the Iran–Iraq War, and the Palestinian issue was sidelined (Qumsiyeh 2011: 135) adding to the sense that the PLO was impotent, and had no strategy for the future, intensifying the feeling that salvation would have to come from within. The organizers of local factions were well aware of these sentiments, and at least one Fatah cadre was preparing to try to spark off a wider uprising at the beginning of 1988 (Y. Sayigh 1997: 614).

In the event, the male youth of the camps and villages who built barricades and used stones and petrol bombs to hold back the Israeli military immediately after 8 December, played an important role as the vanguard of the *intifada*. Their actions, along with the sheer size and number of the demonstrations, signalled something new. The fruits of more than a decade of grassroots mobilization on the ground now weighed in the balance, as committees and organizations set up for social services, public works and empowerment on the one side, and the local political factions on the other (along with the 'prominent personalities' cultivated by the PLO-in-exile), swung into action.

Popular Committees to coordinate activism sprang up in numerous towns and villages, while in January the factions (Fatah, the PFLP, the DFLP and the Palestine Communist Party) established a new leadership, the United National Command (UNC) to coordinate the uprising while affirming allegiance to the PLO. At the same time, Islamists linked to the Muslim Brotherhood in Gaza were also active. The prominent personalities, such as Faisal Husseini, carried out important intermediary roles, between the PLO and local constituencies, holding press conferences and specifying positions.

The UNC started to issue communiques involving political direction and practical guidelines on organization and resistance:

They designated strike days, urged a boycott of Israeli goods, and called for social solidarity. As the uprising gained momentum the appeals formulated the elements of a programme designed to disengage the occupied territories from Israel economically and administratively, in the undeclared hope of readying the population ultimately for outright civilian disobedience (Y. Sayigh 1997: 615).

An organizational basis for the prolongation and coordination of the *intifada* was thus established in a matter of weeks. By January, the goals of the UNC were clearly articulated: an end to settlement building, land-seizure and road blocks, the granting of building permits, the freeing of political prisoners, an end to numerous restrictive measures and above all national self-determination.

In this context, the forms of repression unleashed by the Israelis only seemed to provoke resistance, not to crush it. The Israelis defined the *intifada* as mere 'rioting', and deployed, in the words of Defence Minister Rabin 'force, power and blows' (cited in Qumsiyeh 2011: 137). No Israeli soldiers and more than 200 Palestinians, were killed during the first year of the uprising. The violence from above was not that of napalm or carpet bombing; it was an infrastructure of beating, incarceration and torture: approximately 18,000 Palestinians were injured by Israeli forces during the *intifada* (Tripp 2013: 119). The scope of this policy, far from causing the Palestinians to back down in humiliation as intended, played an important role in bringing in everwider sectors of Palestinian society in support of the uprising. Hunter's work indicates the importance of the rounds of repression in widening the scope of the uprising by February and March of 1988 (Hunter 1993), bringing in merchants and shopkeepers, among others. Peteet's research suggests how surviving incarceration and beating without turning informant enhanced the status and leadership position of newly politicized male youth, while acting to bring to the fore a new generation of younger leaders, side-lining some of the older men. Israeli soldiers' involvement in repression against the unarmed, the female, and children, also acted to dishonour them in the eyes of many Palestinians. Women who were beaten and incarcerated but lived to tell the tale returned to assert their equality in the national struggle (Peteet 1994). Israel's policy of beating and breaking bones, then, especially in the well-organized early months of the *intifada*, only widened the intensity of the activism.

Central to the action was civil disobedience. On the one hand, acts of civil disobedience involved forms of direct action linked to the material fabric of the occupation: they included boycotts of Israeli goods, walking off the job including closing shops (against orders), opening shops (against orders), resigning from administrative posts, refusing to pay taxes (such as the lengthy and courageous tax strike in Beit Sahour, near Bethlehem), refusing to take direct orders from soldiers, the burning of ID cards, the pelting of soldiers and tanks with stones and sometimes molotov cocktails, and baring the chest at soldiers ready to shoot. These acts all symbolized and enacted the visible refusal and defiance of occupation and control. It was a strategy that the Israelis sought to break at all costs (Qumsiyeh 2011: 146), that opposed the logic of direct-domination through defiance. Armed struggle was rejected (but never the right to it) on the basis that it had failed previously to bring about self-determination. This message was reinforced and coordinated at all levels of Palestinian organization.

On the other side, the Palestinians, dissociating themselves from the forms of Israeli domination and the socio-economic structures associated with it, complemented such disobedience with a variety of forms of self-organization. Drawing on the grassroots mobilization of previous years, they started to grow their own food, and manufacture their own goods (especially textiles), and to engage in social provision in order to subsist independently of Israeli control. Empowerment meshed with the languages and practices of the private voluntary organizations that had sprung up in the occupied territoriesover the previous years. Civil disobedience and self-organization had the signal advantage of drawing in the participation and engaging the energies of women: 'women's groups, co-operatives, educational and literary circles, boycott committees, childcare centres and communication networks were central' in the 'infrastructure of resistance that helped to sustain the *intifada*' (Tripp 2013: 203).

These tactics were supposed to disengage the territories from Israeli control, paving the way for the establishment of a state there. The latter possibility was concretized at the level of the PLO on the 'outside' when it agreed to a two-state solution in Algiers in late 1988. It was hoped that the uprising would make the Israeli occupation unsustainable, and weaken the Israeli economy, forcing concessions, while splitting public opinion internationally where a non-violent movement confronted ugly military repression. The PLO aimed to use the *intifada* to lift its flagging fortunes and gain it a place at a negotiating table set up under the auspices of the United States and the Soviet Union.

There were a number of key problems. The damage to the Israeli economy was undoubtedly there, but it could not fundamentally disrupt it. Civil disobedience was extraordinarily costly in terms of lives and livelihoods and thus hard to sustain. And self-organization was not capable of generating the basis for an alternative economy, while Israel controlled the borders that could have created linkages further afield. The mobilizing effects of repression could only last for so long – and, after eighteen months or so, incarceration and beatings started to take their toll, wearing down the resistance. The Israelis, over time, sexualized their modes of repression in order to counter the 'honouring' impact on men that non-sexualized beating and incarceration was having (Peteet 1994). Sexual violations or rumours of such in regard to female prisoners put them, on release, in danger of attack or even death at the hands of their male relatives (Tripp 2013: 212), a grotesque obstacle to female activism. Where concrete gains were few, disputes over strategy created division, and Israel was able to develop its network of informers and collaborators by coercion, sowing mutual suspicion and contributing to the incoherence of the movement. The use of arms crept into the conflict, the killing of informants accelerated, physical attacks on women deemed by Hamas to be unsuitably attired increased, and the central focus on civil disobedience was diluted (Tripp 2013: 204–5). By 1990, the *intifada* was showing signs of weakening and wound down during 1991 and after, with the start of negotiations in Madrid.

The *intifada* was a massive demonstration of the popular Palestinian national will. A sign of its broader international significance was that it caused an Arabic word to enter the English language. Even more remarkably, the word had either a neutral, or even a positive, connotation, illustrating how the near-automatic link between Palestinian resistance and terrorism in the English language was broken by the *intifada*. It was the most important reason for Jordan's renunciation of its claim to the West Bank in 1988. It rescued the PLO from chilly exile, and paved the way for negotiations (starting in Madrid in 1991), which held out the prospect, at least for a time, of a two-state solution to the Israel–Palestine conflict (Hiltermann 1991; Hunter 1993; Lockman and Beinin 1990; Qumsiyeh 2011).

The Oslo process which followed the *intifada* failed. Instead of achieving national self-determination, the Palestinians found themselves faced with ongoing Israeli land colonization, and fragmented in bantustans under a neo-patrimonial interim authority (Roy 2002; Shlaim 2000; Slater 2001; Usher 1995). This was the key context for the break out of the second *intifada* in September 2000, an armed struggle, and the rise and growing popularity of the Islamist movement Hamas during the 1990s and into the 2000s, who had always said against their local secular foes that it was pointless to negotiate with 'infidels' and 'Jews'. On the other hand, other sections of the Palestinian nationalist movement also rejected Oslo, from the DFLP to prominent, secular exiles such as Edward Said. Hamas' rise in popularity among a substantial constituency of Palestinians under occupation, confirmed by its victory in the elections of 2006, depended not just on the failure of Oslo, and on Israeli settlement building and intransigence, but also on the failures of the PLO and Fatah during Oslo and the state-building process in the occupied territories that followed, on the limits of alternative mobilizing projects, and on the strengths of the leadership, organization, strategies and tactics of Hamas itself.

Algeria: from 'bread riots' to civil war, 1988–1995

Il faut bien comprendre que le peuple algérien marche aujourd'hui avec un poignard dans le dos, qu'il a été trahi par ses dirigeants. La confiance était énorme – il n'y a pas de mots pour qualifier cette force et lorsqu'elle retombe, c'est terrible (Yacine Kateb, *L'autre journal*, No. 7: été 1985, cited in Redjala 1988).

On 5 October 1988, thousands of youths, mostly male, secondary-school students and unemployed, ransacked central Algiers. Over the following two days, the movement spread across the country, drawing in broader constituencies and Islamist organizations, and bringing heavy repression from the government. While widespread protests had taken place in the name of the Amazigh/Berbers in 1980 (Tripp 2013: 237–52), the protests of 1988 were more widespread, drew in a wider cross-section of the public, and further fractured the hegemony of the post-independence state. The crowd actions of October 1988, indeed, were the main reason for a turn in Algeria towards elections and a multi-party system, a move which set in train a whole series of events that led into the civil war of the 1990s.

A new generation grew up in the 1980s amid economic problems, problems with corrupt state bureaucracies, dead-end jobs, unemployment and boredom with social and economic amenities and conditions. Many had no direct memory of the war of liberation or of French colonialism. The regime's version of history was increasingly sterile and irrelevant: many were 'sick' of having it rammed down their throat. Official history was more like a millstone, maintaining a discredited elite in place. Third Worldism meant less and less (Malley 1996). Many worried over the place and role of 'the categories of Western culture' (Burgat 2003: 103). While Boumediène liked to depict Algerians as 'austere revolutionaries resolutely committed to the goals of socialism, in reality many of his compatriots were growing weary of the emphasis on heavy industry. Instead of constant sacrifices, they wanted more consumer goods such as hi-fis, household appliances and cars' (Evans and Phillips 2007: 94–5). People were fearful of mass redundancies, frustrated by the lack of a regular water supply, resentful at the absence of many basic foodstuffs in the shops and angry at the sharp rise in the price of school materials (Evans and Phillips 2007: 102). The expansion in educational opportunities, and the rising standard of living that many had enjoyed in the 1960s and 1970s, were much more uneven in the 1980s. Austerity measures had hit Algeria with falling energy prices from the early 1980s onwards. There was also popular opposition to corrupt bureaucrats in the statist economy: the country had oil and gas revenues, but many wondered who exactly was benefitting from them. Linked to this was a powerful resentment at the persistent *hogra* (arrogance) of the generals who brooked no meaningful participation in the state.

The *hittistes* were the unemployed who gathered around walls (Evans and Phillips 2007: 107). They went for walks; they expressed boredom; they chewed mild stimulants – the litter of which small metal cases was ubiquitous on Algerian provincial roads in the late 1980s. This was also the generation of rai music and football. Anti-government slogans and songs became a well-established tradition on the terraces, where young men could express themselves without fear of reprisal: 'at national games President Chadli was so heavily jeered that it became a political embarrassment' (Evans and Phillips 2007: 114).

Young men from the popular quarters, including *hittistes* and football fans, and organized in a wide variety of ways, were the early risers of October 1988. The Palestinian *intifada*, which was given nightly coverage on Algerian television, may have led some to think about collective action in defence of rights (Evans and Phillips 2007: 102). The regime used the coverage to burnish its own pan-Arab credentials and deflect discontent to distant causes, while the rioters brought this logic to bear in places unexpected by the regime. The actions of these youth were stitched in to powerful forms of spontaneous philosophy, common sense and proverbial wisdom. Moral economy, 'moral polity' (Roberts 2002) and popular culture were all at work. First, just as in Egypt in 1977, economic inequality, property and class was at stake. The targets of the rioters included the boutiques on Rue Mourad Didouche, Algiers' commercial high street, department stores, cafés, restaurants, discothèques, the notorious Blue Note night club and other places frequented by the *chi-chis*, the sons and daughters of the privileged, state-connected, commercial elite. A commercial centre on the heights overlooking the capital was looted (Evans and Phillips 2007: 102). Ostentatious wealth contrasted with poverty and struggle, coupled with the widespread notion that such wealth was obtained by dishonest means was a standing provocation to wide sectors of the population.

Second, the exclusionary, corrupt and abusive state, president Chadli, the police and the legal system were also targeted in the Algerian crowd actions of 1988. On one public building, significantly enough, the national flag was symbolically torn down and replaced by an empty couscous sack (Evans and Phillips 2007: 102). In Oran, two hotels, one previously belonging to President Chadli, were ransacked (Evans and Phillips 2007: 102–3). Another chant read: 'Chadli, that's enough vice. Tell your son to return the money.' Banners proclaimed that 'We want our rights' – in part a reference to those social and economic rights that the state had previously guaranteed, but was no longer doing so. In the provincial town of Blida, south of Algiers, in October 1988, 'the law courts were torched and the town centre occupied by protestors'. In Belcourt, a popular Algiers neighbourhood, a police chief was made to strip down to his underwear, and the crowd encouraged to taunt and slap him. In Bab el-Oued, a policeman was forced to parade the streets – shouting 'I am a braggart, I am a betrayer'. Mock trials were staged satirizing the Algerian justice system where 'defendants' accused of abuses of power were all acquitted (Evans and Phillips 2007: 102–3).

Actions against economic and political targets were fortified by popular culture. The slogan 'villa, Honda, blonda' was a swipe at corrupt officials with no sense of the public interest, indulging in luxury, 'decadent' sexuality, and links to the West (Evans and Phillips 2007: 102–42). Masculinist languages were at work: there were banners proclaiming that 'We are men'. Slang phrases mocked leaderships by associating them in coded ways with effeminacy and homosexuality. In some sense, these riots involved a moment of inversion of the social order, enabling 'young male rioters to recover a sense of honour, dignity and manhood'. Slogans, in the form of rhyming couplets in Arabic, ridiculed Chadli as a eunuch, dominated by his wife Halima, and feebly allowing the corruption of his son. As these young men chanted: 'We don't want butter or pepper. We want a leader we can respect.' 'Boumediène, come back to us. Halima has come to dominate us.' Here, the contrast between a weak and effete Chadli and a tough and upright Boumediène was ever present (Evans and Phillips 2007: 103–4). Chadli was seen as the 'Cauliflower President': henpecked, with a shock of bouffant white hair, which made him look like a cauliflower (Evans and Phillips 2007: 114–18).

The repression enacted by the state on the rioters of early October 1988 in Algeria was an intense provocation. While many did not join with the young men on the streets, they could sympathize with many of the grievances that they broached and object to the violent nature of the repression. The targeting of government and property continued into a second day, with pitched battles in central Algiers, the batons and tear gas of police and security forces being opposed to stones and Molotov cocktails. On 6 October, the army declared a state of siege, imposing a curfew and deploying tanks. In the army's view, there was 'no question of dialogue; the rioters were hooligans and looters and had to be brought to heel' (Evans and Phillips 2007: 103–4). This stance implied a free rein to shoot into crowds and torture arrested protestors. Thousands were rounded up and placed in makeshift prison cells. Many were killed. Perhaps fifty, for example, were killed under fire near a mosque in Kouba. The Interior Minister made an appeal for calm, and foodstuffs, butter, semolina, flour and cooking oil suddenly appeared in the shops.

In Egypt, the popular uprising of January 1977 had been comparable in many ways. And it had been put down after two days by the military after socio-economic concessions. Part of the explanation for why in the Algerian case the action was prolonged must lie with the fact that Islamists, who had remained relatively quiet in Egypt, now swung into action in Algeria. On 7 October 1988, taking advantage of the masses of people who turned out as a matter of religious routine and devotion for the Friday prayers, around 8,000 Islamist sympathizers joined, after the prayer, a pitched battle with the police in the Belcourt neighbourhood. Their slogans were 'Allahu Akbar', 'Islamic republic' and 'Chadli murderer' – a reference to the repression of the previous days. This was the 'first appearance of Islamists on the street' (Evans and Phillips 2007: 104–5). Islamists, with some depth in pre-existing organization, and loudly declaring principles and forms of identity that added up to a radical alternative to the existing order, were mobilizing among those horrified by the repression and with a raft of political, economic and social grievances. By joining the physical battle, Islamists aligned themselves with the 'brave and honourable' youth – where actions spoke louder than words.

On the strength of this showing, Islamists moved on 10 October to take control of the protest movement, harnessing its energies, and stitching it into their religious and political project. Ali Belhadj organized a demonstration in which 20,000 marched down Hassiba Ben Bouali Street, one of the largest avenues in Algiers, named after one of the most well-known heroines of the war of independence, and then to the sea front. They were met with a military barricade, and, after shots were fired, the army fired indiscriminately into the crowd killing around fifty persons. Fleeing rioters shouted to journalists: 'They are worse than the Zionists! Zionists do not fire on mosques, you must write this down.' Rioters also shouted to foreign journalists: 'It is worse than South Africa, it is worse than Chile!' (Evans and Phillips

2007: 105). After less than a week, around 500, mostly young, male Algerians were dead. Never before had the post-independence state turned its guns on its own people in this way.

The action, however, had dramatic results. On the night of 10 October 1988, amid the massive repression of the demonstrations, riots and protests of the previous six days, President Chadli appeared on television promising political, institutional and constitutional reform. He stated that he would 'eliminate the current monopoly of responsibility and will permit the official institutions of the State, the Parliament or others, to play their part in the control and monitoring of the state' (Evans and Phillips 2007: 105–6). Many were suspicious, but the protests subsided, and shops re-opened the next day. Two days later, the state of siege was lifted. Less than two weeks later (on 23 October 1988), plans for political reform were published. Their central premise was the separation of the state and the FLN. They paved the way for the development of a multi-party system, which was overwhelmingly approved in a national referendum on 3 November. More pressure from below secured the amendments of February 1989 that would allow elections. Chadli was seeking to distribute the burden of rule more widely within the dominant bloc – while preserving the privileges of the military and winning international approval for democratic reform in the process. It was a move true to Huntington's model (Katsiaficas 2013: 22–9). As elsewhere, popular mobilization linked itself to consequences, through a glass darkly.

Algeria's Islamic movement formed the Fronte Islamique du Salut (FIS) to contest these elections, declaring in Algiers in March 1989 that new moral, spiritual, material and political solutions were necessary at a time when 'the regime in place ... is incapable to manage properly the multidimensional crisis which is shaking the nation in its depths' (FIS Information Bureau 1990s). On 12 June 1990, Algeria held multi-party municipal and provincial elections – the first of their kind in the history of the country. FIS won 32 of the 48 provincial assemblies; the FLN only won 14 assemblies. FIS were to win a landslide victory (188 out of 231 seats) in the parliamentary elections of 26 December 1991.

The FIS took a heavy punishment for its electoral popularity. In spring 1991, the generals moved to alter the electoral law to favour the FLN – leading to demonstrations by Islamists and other political parties. These non-violent protests were answered with repression: Islamists were killed and the two key leaders of FIS, Abbasi Madani

(b. 1931) and Ali Belhadj (b. 1956), were arrested. Still the non-violent tendency in FIS had the upper hand – as evidenced by the Batna Congress in July 1991 – while from November 1991 armed groups appeared 'on the flanks' of Abbasi Madani's supporters (Burgat 2003: 106). Worse was to come. In January 1992, the army annulled the parliamentary elections of December 1991 and disbanded the FIS. Some 20,000 FIS supporters were rounded up and put in 'concentration camps in the southern Sahara desert' (Burgat 2003: 104). Chadli calculated that the electoral process would threaten the dominant bloc more than legitimate it, and thus moved against that process. Many Islamists protested through official channels; others appealed unsuccessfully for international solidarity – but to no avail.

The non-violent mainstream of FIS now took up the 'armed struggle that the radicals had long been fighting' (Burgat 2003: 102). The anti-democratic currents among Algeria's Islamists had long scoffed at elections seen as a sham and un-Islamic. Some were remnants of Mustafa Bouyali's (1940–87) armed Islamic movement, based around Larbaa, south of Algiers, which, before it was repressed, had carried out attacks on the government, girls' schools, libraries, cinemas and restaurants, deemed illicit in Islam, between 1982 and 1987 (Willis 1996). These groups were joined by 'Arab–Afghan' jihadists supported by Madani's opponents in the FIS and forming the basis for the Groupe Islamique Armé (GIA). Forces loyal to the FIS became the Islamic Salvation Army in June 1994. The prominent Palestinian-Jordanian Abu Qatada (b. 1960), supporter of Sunni *jihad* in Salafi colouring, does seem to have issued at least one *fatwa* permitting the killing of women and children in regard to the GIA in Algeria in the mid-1990s. The Salafi cleric Abd Al-Malik Al-Ramadani Al-Jaza'iri issued a robust denunciation of this 'barbarism' and 'savagery' (Jaza'iri 2007). Those advocating violence were handed a major argument by the actions of the generals.

Armed actions targeting the government, foreigners, non-Muslims, economic 'collaborators' and the surviving remnants of French community started to get under way from 1992 onwards (Burgat 2003: 106–7). To begin with, the FIS saw this as legitimate armed struggle aiming to oust the Generals and return the country to elections. But the GIA itself appears to have been taken over by a faction ready to conduct more wholesale massacres of civilians in order to achieve its goals. By 1995, massacres of whole villages, especially of women and children linked to government-organized 'defence units', were being carried out. The security forces themselves, masquerading as Islamists in order to discredit them, also seem to have played a role in this (Burgat 2003: 114). In this way, the credo of a fringe armed group which had been all but eliminated in 1987 came to dominate the Islamist movement in Algeria after 1991. That the state opened the institutional terrain for elections and then clamped down on those who won them clearly played a role in the descent into civil war. The armed struggle was also home-grown, as well as strongly encouraged by the veterans of the Afghan war, and the appropriation of concepts and practices of Sunni *jihad* from Sayyid Qutb to Syria to contemporary Egypt.

The Western press was often silent in regards to issues that were the domain of civil liberties, human rights and democracy, because it perceived them to be trojan horses for the advance of Islamic 'fascism' or because it had imbibed the mantra of stability first. Sometimes even human rights organizations faltered. It took two years for Amnesty International to start reporting the state violence unleashed against the FIS. For example, 1,224 teachers were arrested in 1993, several hundred, at the peak of their careers or fresh from university, 'had been taken by surprise on their doorstep or stolen away in the night, savagely tortured to within an inch of their lives, openly murdered in front of their families or crushed, asphyxiated, electrocuted in the depths of a jail and, predictably, buried out of sight of any television camera' (Burgat 2003: 109).

The official line of the FIS in the 1990s was that the complicity of the West with the human rights violations and anti-democratic moves of the deep state (or *"le pouvoir"*) in Algeria had given credence among MENA populations to the idea that the West held a basic enmity towards Muslims and Islam. The English-language website of the FIS in the mid-1990s hammered this point home:

The non-recognition by the International Community of the people's right to choose freely their political authority and to defend their elected institutions does only radicalize the armed movement ... The expressed desire by western governments to see democracy progress in the Muslim World is not compatible with their silence about, or support of, the repressive tyrannical response dealt to the Islamic movements and populations by most regimes of the region. This attitude only alienates the west further from those Muslim populations and fulfils the theory of western conspiracy against Islam,

a theory held authentic at least since the dawn of European colonialism
(FIS Information Bureau n.d.)

Geopolitics was converted through schemata of interpretation into
history, narrative and a particular project of mobilization. While Leftist activists stressed the way neo-colonialism and capitalism were
responsible for the stance of the West, the FIS interpreted Western
hypocrisy in terms of a basic enmity towards Islam. Given the European and US governments' support for the generals, it was an interpretation that was easier to develop.

The diversionary potential of such forms of nativism and essentialism is exemplified by the way in which Algerian television denounced
the political negotiators of the FIS in January 1995 as dealing with
Christians and Jews. Anwar Haddam was an Algerian nuclear physi-
cist, long-standing Islamist, and a key member of the FIS from its
origins until 2004. He was elected to parliament on a FIS ticket in
1991. Haddam was a key originator and signatory (alongside Abdelhamid Mehri and Hocine Ait Ahmed) of the Sant Egidio Platform,
which demanded a reinstatement of democracy, and was hammered
out in Rome by the main Algerian political parties in January 1995.
The Algerian generals rejected the Platform, and the civil war in the
country intensified. Anwar Haddam himself then stated in an
interview:

Yes. It was really an amazing situation in Rome. There we were sitting in a
church, hammering things out. Then, the Algerian television showed a cross
in the church and said, 'Look at those people who went to the church! They
are dealing with Christians and Jews.' And there we, the FIS delegation, were
discussing peace, hosted by Christians, as we were last February in Stock-
holm (Haddam 1996: 69–80).

Here the (secular) state media in Algeria was attempting to tap into
populist, essentialist sentiments (which had been used by the FIS itself)
to discredit attempts to thrash out political and democratic solutions
for the future of Algeria.

The crowd actions of 1988 were the direct cause of the democratic
opening in Algeria in 1989. When the electoral process, however,
threw up a challenge to privileges at the top of the state, the generals
annulled it. The possibilities that were clearly there for a democratic
Islamism were nipped in the bud, and the armed and anti-democratic
elements in the broader Islamist movement seized the upper hand

through the period 1991–2 – and democratic elements were drowned out or lost heart amid massive repression. The crowd actions of October 1988 were arguably longer lasting in Algeria than in Egypt because they were championed by an organized leadership, the Islamists, who entered the fray after these actions had begun. Between 1989 and 1991, the Islamist movement used and argued in favour of an electoral system in Algeria. It was by no means clear, in default of organized forces emerging from the ranks of the young men of the popular quarters themselves, that any political force had emerged that would clearly reflect the views and grievances that had motivated the rioters in the first place. Moreover, not everyone could be sure that Islamists did not harbour a revolutionary challenge to the secular state that would abandon democracy after instituting it. This lack of clarity was not solely about the vested interests of the dominant bloc or the prejudices of those confronted with the FIS – although these weighed heavily. It also had to do with the acute divisions between the secular state and the Sunni Islamist movement that had been at work in the region since 1954, when Nasser crushed the Muslim Brotherhood. Furthermore, and insofar as any of this was in the gift of FIS itself, it did matter that there was a lack of clarity in their theory of the state – a problem they shared with many other currents in Sunni Islamism. The charge of opportunism against Islamists in the matter of electoral process could not be simply dismissed, because there was a vagueness about the place of electoral and democratic mechanisms in their mobilizing project. Nonetheless, ambiguity has not always been fatal to movements. No such fuzziness characterized Salafi-Wahhabi mobilization, virtually all of which involves an emphatic rejection of democracy as un-Islamic.

Taking on the Far Enemy: Al-Qaʻida and Salafi-Wahhabism

The attack on the World Trade Center on 11 September 2001 was among the most spectacular, and, for the MENA region, catastrophic, single events in its contentious history. The PFLP and Fatah, among others, had attacked targets, including civilian ones, in Europe in the 1970s. Algerian nationalists had mounted attacks in France during the war of liberation (1954–62) and Algerian Islamists did so on one or two occasions in the 1990s. The World Trade Center had been targeted in the early 1990s. But no socio-political movement with its roots in the region (or indeed in any other region) had struck in the heartlands of empire with such devastating effect before. And no group, since the eighteenth century at least, had ever reaped such rewards from a single contentious act. The subsequent invasion of both Afghanistan (2001) and Iraq (2003) by the United States and its allies, and the US-led War on Terror throughout the 2000s (Khalili 2012) was profoundly ineffective in destroying Al-Qa'ida. Instead of eliminating the organization, which had very little organized support in the MENA in 2001 (Gerges 2005), the United States and its coalition partners handed Al-Qa'ida, along with their fellow travellers in the scattered milieu of Salafi and Wahhabi *jihad* movements, an extraordinary political opportunity. They destroyed one of its secular foes – the Iraqi regime. In its place they created a collapsed state (Iraq) adjacent to the Gulf, complete with hundreds of thousands of newly redundant party members, civil servants, and soldiers with ready access to arms (Tripp 2013: 42–5), where Al-Qa'ida and fellow travellers could operate. Not only this, but the US invasion and subsequent political botching and atrocities generated an aggrieved constituency all over the region and beyond, and very much among Iraqi Sunnis, who could be mobilized for the cause (Gerges 2005: 251ff.). By pursuing all these policies under the banners of democracy, the United States made it harder for others to hoist this slogan, as it tarnished it by association – another very substantial political gift to Al-Qa'ida, which always rejected democracy as Western hypocrisy (Rasheed 2006; Gerges 2011; Mitchell 2002).

The (neo-)Orientalist fantasy – that these attacks expressed the ancient, invariant enmity and hatred of 'Islamic civilization' towards the 'Judeo-Christian West' (Huntington 1997) – was much ventilated in the aftermath of the attacks. It was an old, essentialist and exceptionalist thesis, very convenient for the dominant bloc, marking out a tremendous disregard for research-based knowledge. Even the majority of the jihadist movement opposed Al-Qa'ida in the wake of 9/11 (Gerges 2005: 200–28). If anything, it was the Orientalist thesis that was most similar to the worldview maintained by the perpetrators of the attacks, a point illustrating the similarity between the essentialist premises of global jihadist thought, and those of large sections of the elite in Europe and the United States. On the other hand, processual and sometimes rather abstract or structural understandings of these attacks, rooted in the study of modernization, capitalism or globalization, have not always been satisfactory. 9/11 was not a structural inevitability. In order to capture the constructed nature of the contentious politics of 9/11, it is useful to consider the leadership, ideology, organization and repertoires of a particular, armed strand of Wahhabism, distinguishable from other quietist, millenarian or modernist strands of Wahhabism, which in turn was a tradition distinguishable in various ways from the forms of Sunni and Shi'a religious politics in the rest of the region from the 1920s to the 1980s that has been treated so far in this book.

The recent origins of this history lay not in Afghanistan or Iraq (or in US official enemies such as Syria or Iran), but in Saudi Arabia, an ally of the United States since at least the Second World War and of the British since the 1890s. The Saudi state based its legitimacy on Wahhabism, but Wahhabism was not always controllable by the royal house. Especially after 1916, Ibn Saud relied to expand his state on the Ikhwan, highly committed Najdi warrior-tribesmen – drawn from the ranks of the 'Utaybi, the Mutayr and others – organized in special oasis settlements (wherein they were supposed to abandon pastoral-nomadism and turn to agriculture), and bound together in religion and *jihad* by an oath of brotherhood. The Ikhwan were partly difficult to control as 'they had no traditional position in the Saudi power structure but depended instead on the prestige of their ideological goals' (Kostiner 1990: 231). They had no wish to cease expanding the state before the seizure of Kuwait, of 'heretical' Shi'a shrines in Iraq, or the ethnic cleansing of the Shi'a populations in the Eastern provinces, and they objected to non-Wahhabi pilgrims, Ibn Saud's interactions with Westerners, and various unlawful innovations such as the telegraph or the motor vehicle (Hegghammer and Lacroix 2011: 4; Trofimov 2007). Saudi state-building, as well as some of these innovations, which were linked to the expansion of state power, struck at tribal customary rights to trade and raid (Kostiner 1990: 233, 235). Some tribal leaders also felt they deserved more political autonomy (Kostiner 1990: 235) and more secular power in the state than Ibn Saud offered them (Rasheed 2002: 70).

Between 1927 and 1930, the Ikhwan confronted the forces of Ibn Saud and the British air force based out of Iraq. They were decisively defeated by the British machine guns of Ibn Saud's forces in March 1929 at the battle of Sbala in the Najd (Kostiner 1993; Habib 1978). The Al-Saud had their state, and the independent political power of the

tribes was broken. Tribes mostly became patronage networks or intermediaries between local constituencies and the state, where the latter
monopolized sovereignty, coercion, tax-raising and regulatory powers.
Tribal social conservatism in matters of gender and sexuality lived on
in new forms, as did tribal networks and loyalties in altered forms.
More importantly, the question of the relationship between the monarchy and Wahhabism, which could become critical of deviations from
the creed, was by no means fully resolved.

In the early 1960s, as part of a response to the gathering forces of
Nasserism, pan-Arabism and Leftism that threatened its power from
within and without, the Saudi royal house, now in the hands of Faysal,
who sought to be a modernizer, also took the decision to upgrade,
rather than move away from, Wahhabism as a source of legitimacy
(Rasheed 2002: 106). In this the Saudis took a proactive initiative that
King Idris of Libya, who was soon in the dustbin of history, never did.
It was not that the king became an ideologue: a risky strategy at best;
far better to stand back as 'glorious' patron than to get directly
involved. Nor was it simply about rent distribution through patronage
to win loyalty. Instead, the target on the domestic front was the
Wahhabi religious establishment and a wider civil society, all the easier
to define the limits and boundaries of which as substantial new segments could be created from on high. While Nasser courted the Left,
Faisal courted the *Al-Muwahhidun*. Material capital, based on oil-
rents, was converted into spiritual capital (Farquhar 2013). The
existing Wahhabi religious establishment was drawn on and funded
as the main vehicle for this push, but heavily supplemented by other
sources. Universities, schools, the media, radio, publications and
mosques were built up. The Islamic University of Medina, for example,
was founded in 1961 as a proselytizing institution, and drew on
modern social technologies of all kinds, rendering curricula content
transparent to the state, enabling supervision at one remove, and
certifying graduates, for example, who were then in a position to
operate in the wider society as if entirely independent (Farquhar 2013).

On the foreign policy front, King Faisal staked a further claim to
religious integrity by seriously championing the doctrine of Muslim
solidarity as 'an alliance-building tool in the Arab cold war between
Egypt and Saudi Arabia' (Hegghammer 2010: 17). He took on the
mantle of Abdulhamid II. The Muslim World League was founded in
1962 and the Organization of the Islamic Conference during

1969–72 – organizations to promote pan-Islamism which moved from an apolitical focus on humanitarian aid and disaster relief in the 1960s to a more political focus on the suffering of Muslims through war, oppression and discrimination from the late 1970s onwards. Emphasizing pan-Islamic credentials was a way to compete with Iran after 1979 and to divert attention from socio-economic discontent during the low oil prices of the 1980s (Hegghammer 2010: 18–23).

Many of the cadres of this 'Wahhabi expansion', providing key skills, were Muslim Brothers fleeing repression at the hands of the secularists of Egypt and to some extent Syria. One such figure was the Syrian Muslim Brother Muhammad Surur (b. 1938) who took up a teaching post at Burayda, a provincial capital in north-central Saudi Arabia. Another was the brother of Sayyid Qutb. By driving the Brotherhood into exile, Nasser and the Ba'thists were inadvertently doing Saudi bidding – up to a point. But Muslims and preachers ready to embrace and work with (or even contribute to shaping) Wahhabism and find livelihoods, positions, and scholarships in Saudi institutions, such as the Islamic University of Medina, came from many parts of the Muslim world, from Mauretania to Indonesia. By the 1970s, and with the huge increases in rents that were made available for these activities during the oil boom, this re-vamped Wahhabism, which drew on and was shaped by many influences, was increasingly making an impact in the wider region. In complete contrast to the 1960s, by the 1980s there was now very much a Salafi-Wahhabi 'point of view' in Islamist circles in the region and beyond. This was not only because members of the Saudi royal family sometimes sponsored Wahhabi organization abroad; it was also very much because the energies of civil society had been engaged: students and others studying or working in Saudi Arabia, for example, returned to their countries of origin, or moved on to third countries, or started up publishing houses, or preached in mosques, or set up study groups (Farquhar 2013).

Wahhabi-Salafi *da'wa* can be distinguished from popular Shi'ism, the modernist Sunnism of the Muslim Brotherhood, and even the Sunni jihadists who split from the Muslim Brotherhood in the 1960s, 1970s and 1980s, who were influenced in doctrine as well as strategy by Sayyid Qutb. While it used to be thought that Wahhabism was decisively changed by the Muslim Brotherhood, more recent research has done a good deal to show its relative autonomy and distinctiveness (Lacroix 2011). Saudi Wahhabism never became just another offshoot of the Muslim Brotherhood. There were all sorts of differences in doctrine, ritual and comportment. But the Wahhabi focus on purity and communal separateness marked it out; as did its sectarianism regarding all other currents and especially the Shi'a. Sectarianism, long a staple of Wahhabism, was only ramified in the 1960s and 1970s. Perhaps more than other currents, the Wahhabis really did insist on their monopoly on the one true Islam of the pious ancestors (*al-salaf al-salih*). While *salafiyya* movements are a very old thing in the MENA region, Wahhabi Islamists have laid claim to the label 'Salafi' with a tenacity and a vehemence perhaps unmatched in the modern period. It was for this reason that their 'summons' was almost completely rejected in the region as a whole from the mid-eighteenth century until the 1920s (Redissi 2008).

Equally distinctive, compared to the religious politics developed within civil society elsewhere in the region, was the insistence on a *non-political* religion, in the sense that all questions of decision-making in the state were ceded to the *wali al-amr* – the ruler (Meijer 2009). Far from seeking an Islamic state, official Wahhabism, and several of the diverse currents within it, insisted that there already was one. This was the key utility of the cultivation of Wahhabism for the Al-Saud: it was an available creed that could be used and moulded to justify fully an absolutist monarchy. This meant that quite unlike what Hegghammer has styled the 'socio-revolutionary' Muslim Brotherhood and its armed splinter-groups in Egypt, Syria, and other secular states in the region, which had developed against and in conflict with secular states, mainstream Saudi Wahhabis mostly (but not all) conceived that they had no Near Enemy to fight: often they directed their attention outward, with a strongly marked missionary orientation – a summons (*da'wa*) to the faith. In Saudi Arabia, officially speaking, Shari'a was the law of the land, and the king implemented Shari'a in accordance with the wishes of the *ulema*, charged with the interpretation of revelation and law. No further *political* questions were relevant. The domain of the political was very much subsumed, in theory, into the decisions of the monarch, and the implementation of Islamic law.

This set up mandated very intensive doctrinal disputes about the true content of Islamic law – the actual content of creed and jurisprudence, the place of the Hanbali school of law, the role of *ijtihad*, the relative prominence of the *hadith*, or the correctness of different kinds of ritual practice or daily comportment. It also generated relationships between monarch and religious establishment that allowed for lines of influence and real power in both directions. But it did not, in general, provide a reliable or continuous mandate for forms of collective and contentious political action within civil society that would intervene *between* the determination of the law (within the religious establishment), and the use of sovereign state power (by the royal family). Such forms of political action were repeatedly denounced from within the religious establishment, and by various currents within it, not to mention by the monarchy, as "politics". Proper Muslims, it was said, should concentrate on law, doctrine and piety.

Given that the determination of the law was undertaken by *ulema* whose institutions and livelihoods depended on rents distributed by the royal family, legal positions threatening to that royal family, as opposed to positions that influenced policy in particular areas, were powerfully selected against, particularly among the higher *ulema*. Even though the Grand Mufti Bin Baz showed considerable independence, he respected the official line in a crisis such as that of 1979 and increasingly later, and was in any case replaced by a figure of much lowlier stature. In this context, Wahhabism in Saudi Arabia was neither willing nor able to undertake, or gain experience in the war of position and concomitant repertoires of mass mobilization drawing on or blending with notions of nationalism, liberal-constitutionalism, and popular sovereignty that had become common among both Islamic modernists and Shi'a populists alike, whether the Muslim Brotherhood in Egypt before 1952, and again after the mid-1970s, or, say, Hizbullah in Lebanon after 1982. Further, direct influence or exchange of doctrinal content between the politicized, revolutionary and popular Shi'ism of Iran, Iraq, Lebanon and Bahrain on the one hand, and the Wahhabism of Saudi Arabia on the other, was acutely limited, even when Shi'a and Wahhabi renegades were imprisoned together. This was not because Saudi Arabia was a 'closed kingdom' (it was not) or because 'globalization' was insufficiently advanced. It was instead because such connection was ruled out by the extreme lengths to which Wahhabi sectarianism was carried, as well as the interest of the state in repressing the Shi'a in the oil-rich Eastern provinces, and then in opposing as the arch-enemy Khomeini and the Islamic revolution in Iran.

Sources of tension, however, within the forms of hegemony exercised by the Saudi state, there were. In many ways, while rich in instruments of economic patronage, and in sources of legitimacy, the

Saudi state lacked effective means of political hegemony, which it always deemed too threatening to the institution of absolutist monarchy and its grip on power. It looked with great suspicion on unorthodox developments within the religious establishment, while shutting down and arresting those minor forays into the domain of the political that certain groups attempted from time to time, such as the petitioning, faxes, or open letters, or public lectures used by the Sahwa movement in the early 1990s, albeit after a period of toleration. In some respects, the lack of instruments of political incorporation and contestation on the one hand, and the anti-political creed of so many in the various streams of Wahhabism on the other, can help account for the fact that, when challenges to the Saudi state emerged, they were less political, and more coercive – the armed seizure of the Grand Mosque in Mecca in 1979 or the car-bombing in Riyadh of 1995 being cases in point.

The seizure of the Grand Mosque in Mecca in 1979, the petitions and mass meetings of the Sahwa in the early 1990s, and the car-bombing in Riyadh in 1995, eventually followed up by the bombings, assassination attempts and gun battles led by Al-Qa'ida in the Arabian Peninsula of 2003–6, were, respectively, the main contentious manifestations of three different strands of religious opposition within the country and on the wider international stage between the 1970s and the early 2000s. The first was about a millenarian splinter from within an already oppositional Ahl Al-Hadith position within Wahhabism; the second had much more to do with the Sahwa–Muslim Brotherhood-influenced Wahhabism; and the third was decisively affected by its link to the *jihad* movement that had coalesced during the 1980s in Afghanistan. Each movement had a strongly marked intellectual and religious heritage, and a sufficiently distinctive set of interpretations of Salafi-Wahhabism. And each movement selected a repertoire of contention that cohered with its identities, principles, goals and organizational capacities. None of the movements achieved their goals. And, while the first two were repressed or re-incorporated into the Saudi system, the third operated in Afghanistan, Bosnia and Chechnya, shifted gears before launching the attacks of 9/11, before returning to Saudi in the mid-2000s, being repressed, before re-appearing in new guises in Iraq and eventually Syria.

The seizure of the Grand Mosque in Mecca, the holiest site in Islam, took place on 20 November 1979 (1 Muharram 1400). In the morning of that auspicious day, the turn of the new Islamic century, in front of thousands of pilgrims and worshippers, around 300 well-prepared, armed men fired shots in the air, secured the doors of the mosque, and posted snipers in the minarets. The head of their tousled band seized the microphone from the imam and proclaimed the appearance of an Expected Deliverer (Al-Mahdi), who advanced before the crowd. Once some explanatory pamphlets had been distributed, most of those now held hostage were gradually allowed to leave in order to spread what the rebels thought was marvellous news. The insurgents then waited for the battles and signs that would mark the steps towards the prophesied apocalypse. They held the mosque for two weeks against the security forces: their final hold outs in the tear-gassed network of rooms and corridors under the mosque only falling to French commandoes on 3 December 1979. There were hundreds of fatalities, and, of those captured, most were executed. While this contentious episode was shrouded in mystery and conspiracy theory at the time, it has more recently been understood (Hegghammer and Lacroix 2011; Trofimov 2007) as one of the most important domestic challenges, rooted in the tenets of a version of Wahhabism itself, to the Al Saud dynasty since the days of the Ikhwan.

The millenarians were led by Juhayman Al-'Utaybi (mid-1930s– 1980). He grew up in an erstwhile and long-impoverished Ikhwan settlement in the Najd near Riyadh. His father had fought among the defeated Ikhwan. Juhayman remained proud and vocal about his father's exploits. He left school early, and served in the National Guard (Saudi's praetorian force) for almost two decades as a soldier and driver. In the 1970s, he moved to Medina, and attended classes at the Islamic University of Medina. There he joined the ranks of a society, al-Jama'a al-Salafiyya al-Muhtasiba (JSM), that had been growing since the 1960s.

The JSM was the leading organization of a sub-current within Salafi-Wahhabism characterized by its strong rejection of the state and its institutions (Hegghammer and Lacroix 2011: x). The JSM had its origins in an episode of moral vigilantism in 1965, when a small group of religious students who had taken to proselytizing in poor neigh-bourhoods, set about destroying pictures and photographs in public places. The students then formed the movement with the blessing of Ibn Baz (1909–99), who was one of the most respected figures in the Wahhabi religious establishment, and was to serve as Grand Mufti of

Saudi Arabia from 1993 until his death. The JSM was also 'greatly inspired' by the ideas of the influential shaykh Nasir Al-Din Al-Albani (1914–99). Al-Albani hailed from Damascus, and was the self-educated son of a clockmaker, but had taught at the Islamic University of Medina in the early 1960s and became a key figure within Salafi-Wahhabism. He claimed to be more Salafi than the Salafis by advocating a greater reliance on the Qur'an and especially the *hadith* than even the Wahhabis, whom he accused of relying too much on the Hanbali school of law. He was a major advocate of the banning of reason from the interpretation of the *hadith*. He absolutely rejected political activism in the style of the Muslim Brotherhood which he considered damaging to preaching and divisive among Muslims who would unite if only they concentrated on religious science and creed (Hegghammer and Lacroix 2011: 43).

By 1976, the JSM had followers in virtually all of Saudi's cities and a purpose built administrative HQ and forum for classes and conferences, the Bayt Al-Ikhwan, situated in a poor neighbourhood of Medina. The JSM were all men, mostly young and unmarried, and from relatively poor or low-status, often Bedouin, backgrounds. Some Yemenis were involved. They met with Al-Albani, and had links with the Pakistani Ahl-e Hadith and the Egyptian Salafi group Ansar Al-Sunna Al-Muhammadiyya. The JSM hammered away on the importance of *hadith*, rejected the use of identity cards and passports because they 'denoted loyalty to an entity other than God' (Hegghammer and Lacroix 2011: 11), opposed images of living beings on television or on currency, and had unusual views on ritual and prayer. The group denounced the moral laxity and decadence that it saw all around, the appearance of women on the television, for example, and wondered at the failure of the *ulema* to act, and the dereliction of the authorities in allowing it to continue, or even participating in the evil, through trips to the Riviera, clandestine alcohol or illicit sex. Juhayman quickly rose to prominence within the group because of his charisma and readiness to criticize the *ulema*.

In late summer 1977, however, following the intervention of a senior *'alim*, worried about the peculiar interpretations of the JSM, most of the group deserted, leaving Juhayman to dominate a 'smaller and radicalized' JSM (Hegghammer and Lacroix 2011: 12). Fleeing a police crackdown in December 1977, Juhayman ended up in the northern desert regions until the seizure of the mosque. There he developed his ideology and started issuing clandestine pamphlets. Key was the idea of allegiance to fellow Muslims and dissociation from infidels (*al-wala' wa-l-bara'*). Further, he maintained that Al-Saud's non-Qurayshi origins invalidated their right to Islamic leadership. The implication was that Juhayman's followers should 'keep away from state institutions by resigning if they were civil servants or by leaving school or university if they were still students' (Hegghammer and Lacroix 2011: 17). But Juhayman distinguished between the state as an institution, and individual rulers, who could not be excommunicated as long as they called themselves Muslims. Finally, and perhaps above all, Juhayman came to be convinced through dreams that his close companion, Muhammad Al-Qahtani, was the Expected Deliverer, as he possessed several of the key attributes given in the *Hadith*. The dawn of the new century would be the moment for his consecration at the Kaʿba as tradition required.

Millenarianism had been used throughout the nineteenth century in Sunni North Africa to give authority to movements that challenged the *ulema*, often by outsiders mobilizing humbler rural constituencies. Such movements laid claim to a charismatic authority even higher and closer to the divine will than that which the *ulema* could supply. In reviving millenarianism, the first time any such manifestation had been made known in the Sunni MENA since before the First World War, Juhayman was precisely finding a lodestone through which he could judge even the prestigious urban *ulema* who refused to implement the very principles they claimed to hold so dear. Clandestine training for the seizure of the mosque in order to carry out the consecration of the Expected Deliverer began in earnest in late 1978.

The preparation for the moment had been helped by collaboration, high and low, ranging from Bedouin in the desert to Ibn Baz who had previously secured the release of some of Juhaymen's men under suspicion by the authorities. The armed defence of the mosque was well prepared with ammunition, food and water, the effective use of sniping positions, well-trained marksmen, and the use of the network of tunnels under the Grand Mosque for the rearguard action when the above ground fell. The Saudi police and then the army both failed to take back the mosque during the first ten days or so. The movement suffered a heavily disorienting and discouraging blow, however, in the early stages when the Expected Deliverer was fatally injured while trying to throw back an unexploded grenade. He became separated from the group, his fate unknown to them. The fighters were only finally ousted by French commandos after two weeks of fighting. All the main protagonists who survived were executed by January 1980.

Just as armed struggle was declared against the secular state by Islamists in Egypt and Syria, and just as another armed struggle had been announced by Shi'a Islamists against a secular state in Iraq, the most ostensibly religious state in the region – Saudi Arabia – also faced an armed challenge from Islamists. This time, however, the Salafi-Wahhabi Islamists in question were hardly paying attention to the state at all. What was most remarkable about this contentious episode, arguably, was that the anti-political creed of the protagonists was so highly developed that they were capable of acting, and they did act, more or less as if the state was not there. The forceful seizure of the Grand Mosque, and the quick use of deadly force to defend it, was clearly a major challenge to the authorities' secular monopoly of the use of legitimate coercion. By taking control of territory, moreover, it challenged the right of the state to regulate it. By usurping the religious authority of the *ulama*, the movement challenged the state-backed system of legitimacy, and by seizing this piece of holy ground, in some respects the centre of the Islamic world, the challenge was all the greater to the Saudis, who made much of their role of guardian of the holy places. Juhayman and his men were trumpeting to the world that the holiest site of Islam was in deeply corrupted and undeserving hands. Nonetheless, Juhayman's men saw the rulers of the kingdom as Muslims, and not as infidels. It was simply that they owed those rulers no obedience. The attempt to stage the consecration of the Expected Deliverer 'without interference' was in many ways all that Juhayman required of the state. This was a requirement not to be there, not a set of claims or demands made on the government. There was no mass mobilization, no expectation of an uprising from the masses, no polit-ics in this sense, and no question of seizing power or creating a new political system. Instead, there was a set of messianic beliefs in *hadith* prophecies. When this well-organized and efficiently executed plan backfired, Juhayman had no answers, and even issued words of regret when he was pulled from the gas-filled interior, presumably because something had gone wrong in regard to the Expected Deliverer. Thus it was that a profoundly apolitical movement clattered onto the stage of Saudi and global politics.

The foray into political mobilization undertaken by another current within Salafi-Wahhabism, that of the Brotherhood-influenced, 'awakening' movement in the early 1990s, was in many ways a complete contrast with the seizure of the mosque. This time the target was the temporal power of the state and the reform of its political system. This time the identities and principles of the Wahhabi protagonists were influenced not by an Al-Albani but by the heirs of Hasan Al-Banna, the modernist and political Syrian and Egyptian Muslim Brotherhoods, whose members played such an important role in staffing Saudi Arabia's educational system, especially since the 1960s. The social bases of the movement were considerably more affluent, and educated, and its cadres had positions in the state and religious system. And this time the repertoire of contention involved mass meetings, pamphlets, *hadith* competitions, faxes from the exiled (newly minted) Committee for the Defence of Legitimate Rights (CDLR), and a major Memorandum of Advice to the Saudi rulers urging reform, signed by a wide array of Islamists and religious figures across the country.

While this round of contention has been read as a response to the fall in the oil price during the 1980s, or a result of the collapse of the authority of the Saudi state in 1990–1, these structural factors should not be exaggerated. Both factors were important, especially the Gulf crisis, when the Saudi state accepted and Ibn Baz condoned the deployment of around half a million American troops on Saudi soil as part of the operation to oust the Iraqi forces from Kuwait. This factor shook the *status quo* and divided opinion like nothing in the modern history of the kingdom (Meijer 2009: 28). Burgat speaks of '[t]he collapse of the Islamic legitimacy of the Saudi guardians of the holy places of Islam immediately after the 1990 alliance with the US against Iraq and the resulting emergence of a powerful Islamist opposition to the monarchy in Riyad' (Burgat 2003: 53). Certainly, the crisis is probably the best available explanation for the timing of the Sahwa contention, as things turned out. Nonetheless, detailed attention to the identities, principles and social bases of the movement (Lacroix 2011) can better explain how they did what they did, the sorts of claims they made, and the goals they had, and the form taken by their strategies and tactics, and to some extent the nature of their subsequent interactions with the authorities.

It should be noted in this regard, against structural determinism, that certain rivals of the Sahwa, such as a quietist trend that emerged from the remnants of the JSM, bolstered a staunchly apolitical current in the 1990s, a current that insisted that the true vocation of the religious should be to ignore what the state was doing in matters of politics, and bitterly criticized the Sahwa. This group (the jami) thereby offered significant (and much appreciated) support to the Saudi monarchy (Lacroix 2011: 215). Here rivalry (and perhaps opportunism) within the political field was as important as the larger geopolitical situation. Moreover, another Salafi-Wahhabi trend, an heir to a more unrepentant branch of Juhayman's state-rejecting movement, who gathered round a new HQ called Bayt Shubra, were ferociously discontented by Ibn Baz's *fatwa*, but engaged in no significant mobilization to begin with – or certainly led no initiatives on the lines of the Sahwa. Doctrinal 'battles' (Meijer 2009: 21) raged indeed, but these did not always translate into contentious politics.

The contrast between the educated and political reformism of the Sahwa, and the rugged and doctrinal moralism of Juhayman was sharp indeed. The CDLR, for example, was set up by highly educated Saudi professionals in 1993, and operated in London after being exiled within a year. They advanced a clinical and very much legal and rights-based critique of the patrimonialism, despotism, social arrogance, personalism, and organizational and strategic incompetence of the Saudi royals and other powerful members of the political establishment. They argued for root-and-branch political reform. In 1995, they demanded the

immediate and unconditional release of all political prisoners and then the restoration of the legal rights of the people including the rights of freedom of speech and assembly and the right to choose their accountable leaders (Committee for the Defence of Legitimate Rights 1995).

They linked Saudi failings to the submission and incompetence of 1990–1, and American support for Saudi despotism. They mocked the royals by saying that even 'the temperature in Baghdad is forbidden'. What this referred to was that the 'official news channels [in Saudi Arabia] stopped broadcasting the temperature in the capitals of the Arab states accused' of helping Iraq!' (Committee for the Defence of Legitimate Rights n.d.). The CDLR committed themselves to non-violence and persuasion, disseminating their ideas with pamphlets, and a number of lengthy tracts. In exile, they made extensive uses of faxes sent to leaders and ordinary Saudis alike during the mid-1990s.

While the exiles kept up the pressure for a while, on domestic soil the campaign fizzled out as early as 1994. Lacroix argues that this had less to do with repression than might be expected – especially because repression was not as heavy as conventional views presume (Lacroix 2011: 202). His explanation turns on the absence of the development of strongly developed mobilizing structures within the Sahwa movement:

Although the Sahwi protest in principle had the resources necessary for a successful mobilization, the movement's leaders needed the backing of reliable and solid grassroots networks in order for the protest to endure against the regime (Lacroix 2011: 201ff.).

This is a convincing point. But, while Lacroix seems to attribute this lack to the absence of an 'open public sphere' (Lacroix 2011: 226), a factor which must carry some weight, it should be pointed out that the Muslim Brotherhood in Egypt did engage in mass, grassroots organization, as did the Palestinians in the occupied territories, as, to some extent, did Shi'a movements in Iran and elsewhere, in spite of the absence of strongly protected autonomous and legal spaces guaranteed by a liberal state. A further shaping factor thus needs to be taken into account: for all the influence of the Muslim Brotherhood in Saudi Arabia, the key Salafi-Wahhabi activists in the kingdom maintained a doctrinal rejection of politics as conducted by Islamic modernists and secularists alike; their forays into politics may have been transgressive but they were no 'insurrection'; instead, they were limited and tentative; while the Shi'a in the Eastern Provinces were quick to engage in demonstrations, strikes, road-blocks, and even uprisings, in the midst of heavy repression, Salafi-Wahhabis did no such thing. We might usefully therefore accord some status to their identities and principles in explaining the non-mobilizing repertoire of contention that they undertook. If we accept this, then the next flurry of contention in the kingdom is easier to explain.

Just when the Sahwa contention had run out of steam, on 13 November 1995, a car-bomb exploded at a US-run National Guard training facility in Riyadh. Five Americans and two Indians were killed. This was the first major attack of its type on the Al-Saud regime in many years, and it was one of the first spectacular attacks on US interests in the kingdom. The targeting of the attack clearly aimed to indict the alliance between the US military forces and the state. Apart from screening the staged confession of the perpetrators on television, public details about the incident were sparse. The four perpetrators were executed soon after and the attack failed to spark a wider cycle of contention. This very failure was significant, however, because it helped to persuade the international *jihad* movement that richer pickings might be found elsewhere. Within a year, Bin Laden was targeting the United States.

The attack was carried out by a small group of men, drawn from the international *jihad* movement on the one side, and the state-rejecting heirs of Juhayman on the other – their first joint action. The doctrinal vision of the heirs of Juhayman was stitched into the 'men of action' from the Arab–Afghan *jihad*. Three of the executed perpetrators had met while fighting in Afghanistan. The fourth was a rejectionist, who had for a time frequented the Bayt Shubra community and was in personal contact with Al-Maqdisi (Lacroix 2011: 196–7). The latter was an influential and widely known Palestinian shaykh born near Nablus in 1959, but raised in Kuwait, and linked first to Qutbist and then to JSM circles. He had offered an original synthesis of Qutbist and JSM ideas in the 1980s: adopting Juhayman's concept of the community of Abraham, but unlike Juhayman, accepting the doctrine of *takfir* (excommunication) of rulers who do not govern according to God's revelation (Lacroix 2011: 101).

The vital background to this attack was the armed struggle against the Soviet invasion in Afghanistan in the 1980s, during which time a new kind of international *jihad* movement was born, lavishly supported by the CIA, the Pakistanis and the Saudis alike. The Saudi authorities, in the wake of Juhayman's movement, had woken up to the domestic threat, and many considered that exporting their 'fervent youth' to fight a foreign *jihad* would offer an important safety valve. Other Saudis were involved in funding the movement. The most important of these was of course the wealthy scion of a hugely successful contracting company, Ussama Bin Laden, who, more than just sending money, went out to Afghanistan to join the struggle. Lacking religious credentials, Bin Laden 'successfully fostered an image of modesty, austerity, and simplicity' (Gerges 2005: 183). Beyond this, Saudi Arabia did provide the bulk of the volunteers, several thousand at least (Hegghammer 2010: 47), while thousands were also drawn from across the Arab world and beyond (Rasheed 2006). In Afghanistan, the Sunni *jihad*, recently taken up in the Arab secular states against the Near Enemy, now combined with a newly minted Wahhabi *jihad*, aimed at defending Muslims in particular territories around the world wherever they were threatened by invasion or occupation by non-Muslims (Hegghammer 2010: 38ff.). The state-sanctioned pan-Islamist mantle was now donned and turned to armed struggle by its true believers acting beyond official initiative.

Diverse Sunni movements were brought together to some extent by the common experience of fighting the Soviets. On the other hand, issues of leadership, doctrine, and organization remained highly significant in determining unity and fission. Hence the important role played at the junction of these converging streams by certain key figures, activists and religious figures, who acted as articulators between different segments of the movement, providing principles and identities capable of assisting unification. Abdullah Azzam was one of these figures. In 1980, feeling the pressure in Jordan, he had taken a university job in Saudi Arabia, where he 'rubbed shoulders with many of the exiled Muslim Brothers and discussed with them the plight of Muslims around the world, including in his home country of Palestine' (Calvert 2007: 19). He then came out urging *jihad* in Afghanistan as a *fard ayn* – that is, a duty incumbent on every individual Muslim, rather than a decision for a particular political community to take collectively. This was a remarkable position which made every Muslim duty-bound to fight in whichever part of the world Muslims came under occupation. It differed sharply from a more mainstream position, for example among the Wahhabi *ulema*, which asserted that only Muslims in that particular territory were obliged to fight (Hegghammer 2010: 40–2). Azzam said that *jihad* was an immediate duty, just like saving a child from drowning is; one does it regardless of what parents and community leaders might say (Calvert 2007: 50–1). He also argued that women could participate, against the strictures of authorities in Afghanistan. *Mujahidin* who initially saw their involvement in Afghanistan as a launch pad for later operations against the Near Enemy came to be influenced by the view of figures such as Bin Laden who insisted that Muslim solidarity against the Far Enemy was the key (Gerges 2005: 119–50).

When the *jihad* in Afghanistan wound down, having achieved its objectives, it also started to fragment, with many divisions coming to the fore. But the de-mobilized soldiers of this armed struggle then returned to their home countries, ready for more armed struggle in the name of Islam, in Bosnia, Chechnya and elsewhere. Doctrine remained important: for example, for most Saudi jihadists, 'getting militarily involved in Algeria was out of the question because it was an internal conflict, not a classical *jihad* pitting Muslims versus non-Muslims' (Hegghammer 2010: 53). The car-bombing in Riyadh in 1995 was one of the few echoes of the return of the jihadists to the Saudi scene in the 1990s. Skilled in armed struggle, eschewing politics, and having no time for petitions and memoranda of advice, or faxes, although appalled at the repression of the Sahwa, this group went straight to the method of the car-bomb, deploying the extensive training and networks they had built in Afghanistan. The operation was aimed at the US military presence in Saudi Arabia, and also indicted the position of the Saudi royal family in allowing it. But neither the quietists nor the modernists, nor many other conservatives of different stripes, nor of course the official Wahhabi establishment, who taken together were in the overwhelming majority, supported the bombing. Saudi Arabia was not like Algeria, where stolen elections made a modernist FIS ripe for transformation into a *jihad* movement, and where wider cadres and organizations in Francophone Algeria were not nearly so doctrinally savvy as they were in Saudi Arabia. Classical jihadists had no viable organizational base in Saudi Arabia, and lacked religious and theological credentials there (Hegghammer 2010: 97).

It was now that the idea of striking the Far Enemy (the United States) was born in the ranks of Osama Bin Laden's organization, Al-Qa'ida, originally established in Afghanistan in 1988. This was in part about an 'internal upheaval' within the jihadist movement:

Al Qaeda emerged as a direct result of the entropy of the jihadi movement in the ... 1990s and as a desperate effort to alter the movement's route, if not its final destination, and to reverse its decline (Gerges 2005: 24).

In search of a new *raison d'être*, after the failure in Saudi Arabia itself, as well as failures almost everywhere else (Hegghammer 2010: 99), and in order to sustain itself, the movement turned from defending Muslims in this or that territory towards attacking the Far Enemy, the United States, as the 'head of the snake'. Thus developed a new kind of global *jihad*, targeting the United States above all, and sanctioning attacks on Western civilians. Global jihadists built up a real organizational base, complete with military training camps, indoctrination, recruitment networks and increasingly skilled use of the media and the newly appeared Internet in their safe haven in Afghanistan between 1996 and 2001. Al-Qa'ida also had some limited organizational development in Yemen in the late 2000s, and in Saudi Arabia, especially after 2000 (Hegghammer 2010: 99–129). This was particularly possible after the necessary religious and doctrinal backing for global *jihad* appeared in a distinct stream of anti-Sahwa and anti-modernist theology – the Al-Shu'aybi school – which emerged in Saudi Arabia through informal clerical networks from the mid-1990s onwards (Hegghammer 2010: 83–98).

The attacks on the World Trade Center in September 2001 were a propaganda success for Al-Qa'ida, even if they led directly to intense criticism in the Muslim world, and the near destruction of Al-Qa'ida's operational capacity in Afghanistan following the US invasion. The US response to these attacks, driven by a resurgent neo-conservatism, fit perfectly the narrative that the global jihadists had been crafting to vilify the United States itself. The US invasions of Afghanistan and Iraq were read in Islamist circles as confirming its position as a crusading force bent on the humiliation, oppression and destruction of Muslims (Hegghammer 2010: 143ff.). Just as Bin Laden had hoped, the United States lashed out militarily 'against the *ummah*' (Gerges 2005: 271). In the fevered atmosphere that emerged in the early 2000s in Saudi Arabia, Bin Laden, pushed out of Afghanistan, devoted his attention to organizing in Saudi Arabia, giving birth to the campaign of violence waged by Al-Qa'ida in the Arabian Peninsula against US interests and more and more against the Saudi security forces in the mid-2000s. Destroying the Ba'thist regime in Iraq in 2003 by invasion and blundering occupation, the US defeated an implacable enemy of many an Islamist, and inadvertently created a territory in the MENA where Al-Qa'ida could flourish. The subsequent rise of global jihadism among Sunni Muslims and foreign volunteers in Iraq, spearheaded not by Bin Laden, but by the Jordanian Abu Musab Al-Zarqawi (d. 2006), was a new development, as this current had hitherto made little impression there (Gerges 2005: 251ff.). Nonetheless, Al-Qa'ida in Iraq became vulnerable because of its own acute sectarianism: it spent more time killing civilian Shi'a and other 'deviant' Muslims than it did fighting the United States. This paved the way for splits, and dramatic losses of support. In 2010, Al-Qa'ida in Iraq, as well as the organization more generally, was reduced to a tiny rump.

The Arab uprisings of 2011, and more precisely the long- and short-term failures of both the Asad and the Iraqi regime to in any way tackle the chronic need for more participatory and consensual forms of rule, paved the way for the resurgence of Al-Qaʻida – this time in the shape of what was to become known as the Islamic State – amid the bankrupt policies of regional and external powers (Cockburn 2015). The new entity covered important territories in Syria and Iraq, and laid claim to the Caliphate in June 2014. The 'tragic phenomenon of the Afghan Arabs [was to some extent] ... replaced by that of the "Iraqi Arabs"', as Gerges feared long before (Gerges 2005: 269). The movement carried out spectacular killings of Western civilian hostages which drew in airstrikes. The result was bloodshed and insecurity on a wide scale, a situation intended by the Islamic State's strategic 'management of savagery' as a prelude to its goal of imposing a new order. The strategy was capable of generating conflict and bringing volunteers, but it was doubtful whether it could actually establish a new order when its own actions did so much to bring about bloodshed and insecurity.

The reform movement in Iran

In the wake of 1979, the revolution started to devour its children. Like most major revolutions, this one was invaded, and, as in France after 1789 and the Soviet Union after 1917, the Iraqi invasion of March 1980 added great fuel to those seeking to repress and execute 'traitors' and 'spies'. The Iraqi invasion of Iran in 1980, with at the very least a supportive tilt from the United States and its allies (with countries such as West Germany supplying chemical weapons), played an important role in greatly diminishing the pluralistic potential of the newly minted Islamic Republic of Iran. In mobilizing for war against Iraq, and in the clash with the United States, driven by the more radical elements among the Shiʻa revolutionaries, who carried out the hostage taking, the Islamic revolution consolidated power on a theocratic basis:

The seizure of the US embassy in 1979, and the escalation of the war with Iraq during the 1980s facilitated the suppression of internal complaints, including those of the urban poor, in the name of national unity, national security, and the anti-imperialist campaign. Thus open, collective, and audible mobilization was seriously undermined, and the disenfranchised withdrew into backstreet politics (Bayat 1997: 164).

By 1982, much of the political pluralism of the Iranian revolution was extinguished, activists were killed, imprisoned or exiled, and real power in the state was taken by a clerical leadership under Imam Khomeini. The Family Code was repealed, many female civil servants lost their jobs, co-education was banned, all women judges were sacked, and women were barred from various professions. A version of Islam championing property rights and male privilege won out in the corridors of power against more socialist and feminist conceptions.

The reform movement in Iran in the 1990s and 2000s opposed theocracy and sought a more democratic, pluralistic and less male-dominated version of the Islamic Republic than that of the 1980s (Adib-Moghadam 2006; Bayat 2007: 106–35). Reformists were drawn from the usually urban and educated ranks of seminarians, politicians, thinkers, students, women, NGO activists and others. They had appeal among the younger generation that had known nothing except the Islamic republic – and among the politically marginalized middle classes. They had a champion in Khatami (b. 1943), who was president, 1997–2005. Many were drawn from among the most ardent revolutionaries, who now advocated a change of course. A striking role here was played by religious intellectuals (Ashraf and Banuazizi 2001; Kurzman 2001; Mir-Hosseini and Tapper 2006; Sadri 2001). They blended Islamic theology with science, reason and an emphasis on civil liberties and democracy. Many refused the idea of the infallible interpretation of sacred texts, rejecting Khomeini's rule of the jurisprudent as an undesirable and undemocratic innovation. Some carried out woman-centred readings of Islamic texts, advocating for women's equality in the press, and took on masculine domination in matters of divorce and child custody (Tripp 2013: 192–9). Iran's despotism was not blamed on the West. In place of the culture of martyrdom, bravery, discipline, militancy and war, many now emphasized reform, tolerance, plurality and peaceful co-existence. Figures like Akbar Ganji (b. 1960), a leading journalist and intellectual who had been in the Revolutionary Guards, came to oppose the ideologization of the religion, which he argued led into totalitarianism. He was imprisoned during 2001–6 for his views. The reform movement refused binaries of East–West: 'they discerned differentiation, change and hybridity within these worlds, and flow and dialogue between them' (Bayat 2007: 88). The movement made use of the press, and from the late 1990s the Internet and blogs, and displayed their preferences in consumption patterns (e.g. wearing jeans), the use of public space (e.g. mixing men and women in parks), promoting colourful women's clothing or female biking and ski-ing, and in arts, literature, film and music. In some respects, formal forms of movement organization were eschewed. As Reza Delbari, the Islamic Association leader at Amir Kabir University, put it:

The student movement is not a political party, an institution, or a political actor; on the contrary it is the antithesis of such powers. Its objective is to mobilize for democracy and human rights and to reform power (Bayat 2007: 108).

Where the reform movement took aim at civil society, it was fed by diverse leaderships. Where it took aim at the state, Khatami was its oft-acknowledged leader, even if students and others became increasingly disaffected with his apparently timid and legalistic leadership over time. Khatami's legislation aimed at diminishing the powers of theo-cratic Islamic and judicial oversight of elections and presidency. But his bills never got past the Council of Guardians, which threw them out in April and June 2003. Many questioned whether theocrats would ever consent to the erosion of their own power through a legal route, which in turn seemed to owe too much to negotiation and compromise, and through legalism lost the attention of wider constituencies worried about more social and economic issues. Khatami's own constituencies were unsure about his strategies, and wider constituencies were not mobilized by the constitutional question. The election of Ahmadinejad on a more populist and socially conservative platform signalled the end of this political phase of the reform movement. Many of the same *dramatis personae* and ideas, however, were involved in the Green Movement, which rose up to contest the results of a stolen election in 2009 (Tripp 2013: 82–8).

In the 1990s and 2000s, the country that had seen an Islamic revolution now brought forth a more secular set of social trends and movements than was present in any of the *secular* states of the Arab world. This was not simply because the rulers claimed Islamic legitim-acy and thus opposition took a more secular tone; in Saudi Arabia, where rulers also claimed an Islamic legitimacy, opposition took on an even more religious form. It owed something to the intellectual content of the movement, which was partly provided by religious, reformist intellectuals, who risked (and often received) imprisonment for their views. Liberal reformism was re-emerging in other states of the region from the 1990s onwards. The uprising in Bahrain was a case in point.

The uprising in Bahrain in the 1990s

In November 1992, a polite petition, praising the ruling Al-Khalifa family, and signed by many opposition and other prominent figures, was presented to the Amir of Bahrain raising the historic demand for the restoration of the National Assembly that had been dissolved by decree in 1975. When such petitions yielded little fruit, and repression was ratcheted up, protests became mass demonstrations and confrontations with security forces from December 1994 onwards. After September 1995, arson and bombings became more frequent, as well as demonstrations by women. During 1996, boycotts of state services added to the action. It was only in 1998 and 1999 that the uprising subsided – without a National Assembly having been achieved. For at least five years, much of the small island of Bahrain had been a witness to a major uprising that sought to bring a greater measure of political freedom to an island dominated by the sectarian and segmentary logic of a Sunni ruling family and elites. In some respects, this was the latest phase in a decades-old struggle in Bahrain, in which reform had been attempted in 1953–6, sporadically in the 1960s, and again with some short-lived success with the 1973 constitution and the two-year establishment of the National Assembly (Khalaf 1998). It was a demonstration not only of the capacity and unity of reformist forces within the political field under the liberal banners of constitution and parliament, but also of the entrenched and implacable opposition of the dominant bloc, backed by Saudi Arabia and the United States, to meaningful reform of any kind.

A crucial aspect of the background to the uprising was the long-standing failure by the Sunni sectarian regime to allow forms of meaningful political participation through representative institutions, in the face of rounds of contestation that had aimed at this since at least the 1950s and even before. The closure of the National Assembly in 1975 when it started to threaten the power of the dominant bloc, especially because of the incipient alliance there between the religious and secular forms of opposition, was only the most recent demonstration of this. Bypassing representative politics, the regime made selective use of modern forms of tribalism, the support of regional states and rents, and the use of intermediaries through which land, position, citizenship or other gratuities were distributed. Intermediaries were encouraged to intervene on behalf of beneficiaries, generating a form of vertical and segmented politics (Khalaf 1998: 27) through which demands for political representation in the state could be forestalled. Ruthless coercion was meted out to those who sought participation or representation that would violate this politics (Khalaf 1998: 32).

In the run up to the Gulf War of 1990–1, after which Bahrain housed a key US military base, signals from the state-censored media appeared to indicate that political reform was in the offing, as part of a *quid pro quo* for Bahraini participation in the US-led conflict. In the aftermath, Amnesty International reported a relaxation of repression in Bahrain (Khalaf 1998: 39), which encouraged reformists to mobilize around constitutional positions. The amir even met with petitioners (e.g. on 15 January 1993) and promised to study their demands. However, nothing meaningful was done in the way of reform. Hopes raised were disappointed. The consultative body that was created was merely window-dressing. Worse, in the face of these heightened expectations, the regime moved swiftly to crack down on protest gatherings, and some of the demonstrations that appeared, provoking intense grievances. Levels of repression that never rose to a full military assault then only fanned the flames of discontent until 1997, when a more conciliatory strategy on repression was adopted (Lawson 2004). In short, the contradictions and failures of the dominant bloc played an important role in driving the uprising.

Arguably even more important than the failure of the regime was the proactive and unified nature of the reformist contentious mobilization. A wide variety of opposition leaderships and groups came together on a similar platform of political freedom in the early 1990s. All of Bahrain's leading political opposition currents lined up behind the petitions of 1992–4. The Elite Petition, as it was known, of November 1992, for example, included Shaykh Abd Al-Amir Al-Jamri, a Shi'i religious scholar and former member of the National Assembly with a following in the villages; Dr Abd Al-Latif Al-Mahmud, a Sunni religious scholar and university professor; as well as Muhammad Jabir Al-Sabah, a former Leftist member of the National Assembly (Lawson 2004: 96). The armed uprising of 1980 inspired by the Iranian revolution had come to nothing, and was notable only for how it underlined the failures of a revolutionary and externalist strategy, paving the way for a more reformist and domestic stance. Analogously to the Lebano-nization of Hizbullah in the 1990s, the Shi'a parties and groups in Bahrain now sought a place in the political institutions of the local state, which opened very slightly to participation, domesticating their previously more transnational politics (Louër 2008a: 238–9). The broad reformist platform thus united a wide variety of groups: liberals, Shi'a, notables, some Sunni Muslims, elements from the business community (Lawson 2004: 93–4) aggrieved at discriminatory concession granting, Baharna (indigenous Bahrainis), workers blaming the regime for unemployment and poor advancement possibilities at work, and women, who had been politicized as students or discovered gender discrimination at work or ran into regime repression of their newly developing associational life. Among those who signed the petition of November 1994, nearly 20 per cent were women. Another petition sent to the Amir in April 1995 was signed by more than 300 women, 'mainly professionals and/or members of women's associations' (Fakhro 1997: 178), who had often encountered repression. The griev-ances of poorer Shi'a Bahrainis in the labour market regarding hier-archy and the lack of advance at work on the one hand, and the increasingly acute competition of Asian labour on the other, were very much directed at the regime, its discriminatory policies, 'and the cor-ruption of some of its key figures' (Louër 2008b; cf. Bahry 2000: 138). This framing allowed those who were seeking reform at the level of the state to link themselves to the labour grievances of the poor and middling strata, including women, who in turn sought the reform of the state and representation within it. An unemployed workers' dem-onstration, one of the first key demonstrations of the uprising, outside the Ministry of Labour and Social Affairs in June 1994, signalled the role of labour, although the demonstration was dispersed and came to nothing. Petitions were signed by ever larger numbers. In October 1994, for example, a petition demanding greater political freedom was signed by 23,000 persons.

In short, a rising tide of reform, uniting a very broad coalition of forces, came together during 1992–4, with a strong sense of its own historic legitimacy and the reasonableness of its demands and methods. The demand for a constitution was 'the most basic of the popular demands', as the Bahraini Freedom Movement put it, on which 'all sectors of the people agree' (Bahraini Freedom Movement 1995: 1). It was this rising pressure, even more than any sudden crisis afflicting the regime, that lay behind the force of this contentious mobilization. When demonstrations were met with violence and key leaders arrested (as they were in December 1994), protest underwent a scale shift towards mass demonstrations. These demonstrations, seen as 'disturbances' by the authorities, were in turn met with a violent crackdown. Over the next few weeks, 30 were killed, a few hundred injured, and 3,000–5,000 arrests carried out, including that of nearly 30 women and 50 children (between twelve and fifteen years of age). Again, the repression aimed to provoke sectarian conflict, and to paint the uprising in diversionary, sectarian colours – hence all the arrests were among the Shi'a (Fakhro 1997: 181–2). It does not seem particularly puzzling how, under such circumstances, repression led to more transgressive forms, including arson and attacks on government buildings and targets, as well as forms of civil disobedience linked to boycotts of state-provided services such as electricity, and the use in villages of barricades and stone-throwing youth, *intifada*-style, to prevent access by government forces.

The diverse, relatively secular and democratic uprising in Bahrain, like that in the Occupied Palestinian Territories, but unlike that in Egypt in 1977 or Algeria in 1988 or Lebanon in 2005 (as we shall see), was highly sustained. While in Algeria the government had come with concessions, which had demobilized the movement, in Egypt and Lebanon the leadership simply was not present or had different goals and intentions. In Bahrain, just as in the Occupied Palestinian Territories, leaderships were very much involved and able to sustain and coordinate the action for months and even years, albeit without winning political concessions until 1999. Bahraini exiles, of whom there were increasing numbers, did not give up their politics in the face of deportation. Instead, they developed in receiving countries in Europe and North America their networks, media experience, and a broadly appealing rights discourse, documenting and publicizing in reports and electronic bulletins the extensive human rights abuses of the Bahraini regime (Beaugrand 2015). Nonetheless, Western policies were little changed (Mahdi n.d.). The 'United States thought that free elections might bring in a majority of Shi'a fundamentalists, thus leading to a pro-Iran parliamentary policy. Added to this, the United States previously experienced the 1975 parliament, in which the "People's Bloc" opposed any US military presence in Bahrain. Hence ... strategic and commercial interests overruled democracy and human rights ...

causing the United States to stand by the regime' (Fakhro 1997: 183). All the GCC states, moreover, 'supported all the steps taken to quash the uprising'. The Saudi Interior Minister visited Bahrain and declared that 'the security of Bahrain was inseparable from that of Saudi Arabia' (Fakhro 1997: 184).

With such external support, the ruling amir believed that the domestic protest wave could be ridden out. Unlike in Iran in 1979, when even the oil economy was disrupted by strikes, the popular rising did not fundamentally disrupt the political economy of a regime that drew its resources from outside the national economy. On 16 December 1995, the amir insisted in his National Day speech on security, order, the interests of the country and a policy of 'firmness'. He spoke of:

certain incidental adverse events aimed at disrupting the security of citizens, the nation and its prosperity. Such actions are, categorically, far from the nature and spirit of both this nation and various ranks and sectors of the people (Fakhro 1997: 185).

What such a patrimonial dismissal added up to was a refusal to meet all delegates and their petitions, a policy of suppression and a failure to undertake constructive reform. A new minister of education and president of the University of Bahrain was now selected from the ranks of the military. And in 1996 a new system linked the provinces to the Ministry of the Interior (Fakhro 1997: 185). The authorities had a powerful, anti-democratic device: they spoke fancifully of a Shi'a, Iran-backed plot to overthrow the government. But, as Fakhro remarked in 1997, 'they have not produced the evidence to support the case' (Fakhro 1997: 182). Indeed, to the chagrin of the Arab Shi'a, the Persian Shi'a community, 10 per cent of the total population, 'remained neutral and silent' (Fakhro 1997: 183). When ninety-two government employees added their names to a petition calling for political reform in April 1995, the government demanded written apologies under threat of the sack (Fakhro 1997: 178). The combination of economic and state power was formidable.

Nonetheless, the movement's powers of institutional disruption made an impact. The accession of a new ruler in 1999 allowed the government to distinguish between the political and the 'violent' opposition, and to make real political concessions on security laws, political prisoners, exiles, parties and newspapers, and women's suffrage, and to promise a constitutional monarchy complete with parliamentary elections and a new constitution, which was duly promulgated in 2002 (Tripp 2013: 107–8). For a segment of the political opposition, these concessions opened an avenue of political participation. However, the violent repression of the 1990s generated a bitter legacy, heavy-handed tactics continued to be used against demonstrations throughout the 2000s, and structural inequalities remained. The constitution of 2002 also fell short of the demands of the Shi'a, socialist and Arab nationalist opposition parties, who boycotted the elections of 2002. Bahrain's political problems were by no means resolved and protests were to return again.

The independence *intifada* in Lebanon, 2005

In the wake of the dramatic car-bomb assassination of ex-prime minister and Saudi-linked Sunni billionaire Rafiq Al-Hariri on 14 February 2005, a series of protests and street demonstrations against Syrian military control (which was widely blamed for the killing) started to develop, with student activists of the Free Patriotic Movement linked to Michel Aoun, an exiled Maronite ex-general, in the forefront. These protests, involving tens of thousands in all, were countered by a massive Hizbullah-organized demonstration on 8 March 2005. Perhaps half a million were mobilized from many parts of Lebanon. They joined the General Secretary of Hizbullah, Shaykh Hasan Nasrallah, in thanking Syria for providing security in Lebanon and warning against interference by the United States. An even bigger, perhaps million strong, pro-independence demonstration took place in Martyrs' Square in downtown Beirut on 14 March 2005. The demonstration was planned by an emerging pro-'Syria Out' coalition of long-standing Sunni, Christian and Druze politicians, but given substance and force by the more spontaneous energies of almost a quarter of the entire population of the country, a seemingly unbelievable statistic. These protests were hailed for geopolitical reasons in Washington as a 'Cedar Revolution', and many analogies were in the Beltway and beyond to the recent 'people power' protests in Ukraine and elsewhere, which had also, often inadvertently, served US interests. By the end of April 2005, under heavy regional and international pressure, Syria withdrew its troops. The 'independence *intifada*' had achieved its most crucial goal. In the longer term, however, early optimistic assessments (Kassir 2005; Safa 2006) were proved to be largely that. Greater democracy, diminished sectarianism and socio-economic solutions remained elusive in Lebanon – vindicating more disillusioned analyses (Salti 2005). And Lebanon, now closer to the United States and detached from Syria, became vulnerable to the Israeli desire to eliminate Hizbullah: the Israeli aerial bombardment of Hizbullah, the Shi'a, the south and Lebanese infrastructure followed in the summer of 2006, more than a thousand mostly civilians were killed, tens of thousands of homes, shops and schools were destroyed, and perhaps a million from the south were temporarily displaced.

Increasingly isolated on the regional and international stage, Syria, dominating Lebanese politics since the early 1990s, overplayed its hand in 2004. Bashar Al-Asad insisted on an extra-constitutional extension of the term of President Emile Lahoud, who was isolated even among his own Maronite constituency. This insistence was unnecessary as there were many other pro-Syrian Maronites that Syria could have chosen. In the process, moreover, a powerful, Saudi-linked and by no means anti-Syrian figure, Al-Hariri, was snubbed. Although direct evidence is lacking, a Bashar Al-Asad determined to prove his strong-man credentials (Ajami 2005: 25) might well have then been behind the assassination of Al-Hariri in order to pre-empt the latter's drift into the opposition camp and send the message that Syria controlled Lebanon and would brook no dissent. It turned out to be a major blunder. At the time, Al-Asad knew that the only mass-mobilized force on the Lebanese scene was Hizbullah, which was an ally of Syria. But in this there was no thought for what might happen, and no regard to the ways in which contentious mobilization can generate new subjects and forms of politics.

It was not that the US attack on Iraq in 2003 was somehow the key to rising protest in Lebanon. This thesis has been advanced speculatively (Ajami 2005) and without serious evidence that would link such protests to the US War on Terror. Instead, protest against the Syrian military control, interference in political, educational, economic and other aspects of Lebanese life, had been on the rise since the 1990s (Chalcraft 2009: 192–204). By the late 1990s, articles in the press, official and academic studies and reports, meetings, talks and panels aired extensive criticism of the Syrian control in Lebanon. The first anti-Syrian street protests and demonstrations, whose actions were shaped by this critique, were staged in the second week of May 2000. Students linked to the exiled Aoun's Free Patriotic Movement put on a number of innovative campaigns and actions which received wide coverage in the media. In one case, for example, they sold 'Lebanese' produce on the streets – as a show of opposition to the presence of Syrian worker vendors, and urged Lebanese workers to join the 'insurgency' against the Syrian occupation. Syrian control, not labour rights, was their key concern. Until that spring, the word 'occupation' had rarely appeared in the mainstream Lebanese press in regard to Syria. From that time, it started to become increasingly common. The timing of these protests, whether by accident or design, was acute: the Israeli withdrawal from south Lebanon was completed on 23 May 2000. The occupation in the south now over, thanks to the Islamist resistance, it was just the moment for attention to be transferred to occupation from the east, a move spearheaded by new forms of resistance.

These student protests were sometimes met with repression, photos of which were circulated to illustrate Syrian violence. Over time, some communists, other Christian groups, and elements from Walid Jumblatt's Progressive Socialist Party, were drawn towards the opposition camp. It was the assassination of Al-Hariri that then generated another major leadership for the opposition movement, bringing over Al-Hariri's new entourage, extensive business interests and supporters, and fledgling dynasty. This assassination also engaged the more spontaneous energies of broad sections of the population, who could see less and less of a security rationale for the Syrian presence, chafed at the competition for jobs and wages represented by Syrian workers in the country, and hoped for a more democratic and less corrupted and sectarian political system. All of these grievances were expressed in the widespread laments for the slaying of Al-Hariri, who was suddenly depicted as Mr Lebanon – a symbol of national unity and economic and political progress.

This episode of contention involved some of the largest, mass demonstrations in an Arab country that anyone could remember. The protests certainly compared to January 1977 in Egypt or October 1988 in Algeria; they bore family resemblances to the first *intifada* of 1987–91 and the protests and demonstrations in Bahrain during the 1990s. They were more secular than religious; they involved mass demonstrations; they were not completely controlled by any single leadership; they took aim at forms of oppression socio-political not cultural; they politicized new sections of the population, and they owed something to spontaneity. That there were no attacks on the signs of wealthy, luxury and regime power was not an indication of some new threshold of peaceful values imbibed by essentially 'advanced' protestors – in spite of media trumpeting of non-violence. It should more plausibly be linked to the fact that first, the identities, principles and demands espoused by the crowd were not socio-economic, and hence there was no rationale for staging assaults on property, and, second, that there were few high-profile Syrian targets to attack in downtown Beirut, which was instead dominated by Al-Hariri's Ottoman-style mosque and his own glitzy shops and luxury developments, which were very much not the target. Indeed, the visible Syrian 'targets' that did exist were the Syrian workers, a stigmatized, low-paid and hard-working population, who *were* violently attacked: sometimes there were planned assaults using explosives on shanties housing Syrians, and sometimes there were more spontaneous confrontations sparked by bands of Lebanese youth on the streets (Chalcraft 2009: 200–4). Between February and April 2005, Syrian workers lived through the worst violence in Lebanon that they had experienced since the civil war, and many were driven out of the country. This violence took place in back streets and slums and went largely unreported in the media generally.

Martyrs' Square in downtown Beirut came under more or less permanent occupation by protestors during March and April, and urban public space was in an unprecedented way politicized (Haugbolle 2006), a process which built on earlier rounds of protest against Hariri's own exclusionary and corrupt development of downtown Beirut itself in the 1990s. People power protest of this kind was hugely inspiring to wide sections of the Lebanese public, desperate for unity, desiring to put the scars of the civil war behind them, to escape from the dead hand of Syrian control, and to build a more democratic political system. This kind of protest, even against the wishes of the country's most powerful mass movement, Hizbullah, showed its great capacity when Syrian troop withdrawal followed. Before February 2005, few had predicted such an eventuality. When Russians and Saudis alike signalled their unwillingness to back Syrian control, the writing was on the wall: a costly and coercive re-assertion of Syrian military power in Lebanon did not look feasible. People power had played its part: the mass mobilizations of spring 2005 re-asserted the Lebanese national subject and heavily underlined its commitment to independence from Syria – and the costs to the Syrians who would oppose it. This assertion stemmed much from the new politicization of those who demonstrated for the first time, or were suddenly enthused by new possibilities. 'Now, we're not following our leaders', declared one participant, '[o]ur leaders are following us' (cited in Tripp 2013: 129).

Protests of this kind also re-iterated the condition of their success: that there be no systematic military campaign of repression and/or that repression remain low-level and provocative rather than crushing. Indeed, there were many reports of police and security forces in Lebanon allowing protestors to walk through their lines unmolested, a practice which became systematic during this period. And Syria never sent troops to downtown Beirut. Part of the potency of such an uprising, then, was that it presented regimes with a stark choice, bloodbath or capitulation.

On the other hand, the relatively spontaneous aspects of the popular uprising also showed their weakness: where the energies of the masses were not linked systematically to new organic leaderships with a meaningful programme of transformation, pre-existing leaderships, albeit in new guises, could return to the stage, and start to determine the course of events. The Syrian *mukhabarat* were out – this was a real gain, although US influence was increasingly in. But, while the Lebanese elections of June 2005 were among the freest and fairest in Lebanese history (Safa 2006: 1), once the coalitions of 8 March, underpinned by Hizbullah, and that of 14 March, underpinned by the Al-Hariris and the Jumblatts consolidated their positions, with Aoun's movement working between these coalitions, many of the sectarian logics of the Lebanese system re-asserted themselves, albeit on re-formulated bases. These actors, after all, had cut their teeth long before March 2005, their real origins lay in the civil war. They had entered the action during the period of the uprising in order to manoeuvre for position and to advance their interests. These interests were re-formulated and re-coloured, but it cannot be plausibly suggested that they fundamentally changed. Not for the first or last time, then, people power showed its short-term strengths and long-term weaknesses.

The return of liberal and labour protest in Egypt, 2000–2010

As long as the Palestinians were appearing to make progress towards a two-state solution, the inaction of the Mubarak regime on the

Palestinian file could be obscured. But the outbreak of the second *intifada* in September 2000 showed definitively that the Oslo process was broken, vivifying Egypt's complicity with the US and Israeli agenda on the regional stage, especially as the Mubarak regime did nothing meaningful to support the Palestinians. Moreover, with the termination of the Islamist armed struggle in the late 1990s, the lack of progress on democracy in Egypt could no longer be blamed on the need to repress 'fundamentalists'. Instead, the Mubarak regime and the many ways in which it corrupted and manipulated the electoral process, was in the dock. Mubarak fell in line with the Israeli–EU–US siege of Gaza after the elections of 2006 brought Hamas to power – another violation of widely held values – which was widely read as a 'deal': Mubarak would do US–Israeli bidding on Gaza in return for the West turning a blind eye to his 'old man's' attempt to ensure the succession (*tawrith*) of his widely disliked, non-military son Gamal to the presidency. Gamal had his own clique of business cronies whose billions caused resentment and whose networks threatened an old guard in the dominant bloc. Mubarak's capitulation (*istislam*) and inertia on the regional stage were even clearer in the context of the US-led invasion of Iraq in 2003; the Israeli assault on Lebanon in August 2006; the trade and gas treaties with Israel, which were accompanied by regime corruption; and the lack of concrete responses to the Israeli bombardment and massacre of trapped Palestinian civilians in Gaza in 2008 and 2009. In general, the ostentatious wealth and corruption of the very narrow elites that made gains in the context of high levels of GDP growth were more marked than ever before in the Egypt of the 2000s.

Discussions were launched on a more regional level in liberal and educated circles after 2000 about the iniquities of the *gumlukiyyat* – liberal critic Saad Eddin Ibrahim's resonant phrase denoting the mixed form of republic/monarchic rule that now loomed as a threat to the once proud revolutionary republics. A case in point was that of Bashar Al-Asad who succeeded his father in Damascus. The minor political opening in Syria had led to a flurry of liberal and democratic activity and critique in Syria during 2000–1 which was soon repressed and went underground. In Egypt, in late 2000, for the first time, formerly sharply opposed ideological currents (Islamists, liberals, the secular Left and Nasserists) started to organize together to demonstrate support for the Palestinians (Mahdi 2009), an innovation even if these alliances were hardly complete, with co-operation between Islamists and Leftists being particularly fraught (Abdelrahman 2009). Islamists and liberals could find common ground in a search for a more liberal political field. After September 2000, urban protestors started to identify the regime (rather than Israel, the West or capitalism) as the major problem. This meant that the usual 'safety valve' effect, in which domestic regimes were let off the hook amid the criticism of Israel or grand abstractions, ceased to operate. Open criticism of the president, who was initially compared to the then recently discredited and corrupt Suharto in Indonesia, was voiced in demonstrations and in secular terms for the first time in years.

During the 2000s, a number of more senior liberal politicians came out in public as cautious opponents of Mubarak's presidency-for-life. Ayman Nur (b. 1964), founder of the Al-Ghad Party, and member of the parliament, stepped up to become the first to run in an election against Mubarak, winning 7–13 per cent of the vote in the heavily controlled and corrupted 2005 presidential elections. He was soon to be imprisoned until 2009. The stance of these politicians inspired some educated youth to get involved in political activism for the first time.

The Kifaya! ('Enough!') movement emerged from the ranks of the youth during the elections of 2005 protesting in legal, constitutional and democratic terms the proposed transformation of the republic into a hereditary dynasty. This movement involved the more or less active participation of several thousands in signing petitions, attending meetings and some demonstrations. Those involved were mainly urban (chiefly Cairean), educated, secular and relatively high-status youth, new to political action of any kind, many being students or recent graduates (Mahdi 2009). Some were the offspring (in the literal sense) of the now de-mobilized Leftist generation of the 1970s.

Kifaya! did not bequeath a continuous organization: it took a more networked and de-centralized form. This made it weak and insignificant in the eyes of the security forces – but in some respects gave it a certain strength, as there was no vanguard to imprison, headquarters to ransack, newspaper to close, bank account to seize, or chain of command to disrupt. This network was significant in acting to bring new and more secular and human-rights-oriented groups, including elements linked to leading NGOs, into political activism in de-centralized and participatory ways. However, without a permanent organization or clear strategy, or any outreach to subaltern social groups in terms of social demands or organization (de Smet 2012a: 287), the movement lost momentum by 2007.

Meanwhile, the Mubarak regime started to push privatization of Egypt's public sector industries more insistently, especially after July 2004, with the installation of a 'businessmen's cabinet' implementing Washington Consensus economics. State-owned factories and businesses were increasingly sold off to Egyptian, Saudi and other financial interests, and cut backs, job insecurity, redundancies, missed bonuses that had been promised, and deteriorating wages and conditions were the result. In addition, a long-term decline in the wages and conditions of public servants of all kinds, from teachers to tax-collectors, along with cuts to subsidies and rising prices in basic commodities, were all at work.

In the face of this attack on socio-economic rights and protections, and the hardships involved, Egypt's labour movement underwent a resurgence unknown since before 1952. The reports of the Land Center for Human Rights indicate that collective actions, strikes, sit-ins and demonstrations by workers were already becoming more frequent in the early 2000s, with over 100 incidents per year. During 2004–6, more than 200 actions per year were recorded. During 2007, in the wake of the successful strike at Mahalla in December 2006, there were 'a staggering 614' collective actions (Beinin 2009: 77), and then 608 during 2008 (Alexander 2009). During these years, over 1.2 million workers and their families were mobilized (Beinin 2009: 77; de Smet 2012a).

Workers were tenaciously defending their lives and livelihoods and the rights that their moral economy insisted were theirs, and the place that they believed they were entitled to in Egypt's national development (Bassiouni 2007). By late in the decade, as Joel Beinin observed, some workers stopped saying 'Where is the President?' (in order to bring about his intervention) and started invoking the need for democracy, stating even on record that the president and the 'whole regime' must go. The statist union (the Egyptian Trade Union Federation, ETUF) was invariably opposed to strikes. Workers drew strength instead from the renewed 'climate of protest' (Bassiouni 2010) in the country, and the activities of some NGOs set up by veteran activists. Unionists ousted by corrupt elections from the ETUF in 2006 played a role in organizing the strikes and confrontations with the ETUF that followed in December (de Smet 2012a: 284). On the other hand, workers organized mostly locally and informally without national organization or links to political parties (Beinin and Duboc 2013).

The property tax collectors, mobilizing tens of thousands in strikes and sit-ins in downtown Cairo over three months after October 2007, did manage to organize nationally, won a major pay rise (300 per cent), and went on to establish Egypt's first independent trade union (the Property Tax Authority Union) during 2008–9. Teachers, health technicians and pensioners followed suit (de Smet 2012a: 273–81).

The labour movement now inspired elements among the liberal youth to try to develop linkages between urban liberals and workers. This gave birth to the 6 April Youth Movement, some of whose members had cut their teeth in Kifaya!. This group called a 'general strike' to coincide with a workers' strike at Mahalla Al-Kubra on 6 April 2008, but without organizing on the ground. These activists, searching for ways to protest without attracting massive repression, suggested that people stay at home, on strike, to show solidarity with the workers. The Mahalla strike, however, was broken up before it really got going, and the 'general strike' had only a slight visible impact. Workers remained suspicious of the distant agenda (de Smet 2012b: 150) of 'counter-productive' urban activists and their ideologies (Tripp 2013: 159). Calls for a 'Day of Anger' by similar networks in April 2009 largely fizzled out (Alexander 2009). Some linkages, albeit tentative and problematic, between some workers and some urban liberals were nonetheless established for the first time.

Activists started to use blogs and Facebook in increasing numbers to publicize the human rights abuses and corruption of the Mubarak regime, benefitting from the protection against repression that web-based anonymity provided. These bloggers and groups attracted followers and readers in their tens of thousands among the new generation. New forms of theatre, art spaces, cultural clubs, poetry, music, the independent press, certain NGOs and satellite television were also sites in which educated and liberal youth developed their criticism of the regime (Mossallam 2012). These sites developed in leaps and bounds throughout the first decade of the twenty-first century.

In short, during the 2000s, liberal and labour protests in Egypt developed an unmistakable and proactive momentum, generating new forms of leadership, new spaces of mobilization, new forms of organization, and articulating liberal and secular principles as a critique of the sclerotic and authoritarian regime. While hegemonic contraction had played its role, much depended on the constructions of activists themselves. One striking innovation involved the increasing presence of horizontalist styles of organizing and radically democratic doctrines: an emphasis on deliberation, leaderless/leaderfulness, a rejection of doctrinalism, and a striving for egalitarian consensus-building. It is striking that, just as in Bahrain, which itself had witnessed the rise and fall of an armed Islamist challenge in the previous decade, the critique of the regime was no longer couched in primarily religious terms; in Egypt, while the reformist activism of the Muslim Brotherhood continued as before, the novelty was that there were many, newly mobilized constituencies articulating secular and liberal principles. Just as in Bahrain, some of the centrist religious currents had joined hands with liberal currents. In Egypt, the betrayal of 1979 had been read in Islamist terms by small groups of revolutionaries. The cuts of 1977 had been opposed in Nasserist and Arab socialist terms. The inertia and corruption of 2000 onwards was now read in terms more secular, liberal and reformist by increasingly broad constituencies. This new reading owed a great deal to the initiatives and ideational constructions of activists themselves.

It is perhaps noteworthy that repression was arguably more cautious in Egypt than in Bahrain. The Mubarak regime refrained from unleashing the iron fist on workers: these were the 'sons of the nation', not easy to discredit as 'foreign agents', had the power of institutional disruption, and a tenacious strength. Bloody incidents, moreover, might have discouraged foreign investment. The urban youth presented a different problem: high status, enjoying access to global media, technologically savvy, and sometimes linked to wealthy members of the dominant bloc, they were part of the new, open-for-business face that Egypt was attempting to project. This may have made them harder to repress – and these activists in turn sought to protest in ways that avoided open confrontation with security forces. This context and these tactics did offer opportunities for new forms of protest to develop. But they also – at least before the murder by police of Khaled Said in June 2010 in broad daylight in Alexandria – failed to offer the egregious and high-profile violations that might have generated more transgression or activated the energies of wider constituencies. Unlike in Bahrain, wide sectors of the urban poor, who continued to suffer at the hands of the police and the failing economy, stayed away from noisy and overt protests, hunkered down and sought to get by as best they could.

The BDS movement for Palestinian rights

In May 2011, Ehud Barak, an ex-Prime Minister of Israel, who had also been Chief of the General Staff in the Israeli army, spoke to the left-leaning Israeli daily newspaper, *Ha'aretz*:

There are some pretty powerful elements in the world that are active in the matter ... in various organizations of workers, academics, consumers, green parties ... And this drive boils down to a large movement called BDS [boycotts, divestment and sanctions], which is what they did with South Africa. It won't happen all at once. It will begin, like an iceberg, to advance on us from all quarters (Ehud Barak, 9 May 2011, interview in Ha'aretz, cited in Wiles 2013: 222).

In the early 2010s, politicians of the dominant bloc in Israel started to take the BDS movement more seriously. Whether or not the movement was an iceberg, it was certainly highly de-centralized and horizontally organized, with initiatives coming from many quarters and countries. By the early 2010s, activists had been at work for almost a decade. With the lack of progress made by the second *intifada*, the Israeli re-invasion of Jenin in April 2002, and the search for new kinds of non-violent politics that could break the impasse of occupation, colonization and Islamist armed struggle (Tripp 2013: 122–6), a number of Palestinian academics and students, along with half a dozen or so like-minded academics in Britain and France, started to raise the question, in secular and democratic terms, of boycotting the institutions of the Israeli state that were complicit in colonization and occupation (Morrison forthcoming).

Trans-regional solidarity movements extending to the populations of the colonial or ex-colonial centres have hardly played a role in the history of the region; the French Communist Party supported Abd Al-Krim in the 1920s; some French radicals assisted the FLN; British and some other European labour movements in Europe had often had links of various kinds to counterparts in the MENA; early forms of feminism in Egypt had many links to European feminists. But such movements were relatively rare and weak – and had almost never included liberals or democrats, who had either collaborated in imperialism, or played second fiddle to the Left in any critique of imperialism. BDS activists were therefore trying to create something new. In this, they were heavily inspired by what the international BDS movement had achieved in bringing down Apartheid in South Africa in 1994–5 (Wiles 2013). For all the differences between the two cases, Jewish ethnocracy stemming from settler colonization and British colonial sponsorship did bear many resemblances to white racism and Apartheid stemming from settler colonization and British colonial sponsorship in South Africa (Bakan and Abu-Laban 2010; Glaser 2003; Piterberg 2008; Yiftachel 2006, 2009).

From early calls, discussions, union and associational activity in both Palestine and the United Kingdom and to a lesser extent France between 2002 and 2004, well over a hundred Palestinian associations, unions and committees endorsed a general call for boycotts, divestment and sanctions on Israel in 2005. Over the next decade, academics, consumers, students, church groups, workers, unions, co-operatives, campaign groups, and professional associations from Palestine, the United Kingdom, the United States, France and to some extent other countries as diverse as Spain, Australia and Pakistan, their ranks swelling in the wake of Israeli military atrocities in 2006, 2008–9 and 2014, built a movement with thousands of activists (and not much funding) against Israeli racism and human rights violations (Barghouti 2011; Hickey and Marfleet 2010; Morrison forthcoming). The movement scored some success in provoking debate, and in generating boycotts of Israeli academic and cultural institutions, notably by world-famous scientist Stephen Hawking in 2013. It also caused divestment in some cases, such as the major Dutch pension fund PPGM in January 2014, and a loss of contracts worth billions in Europe for companies such as Veolia whose reputations were tarnished by campaigners because they operated in the occupied territories. The movement acted to break down some of the racist, ethnocratic and neo-Orientalist hegemonic scaffolding that fortified the ongoing Israeli colonization of Palestinian land. It also provoked a considerable amount of well-funded activity by Zionists attempting to row back on what they saw at best as the 'de-legitimization' of Israel and at worst an anti-Semitic 'poison pill' (Brackman 2013). The Israeli Knesset passed a Boycott Prohibition Bill in July 2011 which allowed civil prosecutions against individual advocates of boycott (Tripp 2013: 126). The BDS movement has nonetheless made progress in defining the central issues of the conflict in terms of democracy, anti-racism and rights – after a decade in which armed struggle under Islamist banners targeting civilians had been dominant.

In the present, as long as external military intervention, Salafi-Wahhabi Islamism, civil war, and acute regional conflicts between states and their backers intensify or continue, Israel will be able to continue to colonize Palestinian land, business among elites will continue more or less as usual, and the BDS movement will be constrained. If these forms of regional conflict and instability diminish or are resolved, however, the BDS movement will develop, and, because it has the potential to bring in constituencies all over the world under the banners of democracy, self-determination and human rights, could generate unstoppable momentum. At this point, the dominant bloc in Israel and the West would have to think seriously, perhaps for the first time, about the question of Israel and the rights of the Palestinians dispossessed for so long.

The Arab uprisings: the fate of liberals in Egypt, 2011

In July 1908, Abdulhamid II granted a constitution so quickly that the Third Army was kept away, at least for the time being, from dominating the state. In February 2011, the Egyptian president Hosni Mubarak was much more flat-footed, grossly under-estimating the protests, and over-estimating the powers of repression and manipulation wielded by his right-hand man and Interior Minister, Habib Al-Adli. By the time Mubarak started to make concessions, abandoning the succession of his son Gamal and promising not to run in subsequent elections, it was too little, too late. These concessions only confirmed his prior errors to the crowd and boosted their determination to stay put. The protestors successfully 'made their existence as a mobilized, cohesive, political public a reality' (Tripp 2013: 133). The Egyptian army followed the Tunisian example and refused to shoot on the millions of civilians protesting in the full glare of the world's media. This move detached the fate of the military from that of the presidency. The army could not risk the breakdown in its own unity that could well have followed a decision to precipitate a bloodbath.

On 11 February, however, the army seized the initiative, stepping in to unseat Mubarak. The Supreme Council of the Armed Forces (SCAF) set about ruling the country, promising presidential and parliamentary elections and a new constitution. The army could hardly sit on its hands. It was already widely deployed in 'neutral' fashion on the streets. Its vital political and economic interests, along with those of much of the dominant bloc, were under threat from the popular upsurge. The massacre option was off the table. US President Obama, who held some big purse strings, was urging an orderly transition and seeking a new strong-man who could deliver stability and not upset the peace with Israel. And the country was increasingly ungovernable in the face of the regime's own mis-steps (such as withdrawing the police and shutting down Internet and mobile services on 28 January which worried business elites and signalled a revolutionary situation to the entire country) and in the face of the popular uprising, the determined occupation of Tahrir Square, and the strikes that were breaking out in scores up and down the country after 7 February. If the army did not act, then the entire regime really might fall. Perhaps it was the cheering of the crowds that helped give the army the idea that the popularity it had garnered from its neutral stance could propel it (once again) into the very heart of the state – the military character of which had been diluted with the rise of Gamal Mubarak and his clique, and the greater power of the Interior Ministry. The head of the army, Tantawi, after all, had been satirized as the president's poodle. As the chants that urged the army not to shoot went: 'The army and the people are one hand!' (Ketchley 2014). The slogan was tactically clever, as it may have restrained the army, but it was strategically problematic, as it helped to propel an army to power that had no answer to the protestors' problems.

The decision by the army to act as a champion of, and in the place of, the people, and of the leaderships who had helped to organize the uprising was a calculation that paid immediate dividends. The crowd had demanded that the regime fall, but the euphoria unleashed by the resignation of Mubarak was achievement enough for most of these first-time protestors: millions of ordinary people went home after a night of celebration. Some were burning with pride that the brotherly military had stepped in to rescue the honour of the Egyptian nation. To the misery of more revolutionary youth, they sang: 'Hold your head up high, you are Egyptian.' Others were merely content to give the military a chance. Many more experienced liberal and Left activists, although celebrating, were also extraordinarily anxious. They knew that the military had seized the initiative. This sense was underlined when in the following days the SCAF, which was not trusted in these sectors, forcibly cleared the last remaining encampments from Tahrir Square. As the military tried to put the genie back in the bottle, they even declared that 'standing' was forbidden in Tahrir Square – the site of eighteen days of revolution, dignity, solidarity and freedom, during which time even military curfews had meant nothing to the dynamics of the crowds.

The Muslim Brotherhood had long been an important mass organization, and played an important role during the eighteen days, especially in defending Tahrir Square against the thugs of Al-Adli. Workers, already organized, practised and activated in their hundreds of thousands as we have seen, made their mark by demonstrating and then striking in their tens, possibly hundreds, of thousands, both advancing socio-economic demands and declaring their solidarity with the goals of the revolution, and threatening the business interests of the military directly (Alexander and Bassiouny 2014; Clément et al. 2011; de Smet 2012a: 461ff.). The real estate tax workers, teachers, health professionals and pensioners formed a new independent trade union federation (EFITU) on 30 January 2011 which called without immediate success for a general strike (Clément et al. 2011: 9), but signalled the presence of organized labour in Tahrir Square.

The activism of the educated youth, building on the development of their protests and networks since 2000, also played an important role (Gunning and Baron 2013). The youth had already developed tactical expertise and savvy over a decade. They had maintained over years a space for street protest against heavy repression. They had appropriated new sites of mobilization and communication in social media, that had facilitated anonymity and kept the regime flat-footed. They had brought news of regime human rights abuses to thousands in Egypt. They cleverly picked the day of the uprising, National Police Day, activating a very wide-range of grievances against the hated police who had intruded heavily into everyday lives. The liberals' insistence on non-violence may well have been an important element in maintaining the neutrality of the army. Their tactic of starting mobilizations in backstreets and then moving into main thoroughfares and public squares proved effective.

Three further broad and overlapping segments of the population surged into action during the eighteen days in a relatively spontaneous fashion. The first were the low-status young men of the popular quarters who had faced brutality, torture and humiliation at the hands of the increasingly paramilitarized, invasive and corrupt police force over the previous two or three decades, when Cairo's 'informal areas' swelled (Ismail 2006). These men rose up to join pitched battles against the police, which played a vital role in degrading one of the key pillars of the regime (Ismail 2012). The second was a broader layer of the urban poor, struggling to get by and construct functioning markets and livelihoods in the survivalist sector of the so-called informal economy (Elyachar 2005). They saw their fate writ large in the new Tunisian hero, Muhammad Bouazizi. They joined others in disgust and protest against the corruption and restrictions of a neo-liberal order that had not delivered the gains they were told to expect (Chalcraft 2012). Third, women from all walks of life appeared in public demonstrations in very large numbers, and a space for women's participation opened insofar as revolutionary *communitas* temporarily neutralized familiar patterns of sexual harassment: male honour was now engaged in 'protective' mode. These spontaneous protestors provided a good quantity of the disruptive force of the uprising in Egypt. They were a crucial part of the strength and mass character of the uprising.

After 11 February 2011, however, the unity of this extremely broad and diverse revolutionary coalition broke up, and no single group or leadership was present or stepped up with the capacity to lead a revolutionary transformation. The workers pushed forward with vital socio-economic demands, mounting extremely numerous strike actions in a highly tenacious fashion. Organizational links with the parties or vanguards of the urban, liberal or Left remained embryonic at best and a national leadership was lacking (de Smet 2012a: 472). In some respects, the workers did not need, or at least did not think they needed, such urban groups with their agenda, internal arguments, and ideology, in order to press successfully their demands. In many cases, socialists and liberals, sometimes sought to use workers for their own ends, and did not necessarily agree on ideology or strategy. There were splits and disagreements. The Muslim Brotherhood went with a strategy of mobilizing for elections, negotiating with the SCAF, and trying to find with the re-writing of the constitution a place in the state which it had long been denied. It drew away from street protests, the sponsorship of which would have jeopardized both its evolving *modus vivendi* with the SCAF and its respectable, orderly and pious image. New political parties scrambled into action. More than one Salafi party, drawing much funding from the GCC, and shedding key Salafi-Wahhabi principles, organized a political party and started making organizational links especially to rural constituencies, embracing the SCAF-led 'transition' in the process. The urban poor, the young men from the popular quarters and those in the informal sector increasingly melted away from demonstrations. Many trusted the military. Others felt that ongoing protests would disrupt the economy and the tourist industry even further. Others believed that application and hard work (rather than protesting) would set the economy right again. Others feared that protests would bring more insecurity and criminality, which had undoubtedly risen. Committed female activists may not have been put off by high-profile instances of sexual harassment on the streets, including military-initiated 'virginity tests' designed to shame women into returning home for fear of being branded sexually immodest, but women more generally may well have been discouraged by these patterns, which made public protest more burdensome. Most of the popular committees that had sprung into existence to protect neighbourhoods when the police disappeared from the streets on 28 January either disbanded or lost their contentious character.

The revolutionary youth, who in many ways felt ownership of what they saw as a real revolution in-the-making, faced very difficult circumstances – at the moment of what had briefly seemed like a great victory. It became increasingly clear that military rule was unacceptable. It would allow the *ancien regime* to re-group, and the intelligence and police to re-organize. It would compromise the electoral process and the new constitution, a fact which diminished the attractiveness of organizing political parties. The revolutionary youth had not risked their lives only to engage in workaday electoral politics in any case. Or, if they had, the eighteen days had raised their aspirations much higher. The doors of the SCAF, unsurprisingly, did not swing open. Those who did speak to the SCAF were seen, not without justification, as sell-outs or as naïve for imagining that the SCAF would listen. But protesting military rule was difficult, as this alienated the liberal youth from wider constituencies who acquiesced in military stewardship. The revolutionary youth were not even that popular among the middle and upper classes from which they were drawn, as the economic slowdown was felt. These youth organized demonstrations in the name of the continuing revolution, which increasingly came into conflict with the military regime. They found allies among the Ultras football fans, the only organized, politicized forms in which the urban poor were enrolled, and thus one of the only bridges between the revolutionary liberals and the larger population. The Ultras were effective forces on the streets. But, without larger forms of support, and particularly in the absence of the Muslim Brotherhood, the tenacious battles of Muhammad Mahmoud St in November 2011 calling for the overthrow of the military government were lost. There was to be no overthrow of the SCAF. In the wake of November 2011, when electoral politics became the only game in town, many of the revolutionary youth realized that they had been outflanked by more pyramid-like organized political forces, and thus could not effectively compete in the political field.

It is clear that the liberal revolutionaries had been dealt a difficult hand. To what extent had their fate and fortunes been in their own hands? In some respects, these groups had stumbled into a revolutionary situation. They did not long plan for or expect a revolutionary seizure of power. They did not predict the moves of the military. They did not realize that the force of the urban poor would be required to degrade the police (for this purpose instead ineffective roses were to be distributed). There was no strategy for seizing or neutralizing at the operative moment the presidential palace, the praetorian guard, the Ministry of the Interior or the state TV at Maspero. There was no countenancing of the use of force. They did not have a blueprint for post-revolutionary transformation. They did not have a political, economic or social programme capable of having mass appeal. They had organized around human rights, and the attempt to block dynastic rule, and the reform of the state. Their key demand in November 2011 that imminent general elections be postponed came across as confusing, against this background, and lacked wider appeal (Tripp 2013: 105). They had no theory of the state that could thoroughly replace the existing state of affairs or act as a concrete guide to action. Nor did they have a figurehead or leader around whom to group. Some of their anonymous leaders, like Wael Ghonim, once outed, more or less disappeared from the political scene, exchanging revolutionary leadership for a lucrative book deal, talk shows, and an NGO start up or two. There was little or no meaningful move by a substantial and unifying leadership to build a mass organization or platform, whether a political party or something more innovative, that was capable of mobilizing the energies of the masses and building links to the constituencies that moved during the eighteen days. Many of the great anxieties that the revolutionary youth, often justifiably, had about representation, collaboration, co-optation, the discredited parties and

unions, doctrinalism, and the cult of the sole leader, turned into fetters
when it came to the need to build new forms of organization. Activism
using the new media had been effective in building support for an
uprising, but it was no substitute for face-to-face and on-the-ground
organization in the towns and villages of Egypt. In other words, the
would-be revolutionaries of Egypt in 2011 were not prepared for the
revolutionary situation in which they found themselves. In every
respect, they differed from the strong leadership that Khomeini and
revolutionary Shi'ism had provided in Iran in 1978–9. In other words,
there were many features of the leadership and mobilizing project of
the revolutionary youth that played a role in the outcomes. These
leaderships were not capable of uniting the forces of the revolution
and enacting a revolutionary overthrow of the existing order.

These precise patterns were not necessarily repeated in other parts of
the Arab world, where outcomes and national contexts were different.
But, in all cases, the nature and strategies of the different mobilizing
projects in interactions with different forms of elite collective action
that re-organized existing forms of hegemony made key differences to
the course of change. In Tunisia, the grassroots of the UGTT union,
now joined by most of its leaderships, were able to play a real role, and
modernist Islamists managed to pursue a less divisive strategy there
than the Muslim Brotherhood in Egypt. In Libya, the hard core of the
state was shattered by the NATO intervention, and contentious mobilization radically de-centralized, undermining the capacity of new,
would-be national leaderships to steer the new dispensation. It is
noteworthy for our grasp of what difference forms of contestation
make, to point out that, had the protests in Libya been joined under
Islamist banners, a military intervention in their 'favour' by the West
would have been very unlikely. In Yemen, there were a wide variety of
mobilizations, which the old regime was able to divide and play in such
a way as to secure much of its power in an orderly transition to a scion
of the Saleh family. In Bahrain, the role for non-violent mass mobilization initially demanding political reform in the tradition of the 1990s
and before, was radically curtailed by the massive suppression accompanying the deployment of Saudi troops there in March 2011 (Tripp
2013: 106–16). In Syria, there was never a unified or cohesive revolutionary movement. Armed protest was propelled there from mid-2011
as much by self-defence and conscript-defection in the face of the ultra-
violence of the regime as by the forward capacities and decisions of this

or that political force. Minorities there preferred to stick with the devil they knew or, like Kurdish parties, had their own agenda. Urban spaces could not be occupied for any period because of the massive use of force against them. Amid the onslaught, fighters linked to Salafi-Wahhabi trends who had cut their insurgent teeth in Iraq after 2003 were able to gain the upper hand, with some help from the Asad regime itself, generating a complex impasse out of which came the Arab world's first Islamic state. Jordan and Morocco weathered the upsurge with some political reforms and containment strategies. Countries with hydrocarbons – from the GCC to Algeria – ratcheted up selective and non-selective distribution to win acquiescence. Egypt's first Islamist government and elected presidency between 2012 and 2013 lost the support of civil society by trying to monopolize power, was subverted by forces in the state that it thought it had conquered, and became vulnerable to the mass uprising of 30 June and a decisive military coup on 3 July 2013. Egypt then witnessed the largest, public massacre of civilian protestors in the region for many decades. Overall, by 2013, the liberals had lost the initiative almost everywhere. It was a major setback, but, with the bankruptcy of the Islamist revolutionary alternative, and the failure of counter-revolutionary elites to offer new forms of participatory hegemony on the political stage, these setbacks did not by any means spell the end of the advance of liberal politics that had mattered in most parts of the region since the late 1980s. The Arab uprisings had given rise to new and democratic aspirations, and the consequences of this would be felt in the region for a long time to come. They had presented a major challenge to the old order, but gave birth to no decisively new forms of hegemony. Real change would have to wait.

Conclusion

Between 1977 and 2011, amid the exhaustion of the promise of the military men, single parties and increasingly dynastic autocrats that ruled the secular state, revolutionary Islamism, popular uprisings, many a defensive protest, and, more recently, a wide variety of liberal and democratic protests emerged on the regional stage. In Iran came one of the most extraordinary revolutionary successes in the history of the region. The US-allied authoritarian Pahlavi monarchy was swept away and replaced with an Islamic republic headed by a jurisprudent from the seminary in Qom. An array of new political institutions was brought into being, amid sweeping economic and social change. The revolution unleashed an Iraqi invasion, gave rise directly to new forms of Shi'a popular activism from Lebanon to the Persian Gulf, and indirectly inspired a generation of Sunni Islamist revolutionaries, who radicalized their methods and goals.

Sunni Islamists had a broad impact on culture and society in the Arab world, playing a role in the resurgence of new forms of pious comportment and social conservatism. Islamists re-wrote the dominant terms of a widely held secular worldview, dismantling ideas of progress and reaction in favour of the idea of authentic and endogenous Islamic and Arab society that was under threat from corrupted and exogenous forces associated with the West. Imperialism was redefined for many as being a matter of cultural corruption and a clash of values rather than of economic exploitation and a clash of material interests. The Islamists had their impact in defining problems in identitarian rather than socio-economic terms. In Iraq after 2003, Islamists and other forms of resistance prevented the United States from controlling the country, or installing a secure client regime there. Hizbullah was the first non-state mobilizing project to force the Israelis to withdraw from occupied territory in May 2000. Hizbullah was also able to foil a sustained Israeli attempt to destroy them by military force in the summer of 2006.

While statist provision was in retreat, especially reformist Sunni Islamist movements provided goods, services and new forms of social life to probably millions of poor. They also won mostly symbolic concessions from secular regimes, who sometimes competed with Islamists to try to re-claim the moral high ground on issues of sexuality in particular. In some cases, especially where reformist Islamists ran for elections, such as in Algeria between 1989 and 1992 (but also in Jordan, Yemen and Egypt to varying extents), the effect, albeit not necessarily long-lasting, was to deepen and popularize forms of albeit truncated democratic electoral practice, and define Islamism in more democratic terms.

Those who protested in more defensive terms the unravelling of statist developmentalism and socio-economic provision, and this included the 1977 *intifada* in Egypt, as well as 'bread riots' in Morocco in 1981 and in Morocco and Tunisia in 1984 (Tripp 2013: 150–1), were able to win socio-economic concessions in many cases and slow the course of neo-liberal advance. The uprising in Algeria in

October 1988 was the direct cause of a remarkable move by *le pouvoir* in Algeria to announce a turn towards multi-party elections. The labour movement in Egypt was clearly able to blunt the course of privatization, up to a point, during the 2000s. Power-holders could not afford to be insensitive to this kind of protest, partly because they did not want to frighten foreign investors, partly because workers still had powers of institutional disruption, and partly because it was harder to depict workers who were clearly struggling to get by and not attached to any particular political current as inauthentic, or subversive, or as agents of foreign interests. The grassroots activists of the UGTT union in Tunisia played a role in defending labour rights throughout the period, beginning with the strikes of 1977 and culminating in a general strike in 1978 (Tripp 2013: 150), and helped to develop the powers of the uprising of 2010–11 that unseated Ben Ali. The mass demonstrations in Lebanon in 2005, involving perhaps a quarter of the total population of the country, were the direct cause of the withdrawal from the country of Syrian troops, whose occupation had begun in 1976. The uprisings of 2011, more generally, removed four dictators, directly (in Tunisia and Egypt) and indirectly (in Libya and Yemen), and shook the *status quo* in the entire region, politicizing a new generation, and winning new socio-economic concessions for populations from *rentier* states, and some political concessions elsewhere.

The 'first' *intifada* of 1987–91, a popular uprising involving a remarkably sustained campaign of civil disobedience against Israeli occupation and settler colonization in the name of Palestinian national self-determination, rescued the PLO-in-exile, re-asserted the strength of Palestinian national identity, transformed the hitherto terrorist-dominated European image of Palestinians, led directly to Jordan renouncing its claim on the West Bank, and was a key element in bringing the Israelis to the negotiating table in 1991. The *intifada* also illustrated the possibilities of mass-based forms of direct action and institutional disruption as a strategy. It paved the way for the Oslo Accords of 1993, which many hoped would bring a two-state solution to the Israeli–Palestinian conflict.

Reformists were able to pluralize the political space in Iran, at least between 1997 and 2005, while putting the government on notice after 2009 that fraudulent elections would be the cause of massive protest. Likewise, protests in Bahrain in the 1990s and from 2011 onwards demonstrated that the country would not be stable unless concessions

were made on questions of constitution, parliament, and discrimination against the Shi'a. The long-standing movement for women's
rights in Morocco, based in various NGOs founded since the 1980s,
and focused on petitioning the king, gathering signatures, and press
campaigning, won an important victory in the teeth of mainly Islamist
opposition when the king used his immense authority to steer through
a New Family Code in 2003–4: wives won joint responsibility within
the family, women were no longer required to have a guardian after the
age of 18, and women's rights regarding polygamy and divorce were
improved (Tripp 2013: 181–92). The Kifaya! movement in Egypt
contributed to defining the succession in Egypt as a real question for
the dominant bloc, and Egypt's militant bloggers and liberal movements played important leadership roles in the uprising of 2011. New
liberal movements have very much put on the table the question of
how to develop new forms of leadership and organization that do not
lead into hierarchy and authoritarianism.

Sunni Islamist revolutionary projects, for all their vast energies, only
produced one state (the Islamic State in parts of Iraq and Syria in 2013)
during the entire period. This state was a violent and bitterly sectarian
entity that provoked and attracted violent repression from external
powers. Indeed, revolutionary forms of Islamism, especially those
ready to engage in armed confrontations with secular regimes, very
often attracted repression and violence, contributing inadvertently to
the ever more ramified development of the security state, and failing to
bring about the wished-for Islamic state. Armed Islamists gave secular
regimes a chance to posture to domestic and international audiences as
the only forces for 'stability' amid a 'chaotic' and 'violent' region. They
gained rents from outside and garnered legitimacy from posing as a
kind of necessary evil. They turned such support to repressive account
in crushing popular mobilization in general, repression which did not
always extend to the very Islamist groups that fitted the caricature most
closely. As Burgat argued, in Iraq, Palestine and the Arabian peninsula,
'[u]nrepresentative Arab states would be unable to withstand domestic
pressure to reform were they not beneficiaries of the West's unconditional support in their "struggle against fundamentalism [read local
dissidents]"' (Burgat 2003: xiii–xiv). Many of these armed Islamists
turned out to be 'useful idiots' for the repressive and narrowly self-
interested aspects of the policies of the dominant bloc in the region and
internationally.

The rise of Islamism owed something to the support of states, above all on the international stage. It was not so much that, domestically, states repressed the Left, while supporting domestic Islamists or leaving them unscathed. There are, of course, numerous examples of states suppressing the domestic Left: for example, the repression and exile of the communists in Iraq in the 1960s and 1970s 'left the disadvantaged of the capital with no organized means of protest and produced a void in the underground which the Da'wah and Mujahidin hastened to fill' (Batatu 1981: 583). Another example comes from Bahrain in 1973 with the suppression of the Popular Front for the Liberation of Bahrain (Fakhro 1997: 179–80). There are also examples of states and rulers supporting local Islamists. In the 1950s, King Husayn viewed Islamists as a strategic ally against Arab nationalist and socialist critics. In the early 1970s, Anwar Al-Sadat released Islamists from prison to counter Nasserism. In the early 1980s, Chadli Benjedid facilitated the rise of the Islamist movement as an auxiliary force for his policies in a purge of Leftists and Boudmediennists. Through the 1990s, the Yemeni president, Ali Abdullah Salih, pitted Islamists against socialists to weaken the influence of the latter (Browers 2009: 2–3). Bourguiba did something similar in Tunisia (Burgat 2003: 23).

However, there are just as many examples of state repression against Islamists. Bourguiba, for example, made 6,000 summary arrests of Islamists, having been unnerved by the April 1989 election results (Burgat 2003: 78). Hundreds were killed and executed in the repression of Juhayman's movement in 1979. In Syria, the torture of Islamists was widespread, and in Hama in 1982 between 10,000 and 30,000 people, including many members of the Muslim Brotherhood, were killed (Lefèvre 2013: 110–15). Thousands of Islamists were killed by the Algerian security forces in the 1990s. And one of the largest single massacres of peaceful protestors in Egypt's history took place in August 2013 at the hands of the Egyptian security forces: on this occasion, up to 1,000 Muslim Brotherhood supporters were killed. It may well be true that Islamists have a more extensive record of being arrested, tortured and executed at the hands of the state since the 1970s than the Left. This itself is a remarkable indication of the way repression does not determine the identities and principles of protest in any deterministic or linear way.

On the other hand, the Left has had little or no meaningful support or sponsorship from states since the 1970s, whereas Islamists have, both domestically, and above all internationally. The willingness of states to sponsor movements beyond their borders weighed in the fortunes of secular and Left nationalism in the 1950s and 1960s, and this has mattered in the waxing fortunes of Islamists in the more recent period. Iran sought to export the revolution, and had an impact through Hizbullah in Lebanon in the 1980s. Saudi Arabia has exported by means subtle and less subtle forms of Salafi-Wahhabism, from Afghanistan in the 1980s through to Sunni militancy in Lebanon since 2005 and Syria since 2011. Qatar has followed a line sympathetic to the Muslim Brotherhood, distinctively through Al-Jazeera, and arguably played a role in initial Brotherhood ascendancy after 2011. These foreign policies can be sharply contrasted with the notable lack of support by regional and external states during this period for meaningfully democratic, let alone Leftist movements.

More important, nonetheless, in explaining contentious mobilization since the 1970s, are the multiple failures of the dominant bloc in the secular states, their jealous monopolization of the political field, and the forms of hegemonic contraction at work therein. We must also attend to the agency and intellectual labour involved in the fact that many of those who seized the initiative defined their normative invest-ment in terms of Islamic identities, principles and frames. Just as in earlier periods, there is no way to explain fully why those defining things in Islamist terms were the ones who seized the activist initiative, while those defining things in other ways did not. But we can note that those who did seize the initiative, for whatever reason, drew on the elaborations and constructions of intellectuals, lay and clerical, who proposed a new reading of the region's problems, and new ways to tackle them. In other words, the rise of Islamism as a radical alternative to the *status quo* was no different in explanatory terms to the rise of revolutionary nationalism in the 1950s and 1960s, or that of liberals in the previous or more recent period, or that of neo-Sufis or millenarians in the period before that. Amid conditions of acute crisis, certain groups seized the initiative, borrowing from the thought of those who offered untarnished revolutionary alternatives. While post-1967 democratic trends on the Left did try to define revolutionary alterna-tives to the secular state, they were not that successful in doing so, were often heavily divided, and only rarely engaged in real mass mobiliza-tion to promote their vision. As we have seen, the Left in Egypt in 1977 was limited in this regard. The only current in the region that had always maintained that the secular state was a catastrophic betrayal of the promise of anti-colonial liberation was the Islamist one.

The fate and fortunes of Islamist projects owed a great deal to the forms of leadership they developed, and the extent to which they were capable of winning consent. The reformist Muslim Brotherhood in Egypt, which adopted an accommodationist stance towards the secular regime, and engaged in mass mobilization of a serious kind, was able to win a real social base. On the other hand, the small *takfiri* groups encountered both massive repression, and did not engage in mass mobilization beyond propaganda of the deed. They were not successful. The only group that scored a success following spectacular violence was Al-Qaʻida, who either predicted very well the almost unhinged response of the United States to 9/11 (i.e. to mount a massive attack on Iraq, which had nothing to do with 9/11), or simply got lucky. By attacking Iraq, the United States provided Al-Qaʻida with a collapsed state and aggrieved constituencies in the heart of the MENA in which to operate. Popular Shiʻism in Iran, which was able to unite a far broader constituency than any Sunni Islamist revolutionary group, and which unusually combined such broad appeal with a revolutionary agenda, was able to make far greater gains – especially where the shah did everything to hand the initiative to them, and the cards fell in a fortuitous way.

The dynamic interactions between the Left and the Islamists in the Arab world often acted to undercut the capacity of the Left to organize a constituency capable of confronting the secular regimes. This was partly because the Left often chose to stick with the state against the Islamists – as the lesser of the two evils. This dynamic rather reinforced the undemocratic nature of much of the Left, and acted against Left attempts to evolve in a more democratic direction, especially as the Islamists were increasingly perceived to rule the arena of mass mobilization. The Algerian Parti de l'Avant-Garde Socialiste, founded in 1966 as an heir to the Algerian Communist Party, was reconstructed in 1993 as Ettehadi. During the Algerian civil war, Ettehadi strongly opposed the Islamists and supported the banning of FIS, linking itself to the 'eradicating line' of the Algerian generals whose absolutism it once challenged (Burgat 2003: 53). Mohamed Boudiaf (1919–92), one of the historic founders of the FLN, returned from exile in 1992 to become chairman of the Algerian High Council of State, a figurehead body for the military junta, following the annulment of the election results in which Islamists had won. He was assassinated by a body-guard, apparently an Islamist sympathizer acting alone, shortly there-after. In Tunisia, the Mouvement Tunisien des Démocrates Socialistes gradually renounced the fight against Bourguiba's authoritarianism, and preferred, 'without shame', to rally round the regime with weapons and supplies. In Egypt, the Tagammu' (National Progressive Unionist Party), founded in 1977 by former Free Officer and promin-ent Leftist figure under Nasser, Khaled Muhieddin (b. 1922), refused in 1991 to be associated with the Muslim Brotherhood-led boycott of obviously rigged elections (Burgat 2003: 52–3). While this pattern was not completely general, it did act to draw the Left closer to the secular regimes and pushed the Islamists to rely more on their constituencies.

The rise of significant, organized, liberal currents from the 1990s onwards must surely owe something to the fact that liberals, for the most part, started to take the initiative to undertake mass mobilization, especially as armed Islamism subsided on the domestic stage. Liberals made key contributions to the 25 January 2011 uprising in Egypt, as we have seen.

Arguably, then, it was far more the dynamics of hegemony and leadership that contributed to the shape and outcomes of mass mobil-ization in the region since the 1990s than, for example, the existence of the new media – satellite TV, social media and mobile phones. While these forms did help break down the state's monopoly of the media, and they can help us understand the new modes of organization (and some of the strategies and tactics) that activists of all stripes were able to use, they struggle to account for which groups came to the fore, for the fact that activism was much less mass-based or sustained in the key *rentier* states (from Algeria to Saudi Arabia), the content of principles and identities mobilized (e.g. Islamist versus secular), and a great many of the strategies and tactics used. All political tendencies used the new media. What mattered was the nature of these tendencies, not the means they used. That activism was linked to path dependencies, differed by national context, and did not exhibit any linear relationship to the depth of Internet penetration, are all factors that tend to reinforce this thesis. The new media played many roles, but what mattered was who was using it, and to what end.

Conclusion

This book has aimed to demonstrate that the history of the Middle East and North Africa since the eighteenth century cannot be understood without paying attention to the role played by contentious mobilization. From the uprising in Ottoman Egypt against the French occupation of 1798–1801 to the Arab uprisings of 2011, a wide variety of mobilizing projects have reinforced fragile or brought into being new collective actors and thereby weighed heavily in the region's political dynamics and settlements. This history cannot be captured by solely top-down or power-institutional accounts.

The first part of the book argued that the long crisis of the dynastic and Islamic state from 1798 to 1914 cannot be understood without taking into account a wide variety of revolutionary, reformist, autonomist and defensive mobilizing projects. Such movements were sometimes able to carve out spheres of autonomy and to promote forms of justice and equality in the operations of the political order – at least in certain times and places. Sufi orders and tribal notables kept the French at bay in many ways in Algeria. Or, petitioners and mobilization around elections for village and guild heads in Egypt in the 1870s were sometimes successful, and deepened these sites of articulation at least until the period of British rule, which dismantled them. Weapons of the weak could blunt the force of the burdens imposed by the centralizing states. Reformists established the principle of representation in the state on at least three occasions – in Egypt during 1881–2, in Iran in 1905 and in Istanbul in 1908 – although on each occasion the effort was knocked back. Revolutionaries under the banners of Islam brought two new states into being, one in Sudan, the other in Arabia, while Abd Al-Qadir in Algeria and Al-Hiba in Morocco also brought temporary, new forms of statehood. In all cases, though, these new states were either destroyed, or accommodated themselves with imperialism.

The crisis of the Alawi, Ottoman and Qajar states was not brought about solely by European pressure or the activities of the dominant bloc. One of the most important contributions that mobilizing projects made to this crisis was unintended: they regularly acted to provide the pretext for, and even more actively to draw in European imperial intervention from outside. This took place in the Balkans from at least the 1820s onwards, southern Algeria, Morocco and Tunisia after the 1840s, on Mount Lebanon after 1858–60, in Egypt in 1882, in Sudan in the 1880s and 1890s, and in Iran in 1911. Not for nothing did people in Egypt mutter 'ya 'Urabi ya khurrabi' ("Urabi you destroyer') after his movement played a role in precipitating the British invasion of 1882. Where contentious mobilization was unable to challenge British clients, as in the Persian Gulf, highly indirect imperial rule remained the norm. Uprisings playing an important role in pushing out colonial occupation, such as that in Egypt in 1798–1801, were the exception rather than the rule. On the other hand, colonial invasion occasionally took place without any relevant preceding mobilization at all – Egypt in 1798 and Algeria in 1830 were two cases in point. In many ways, the nineteenth century, at least compared to the period 1914–76, left a bitter harvest in terms of the achievements of contentious mobilization. Contentious movements were neither able completely to replace, escape, sustainably reform nor adequately defend the state and its forms of hegemony. The tenacity of their failed attempts, nonetheless, contributed significantly to the crisis of dynastic states guaranteed by divine favour, Islamic law, sultanic justice and customary autonomy – and to the ways in which the failures of these states were judged.

The second part of the book argued that, when the existing absolutist, dynastic and religious order was finally broken down in the years surrounding the First World War – above all by colonial invasion and the First World War in combination with the enormous power of Turkish nationalism – liberal nationalists in the Arabic-speaking world were able to hegemonize broad constituencies and make a significant contribution to the construction of a new form of national political community and to at least briefly and tenuously establish principles of liberal representation within the state. Reformist, defensive and autonomist traditions of protest converged to give nationalism a force that it would not otherwise have had. Without an understanding of this activism, it would be impossible to understand why amid shattered dynastic and Islamic states the political field was constructed anew on national and partially liberal lines. Moreover, the development of nationalist, Islamist, socialist and liberal ideologies during these years were productive in the making of a new kind of national political field, based on the institutionalization of popular political participation in the politics of the centralized state.

The struggles of these years, in contrast to the nineteenth century, were able to push back against direct forms of imperial rule, creating more indirect forms, whether in Syria (1918–20, and again after 1927), in Iraq (1917–21), Transjordan (after 1921), Egypt (1919–22) and the Moroccan Rif after 1926. The armed struggle in Palestine during 1936–9 played a role in causing the British to abandon their official policy of sponsoring a Jewish national home. In Cyrenaica in the 1920s, there were Italian fascist concentration camps and extermination, although the leaderships of the armed struggle were called up by the UN to form the first post-independence government in 1951.

The later 1930s and the Second World War, however, involved above all more direct forms of colonial rule as the capacity to engage in nationalist mobilization dwindled as divisions set in between different contenders within the political field. Settler colonialism went ahead in Algeria, in what became Libya, and in Mandate Palestine – leading to the catastrophic dispossession of the Palestinians at the hands of Zionism in 1948–9.

The third part of the book argued that contentious mobilization during the period 1952–76 played a substantial role in bringing about national liberation, state-building, and far-reaching social and economic change. The armed struggles in Algeria (1954–62) and in South Yemen (1963–7) made major contributions to the end of French and British colonial rule in both countries. Revolutionary coups in Egypt (1952), Iraq (1958), North Yemen (1962) and Libya (1969) were decisive in bringing national independence in these states and putting an end to client monarchies there. Military men were only able to seize the initiative in a ruling order shaken loose by more mass-based forms of mobilization, domestically in the case of Egypt and Iraq, and more regionally in the case of North Yemen and Libya. The social reforms that single parties and military men then put into place drew their content from the principles, identities and demands of Leftist and nationalist mobilization. They drew strength from the major challenges to neo-feudal forms of power posed by a wide variety of mobilizations. The anti-colonial posture adopted by Nasser in 1956 and later owed something to the ideas and energies of the Left movements that he sought to hegemonize and control. On the other hand, Leftist and nationalist mobilization on the Arabian peninsula (apart from South Yemen) was defeated, and only left its mark in the rent price of the subsequent co-optation of small national populations. Pan-Arabism was not an effective force in preventing the out-sourcing of stigmatized and exploited labour to Asians in their millions. Further, Leftism contributed, only partly inadvertently, to the construction of single-party, military and authoritarian rule.

The fourth part of the book argued that the period from 1977 to 2011, at least in the Arab states, looked more like the long nineteenth century than the short twentieth in terms of the results achieved. Islamist revolution, for all its vast energies, only produced one state (the Islamic State in parts of Iraq and Syria in 2013) during the entire period, and this was a violent and bitterly sectarian entity that provoked and attracted violent repression from external powers. The picture was different in Iran, where popular Shi'ism led during 1978–82 to a thoroughgoing revolution in one of the three historically most powerful and populous and important states of the region. This revolution completely changed the geopolitical posture of Iran and brought about sweeping, rapid, domestic change. Revolutionary Islamism in the Arab world won symbolic concessions from secular rulers, and had an impact on wider social mores and culture. More reformist forms of Islamism at least delivered significant levels of non-state social and economic provision to disenfranchised constituencies. They worked to define basic categories of oppression, resistance and emancipation. For the most part, however, Islamism of all stripes attracted repression and violence, contributed to the ever more ramified development of the security state, and failed to achieve many of its basic goals. These dialectics did contribute in important ways to the crisis of the secular states in the region, while being unable to replace them.

Those who in more Leftist and autonomist forms fought to defend the statist and provisionist *status quo ante* in the face of neo-liberal revolution from above were able to extract some socio-economic concessions here and there; while those who adopted weapons of the weak could at least carve out their own forms of autonomy and avoid repression; these forms of 'quiet encroachment' did work to undermine the ideological hegemony of the state, and thus fed indirectly into the mass uprisings of 2011. The results of emerging liberal and democratic mobilizing projects were also mixed, and in particular were not very successful in capitalizing on the Arab uprisings of 2011, at least outside of Tunisia, where secular, Leftist and reformist Islamic mobilizing projects were stronger. Nonetheless, liberal and democratic principles advanced, in spite of setbacks, in the Iranian reform movement, in the first *intifada* in the Occupied Palestinian Territories during 1987–91, in Algeria during 1988–92, in Bahrain during the 1990s, in the Iranian reform movement in the 1990s and early 2000s, in Damascus in 2000–1, in the independence *intifada* in Lebanon in 2005, in the Kifaya! movement in Egypt, and then during the Arab uprisings. The fact that these projects enjoyed only very limited success in achieving their goals in some ways echoes their failures in the region just before the First World War. Overall, the period since 1977, at least compared to the previous two periods, has been one of gathering crisis and impasse, a time of 'morbid symptoms' in Gramsci's striking phrase.

Overall, the crises of the state in the nineteenth century, and in the late twentieth and twenty-first, along with the making of a national political community, the achievement of national independence, and significant measures of socio-economic reform between 1914 and 1976, cannot be understood without serious attention to the role played by contentious mobilization. Conversely, colonial rule in the nineteenth century, and authoritarianism since 1952, cannot be properly grasped without the more negative contribution made to them by contentious mobilization itself, both in attracting invasion during the nineteenth century, and, in the case of Leftists and Islamists alike, using means and principles that were undemocratic.

In other words, contentious mobilization, unlike in the dominant accounts reviewed by Tilly in regard to eighteenth- and nineteenth-century Britain (Tilly 1995: 18–19), cannot be pictured simply in terms of the positive role it has played in generating progress. But nor can it be shunted uncomprehendingly into a neo-Orientalist account of chaos, violence, security, and 'ugly movements'. Instead, the history given here in some respects echoes Tilly's understanding of the history of protest in Britain:

the creation of mass national politics in Britain [w]as a by-product of great struggles and provisional settlements in the course of which all parties had programmes and interests but no one intended to create the political arrangements that actually emerged (Tilly 1995: 18–19).

This conception of unintended consequences, and the way in which mobilizing projects fitted into a larger history is affirmed here. 'Urabi was desperately trying to avoid a British invasion, but that invasion came; Palestinians did not seek a neo-patrimonial state-in-waiting, but that is what they got after 1982; Ba'thists in the 1940s would have been horrified to think that they were creating a one man dictatorship, but both Syria and Iraq became such; the Lebanese National Movement hoped for a democratic and socialist Lebanon, but played a role in precipitating a civil war; and the FIS in Algeria were running for elections and touting the virtues of democracy and the line of 'no compulsion in religion' during 1988–92, but they did not expect or hope for the bloody civil war that ensued. In other words, unintended consequences were a standard part of this history. Transformation was never brought about by mobilizing projects alone, but their gathering force weighed in interaction with other actors. This argument concedes no ground to histories which leave out the vital dynamics of contentious mobilization, with its many forms of articulation and re-articulation. Many of the actions of elites, even the migration, *rentier* and educational policies of the GCC countries, can only be fully understood in terms of the opposition movements that absolutist monarchs sought to neutralize, prevent or co-opt.

Only during the period 1914–52, however, can we speak of something like the rise of mass national politics. This period saw the rise of a political field structured around the national political community, complete with mass organizations (parties, unions, mass societies) linking elements (sometimes defectors) from the dominant bloc on a more or less continuous basis to subaltern groups. Otherwise, mass organizations of the continuous type, with their autonomy legally guaranteed, have either played a less significant role or not been linked to nationalism (1798–1914), or they have been repressed (1952–2011). The mass, national politics of the inter-war period was in some ways usurped by the military and single-party rule that followed. Further, nationalism (as opposed to statehood) was only the central feature of contentious mobilization during the period 1914–52. On the other hand, the state, and the political community guaranteed by it, played a crucial role throughout this study. The centralization of the state was a basic contextual factor during 1798–1914. But the state as such did not 'rise' or come into existence during this period: the history of state-building in the MENA was highly developed before 1798. Finally, mass politics weighed through-out the period: as we have seen, and whether power-holders liked it or not, commoners and people continuously intervened in transgressive ways in the political field, whether in Egypt in 1798, Istanbul in 1807, or in Tunisia in 2011. During the period 1914–76, the idea of the modern, and of progress, played a key role in mobilizing projects: it anchored a wide variety of claims and projects that sought to challenge the *status quo*, with a centrality that was not present, although often back-projected, before 1914. Since the 1970s, however, the centrality of the implicit or explicit claim to modernity and progress was broken. These forms of post-modernity, of whatever kind, were certainly not the simple imposition of the West. This history has shown how deeply erroneous, even absurd, such an understanding would be. Nor were they a resurgence of the global South against the North. The diverse forms of the post-modern in the region owed a great deal to conten-tious mobilization in the face of the crises of the secular state. The study of the state and the political community, not global abstractions, grand processes or cultural essences, are ultimately the most plausible anchors for the study of contentious politics. Overall, contentious mobilization played a key and in many ways unintended role in the rise and fall of hegemony, but cannot be pictured as the result of a grand modernizing uni-directional escalator of transformation.

The limits on popular politics during this history have been readily on display. While popular politics played a role in cracking the dynas-tic states of the nineteenth century, it was colonialism that delivered the final blow. While popular politics played a major role in national independence, its place was usurped by small groups of military offi-cers, single parties, sole leaders and the securitocracy. And, while popular politics played a major role in undermining the hegemony of the secular state in recent times, it was again external intervention that played the lead role in actually shattering the hard core of the secular state on the two occasions where this actually happened (Iraq in 2003 and Libya in 2011). This history contrasted with that of Iran in 1979 and Turkey in the early 1920s, when mass-based and revolution-ary activity was able to come to power.

Without aiming to exaggerate the role of popular politics, then, the account offered here offers a corrective to those who have written the history of the region solely in terms of the views and policies of the dominant bloc, histories that have in recent times revolved around the question of succession, the internal dynamics of the securitocracy, the activities of crony capitalists, the actions of modernizing elites, the work of embassies, foreign governments, consultants and security advisors. Top-down accounts, while vital in understanding the many and important forms of elite collective action, are insufficient on their own. They can even collaborate in the dessication of forms of hegemony itself, given that meaningful forms of hegemony must always pay attention to consent, a term that cannot be understood without reference to the subaltern population and the projects mobilizing it. The state, by virtue of the fact that it must stitch together material interests, coercion *and* consent in order to create a viable political community can only be fully comprehended when the dynamics of hegemonic contestation are taken into account. Just as in other regions of the world, power-holders had to supplement coercion with consent in order to endure.

This book has challenged the three most basic existing frameworks within which protest has been understood: the (neo-)Orientalist position in which protestors are above all Muslims and Arabs reacting against the West; the position derived from theories of capitalism and modernization that understands mobilization above all in terms of socio-economic change; and the position rooted in post-colonial theory that sees protest as an effect of colonial discursive inscription. There is no evidence in the historical record presented here that can support or sustain the claims of the Orientalist vulgate, that protest is driven in the Arab and Muslim world by recalcitrance, hatred, backwardness, sexual repression, the love of violence and so on. These features were no more present in the mobilizing projects of the MENA than they were in other parts of the world undergoing similar conflicts. They are racist caricatures resting ultimately on incomprehension. Islamism is not primordial or congenital but constructed and diverse. Otherwise, it would not be possible to account for the conversions to Islamism by diverse figures, from Sayyid Qutb, originally a liberal nationalist, to Rashid Al-Ghannushi, originally a francophone who knew little about Islam, to the Australians and British convert-fighters for the Islamic State in Syria and Iraq in 2013. Nor is it possible to grapple with the many secular forms of mobilization that have repeatedly made headway and sometimes dominated the region for decades at a time through an essentialist lens. Likewise, no neo-Orientalist predicted that the Muslim Brotherhood would be swept from power by a popular anti-Islamist uprising and a secularist military coup in Egypt in June and early July 2013. Islamism, moreover, is not singularly undemocratic: there have been many undemocratic social movements in the history of the region and the wider world, under banners fascist, communist and xenophobic. Shiʿa populism and Islamic modernism alike incorporated democratic forms into their practice and in the first case into their theory of the state.

The victory of President Khatami in Iran meant that, ironically, the 'theocratic dictatorship' founded by Khomeini was the very first state in the region to witness a credible change in leadership through the ballot box. All the 'modernist' generals who ruled secular countries such as Algeria, Egypt and Tunisia, failed to achieve such a feat (Burgat 2003: xv).

Armed struggle has been a feature of contentious mobilization in the region throughout the period: it was not the special preserve of Muslims or Arabs; it was a construction of movements, often amid crises of authority. Since the 1970s, the new religious politics of Islam has been mirrored in other parts of the world by new forms of religious politics among Jews, Christians, Hindus and others. Terror tactics have been deployed by a wide variety of movements, some Islamist, some not, some MENA-based, others not. Terror tactics have also been used by governments of many political stripes and persuasions. We recall here the villagers of Lower Egypt in 1798 who tried to resist non-violently by refusing to provide the French occupiers with provisions: these villagers were massacred *en masse* by the occupiers, and their villages destroyed. Armed struggle has to be read in terms of the dessication of hegemony, and in the agency of movements, not in terms of enduring cultural essences.

Marxism and historical sociology has been faulted throughout the book for paying insufficient attention to politics and culture. Sociological groups defined by their relationship to the means of production had diverse politics. Workers have been Salafi-Wahhabis as well as Leftists as well as of no political persuasion. Conversely, political groups struggling together in the same trench often had a diverse sociology: communists have been technicians and teachers as well as workers and peasants, and Islamists have been poor, rural–urban migrants as well as doctors and engineers. Social and economic changes undoubtedly formed and shaped political mobilization. But their explanatory value has too often been exaggerated in historical sociology – and more recently in some accounts stressing globalization. These changes do not explain the identities, frames, principles, goals, modes of organization, strategies or tactics that movements take up. Vested interests were permanently at stake in one way or another. But they do not by themselves give content to a politics of articulation, which is also comprised of coercion, consent, leadership and contentious mobilization. It has not been the rise of new social classes in themselves, on its own, that has discredited hegemony or generated contention, but the intersection between new configurations of interest and ways of life and the existing political field.

The book has also maintained throughout that cultural history has not done justice to the fact that interpretive context shapes but does not account for or properly explain the dynamics of contention amid changing forms of hegemony, in which coercion and material interests play vital roles, and the forms of consent at work are not merely cultural, but also political, economic and social. Discursive determinism, moreover, has been faulted for its erasure of struggle, contradiction and subalternity. It is certainly unable to account for the moments at which powerful forms of hegemony start to break down. We have seen such major crises when entire worldviews start to cease to make sense at least three times in this history, during the nineteenth century, from the 1930s to the 1960s, and since the 1970s.

The main argument marshalled here with respect to theories of social movements of all kinds is that they are insufficient tools for connecting contentious mobilization to larger questions of power, historical context and change, and they pay insufficient attention to the all-important work of the construction of the collective subject. The way that classical social movement theory has multiplied intervening variables to account for the gap between grievance and action has actually left the link between the larger context and contention ever more difficult to fathom, as intervening variables become ever more numerous and un-prioritized. There is no way to know which variable to pick or why it should be so picked. The lack of an overall explanatory theory tends to collapse our ability to connect contention to the structures and grand transformations that are undoubtedly present in the political field, as a result of both political settlements and the unequal distribution of wealth, position and status honour. The notion of political opportunity is a thin reed on which to lean the entirety of the link to wider context. This history has shown over and over again that political opportunities subjective and/or objective, even assuming we can clearly define them, are not reliable predictors of contentious mobilization. Repression has stimulated protest, or crushed it; and institutional openings have co-opted and/or energized challengers.

This history has not been able to make use of the DOC programme's concept of mechanisms except as a useful descriptor of things-which-happen during protest. The causal status of mechanisms is simply not clear. Shapeless interaction has not been a key feature of this history. Some mobilizing projects were a lot more organized and effective than others: compare Hizbullah in the 1980s and 1990s with the revolutionary youth of Cairo in 2011–13. Some elites have been brutally efficient in crushing protest, such as Hafez Al-Asad in 1982, while others have bungled and vacillated, such as the Shah of Iran in 1978–9. Perhaps the clash between an historical approach and a universalizing one is inevitable. But the need to write history into contention and *vice versa* remains a pressing problem in the field of social movement studies.

Drawing on the research of others, and where possible from historical sociology, cultural history, theories of social movements, and a non-teleological and non-economistic Gramsci, the book has made sense of this history of contestation in terms of forms of hegemonic expansion and contraction on the one hand, and forms of leadership and mobilizing projects on the other. This framework has offered answers to the questions posed at the outset of this study: how to explain protest without explaining it away, or explaining it by simply referring back to previous rounds of protest; the extent to which the fate and fortunes of movements rested in the hands of their leaderships; and how to specify the role of contentious mobilization in the history of the region as a whole.

The history of the MENA offers a vast amount of evidence in regard to the utility of hegemony, the fortification of coercion with consent, for the dominant bloc and its capacity to get things done. Even in imperial armies, consent played a role. Allow a single illustration here. One of the Spanish pilots 'responsible for dropping the most lethal of the mustard gas bombs' on the Rif mountains in the 1920s who came to believe that the campaign was 'truly despicable' confessed in 1961 that 'not for one second did it occur to me [at the time] that the mission I had been given was an abomination or a crime ... it is incredible how naturally one can commit the greatest barbarities when one has a certain mentality.' This pilot's subject-hood was a social construct, not a psychological condition, and only in the most superficial and ahistorical sense a rational choice. It was a subjectivity informed and moulded by church and army, a bitter military campaign following a major defeat, and the notion of the Moor as enemy of Spain, and as uncivilized and 'racially inferior' (Balfour 2002: 137–8). In this case, the pilot 'admitted that he only began to realize the enormity of what he and his fellow pilots had done was when he heard about the Italian chemical war against the Abyssinians in 1935. His first reaction was a sense of indignation at the atrocity the Italians were committing, until it dawned on him that he had taken part in the same sort of atrocity in Morocco' (Balfour 2002: 137). This is a good illustration of the power of forms of hegemony in ensuring the coordination and control of the actions of those (such as this pilot) doing the bidding of the dominant bloc. It is also a striking example of how even the most tightly wound tissues of consent can be unpicked and broken over time and under changing circumstances.

Hegemonic articulation, indeed, is a double-edged sword because it involves downward as well as upward delegation. While forms of adherence and loyalty are granted by subordinates in an upward direction, resources and capacities are also distributed downwards to consenting subordinates. This does not just involve the control of aeroplanes, which could be piloted towards defection, as in the case of some elements of the Libyan air force in 2011. At a different level, Isma'il's Chamber of Deputies delegated after 1866 the power to speak before the ruler to a group of provincial notables. When authorities, however, moved to break up these sites of downward delegation and consent, without replacing them with adequate alternatives, or where they did not multiply such sites in order to keep pace with new demands, they paved the way for resistance by generating disaffected subordinates often commanding resources and capacities which could be re-directed to new ends. In many ways, this was what happened in Egypt to the Chamber of Deputies between 1879 and 1882 as we have seen, with the advent of the Khedive Tawfiq and the attempts by the European debt controllers to curb the Chamber's power. We have also noted the prominence of former members of the prorogued Bahraini National Assembly in writing the reformist petitions of 1992–4. These were leaderships trying to recover a role in the state that they had previously enjoyed. These forms of hegemonic contraction, often brought about by elites themselves, whether by blundering and the arrogance of power, or through the search to maintain the cohesion of the dominant bloc, or in order to protect or further narrow interests, have paved the way for contentious mobilization based around re-articulation throughout the history of the region.

It is worth underlining some further examples of hegemonic contraction here. We have seen, for example, in Syria in the 1960s and 1970s, how much harder it was for the liberal and modernist wing of the Muslim Brotherhood to continue to cleave to its liberal position because, first, the state closed down all forms of liberal and participatory politics, which defeated any liberal strategy, and, second, it actually went on the offensive against the liberal sections of the movement, either destroying them physically, handing the initiative to the proponents of *jihad*, or making it far easier for them or their constituencies to accept the arguments of the jihadists which maintained that the state was utterly corrupted. In this case, it was hegemonic contraction associated with the repression of liberal possibilities that paved the way for more violent forms of protest. We have seen, moreover, how this process operated in Algeria when the elections of 1991 were cancelled. We have also seen how the catastrophe of 1948 radicalized a whole generation, because it undercut a key basis of the legitimacy of the existing monarchies and regimes, which was their proclaimed ability to protect the Arab nation and Arab brothers against external foes, a cause for which they had extracted consent. The defeat of 1967 had similar effects, undercutting a key basis of regime legitimacy in Syria and Egypt above all, while inadvertently bolstering that of those states, such as Morocco or Oman, who had stayed out of the conflict. We have also seen how the failures of the Wafd and its forms of hegemony paved the way for Nasser's assault on them. Conversely, we note that the Sunnis of Iraq were one of the few major groups of Sunnis in the MENA who were only slightly affected by the rise of Sunni Islamism between the 1970s and 2003. There is surely some legitimate reason to associate this with the expansive ways in which they were integrated into the hegemony of the Ba'thist state. By the same token, the spread of various strands of Sunni Islamism among this constituency in Iraq *after* 2003, when these forms of hegemony were broken up by US occupation and the ascendancy of Kurds and Shi'a, was dramatic. Finally, consider the instantaneous reaction in Egypt to the price rises that Sadat's government announced on January 1977. It was on the very day that the price rises came into effect (18 January) that protestors, anticipating the hardship that the measures would bring (but not having yet experienced it), filled the streets: social and economic rights they had come to believe were theirs were being snatched away by the state that was supposed to provide them.

This history, nonetheless, has not justified a lock-step causal relationship between hegemonic contraction and contentious mobilization – and has not intended to. Initiative counted. Hegemonic contraction by no means determined the content (identities etc.), the type (defensive, reformist and so on), or the extent of transgression, or the strategies and tactics, or even the modes of organization that new mobilizations would adopt. Nor even did it always cause contentious mobilization. The evidence seems to show a relationship between the break-up of sites of contained contention, and the rise of transgressive contention, but to assert that this is a universal cause goes too far in a nomothetic direction. For example, the Muslim Brotherhood in Egypt did *not* turn to the use of armed struggle in spite of the extreme provocations posed by the coup against an elected president in July 2013 and the massacres of August 2013. Determinism here must be avoided.

What this study has seen evidence for, and has argued for throughout, is that intellectual production plays a mediating role between hegemonic contraction and the content and repertoires of the mobilizing project. What intellectuals have done is helped define the meaning of hegemonic contraction, and diagnose what is to be done about it. Ali Shariati, for example, helped to define what it meant that the shah was repressing political freedoms, and aggregating wealth to a small elite circle. Khomeini and other Shi'a clerics, by elaborating their theory of the Islamic state, helped to define what goals mobilization should adopt. A dramatic illustration of the huge diversity of interpretation in the face of crisis can be derived from views of 1948. While many saw it in terms of the corruption and ambition of contemporary rulers and an indictment of the feudal system in which they were rooted, Nabahani, the founder of Hizb Al-Tahrir, saw it as a direct result of the fall of the Caliphate in 1924, and sought to organize a party that would recover that Caliphate. Likewise, 1967 signalled to some the dereliction of secularism; to large sections of the Left, however, it signalled something different: the crisis of military society which had failed to institute popular democracy. In other words, hegemonic contraction did not pre-define its own meaning, and, in answering the question 'what is to be done', among those so minded to pose it, much depended on interpretation. As Gramsci put it in the *Prison Notebooks*:

What matters is the criticism to which such an ideological complex is subjected by the first representatives of the new historical phase. This criticism makes possible a process of differentiation and change in the relative weight that the elements of the old ideologies used to possess. What was previously secondary and subordinate, or even incidental, is now taken to be primary – becomes the nucleus of a new ideological and theoretical complex (Gramsci 1971: 195; Mouffe 1979: 191).

This book has aimed to expose how critical intellectual mediation of this kind, which was no respecter of prison walls, or regional, cultural, class or national borders, played a role in the history of the MENA, shaping the content of activist initiatives.

Especially in the early stages of movements, inspiring ideas and normative commitments have helped to motivate adherents and leaderships, and shaped identities, frames, goals, and even strategies and tactics. We have seen how Shi'a popular Islamism acted in this way in the origins of Hizbullah. It was also made clear that Juhayman's tactics in 1979 (seizing the Grand Mosque in Mecca at the turn of the Islamic century in order to announce the Expected Deliverer) stemmed very directly from his millenarian conceptions. We note further that Juhayman only discovered the existence of millenarianism through his devotion to *hadith* studies, which in turn was driven by his Al-Albani-influenced Ahl Al-Hadith beliefs. We recall the normative backbone at the centre of the Mahdiyya in the 1880s. When the world's largest empire tried to co-opt this son of a boat-builder, who was backed by a cattle-herding tribe, he replied magisterially that as, 'the Expected Mahdi, the Successor of the Apostle of God', he had 'no need of the sultanate, nor of the kingdom of Kordofan or elsewhere, nor of the wealth of this world and its vanity' (Holt 1970: 93). The commitment to negotiation and the reformism of Sa'd Zaghlul and the Wafd in Egypt in the early 1920s, at the other end of the spectrum, can help account for the fact that they went along with a British-designed constitution in 1922–4, one which made the king far too powerful to make the document meaningful. Finally, we note how the use of

attacks on international targets ('external operations') on the part of
the DFLP in the late 1960s and early 1970s was linked to their belief
that Israel was stitched into global capitalism, and thus the symbols
and bastions of global capitalism, even if located far from Israel, were
legitimate targets in the struggle against Zionism. On the other hand,
there is no reason to believe that ideas actually cause activism to
happen in any nomothetic sense. Here initiative weighs in the balance.
This study can see no way to explain deterministically such initiatives,
and sees no virtue in explaining them away. When such initiatives were
undertaken, however, they were shaped by the available mobilizing
discourses.

Once mobilizing projects got under way, intellectual schemes
became less crucial as the drivers of innovation in the face of political,
strategic and other factors pressing on all sides. New identities, principles, goals, organization, strategy and so on now stemmed from
projects' need to ensure cohesion and to win consent and adherents
and manoeuvre for advantage amid the 'grind and spark' of political
struggle. This study has argued that nationalism, for example, became
the term that could allow cohesion between diverse constituencies
in Egypt, Iraq, Morocco, Palestine and Syria in the aftermath of the
First World War. It was also a way for pre-war patriots and reformers
to hegemonize a diverse political field. No one had spotted this in
advance, least of all the British, in part because this mode of articulation was an innovation: it did not just borrow from the intellectual
work of elites, but the exigencies of integration. What few could
predict in advance was how nationalism would suddenly play this
mediating role and thus become central. Hence the proper surprise,
that beyond Orientalism, was on display in different parts of the
political field amid the inspiring upsurges of the post-1918 period.
Or, the rapid appropriation of the Tunisian model for overthrowing
a dictator in 2011 served as an integrating idea for diverse disaffected
constituencies and an effective repertoire for many a frustrated citizen.
We have seen, thanks to the research of Lockman, how liberal nationalists actively drew on notions of the working class in order to find a
constituency to represent and mobilize in their struggle against
the British in early twentieth-century Egypt (Lockman 1994b). We
have seen how reforming societies, political parties, underground cells
and trade unions have all been built up in the course of mobilization.
Specific tactics, such as the general strike, have been quickly

appropriated across borders: in Egypt in 1919, in Syria in 1936 and then in Palestine in the same year, for example. Necessity has been the mother of invention (and appropriation) in contentious mobilization as elsewhere. This point is vitally important for this study because it helps to make clear how contentious mobilization can play an historical role in its own right: by developing new frames, identities, goals, forms of social association and so on and confronting the larger political field with them.

Agency has been possible in mobilization through the development of cohesion, which depends on subordinated subjects getting out of old places and finding new ones, i.e. on politicization, recombination and mobilization. The challenge for labour activism, for example, in the oil fields of Al-Hasa province in the 1950s was not limited to engaging in strategic organization that would allow immanent contradictions and pre-existing material interests to express themselves in politics. Instead, the challenge was about stitching together a diverse sociology: the teachers and skilled workers, some with university degrees, from various nationalities and origins had in some way to win the trust of, and become the *porte-parole* of poor Shi'a from oases or from tribal backgrounds. This bloc had in turn to link to the press, to figures in the Ministries, to conquer the institutional and political terrain, and thus to build up an assemblage with capacity. Such collective subject formation required a set of identities and principles, an ideological project to coordinate this diversity, and to do the work of stitching it together. Moreover, the very stuff and substance of coordination also involved consent for this or that evidently political gesture, whether to petition now or later, whether to strike in this or that way, what tactics to use and so on. For these reasons, the forms of politics and ideology were inherent to the subject formation in these strikes and protests, not epiphenomenal to it. The task of this activist subject was to politicize: to turn subjects who were previously minding their own business, 'not involved', trying to make money, and so on, into those who are signed up to, and offering some agency and powers of delegation, to the new or fragile subject. In this way, politicization and the mobilization of new constituencies is able to generate capacity and forcefulness in regard to a given project where there was none.

There have been plenty of examples in the foregoing, moreover, that can help explain why it is that ruling elites, who wield immense power, cannot always simply crush or destroy the innovations that mobilizing projects are capable of throwing up. It is not just that elites are sometimes taken by surprise and forced onto the back foot, although this element has counted in this history. It is also that elites are constrained by their vested interests, and/or by the need to maintain the cohesion of the dominant bloc. This makes them vulnerable to certain strategies of contention (and not others). One example of this kind of constraint refers to the decision of the Egyptian army not to shoot on masses of civilian protestors in late January 2011. First of all, the risk of generating a split between president and army was there in regard to any presidential order to use massive lethal force. Second, any decision by the top brass of the army to use lethal force risked a split in the army stemming from a mutiny of officers refusing to shoot. There were constraints, in other words, on the use of the military option, imposed by the need to maintain the cohesion of the dominant bloc, the vested interests of which are not always entirely unified, because they do not all have the same relationship to the accumulation, the state, and social honour. Whether or not the dominant bloc in Egypt would have split had the army used massive force is another matter. But, in this case, the risks of such a split informed the actions of those on the ground and imposed a constraint on elite collective action.

It has also been shown that leadership and initiative, and the nature of the mobilizing project itself, have weighed heavily in the balance. The fate and fortunes of mobilizing projects were to some extent in the hands of activists themselves. The words of Brutus, in *Julius Caesar*, may be oft-quoted, but they certainly capture part of this point:

> There is a tide in the affairs of men
> Which, taken at the flood, leads on to fortune
> Omitted, all the voyage of their life
> Is bound in shallows and in miseries
> On such a full sea are we now afloat
> And we must take the current when it serves
> Or lose our ventures.

Such a 'tide' comes into play at moments of heightened uncertainty, which can be generated by hegemonic contraction and by the actions of activists themselves. This is not to say that the 'tide' can always be read effectively, as Brutus' own failure suggests. The unwavering and inclusive nature of Khomeini's leadership proved important in Iran in the 1970s. It is also instructive to compare the lack of sustainability of the uprising in Egypt in 1977, with the way mobilization was sustained in the wake of the uprising in Algeria in October 1988. The timidity of the Left in Egypt in terms of its lack of mass mobilization contrasted strongly with the immediate energies of the Islamist movement in Algeria, which moved in to hegemonize the young men on the streets. The Muslim Brotherhood was a more effective organizer in Egypt after February 2011 than the revolutionary youth, and the former reaped the rewards in election victories. The Wafd in Egypt chose international diplomacy over mass mobilization between 1919 and 1921 when all of Egypt was at its feet: this move was a failure. Hajj Amin did not need to reject the British White Paper of 1939, while Abd Al-Krim might not have attacked the French in 1925. This book has also attempted to explain the prolongation of the first *intifada* of 1987–91, and the force of the uprising in Bahrain in the 1990s in terms of leadership and mass mobilization. It has been argued also that the strategies of mass mobilization by Hizbullah launched in the 1980s and greatly developed thereafter contributed very much to the group's stability and continuity after 2000 when it lost a key part of its *raison d'être* because it achieved its most basic goal, the withdrawal of Israel from southern Lebanon.

In the same vein, this study has suggested that the lack of inclusiveness of the Muslim Brotherhood in Egypt in the 1970s and subsequently on the social question may have limited its appeal compared to Shi'ism in Iran, which always took up social and economic questions. The lack of a clear or developed theory of the state almost anywhere in Sunni Islamism, especially when it is compared to Shi'a popular currents, has been striking since the inertia of the bulk of the mostly propertied Sunni *ulema* in the long nineteenth century.

Conversely, the acquisition of vested interests, through the lifetime of a movement, starts to shape the action of the movement, making it more predictable over time. It can lead, for example, into a situation where that movement continues, even when the basic *raison d'être* is gone as in Hizbullah, which lost over time both the possibility of creating an Islamic state in Lebanon and the eviction of Israel from occupied territory. The group did not dissolve, however, but turned more to domestic Lebanese politics, with mixed success.

Overall, there is much in this history to support an interpretive framework in which mobilizing projects intervene to shape the relationship of articulation between the dominant bloc and the subaltern population, altering the dynamics of the political field, the balance of coercion and consent, and re-negotiating the way vested interests intersect with the political field. Of crucial interest has been the vector of politicization: the transgressive dynamic involved when citizens, commoners and subaltern social groups aggregate to themselves the right to act politically and thus come to weigh in innovative ways in the political field, whose boundaries cannot always be effectively policed.

What can such a history say to the present and the future? One of the important lessons of this study has to do with the strictures it offers on any romanticization of informalism and spontaneity. The lesson of the Arab uprisings is that even the power of millions can dissipate almost as rapidly as it appears. It should be admitted that this harsh reality has been present throughout the history of the region – in January 1952 (the Cairo fire), January 1977 in Egypt and 2005 in Lebanon, for example. Organization is indispensable, whether or not it comes out of the grind and spark of the action itself, or pre-dates it. But there is no doubt that this is a vicious dilemma in a region where most forms of organization are quickly crushed by a security state backed by external powers. This fact, the virtual abolition of the political field by the manipulative, violent and repressive actions of states throughout the region, typically with the connivance of their external backers, has been one of the central causes of the impasse and successive crises of recent decades. Meaningful articulation and re-articulation have been radically curtailed by state violence. Nor can the historian ever afford to be too dismissive in regard to the 'timidity' of reformists: again and again, the history has shown cases where outright assault on the established order has been crushed with massive repression. The case of the Palestinian uprising of 1936–9 is just one example of many. Mass mobilization is always difficult to coordinate and requires resources which may not always be forthcoming. The use of state sponsors is no magic wand, as those states may then go on to impose their own agenda. The PLO was remarkably skilled at navigating this terrain between the 1960s and the 1980s. Other movements have been less effective, and have become the pawns of their sponsors. It should even be conceded that those who argue that protest leads to violent conflict and unleashes manipulative and opportunistic behaviour by the powerful are not just repeating essentialist mantras, as some support can be found in the history of the region for these claims, above all where protest has attracted imperial intervention.

The emphasis on consent that runs throughout this book has to do with the fact that the tissues of consent are the sites where contestation can happen: there is no intention to diminish the key importance of coercion and vested interests. The bleaker parts of this history have illustrated their importance. It is more that coercion and vested interests enter the question of contestation through a glass darkly: they are always present as constraints, and as backbone in the case of more routinized and developed movements, and yet they are very poor at explaining the dynamics of articulation and forms of creativity rooted in contentious mobilization.

Finally, the progress that contentious mobilization achieved in the region between the First World War and the 1960s came after many years of crisis. Since the 1970s, the Arab world, although not Iran, has likewise been undergoing many years of crises of authority. The forms of Islamism that came into the ascendancy through the Saudi state, the *jihad* in Afghanistan, Al-Qa'ida in Iraq, and in regards to the Islamic State, only spell violence and destruction. Their vacuous, Manichean sectarianism, which also owed much to the policies of states, from Saudi Arabia to the United States, is almost freakishly fringe compared to the great bulk of contentious mobilization in the region and its history, but global elites have allowed such miniscule groups to attract the lion's share of their attention, and even ensnared them into restricting civil liberties at home and pushed their foreign policies all over the place, with catastrophic results. Perhaps this does give some credence to the DOC project's claim that transgressive contention really does bring the most dramatic results. What would be unsurprising in the present moment would be that regional powers will bolster their securitocracies, suppressing the political field, and treating their own populations with contempt and violence; Israel will press on with expansionism and settler colonialism; and external powers will react with their own combination of cynical machination and war. Coercion will continue to outweigh consent in the social formation as a whole, except where *rentier* distribution wins consent of the socio-economic kind. Such is the cynically predictable state of the present, informed by a bitter history in which so many great, popular, collective endeavours have been violently cut down by local or colonial elites.

Nonetheless, crises have been unjammed before. This history has argued that we cannot predict what is next with any confidence.

Perhaps the forms of liberal and democratic activism that have been on the rise in the region since the 1970s – from the democratic socialism of Kamal Jumblatt to the secular, liberal, labour movements in Egypt in the 2000s – will develop further into the nucleus of a revolutionary alternative anchored in radical democracy itself. This would be a major innovation. In the history of the MENA, alternative hegemony has never had the post-1968 idea of radical democracy, as opposed to the nineteenth-century liberal idea of representation in the state, as its lead term. Just as the liberal reformists of the pre-1914 MENA came later to hegemonize wider constituencies through forms of more thoroughgoing nationalism, perhaps the often failed and frustrated liberals and democrats of the present moment will be able to hegemonize wider constituencies, through the embrace of an entirely uncompromising participatory democracy, fortified by the embrace of multi-form identities, in the future. Certainly, there are many disgusted with the sectarianism and sterility to which revolutionary Islamism has finally been reduced, and many ordinary people in the MENA do not currently believe that the United States holds a monopoly on the interpretation of democracy. The socio-economic crisis, outside of the states rich in 'buried sunshine', is ongoing. And there are many potential political crises on the horizon, and many sources of inspiration: the eighteen days in Tahrir Square, the humanism of an Edward Said, the liberal fortitude of a Raja Shehadeh, the Leftism of the grassroots activists of the Tunisian UGTT, the feminism of the tiny Cairo collectives, the horizontalism and egalitarianism of this or that intellectual or of co-eval movements in Latin America and beyond, the transregional and institutionally disruptive strategy of the democratic BDS movement, and the deep intellectual, literary, poetic and artistic talents of the MENA region. Perhaps such a project would develop as a revolutionary alternative to the corrupted securitocracies, absolutist monarchies, Islamist essentialism, crony capitalism, *rentier*-ism, ethnocratic Zionism and imperialism that mark the present, proceeding through a wide range of mass-based, transnational and de-centralized direct actions generating real institutional disruption, and developing new organizations and popular assemblies capable of making democratic decisions, building up new forms of politics, and providing and generating goods and services for wide constituencies. It may be, on the other hand, that *rentier* and distributive forms of consent-winning will continue to garner the resources from oil or rents that enable them to reproduce themselves and their anti-democratic ideological out-works for a long time yet. Where such rents are not available, more political or ideological forms of hegemony will have to be developed. If liberals and democrats sit on their hands, and fail to act amid hegemonic contraction, then other forces will reap the rewards. Leadership and activism will count in the future, as in the past. In the end, we must expect to be surprised. We do not know what form the next viable alternative hegemony will take once Islamism has run its course. But the history offered here at least suggests that there will be one, eventually.

References

Abbas, Ra'uf. 1967. *Al-Haraka al-'Ummaliyya fi Misr 1899–1952* (The Labour Movement in Egypt, 1899–1952). Cairo: General Egyptian Book Organization.

Abd Al-Malek, Anwar. 1968. *Egypt: Military Society: The Army Regime, the Left, and Social Change under Nasser.* New York: Random House.

— ed. 1983. *Contemporary Arab Political Thought.* Trans. Michael Pallis. London: Zed Books.

Abd Al-Qadir. 1849. *L'Emir AbdelKader autobiographie: ecrite en prison (France) en 1849 et publiée pour la première fois.* Trans. H. Benmansour. Paris: Dialogues Editions.

Abd Al-Raziq, Husayn. 1979. *Misr fi 18, 19, Yanayir: dirasa siyasiyya watha'iqiyya* (Egypt on 18–19 January: A Documented Political Study). Beirut: Dar Al-Hikma li-l-Nashr.

Abdallah, Ahmad. 2009. *The Student Movement and National Politics in Egypt, 1923–1973.* Cairo: American University in Cairo Press.

Abdelrahman, Maha. 2009. '"With the Islamists? – Sometimes. With the State? – Never!" Cooperation between the Left and Islamists in Egypt'. *British Journal of Middle Eastern Studies,* 36, 1 (April): 37–54.

Abdul-Jabar, Falah. 2002. *Ayatollahs, Sufis and Ideologues: State, Religion and Social Movements in Iraq.* London: Saqi.

— 2003. *The Shi'ite Movement in Iraq.* London: Saqi.

Abir, Mordechai. 1971. 'The "Arab Rebellion" of Amir Ghalib of Mecca (1788–1813)'. *Middle Eastern Studies,* 3: 185–200.

— 1993. *Saudi Arabia: Government, Society and the Gulf Crisis.* London: Routledge.

Abisaab, Malek. 2009. *Militant Women of a Fragile Nation.* Syracuse, NY: Syracuse University Press.

Abou-El-Fadl, Reem. 2015. 'Neutralism Made Positive: Egyptian Anticolonialism on the Road to Bandung'. *British Journal of Middle Eastern Studies,* 42, 2 (April): 219–40.

Abrahamian, Ervand. 1982. *Iran between Two Revolutions.* Princeton, NJ: Princeton University Press.

1993. 'The Crowd in the Persian Revolution'. In *The Modern Middle East: A Reader*. Albert Hourani, Philip S. Khoury and Mary C. Wilson eds. London: I. B. Tauris, pp. 289–309.

2001. 'The 1953 Coup in Iran'. *Science & Society*, 65, 2 (summer): 182–215.

Abu Fakhr, Saqr. 2010. *Anis Al-Naqqash: asrar khalaf al-astar'* (Anis Al-Naqqash: Secrets behind the Curtains). Beirut: Al-Mu'assasa Al-'Arabiyya.

Abu-Lughod, Lila ed. 1998. *Remaking Women: Feminism and Modernity in the Middle East*. Princeton, NJ: Princeton University Press.

Abu-Rabi, Ibrahim. 1996. *Intellectual Origins of Islamic Resurgence in the Modern Arab World*. Albany, NY: State University of New York Press.

Abul-Magd, Zeinab. 2013. *Imagined Empires: A History of Revolt in Egypt*. Berkeley, CA: University of California Press.

Abun-Nasr, Jamil M. 1987. *A History of the Maghrib in the Islamic Period*. Cambridge: Cambridge University Press.

Achcar, Gilbert. 2010. *The Arabs and the Holocaust: The Arab–Israeli War of Narratives*. Trans. G. M. Goshgarian. London: Saqi Books.

2013a. *The People Want: A Radical Exploration of the Arab Uprising*. London: Saqi Books.

2013b. *Marxism, Orientalism, Cosmopolitanism*. London: Saqi Books.

Adib-Moghadam, Arshin. 2006. 'The Pluralistic Momentum in Iran and the Future of the Reform Movement'. *Third World Quarterly*, 27, 4: 665–74.

Afary, Janet. 1996. *The Iranian Constitutional Revolution, 1906–1911: Grassroots Democracy, Social Democracy, and the Origins of Feminism*. New York: Columbia University Press.

Aflaq, Michel. 1977. *Choice of Texts from the Ba'th Party Founder's Thought*. Florence: Cooperativa Lavoratori.

Ahmad, Feroz. 1991. 'Politics and Islam in Modern Turkey'. *Middle Eastern Studies*, 27, 1 (January): 3–21.

1995. 'The Development of Class-Consciousness in Republican Turkey, 1923–45'. In *Workers and the Working Class in the Ottoman Empire and the Turkish Republic, 1839–1950*. Donald Quataert and Erik Jan Zürcher eds. London: I. B. Tauris, pp. 75–94.

Ahmed, Leila. 1992. *Women and Gender in Islam: Historical Roots of a Modern Debate*. New Haven, CT: Yale University Press.

Ajami, Fouad. 2005. 'The Autumn of the Autocrats'. *Foreign Affairs*, 84, 3 (May–June): 20–35.

Akarlı, Engin. 1987. 'Gedik: Implements, Mastership, Shop Usufruct and Monopoly among Istanbul Artisans, 1750–1850'. In *Wissenschaftskolleg Jahrbuch 1985/6*. Munich: Siedler Verlag.

2004. 'Gedik: A Bundle of Rights and Obligations for Istanbul Artisans and Traders, 1750–1840'. In *Law, Anthropology and the Constitution of the Social: Making Persons and Things*. Alain Pottage and Martha Mundy eds. Cambridge: Cambridge University Press, pp. 166–200.

Ali, Nadje Al-. 2000. *Secularism, Gender and the State in the Middle East: The Egyptian Women's Movement*. Cambridge: Cambridge University Press.

2002. 'The Women's Movement in Egypt, with Selected References to Turkey'. UNRISD: Civil Society and Social Movements, Paper No. 5: 1–42. www.unrisd.org/80256B3C005BCCF9/search/9969203536 F64607C1256C08004BB140?OpenDocument.

Alexander, Anne. 2009. 'Egypt's Strike Wave: Lessons in Leadership', Research Briefing, ESRC Non-Governmental Public Action Programme.

Alexander, Anne and Mustafa Bassiouny. 2014. *Bread, Freedom, Social Justice: Workers and the Egyptian Revolution*. London: Zed Books.

Alianak, Sonia. 2007. *Middle Eastern Leaders and Islam: A Precarious Equilibrium*. New York: Peter Lang.

Allal, Amin. 2013. 'Becoming Revolutionary in Tunisia, 2007–2011'. In *Social Movements, Mobilization, and Contestation in the Middle East and North Africa*. Joel Beinin and Frédéric Vairel eds. Stanford, CA: Stanford University Press, pp. 185–204.

Amin, Mohammed Nuri El-. 1987. 'The Role of the Egyptian Communists in Introducing the Sudanese to Communism in the 1940s'. *International Journal of Middle East Studies*, 19: 433–54.

Anderson, Charles W. 2013. 'From Petition to Confrontation: The Palestinian National Movement and the Rise of Mass Politics, 1929–1939'. Unpublished Ph.D. Dissertation, New York University.

Anderson, Perry. 1977. 'The Antinomies of Antonio Gramsci'. *New Left Review*, 100: 5–78.

Antonius, George. 1939. *The Arab Awakening: The Story of the Arab National Movement*. Philadelphia: J. B. Lippincott.

Archives du Ministère des Affaires Étrangères: Maroc, 1944–1955, Nos. 61ff.

Arjomand, Said Amir. 1989. *The Turban for the Crown: The Islamic Revolution in Iran*. Oxford: Oxford University Press.

Ashraf, Ahmad and Ali Banuazizi. 2001. 'Iran's Tortuous Path toward "Islamic Liberalism"'. *International Journal of Politics, Culture, and Society*, 15, 2: 237–56.

Atkinson, David. 2000. 'Nomadic Strategies and Colonial Governance: Domination and Resistance in Cyrenaica, 1923–32'. In *Entanglements of Power: Geographies of Domination / Resistance*. Joanne P. Sharp, Paul Routledge, Chris Philo and Ronan Paddison eds. London: Routledge, pp. 93–121.

Ayache, Germain. 1981. *Les origines de la guerre du Rif.* Paris and Rabat: Les Editions de la Sorbonne, SMER.

Ayubi, Nazih N. 1995. *Over-stating the Arab State: Politics and Society in the Middle East.* London: I. B. Tauris.

Aziz, T. M. 1993. 'The Role of Muhammad Baqir Al-Sadr in Shi'i Political Activism in Iraq from 1958 to 1980'. *International Journal of Middle East Studies*, 25, 2 (May): 207–22.

Badimon, Montserrat Emperador. 2011. 'Unemployed Moroccan University Graduates and Strategies for "Apolitical" Mobilization'. In *Social Movements, Mobilization, and Contestation in the Middle East and North Africa.* Joel Beinin and Frédéric Vairel eds. Stanford, CA: Stanford University Press, pp. 217–36.

Baer, Gabriel. 1964. *Egyptian Guilds in Modern Times.* Jerusalem: Hebrew University Press.

1969. *Studies in the Social History of Modern Egypt.* Chicago: University of Chicago Press.

1977. 'Popular Revolt in Ottoman Cairo'. *Der Islam*, 54: 213–42.

Bahrain Government Annual Reports, 1924–1956. 1986. Vols. 1–5. Gerrards Cross: Archive Editions.

Bahri, Luayy. 2000. 'The Socioeconomic Foundations of the Shiite Opposition in Bahrain'. *Mediterranean Quarterly*, 11, 3 (summer): 129–43.

Bakan, Abigail B. and Yasmeen Abu-Laban. 2010. 'Israel/Palestine, South Africa and the "One-State Solution": The Case for an Apartheid Analysis'. *Politikon: South African Journal of Political Studies*, 37, 2–3: 331–51.

Baldwin, James. 2010. 'Islamic Law in an Ottoman Context: Resolving Disputes in Late 17th/Early 18th Century Cairo'. Ph.D. Dissertation, New York University.

Balfour, Sebastian. 2002. *Deadly Embrace: Morocco and the Road to the Spanish Civil War.* Oxford: Oxford University Press.

Bardawil, Fadi A. 2010. 'When All This Revolution Melts into Air: The Disenchantment of Levantine Marxist Intellectuals'. Unpublished Ph.D. Dissertation, Columbia University.

Barghouti, Omar. 2011. *Boycott, Divestment, Sanctions: The Global Struggle for Palestinian Rights.* Chicago: Haymarket Books.

Barker, Colin, Laurence Cox, John Krinsky and Alf Grunvald Nilsen eds. 2013. *Marxism and Social Movements.* Leiden: Brill.

Baron, Beth. 2007. *Egypt as a Woman: Nationalism, Gender, and Politics.* Berkeley, CA: University of California Press.

Bassiouni, Mustafa. 2007. *Rayat al-Idrab fi Sama' Misr: 2007 Harakat 'Ummaliyya Jadida* (Banners of the Strike in the Skies of Egypt: A New Labour Movement in 2007). Cairo: Center for Socialist Studies.

2010. Author Interview, Cairo (21 June).

Batatu, Hanna. 1978. *The Old Social Classes and the Revolutionary Movements of Iraq*. Princeton, NJ: Princeton University Press.

1981. 'Iraq's Underground Shi'a Movements: Characteristics, Causes, Prospects'. *Middle East Journal*, 35 (autumn): 578–94.

1999. *Syria's Peasantry, the Descendants of Its Lesser Rural Notables, and Their Politics*. Princeton, NJ: Princeton University Press.

Bayat, Asef. 1987. *Workers and Revolution in Iran: A Third World Experience of Workers' Control*. London: Zed Books.

1997. *Street Politics: Poor People's Movements in Iran*. New York: Columbia University Press.

2007. *Making Islam Democratic: Social Movements and the Post-Islamist Turn*. Stanford, CA: Stanford University Press.

Baylouny, Anne Marie. 2013. 'Hizbullah's Women: Internal Transformation in a Social Movement and Militia'. In *Social Movements, Mobilization, and Contestation in the Middle East and North Africa*. Joel Beinin and Frédéric Vairel eds. 2nd edn. Stanford, CA: Stanford University Press, pp. 86–104.

Bazzaz, Abd Al-Rahman Al-. 1967 [1954]. *Al-'Iraq min al-Ihtilal hatta al-Istiqlal* (Iraq from Occupation to Independence). Baghdad: Al-'Ani.

Beaugrand, Claire. 2015. 'In and Out Moves of the Bahraini Opposition: How Years of Political Exile Led to the Opening of an International Front during the 2011 Crisis in Bahrain'. In *Transit States: Labour, Migration and Citizenship in the Gulf*. Abdulhadi Khalaf, Omar AlShehabi and Adam Hanieh eds. London: Pluto Press, pp. 198–219.

Beblawi, H. 1990. 'The Rentier State in the Arab World'. In *The Arab State*. G. Luciani ed. London: Routledge, pp. 85–98.

Bedri, Babikr. 1969. *The Memoirs of Babikr Bedri*. Trans. from the Arabic by Yousef Bedri and George Scott, with an introduction by P. M. Holt. London: Oxford University Press.

Beinin, Joel. 1988. 'Islam, Marxism, and the Shubra al-Khayma Textile Workers: Muslim Brothers and Communists in the Egyptian Trade Union Movement'. In *Islam, Politics and Social Movements*. Edmund Burke III and Ira M. Lapidus eds. Berkeley, CA: University of California Press, pp. 207–27.

1989. 'Labor, Capital, and the State in Nasserist Egypt, 1952–1961'. *International Journal of Middle East Studies*, 21, 1 (February): 71–90.

1994. 'Will the Real Egyptian Working Class Please Stand Up?'. In *Workers and Working Classes in the Middle East: Struggles, Histories, Historiographies*. Zachary Lockman ed. Albany, NY: State University of New York Press, pp. 247–70.

2001. *Workers and Peasants in the Modern Middle East*. Cambridge: Cambridge University Press.

2003. 'Is Terrorism a Useful Term in Understanding the Middle East and the Palestinian–Israeli Conflict?'. *Radical History Review*, 85 (winter): 12–23.

2009. 'Workers' Struggles under "Socialism" and Neoliberalism'. In *Egypt: The Moment of Change*. Rabab El-Mahdi and Phil Marfleet eds. London: Zed Books, pp. 68–86.

2011. 'A Workers' Social Movement on the Margin of the Global Neoliberal Order, Egypt 2004–2009'. In *Social Movements, Mobilization, and Contestation in the Middle East and North Africa*. Joel Beinin and Frédéric Vairel eds. Stanford, CA: Stanford University Press, pp. 181–201.

Beinin, Joel and Marie Duboc. 2013. 'A Workers' Social Movement on the Margins of the Global Neoliberal Order, Egypt 2004–2012'. In *Social Movements, Mobilization, and Contestation in the Middle East and North Africa*. Joel Beinin and Frédéric Vairel eds. 2nd edn. Stanford, CA: Stanford University Press, pp. 205–27.

Beinin, Joel and Zachary Lockman. 1993. '1919: Labor Upsurge and National Revolution'. In *The Modern Middle East: A Reader*. Albert Hourani, Philip S. Khoury and Mary C. Wilson Eds. London: I. B. Tauris, pp. 395–428.

1998 [first published 1987]. *Workers on the Nile: Nationalism, Communism, Islam and the Egyptian Working Class*. Princeton, NJ: Princeton University Press.

Beinin, Joel and Frédéric Vairel eds. 2013. *Social Movements, Mobilization, and Contestation in the Middle East and North Africa*. Stanford, CA: Stanford University Press.

Benford, Robert and David Snow. 2000. 'Framing Processes and Social Movements: An Overview and Assessment'. *Annual Review of Sociology*, 26: 611–39.

Berque, Jacques. 1972. *Egypt: Imperialism and Revolution*. Trans. Jean Stewart. London: Faber and Faber.

Biancani, Francesca. 2011. 'Let Down the Curtains around Us: Sex Work in Colonial Cairo, 1882–1952'. Unpublished Ph.D. Thesis, London School of Economics and Political Science (LSE).

Bill, James A. and Carl Leiden. 1979. *Politics in the Middle East*. Boston: Little, Brown and Company.

Bishri, Tariq Al-. 1981 [1972]. *Al-Haraka al-Siyasiyya fi Misr, 1945–51* (The Political Movement in Egypt, 1945–51). Cairo: General Egyptian Book Organization.

Blumer, Herbert. 1951. 'Social Movements'. In *Principles of Sociology*. A. McClung Lee ed. 2nd edn. New York: Barnes and Noble.

Bourdieu, Pierre. 1991. *Language and Symbolic Power*. John B. Thompson ed. Trans. Gino Raymond and Matthew Adamson. Cambridge: Polity Press.

1999. *The Weight of the World: Social Suffering in Contemporary Society*. Stanford, CA: Stanford University Press.

Bowden, Tom. 1975. 'The Politics of the Arab Rebellion in Palestine 1936–9'. *Middle Eastern Studies*, 11, 2 (May): 147–74.

Boyd, Douglas A. 1975. 'Development of Egypt's Radio: "Voice of the Arabs" under Nasser'. *Journalism & Mass Communication Quarterly*, 52: 645–53.

Brackman, Harold. 2013. 'Boycott, Divestment, Sanction (BDS) against Israel – an Anti-Semitic Anti-Peace Poison Pill'. Simon Wiesenthal Centre (March) www.wiesenthal.com/atf/cf/%7B54d385e6-f1b9–4e9f-8e94–890c3e6dd277%7D/REPORT_313.PDF.

Brand, Laurie. 1988. *Palestinians in the Arab World: Institution Building and the Search for State*. New York: Columbia University Press.

Brower, Benjamin Claude. 2009. *A Desert Named Peace: The Violence of France's Empire in the Algerian Sahara, 1844–1902*. New York: Columbia University Press.

Browers, Michaelle L. 2009. *Political Ideology in the Arab World: Accommodation and Transformation*. Cambridge: Cambridge University Press.

Brown, Nathan J. 1990a. *Peasant Politics in Modern Egypt: The Struggle against the State*. New Haven, CT: Yale University Press.

1990b. 'Brigands and State Building: The Invention of Banditry in Modern Egypt'. *Comparative Studies in Society and History*, 32: 258–81.

Budeiri, Musa K. 2010 [1979]. *The Palestine Communist Party 1919–1948: Arab and Jew in the Struggle for Internationalism*. Chicago: Haymarket Books.

Burdett, A. L. P. 1997. *Records of Saudi Arabia, 1961–1965*. 5 vols. Chippenham: Archive Editions.

2004. *Records of Saudi Arabia, 1966–1971*. 6 vols. Chippenham: Archive Editions.

Burgat, François. 2003. *Face to Face with Political Islam*. London: I. B. Tauris.

Burke, Edmund III. 1972. 'Pan-Islam and Moroccan Resistance to French Colonial Penetration, 1900–1912'. *Journal of African History*, 13: 97–118.

1976. *Prelude to Protectorate in Morocco: Precolonial Protest and Resistance, 1860–1912*. Chicago: University of Chicago Press.

Burke, Edmund III and Ira M. Lapidus eds. 1990. *Islam, Politics, and Social Movements*. Berkeley, CA: University of California Press.

Bustani, Butrus Al-. 1987. *Muhit al-Muhit: Qamus Mutawwal li-lugha al-ʿArabiyya* (The Ocean: Dictionary of the Arabic Language). New edn. Beirut: Maktabat Lubnan Nashirun.

1999. *Khuttab fi al-Hayʾa al-Ijtimaʿiyya wa al-Muqabila bayn al- ʿAwaʾid al-Arabiyya wa al-Afranjiyya* (Discourse on Society and the Comparison between Arab and Western Customs). Beirut: Kaslik.

Calvert, John. 2007. 'The Striving Shaykh: Abdullah Azzam and the Revival of Jihad'. *Journal of Religion and Society*, Supplement Series 2 http://moses.creighton.edu/JRS/2007/2007-6.html.

2010. *Sayyid Qutb and the Origins of Radical Islamism*. London: Hurst.

Carré, Olivier. 1991. *L'Utopie Islamique dans l'Orient arabe*. Paris: Fondation Nationale des Sciences Politiques.

Castells, Manuel. 2000. *The Rise of the Network Society: Economy, Society and Culture*. Vol. 1. Oxford: Wiley-Blackwell.

2012. *Networks of Outrage and Hope: Social Movements in the Internet Age*. Cambridge: Polity Press.

Chalcraft, John. 2001. 'The Coal-Heavers of Port Saʿid: State-Building and Worker Protest, 1869–1914'. *International Labour and Working Class History*, 60 (fall): 110–24.

2004. *The Striking Cabbies of Cairo and Other Stories: Crafts and Guilds in Egypt, 1863–1914*. Albany NY: State University of New York Press.

2005a. 'Engaging the State: Peasants, Petitions, Justice and Rights on the Eve of Colonial Rule in Egypt'. *International Journal of Middle East Studies*, 37, 3 (August): 303–25.

2005b. 'Pluralising Capital, Challenging Eurocentrism: Toward PostMarxist Historiography'. *Radical History Review*, 91 (winter): 13–39.

2007. 'Counterhegemonic Effects: Weighing, Measuring, Petitions, and Bureaucracy in Nineteenth Century Egypt'. In *Counterhegemony in the Colony and Postcolony*. John Chalcraft and Yaseen Noorani eds. Houndmills: Palgrave Macmillan, pp. 179–203.

2009. *The Invisible Cage: Syrian Migrant Workers in Lebanon*. Stanford, CA: Stanford University Press.

2011a. 'Migration and Popular Protest in the Arabian Peninsula and the Gulf in the 1950s and 1960s'. *International Labor and Working Class History*, 79 (spring): 28–47.

2011b. 'Labour Protest and Hegemony in Egypt and the Arabian Peninsula'. In *Social Movements in the Postcolonial*. Alf Nilsen and Sara Motta eds. Houndmills: Palgrave Macmillan, pp. 35–59.

2012. 'Egypt's Uprising, Mohammed Bouazizi, and the Failure of Neoliberalism'. *The Maghreb Review*, 37, 3–4: 195–214.

Chalcraft, John and Yaseen Noorani eds. 2007. *Counterhegemony in the Colony and Postcolony*. Houndmills: Palgrave Macmillan.

Chamberlin, Paul Thomas. 2012. *The Global Offensive: The United States, The Palestine Liberation Organization, and the Making of the Post-Cold War Order*. Oxford: Oxford University Press.

Chatterjee, Kingshuk. 2011. *'Ali Shariati and the Shaping of Political Islam in Iran*. New York: Palgrave Macmillan.

Chatterjee, Partha. 1986. *Nationalist Thought and the Colonial World: A Derivative Discourse?*. Minneapolis, MN: University of Minnesota Press.

Clancy-Smith, Julia. 1994. *Rebel and Saint: Muslim Notables, Populist Protest, Colonial Encounters (Algeria and Tunisia, 1800–1904)*. Berkeley, CA: University of California Press.

Clark, Janine. 2004. *Islam, Charity, and Activism: Middle Class Networks and Social Welfare in Egypt, Jordan, and Yemen*. Bloomington, IN: Indiana University Press.

Clegg, Ian. 1971. *Workers' Self-Management in Algeria*. London: Allen Lane.

Clément, Anne. 2012. 'Fallahin on Trial in Colonial Egypt: Apprehending the Peasantry through Orality, Writing, and Performance (1884–1914)'. Unpublished Ph.D. Dissertation, University of Toronto.

Clément, Françoise, Marie Duboc and Omar El Shafei. 2011. 'Le rôle des mobilisations des travailleurs et du mouvement syndical dans la chute de Moubarak'. *Mouvements*, 2, 66: 69–78.

Cleveland, William. 2004. *A History of the Modern Middle East*. 3rd edn, Boulder, CO: Westview.

Clogg, Richard. 1973. 'Aspects of the Movement for Greek Independence'. In *The Struggle for Greek Independence*. Richard Clogg ed. London: Macmillan, pp. 1–40.

Coates-Ulrichsen, Kristian. 2007. 'The British Occupation of Mesopotamia, 1914–1922'. *Journal of Strategic Studies*, 30, 2 (April): 349–77.

Cockburn, Patrick. 2015. *The Rise of Islamic State: ISIS and the New Sunni Revolution*. London: Verso.

Cole, Juan R. I. 1999. *Colonialism and Revolution in the Middle East: Social and Cultural Origins of Egypt's 'Urabi Movement*. Cairo: American University in Cairo Press.

    2007. *Napoleon's Egypt: Invading the Middle East*. New York: Palgrave Macmillan.

Colla, Elliott, Daniel Gumbiner and Diana Abouali. 2012. *Now That We Have Tasted Hope: Voices from the Arab Spring*. Kindle Edn, Byliner Inc.

Committee for the Defence of Legitimate Rights in Saudi Arabia. 1995. 'Political Explosion in Riyadh'. Communiqué 41. Trans. into English

(14 November). Islamic Fundamentalism Collection ca 1980–2002: Box 4. Archives of the Hoover Institution, Stanford, CA.

n.d. *Al-Hajj: Fi Dhull al-Hukm al-Sa'udi* (The Hajj: In the Shadow of Saudi Rule). Islamic Fundamentalism Collection ca. 1980–2002: Box 4. Archives of the Hoover Institution, Stanford, CA.

Connelly, Matthew. 2001. 'Rethinking the Cold War and Decolonization: The Grand Strategy of the Algerian War for Independence'. *International Journal of Middle East Studies*, 33: 221–45.

2002. *A Diplomatic Revolution: Algeria's Fight for Independence and the Origins of the Post-Cold War Era*. Oxford: Oxford University Press.

Correspondence Politique Turquie (CPT). 1827–9. Microfilm P652. Vols. 257–8. Ministère des Affaires Étrangères, Archives Diplomatiques, La Courneuve, France.

Cronin, Stephanie. 2010. 'Popular Politics, the New State and the Birth of the Iranian Working Class: The 1929 Abadan Oil Refinery Strike'. *Middle Eastern Studies*, 46, 5 (September): 699–732.

Cuno, Kenneth M. 1994 [1992]. *The Pasha's Peasants: Land, Society and Economy in Lower Egypt, 1740–1858*. Cairo: American University in Cairo Press.

Dahir, Mas'ud. 1988. *Al-Intifadat al-Lubnaniyya did al-Nizam al-Muqata'ji* (Lebanese Uprisings against the Regime of the Nobles). Beirut: Dar Al-Farabi.

Dallal, Ahmad. 1993. 'The Origins and Objectives of Islamic Revivalist Thought, 1750–1850'. *Journal of the American Oriental Society*, 113, 3 (July–Sepember): 341–59.

Danzinger, Raphael. 1980. 'From Alliance to Belligerency: Abd Al-Qadir in Morocco, 1843–1847'. *The Maghreb Review*, 5, 2–4 (March–August): 63–74.

Darling, Linda T. 2012. *A History of Social Justice and Political Power in the Middle East: The Circle of Justice From Mesopotamia to Globalization*. London: Routledge.

Davis, Eric. 1983. *Challenging Colonialism: Bank Misr and the Egyptian Industrialization, 1920–1941*. Princeton, NJ: Princeton University Press.

2005. *Memories of State: Politics, History, and Collective Identity in Modern Iraq*. Berkeley, CA: University of California Press.

Davis, Mike. 2002. *Late Victorian Holocausts: El Nino Famines and the Making of the Third World*. London: Verso.

2007. *Planet of Slums*. London: Verso.

De Smet, Brecht. 2012a. 'The Prince and the Pharaoh: The Collaborative Project of Egyptian Workers and Their Intellectuals in the Face of Revolution'. Unpublished Ph.D. Thesis, University of Utrecht.

2012b. 'Egyptian Workers and "Their" Intellectuals: The Dialectical Pedagogy of the Mahalla Strike Movement'. *Mind, Culture, and Activity*, 19, 2: 139–55.

Deeb, Lara. 2006. *An Enchanted Modern: Gender and Public Piety in Shi'i Lebanon*. Princeton, NJ: Princeton University Press.

Del Boca, Angelo. 2010. *Mohamed Fekini and the Fight to Free Libya*. Trans. Antony Shugaar. Houndmills: Palgrave Macmillan.

Denoeux, Gilles. 1993. *Urban Unrest in the Middle East: A Comparative Study of Informal Networks in Egypt, Iran, and Lebanon*. Albany, NY: State University of New York Press.

Dib, Mohamed Fathi Al-. 1985. *Abdel Nasser et la Révolution Algérienne*. Paris: Editions Harmattan.

Dobbin, Christine. 1983. *Islamic Revivalism in a Changing Peasant Economy: Central Sumatra, 1784–1847*. London: Curzon Press.

Dobry, Michel. 1986. *Sociologie des crises politique: les dynamiques des mobilisations multi-sectorielles*. Paris: Presses de la Fondation Nationale des Sciences Politiques.

2009. 'Critical Processes and Political Fluidity: A Theoretical Appraisal'. *International Political Anthropology*, 2, 1: 74–90.

Doumani, Beshara. 1995. *Rediscovering Palestine: Merchants and Peasants in Jabal Nablus, 1700–1900*. Berkeley, CA: University of California Press.

Duboc, Marie. 2011. 'Egyptian Leftist Intellectuals' Activism from the Margins: Overcoming the Mobilization/Demobilization Dichotomy'. In *Social Movements, Mobilization, and Contestation in the Middle East and North Africa*. Joel Beinin and FrédéricVairel eds. Stanford, CA: Stanford University Press, pp. 61–82.

Dunn, Ross E. 1977. *Resistance in the Desert: Moroccan Responses to French Imperialism 1881–1912*. Madison, WI: University of Wisconsin.

Edwards, Gemma. 2014. *Social Movements and Protest*. Cambridge: Cambridge University Press.

Eley, Geoff. 2005. *A Crooked Line: From Cultural History to the History of Society*. Ann Arbor, MI: University of Michigan Press.

Elyachar, Julia. 2005. *Markets of Dispossession: NGOs, Economic Development, and the State in Cairo*. Durham, NC: Duke University Press.

Evans, Martin and John Phillips. 2007. *Algeria: Anger of the Dispossessed*. New Haven, CT: Yale University Press.

Evstatiev, Simeon. 2013. 'The Qādīzādeli Movement and the Spread of Islamic Revivalism in the Seventeenth and Eighteenth Century Ottoman Empire: Preliminary Notes'. CAS Sofia Working Paper Series, No. 5, www.ceeol.com (accessed 27 March 2015).

Fahmy, Khaled. 1997. *All the Pasha's Men*. Cambridge: Cambridge University Press.

Fahmy, Ziad. 2011. *Ordinary Egyptians: Creating the Modern Nation through Popular Culture, 1870–1919*. Cairo: American University in Cairo Press.

Fakhro, Munira A. 1997. 'The Uprising in Bahrain: An Assessment'. In *The Persian Gulf at the Millennium: Essays in Politics, Economy, Security, and Religion*. Gary G. Sick and Lawrence G. Potter eds. New York: St Martin's Press.

Faraj, Muhammad Abd Al-Salam. 1980. *Al-Jihad: Al-Faridah al-Ghaiba* (The Neglected Obligation). Publications of the Islamic Movement in Egypt. Islamic Fundamentalism Collection ca. 1980–2002: Box 1, Archives of the Hoover Institution, Stanford, CA.

Farquhar, Michael. 2013. 'Expanding the Wahhabi Mission: Saudi Arabia, the Islamic University of Medina and the Transnational Religious Economy'. Unpublished Ph.D. Thesis, LSE.

Femia, Joseph V. 1981. *Gramsci's Political Thought: Hegemony, Consciousness, and the Revolutionary Process*. Oxford: Clarendon Press.

Filippini, Michele. 2012. 'Antonio Gramsci e la scienza politica della crisi'. In *Domande dal presente. Studi su Gramsci*. Lea Durante and Guido Liguori eds. Rome: Carocci editore, pp. 53–66.

FIS Information Bureau. 1990s. 'Journey through Time'. Islamic Fundamentalism Collection ca. 1980–2002: Box 3, Archives of the Hoover Institution, Stanford, CA.

n.d. [mid-1990s]. Islamic Fundamentalism Collection ca. 1980–2002: Box 3, Archives of the Hoover Institution, Stanford, CA.

Fleischmann, Ellen L. 1999. 'The Other "Awakening": The Emergence of Women's Movements in the Modern Middle East, 1900–1940'. In *Social History of Women and Gender in the Modern Middle East*. Margaret L. Meriwether and Judith E. Tucker eds. Boulder, CO: Westview Press, pp. 89–140.

Front de Libération Nationale (FLN). 1954. 'Proclamation of the Algerian National Liberation Front' (1 November). Islamic Fundamentalism Collection ca. 1980–2002, Archives of the Hoover Institution, Stanford, CA.

Fu'ad, Sa'd Zaghlul. 2001. *Mudhakkirat Fida'i Misri: ma'arik sha'b misr li-l-taharrur al-watani wa al-dimuqrati* (Memoirs of an Egyptian Guerrilla: Battles of the Egyptian People for National and Democratic Liberation). Cairo: Maktab al-Misri al-Hadith.

Gamson, William A. 1975. *The Strategy of Social Protest*. Homewood, IL: The Dorsey Press.

Gasper, Michael. 2009. *The Power of Representation: Publics, Peasants, and Islam in Egypt*. Stanford, CA: Stanford University Press.

Gazzini, Claudia Anna. 2004. 'Jihad in Exile: Ahmad al-Sharif Al-Sanusi, 1918–1933'. Unpublished MA Dissertation, Princeton University.

Gelvin, James L. 1998. *Divided Loyalties: Nationalism and Mass Politics in Syria at the Close of Empire*. Berkeley, CA: University of California Press.

2005. *The Modern Middle East: A History*. New York: Oxford University Press.

Gerges, Fawaz. 2005. *The Far Enemy: Why Jihad Went Global*. Cambridge: Cambridge University Press.

2011. *The Rise and Fall of Al-Qaeda*. Oxford: Oxford University Press.

ed. 2013. *The New Middle East: Protest and Revolution in the Arab World*. Cambridge: Cambridge University Press.

Gershoni, Israel and James Jankowski. 2010. *Confronting Fascism in Egypt: Dictatorship Versus Democracy in the 1930s*. Stanford, CA: Stanford University Press.

Ghannam, Farha. 2002. *Remaking the Modern: Space, Relocation, and the Politics of Identity in a Global Cairo*. Berkeley, CA: University of California Press.

Ghazaleh, Pascale. 1999. *Masters of the Trade: Crafts and Craftspeople in Cairo, 1750–1850*. Cairo: American University in Cairo Press.

Ghazali, Salah Muhammad 'Aisa Al-. 2007. *Al-Jama'at al-Siyasiya al-Kuwaytiya fi Qarn 1910–2007: Dusturiyin, Islamiyyin, al-Shi'a, al-Qawmiyyin* (Political Organizations in Kuwait, 1910–2007: Constitutionalists, Islamists, Shi'a and Arab Nationalists). Kuwait.

Gilsenan, Michael. 1996. *Lords of the Lebanese Marches: Violence and Narrative in an Arab Society*. Berkeley, CA: University of California Press.

Glaser, Daryl. 2003. 'Zionism and Apartheid: A Moral Comparison'. *Ethnic and Racial Studies*, 26, 3: 403–21.

Goldberg, Ellis. 1992. 'Peasants in Revolt – Egypt 1919'. *International Journal of Middle East Studies*, 24, 2 (May): 261–80.

ed. 1996. *The Social History of Labor in the Middle East*. Boulder, CO: Westview Press.

Goldschmidt, Arthur, Amy J. Johnson, Barak A. Salmoni eds. 2005. *Re-Envisioning Egypt, 1919–1952*. Cairo: American University in Cairo Press.

Goodwin, Jeff and James M. Jasper. 1999. 'Caught in a Winding, Snarling Vine: The Structural Bias of Political Process Theory'. *Sociological Forum*, 14: 27–54.

Gordon, Joel. 1997. *Nasser's Blessed Movement: Egypt's Free Officers and the July Revolution*. Cairo: American University in Cairo Press.

Gordon, Lady Duff. 1969. *Letters from Egypt (1862–1869)*. London: Routledge and Kegan Paul.

Gramsci, Antonio. 1971. *Selections from the Prison Notebooks of Antonio Gramsci*. Ed. and trans. Quintin Hoare and Geoffrey Nowell Smith. London: Lawrence and Wishart.

Griswold, William J. 1983. *The Great Anatolian Rebellion: 1000–1020/ 1591–1611*. Berlin: Klaus Schwarz Verlag.

Guha, Ranajit. 1983. *Elementary Aspects of Peasant Insurgency in Colonial India*. New Delhi: Oxford University Press.

  1997. *Dominance without Hegemony: History and Power in Colonial India*. Cambridge, MA: Harvard University Press.

Gunning, Jeroen. 2012. 'Seeing the Egyptian "Revolution" through Social Movement Glasses: Networks, Frames, Protest Cycles and Structural Changes'. Unpublished paper delivered at Brismes Annual Conference, London School of Economics and Political Science, London, 26–8 March.

Gunning, Jeroen and Ilan Zvi Baron. 2013. *Why Occupy a Square? People, Protests and Movements in the Egyptian Revolution*. London: Hurst.

Gurr, Ted. 1970. *Why Men Rebel*. Princeton, NJ: Princeton University Press.

Habib, John. 1978. *Ibn Saud's Warriors of Islam: The Ikhwan of Najd and their Role in the Creation of the Saudi Kingdom, 1910–1930*. Leiden: Brill.

Haddam, Anwar N. 1996. 'An Islamist Vision for Algeria'. *Middle East Quarterly*, 3, 3 (September): 69–80.

  1998. *The FIS Approach to the Algerian Crisis*. FIS Information Bureau [12 pages].

Hafez, Mohammed M. 2000. 'Armed Islamist Movements and Political Violence in Algeria'. *Middle East Journal*, 54, 4 (autumn): 572–91.

  2003. *Why Muslims Rebel: Repression and Resistance in the Islamic World*. Boulder, CO: Lynne Rienner.

Hall, Stuart. 1981. 'Notes on Deconstructing the Popular'. In *People's History and Socialist Theory*. Raphael Samuel ed. London: Routledge and Kegan Paul, pp. 227–40.

  1987. 'Gramsci and Us'. *Marxism Today* (June): 16–21.

Halliday, Fred. 1974. *Arabia without Sultans*. London: Penguin.

  2000. *Nation and Religion in the Middle East*. London: Saqi Books.

  2003. *Islam and the Myth of Confrontation*. 2nd edn. London: I. B. Tauris.

Halliday, Fred and Hamza Alavi eds. 1988. *State and Ideology in the Middle East and Pakistan*. New York: Macmillan.

Halpern, Manfred. 1963. *The Politics of Social Change in the Middle East and North Africa*. Princeton, NJ: Princeton University Press.

Hamas Covenant. 1988. Islamic Fundamentalism Collection ca. 1980–2002: Box 3, Archives of the Hoover Institution, Stanford, CA.

Hanf, Theodor. 1993. *Coexistence in Wartime Lebanon: Decline of a State and Rise of a Nation*. Trans. John Richardson. London: I. B. Tauris.

Hanioğlu, Şükrü. 1995. *The Young Turks in Opposition*. Oxford: Oxford University Press.

2001. *Preparation for a Revolution: The Young Turks, 1902–1908*. Oxford: Oxford University Press.

Hanna, Abdullah. 1973. *Al-Haraka Al-'Ummaliyya fi Suriya wa Lubnan, 1900–1945* (The Labour Movement in Syria and Lebanon, 1900–1945). Damascus.

Hannigan, John A. 1990. 'Apples and Oranges or Varieties of the Same Fruit? The New Religious Movements and theNew Social Movements Compared'. *Review of Religious Research*, 31, 3 (March): 246–58.

Harakat Ahrar Al-Bahrayn Al-Islamiyya (Bahraini Islamic Freedom Movement). 1995. *'Am al-Tadhiyyat wa-l- 'Amal: yawmiyyat al-intifada al-dusturiyya fi-l-Bahrayn Disambar 1994 – Nufimbar 1995* (Year of Victims and of Hope: Diary of the Constitutional Intifada in Bahrain, December 1994–November 1995). London, Islamic Fundamentalism Collection ca. 1980–2002: Box 2, Archives of the Hoover Institution, Stanford, CA.

Harb, Mona. 2008. 'Faith-Based Organisations as Effective Development Partners: Hezbollah and Post-War Reconstruction in Lebanon'. In *Development, Civil Society and Faith-Based Organizations – Bridging the Sacred and the Secular*. G. Clarke and M. Jennings eds. Basingstoke: Palgrave Macmillan.

Harb, Mona and Reinoud Leenders. 2005. 'Know Thy Enemy: Hizbullah, "Terrorism" and the Politics of Perception'. *Third World Quarterly*, 26, 1: 173–97.

Hardt, Michael and Antonio Negri. 2004. *Multitude: War and Democracy in the Age of Empire*. London: Penguin.

Hart, David M. 1976. *The Aith Waryaghar of the Moroccan Rif*. Tucson, AZ: University of Arizona Press.

Hasso, Frances. 2005. *Resistance, Repression, and Gender Politics in Occupied Palestine and Jordan*. Syracuse, NY: Syracuse University Press.

Hatem, Mervat F. 1992. 'Economic and Political Liberation in Egypt and the Demise of State Feminism'. *International Journal of Middle East Studies*, 24: 231–51.

Haugbolle, Sune. 2006. 'Spatial Transformations in the Lebanese "Independence Intifada"'. *Arab Studies Journal*, 14, 2 (fall): 60–77.

Havemann, Axel. 1991. 'The Impact of Peasant Resistance on Nineteenth-Century Mount Lebanon'. In *Peasants and Politics in the Modern Middle East*. Farhad Kazemi and John Waterbury eds. Miami: Florida International University Press, pp. 85–100.

Hawrani, Akram Al-. 2000. *Mudhakkirat Akram al-Hawrani* (Memoirs of Akram al-Hawrani). 4 vols. Cairo: Madbuli.

Haykel, Bernard. 2003. *Revival and Reform in Islam: The Legacy of Muhammad al-Shawkani*. Cambridge: Cambridge University Press.

Heard-Bey, Frauke. 1982. *From Trucial States to United Arab Emirates: A Society in Transition*. London: Longman.

Hegghammer, Thomas. 2010. *Jihad in Saudi Arabia: Violence and Pan-Islamism since 1979*. Cambridge: Cambridge University Press.

Hegghammer, Thomas and Stéphane Lacroix. 2011. *The Meccan Rebellion: The Story of Juhayman al-'Utaybi Revisited*. Bristol: Amal Press.

Held, David and Anthony G. McGrew, David Goldblatt and Jonathan Perraton. 1999. *Global Transformations: Politics, Economics, and Culture*. Stanford, CA: Stanford University Press.

Hickey, Tom and Phil Marfleet. 2010. 'The "South Africa Moment": Palestine, Israel and the Boycott'. *International Socialism*, 128. www.isj.org.uk/index.php4?id=680&issue=128.

Hill, Christopher. 1996. *Liberty against the Law: Some Seventeenth Century Controversies*. London: Allen Lane.

Hiltermann, Joost R. 1991. *Behind the Intifada: Labor and Women's Movements in the Occupied Territories*. Princeton, NJ: Princeton University Press.

Hilw, Yusuf Khattar Al-. 1979. *Al- 'Ammiyyat Al-Sha'biyya fi Lubnan* (Popular Uprisings in Lebanon). Beirut: Dar al-Farabi.

Hizb Al-Da'wa Al-Islamiyya (The [Iraqi] Party of the Islamic Call). 1992. *Burnamijuna: al-bayan wa-l-burnamij al-siyasi li-hizb al-da'wa al-islamiyya* (Our Programme: The Statement and the Political Programme of the Party of the Islamic Call). London, Islamic Fundamentalism Collection ca. 1980–2002: Box 1, Archives of the Hoover Institution, Stanford, CA.

Hmed, Choukri. 2012. 'Réseaux dormants, contingence et structures'. *Revue Française de Science Politique*, 62, 5: 797–820.

Hobsbawm, Eric. 1988. *The Age of Revolution: Europe 1789–1848*. London: Abacus Books.

Holt, P. M. 1966. *Egypt and the Fertile Crescent, 1516–1922: A Political History*. Ithaca, NY: Cornell University Press.

1970. *The Mahdist State in the Sudan, 1881–1898: A Study of its Origins, Development and Overthrow*. 2nd edn. Oxford: Clarendon Press.

Hourani, Albert. 1962. *Arabic Thought in the Liberal Age 1798–1939*. Cambridge: Cambridge University Press.

1991. *A History of the Arab Peoples*. London: Faber and Faber.

1994. 'The Politics of the Notables'. In *The Modern Middle East: A Reader*. Albert Hourani *et al.* eds. London: I. B. Tauris, pp. 83–110.

Hudson, Michael C. 1977. *Arab Politics: The Search for Legitimacy*. New Haven, CT: Yale University Press.

Hunter, F. Robert. 1993. *The Palestinian Uprising: A War by Other Means*. 2nd edn. Berkeley, CA: University of California Press.

1999 [1984]. *Egypt under the Khedives, 1805–1879: From Household Government to Modern Bureaucracy*. Cairo: American University in Cairo Press.

Huntington, Samuel P. 1968. *Political Order in Changing Societies*. New Haven, CT: Yale University Press.

1997. *The Clash of Civilizations and the Remaking of World Order*. London: Simon and Schuster.

Hussein, Mahmoud. 1973. *Class Conflict in Egypt, 1945–1970*. New York: Monthly Review Press.

Ibrahim, Saad Eddin. 1982. *The New Arab Social Order: A Study of the Social Impact of Oil*. Boulder, CO: Westview Press.

Irving, Sarah. 2012. *Leila Khaled: Icon of Palestinian Liberation*. London: Pluto.

Isma'il, Hamada. 2005. *Intifadat 1935: bayn wuthbat al-Qahira wa ghadbat al-aqalim* (The Uprising of 1935: Between the Upsurge in Cairo and the Anger of the Provinces). Cairo: Dar Al-Shuruq.

Ismail, Salwa. 2006. *Political Life in Cairo's New Quarters*. Minneapolis, MN: University of Minnesota Press.

2012. 'The Egyptian Revolution against the Police'. *Social Research*, 79, 2: 435–62.

Izz Al-Din, Amin. 1967–71. *Ta'rikh al- 'Amila al-Misriyya* (The History of Egyptian Labour). 3 vols. Cairo: Dar al-Sha'b.

Jabarti, Abd Al-Rahman Al-. 1993 [1798]. *Napoleon in Egypt: Al-Jabarti's Chronicle of the First Seven Months of the French Occupation of Egypt, 1798*. Trans. Shmuel Moreh, intro. by Robert Tignor. Princeton, NJ: Markus Wiener.

Jackson Lears, T. J. 1985. 'The Concept of Cultural Hegemony: Problems and Possibilities'. *American Historical Review*, 90, 3 (June): 567–93.

Jahhaf, Lutf Allah. 1975. *Nusus Yamaniya 'an al-Hamla al-Faransiyya 'ala Misr* (Yemeni Texts on the French Campaign in Egypt). Ed. Sayyid Mustafa Salim. Cairo: Markaz al-Dirasat al-Yamaniyya.

James, C. L. R. 2001. *The Black Jacobins: Toussaint L'ouverture and the San Domingo Revolution*. London: Penguin.

Jameson, Frederic. 1992. *Postmodernism: Or, the Cultural Logic of Late Capitalism*. London: Verso.

Jaza'iri, Abd Al-Malik Al-Ramadani Al-. 2007. *The Savage Barbarism of Abu Qatada*. SalafiManhaj, www.salafimanhaj.com/pdf/SalafiManhaj Qataadah.pdf.

Johnson, Michael. 1986. *Class & Client in Beirut: The Sunni Muslim Community and the Lebanese State, 1840–1985*. Reading: Ithaca Press.

2002. *All Honourable Men: The Social Origins of War in Lebanon*. London: I. B. Tauris.

Jones, Toby Craig. 2006. 'Rebellion on the Saudi Periphery: Modernity, Marginalization and the Shi'a Uprising of 1979'. *International Journal of Middle East Studies*, 38, 2 (May): 213–33.

Joyce, Patrick. 1993. *Visions of the People: Industrial England and the Question of Class, c. 1848–1914*. Cambridge: Cambridge University Press.

Jumblatt, Kamal. 1982. *I Speak for Lebanon*. Trans. Michael Pallis. Recorded by Philippe Lapousterle. London: Zed Books.

Kafadar, Çemal. 2007. 'Janissaries and Other Riffraff of Ottoman Istanbul: Rebels without a Cause?'. In *Identity and Identity Formation in the Ottoman World: A Volume of Essays in Honor of Norman Itzkowitz*. Baki Tezcan and Karl K. Barbir eds. Madison, WI: University of Wisconsin Press, pp. 113–34.

Kamrava, Mehran. 2005. *The Modern Middle East: A Political History since the First World War*. Berkeley, CA: University of California Press.

Karakişla, Yavuz Salim. 1995. 'The Emergence of the Ottoman Industrial Working Class, 1839–1923'. In *Workers and the Working Class in the Ottoman Empire and the Turkish Republic, 1839–1950*. Donald Quataert and Erik Jan Zürcher eds. London: I. B. Tauris.

Kartodirdjo, Sartono. 1966. *The Peasants Revolt of Banten in 1888*. Gravenhage: Martinus Nijhoff.

Kassir, Samir. 2005. *Intifadat al-istiqlal ka-ma rawaha* (The Independence Uprising as It Was Seen). Beirut: Dar al-Nahar.

Katsiaficas, George. 2013. *Asia's Unknown Uprisings: People Power in the Philippines, Burma, Tibet, China, Taiwan, Bangladesh, Nepal, Thailand and Indonesia, 1947–2009*. Oakland, CA: PM Press.

Keddie, Nikki. 1988. 'Iranian Revolutions in Comparative Perspective'. In *Islam, Politics, and Social Movements*. Ira Lapidus and Edmund Burke eds. Berkeley, CA: University of California Press, pp. 298–313.

1998. 'The New Religious Politics: Where, When, and Why Do "Fundamentalisms" Appear?'. *Comparative Studies in Society and History*, 40, 4 (October): 696–723.

Kepel, Gilles. 1985. *The Prophet and Pharaoh: Muslim Extremism in Egypt*. London: El Saqi Books.

Kerr, Malcolm H. 1971. *The Arab Cold War: Gamal Abd al-Nasir and His Rivals, 1958–1970*. 3rd edn. Oxford: Oxford University Press.

Ketchley, Neil. 2014. '"The Army and the People Are One Hand!": Fraternization and the 25th January Egyptian Revolution'. *Comparative Studies in Society and History*, 56, 1 (January): 155–86.

Khafaji, Isam Al-. 2004. *Tormented Births: Passages to Modernity in Europe and the Middle East.* London: I. B. Tauris.

Khalaf, Abdulhadi. 1998. 'Contentious Politics in Bahrain: From Ethnic to National and Vice Versa'. Paper presented at the fourth Nordic conference on Middle Eastern Studies: The Middle East in globalizing world. Oslo, 13–16 August.

Khalaf, Issa. 1997. 'The Effect of Socio-Economic Change on Arab Societal Collapse in Mandate Palestine'. *International Journal of Middle East Studies*, 29, 1: 93–112.

Khalaf, Samir. 1987. *Lebanon's Predicament.* New York: Columbia University Press.

Khaled, Leila. 1973. *Mon Peuple Vivra.* Trans. Michel Pagnier. Paris: Gallimard.

Khalidi, Rashid. 1997. *Palestinian Identity: The Construction of Modern National Consciousness.* New York: Columbia University Press.

Khalidi, Walid. 1988. 'Plan Dalet: Masterplan for the Conquest of Palestine'. *Journal of Palestine Studies*, 18, 1: 4–33.

Khalili, Laleh. 2007a. *Heroes and Martyrs of Palestine: The Politics of National Commemoration.* Cambridge: Cambridge University Press.

2007b. '"Standing with My Brother": Hizbullah, Palestinians, and the Limits of Solidarity'. *Comparative Studies in Society and History*, 49: 276–303.

2012. *Time in the Shadows: Confinement in Counterinsurgencies.* Stanford, CA: Stanford University Press.

Khater, Akram Fouad. 1996. '"House" to "Goddess of the House": Gender, Class, and Silk in 19th Century Mount Lebanon'. *International Journal of Middle East Studies*, 28: 325–48.

Khoury, Philip. 1984. 'Syrian Urban Politics in Transition: The Quarters of Damascus during the French Mandate'. *International Journal of Middle East Studies*, 16: 507–40.

1987. *Syria and the French Mandate.* Princeton, NJ: Princeton University Press.

Khuri, Fuad. 1980. *Tribe and State in Bahrain: The Transformation of Social and Political Authority in an Arab State.* Chicago: University of Chicago Press.

Khuri-Makdisi, Ilham. 2010. *The Eastern Mediterranean and the Making of Global Radicalism, 1860–1914.* Berkeley, CA: University of California Press.

Kienle, Eberhard ed. 2003. *Politics from Above, Politics from Below: The Middle East in the Age of Economic Reform.* London: Saqi Books.

Knei-Paz, Baruch. 1978. *The Social and Political Thought of Leon Trotsky.* Oxford: Oxford University Press.

Kostiner, Joseph. 1990. 'Transforming Dualities: Tribe and State Formation in Saudi Arabia'. In *Tribes and State Formation in the Middle East.* Philip S. Khoury and Joseph Kostiner eds. Berkeley, CA: University of California Press, pp. 226–51.

1993. *The Making of Saudi Arabia 1916–1936.* Oxford: Oxford University Press.

Kurzman, Charles. 2001. 'Critics Within: Islamic Scholars' Protests against the Islamic State in Iran'. *International Journal of Politics, Culture, and Society*, 15, 2: 341–59.

2004. *The Unthinkable Revolution in Iran.* Cambridge, MA: Harvard University Press.

2008. *Democracy Denied, 1905–1915: Intellectuals and the Fate of Democracy.* Cambridge, MA: Harvard University Press.

Lackner, Helen. 1978. *A House Built on Sand: A Political Economy of Saudi Arabia.* London: Ithaca Press.

Laclau, Ernesto and Chantal Mouffe. 1985. *Hegemony and Socialist Strategy: Towards a Radical Democratic Politics.* London: Verso.

Lacroix, Stéphane. 2011. *Awakening Islam: The Politics of Religious Dissent in Contemporary Saudi Arabia.* Trans. George Holoch. Cambridge, MA: Harvard University Press.

Ladjevardi, Habib. 1985. *Labor Unions and Autocracy in Iran.* Syracuse, NY: Syracuse University Press.

Lambton, Ann K. S. 1977. 'The Tribal Resurgence and the Decline of the Bureaucracy in the Eighteenth Century'. In *Studies in Eighteenth Century Islamic History.* Thomas Naff and Roger Owen eds. Carbondale, IL: Southern Illinois University Press, pp. 108–29.

Lapidus, Ira M. 1988. *A History of Islamic Societies.* Cambridge: Cambridge University Press.

Laroui, Abdallah. 1977. *Les origines sociales et culturelles de nationalisme Marocain, 1830–1912.* Paris: Maspero.

Lawrence, Adria K. 2013. *Imperial Rule and the Politics of Nationalism: Anti-Colonial Protest in the French Empire.* Cambridge: Cambridge University Press.

Lawson, Fred H. 1981. 'Rural Revolt and Provincial Society in Egypt, 1820–1824'. *International Journal of Middle East Studies*, 13: 131–53.

2004. 'Repertoires of Contention in Contemporary Bahrain'. In *Islamic Activism: A Social Movement Theory Approach.* Bloomington, IN: Indiana University Press, pp. 89–111.

Le Bon, Gustave. 2014 [1896]. *The Crowd: A Study of the Popular Mind.* Createspace, https://www.createspace.com.

Le Tourneau, Roger, Maurice Flory, and René Duchac *et al.* 1972. 'Revolution in the Maghreb'. In *Revolution in the Middle East and Other*

Case Studies. P. J. Vatikiotis ed. London: George Allen and Unwin, pp. 73–119.

Lee, Christopher J. 2010. *Making a World after Empire: The Bandung Moment and its Political Afterlives*. Athens, OH: Ohio University Press.

Leenders, Reinoud. 2013. '"Oh Buthaina, Oh Sha'ban – the Hawrani is not Hungry, We Want Freedom!": Revolutionary Framing and Mobilization at the Onset of the Syrian Uprising'. In *Social Movements, Mobilization, and Contestation in the Middle East and North Africa*. Joel Beinin and FrédéricVairel eds. Stanford, CA: Stanford University Press, pp. 246–64.

Lefèvre, Raphaël. 2013. *Ashes of Hama: The Muslim Brotherhood in Syria*. London: Hurst.

Lerner, Daniel. 1958. *The Passing of Traditional Society: Modernizing the Middle East*. New York: The Free Press.

Levtzion, Nehemia and John O. Voll eds. 1987. *Eighteenth-Century Renewal and Reform in Islam*. Baltimore, MD: Syracuse University Press.

Lewis, Bernard. 1961. *The Emergence of Modern Turkey*. Oxford: Oxford University Press.

   1990. 'The Roots of Muslim Rage'. *Atlantic Monthly*. www.theatlantic .com/magazine/archive/1990/09/the-roots-of-muslim-rage/304643.

Lia, Brynjar. 1998. *The Rise of an Islamic Mass Movement, 1928–1942*. Reading: Ithaca Press.

Linebaugh, Peter and Marcus Rediker. 2000. *The Many-Headed Hydra: Sailors, Slaves, Commoners, and the Hidden History of the Revolutionary Atlantic*. New York: Beacon Press.

Lockman, Zachary. 1994a. 'Imagining the Working Class: Culture, Nationalism and Class Formation in Egypt 1899–1914'. *Poetics Today*, 15: 157–90.

   1994b. 'Introduction'. *Workers and Working Classes in the Middle East: Struggles, Histories, Historiographies*. Zachary Lockman ed. Albany, NY: State University of New York Press, pp. xi–xxxi.

   1996. *Comrades and Enemies: Arab and Jewish Workers in Palestine, 1906–1948*. Berkeley, CA: University of California Press.

   2004. *Contending Visions of the Middle East: The History and Politics of Orientalism*. Cambridge: Cambridge University Press.

Lockman, Zachary and Joel Beinin eds. 1990. *Intifada: The Palestinian Uprising against Israeli Occupation*. London: I. B. Tauris.

Louër, Laurence. 2008a. *Transnational Shia Politics: Religious and Political Networks in the Gulf*. London: Hurst & Company.

   2008b. 'The Political Impact of Labor Migration in Bahrain'. *City & Society*, 20, 1: 32–53.

Luciani, Giacomo ed. 1990. *The Arab State*. Berkeley, CA: University of California Press.

Lynch, Marc. 2007. *Voices of the New Arab Public: Iraq, Al-Jazeera, and Middle East Politics Today*. New York: Columbia University Press.

McAdam, Doug. 1982. *Political Process and the Development of Black Insurgency, 1930–1970*. Chicago: Chicago University Press.

1983. 'Tactical Innovation and the Pace of Insurgency'. *American Sociological Review*, 48, 6 (December): 735–54.

McAdam, Doug, John D. McCarthy and Mayer N. Zald. 1996. *Comparative Perspectives on Social Movements: Political Opportunities, Mobilizing Structures, and Cultural Framings*. Cambridge: Cambridge University Press.

McAdam, Doug and William H. Sewell. 2001. 'Temporality in the Study of Social Movements and Revolutions'. In *Silence and Voice in Contentious Politics*. Ronald R. Aminzade *et al.* Cambridge: Cambridge University Press.

McAdam, Doug, Sidney Tarrow and Charles Tilly. 2001. *Dynamics of Contention*. Cambridge: Cambridge University Press.

Mahdi, Muhammad. n.d. *Al-Bahrain: intihakat huquq al-insan 1979–1990* (Bahrain: Human Rights Abuses 1979–1990), Islamic Fundamentalism Collection ca. 1980–2002: Box 2, Archives of the Hoover Institution, Stanford, CA.

Mahdi, Rabab El-. 2009. 'The Democracy Movement: Cycles of Protest'. In *Egypt: The Moment of Change*. Rabab El-Mahdi and Phil Marfleet eds. London: Zed Books, pp. 87–102.

Mahmood, Saba. 2004. *Politics of Piety: The Islamic Revival and the Feminist Subject*. Princeton, NJ: Princeton University Press.

Makdisi, Ussama. 2000. *The Culture of Sectarianism: Community, History, and Violence in Nineteenth Century Ottoman Lebanon*. Berkeley, CA: University of California Press.

Makiya, Kanan. 1998. *Republic of Fear: The Politics of Modern Iraq*. Updated edn. Berkeley, CA: University of California Press.

Mallat, Chibli. 1993. *The Renewal of Islamic Law: Muhammad Baqir as-Sadr, Najaf and the Shi'i International*. Cambridge: Cambridge University Press.

Malley, Robert. 1996. *The Call from Algeria: Third Worldism, Revolution, and the Turn to Islam*. Berkeley, CA: University of California Press.

Mandel, Ernest. 1975. *Late Capitalism*. London: Humanities Press.

Mann, Michael. 1986. *The Sources of Social Power: A History of Power from the Beginning to AD 1760*. Vol. 1. Cambridge: Cambridge University Press.

Mao Tse-Tung. 1937. *Yu Chi Chan* (On Guerrilla Warfare) http://www .marines.mil/portals/59/publications/FMFRP%2012-18%20%20 Mao%20Tse-tung%20on%20Guerrilla%20Warfare.pdf.

Marsot, Afaf Lutfi Al-Sayyid. 1966. 'Review of Gabriel Baer's Egyptian Guilds in Modern Times'. *Middle Eastern Studies*, 2 (April): 275–6.

1984. *Egypt in the Reign of Muhammad Ali*. Cambridge: Cambridge University Press.

Massad, Joseph. 2001. *Colonial Effects: The Making of National Identity in Jordan*. New York: Columbia University Press.

2007. *Desiring Arabs*. Chicago: University of Chicago Press.

Mattar, Philip. 1988. *The Mufti of Jerusalem: al-Hajj Amin al-Husayni and the Palestinian National Movement*. New York: Columbia University Press.

Matthews, Weldon. 2006. *Confronting an Empire, Constructing a Nation: Arab Nationalists and Popular Politics in Mandate Palestine*. London: I. B. Tauris.

Mdairis, Falah Abdallah Al-. 2004. *Al-Harakat wa-l-Jama'at al-Siyasiyya fi-l-Bahrain 1938–2002* (Political Organizations and Movements in Bahrain 1938–2002). Beirut.

Meijer, Roel ed. 2009. *Global Salafism: Islam's New Religious Movement*. London: Hurst & Co.

Mercier, Ernest. 1901. 'Le Bach Ag'a Mokrani et les causes de l'insurrection indigène de 1871'. In *Extrait du Bulletin de la Réunion d'Etudes Algériennes*. Paris: 12, Galerie D'Orléans, pp. 31–2.

Mir-Hosseini, Ziba and Richard Tapper. 2006. *Islam and Democracy in Iran: Eshkevari and the Quest for Reform*. London: I. B. Tauris.

Mirza, Mansoor Ahmed. 2014. 'Between 'Umma, Empire and Nation: The Role of the 'Ulama in the 'Urabi Revolt and the Emergence of Egyptian Nationalism'. Unpublished Ph.D. Thesis, LSE.

Mitchell, Richard. 1969. *The Society of the Muslim Brothers*. Oxford: Oxford University Press.

Mitchell, Timothy. 1988. *Colonising Egypt*. Cambridge: Cambridge University Press.

2002. 'McJihad: Islam in the US Global Order'. *Social Text*, 20, 4 (winter): 1–18.

Moghadam, Valentine. 1993. *Modernizing Women: Gender and Social Change in the Middle East*. Boulder, CO: Lynne Rienner.

Morrison, Suzanne. Forthcoming. 'The Boycott, Divestment, and Sanctions Movement: Border-Crossing Contentious Politics for Palestinian Justice'. In *Contentious Politics in the Middle East*. Fawaz Gerges ed. New York: Palgrave Macmillan.

Morton, A. L. 1938. *A People's History of England*. London: Lawrence and Wishart.

Mossallam, Alia. 2012. *Democratic Transition in the Middle East: Unmaking Power*. Larbi Sadiki ed. London: Routledge.

2013. 'Hikayat Sha'b – Stories of Peoplehood: Nasserism, Popular Politics and Songs in Egypt, 1956–1973'. Unpublished Ph.D. Thesis, LSE.

Mottahedeh, Roy P. 1996. 'Shi'ite Political Thought and the Destiny of the Iranian Revolution'. In *Iran and the Gulf: A Search for Stability*. Jamal S. Al-Suwaidi ed. Abu Dhabi: The Emirates Center for Strategic Studies and Research.

Mouffe, Chantal. 1979. 'Hegemony and Ideology in Gramsci'. In *Gramsci and Marxist Theory*. Chantal Mouffe ed. London: Routledge and Kegan Paul, pp. 168–203.

Munib, Abd Al-Mun'im. 2010. *Muraji'at al-Jihadiyyin: Al-Qissa al-Khaffiya li-Muraji'at al-Jihad wa-l-Jama'a al-Islamiyya Dakhil wa Kharij al-Sijun* (The Recantation of the Holy Warriors: The Hidden Story of the Recantation from Holy War and the Islamic Group in and out of Prison). Cairo: Madbuli.

Muslim Brotherhood. 1990s. Statements, Pamphlets, and Website Material, Islamic Fundamentalism Collection ca. 1980–2002: Box 3, Archives of the Hoover Institution, Stanford, CA.

Muslim Brotherhood in Jordan. 1997. *Official Statement on the Boycott of 1997 Elections*. Trans. into English. Amman: Muslim Brotherhood.

Nafi, Basheer M. 1997. 'Shaykh Izz al-Din al-Qassam: A Reformist and a Rebel Leader'. *Journal of Islamic Studies*, 8, 2: 185–215.

Nakash, Yitzhak. 1994. *The Shi'is of Iraq*. Princeton, NJ: Princeton University Press.

Nasser, Gamal Abdul-. 1973. 'Memoirs of the First Palestine War'. *Journal of Palestine Studies*, 2, no. 2 (winter): 3–32.

National Liberation Front (Central Organizing Committee). 1968. 'How Do We Understand the Experiment of the People's South Yemen?'. Beirut: Dar Al-Tali'a (24 August), pp. 96. National Liberation Front [Yemen] Issuances, 1955–1968. Archives of the Hoover Institution, Stanford, CA.

National Liberation Front (General Command). 1969. 'Programme for the Implementation of the Phase of National Democratic Liberation', Approved by in ordinary meeting held 7–11 October 1968, p. 20.

National Liberation Front [Yemen] Issuances, 1955–68. Archives of the Hoover Institution, Stanford, CA.

Nelson, Cynthia. 1996. *Doria Shafik Egyptian Feminist: A Woman Apart*. Miami: Florida University Press.

Neyzi, Leyla. 2005. *Amele Taburu: The Military Journal of a Jewish Soldier in Turkey during the War of Independence*. Istanbul: Isis Press.

Nimr, Sonia Fathi El-. 1990. 'The Arab Revolt of 1936–1939 in Palestine: A Study Based on Oral Sources'. Ph.D. Thesis, University of Exeter.

Noorani, Yaseen. 2007. 'Redefining Resistance: Counterhegemony, the Repressive Hypothesis and the Case of Arabic Modernism'. In *Counterhegemony in the Colony and Postcolony*. John Chalcraft and Yaseen Noorani eds. Houndmills: Palgrave Macmillan, pp. 75–99.

2010. *Culture and Hegemony in the Colonial Middle East*. London: Palgrave Macmillan.

Norton, Augustus R. 1987. *Amal and the Shi'a: Struggle for the Soul of Lebanon*. Austin, TX: University of Texas Press.

2007. *Hizbullah: A Short History*. Princeton, NJ: Princeton University Press.

O'Brien, Kevin. 2002. 'Neither Transgressive nor Contained: Boundary-Spanning Contention in China'. *Mobilization: An International Quarterly*, 8, 1 (October): 51–64.

O'Fahey, Rex S. 1990. *Enigmatic Saint: Ahmad Ibn Idris and the Idrisi Tradition*. London: Hurst.

O'Fahey, Rex S. and Ali Salih Karrar. 1987. 'The Enigmatic Imam: The Influence of Ahmad Ibn Idris'. *International Journal of Middle East Studies*, 19: 205–20.

O'Fahey, Rex S. and Bernd Radtke. 1993. 'Neo-Sufism Reconsidered'. *Der Islam*, 70, 1: 52–87.

Opp, Karl-Dieter. 2009. *Theories of Political Protest and Social Movements: A Multidisciplinary Introduction, Critique, and Synthesis*. London: Routledge.

Osterhammel, Jürgen. 2005. *Colonialism: A Theoretical Overview*. Princeton, NJ: Marcus Wiener.

Owen, Roger. 1981. *The Middle East in the World Economy, 1800–1914*. London: I. B. Tauris.

2004a. *State, Power and Politics in the Modern Middle East*. 3rd edn. London: Routledge.

2004b. *Lord Cromer: Victorian Imperialist, Edwardian Proconsul*. Oxford: Oxford University Press.

2012. *The Rise and Fall of Arab Presidents for Life*. Cambridge, MA: Harvard University Press.

Oxford Dictionary of National Biography. 'James Augustus St John'. www.oxforddnb.com/view/article/24498?docPos=3 (accessed 27 April 2015).

Özok-Gündoğan, Nilay. n.d. 'A Peripheral Approach to the 1908 Revolution in the Ottoman Empire: Land Disputes in Peasant Petitions in Post-Revolutionary Diyarbekir'. Unpublished paper, Binghamton University.

Paidar, Parvin. 1995. *Women and the Political Process in Twentieth Century Iran*. Cambridge: Cambridge University Press.

Palestine Royal Commission Report. 1937. London, http://unispal.un.org/pdfs/Cmd5479.pdf (accessed 8 May 2014).

Pankhurst, Reza. 2013. *The Inevitable Caliphate? A History of the Struggle for Global Islamic Union, 1924 to the Present*. London: Hurst.

Pappé, Ilan. 2006. *The Ethnic Cleansing of Palestine*. Oxford: Oneworld Publications.

Patnaik, Arun K. 1987. *Gramsci's Concept of Commonsense: Towards a Theory of Subaltern Consciousness in Hegemony Processes*. Calcutta: Centre for Studies in Social Sciences.

Pennell, Charles Richard. 1986. *A Country with a Government and a Flag: The Rif War in Morocco, 1921–1926*. Wisbech: Middle East and North African Studies Press.

Perlmutter, Amos. 1970. 'The Arab Military Elite'. *World Politics*, 22 (January): 269–300.

Peteet, Julie. 1994. 'Male Gender and Rituals of Resistance in the Palestinian "Intifada": A Cultural Politics of Violence'. *American Ethnologist*, 21, 1 (February): 31–49.

Peters, Rudolf. 1979. *Islam and Colonialism: The Doctrine of Jihad in Modern History*. The Hague: Mouton Publishers.

PFLP. 1970. *Rihlat al-Istislam min Qarar Majlis al-Amn ila Mushru' Rogers* (The Journey of Submission from the Security Council Resolution to the Rogers Plan). PFLP.

n.d. *Al-Jabhat al-Sha'biyya wa-l-'Amaliyyat al-Kharijiyya* (The Popular Front and External Operations). Beirut: Kitab al-Hadaf.

Picard, Elizabeth. 2002. *Lebanon: A Shattered Country: Myths and Realities of the Wars in Lebanon*. Teaneck, NJ: Holmes and Meier.

Pinson, Mark. 1975. 'Ottoman Bulgaria in the First Tanzimat Period – The Revolts in Nish (1841) and Vidin (1850)'. *Middle Eastern Studies*, 11 (May): 103–46.

Piot, Oliver. 2011. *La revolution tunisienne: dix jours qui ébranlèrent le monde arabe*. Paris: Les Petit Matins.

Piterberg, Gabriel. 2008. *The Returns of Zionism: Myths, Politics and Scholarship in Israel*. London: Verso.

Porath, Yehoshua. 1966. 'The Peasant Revolt of 1858–1861 in Kisrawan'. *Asian and African Studies*, 2: 77–157.

Posusney, Marsha Pripstein. 1993. 'The Moral Economy of Labor Protest in Egypt'. *World Politics*, 46, 1: 83–120.

1994. 'Collective Action and Workers' Consciousness in Contemporary Egypt'. In *Workers and Working Classes in the Middle East: Struggles, Histories, Historiographies*. Zachary Lockman ed. Albany, NY: State University of New York Press, pp. 211–46.

1997. *Labor and the State in Egypt*. New York: Columbia University Press.

2003. 'Globalization and Labor Protection in Oil-Poor Arab Countries: Racing to the Bottom?'. *Global Social Policy*, 3, 3 (December): 267–97.

Prashad, Vijay. 2012. *Arab Spring, Libyan Winter*. Oakland, CA: AK Press.

Prochaska, David. 1986. 'Fire on the Mountain: Resisting Colonialism in Algeria'. In *Banditry, Rebellion, and Social Protest in Africa*. Donald Crummey ed. London: James Currey, pp. 230–5.

Provence, Michael. 2005. *The Great Syrian Revolt and the Rise of Arab Nationalism*. Austin, TX: University of Texas Press.

Qassem, Naim. 2010. *Hizbullah: The Story from Within*. Trans. Dalia Khalil. London: Saqi.

Qawuqji, Fawzi Al-. 1995 [1975]. *Mudhakkirat Fawzi al-Qawuqji*. Khayriyya Qasimiyya ed. Damascus: Dar al-Namir.

Quandt, William B. 1969. *Revolution and Political Leadership: Algeria, 1954–1968*. Cambridge, MA: MIT Press.

Quataert, Donald. 1995. 'The Workers of Salonica, 1850–1912'. In *Workers and the Working Class in the Ottoman Empire and the Turkish Republic, 1839–1950*. Donald Quataert and Erik Jan Zürcher eds. London: I. B. Tauris, pp. 59–74.

    2006. *Miners and the State in the Ottoman Empire: The Zonguldak Coalfield, 1822–1920*. New York: Berghahn Books.

Quataert, Donald and Yüksel Duman. 2001. 'A Coal Miner's Life in the Late Ottoman Empire'. *International Labor and Working-Class History*, 60 (October): 153–79.

Quataert, Donald and Erik Jan Zürcher eds. 1995. *Workers and the Working Class in the Ottoman Empire and the Turkish Republic, 1839–1950*. London: I. B. Tauris.

Qumsiyeh, Mazin B. 2011. *Popular Resistance in Palestine: A History of Hope and Empowerment*. London: Pluto Books.

Ramadan, Abd al-'Azim. 1985. *Al-Ghazwa al-Isti'mariyya li-l-'Alam al-'Arabi wa Harakat al-Muqawama* (The Colonial Attack on the Arab World and Resistance Movements). Cairo: Dar al-Ma'arif.

Ramdani, Nabila. 2013. 'Women in the 1919 Egyptian Revolution: From Feminist Awakening to Nationalist Political Activism'. *Journal of International Women's Studies*, 14, 2: 39–52.

Rasheed, Madawi Al-. 1996. 'Saudi Arabia's Islamist Opposition'. *Current History*, 95, 597: 16–22.

    2002. *A History of Saudi Arabia*. Cambridge: Cambridge University Press.

    2006. *Contesting the Saudi State: Islamic Voices from a New Generation*. Cambridge: Cambridge University Press.

Raymond, André. 1958. 'Les porteurs d'eau du Caire'. *Bulletin de l'Institut Français d'Archéologie Orientale*, 57: 183–203.

    1968. 'Quartiers et mouvements populaires au Cairo au XVIIIe siècle'. In *Political and Social Change in Modern Egypt*. P. M. Holt ed. London: Oxford University Press.

1973. *Artisans et commerçants au Caire au XVIIIe siècle.* 2 vols. Damas: Institut Français de Damas.

Redissi, Hamadi. 2008. 'The Refutation of Wahhabism in Arabic Sources, 1745–1932'. In *Kingdom without Borders: Saudi Political, Religious and Media Frontiers.* Madawi Al-Rasheed ed. London: Hurst, pp. 157–82.

Redjala, Ramdane. 1988. *L'opposition en Algérie depuis 1962.* Vol. 1. Paris: Editions Harmattan.

Renton, James. 2007. 'Changing Languages of Empire and the Orient: Britain and the Invention of the Middle East, 1917–1918'. *Historical Journal,* 50, 3 (September): 645–67.

Reynolds, Nancy. 2012. *A City Consumed: Urban Commerce, the Cairo Fire, and the Politics of Decolonization in Egypt.* Stanford, CA: Stanford University Press.

Richards, Alan and John Waterbury. 1990. *A Political Economy of the Middle East.* Boulder, CO: Westview Press.

Rizk, Yunan Labib. 2004. 'Because of the British'. *Al-Ahram Weekly,* 710 (30 September–6 October), http://weekly.ahram.org.eg/2004/710/chrncls.htm (accessed 21 August 2013).

Roberts, Hugh. 2002. 'Moral Economy or Moral Polity? The Political Anthropology of Algerian Riots'. Crisis States Programme, Working Papers Series No. 1. London: London School of Economics and Political Science.

2003. *The Battlefield Algeria 1988–2002: Studies in a Broken Polity.* London: Verso.

2014. *Berber Government: The Kabyle Polity in Pre-Colonial Algeria.* London: I. B. Tauris.

Rosefsky Wickham, Carrie. 2002. *Mobilizing Islam: Religion, Activism, and Political Change in Egypt.* New York: Columbia University Press.

Roy, Olivier. 1994. *The Failure of Political Islam.* Trans. Carol Volk. London: I. B. Tauris.

Roy, Sara. 1995. *The Gaza Strip: The Political Economy of De-development.* Beirut: Institute for Palestine Studies.

2002. 'Why Peace Failed: An Oslo Autopsy'. *Current History* (January): 8–16.

Rubin, Barry. 2002. *Islamic Fundamentalism in Egyptian Politics.* Updated edn. Houndmills: Palgrave Macmillan.

Saad, Reem. 1999. 'State, Landlord, Parliament and Peasant: The Story of the 1992 Tenancy Law in Egypt'. In *Agriculture in Egypt from Pharaonic to Modern Times.* Alan Bowman and Eugene Rogan eds. Oxford: Oxford University Press, pp. 387–404.

Sa'adawi, Nawal Al-. 1980. *The Hidden Face of Eve: Women in the Arab World.* Trans. Sherif Hetata. London: Zed Books.

Sadiki, Larbi. 2000. 'Popular Uprisings and Arab Democratization'. *International Journal of Middle East Studies*, 32, 1 (February): 71–95.

Sadowski, Yahya. 1993. 'The New Orientalism and the Democracy Debate'. *Middle East Report*, 183, Political Islam (July–August): 14–21 and 40–1.

Sadri, Ahmad. 'The Varieties of Religious Reform: Public Intelligentsia in Iran'. *International Journal of Politics, Culture, and Society*, 15, 2: 271–82.

Safa, Oussama. 2006. 'Lebanon Springs Forward'. *Journal of Democracy*, 17, 1 (January): 22–37.

Safran, Nadav. 1961. *Egypt in Search of Political Community*. Cambridge, MA: Harvard University Press.

Said, Edward. 1994. *Culture and Imperialism*. London: Vintage.

    1995. *The Politics of Dispossession: The Struggle for Palestinian Self-Determination, 1969–1994*. London: Vintage.

    1997. *Covering Islam: How the Media and the Experts Determine how We See the Rest of the World*. London: Vintage.

Said, Edward and Christopher Hitchens eds. 1988. *Blaming the Victims: Spurious Scholarship and the Palestinian Question*. London: Verso.

St John, J. A. 1845. *Egypt and Nubia*. London: Chapman and Hall.

Salem, Paul. 1994. *Bitter Legacy: Ideology and Politics in the Arab World*. Syracuse, NY: Syracuse University Press.

Salibi, Kemal. 1976. *Crossroads to Civil War: Lebanon 1958–1976*. New York: Caravan Books.

Salim, Latifa Muhammad. 1981. *Al-Quwa al-Ijtima'iyya fi al-Thawra al-'Urabiyya* (Social Power in the 'Urabi Revolution). Cairo: General Egyptian Book Organization.

Salt, Jeremy. 2009. *The Unmaking of the Middle East: A History of Western Disorder in Arab Lands*. Berkeley, CA: University of California Press.

Salti, Rasha. 2005. 'Beirut Diary: April 2005'. *Middle East Report*: 236 (fall), www.merip.org/mer/mer236/beirut-diary-april-2005.

San Juan, E. Jr. 2009. *Critique and Social Transformation: Lessons from Antonio Gramsci, Mikhail Bakhtin, and Raymond Williams*. Lewiston, NY: Edwin Mellen Press.

Sanagan, Mark. 2013. 'Teacher, Preacher, Soldier, Martyr: Rethinking 'Izz al-Din al-Qassam'. *Die Welt des Islams*, 53, 3–4: 315–52.

Sanbonmatsu, John. 2003. *The Postmodern Prince: Critical Theory, Left Strategy, and the Making of a New Political Subject*. New York: Monthly Review Press.

Sankari, Jamal. 2005. *Fadlallah: The Making of a Radical Shi'ite Leader*. London: Saqi.

Santarelli, Enzo, Giorgio Rochat, Romain Rainero and Luigi Goglia. 1986. *Omar Al-Mukhtar: The Italian Reconquest of Libya*. Trans. John Gilbert. London: Darf Publishers.

Sarkar, Sumit. 2000. 'The Decline of the Subaltern in Subaltern Studies'. In *Subaltern Studies and the Postcolonial*. Vinayak Chaturvedi ed. London: Verso, pp. 300–22.

Sartre, Jean-Paul. 2001 [1964]. *Colonialism and Neocolonialism*. Trans. Azzedine Haddour, Steve Brewer and Terry McWilliams. London: Routledge.

Sassoon, Anne Showstack. 1987 [1980]. *Gramsci's Politics*. 2nd edn. London: Hutchinson.

Sayigh, Rosemary. 1979. *The Palestinians: From Peasants to Revoutionaries*. London: Zed Books.

1994. *Too Many Enemies: The Palestinian Experience in Lebanon*. London: Zed Books.

Sayigh, Yezid. 1986. 'Palestinian Armed Struggle: Means and Ends'. *Journal of Palestine Studies*, 16, 1 (autumn): 95–112.

1997. *Armed Struggle and the Search for State: The Palestinian National Movement 1949–1993*. Oxford: Oxford University Press.

Schleifer, Abdullah. 1993. 'Izz al-Din al-Qassam: Preacher and Mujahid'. *Struggle and Survival in the Modern Middle East*. Edmund Burke III ed. Berkeley, CA: University of California Press, pp. 164–78.

Schölch, Alexander. 1981. *Egypt for the Egyptians! The Socio-Political Crisis in Egypt 1878–1882*. London: Ithaca Press.

Schreier, Joshua. 2010. *Arabs of the Jewish Faith: The Civilizing Mission in Colonial Algeria*. New Brunswick, NJ: Rutgers University Press.

Schulze, Reinhard C. 1991. 'Colonization and Resistance: The Egyptian Peasant Rebellion, 1919'. In *Peasants and Politics in the Modern Middle East*. Farhad Kazemi and John Waterbury eds. Miami: Florida International University Press, pp. 171–202.

Schwedler, Jillian. 2006. *Faith in Moderation: Islamist Parties in Jordan and Yemen*. Cambridge: Cambridge University Press.

Seale, Patrick. 1992. *Abu Nidal: A Gun for Hire*. New York: Random House.

Seccombe, Ian J. 1983. 'Labor Migration to the Arabian Gulf: Evolution and Characteristics, 1920–1950'. *Bulletin of British Society for Middle Eastern Studies*, 10, 1: 3–20.

Shabbi, Muhammad Al-Mas'ud Al-. 1966. *Hawl Istratijiyya al-Thawra al-'Arabiyya* (Towards the Strategy of the Arab Revolution). Beirut: Manshurat Dar al-Tali'a.

Shafik, Doria. 1996. *Doria Shafik, Egyptian Feminist: A Woman Apart*. Cairo: American University in Cairo Press.

Shafir, Gershon. 1996. *Land, Labor and the Origins of the Israeli–Palestinian Conflict, 1882–1914*. Berkeley, CA: University of California Press.

Shakibi, Zhand. 2007. *Revolutions and the Collapse of Monarchy: Human Agency and the Making of Revolution in France, Russia and Iran*. London: I. B. Tauris.

Shakry, Omnia El. 1998. 'Schooled Mothers and Structured Play: Child-Rearing in Twentieth Century Egypt'. In *Remaking Women: Feminism and Modernity in the Middle East*. Lila Abu Lughod ed. Princeton, NJ: Princeton University Press.

2006. 'Cairo as Capital of Socialist Revolution?'. In *Cairo Cosmopolitan: Politics, Culture, and Urban Space in the New Globalized Middle East*. Diane Singerman ed. Cairo: American University in Cairo Press, pp. 73–98.

2007. *The Great Social Laboratory: Subjects of Knowledge in Colonial and Postcolonial Egypt*. Stanford, CA: Stanford University Press.

Sharara, Waddah. 1980. *Al-Salm Al-Ahali Al-Barid: Lubnan Al-Mujtami' wa-l-Dawla, 1964–1967* (The Cold Peace: Lebanon, State and Society 1964–1967). 2 vols. Tripoli, Libya: Ma'had Al-Anma' Al-'Arabi.

Shaw, Stanford. 1976. *History of the Ottoman Empire and Modern Turkey: Volume I: Empire of the Gazis: The Rise and Decline of the Ottoman Empire, 1280–1808*. Cambridge: Cambridge University Press.

1977. *History of the Ottoman Empire and Modern Turkey: Volume II: Reform, Revolution and Republic, The Rise of Modern Turkey 1808–1975*. Cambridge: Cambridge University Press.

Shields, Sarah D. 2011. *Fezzes in the River: Identity Politics and European Diplomacy in the Middle East on the Eve of World War II*. Oxford: Oxford University Press.

Shlaim, Avi. 2000. *The Iron Wall: Israel and the Arab World*. London: Penguin Books.

Singerman, Diane. 1995. *Avenues of Participation: Family, Politics and Networks in Urban Quarters of Cairo*. Princeton, NJ: Princeton University Press.

Skocpol, Theda. 1979. *States and Social Revolutions: A Comparative Analysis of France, Russia, and China*. Cambridge: Cambridge University Press.

1982. 'Rentier State and Shi'a Islam in the Iranian Revolution'. *Theory and Society*, 11, 3 (May): 265–83.

Slater, Jerome. 2001. 'What Went Wrong? The Collapse of the Israeli–Palestinian Peace Process'. *Political Science Quarterly*, 116, 2 (summer): 171–99.

Smelser, Neil. 1962. *Theory of Collective Behaviour*. New York: Free Press.

Smilianskaya, Irena. 1966. 'The Disintegration of Feudal Relations in Syria and Lebanon in the Middle of the Nineteenth Century'. In *The Economic History of the Middle East, 1800–1914*. Charles Issawi ed. Chicago: Chicago University Press.

Smith, Pamela Ann. 1984. *Palestine and the Palestinians, 1876–1983*. New York: St Martin's Press.

Spivak, Gayatri Chakravorty. 1988. 'Can the Subaltern Speak?'. In *Marxism and the Interpretation of Culture*. Ed. and with an introduction by Cary Nelson and Lawrence Grossberg. Basingstoke: Macmillan Education.

Stora, Benjamin. 1987. *Nationalistes algériens et révolutionnaires français au temps du front populaire*. Paris: Harmattan.

Swedenberg, Ted. 1993. 'The Role of the Palestinian Peasantry in the Great Revolt (1936–1939)'. In *The Modern Middle East: A Reader*. Albert Hourani, Philip S. Khoury and Mary C. Wilson Èds. London: I. B. Tauris, pp. 467–502.

2003. *Memories of Revolt*. Fayetteville, AK: University of Arkansas Press.

Takriti, Abdel Razzaq. 2013. *Monsoon Revolution: Republicans, Sultans, and Empires in Oman, 1965–1976*. Oxford: Oxford University Press.

Tarrow, Sidney. 2005. *The New Transnational Activism*. Cambridge: Cambridge University Press.

Tauber, Eliezer. 1995. *The Formation of Modern Syria and Iraq*. Ilford: Frank Cass.

Temimi, Abdeljelil. 1978. *Le Beylik de Constantine et Hadj Ahmed Bey, 1830–1837*. Tunis: Société Tunisienne des Arts Graphiques.

Tétrault, Mary Anne. 2000. *Stories of Democracy: Politics and Society in Contemporary Kuwait*. New York: Columbia University Press.

Thomas, Peter D. 2010. *The Gramscian Moment: Philosophy, Hegemony and Marxism*. Chicago: Haymarket Books.

Thompson, E. P. 1971. 'The Moral Economy of the English Crowd in the Eighteenth Century'. *Past and Present*, 50 (February): 76–136.

1978. 'Eighteenth Century English Society: Class Struggle without Class?'. *Social History*, 3, 2 (May): 133–65.

2009. *Customs in Common*. Torfaen: The Merlin Press.

Thompson, Elizabeth. 2000. *Colonial Citizens: Republican Rights, Paternal Privilege, and Gender in French Syria and Lebanon*. New York: Columbia University Press.

Tignor, Robert L. 1966. *Modernization and British Colonial Rule in Egypt, 1882–1914*. Princeton, NJ: Princeton University Press.

Tilly, Charles. 1977. *From Mobilization to Revolution*. CRSO Working Paper No. 156. University of Michigan.

1995. *Popular Contention in Great Britain, 1758–1834*. Cambridge, MA: Harvard University Press.

2004. 'Terror, Terrorism, Terrorists'. *Sociological Theory*, 22, 1 (March): 5–13.

2006. *Regimes and Repertoires*. Chicago: University of Chicago Press.

Tilly, Charles and Sidney Tarrow. 2012. *Contentious Politics*. New York: Oxford University Press.

Toledano, Ehud. 2003. *State and Society in Mid-Nineteenth-Century Egypt*. Cambridge: Cambridge University Press.

Touraine, Alain. 1971. *The Post-Industrial Society. Tomorrow's Social History: Classes, Conflicts and Culture in the Programmed Society*. New York: Random House.

Traboulsi, Fawwaz. 2007. *A History of Modern Lebanon*. London: Pluto Press.

Tripp, Charles. 2000. *A History of Iraq*. Cambridge: Cambridge University Press.

    2013. *The Power and the People: Paths of Resistance in the Middle East*. Cambridge: Cambridge University Press.

Trofimov, Yaroslav. 2007. *The Siege of Mecca*. New York: Doubleday.

Trotsky, Leon. 1997 [1932–3]. *The History of the Russian Revolution*. Trans. Max Eastman, introduction by Tony Cliff. London: Pluto Press.

Tschacher, Torsten. 2011. '"Walls of Illusion": Information Generation in Colonial Singapore and the Reporting of the Mahdi-Rebellion in Sudan, 1887–1890'. In *Singapore in Global History*. Derek Heny and Syed Muhd Khairudin Aljunied eds. Amsterdam: Amsterdam University Press, pp. 67–88.

Tucker, Judith. 1985. *Women in Nineteenth Century Egypt*. Cambridge: Cambridge University Press.

Tuğal, Cihan. 2009. *Passive Revolution: Absorbing the Islamic Challenge to Capitalism*. Stanford, CA: Stanford University Press.

Ulloa, Marie-Pierre. 2007. *Francis Jeanson: A Dissident Intellectual from the French Resistance to the Algerian War*. Trans. Jane Marie Todd. Stanford, CA: Stanford University Press.

United States Government. 1970. 'The Palestine Resistance Movement through 30 June 1970'. Typescript. 187 pages. Collection Number 77106. Archives of the Hoover Institution, Stanford, CA.

Urbinati, Nadia. 1998. 'From the Periphery of Modernity: Antonio Gramsci's Theory of Subordination and Hegemony'. *Political Theory*, 26, 3 (June): 370–91.

Usher, Graham. 1995. *Palestine in Crisis: The Struggle for Political Independence after Oslo*. London: Pluto Press.

Vatikiotis, P. J. 1969. *The Modern History of Egypt*. London: Weidenfeld and Nicolson.

Vatter, Sherry. 1994. 'Militant Journeymen in Nineteenth-Century Damascus: Implications for the Middle Eastern Labor History Agenda'. In *Workers and Working Classes in the Middle East: Struggles, Histories,*

Historiographies. Zachary Lockman ed. Albany, NY: State University of New York Press, pp. 1–21.

Vitalis, Robert. 2006. *America's Kingdom: Mythmaking on the Saudi Oil Frontier*. Stanford, CA: Stanford University Press.

Voll, John. 1975. 'Muhammad Hayya al-Sindhi and Muhammad Ibn Abd al-Wahhab: An Analysis of an Intellectual Group in Eighteenth-Century Madina'. *Bulletin of the School of Oriental and African Studies*, 38, 1: 32–9.

2008. 'Neo-Sufism: Reconsidered Again'. *Canadian Journal of African Studies /Revue Canadienne des Études Africaines*, 42, 2/3 (January): 314–30.

Von Sivers, Peter. 1982. 'Insurrection and Secular Anxieties and Religious Righteousness: The Origins of the Insurrection of 1881 in the Nomadic and Sedentary Communities of the Algerian Southwest'. *Peuples Méditerranéens*, 18: 145–62.

1983. 'Alms and Arms: The Combative Saintliness of the Awlad Sidi Shaykh in the Algerian Sahara, Sixteenth-Nineteenth Centuries'. *The Maghreb Review*, 8, 5–6:113–23.

1988. 'Rural Uprisings as Political Movements in Colonial Algeria, 1851–1914'. In *Islam, Politics and Social Movements*. Edmund Burke III and Ira M. Lapidus eds. Berkeley, CA: University of California Press, pp. 39–59.

Wahab, Muhammad Yunus Al-Sayyid Abd Allah. 1967. *Ahammiyat Tala'far fi Thawrat al- 'Iraq al-Kubra* (The Importance of Tala'far in the Great Iraqi Revolt of 1921). Mawsil: Matba'at al-Jumhuriya.

Walton, John and David Seddon. 1994. *Free Markets and Food Riots: The Politics of Global Adjustment*. Oxford: Blackwell.

Watt, D. C. 1962. 'Labor Relations and Trades Unionism in Aden, 1952–60'. *Middle East Journal*, 16: 443–56.

Wedeen, Lisa. 1999. *Ambiguities of Domination: Politics, Rhetoric, and Symbols in Contemporary Syria*. Chicago: University of Chicago Press.

White, Jenny. 2002. *Islamist Mobilization in Turkey: A Study in Vernacular Politics*. Seattle: University of Washington Press.

White, Sam. 2011. *The Climate of Rebellion in the Early Modern Ottoman Empire*. Cambridge: Cambridge University Press.

Wiktorowicz, Quintan ed. 2004. *Islamic Activism: A Social Movement Theory Approach*. Bloomington, IN: Indiana University Press.

Wiles, Rich ed. 2013. *Generation Palestine: Voices from the Boycott, Divestment and Sanctions Movement*. London: Pluto.

Wiley, Joyce N. 1992. *The Islamic Movement of Iraqi Shi'as*. London: Lynne Rienner.

Williams, Raymond. 1977. *Marxism and Literature*. Oxford and New York: Oxford University Press.

Willis, Michael. 1996. *The Islamist Challenge in Algeria: A Political History*. London: Ithaca Press.

Wilson, Jacob Chacko. 2011. *Working out Egypt: Effendi Masculinity and Subject Formation in Colonial Modernity, 1870–1940*. Durham, NC: Duke University Press.

Woolman, David S. 1969. *Rebels in the Rif: Abd el Krim and the Rif Rebellion*. Stanford, CA: Stanford University Press.

Yaphe, Judith S. 2004. 'The View from Basra: Southern Iraq's Reaction to the War and Occupation, 1915–1925'. In *The Creation of Iraq, 1914–1921*. Reeva Spector Simon and Eleanor H. Tejirian eds. New York: Columbia University Press, pp. 19–35.

Yapp, Malcolm E. 1987. *The Making of the Modern Near East 1792–1923*. London: Longman.

    1991. *The Near East since the First World War: A History to 1995*. London: Longman.

Yiftachel, Oren. 2006. *Ethnocracy: Land and Identity Politics in Israel/ Palestine*. Philadelphia, PA: University of Pennsylvania Press.

    2009. 'Voting for Apartheid: The 2009 Israeli Elections'. *Journal of Palestine Studies*, 38, 3 (spring): 72–85.

Zahid, Muhammed and Michael Medley. 2006. 'Muslim Brotherhood in Egypt and Sudan'. *Review of African Political Economy*, 33, 110 (September): 693–708.

Zeldin, Theodore. 1997. *The French*. London: Vintage.

Zubaida, Sami. 1993. *Islam, the People and the State: Political Ideas and Movements in the Middle East*. London: I. B. Tauris.

Index